Management for Professionals

More information about this series at http://www.springer.com/series/10101

Jan vom Brocke • Jan Mendling
Editors

Business Process Management Cases

Digital Innovation and Business Transformation in Practice

Springer

Editors
Jan vom Brocke
Institute for Information Systems
University of Liechtenstein
Vaduz, Liechtenstein

Jan Mendling
Institute for Information Business
Vienna University of Economics & Business
Vienna, Austria

ISSN 2192-8096 ISSN 2192-810X (electronic)
Management for Professionals
ISBN 978-3-319-58306-8 ISBN 978-3-319-58307-5 (eBook)
DOI 10.1007/978-3-319-58307-5

Library of Congress Control Number: 2017947893

Printed on acid-free paper

This Springer imprint is published by Springer Nature
The registered company is Springer International Publishing AG
The registered company address is: Gewerbestrasse 11, 6330 Cham, Switzerland

Foreword

It is a pleasure to write the introduction to this wonderful book on Business Process Management (BPM) cases. On the one hand, the BPM cases illustrate the maturity of the field. On the other hand, the book also shows that there are still many open challenges. In fact, there is a continuous need to show that BPM indeed adds value and helps organizations to improve. The editors, Jan vom Brocke and Jan Mendling, understand this perfectly and did a great job in bringing together a range of authors and experiences.

In this foreword, I would like to briefly reflect on developments in the field. In 2003 we organized the first International Conference on BPM in Eindhoven. This was the time were BPM was an emerging topic following the workflow management wave of the 1990s. The conference was an immediate success and this year we are celebrating the 15th edition of the BPM conference in Barcelona. BPM is no longer a "hot topic", but has become the "new normal". Process orientation, something which was previously seen as something exotic, has become commonplace for most organizations. Moreover, BPM has become more much evidence-based, exploiting the abundance of event data available. However, the actual practice of BPM is scarcely documented in literature. Scientific papers tend to focus on a particular aspect or technique. Articles written by practitioners or so-called "opinion leaders" are often shallow and just a concatenation of buzzwords. Therefore, this book is a very welcome addition!

Clarence "Skip" Ellis (1943–2014) gave a keynote at the first BPM conference in 2003. He was one of the pioneers in Workflow Management, Computer-Supported Cooperative Work, and BPM. Skip Ellis developed office automation prototypes such as Officetalk-Zero and Officetalk-D at Xerox PARC in the late 1970s. These systems used Information Control Nets, a variant of Petri nets, to model processes. In a way the basics are the same, e.g., there is still a focus on process diagrams and process automation. However, looking at the BPM cases in this book demonstrates that also many things have changed dramatically. Real-life projects show that modeling and automation are not the ultimate goal. BPM needs to add value and help organizations to continuously improve and disruptively innovate their processes.

The BPM cases in this book relate to different core elements of BPM, namely Strategic and Governance (Part I), Methods (Part II), Information Technology (Part

III), and People and Culture (Part IV). The contributions cover different parts of the BPM lifecycle. These actual cases also nicely relate to my own 20 BPM Use Cases elaborated in the survey paper "Business Process Management: A Comprehensive Survey" (ISRN Software Engineering, 2013, http://dx.doi.org/10.1155/2013/507984). Whereas the 20 BPM Use Cases identify the core BPM building blocks, the cases in this book aim to describe end-to-end BPM projects. The first chapter provides a nice taxonomy to position the 31 real-world BPM cases. Different angles are used to show the richness of the BPM discipline. The cases are presented in a unified format, making them accessible and easy to comprehend.

How about the future of BPM? I strongly believe that the spectacular growth of event data is rapidly changing our BPM discipline. It makes no sense to focus on process modeling (including model-based analysis and model-based process automation) without considering the torrents of factual data in and between today's organizations. Recent developments in process mining make it possible to use process models as the "lens" to look at (low) level event data. Such a "process lens" helps to understand and solve compliance- and performance-related problems. The focus on data analysis is good, but should not frustrate process-orientation. In the end, good processes are more important than information systems and conventional analytics. The old phrase "It's the process stupid" is still valid.

I hope you enjoy reading the book and learn from the many practical experiences condensed in the 31 real-world BPM cases reported.

Eindhoven, The Netherlands
March 2017

Wil van der Aalst

Preface

Business Process Management (BPM) is an important and timely topic. For many companies, BPM is the key for mastering digital transformation and for innovating their business models. The fast pace of change has also taken a grip on concepts and techniques of BPM, with various new ideas emerging from research and practice. Several excellent sources exist that summarize established concepts of BPM. So far, however, a collection of real-world cases making available the experience of organizations applying BPM for various objectives was missing. It is the aim of this book to close this gap and to increase knowledge exchange based on real-world BPM projects for fostering both BPM education and practice.

For this book, we have gathered 31 cases on how companies use business process management to achieve outstanding operational results. Each of these cases is organized according to a uniform structure including the following parts:

- Introduction—What is the story of the case? The authors give a brief narrative of the entire story to grasp your interest in the case. This part includes a summary of the key figures of the company.
- Situation faced—What was the initial problem situation? What situation led to the action taken? The authors specify the context of the case as to needs, constraints, incidents, objectives, and beyond.
- Action taken—What has been done? What measures have been taken, as e.g. regarding the process redesign or process innovation? Which methods and approaches have been used? The authors provide a factual passage of the course of events.
- Results achieved—What effects could be observed resulting from the action taken? This could be changes in performance measures as well as qualitative statements from employees, customers, or other business partners. Here, the authors also discuss how far expected results materialize and how far expectations were met or not met.
- Lessons learned—Reflecting the overall case, what can others learn from it? The authors derive around five lessons learned, which are grounded in the case and which are interesting for others to take as an example.

The cases of this book are grouped into four major blocks, which are inspired by the six core elements of BPM by de Bruin and Rosemann. Part I contains cases that relate to strategy and governance. The cases stem from SAP in Germany, S-Y Systems Technologies in Germany, Autogrill in Italy, the Dompe eHospital in Sri Lanka, a leading telecommunications provider in the Middle East, and the Slovene public service company Snaga. Part II presents cases on BPM methods. These cases relate to "Die Mobiliar" from Switzerland, Queensland University of Technology in Australia, the City of Ghent in Belgium, a Brazilian insurance company, the telecommunications provider 3 in Germany, Bolzano Hospital in Italy, an Australian insurance company, Software AG in Germany, and St. Andrew's War Memorial Hospital in Australia. Part III discusses cases on information technology and BPM. The cases refer to CrowdStrom in Germany, MELOS in Germany, Deutsche Bank in Germany, BRFkredit in Denmark, a German manufacturing company, Zalando in Germany, Adler Moden in Germany, a Slovak logistics provider, and HEYCO-WERK in Germany. Part IV discusses BPM-related issues of people and culture. It builds on cases from Lufthansa Technik in Germany, 1&1 Internet in Germany, TCE-PE from Brazil, Jade University of Applied Science in Germany, and a Norwegian company in the Oil and Gas sector.

The material presented in this book is complemented by online material for teaching, training, and advisory. The website

http://www.bpm-cases.com

makes available slides and additional content that can be helpful for using the cases both in teaching BPM and in preparing for BPM projects in practice.

We thank the following people and institutions for their continuous support toward the compilation of this book.

- First, we thank our research teams both in Liechtenstein and in Vienna. There have always been strong ties between Liechtenstein and Vienna not only in BPM but in history, and we emphasize this connection with our book cover that refers to the pattern of the parquet floor of one room in the Palais Liechtenstein in Vienna.
- Second, we thank the organizers of the BPM Conference in Innsbruck 2015 who gave us the chance to bring together many of the case authors of this book by inviting us to organize the industry program of the conference. In Innsbruck, half way between Liechtenstein and Vienna, the idea of this book emerged.
- Third, we thank our colleagues and friends who served on the editorial board of this book and who have dedicated much time and effort in multiple rounds of reviews to further develop the cases presented in this book.
- Fourth, we thank our BPM research colleagues for their continuous inspiration and support, specifically at QUT Brisbane, TU Eindhoven, VU Amsterdam, Uni Tartu, HPI Potsdam, to name but a few.
- Finally, special thanks go to our colleagues from the University of Münster who initiated and coordinate the ERCIS network [European Research Center for Information Systems (ERCIS)]. Stemming from this network, we also have the opportunity to collaborate with many of our BPM colleagues and friends, in the EU Horizon 2020 project RISE_BPM, provided by the European Commission under the Marie Sklodowska-Curie grant agreement No. 645751 and the

Liechtenstein Government. We are grateful for the financial support through this project, which was essential in making the idea of the BPM Cases Book come to life.

We hope you will enjoy reading the book and working with the cases, and we look forward to hearing from you related to any possible feedback!

Vaduz, Liechtenstein — Jan vom Brocke
Vienna, Austria — Jan Mendling

Editorial Board

Contents

Frameworks for Business Process Management: A Taxonomy for Business Process Management Cases

Jan vom Brocke and Jan Mendling

Abstract

While the body of knowledge on business process management has matured during the past decades (Dumas et al., Fundamentals of business process management. Berlin: Springer, 2013; vom Brocke and Rosemann, Handbook on business process management. Berlin: Springer, 2015), few real-world cases are available that provide practical experiences from BPM projects. This book presents a diverse set of 31 real-world BPM cases, all reported using a unified schema so the knowledge contained in these cases can be accessed readily.

1 What Is Business Process Management?

While early contributions to the field of business process management (BPM) focused on the (re-)design of single processes, contemporary research calls for a more holistic view of the management of organizational processes. To that end, BPM uses an integrated set of corporate capabilities, including strategic alignment, governance, methods, technology, people, and culture, to analyze, design, implement, continuously improve, and disruptively innovate organizational processes (vom Brocke and Rosemann 2014).

BPM's roots in early studies of organizational design (e.g., Taylor 1911) then developed into the broader discipline of industrial engineering and has since remained focused on the analysis of operational activities in the dominant manufacturing sector. An increase in the significance of services, the growing

J. vom Brocke (✉)
University of Liechtenstein, Vaduz, Liechtenstein
e-mail: jan.vom.brocke@uni.li

J. Mendling
Wirtschaftsuniversität Wien, Vienna, Austria
e-mail: jan.mendling@wu.ac.at

J. vom Brocke, J. Mendling (eds.), *Business Process Management Cases*,
Management for Professionals, DOI 10.1007/978-3-319-58307-5_1

importance of information technology for the design of processes, and the overall recognition that processes are a critical corporate asset have elevated this domain into a discipline.

According to Hammer (2010), the genesis of BPM as a management discipline is characterized by two developmental paths: process improvement and process development.

- *Process Improvement*: Earlier studies in the field focused on analyzing existing business processes in pursuit of continuous or incremental process improvement. Examples of developments on this path are Total Quality Management (Juran 1988; Crosby 1979), Lean Management (Womack and Jones 2003), and Kaizen (Imai 1986). For example, Deming's (1986) studies on statistical process control provided basic principles by conducting systematic analyses of processes using both quantitative and qualitative criteria.
- *Process Reengineering*: Hammer and Champy (1993) presented an approach that questioned existing business processes and demanded the radical redesign of extant processes from end-to-end in light of organizational goals, particularly capitalizing on the potential of information technology (IT) as a major driver of innovation (Davenport 1993).

BPM has emerged as a consolidation of disciplines that leverage process orientation to increase performance. Today, BPM has evolved into a widely deployed and comprehensively studied discipline. Universities have increasingly integrated BPM capabilities into both management and information systems education (vom Brocke 2017), responding to the strong demand of BPM experts in practice to appropriate contemporary technology in order to foster value creation in all sectors, including production, banking, retail, health, government, entrepreneurship, and others.

In course of this development, BPM has matured as an academic and professional discipline. Textbooks (Dumas et al. 2013) and handbooks (vom Brocke and Rosemann 2015) alike have documented the body of knowledge. Professional associations, conferences, journals, and forums are available for both academics and professionals to discuss the discipline's development, and BPM has been recognized and further developed as a way to drive innovation, particularly digital innovation (vom Brocke and Schmiedel 2015). However, with the emergence of the rich set of opportunities associated with digitization, the established, analysis-intensive BPM methods and tools are no longer capitalizing fully on the affordances of contemporary information systems. As a result, BPM has started to develop its intellectual core and methodological basis to strengthen its exploratory, opportunity-driven capabilities in addition to the rich set of exploitative, problem-driven capabilities. Colleagues have coined the term "ambidextrous BPM" (Rosemann 2015) to express the need to combine both exploration and exploration in BPM (vom Brocke et al. 2015a).

2 How to Structure Business Process Management

This book uses well-established BPM frameworks to characterize the cases it presents based on a shared language. We use the BPM Six Core Elements Model (Rosemann and vom Brocke 2015), the BPM Lifecycle Model (Dumas et al. 2013), and the BPM Context Framework (vom Brocke et al. 2015b).

2.1 The BPM Six Core Elements Model

The BPM Six Core Elements Model describes organizational capability areas that are relevant to BPM. The model helps decision makers to classify the actions an organization undertakes in conducting BPM by conceptualizing six BPM capability areas: strategic alignment, governance, methods, IT, people, and culture. This model expands BPM from a technical concept to a holistic management discipline (Fig. 1).

- **Strategic Alignment**: BPM contributes to the organization's superordinate, strategic goals. Related capabilities include the assessment of processes and process management initiatives according to their fit with the overall corporate strategy.
- **Governance**: BPM must be implemented in the organizational structure. Related capabilities include the assignment of BPM-related tasks to stakeholders and applying specific principles and rules to define the required responsibilities and controls along the entire business-process lifecycle.
- **Methods**: BPM must be supported by methods for process design, analysis, implementation, execution, and monitoring. Related capabilities include

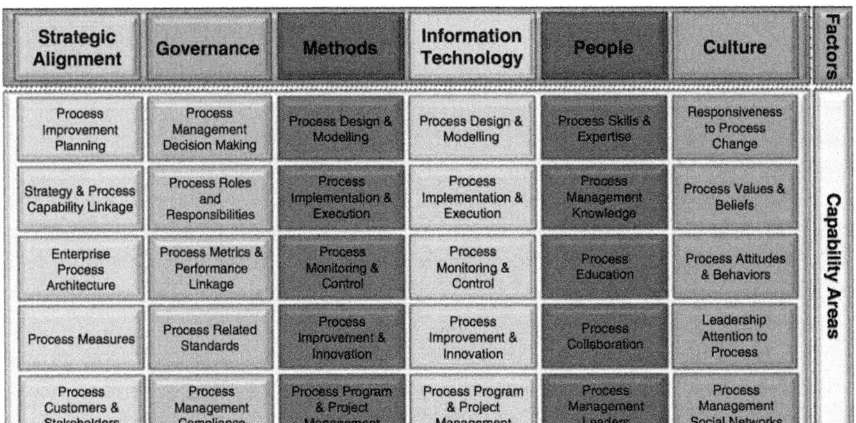

Fig. 1 Six BPM core elements (Rosemann and vom Brocke 2015)

selecting the appropriate BPM methods, tools, and techniques and adapting and combining them according to the organization's requirements.

- **Information Technology**: BPM must use technology, particularly process-aware information systems (PAIS), as the basis for process design and implementation. Related capabilities include the ability to select, implement, and use relevant PAIS solutions that covering, for example, workflow management, adaptive case management, or process-mining solutions.
- **People**: BPM must consider employees' qualifications in the discipline of BPM and their expertise with relevant business processes. Related capabilities include assessing the human-resources impact of BPM-related initiatives and programs that facilitate the development of process-related skills throughout the organization.
- **Culture**: BPM must be met with a common value system that supports process improvement and innovation. Related capabilities include the ability to assess the organizational culture's values and the ability to derive measures to develop these values accordingly.

Research has shown that all six elements must be present if a BPM initiative is to meet its objectives.

2.2 The BPM Lifecycle Model

The BPM lifecycle model describes the phases in managing business processes and illustrates how a BPM project or a BPM initiative can be organized to arrive at an improved process by means of six major steps: process identification, process discovery, process analysis, process redesign, process implementation, and process monitoring and controlling (Fig. 2).

- **Process Identification**: Process identification is concerned with setting up the BPM initiative, including a high-level description of the organization's major processes and an assessment of their current state. The main result of this phase is a "process architecture," which identifies the organization's main processes, describes the relationships between them, and defines criteria for prioritizing them.
- **Process Discovery**: With process discovery, the cycle shifts the focus from the organization's overall portfolio of processes (often also called multi-process management) to one specific process. The process discovery phase produces detailed descriptions of a business process in its current state. This description is referred to as an as-is process model.
- **Process Analysis**: Analytical tools and techniques are applied during process analysis to determine weaknesses in the as-is process and the impact of each weakness.
- **Process Re-design**: Process redesign addresses the most important weaknesses in the process and delivers a reworked design for the process, called the to-be

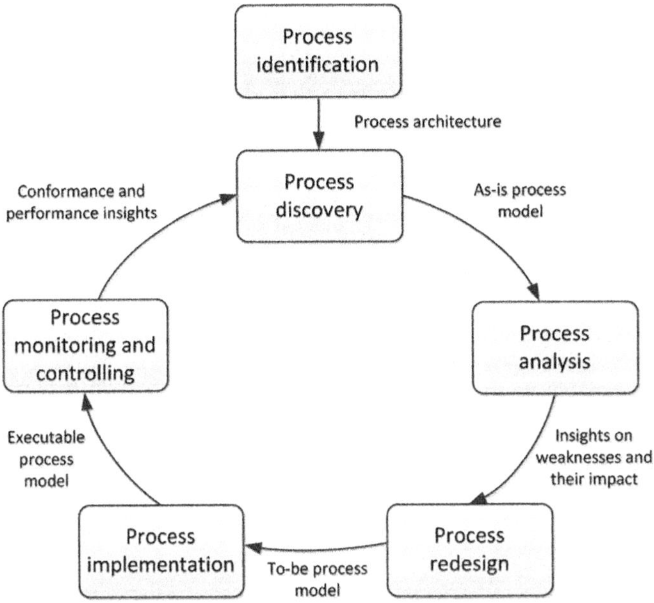

Fig. 2 The BPM lifecycle (Dumas et al. 2013)

process model. This model is subsequently used as the basis for process implementation.

- **Process Implementation**: Process implementation typically includes information system implementation and measures to facilitate organizational change.
- **Process Monitoring and Controlling**: Once the redesigned process is implemented, the process monitoring and controlling phase collects and analyzes execution data continually for their compliance with performance and conformance objectives. Deviations from these objectives and changes in the business environment or the company's goals trigger a new iteration of the BPM lifecycle.

The six phases are seldom executed exactly in this idealistic, sequential way, and the circle is not always closed. For example, a company might decide only to document its processes without considering redesign. Still, the BPM lifecycle is helpful in clarifying how BPM-related activities relate to one another and how they contribute to BPM in a holistic way.

2.3 The BPM Context Framework

The BPM context framework describes the factors in the context of BPM that are relevant to BPM projects based on their settings (vom Brocke et al. 2016). The model helps to characterize a BPM initiative according to factors like its goals, the

Contextual factors	Example characteristics		
Goal-dimension:			
Focus	Exploitation (Improvement, Compliance)	Exploration (Innovation)	
Process-dimension:			
Value contribution	Core process	Management process	Support process
Repetitiveness	Repetitive	Non-repetitive	
Knowledge-intensity	Low knowledge-intensity	Medium knowledge-intensity	High knowledge-intensity
Creativity	Low creativity	Medium creativity	High creativity
Interdependence	Low interdependence	Medium interdependence	High interdependence
Variability	Low variability	Medium variability	High variability
Organization-dimension:			
Scope	Intra-organizational process	Inter-organizational process	
Industry	Product industry	Service industry	Product & Service industry
Size	Start-up	Small and medium enterprise	Large organization
Culture	Culture highly supportive of BPM	Culture medium supportive of BPM	Culture non-supportive of BPM
Resources	Low organizational resources	Medium organizational resources	High organizational resources
Environment-dimension:			
Competetiveness	Low competitive environment	Medium competitive environment	High competitive environment
Uncertainty	Low environmental uncertainty	Medium environmental uncertainty	High environmental uncertainty

Fig. 3 The BPM context framework (vom Brocke et al. 2015b)

process's characteristics, and the organization's and external environment's characteristics. The key contribution of the framework is to capture the situation around the BPM initiative so it can be aligned to the organization's specific context. The BPM context framework helps in assessing this context (Fig. 3).

The BPM context framework captures four contextual dimensions:

- **Goal Dimension**: The goal a BPM project is targeting has a major influence on the BPM-related actions to be planned. The difference between exploitation and exploration may serve as an example, as the first fosters optimization, and the second fosters innovation.
- **Process Dimension**: BPM can be applied to a number of processes, so the process characteristics affect the appropriate BPM methodology. Examples of factors include the knowledge-intensity, complexity, creativity, and variability involved in a process.
- **Organizational Dimension**: BPM serves many organizations, but the characteristics of the organization determines the right BPM approach. Organizational factors include industry, size, and culture.
- **Environmental Dimension**: BPM can also be applied in a variety of environments, which are characterized by, for example, differing levels of competitiveness or uncertainty. Considering the dynamics of the environment is important in scoping and positioning a BPM initiative.

A BPM project must identify its contexts in order to plan appropriate BPM-related actions (vom Brocke et al. 2014).

3 Introducing Cases of Business Process Management

In addition to the body of knowledge about BPM, this book brings together the experience of organizations that have adopted BPM. The focus is neither on academic case studies nor on offerings from consulting companies but on the lessons the adopting organizations learned from using BPM. That said, both academic institutions and consulting companies have been involved, at least in part, in the analysis of these cases.

Cases and case-based learning provides advantages over other approaches to facilitating learning (Srinivasan et al. 2007). First, cases offer a rich account of a specific situation, the actions taken, and the results achieved, which helps the reader to explore ambiguity and variation. Second, cases help the reader to focus on what matters, as they are challenged to reflect on their assumptions. Third, cases are an effective way to stimulate additional reading and research on the management of business processes.

3.1 How to Read the Cases

All cases follow a unified structure that makes the case knowledge easily accessible and transferrable to other contexts and helps readers find and compare the most important parts of the cases. Each of the cases is structured with an introduction, follows by descriptions of the situation faced, the actions taken, the results achieved, and the lessons learned.

- **Introduction**: What is the story of the case? A brief narrative of the entire case informs readers by summarizing its key aspects.
- **Situation faced**: What was the initial problem that led to the action taken? The context of the case is specified concerning needs, constraints, incidents, and objectives.
- **Action taken**: What was done? What measures were undertaken, such as in regard to process redesign or process innovation? What methods and approaches were used?
- **Results achieved**: What effects resulted from the actions taken? Results could take the form of changes in performance measures and/or qualitative statements from employees, customers, and other business partners. To what degree were expectations met or not met?
- **Lessons learned**: What did the organization learn from the case? What can others learn? Lessons learned are grounded in the case and serve as example for others.

3.2 Cases and Industry Sectors

All cases are structure using the framework presented above. The book includes cases that focus on all of BPM's core elements, cover all steps of the BPM lifecycle, and deal with diverse subsets of BPM contexts. The broad set of industries addressed includes nineteen industries, sorted by ISIC code (United Nations Statistics Division 2008):

- 06: Extraction of crude petroleum and natural gas
- 27: Manufacture of electrical equipment
- 28: Manufacture of machinery and equipment
- 32: Other manufacturing
- 35: Electricity, gas, steam, and air conditioning supply
- 36: Waste collection, treatment and disposal activities; materials recovery
- 41: Construction of buildings
- 47: Retail trade, except of motor vehicles and motorcycles
- 49: Land transport and transport via pipelines
- 51: Air transport
- 56: Food and beverage service activities
- 61: Telecommunications
- 62: Computer programming, consultancy, and related activities
- 64: Financial service activities, except insurance and pension funding
- 65: Insurance, reinsurance, and pension funding, except compulsory social security
- 82: Office administrative, office support, and other business support activities

- 84: Public administration and defense; compulsory social security
- 85: Education
- 86: Human health activities

3.3 Cases and BPM Core Elements

The cases in the book relate to the core elements of BPM and are classified in terms of their primary contributions.

Figure 4 shows that 8 of the 31 cases relate primarily to method and 9 to IT, confirming that most companies focus on these two areas of capability when conducting BPM (vom Brocke and Rosemann 2015). However, four cases relate to the people-related aspects of BPM, one of BPM's core elements that often receives little attention (Müller et al. 2014). Five chapters contribute primarily to governance and three to strategic alignment. Since culture has only recently been recognized and conceptualized in the BPM body of knowledge (Schmiedel et al. 2015), only two of the cases primarily address issues on culture in BPM. In summary, each core element is addressed in multiple cases, which makes this book useful in extending our understanding of BPM.

Table 1 Summarizes the cases per BPM core element.

3.4 Cases and BPM Lifecycle Phases

The cases reported in this book relate to a diverse set of the BPM lifecycle phases (Fig. 5). Eight of the cases report on process redesign, while seven are on process discovery, six address process implementation, five deal with process identification, three relate to process monitoring and controlling, and two focus on process analysis. The thorough coverage of the lifecycle phases addresses Recker and Mendling's (2016) observation of a gap in process redesign research, as the focus on process redesign demonstrates the innovative and transformative power of BPM, its role to leveraging digital innovation vom Brocke and Schmiedel (2015), and the importance of process improvement in practice (Vanwersch et al. 2016).

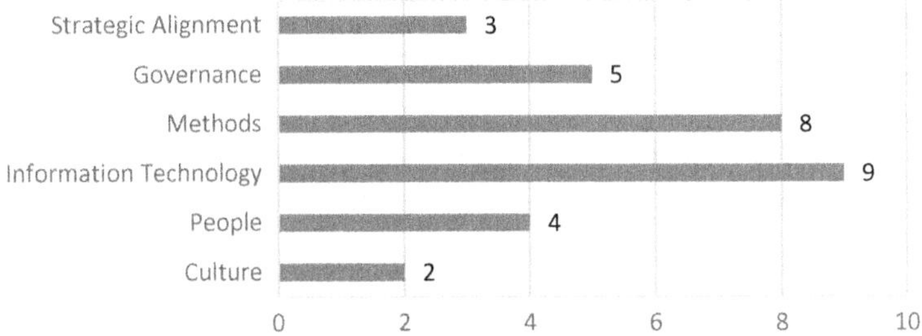

Fig. 4 BPM cases and BPM core elements

Table 1 BPM core elements with corresponding cases

Element	Cases
Strategic alignment	Woliński and Bala (2017)
	Bandara et al. (2017)
	Viaene and Van den Bergh (2017)
Governance	Reisert et al. (2017)
	Blasini et al. (2017)
	Czarnecki (2017)
	Kovačič et al. (2017)
	Kim et al. (2017)
Methods	Rosemann (2017)
	Van Looy and Rotthier (2017)
	Cereja et al. (2017)
	Karle and Teichenthaler (2017)
	Marengo et al. (2017)
	Andrews et al. (2017b)
	Thaler et al. (2017)
	Andrews et al. (2017a)
IT	Matzner et al. (2017)
	Duelli et al. (2017)
	Rau et al. (2017)
	Debois et al. (2017)
	Becker et al. (2017)
	Schrepfer et al. (2017)
	Leitz et al. (2017)
	Suchy et al. (2017)
	Schindlbeck and Kleinschmidt (2017)
People	Kloppenburg et al. (2017)
	Imgrund et al. (2017)
	Russack and Menges (2017)
	Krogstie et al. (2017)
Culture	Bührig et al. (2017)
	Alves et al. (2017)

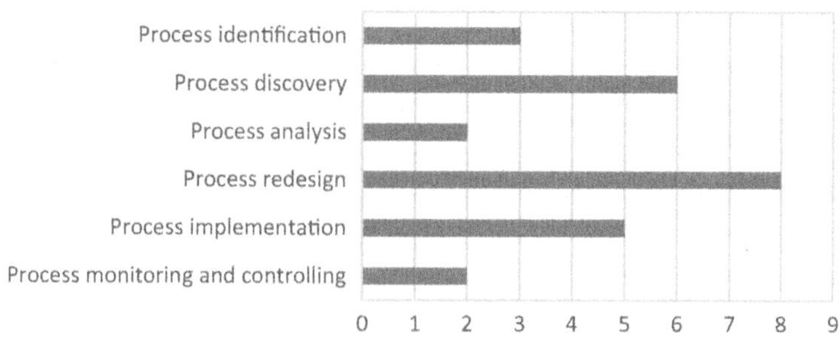

Fig. 5 BPM cases and BPM lifecycle phases

Even though only two cases contribute primarily to process analysis, most of the cases include process analysis—for example, when they discuss process redesign—which shows that the case companies went beyond process analysis and did saw the analysis as a means to an end, not as end in itself. These cases, then, help to advance the body of knowledge past what prior research on BPM has reported regarding organizations whose BPM initiatives have failed because they focused too much on analysis of processes and fell short in delivering business value through actual process improvement (vom Brocke et al. 2014). Table 2 summarizes the cases in terms of the lifecycle phase they address.

Table 2 BPM Lifecycle Phases with corresponding cases

Lifecycle phase	Cases
Process identification	Alves et al. (2017)
	Bührig et al. (2017)
	Imgrund et al. (2017)
	Debois et al. (2017)
	Viaene and Van den Bergh (2017)
Process discovery	Cereja et al. (2017)
	Suchy et al. (2017)
	Reisert et al. (2017)
	Andrews et al. (2017b)
	Andrews et al. (2017a)
	Thaler et al. (2017)
	Becker et al. (2017)
Process analysis	Matzner et al. (2017)
	Schrepfer et al. (2017)
Process redesign	Woliński and Bala (2017)
	Duelli et al. (2017)
	Van Looy and Rotthier (2017)
	Schindlbeck and Kleinschmidt (2017)
	Marengo et al. (2017)
	Czarnecki (2017)
	Karle and Teichenthaler (2017)
	Rosemann (2017)
Process implementation	Duelli et al. (2017)
	Bandara et al. (2017)
	Russack and Menges (2017)
	Kloppenburg et al. (2017)
	Rau et al. (2017)
	Krogstie et al. (2017)
Process monitoring and controlling	Leitz et al. (2017)
	Blasini et al. (2017)
	Kovačič et al. (2017)

3.5 Cases and the BPM Context Framework

The BPM context framework provides dimensions for classifying BPM in general and the cases reported in this book specifically. Under the category of the goal dimension, 23 cases focus on exploitation scenarios, such as improvement of existing processes, while seven address exploration scenarios that seek novel ways of doing processes, and one case covers exploration and exploitation equally (Fig. 6).

Regarding the process dimension, most of the cases (22) focus on core processes (22), while 11 also deal with management processes and 10 deal with support processes. There are 27 of the cases work on repetitive processes, and four tackle non-repetitive processes. The knowledge-intensity of processes is at a medium level in 20 cases, low in 7 cases, and high in 9 cases. Similarly, creativity is at a medium level in 15 cases, a low level in 14 cases, and high in 6 cases. Interdependence is at a

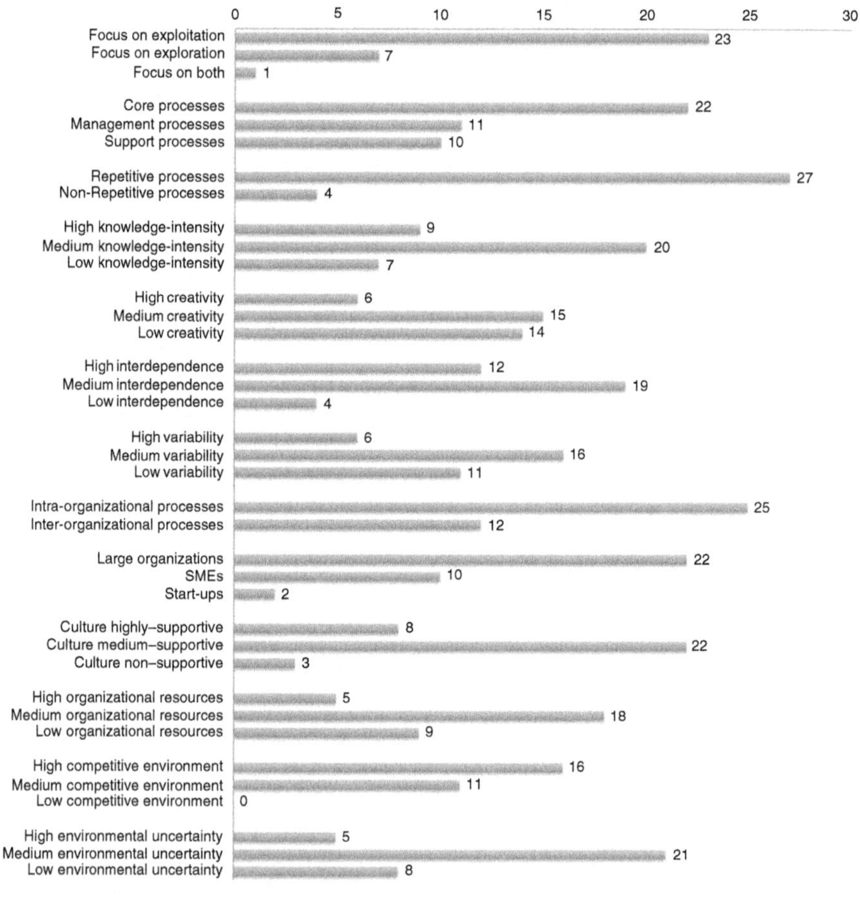

Fig. 6 BPM cases and BPM context

medium level in 19 cases, a low level in 4 cases and high in 12 cases, confirming that process work should be holistic in scope. Finally, variability is at a medium level in 16 cases, a low level in 11 cases, and high in 6 cases.

As for the organizational dimension, 25 cases focus primarily on intra-organizational processes, while 12 address inter-organizational challenges. There are 22 cases from large organizations, 10 are from small and medium-sized companies, and 2 are from start-ups. The culture in the case organizations has a medium level of support for BPM in 22 cases, is highly supportive in 8 cases, and is non-supportive in 3 cases, documenting the emerging role of culture in BPM. Organizational resources spent on the cases are at a medium level in 18 cases, a low level in 9 cases, and high in 5 cases.

Regarding the environmental dimension, about half of the cases (16) report on a highly competitive environment, supporting the notion that BPM is perceived as a way to increase competitiveness. There are 11 cases that report a medium level of competitiveness in their environments, and 6 cases report a low level of competitiveness. Most cases deal with uncertainty in business, as 21 of the cases report a medium level of uncertainty, five report a high level of uncertainty, and eight report a low uncertainty.

4 Conclusions

This book uses the BPM framework to classify the cases it presents. The classification reveals the broad spectrum and richness in the topical focus of cases collected here. We believe that this collection will be inspiring for students, teachers, practitioners, and researchers who are interested in the state of the art of BPM.

The remainder of this book is structured in four major parts. Part I gathers the eight BPM cases that are related primarily to strategy and governance, Part II presents eight BPM cases that focus on methods, Part III contains nine BPM cases that address IT, and Part IV introduces six BPM cases that highlight people and culture.

References

Alves, C., Jatoba, I., Valença, G., & Fraga, G. (2017). Exploring the influence of organizational culture on BPM success—The experience of the Pernambuco Court of Accounts. In J. vom Brocke & J. Mendling (Eds.), *Business process management cases: Digital innovation and business transformation in practice*. Cham: Springer.

Andrews, R., Suriadi, S., Wynn, M., ter Hofstede, A. H. M., & Rothwell, S. (2017a). Improving patient flows at St. Andrew's War Memorial Hospital's emergency department through process mining. In J. vom Brocke & J. Mendling (Eds.), *Business process management cases: Digital innovation and business transformation in practice*. Cham: Springer.

Andrews, R., Wynn, M., ter Hofstede, A. H. M., Xu, J., Horton, K., Taylor, P., & Plunkett-Cole, S. (2017b). Exposing insurance claims processing impediments: Compulsory third party insurance in Queensland. In J. vom Brocke & J. Mendling (Eds.), *Business process management cases: Digital innovation and business transformation in practice*. Cham: Springer.

Bandara, W., Syed, R., Ranathunga, B., & Sampath Kulathilleka, K. B. (2017). People-centric, ICT-enabled process innovations via community, public and private sector partnership, and e-leadership: The case of the Dompe eHospital in Sri Lanka. In J. vom Brocke & J. Mendling (Eds.), *Business process management cases: Digital innovation and business transformation in practice*. Cham: Springer.

Becker, J., Clever, N., Holler, J., & Neumann, M. (2017). Business process management in the manufacturing industry: ERP replacement and ISO 9001 recertification supported by the icebricks method. In J. vom Brocke & J. Mendling (Eds.), *Business process management cases: Digital innovation and business transformation in practice*. Cham: Springer.

Blasini, J., Leist, S., & Merkl, W. (2017). Developing and implementing a process-performance management system—Experiences from S-Y systems technologies Europe GmbH—A global automotive supplier. In J. vom Brocke & J. Mendling (Eds.), *Business process management cases: Digital innovation and business transformation in practice*. Cham: Springer.

Bührig, J., Schoormann, T., & Knackstedt, R. (2017). Business process management in German Institutions of higher education—The case of Jade University of Applied Science. In J. vom Brocke & J. Mendling (Eds.), *Business process management cases: Digital innovation and business transformation in practice*. Cham: Springer.

Cereja, J. R., Santoro, F. M., Gorbacheva, E., & Matzner, M. (2017). Application of the design thinking approach to process redesign at an Insurance Company in Brazil. In J. vom Brocke & J. Mendling (Eds.), *Business process management cases: Digital innovation and business transformation in practice*. Cham: Springer.

Crosby, P. (1979). *Quality is free*. New York: McGraw-Hill.

Czarnecki, C. (2017). Establishment of a Central Process Governance organization combined with operational process improvements. Insights from a BPM Project at a leading telecommunications operator in the Middle East. In J. vom Brocke & J. Mendling (Eds.), *Business process management cases: Digital innovation and business transformation in practice*. Cham: Springer.

Davenport, T. (1993). *Process innovation*. Boston, MA: Harvard Business School Press.

Debois, S., Hildebrandt, T., Marquard, M., & Slaats, T. (2017). Hybrid process technologies in the financial sector—The case of BRFkredit. In J. vom Brocke & J. Mendling (Eds.), *Business process management cases: Digital innovation and business transformation in practice*. Cham: Springer.

Deming, W. E. (1986). *Out of the crisis*. MIT-Press.

Duelli, C., Keller, R., Manderscheid, J., Manntz, A., Röglinger, M., & Schmidt, M. (2017). Enabling flexible laboratory processes—Designing the laboratory information system of the future. In J. vom Brocke & J. Mendling (Eds.), *Business process management cases: Digital innovation and business transformation in practice*. Cham: Springer.

Dumas, M., La Rosa, M., Mendling, J., & Reijers, H. (2013). *Fundamentals of business process management*. Berlin: Springer.

Hammer, M. (2010). What is business process management? In J. vom Brocke & M. Rosemann (Eds.), *Handbook on business process management: Introduction, methods and information systems* (Vol. 1, pp. 3–16). Berlin: Springer.

Hammer, M., & Champy, J. (1993). *Reengineering the corporation. A manifesto for business revolution*. New York: Harper Business.

Imai, M. (1986). *Kaizen: Der Schlüssel zum Erfolg der Japaner im Wettbewerb*. Frankfurt/M.

Imgrund, F., Janiesch, C., & Rosenkranz, C. (2017). "Simply modeling"—BPM for everybody—Recommendations from the viral adoption of BPM at 1&1. In J. vom Brocke & J. Mendling (Eds.), *Business process management cases: Digital innovation and business transformation in practice*. Cham: Springer.

Juran, J. M. (1988). *Juran on planning for quality*. New York: Free Press.

Karle, T., & Teichenthaler, K. (2017). Collaborative BPM for business transformations in telecommunications—The case of "3". In J. vom Brocke & J. Mendling (Eds.), *Business process management cases: Digital innovation and business transformation in practice*. Cham: Springer.

Kim, T. T. T., Weiss, E., Ruhsam, C., Czepa, C., Tran, H., & Zdun, U. (2017). Enabling flexibility of business processes using compliance rules. The case of Mobiliar. In J. vom Brocke & J. Mendling (Eds.), *Business process management cases: Digital innovation and business transformation in practice*. Cham: Springer.

Kloppenburg, M., Kettenbohrer, J., Beimborn, D., & Bögle, M. (2017). Leading 20,000+ employees with a process-oriented management system—Insights into process management at Lufthansa Technik Group. In J. vom Brocke & J. Mendling (Eds.), *Business process management cases: Digital innovation and business transformation in practice*. Cham: Springer.

Kovačič, A., Hauc, G., Buh, B., & Štemberger, M. I. (2017). BPM adoption and business transformation at Snaga, a public company—Critical success factors for five stages of BPM. In J. vom Brocke & J. Mendling (Eds.), *Business process management cases: Digital innovation and business transformation in practice*. Cham: Springer.

Krogstie, J., Heggset, M., & Wesenberg, H. (2017). Business process modeling of a quality system in a Petroleum Industry Company. In J. vom Brocke & J. Mendling (Eds.), *Business process management cases: Digital innovation and business transformation in practice*. Cham: Springer.

Leitz, R., Solti, A., Weinhard, A., & Mendling, J. (2017). Adoption of RFID technology—The case of Adler. A European Fashion Retail Company. In J. vom Brocke & J. Mendling (Eds.), *Business process management cases: Digital innovation and business transformation in practice*. Cham: Springer.

Marengo, E., Dallasega, P., Montali, M., Nutt, W., & Reifer, M. (2017). Process management in construction expansion of the Bolzano Hospital. In J. vom Brocke & J. Mendling (Eds.), *Business process management cases: Digital innovation and business transformation in practice*. Cham: Springer.

Matzner, M., Plenter, F., Betzing, J. H., Chasin, F., von Hoffen, M., Löchte, M., Pritzl, S., & Becker, J. (2017). CrowdStrom—Analysis, design, and implementation of processes for a peer-to-peer service for electric vehicle charging. In J. vom Brocke & J. Mendling (Eds.), *Business process management cases: Digital innovation and business transformation in practice*. Cham: Springer.

Müller, O., Schmiedel, T., Gorbacheva, E., & vom Brocke, J. (2014). Toward a typology of business process management professionals: Identifying patterns of competences through latent semantic analysis. *Enterprise Information Systems, 10*(1), 50–80.

Rau, I., Rabener, I., Neumann, J., & Bloching, S. (2017). Managing environmental protection processes via BPM at Deutsche Bahn. In J. vom Brocke & J. Mendling (Eds.), *Business process management cases: Digital innovation and business transformation in practice*. Cham: Springer.

Recker, J., & Mendling, J. (2016). The state of the art of business process management research as published in the BPM conference – Recommendations for progressing the field. *Business and Information Systems Engineering, 58*(1), 55–72.

Reisert, C., Zelt, S., & Wacker, J. (2017). How to move from paper to impact in business process management. The journey of SAP. In J. vom Brocke & J. Mendling (Eds.), *Business process management cases: Digital innovation and business transformation in practice*. Cham: Springer.

Rosemann, M. (2015). Preface. In J. vom Brocke & T. Schmiedel (Eds.), *BPM – Driving innovation in a digital world*. Heidelberg: Springer.

Rosemann, M. (2017). The NESTT—Rapid process redesign at Queensland University of technology. In J. vom Brocke & J. Mendling (Eds.), *Business process management cases: Digital innovation and business transformation in practice*. Cham: Springer.

Rosemann, M., & vom Brocke, J. (2015). Six core elements of business process management. In J. vom Brocke & M. Rosemann (Eds.), *Handbook on business process management: Introduction, methods, and information systems (International handbooks on information systems)* (Vol. 1, 2nd ed., pp. 105–122). Berlin: Springer.

Russack, T., & Menges, S. (2017). Supporting process implementation with the help of tangible process models. In J. vom Brocke & J. Mendling (Eds.), *Business process management cases: Digital innovation and business transformation in practice*. Cham: Springer.

Schindlbeck, B., & Kleinschmidt, P. (2017). Integrate your partners into your business processes using interactive forms—The case of Automotive Industry Company HEYCO. In J. vom Brocke & J. Mendling (Eds.), *Business process management cases: Digital innovation and business transformation in practice*. Cham: Springer.

Schmiedel, T., vom Brocke, J., & Recker, J. (2015). Culture in business process management: How cultural values determine BPM success. In J. vom Brocke & M. Rosemann (Eds.), *Handbook on business process management: Strategic alignment, governance, people and culture (International handbooks on information systems)* (Vol. 2, 2nd ed., pp. 649–663). Berlin: Springer.

Schrepfer, M., Kunze, M., Obst, G., & Siegeris, J. (2017). Why are process variants important in process monitoring? The case of Zalando SE. In J. vom Brocke & J. Mendling (Eds.), *Business process management cases: Digital innovation and business transformation in practice*. Cham: Springer.

Srinivasan, M., Wilkes, M., Stevenson, F., Nguyen, T., & Slavin, S. (2007). Comparing problem-based learning with case-based learning: Effects of a major curricular shift at two institutions. *Academic Medicine, 82*(1), 74–82.

Suchy, J., Suchy, M., Rosik, M., & Valkova, A. (2017). Automate does not always mean optimize. Case study at a logistics company. In J. vom Brocke & J. Mendling (Eds.), *Business process management cases: Digital innovation and business transformation in practice*. Cham: Springer.

Taylor, F. W. (1911). *The principles of scientific management*. New York: Harper & Brothers.

Thaler, T., Norek, S., De Angelis, V., Maurer, D., Fettke, P., & Loos, P. (2017). Mining the usability of process-oriented business software—The case of the ARIS designer of Software AG. In J. vom Brocke & J. Mendling (Eds.), *Business process management cases: Digital innovation and business transformation in practice*. Cham: Springer.

United Nations Statistics Division. (2008). *International Standard Industrial Classification of All Economic Activities (ISIC)*, Rev. 4.

Van Looy, A., & Rotthier, S. (2017). Kiss the documents! How the City of Ghent digitizes its service processes. In J. vom Brocke & J. Mendling (Eds.), *Business process management cases: Digital innovation and business transformation in practice*. Cham: Springer.

Vanwersch, R. J. B., Shahzad, K., Vanderfeesten, I. T. P., Vanhaecht, K., Grefen, P. W. P. J., Pintelon, L., Mendling, J., Merode, G. G. v., & Reijers, H. A. (2016). A critical evaluation and framework of business process improvement methods. *Business and Information Systems Engineering, 58*(1), 43–53.

Viaene, S., & Van den Bergh, J. (2017). Fast fish eat slow fish: Business transformation at autogrill. In J. vom Brocke & J. Mendling (Eds.), *Business process management cases: Digital innovation and business transformation in practice*. Cham: Springer.

vom Brocke, J. (2017). *Where to study business process management? A global perspective based on EDUglopedia.org*. Notes. BPTrends (1–11), 2017.

vom Brocke J, Rosemann M (2014) Business process management. In: Wiley encyclopedia of management, vol 7. Management information systems. doi:10.1002/9781118785317.weom070213

vom Brocke, J., & Rosemann, M. (Eds.). (2015). *Handbook on business process management (International handbooks on information systems)* (Vol. 1 and 2, 2nd ed.). Berlin: Springer.

vom Brocke, J., & Schmiedel, T. (Eds.). (2015). *BPM – Driving innovation in a digital world*. Berlin: Springer.

vom Brocke, J., Schmiedel, T., Recker, J., Trkman, P., Mertens, W., & Viaene, S. (2014). Ten principles of good business process management. *Business Process Management Journal (BPMJ), 20*(4), 530–548.

vom Brocke, J., Seidel, S., & Tumbas, S. (2015a, April). The BPM curriculum revisited. *BPTrends, Class Notes*, 1–7.

vom Brocke, J., Zelt, S., & Schmiedel, T. (2015b, November). Considering context in business process management: The BPM context framework. *BPTrends, Class Notes*, 1–12.

vom Brocke, J., Zelt, S., & Schmiedel, T. (2016). On the role of context in business process management. *International Journal of Information Management, 36*(3), 486–495.

Woliński, B., & Bala, S. (2017). Comprehensive business process management at Siemens. Implementing business process excellence. In J. vom Brocke & J. Mendling (Eds.), *Business process management cases: Digital innovation and business transformation in practice*. Cham: Springer.

Womack, J. P., & Jones, D. T. (2003). *Lean thinking: Banish waste and create wealth in your corporation*. New York: Free Press.

Jan vom Brocke is head of the BPM group in Liechtenstein. He is Professor of Information Systems, the Hilti Endowed Chair of Business Process Management, Director of the Institute of Information Systems, Director of the Ph.D. Program in Information and Process Management, and Vice President Research and Innovation at the University of Liechtenstein. Jan has conducted over 300 studies in the area of IT and BPM, published in renowned outlets, including MIT Sloan Management Review, MIS Quarterly (MISQ), Journal of Management Information Systems (JMIS), European Journal of Information Systems (EJIS), Information Systems Journal (ISJ), and Business Process Management Journal (BPMJ). He has authored and edited over 30 books, including the International Handbook on Business Process Management, BPM: Driving Innovation in a Digital World and Green BPM: Towards the Sustainable Enterprise. Jan is an invited speaker and trusted advisor on BPM serving many organizations around the world.

Jan Mendling is a Full Professor with the Institute for Information Business at Wirtschaftsuniversität Wien (WU Vienna), Austria. His research areas include Business Process Management, Conceptual Modelling and Enterprise Systems. He has published more than 300 research papers and articles, among others in ACM Transactions on Software Engineering and Methodology, IEEE Transaction on Software Engineering, Information Systems, Data and Knowledge Engineering, and Decision Support Systems. He is member of the editorial board of seven international journals, board member of the Austrian society for process management (http://www.prozesse.at), one of the founders of the Berlin BPM Community of Practice (http://www.bpmb.de), organizer of several academic events on process management, and member of the IEEE Task Force on Process Mining. His Ph.D. thesis has won the Heinz-Zemanek-Award of the Austrian Computer Society and the German Targion-Award for dissertations in the area of strategic information management.

Part I

Strategy and Governance

How to Move from Paper to Impact in Business Process Management: The Journey of SAP

Corinne Reisert, Sarah Zelt, and Joerg Wacker

Abstract

(a) **Situation faced**: In order to produce innovative solutions faster and more simply, SAP started in 2008 to transform its research and development processes. SAP moved away from complex and static project methods toward agile and simple processes, thereby significantly reducing the throughput time of the standard innovation cycle. Based on the experience of this transformation and optimization, the first at that time in a global company of knowledge workers, SAP decided to increase the emphasis on Business Process Management (BPM). Therefore, BPM initiatives were implemented on a company-wide level in the effort to establish a process infrastructure and a process improvement culture.

(b) **Action taken**: The Productivity Consulting Group (PCG) was founded with the mission of strengthening the importance of BPM throughout the company. The SAP Process Map was established to create transparency in SAP's key processes, roles, and responsibilities. The SAP Process Maturity Model was created with the aim of constantly increasing the maturity of SAP's processes. An approach to performance measurement and process improvement and a portfolio of BPM-related services were introduced to support Process Managers on their way to reaching process excellence. In addition, activities were introduced to strengthen the BPM community, the foundation for BPM at SAP.

(c) **Results achieved**: Implementing BPM at SAP was an important step toward overcoming the complexities that plague our businesses, a step that was important to both SAP and its customers. Following the operating principle "Run Simple," SAP developed a process-management

C. Reisert (✉) • S. Zelt • J. Wacker
SAP SE, Walldorf, Germany
e-mail: corinne.reisert@sap.com; sarah.zelt@sap.com; joerg.wacker@sap.com

J. vom Brocke, J. Mendling (eds.), *Business Process Management Cases*,
Management for Professionals, DOI 10.1007/978-3-319-58307-5_2

infrastructure throughout the company that led to transparency in SAP's key processes and measurable process improvements.

(d) **Lessons learned**: The key success factor in SAP's journey from BPM concepts and ideas to measurable impact—that is, from paper to impact—was the strategic alignment of BPM with top management support. Strong governance with the SAP Process Map, the SAP Process Maturity Model, and BPM standards enabled the company to strive toward process excellence.

However, a lively and engaged BPM community was as important as having the right methods or tools at hand. Implementing BPM from a top-down perspective helped to some extent, but building an understanding of BPM and its value from the bottom-up using a variety of mechanisms (introduced in this article) was also required.

1 Introduction

As the market leader in enterprise application software, SAP is at the center of today's business and technology revolution. SAP has a 44 year history of innovation and growth as a true industry leader, has an annual revenue (IFRS) of 20.793 billion euros, and employs more than 77,000 employees in more than 130 countries (SAP Global Corporate Affairs 2016). SAP's innovations enable more than 300,000 customers in 190 countries to work together more efficiently and use business insights more effectively. SAP's intention is to help organizations of all sizes and in all industries overcome the complexities that plague our businesses, our jobs and our lives (SAP SE 2016).

"Run Simple—If we simplify everything, we can do anything" is not only the SAP's key external message but also its operating principle. Simplifying processes is also a key request from SAP's employees. The employee survey (the "people survey") contains a set of questions to measure employees' satisfaction with processes and to collect feedback on specific process improvements. The Chief Operating Officer (COO) is responsible for the company's process office, and the COOs of each of SAP's business units, who form the company's virtual COO network, agree on the joint execution of the SAP strategy and a common portfolio of process improvements.

In order to produce innovative solutions faster and more simply, in 2008 SAP started an initiative to transform its research and development processes to move away from complex and static project methods toward agile and simple processes. As the transformation significantly reduced the standard innovation cycle's throughput time, SAP decided to build on this success and founded the Productivity Consulting Group (PCG), which acts as process office with direct oversight of SAP corporate functions in all regions throughout the globe.

During the past couple of years, BPM's role was strengthened through a variety of BPM initiatives, including the development of the SAP Process Map, the SAP

Process Maturity Model, approaches to measuring process performance and process improvements, and a portfolio of BPM-related services. This chapter summarizes SAP's BPM journey from paper to impact and presents a case that shows how BPM can be set up in organizations. As such, this chapter focuses primarily on the governance capability area of BPM's six core elements (Rosemann and vom Brocke 2015). A variety of initiatives is required for the successful implementation of BPM (which will be explained in the course of this paper) that relate to the phases of the BPM Lifecycle (Dumas et al. 2013). After a description of the situation that SAP faced (Sect. 2), Sect. 3 introduces all BPM-related actions that have been undertaken, ranging from strong governance to establishing a lively BPM community. The results achieved are discussed in Sect. 4, and the lessons learned are summarized in Sect. 5.

2 Situation Faced

SAP started to improve processes systematically in 2008. At that point, SAP's core software development process was a waterfall process that was implemented in the late 1990s. The waterfall process introduced customer validation, quality gates, and compliance with standards, thus ensuring that the products being shipped were compliant with an ever-growing set of formal and quality requirements. However, the process was built on a globally distributed functional setup based on a division of labor, which created long decision times, long development cycle times, and developers who identified poorly with the whole process. Customers complained about limited usability and medium levels of quality, which resulted in a low adoption. Unhappy customers and an inefficient work environment also influenced SAP's numbers. While single departments had always had approaches with which to optimize processes, there was no central team or organizational setup that was responsible for managing processes comprehensively. Therefore, this situation had to be changed in favor of an approach that increased efficiency (reduced time, resources, and costs) and the quality of products and solutions (ease of consumption and superior user experience).

SAP decided to strive for efficiency and effectiveness in its entire product development process by implementing a development model that follows lean principles (Lean Development Model) and is based on agile practices. Scrum, an iterative and incremental software-development framework, was introduced at the team level. Teams were built to cover cross-functional requirements to define, build, and deliver products and functions in short cycles of 2–4 weeks. Each cycle ends with a review and team retrospective. Issues and obstacles identified in the retrospective were integrated into a continuous-improvement process. This effort resulted in constant improvement of throughput time, on-time delivery, productive capacity, product adoption, number of deliveries, sustainable pace, and workload, and is now building a solid foundation for an even more innovative delivery process for cloud products.

Based on the success of this transformation and optimization, management decided to extend the approach to all of the company's business units. Employees had expressed their dissatisfaction with complicated internal processes via the yearly "people survey" at the same time that the need for standardization (e.g., triggered by implementing Shared Service Centers) increased. Therefore, SAP's intention was to build on the experiences from the research and development transformation to widen the scope to the organization as a whole. This effort required a central organization with strong governance and a process improvement culture that could drive Lean thinking, operational excellence, and BPM initiatives.

3 Action Taken

After the decision was made to enhance the success of the recent transformation in research and development, the PCG was founded as a process office with direct oversight over SAP's corporate functions throughout all regions. The PCG is responsible for establishing a process infrastructure in the company, including process governance, idea management, and improvement services. The PCG is located in the area of SAP's COO, which facilitates a direct connection between the PCG's portfolio and the corporate strategy. By grouping PCG with an organizational unit called Business Insight and Technology, the company ensures a close relationship with IT projects and innovations.

In contributing to SAP's strategy, the PCG increases the organization's efficiency and effectiveness by implementing governing processes and standards, the Lean methodology, and continuous improvement and by providing transparency for sound decision-making. The components of BPM at SAP follow many phases of the BPM Lifecycle (i.e., process identification, discovery, analysis, redesign, implementation, monitoring and controlling) (Dumas et al. 2013) and include the SAP Process Map, the BPM community, continuous process improvement, the SAP Process Maturity Model, performance measurement, and improvement and productivity services and strategic projects.

3.1 SAP Process Map

A process map typically results from the process-identification phase of the BPM Lifecycle (Dumas et al. 2013). SAP's processes are reflected in the SAP Process Map (shown in Fig. 1), which serves as the primary top-down process perspective and is the single source of internal process information. The SAP Process Map is closely linked to the corporate strategy and is the basis for audits and external certification and the starting point for business-driven process management and improvement projects. It is accessible to all SAP employees via the intranet (corporate portal). According to established process-classification frameworks (Dumas et al. 2013), the processes are structured as *management processes*, which are used to plan, diagnose, and manage core and support processes; *core processes*, which create direct value for SAP's customers' and *support processes*, which provide the necessary resources and infrastructure for core processes.

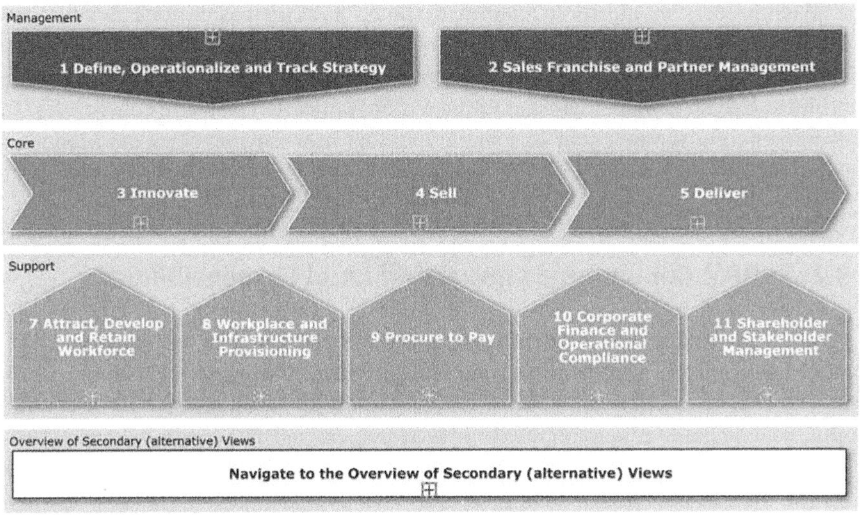

Fig. 1 SAP process map

The SAP Process Map is a hierarchical composition that consists of multiple high-level processes and corresponding sub-processes (Dumas et al. 2013). Processes on the highest level, called Level 1 processes, are directly visible on the Process Map. Level 2 processes break the Level 1 processes into more detail, while Level 3 process documentations describe the process flow, the responsibilities, and input and output documents.

Establishing strong governance mechanisms ensures that there are clear rules for including processes in the SAP Process Map, for consistent naming, and for modelling. A process can be included as a Level 3 process only if it if it has process costs of 1 million euros or if it impacts 1 million euros in revenue, and/or it follows certain compliance standards (e.g., SOX compliance), and/or it directly supports a core process.

Processes on Level 3 are named according to certain rules, which follow established guidelines (e.g., Dumas et al. 2013; Mendling et al. 2010).

- Use the pattern < Imperative Verb + Noun in Singular > unless there is a common name or business terminology (e.g., from ITIL or ISO standards).
- Avoid abbreviations.
- Names should reflect generally accepted common usage and be short and concise.
- Names should reflect the company's terminology.
- Verbs like manage, perform, coordinate, and execute should have concrete definitions that are used consistently.

Each process should serve a purpose, should have a measure for efficiency, and should continuously be improved. The focus of process documentation is to deliver valuable information for the people who execute the process and to be the basis for business-driven management and improvement projects. To ensure consistency, the documentation should occur in a single tool that uses Business Process Model and Notation 2.0.

3.2 BPM Community: Central and Local Responsibilities

People and culture are core elements of BPM (Rosemann and vom Brocke 2015). PCG manages the SAP Process Map and provides SAP-wide BPM standards on how to design, measure, and improve processes. It also manages the BPM community, which entails educating the Process Managers on BPM methodology. Process Managers are responsible for defining, operating, and improving processes, so they pursue the business goals, strategies, and objectives defined by Business Owners. As shown in Fig. 2, the responsibility for a process's design, documentation, and improvement lies with the business unit that is responsible for the process's

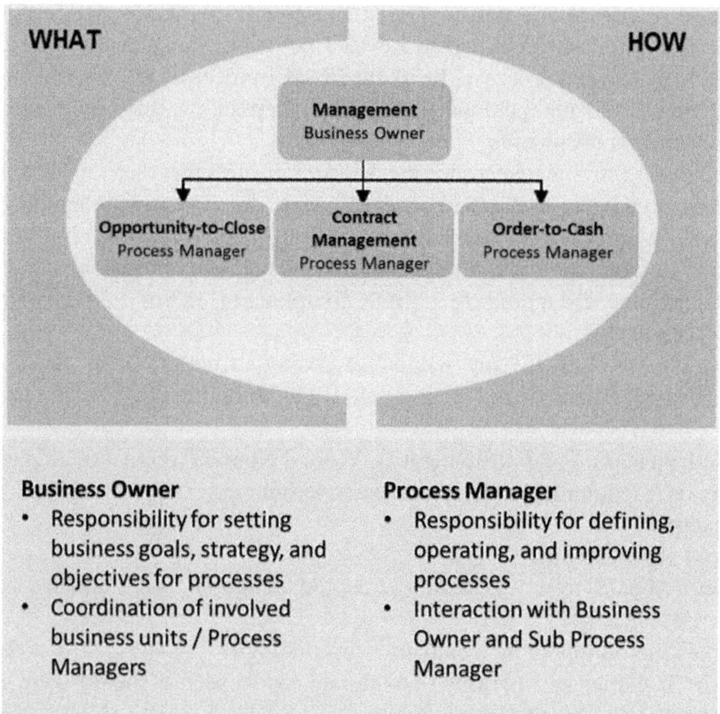

Fig. 2 Main responsibilities of Business Owner and Process Manager

business outcome. Therefore, the Business Owner and the Process Manager for each process are based in the respective business unit, not in the central PCG.

A key element for successful BPM is a vibrant BPM community (Fig. 3). Since this community is not necessarily defined by organizational structures, creating its own identity is important. The PCG supports a series of communication and enablement activities in order to establish a solid relationship with the BPM community based on the aligned collaboration model between Process Managers, the COOs of the various business units, and the PCG. These activities include:

- **SAP Process Excellence Newsletter**: Bi-monthly issues that contain training offers, information on upcoming events and success stories on process improvement

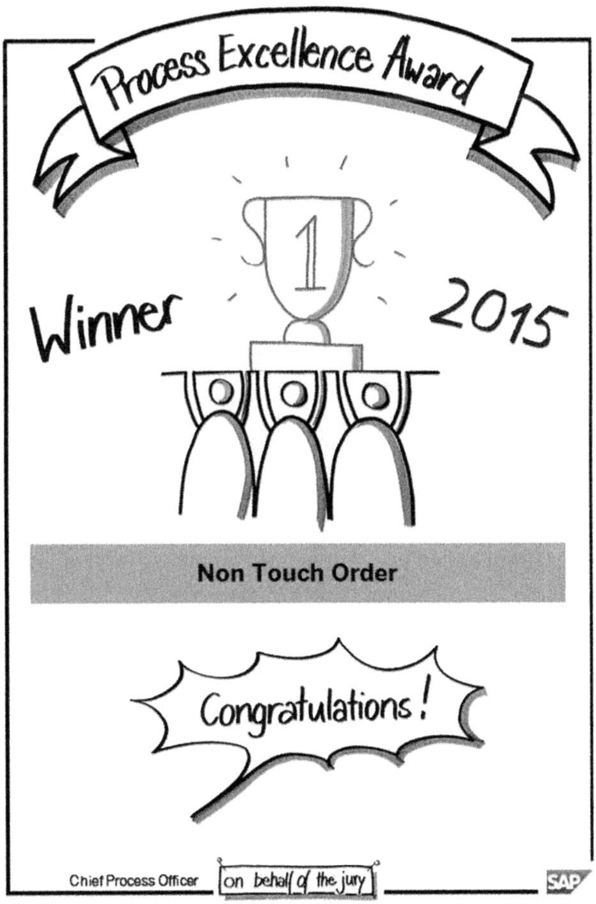

Fig. 3 Process excellence award 2015

- **Process Manager Information Sessions**: Bi-monthly sessions for Process Managers to share best practices and roll out information about BPM standards
- **Process Management Training**: Classroom and virtual training sessions on the BPM methodology, tools, and best practices (from Process Managers for Process Managers)
- **SAP Process Summit**: Annual event where all Process Managers come together to exchange best practices, get inspiration from external speakers, and learn about new topics related to BPM
- **SAP Process Excellence Award**: Increases the visibility of excellent processes and provides a platform for employees who are working on process improvement by rewarding outstanding processes that accomplish measurable process improvements and have a positive impact on the company.

3.3 Continuous Process Improvement

The primary target of BPM at SAP is to improve processes continuously. Process improvements can result from following the phases of the BPM Lifecycle (Dumas et al. 2013) or can be triggered by strategic initiatives. Although the triggers for actual process improvement can be numerous, the process activities involved in improving a process is standardized and, as such, is documented in the SAP Process Map.

The Process Manager is responsible for defining the process improvement goal (with approval from the Business Owner), which is typically derived from the SAP strategy (improvement portfolio, strategic objectives), from a current issue in the process (impediment, audit finding), or from an idea from the SAP idea management initiative. Process Managers define process improvements by reusing existing process definitions, thus following an evolutionary re-design approach (Dumas et al. 2013). They state the benefits of an improvement initiative for the business, as well as the improvement's impact on the process itself and on the process performers. The actual activities involved can be numerous and diverse, depending on the process and the character of the improvement. For example, improvements can:

- Result from following the phases of the BPM Lifecycle (Dumas et al. 2013): process discovery, analysis, redesign, implementation, monitoring and control
- Be strategic projects/programs/initiatives
- Be initiated through process improvement services provided by PCG
- Be part of continuous improvement (e.g., by establishing a regular feedback cycle/group)

The effect of the process's changes are measured according to Process Performance Indicators (PPIs), which include throughput time, customer satisfaction, and cost per unit output. These PPIs are measured by the Process Manager and compared with previously defined success criteria.

3.4 SAP Process Maturity Model

As another aspect of BPM governance (Rosemann and vom Brocke 2015), SAP uses its own process maturity model that has been tailored to the company's needs and business model. It follows the idea of generic maturity models [e.g., Capability Maturity Model Integration (CMMI) (CMMI Product Team 2002)], which is to offer a consistent, well-defined methodology to measure a process's maturity in a comparable way (SAP Process Governance Team and Konhaeuser 2015). The SAP Process Maturity Model distinguishes four maturity levels, from Level 0 (the lowest) to Level 3. Processes on Level 0 are neither transparent nor managed, while a set of predefined criteria define each of the higher maturity levels:

- **Maturity Level 0**: The process is neither transparent nor managed.
- **Maturity Level 1**: The process is transparent.
  - Basic process documentation (included in the SAP Process Map) is available.
  - An accountable Process Manager and Business Owner are named.
  - The degree of process standardization is transparent [e.g., is this process a global process applicable to all of SAP's local Market Unit or are there local variants (e.g., to reflect local legal regulations)?]
  - Knowledge transfer through such efforts as internal training and process handbooks is available to ensure that process participants have the required knowledge to execute the process.
- **Maturity Level 2**: The process is managed.
  - Process operation, input and output is measured, monitored, and transparent to decision-makers.
  - PPIs are regularly monitored using SAP standard software.
  - "Customers" of the process are named—for example, a Manager who is looking for a new hire is the customer of the HR recruitment process—and their top three requirements are defined.
  - Detailed process documentation is available (included/linked in the SAP Process Map).
  - Process variants are documented.
  - Risk assessment is performed.
- **Maturity Level 3**: The process is on a high level of optimization and is continuously improved.
  - The process vision is defined.
  - Annual improvement targets are defined.
  - Service level agreements are established.
  - SAP standard systems are applied to support the process's execution.
  - Online real-time process data is available for processes that are supported by SAP tools.

- Accountability for the process output is ensured.
- A continuous improvement process is established.
- Process standardization is higher than 80%.

Since SAP strives for process excellence through continuous increases in its processes' maturity, the processes' maturity is monitored centrally.

3.5 Performance Measurement

Process monitoring and controlling are critical phases of the BPM Lifecycle (Dumas et al. 2013), so a central element of maturity Level 2 is the measurement of process performance. The importance of performance measurement is based on the assumption that one can only manage what one can measure. The inability to measure basic PPIs like the number of process instances or a process's throughput time, working time, or costs per output makes it difficult to judge a process's quality, not to mention the effect of changing a process.

Setting up performance measurement for a process requires significant effort and thorough discussion beforehand. What are the right indicators? How and how often should they be measured? What is a reasonable sample size (if continuous measurement is impracticable)? SAP introduced six basic PPIs have been introduced at SAP to simplify process measurement, all of which refer to processes' input, operations, and output:

- Input
  - Number of requests per year (how many instances of the process occur per year?)
  - Number of people involved (how many employees are required to execute the process?
- Operations
  - Throughput time (How much time does it take to complete one instance of the process?)
  - Working time (how much working time is required to complete one instance of the process?)
- Output
  - Cost per output
  - Customer satisfaction

This basic set of PPIs is often the starting point and can be extended through area-specific PPIs that cover more business-specific needs that depend on such factors as the process's purpose and nature and organizational and environmental factors (vom Brocke et al. 2016).These business-specific needs serve as a fact-based instrument that support Process Managers in discussions with stakeholders, such as higher-level managers or process customers.

3.6 Improvement and Productivity Services and Strategic Projects

In addition to the BPM initiatives introduced above, the PCG offers a portfolio of well-structured, innovative services that can support BPM experts in their efforts to improve processes. These services contain classic process-improvement support services and services that increase the efficiency and effectiveness of individual roles and business units. The services of PCG are clustered along primary improvement dimensions and levels of intensity, as depicted in Fig. 4.

The standardization of the PCG services facilitates means that a PCG employee can use the service description to prepare for their first service delivery with an experienced colleague and later deliver the service on their own. The standardization of services also supports the measurement of results and simplifies collaboration with internal customers. Project results are assessed jointly and measured with respect to their value and customer satisfaction. Collaboration between the PCG and internal customers is voluntary, driven by the internal customer's need for support in improving a process or analyzing a problem. The standardization of the services, the customer's equal representation in the project team, and the measurement of the results help to prevent misuse of the services the PCG offers.

The PCG services focus on analyzing an organizational unit's process and understanding its business roles. In order to get a complete picture of the "life" of a business unit, one must understand the people who work on the processes. An organizational unit needs to ensure that employees are qualified for their roles so they can do their jobs. Taking into account the employees' backgrounds, education, and day-to-day work reality is part of designing excellent processes. Typically, employees want to do their jobs and focus on their key tasks, but badly designed

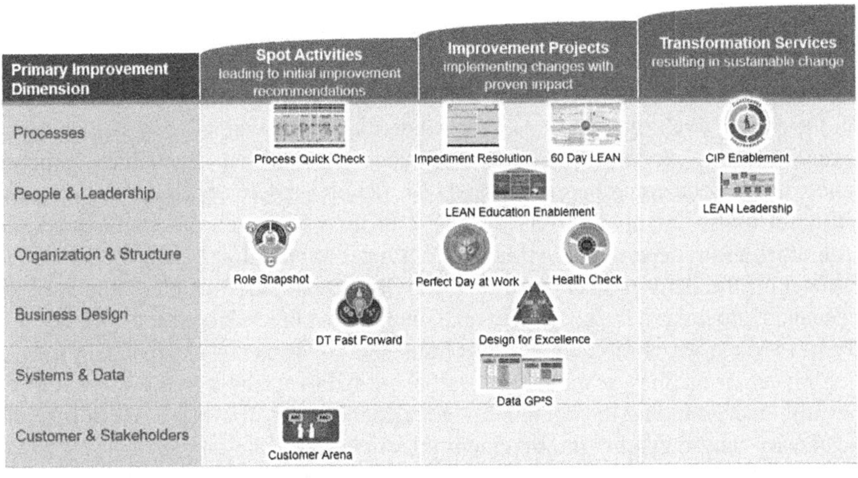

Fig. 4 PCG service catalog

processes, lack of education, and misassumptions hinder them from doing so. To change this situation, the PCG designed two services that focus on the roles that are involved in process execution: the role snapshot and the perfect day at work.

- **Role Snapshot**: This service contains an easy and intuitive Lean approach to analyzing a role. It identifies opportunities to increase a process role's efficiency, which contributes to improved productivity during the employee's workday and improves his or her work/life balance. The Role Snapshot service provides an initial assessment and concrete recommendations for improvement but does not develop or implement these improvements.
- **Perfect Day at Work**: The role-based service, "Perfect Day at Work," offers a comprehensive analysis to determine whether employees have the skills they need to do their job. The analysis provides a 360° view of all of the major aspects of a perfect day at work. Concrete recommendations are worked out and then implemented and measured during the project.

4 Results Achieved

The unique combination of strategic initiatives based on the corporate strategy, standardized service delivery, and sound process infrastructure enabled the PCG to simplify internal processes and raise overall productivity. Success for SAP's BPM activities is defined as creating measurable and sustainable positive impact by which it contributes significantly to the corporate strategy.

With the implementation of the SAP Process Map and easy-to-use tools for process documentation, process modeling has become an important part of Process Managers' jobs. Currently, 626 employees have an editor user for process modeling, and more than 1200 employees are enrolled in internal training that helps them to design and leverage processes at SAP. Today, 92% of all Level 3 processes are documented and published in the SAP Process Map, and 1023 processes on Level 3 and below are documented.

A documented process as part of the SAP Process Map helps Process Managers in their daily work by enabling quick onboarding of new employees and ensuring execution of a process independent of who undertakes it. It enables common understanding on common executions, so it facilitates delivery of the same results with consistent quality. As one of SAP's Process Managers in the Finance and Administration department explained, "[Process modelling] actually made an impact on the daily project work of the GCMS Team, as it changed the way we visualize processes. It accelerated and improved our collaboration...." As this Process Manager made clear, Process Managers' opinion has changed from viewing process modelling as an administrative burden to seeing it as a critical activity in fully understanding the complexity and dependencies of processes as a first and necessary step in process improvement initiatives.

The SAP Process Map is important to the daily work of individual Process Managers, but it also creates transparency in SAP's key processes, roles, and responsibilities for the whole organization. All SAP employees have access to the SAP Process Map and can view all published processes, which helps them to understand the "big picture" of which their work is part, their work's interfaces to other processes, and the people they can contact if they have questions or plan improvement projects. The SAP Process Map also serves as a reference structure for a broad variety of IT projects, the enterprise architecture, idea management, business continuity, and the data privacy and protection office.

As an example, several IT implementation projects at SAP have used the SAP Process Map to structure their projects along end-to-end processes. This approach helped project managers to define the exact scope of their projects (i.e., the processes that are included or excluded) and to divide their projects into several work streams. The SAP Process Map has been a meaningful reference structure for discussions, as it ensures that Process Managers who are responsible for process execution are involved in the project. In addition, the SAP Process Map enables project managers to identify and consider dependencies on other processes or business areas, thereby linking the project more closely to the day-to-day operation. It also helped project managers to derive IT requirements and to monitor project deliverables with a clear reference to critical processes.

Another example of SAP's use of the Process Map is the company-wide idea management, which is also structured along the SAP Process Map. SAP employees can submit their improvement ideas via a tool that links the ideas to processes and the responsible Process Manager. Using the SAP Process Map as reference structure for idea management ensures clear responsibilities and fast examination and implementation of ideas.

In addition to the SAP Process Map, strong governance and BPM standards for process maturity, measurement, and improvement support Process Managers in their efforts to achieve process excellence. As a result, since the performance indicators were established, the feedback from Process Managers has been overwhelmingly positive, as they finally they have a fact-based instrument that supports them in discussions with management and process customers and that helps them to measure business performance.

While the immediate value of a Process Map and strong process governance is difficult to measure, the impact of process improvement projects is not. Based on a sample of 100 projects per year, SAP currently achieves a typical result of 20:1 payback and a customer satisfaction that exceeds 75%. In addition, many processes' processing time has been reduced significantly, including a process in marketing services team that eliminated eleven process steps and reduced processing time by up to 74%.

Another example of process improvement is a recent project undertaken with Global Facility Management to simplify and increase the efficiency of SAP's internal food-counter processes. (This improvement project shows the wide range of fields to which BPM activities can be applied.) The project resulted in significant shortening of the waiting time for lunch and gave the PCG a chance to demonstrate to Global Facility Management the value of process management with tangible results.

5 Lessons Learned

The implementation of BPM in SAP has moved a long way from the concepts and ideas of BPM to measurable impact—in short, from paper to impact. BPM initiatives have moved from being an administrative burden to creating a real impact, the company's perceptions of BPM experts has improved significantly, and there is a high demand for the improvement services offered by the PCG. While BPM activities had been perceived as push activities that were driven centrally, they are now seen more as pull activities, where employees request services or strive toward process improvement. Moving from paper to impact in BPM could only be realized with the help of four primary success factors.

First, as is the case with most organizational activities, strategic alignment and top management support are important determinants of successful BPM implementation. Therefore, creating a central team that was responsible for the process management infrastructure, process governance, and improvement services and that collaborates with the various organizational units took precedence. The organizational set-up of this central team as part of the COO function plays an important role in ensuring a direct connection between the PCG's portfolio and the corporate strategy. The close collaboration with the COOs of SAP's business units helped to align the process-management effort with activities in the lines of businesses to create measurable benefit and promote process management across the company.

Second, establishing strong governance was important. One important driver was setting up the SAP Process Map as the central repository of process documentation, which created transparency in organizational activities, roles, and responsibilities. It was also important to set standards for how to document, measure, and improve processes. The SAP Process Map also serves as a central infrastructure for areas like risk management and data protection, which increases its usefulness. The implementation of the SAP Maturity Model supports the goal of process improvement and increasing process orientation in the company.

Third, the implementation of the PCG service catalog ensured the delivery of standardized process improvements. With the help of these services, it was possible for internal customers to focus on and resolve dedicated process issues and to understand the services' expected deliverables, scope, and duration. The process-improvement projects followed standardized service descriptions, and delivery was more efficient than it was in comparable projects. Each service delivery also included a concrete measurement of the benefit achieved, which helped to prove the value of the project and demonstrated the benefit of the process-management effort.

Fourth, experience has shown that a top-down goal to increase process maturity can motivate Process Managers only to a certain extent. In order to achieve a sustainable increase in process maturity, the added value of a managed process has to be communicated. To promote investment in increasing process maturity, Process Managers regularly share their experiences in information sessions and the yearly SAP Process Summit.

A strong BPM community and a culture that supports BPM initiatives, where every single employee contributes to process improvement, are essential. SAP established the Process Excellence Award, process management events, and other activities that contribute to the creation of a process management culture and a deeper understanding of the value of BPM.

References

CMMI Product Team. (2002). *Capability maturity model® integration (CMMI), Version 1.1 – continuous representation.*

Dumas, M., La Rosa, M., Mendling, J., & Reijers, H. (2013). *Fundamentals of business process management.* Berlin: Springer.

Mendling, J., Reijers, H. A., & van der Aalst, W. M. (2010). Seven process modeling guidelines (7PMG). *Information and Software Technology, 52*(2), 127–136.

Rosemann, M., & vom Brocke, J. (2015). Six core elements of business process management. In J. vom Brocke & M. Rosemann (Eds.), *Handbook on business process management: Introduction, methods, and information systems* (Vol. 1, 2nd ed., pp. 105–122). Berlin: Springer.

SAP Global Corporate Affairs. (2016). *SAP corporate fact sheet.* Retrieved April 13, from http://www.sap.com/bin/sapcom/en_us/downloadasset.2015-04apr21-01.SAP-Corporate-Fact-Sheet-en-20150421-pdf.bypassReg.html

SAP Process Governance Team, & Konhaeuser, M. (2015, April). *SAP process excellence handbook.*

SAP SE. (2016). *Company information.* Retrieved April 13, from http://go.sap.com/corporate/en/company.html

vom Brocke, J., Zelt, S., & Schmiedel, T. (2016). On the role of context in business process management. *International Journal of Information Management, 36*(3), 486–495.

Corinne Reisert currently serves as Head of Process Governance. In this role she drives the company wide Process management and process improvement efforts enabling the digital transformation of the company. She is responsible for defining SAP's process management standards on how to design, measure and improve processes. She started working at SAP in 1998 and held several positions in Solution Management for the Public Sector market, before she joined the SAP Process Office in 2012. She holds a degree in public administration from the University of Applied Sciences Kehl and an Executive MBA from the Mannheim Business School.

Sarah Zelt is senior HR consultant at SAP SE in Walldorf, Germany. From 2011 until 2016, she worked as a process consultant within SAP's Human Resources department consulting process managers on various aspects of process management (e.g. process modelling, process improvement, process measurement). She holds a diploma in Psychology from the University of Mannheim, Germany, and a Ph.D. in business economics from the University of Liechtenstein. Her Ph.D. thesis focused on context-sensitive business process management which requires the consideration of contextual factors in the analysis and management of business processes. In particular, she investigated the role that process characteristics play for business process management.

Joerg Wacker is Chief Consultant at SAP SE Productivity Consulting Group. He has a track record in Software Development, Project and Program Management. In particular, he is an approved Leader for IT Transformation, Agile and LEAN Management Practices, Operational Change Management, BPM and LEAN SixSigma. As Design Thinking Coach he ensures innovative solutions to optimize customer value. He holds a degree in Computer Science and started his career at Siemens AG 1989 before he joined SAP SE in 1993.

Developing and Implementing a Process-Performance Management System: Experiences from S-Y Systems Technologies Europe GmbH—A Global Automotive Supplier

Josef Blasini, Susanne Leist, and Werner Merkl

Abstract

(a) **Situation faced**: S-Y Systems Technologies Europe GmbH develops, manufactures, and distributes worldwide wire harnesses and associated components for automotive electronic distribution systems. Problems occurred with some automotive manufacturers' ordering wire harnesses, who sent ordering files to the intermediate S-Y Systems to be converted, interpreted, enriched, and forwarded. Errors occurred even in the first steps of data processing errors (e.g., name, format, structure, content), but the exact allocation of errors in the process, the reasons for the errors, and their origin were not apparent. Therefore, S-Y Systems faced the challenge of investigating the processing errors, hoping to prove that the reason for most of these errors lay elsewhere.

(b) **Action taken**: S-Y Systems decided to monitor their operative IT processes and started a Process Performance Management (PPM) project. PPM uses performance measurements to improve the performance of processes. Performance planning, monitoring, and controlling actions in PPM are strongly supported by process-oriented key performance indicators (KPIs) and IT systems. Our case describes a PPM approach to developing and implementing PPM systems and the results of applying this approach at S-Y Systems.

(c) **Results achieved**: The findings from the case refer to the importance of a structured, top-down-oriented development procedure and provide concrete

J. Blasini • S. Leist (✉)
University of Regensburg, Regensburg, Germany
e-mail: email@josef-blasini.de; susanne.leist@ur.de

W. Merkl
it-motive BCS GmbH, Business and Consulting Services, Regensburg, Germany
e-mail: werner.merkl@it-motive-bcs.com

J. vom Brocke, J. Mendling (eds.), *Business Process Management Cases*,
Management for Professionals, DOI 10.1007/978-3-319-58307-5_3

indications about the appropriate, goal-oriented, and useful KPIs of the processes to be monitored.

(d) **Lessons learned**: The case reveals a clear risk of PPM projects' losing their focus on the intrinsically relevant processes, the tasks in the processes, and particularly the overall initial goal of the project. Losing focus explains why many projects generate too many or inappropriate KPIs. The PPM approach presented in this paper helps to keep the focus on the overall goal and enables companies to develop a PPM system, including the appropriate KPIs.

1 Introduction

Process performance management (PPM) helps to monitor and manage business processes using process-oriented key performance indicators (KPIs) (Heß 2004; Jeston and Nelis 2008; Heckl and Moormann 2010; Cleven et al. 2010). Even though PPM has long been applied in business practice, companies still struggle with its challenges. The search for process KPIs that are appropriate for their businesses and their underlying processes is particularly challenging. Although several PPM methods and concepts ask for a top-down procedure, most companies try to identify useful, process-oriented KPIs using an unstructured, bottom-up approach.

The challenge of PPM application arises from the fact that there is no one-fits-all PPM solution (Blasini et al. 2011). PPM has to be adapted to each company based on (1) the company's industry, (2) the company's role in its industry (e.g., service integrator, service provider, or intermediate), and particularly (3) the company's underlying processes and services. Moreover, process KPIs have to be implemented in keeping with the company's vision and strategy in order to enable it to monitor performance consistently, right down to the processes. Thus, the characteristics of the individual company strongly influence the application of PPM and the selection of appropriate process KPIs (Blasini and Leist 2013).

This case deals with the development and implementation of a PPM system at a German automotive supplier, S-Y Systems Technologies Europe GmbH (S-Y Systems). Founded in 2001, S-Y Systems was a joint venture between the two major, globally active companies Continental and Yazaki Europe Ltd. In 2013, Yazaki acquired all of S-Y Systems' shares.

At the time of our case study, S-Y Systems had about 280 employees, generated a turnover of 420 million euros, and operated in seven sales and development locations and six logistic centers. S-Y Systems offers integrated solutions to complex problems in the automotive industry's electrical and electronic distribution systems (EEDS) market (S-Y Systems Technologies Europe GmbH 2012). The company identifies and analyzes interdependencies between EEDS to optimize its customers' electric vehicle architecture and develops and produces wire harnesses and associated components for automotive electronic distribution systems. Its portfolio of services also includes marketing and distribution, logistics, production planning, and quality management, while Yazaki takes care of assembling the wire harnesses.

In 2012, S-Y Systems conducted a project in cooperation with the University of Regensburg that sought to control its operative IT processes; as a result, the company implemented the PPM system. The operative IT processes were comprised of IT service management processes such as help desk services according to the Information Technology Infrastructure Library (ITIL), and data transmission processes, especially electronic data interchange (EDI) processes. The development and implementation of a PPM system to monitor EDI processes constituted the project's first challenges.

This case describes the application and results of applying a PPM approach that had been developed and implemented at companies in the energy industry, the manufacturing sector, and the banking industry some years before the project at S-Y Systems began.

After a description of the automotive supplier in Sect. 2, Sect. 3 introduces the approach used to develop and implement PPM systems and describes its application at S-Y Systems. Section 4 provides a brief overview of the project's results, and Sect. 5 summarizes the lessons learned.

2 Situation Faced

Although S-Y Systems is the market leader in the field of EEDS optimization, the company has been strengthening its position in the system business by incorporating mechanical, electrical, and electronic solutions. Innovations in the areas of automotive information and energy management for EEDS systems highlight the company's role as a system integrator. S-Y Systems extended its presence with offices in Spain, France, the UK, Romania, and Turkey.

The company's goal is to maximize customer satisfaction, so it must provide excellent customer service. Small, flexible teams work closely with the customers; analyze their needs, opportunities, and risks; and adapt their concepts to the customers' requirements. Quality is a key factor for the company, and its goal of "zero defects" can be achieved only through advanced planning and the consistent implementation of all necessary measures to be described later on in the paper. To achieve its goal of zero defects, the company continuously improves its products and processes in both R&D and production in order to offer the highest-quality products and services. Hence, measuring process performance by implementing a PPM system was necessary to identify potential areas for optimization.

Since the PPM system focuses on IT operative processes, S-Y Systems' IT department, called Central IT, was responsible for conducting the PPM project. Central IT not only provides IT support for other departments, such as help desk services, but also makes considerable contributions to the company's value chain. As the link between automobile manufacturers' ordering the wire harnesses and Yazaki's assembling them, the IT department is in charge of the order monitoring, that is, sending, converting, and receiving files like orders and invoices. Since these communication processes are highly automated, and only processing errors require manual intervention, the overall process performance depends heavily on the performance of the IT systems and their underlying processes.

The initial situation was that problems had occurred with the orders of some automotive manufacturers that had ordered wire harnesses from Yazaki, so ordering files were sent to the intermediate, S-Y Systems, to be converted, interpreted, enriched, and forwarded. Errors occurred even during the first steps of data processing (e.g., name, format, structure, content), but the exact location of the errors within the process and the reasons for the errors were not apparent. Most important, the errors' origins were not clear: The automotive manufacturer that had sent the files might have made a mistake when creating the files, or S-Y Systems could have been responsible for the mistake when receiving and editing the files. S-Y Systems needed to monitor their processes to demonstrate that the reason for most of the processing errors lay elsewhere.

Therefore, S-Y Systems decided to monitor its operative IT processes, particularly EDI processes, and started a process-oriented measurement project. Prior to the project, the company had not attempted to collect data on its IT processes, so it had gained no theoretical or practical experience in applying PPM. As a result, a structured procedure for implementing a PPM system for monitoring the EDI processes was needed.

PPM systems that support the operative tasks of PPM are computer-supported tools for the execution of the three phases in PPM: planning, monitoring, and controlling the performance of processes. The pivotal points are process KPIs that enable process managers to compare the actual and the target performances of business processes like S-Y Systems' EDI processes.

EDI is the electronic movement of business documents between or within firms (including their agents and intermediaries) in a structured, machine-retrievable data format that permits data to be transferred without rekeying from a business application in one location to a business application in another (Hansen and Hill 1989). Ritz (1995) and Choudhary et al. (2011) define EDI in terms of four elements: (1) the electronic transmission (2) of structured data (business documents) (3) in a standardized, machine-readable format (4) between trading partners' computer systems. Its benefits are reduced paperwork and inventories, reduction in transaction times, improvements in data-entry activity, and improved communications (Chen and Williams 1998; Choudhary et al. 2011; Hansen and Hill 1989). Therefore, companies almost always adopt EDI for the same reasons: to enable quick response and access to information, to gain cost efficiency, to respond to a customer's request, and/or to reduce paperwork and improve accuracy (Weber and Kantamneni 2002; Hansen and Hill 1989).

As the EDI processes are time-critical, and as business processes that exchange documents with other trading partners depend on them, the processes should be measured and monitored. Therefore, the implementation of a PPM system is the first step in analyzing and optimizing EDI processes.

3 Action Taken

Against this background, a PPM project was conducted as part of a student seminar over 4 months in 2012. Two groups of two students each were involved, guided by a Ph.D. student. The goal of the project was to develop a PPM system for the implemented ITIL and EDI processes for which the IT division of S-Y Systems was responsible. Although the project achieved this development and led to useful findings regarding the implementation of the PPM system for both process areas, the case reported in this paper focuses on the EDI processes. In what follows, we introduce the general approach to developing and implementing a PPM system and explain its application in the case.

3.1 The Approach to Developing and Implementing a PPM System

In order to implement a PPM system successfully, a structured top-down procedure must be applied to ensure that the system monitors all the necessary aspects of the processes that the user wants to monitor. A seven-step PPM approach was developed to ensure the design and implementation of a PPM system was done in a structured and methodically consistent way.

Step 1: Define the goal of the PPM project: Without a clearly stated goal, the original objective of the project may get lost and important KPIs may get less attention than necessary, while inappropriate KPIs accidentally become part of the PPM system. Therefore, the first step of developing a PPM system is to define the overall goal. Examples of such goals are to improve the performance of all customer-related processes within 18 months in order to increase customer satisfaction or to demonstrate within 6 months that the company complies with service-level agreements (SLAs) with another company.

Step 2: Ensure a solid basis of information: All important information—including the company's strategy and related success factors, its organizational structure (organizational charts), its IT architecture, its process map, and any relevant process models that exist—must be gathered to create a solid basis for further steps.

Step 3: Select and model the process: The output of this step is a complete and current model of the process selected for monitoring and performance improvement. For this purpose, all existing process models must be checked for timeliness and refined or enriched with missing information. If the selected process has not been modeled as a process model, the process flow must be identified by analyzing documents and interviewing the staff involved and then by modeling it.

Step 4: Determine the goal of the process: Determining the process's goal helps to identify the process's relevant KPIs. Process goals are either generic and qualitative, such as "customer orientation and satisfaction," or specific and quantitative, such as "reaching the minimum threshold of concluded contracts."

Step 5: Identify the process's critical success factors (CSFs): Examples of success factors are time, quality, costs, and energy consumption. Depending on the process's goal, the process's success factors specify the dimensions in which the process KPIs are derived in the next step.

Step 6: Identify process KPIs: The central and perhaps most difficult aspect of developing a PPM system is identifying the necessary and appropriate process KPIs. Following steps 1–5 helps to ensure that only KPIs that are in accordance with the process's CSFs, the company's strategy, and the overall PPM goal are identified.

All relevant information about every KPI must be laid down in a KPI description, including:

- the point of measurement in the process model
- data sources, calculation algorithm, and graphic visualization
- thresholds and/or target values based on experience, previous data, SLAs, and/or legal regulations
- staff members who are responsible for the KPI and for monitoring it
- staff members who are to be informed about violations of thresholds

There is an obvious risk of choosing KPIs that not closely interrelated and, thus, do more to confuse than to support the monitoring and management of the process's performance. The process KPIs that are identified are be implemented in a PPM system that consists of an IT system and that supports the PPM by calculating and graphically representing the KPIs automatically. A PPM system provides a dashboard view for the system user and visualizes the past and/or present performance of the underlying processes by means of suitable diagrams, such as tachometers and RAG ratings. To ensure that the process KPIs are correctly calculated and that the PPM system works reliably, continuous quality assurance must be conducted on both KPIs and the PPM system. The effort required to develop, implement, and test even a single process KPI is often underestimated and may lead to project delays.

Step 7: Implement organizational integration: To ensure that the PPM system is regularly used and that the necessary information about past and current process performance reaches the staff members responsible for the process, the PPM system must be well integrated into the organization: it has to be documented who is responsible for the operationalization of the PPM and each single KPI (see KPI description in step 6), and for the development of the PPM system and its KPIs.

The PPM approach has a two-sided relationship with the six phases of the BPM Lifecycle. The most obvious relationship is that the approach specifies the "process monitoring and controlling" phase of the BPM Lifecycle and defines how to monitor and control a process systematically and in a goal-oriented manner. In addition, the BPM Lifecycle phases of "process identification" and "process discovery" provide concretion for step 3 of the PPM approach and help to support modeling the process that is to be monitored and controlled. Finally, as a result of the application of the PPM approach, a new process, "Monitor and control the EDI process," is designed and implemented. Therefore, the BPM Lifecycle describes the new process's lifecycle phases of design, analysis, implementation, and monitoring and controlling.

3.2 Application of the Approach at S-Y Systems

This section describes the application of all seven steps of the PPM approach in the IT division of S-Y Systems and presents the results of the project.

Step 1: Define the goal of the PPM project: The goal of the PPM project was to overcome the existing deficits in process monitoring to demonstrate that the fault for most of the EDI processing errors did not lie with S-Y Systems but that the performance of their processes was in keeping with agreements. The company also wanted to strengthen its relationship with its customers. The duration of the PPM project was planned to be 4–6 months.

Step 2: Ensure a solid basis of information: The basis for the next development steps consisted of information about the company's strategy, success factors, its organizational structure, its IT architecture, and its processes, preferably documented as models. This basis of information basis was necessary to limit the enormous number of possible KPIs to a small number of goal-related and case-specific KPIs.

Regarding the company's strategy, S-Y Systems' strategic orientation is based on customer satisfaction. To react quickly to arising problems, S-Y Systems sets great store by being as close to its customers as possible in terms of both time spent and geographic proximity. Quality is also a strategic top-goal, as S-Y Systems aims at zero defects for its products and processes. In short, S-Y Systems tries to offer the best possible quality at the lowest possible price and to satisfy its customers completely with regard to its services and products. The company's IT department provides the support required to reach these strategic goals.

A closer look at S-Y Systems' success factors underscores the company's focus on quality and customer satisfaction. The most important success factor is quality, manifesting as freedom from errors. As customer satisfaction decreases with every error, such as errors in products received or in EDI files, S-Y Systems cannot offer mediocre quality. Therefore, the company has to optimize its process and product quality by eliminating errors and by continuously monitoring the quality of its operative IT processes. Responsiveness is the second important success factor, as fast responses to customer problems helps to ensure customer satisfaction and adds to the company's positive image. For S-Y Systems, responsiveness also includes the more generic ability to react more quickly to changes in the business environment than other companies do, a goal that may not be measurable.

Finally the information basis for the project at S-Y Systems has to be complemented by its organizational structure, IT architecture, and processes:

- The organizational chart helped to clarify the company's organizational structures, but information about the external organizations that were involved had to be added for the subsequent steps of the PPM approach. After all, the company's role as an intermediary (a service provider between two companies) strongly influenced the selection of appropriate KPIs. Since the IT processes of S-Y Systems depended significantly on the quality of the incoming EDI files, a distinction had to be made between external errors caused by external (customer) companies that occur at the start of the EDI processes and subsequent internal processing errors for which S-Y Systems was responsible.
- A graphic representation of the IT architecture, particularly all relevant IT systems of the EDI section, for use in the subsequent process-modeling steps, could be modeled from interviews with the employees responsible for them. The IT architecture at S-Y Systems consists primarily of two IT systems (Fig. 3). The Seeburger Business Integration Server (BIS) is responsible for receiving and sending EDI files from and to customer companies. The BIS also prepares the EDI files for internal use, that is, for the second main IT system, SAP. In addition, there are three main connections: the Integrated Services Digital Network (ISDN) and the European Network Exchange (ENX) network for partner companies and an intranet (TCP/IP) connection to the company's corporate parent, Yazaki.
- Since neither a process map of the EDI processes nor detailed process models existed, they were modeled in the next step.

Step 3: Select and model the process: To model the process map, the project team interviewed staff members and analyzed existing documentation. The resulting process map (Fig. 1) is comprised of four EDI core processes extending over

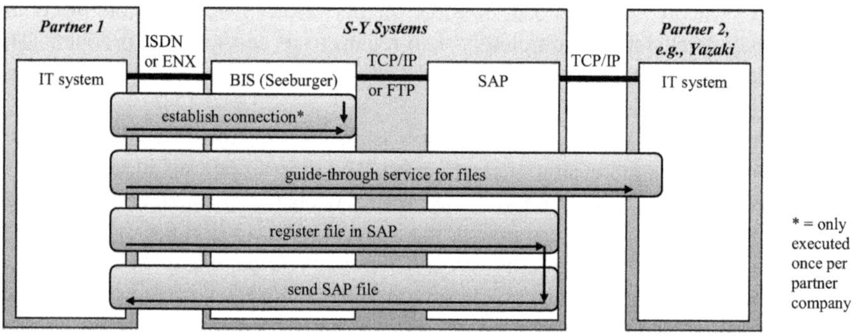

Fig. 1 Process map, including the IT architecture

three types of companies (the file-sending company, S-Y Systems, and the file-receiving company) and the two IT systems at S-Y Systems (BIS and SAP).

The EDI process "establish connection" (Fig. 1) is the only one of the four EDI processes that is executed only once for every partner. This process, which is the basis of the other three processes, establishes a reliable ISDN, ENX, or TCP/IP connection to the customer companies' IT systems. After the connection is tested, files can be exchanged between S-Y Systems and its customers. For certain processes, S-Y Systems acts as an intermediary service provider for Yazaki to process EDI files, receiving the files of one of Yazaki's partners and converting them so Yazaki's application systems can process them—and vice versa. This process is called "guide-through service for files." The last two main processes are "register file in SAP," which includes processing incoming EDI files, and "send SAP file," which includes preparing and sending an outgoing EDI file. Since S-Y Systems could provide process models for only a few parts of the four EDI processes, most of the processes that the company intended to monitor had to be modeled first. The project team used Business Process Model and Notation (BPMN) (Fig. 3), a standard for business process modeling, as the graphical process modeling language.

We focus on the third process, "register file in SAP," because it shows the difference between external and internal errors within the process. The "register file in SAP" process starts when a partner sends an EDI file to S-Y Systems. After receiving and archiving the EDI file, the BIS checks the name of the EDI file, and specific receiving rules are activated based on the partner. These rules determine which mapping is used to create proprietary SAP format files (IDocs) from the received file. Once the IDocs are created, they are sent to the SAP system either via the intranet or, if the file is too large, via an FTP server. Once the IDocs have been sent, the BIS archives them again, and the SAP system interprets and registers them for further use.

Step 4: Determine the goal of the process: Since every process can—and usually does—have its own goal, all processes must be analyzed individually. The generic, quantitative goal of "register file in SAP" is "fast processing without errors according to the customers' needs." The EDI process is automated, and manual interventions are necessary only if there are processing errors, but a fast and reliable run through this process must be ensured, as the customers expect it.

Step 5: Identify the process's critical success factors: Based on the process's goal of "fast processing without errors according to the customers' needs," quality and time were identified as the process's CSFs. To improve quality and to be in accordance with the strategic goal of zero defects, S-Y Systems focused on eliminating errors. Interruptions in the process flow and failures in processing activities that were causing delays in the process had to be eliminated. Errors that were not caused by S-Y Systems but by their business partners had to be identified and reported to the partner company to improve process quality in the long term. Time-related aspects of the process also had to be included in the measurement of the business processes to meet the customers' expectations and ensure compliance with agreements, so it was necessary to examine the processes' internal performance by means of time-related process KPIs. The focus of measurement lay particularly on manual interventions in the process.

Step 6: Identify process KPIs: After steps 1–5 were completed, detailed process KPIs that related to the CSFs of quality and time had to be identified. For the "register file in SAP" process, it was not the successful processing of the tasks but the appearance of processing errors that had to be measured. Since most of the process tasks were executed automatically, their monitoring had to focus on the parts of the process where the errors actually occurred and on actions to resolve these errors.

Thus, KPIs concerning five dimensions of time and quality were identified. The first three dimensions support the CFS of quality, while the last two dimensions focus on time.

- Type of error: Errors can be classified into "decider errors," "mapping errors," and "stop errors. (These errors are described in Table 1 and located within the process in Fig. 3.)
- Reason: The reason for an error refers to whether it is an internal failure or caused by an external partner (Table 1). "Stop errors" are always internal errors because they indicate a problem with the in-house connection between the IT systems BIS and SAP.
- Partner company: To react quickly when one a partner company sends many incorrect files within a short time, the number or frequency of errors per partner must be tracked in order to focus on this partner company and analyze the reason for the errors. In any case, when an error occurs, it must be resolved quickly. Bound by contract, S-Y Systems pays a penalty if the process delay exceeds a certain time because of an error. Therefore, monitoring the time-related aspects of the resolution to an error helps to improve the overall process performance and to avoid the need to pay contractual penalties.

Table 1 Overview of possible errors

Error type	Description	Reason
Decider error	No receiving rule can be found for the incoming file, or the receiving rule found does not match the incoming file. The process stops	External: New file sent without having a receiving rule, or the name of a file has been changed Internal: Misspelling within a receiving rule; receiving rule is inactive
Mapping error	The receiving rule is active, but the mapping of the data causes an error	External: Wrong data type for an area; no value for an area; changes in the logical structure of the file Internal: Incomplete mapping document
Stop error	The file cannot be sent or is not accepted by the following system	Only internal: Wrong file name or structure; errors within the connection; interface used by other files

- Time: The weekly average time for a particular error is compared with the weekly average time for similar errors, and the error is examined in more detail if the time taken deviates from the average of similar errors. The time per error can be split into two other KPIs: reaction time (the time between the occurrence of the error and the start of the resolving actions) and the time needed to resolve the error.
- Priority according to file content: The errors can be classified into four categories of priority according to the criticality of the EDI file's content: low, medium, high, and critical. According to this priority rule, the staff has to react within a specified period of time from a day to within 30 min, depending on the priority level. If this period of time is exceeded, the IT management is informed so it can react quickly.

For each KPI, a KPI description is made. These descriptions inform the PPM system users about what each KPI means, what it measures, where the measuring points are located, what problems and interrelationships exist, and so forth.

After the process KPIs were identified, a visual prototype of the PPM system was implemented. The prototype consisted of a PPM dashboard showing the process KPIs along the process models and used dummy data to calculate dummy values for them.

Step 7: Implement organizational integration: Since this step requires detailed organizational information and the power to enforce organizational changes in the company, S-Y Systems itself ensured the organizational integration of the developed and implemented PPM system and the assignment of responsibilities.

4 Results Achieved

To summarize the results of the PPM project, Fig. 2 shows an overview of the findings of each step of the proposed PPM procedure, which led to appropriate KPIs that fully support the company's vision and goals.

As Fig. 2 shows, each step of the approach uses the information collected in the previous steps, making this top-down procedure structured, consistent, and firmly interconnected.

Since the main result of the project was the PPM system prototype, more explanations are provided in the following paragraphs. The PPM consisted of two levels of aggregation.

On the initial level, a process map showed the four processes of the IT department. Traffic lights were allocated to each of the processes, indicating the overall status of each process, including all of its underlying KPIs. System users could choose one of the four processes and the system led them to the second level, where the selected process was graphically represented as a process model (modeled with BPMN).

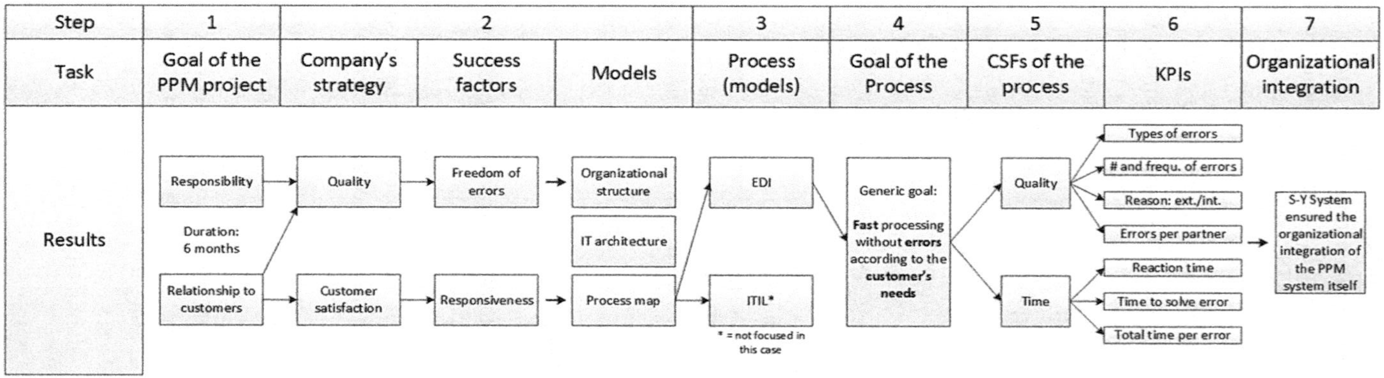

Fig. 2 Summary of the PPM project results

Figure 3 shows the second-level view of the process "register file in SAP." The status of the KPIs at S-Y Systems regarding the three types of errors were allocated to the related task in the process model using traffic lights according to the identified thresholds in the KPI descriptions. In contrast to other dashboards, the process and its related process model was the focus of the PPM dashboard. The KPIs were allocated to the corresponding task within the process model, which emphasized the importance of the graphic visualization connected to the process flow. This process-oriented representation of KPIs differed fundamentally from other dashboards, which usually present KPIs only as tables or independent charts, losing any link to the underlying process.

For example, to monitor decider errors, a set of KPIs (e.g., number of errors, number of errors per partner) are defined and represented with traffic lights next to the task "Check name of EDI file" in the process model. This task checks whether there is a receiving rule for the incoming file. If there is a receiving rule, the process continues; otherwise, the process stops and a decider error occurs. For instance, a red traffic light can indicate that the defined threshold for the number of internal decider errors has been exceeded, providing the analyst at first view of possible reasons for the decider error (e.g., the receiving rule contains spelling mistakes), which can be analyzed and corrected promptly.

The implemented PPM dashboard represents KPIs as separate bar charts when the traffic lights are clicked (Fig. 4). The bar charts in Fig. 4 represent different combinations of the dimensions of number and frequency of errors, reason for errors (internal and external), frequency of errors per partner company, average reaction time according to the level of priority, average time needed to solve errors, and average total time of errors.

Based on the defined KPIs, the allocation of errors within the process, the reasons for the errors, and their origin are traceable. The reports derived from this information serve as the basis for reviews with the partner companies to reduce the number and frequency of errors.

5 Lessons Learned

A review of the PPM project and its results reveals several lessons learned.

Top-Down Approach There is no one-size-fits-all solution when implementing a PPM system, so many companies face difficulties when trying to establish a monitoring system. As most companies follow an unstructured, bottom-up approach, they often monitor inappropriate KPIs and, consequently, define unnecessary measuring points. A structured, top-down approach builds a reliable basis for a PPM system, as the results of this case show.

Internal and External Errors Because of S-Y Systems' intermediary role, appropriate process KPIs were related primarily to quality. Errors were of particular interest, especially in terms of whether they were externally or internally caused. In

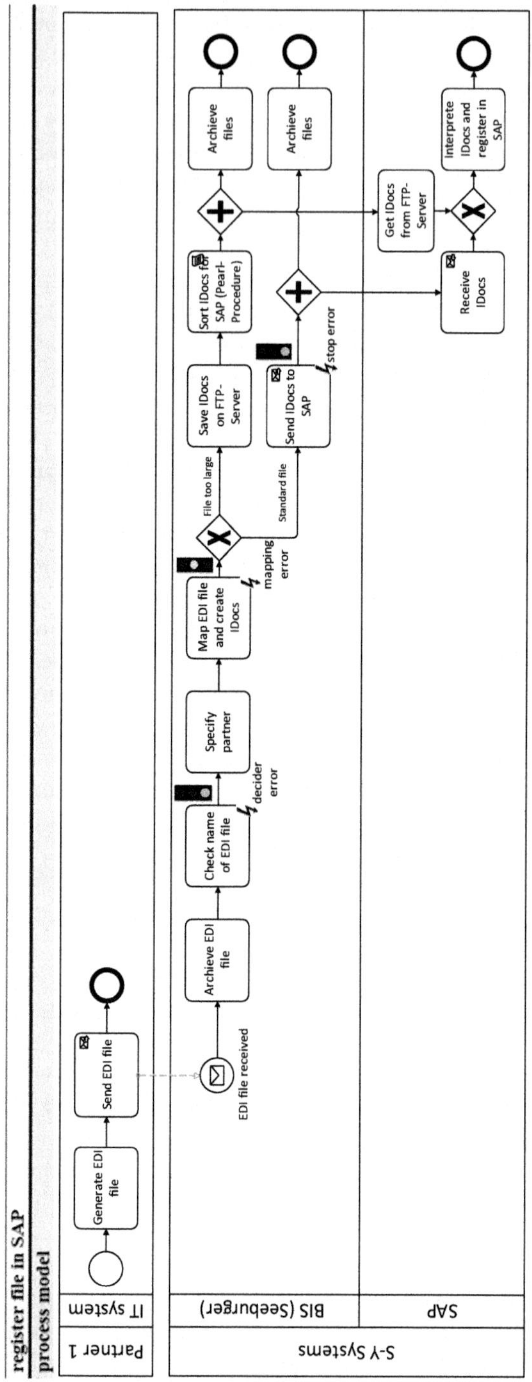

Fig. 3 Prototype of the PPM dashboard

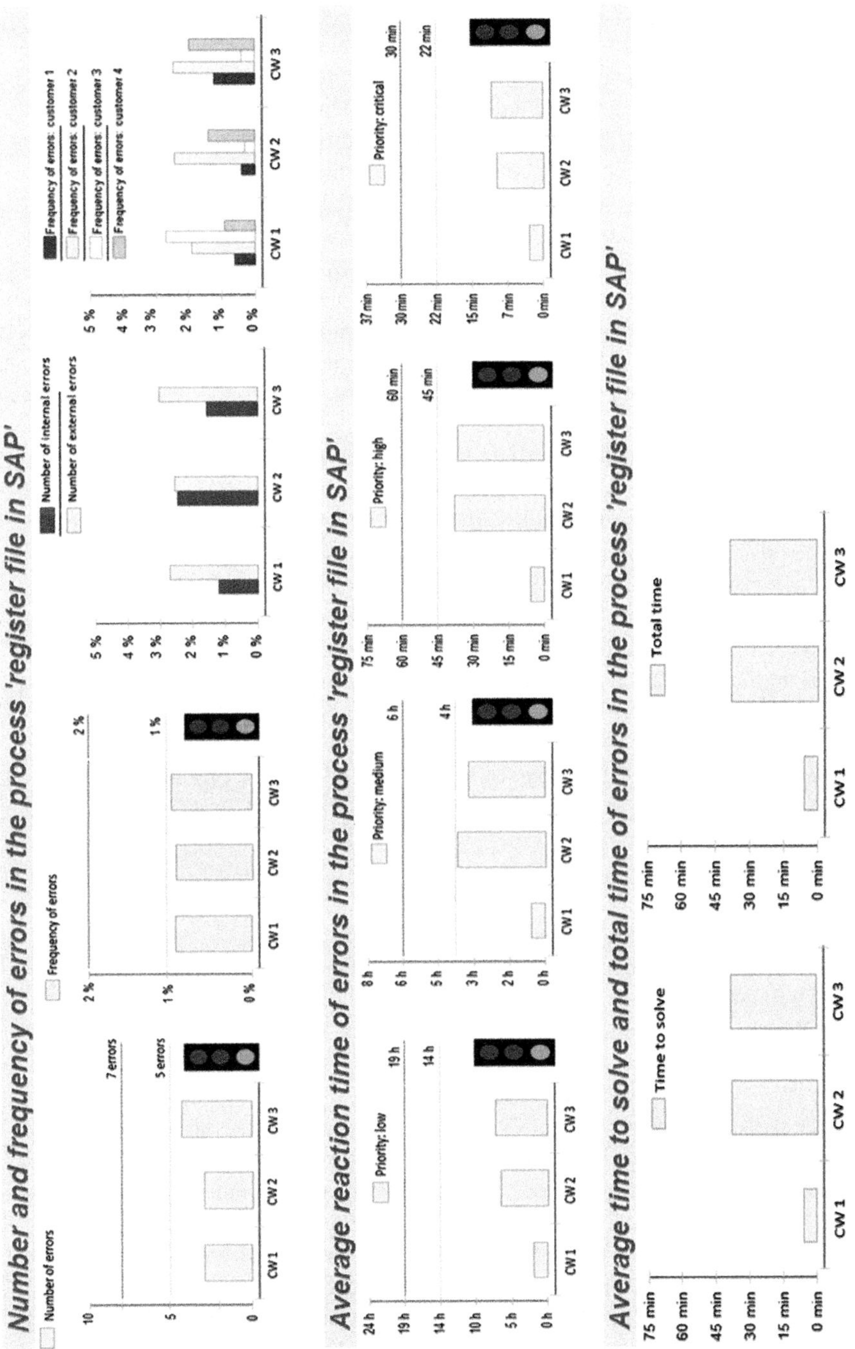

Fig. 4 Bar charts of the PPM cockpit (CW = Calendar Week)

general, whenever a process starts at an external process participant (company), the quality of the first process tasks depends on that participant, so errors in these tasks are mainly caused externally. In contrast, monitoring the performance of the following tasks deals primarily with the internal quality, for which the focal company is fully responsible. Therefore, KPIs that refer to quality are distinguished based on whether they are external or internal. This view affects improvement efforts because internal process performance improvement is much easier than improving the process performance of external partners.

Risk of Losing Focus on the Process While carrying out the PPM project, especially while developing the prototype of the PPM dashboard, the students occasionally strayed too far from the process. For example, they lost focus on the initial process by trying to advance the modeling and monitoring of subsequent processes, and they first presented KPIs in separate diagrams and tables with no visual relationship to the underlying processes.

Consideration of Time Restrictions when Measuring Time-Related KPIs In general, KPIs that relate to the operating time must take several assumptions into account because employees do not work 24×7. Calculations should relate only to the enterprise's contractual working hours, which was the case at S-Y Systems. Problems can also arise if the company has offices in multiple countries with differing holidays. For example, in Turkey (where one of S-Y Systems' affiliates is based), December 25 is not a public holiday as it is in Germany. A PPM system's skipping that day in the calculation would deliver process-performance values that were too positive and distort the KPIs when comparing performance across countries.

Problem of Variants The issue of too many KPIs is a problem caused by several dimensions:

- Process and task
- Type of error and reason for the error
- Partner company (customer)
- Priority of errors because of the priority of the EDI file
- Time interval
- Other possible dimensions, such as type of connection (ISDN vs. ENX vs. TCP/IP)

Since there are several possible values for each dimension, the combination of these dimensions results in a high number of possible KPIs. For example, the information about the number of "Internal high-priority mapping errors within 'register file in SAP' received from customer 1 in November" requires integrating five dimensions (process, type of error, customer, priority of error, time interval) into the calculation, and many KPIs can be defined just for the "time interval" dimension (e.g., processing time, waiting, time, response time, problem solving time, total time). Therefore, combinations of dimensions result in a large number of KPIs. To reduce the number of combinations and avoid losing focus, the PPM system at S-Y Systems specifies the "process" dimension by going from the process map on level 1 to the process model on level 2. The types of errors are located in the process model, and the other dimensions—"reason for error," "partner company," "priority," and "time" are handled by means of separate bar charts below the process model (Fig. 4). A detached button enables the user to select the time interval used for calculating the KPIs.

An outlook on further activities and research projects at S-Y Systems reveals two primary opportunities for future improvements in their PPM.

Performance Measurement across the Complete Process and across Companies To achieve transparency beyond company borders, the complete end-to-end process must be monitored. (See, e.g., the EDI process "guide-through service for files.") Such a cross-company PPM system requires synchronized data input from all participating companies in order to give them instant information about early or late parts of a process. In the case of S-Y Systems, its business partners that were sending EDI files could see how many files were running on failure at S-Y Systems because of their own bad process performance (e.g., sending S-Y Systems files with incomplete data values and causing mapping errors).

Subsequent Student PPM Projects Other student projects will intensify the monitoring within the BIS processes at S-Y Systems and use our university's computer center and the PPM approach to improve all customer-related IT processes, thereby improving customer satisfaction. For the latter purpose, a PPM system that focuses on time measurement will be developed and implemented. Another KPI focus of the project could relate to energy consumption in order to establish green processes.

References

Blasini, J., & Leist, S. (2013). Success factors in process performance management for services—Insights from a multiple-case study. In *HICSS*.

Blasini, J., Leist, S., & Ritter, C. (2011). Successful application of PPM—An analysis of the German-speaking banking industry. In *ECIS* 2011.

Chen, J.-C., & Williams, B. C. (1998). The impact of electronic data interchange (EDI) on SMEs: Summary of eight British case studies. *Journal of Small Business Management, 36*(4), 68–72.

Choudhary, K., Pandey, U., Nayak, M.K., & Mishra, D.K. (2011). Electronic data interchange: A review. In *Proceedings of the 2011 Third International Conference on Computational Intelligence, Communication Systems and Networks* (pp. 323–327).

Cleven, A., Wortmann, F., & Winter, R. (2010). *Process performance management—Identifying stereotype problem situations as a basis for effective and efficient design research* (pp. 302–316). St. Gallen: Desrist.

Hansen, J. V., & Hill, N. C. (1989). Control and audit of electronic data interchange. *MIS Quarterly, 13*(4), 403–413.

Heckl, D., & Moormann, J. (2010). Process performance management. In J. vom Brocke & M. Rosemann (Eds.), *Handbook on business process management* (Vol. 2, pp. 115–135). Berlin: Springer.

Heß, H. (2004). Marktführerschaft durch Process Performance Management: Konzepte, Trends und Anwendungsszenarien. In A.-W. Scheer, F. Abolhassan, H. Kruppke, & W. Jost (Eds.), *Innovation durch Geschäftsprozessmanagement—Jahrbuch Business Process Excellence 2004/2005* (pp. 119–136). Berlin: Springer.

Jeston, J., & Nelis, J. (2008). *Management by process: A roadmap to sustainable business process management*. Oxford: Elsevier Linacre House.

Ritz, D. (1995). *The start-up of an EDI network a comparative case study in the air cargo industry*. Dissertation, Hochschule St. Gallen.

S-Y Systems Technologies Europe GmbH. (2012). *Company brochure*. Retrieved October 05, 2012, from http://www.systech-eu.com/fileadmin/user_upload/downloads/SY-Image broschu__re_EN_Internet.pdf

Weber, M. M., & Kantamneni, S. P. (2002). POS and EDI in retailing: Underlying benefits and barriers. *Supply chain Management: An International Journal, 7*(5), 311–317.

Josef Blasini studied Management Information Systems at the University of Regensburg from October 2002 to March 2007. From April 2007 to December 2013, he worked as a research assistant at the chair of Management Information Systems III—Business Engineering—at the University of Regensburg, where he also received his doctoral degree (Dr. rer. Pol., title of his doctoral thesis: "Process Performance Management—an empirical investigation of critical success factors") in November 2013.

Susanne Leist is Professor of Information Systems at the University of Regensburg, Germany. She is the author of numerous articles in scientific journals, for conferences and books (e.g., Business and Information Systems Engineering (BISE), Business Process Management Journal (BPMJ), Information Systems and e-Business Management (ISeB), Electronic Markets (EM), Managing Service Quality (MSQ), International Conference on Information Systems (ICIS), European Conference on Information Systems (ECIS)). She is a member of the Editorial Boards of the Enterprise Modeling and Enterprise IS department of the international journal BISE, the international journal EM, the quarterly magazine "BIT Banking and Information Technology", and the Regensburg University research magazine "Blick in die Wissenschaft". She has also been acting as an editor or reviewer in several international committees.

Werner Merkl, Director Central IT at S-Y Systems Technologies Europe GmbH until 2013, initiated the company's cooperation with the University of Regensburg and was the project leader on the part of S-Y Systems. Presently Werner Merkl is CEO of the it-motive BCS GmbH in Regensburg, which he founded together with the it-motive AG. He advises customers on Business Model Design, IT Strategy, Industry 4.0 topics and BPM. From 2013 till 2015 he was responsible for Quality, Environmental, Health and Safety and the internal Project Management System for Yazaki Limited Europe, which is the leading global wiring harness manufacturer in the automotive industry. From 2002 till 2013 he was responsible for IT in a Joint Venture of Yazaki and Continental. Prior to this he worked as Manager and Project Manager in the telecommunications and engineering sector. In 2012 he received the Handelsblatt IT Strategy Award.

Establishment of a Central Process Governance Organization Combined with Operational Process Improvements

Insights from a BPM Project at a Leading Telecommunications Operator in the Middle East

Christian Czarnecki

Abstract

(a) **Situation faced**: Because of customer churn, strong competition, and operational inefficiencies, the telecommunications operator ME Telco (*fictitious name due to confidentiality*) launched a strategic transformation program that included a Business Process Management (BPM) project. Major problems were silo-oriented process management and missing cross-functional transparency. Process improvements were not consistently planned and aligned with corporate targets. Measurable inefficiencies were observed on an operational level, e.g., high lead times and reassignment rates of the incident management process.

(b) **Action taken**: The project was structured into three phases. First, countermeasures were identified and planned based on an analysis of the current situation. Second, a new organizational unit responsible for a central BPM was established and equipped with BPM methods and tools. Based on the reference model *enhanced Telecom Operations Map* (eTOM), a company-wide process framework was defined. A process ownership model linked the central governance with the execution. As a pilot implementation, the incident management was improved on an operational level. The project was accompanied by continuous communication and training. Third, the project results were monitored and transferred to daily operations.

(c) **Results achieved**: Quantitative performance improvements in the incident management process were achieved, such as reducing the average lead time from 13.0 days to 3.6 days. Those results confirmed the BPM artifacts that were developed. All of the artifacts (methods, tools, process framework, and process models) were officially accepted and communicated. The new

C. Czarnecki (✉)
Hochschule für Telekommunikation Leipzig, Leipzig, Germany
e-mail: czarnecki@hft-leipzig.de

J. vom Brocke, J. Mendling (eds.), *Business Process Management Cases*,
Management for Professionals, DOI 10.1007/978-3-319-58307-5_4

BPM department was staffed with eight employees. The process ownership was implemented through nominations of responsible persons. In total 290 employees were trained in the new BPM methods and operational process changes. A company-wide repository was introduced that contains the process framework and all detailed process models.

(d) **Lessons learned**: (1) Process content is an important success factor in a BPM implementation. (2) Process ownership requires consideration of the various BPM elements. (3) Early involvement of stakeholders from top management to the operational level is essential for successful implementation. (4) Customization of reference models requires a transparent approach to decision making. (5) General BPM governance and methods are important for an operational process improvement.

1 Introduction

The telecommunications industry is going through a major transformation (Grover and Saeed 2003; Picot 2006). New, innovative players have entered the telecommunications market, leading to a restructuring of the whole telecommunications industry (Pousttchi and Hufenbach 2011; Wulf and Zarnekow 2011). As a result, many telecommunications operators have launched extensive transformation programs to adapt their structures to the changed market conditions (Czarnecki et al. 2012; Czarnecki and Dietze 2017). This case describes a Business Process Management (BPM) project undertaken by the integrated telecommunications operator *ME Telco*[1] in the Middle East. More than 100 million customers make *ME Telco* a leading telecommunications operator with a strong footprint in the region. Once a monopolist, the company now must cope with strong competition and the need for ongoing innovation. Declining customer satisfaction has led to the risk of customer churn. Furthermore, internal inefficiencies on an operational level were observed. The project described here is part of the company's strategic transformation program with the objective to increase its competitive advantage, customer satisfaction, and operational efficiency.

The project started with an analysis of the existing situation related to BPM, identification of major problems, and definition of countermeasures. In particular, central process governance and continuous process improvement were missing. Therefore, a new organizational unit—*BPM department*—was established that is responsible for the overall management of processes, comparable with the *BPM Center of Excellence* proposed by Dumas et al. (2013). Establishing this department included introducing BPM methods and staffing new positions in the department. Based on the industry-specific reference process model *enhanced Telecom Operations Map* (eTOM) (Kelly 2003; Czarnecki et al. 2013), a company-wide

[1]For reasons of confidentiality, ME Telco, an abbreviation for Middle East Telecommunications Company, is a fictitious name.

process framework was developed, and its organizational implementation was assured through a detailed process ownership model. Improvement of the incident management process was conducted as a pilot implementation, which led to measureable performance improvements on an operational level, such as reducing the lead time from 13.0 days to 3.6 days. The whole project was accompanied by continuous communication and training, based on the identification of stakeholder groups and their information needs. In total 290 employees were trained according to their roles. The last project phase was the transition from the project to daily operations as well as the monitoring of the achieved results. The project lasted 8 months.

The case illustrates the interrelation between central governance combined with BPM methods, mapping to organizational responsibilities, and resulting quantitative improvements in efficiency. It also shows the reuse of a reference process model and its customization through a transparent approach. The case shows the interrelation between BPM methods and concrete process content. The identification of relevant stakeholders and their involvement throughout the project is explained as an important success factor. The case can be linked to the BPM lifecycle (Dumas et al. 2013) with concrete artifacts related to a broad range of BPM elements (Rosemann and vom Brocke 2010).

From a general perspective, the case can be used as an exemplary reference for structuring and planning company-wide BPM implementations, especially when existing reference process models are used. With respect to the telecommunications industry, the case illustrates an example of the intensive transformations that are currently typical for this industry (e.g. Grover and Saeed 2003; Bub et al. 2011; Czarnecki et al. 2012; Czarnecki and Dietze 2017).

The situation faced (cf. Sect. 2), the action taken (cf. Sect. 3), and the results achieved (cf. Sect. 4) are a summarized description based on the author's observations as a consultant on the project as well as official project documentations. The lessons learned (cf. Sect. 5) are a retrospective discussion of the case based on general BPM concepts and literature. In addition, some of the actions taken are related to the reuse of the industry specific reference process model eTOM. The author has been involved in the development of those artifacts following the design science research paradigm (Hevner et al. 2004), see Czarnecki et al. (2013) for further details.

2 Situation Faced

The subject of this case is the vertically integrated telecommunications operator ME Telco, which offers fixed and mobile telephony, Internet, IPTV, and business solutions to residential and business customers in the Middle East, Asia, and Africa. The company held a monopoly for a long time, but it is now facing competition from other local telecommunications operators and IP-based Over-the-Top (OTT) providers.

Regular customer surveys indicated that customer satisfaction was declining. From a market perspective, the company's top management needed to avert the risk of customer churn and the resulting loss of revenue. In addition, competition and ongoing innovation of communication technologies led to a race to launch new products and to realize additional product propositions. From an internal perspective, ME Telco was experiencing inefficiencies on an operational level. For example, the lead times for answering requests and incident resolutions were not meeting targets, and unclear responsibilities had led to reassignments of tasks. Those problems were intensified by the ongoing need for product innovations. The launch of a new IPTV offer was planned which might increase the operational problems through additional complexity. In short, ME Telco faced the typical problems of telecommunications operators with historically grown structures and systems (e.g., Grover and Saeed 2003; Czarnecki et al. 2010; Bub et al. 2011). The organization followed a functional structure that was grouped around specifics of the technical infrastructure. But competition and technical innovations required fast changes on an operational level. The growing complexity was no longer manageable through the existing structures.

Therefore, ME Telco started a strategic transformation program with the goal of improving its competitive advantage, customer satisfaction, and internal efficiency. This strategic program included several initiatives that were managed as separate projects, each of which had a high level of management attention with a dedicated sponsor from the executive board. The management of processes was identified as one topic, with the general idea of supporting the overall objectives of customer satisfaction and internal efficiency through the establishment of a BPM. However, there had been no clear evaluation of the existing situation with respect to BPM. Therefore, as a first step, a high-level analysis—called *BPM diagnostics*—was performed to identify problems and define the high-level project focus and detailed solutions.

The results of the BPM diagnostics helped to clarify the situation the company faced. Therefore, their results are anticipated in this section, even though they are an outcome of project phase 1 (cf. Sect. 3). Processes were managed largely in a silo-oriented manner, so different departments had their own way of managing their processes. The responsibility for processes was only defined on an operational level. A cross-functional transparency and awareness of processes was not established. Hence, processes were not aligned with corporate targets, and their improvement was not followed-up from an overall perspective. The exemplary analysis of the incident management process showed those problems on an operational level (cf. Fig. 1): activities between departments were not aligned. A major effort of the incident management process was searching for the responsible person. A high number of reassignments and long lead times were the result. With respect to the overall strategic objectives, both customer satisfaction and internal efficiency were impacted negatively.

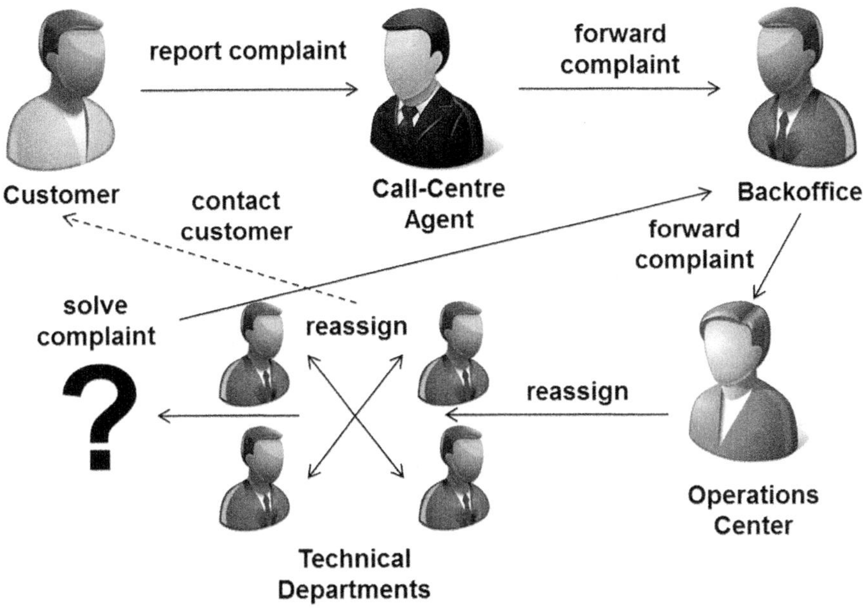

Fig. 1 Exemplary illustration of the incident management process (as-is)

3 Action Taken

This section describes the actions taken based on observations during the project and documented deliverables. The artifacts explained are related to design decisions based on specific, practical requirements and the consensus of the executives and team members involved. Therefore, the structure and terminology might differ from those of general BPM references. In order to facilitate a common understanding, the BPM lifecycle (Dumas et al. 2013) and the six core BPM elements (Rosemann and vom Brocke 2010) are mapped ex post to the project (cf. Fig. 2). The case is also reflected based on these references in the lessons learned section.

The project began with the vague objective of improving how business processes are managed and executed. At this early stage, the concrete scope and objectives were not defined yet. As a first step, the project's organization was defined as consisting of a steering committee, a project management team, a core team, and dedicated functional experts. The project management team and the project core team consisted of both internal employees and external experts. The project management team reported to the steering committee that was staffed with board members and selected senior executives. The core team ensured involvement of ME Telco employees, and additional external experts were involved for selected topics.

The project was structured into three phases (cf. Fig. 3). The first phase was a high-level diagnostics study of the current situation with respect to BPM. The

Project Case		General BPM References	
		BPM Lifecycle (Dumas et al. 2013)	Six BPM Core Elements (Rosemann and vom Brocke 2010)
Phase 1: BPM Diagnostics		process identification; process discovery; process analysis (high-level)	strategic alignment
Phase 2: Design, Implementation and Improvement	A: Process Framework & BPM	process identification; process discovery; methodical basis for the whole lifecycle	strategic alignment, methods, governance
	B: Process Analysis & Design	process analysis, process redesign	methods, information technology, people
	C: Process Implementation	process implementation	methods, information technology, people
	D: Project Management & Communication	not applicable	governance, people, culture
Phase 3: Monitoring and Hand-over		process monitoring and controlling	strategic alignment, governance, methods, information technology

Fig. 2 Mapping between project case and BPM references

objective was to identify and prioritize pain points and respective countermeasures. The scope of phases 2 and 3 was defined based on the findings from phase 1. The second phase covered the detailed design and implementation of the defined countermeasures, which were the core parts of the project and are the focus of this case study. The third phase was the monitoring of results and transition to the line organization—that is, the shift from project execution to daily operations. The monitoring results are described in the next section.

The BPM diagnostics of phase 1 served as a preliminary assessment with a focus on the evaluation of the existing situation based on general maturity criteria. A structured evaluation sheet related to the dimensions of design, performers, owner, infrastructure, and metrics was used (Hammer 2007). The analysis covered the organizational responsibilities of BPM, methods and tools used for BPM, the existing process framework, and a deep dive for selected processes. The work on this analysis took 4 weeks. The detailed analysis findings were prioritized according to the required effort and expected impact. In summary, the findings were mainly related to process ownership, alignment with strategic targets, and planning as well as realization of improvement measures. Based on these findings, the focus of phase 2 was on three

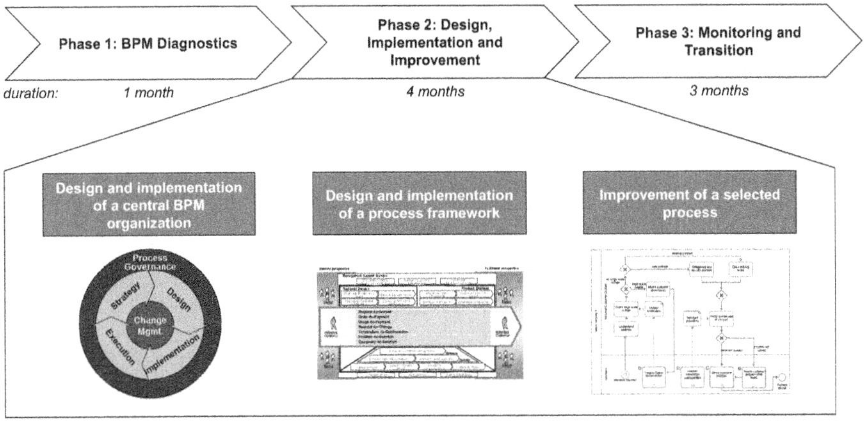

Fig. 3 Project overview

topics (cf. Fig. 3), including the implementation of detailed countermeasures for each topic:

1. *Development and implementation of a central BPM department*: The goal was to establish an organizational entity that is responsible for the management and methodical governance of business processes. Its activities are comparable with the BPM lifecycle (Dumas et al. 2013). The development covered defining an organizational structure for this BPM department, defining roles and responsibilities, developing policies and templates, and selecting the required tools. The implementation included staffing the required job positions, nominating people for additional roles in the organization (e.g., process owners), and conducting training based on the developed policies, templates, and tools.
2. *Development and implementation of a company-wide process framework*: The process framework was based on the industry-specific reference process model eTOM which was customized according to ME Telco's specific requirements. The framework followed a hierarchical process structure that was detailed to level 2 process descriptions for the whole company. A major part of the development was identifying and involving appropriate organizational entities and their formal acceptance. The implementation included final approval by the executive board, communication to all employees, changing affected documents, and detailed employee training.
3. *Improvement of a selected process*: As a proof of concept, a process was improved based on the newly introduced concepts (e.g., process framework, BPM department). The incident management process was selected for this part of the project. After a process analysis was performed on an operational level, the target process was designed based on the reference process model eTOM. Then the target process was implemented through training and changes of existing applications.

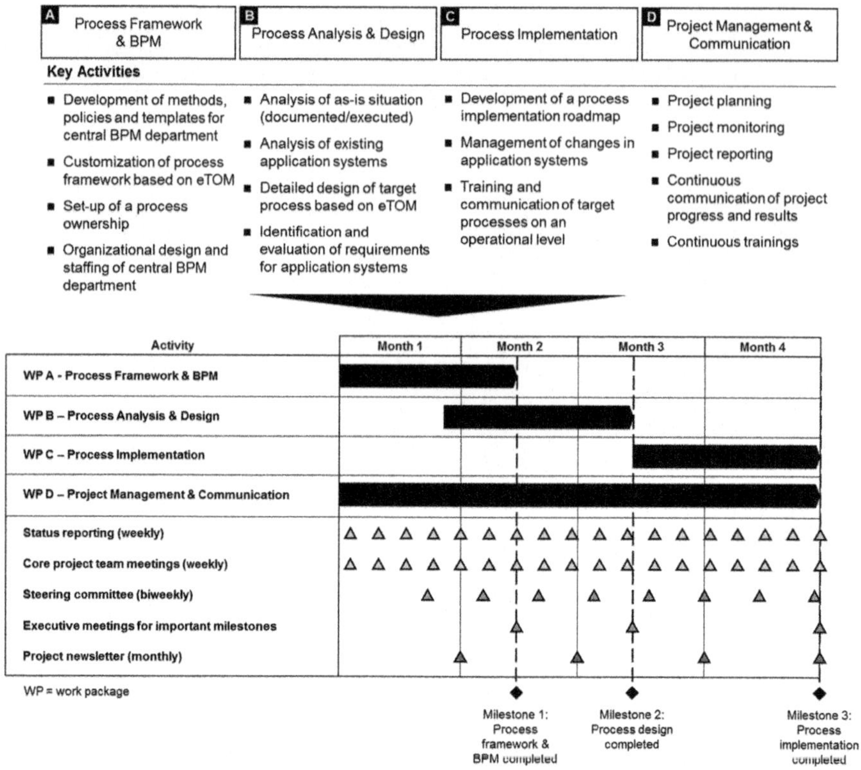

Fig. 4 Work packages and project plan of phase 2

A major structural element for the overall project was the differentiation between the methodical prerequisites of BPM and the design and improvement of a concrete operational process. Phase 2 was structured into four work packages (WP) (cf. Fig. 4). *WP A* covered the development and implementation of the BPM department in combination with the development of the process framework. *WP B* included the detailed design of the target incident management process. The implementation of this target process was part of *WP C*. All of these tasks were accompanied by continuous project management and communication, which was covered in *WP D*. All four work packages in phase 2 were conducted within 4 months.

The project included weekly status reports and core team meetings. The steering committee was involved on a biweekly basis. The project results were divided into three major milestones: (1) process framework and BPM completed, (2) process design completed, and (3) process implementation completed. For those three milestones the project progress and results were presented to the executive board. In addition, all employees received a monthly project newsletter.

According to the above project plan, first, the activities of the central BPM department were defined. Detailed guidelines and templates were developed for all required BPM tasks. Existing blueprints of similar projects were used as references. The major focus was on the overall management and governance.

Six primary tasks were defined for the new BPM department:

(a) Assure processes' compliance with industry-specific reference models (e.g., eTOM).
(b) Manage the detailed design of process flows in all functional areas.
(c) Define and monitor process performance indicators and their respective performance targets.
(d) Manage process implementation initiatives.
(e) Develop and conduct process-related trainings and communications.
(f) Continuously improve processes based on performance figures.

A major challenge was distinguishing between the central governance of processes from a methodical perspective and the responsibility for the design and execution of individual processes. Therefore, a detailed ownership model was developed in order to ensure that the responsible persons from the line organization were involved (cf. Fig. 5). The ownership model followed a top-down approach

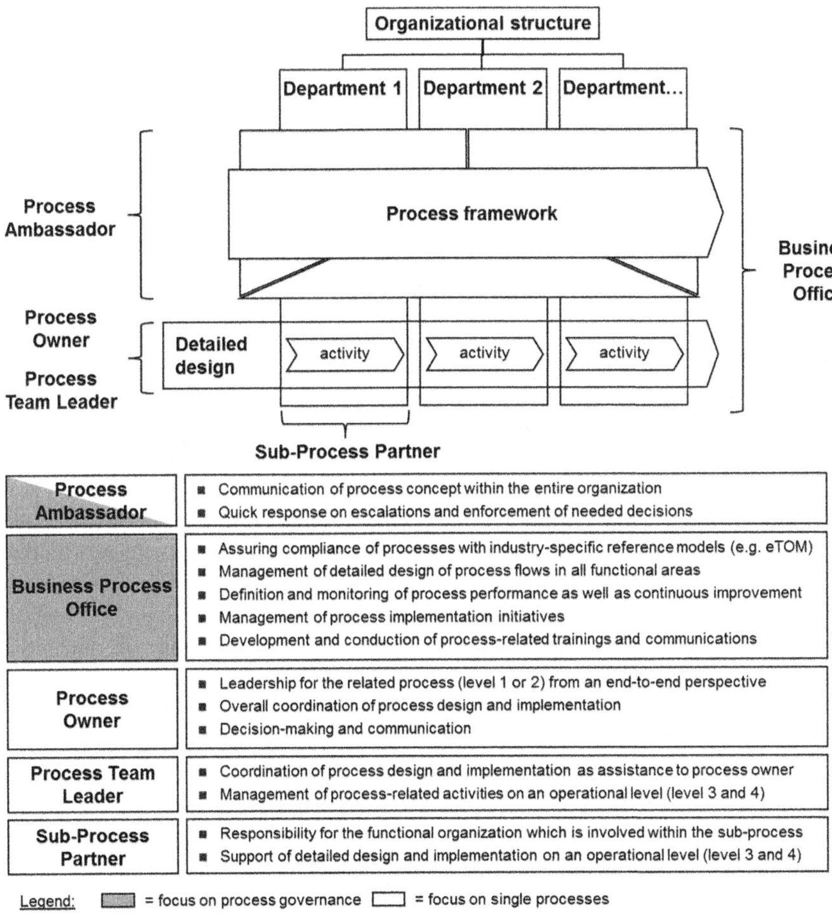

Fig. 5 Ownership model

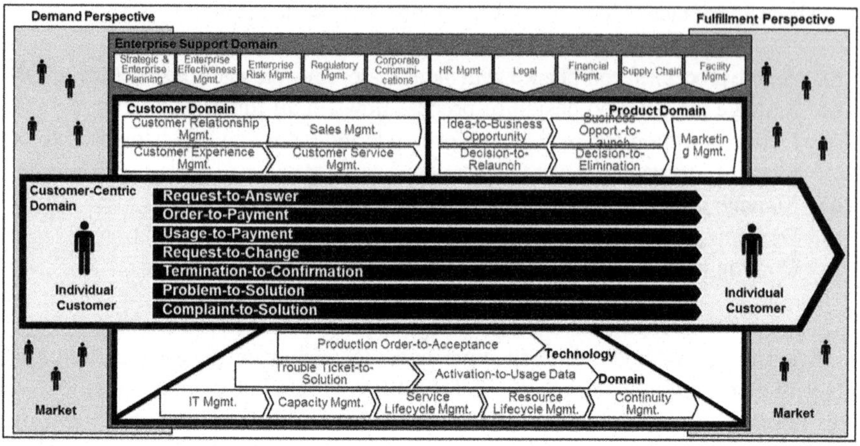

Fig. 6 Process framework

based on the organizational hierarchies. On the top-management level, *process ambassadors* were responsible for communication and required escalations. The *process owners* were senior managers who had functional responsibility for processes from an end-to-end perspective; for example, the Call Center Director was the process owner for the request-to-answer process. For each of these processes, a team consisting of a *process team leader* and several *sub-process partners* was defined. This team was responsible for the detailed design and implementation on an operational level. The central BPM department, the *business process office*, was responsible for the overall governance.

As second step (in phase 2), a cross-functional process framework was developed that forms the bridge between the central BPM department and the operational processes. The process framework provides a high-level definition of all processes (cf. Fig. 6) based on the reference process model eTOM (Kelly 2003). Five process domains were used as a high-level structure (Czarnecki et al. 2013):

- *The customer-centric domain* contains all primary activities, such as sales and customer service. These processes were defined from an end-to-end perspective, always starting and ending with the customer.
- *The technology domain* covers the roll-out, extension, operations, and maintenance of the network infrastructure, as well as the development and realization of telecommunications services.
- *The product domain* contains the development and launch of telecommunications products based on the services provided by the technology domain.
- *The customer domain* focuses on marketing activities, such as market research and campaigns. Unlike the customer-centric domain, the customer domain's processes support customer-related activities like preparing successful sales through marketing campaigns.
- *The support domain* contains all general support activities, such as finance and human resource management.

Each process domain was detailed through end-to-end process flows. For example, the customer-centric domain contains, in addition to others, the *order-to-payment* process flow (Czarnecki et al. 2013). This process framework, which was defined up to level 2 process descriptions for all of ME Telco's processes, provided the topical view that was required to implement the central BPM department's methodical elements. For example, the process domain was used as a structure for defining process ambassadors.

As third step (in phase 2), the incident management process was designed, improved, and implemented on an operational level. This task was performed using the general concepts of the new BPM department. As a starting point, the *problem-to-solution* reference process flow of the process framework was mapped to the as-is situation. According to eTOM, the process starts with the customer contact management that allows the reporting of incidents through various contact channels (e.g., call center, shops) (Czarnecki et al. 2013). Then the incident is analyzed and resolved. Based on the type of incident, these activities are divided between the contact channels, a specialized back office, and technical experts. Providing clear responsibilities and routing the incident to the right person are typically key challenges in this process. After the incident resolution, the billing process might be involved, if, for example, a credit note for a service downtime is issued. The as-is situation for these process steps was analyzed, considering both the existing process documents and the real-life process execution (Hammer 2010). The findings of the as-is analysis were documented. However, detailed as-is process models were not designed. The detailed design of the target process was based on eTOM with consideration given to the capabilities of the existing application systems (e.g., the trouble ticket system). Top management excluded the possibility of replacing the current systems completely from the beginning, so changes in the existing application systems were analyzed and considered in designing the target process.

A major part of phase 2 was the reuse and customization of reference models, which required a great amount of design decisions. From a general perspective, a gap between the reference model and the current situation might require either deviating from the reference or changing the current situation. Since the goal of the implementation is execution of the target models by the line organization, evaluating the specific requirements and involving the line organization should be managed from the beginning (Schermann et al. 2008). All activities and responsibilities, from identification of the relevant stakeholders to formal acceptance of the target models, were clearly defined. The following step-wise approach was officially agreed by the steering committee and communicated as binding for the whole project:

1. *Identify and nominate relevant stakeholders in ME Telco*: The reference models were mapped to the existing organizational structure in order to identify the relevant stakeholders. They were responsible for the provisioning of specific requirements, the formal acceptance of the target design, and the subsequent implementation. These stakeholders were officially nominated by the steering committee.

2. *Nominated stakeholders provide the specific requirements*: The specific requirements were identified through interviews and existing documents. It was carefully distinguished between the currently executed situation, existing but not implemented concepts, and new ideas for further improvements (Hammer 2010). All of these specific requirements were evaluated with respect to their strategic fit, required implementation effort, and improvement potential.
3. *Design first-draft target models*: The required target models were grouped according to their topical focus and assigned to external subject matter experts; for example, the call center part of the incident management process was designed by a dedicated expert in this topic. Starting point for the target models were the relevant reference models, which were customized based on the specific requirements, and their evaluation.
4. *Hold feedback workshops with nominated stakeholders*: The first-draft target models were presented and discussed in workshops (Schermann et al. 2008). Important objective of these workshops was to collect all additional requirements and change requests. The feedback was documented and agreed upon by all participants.
5. *Finalize and formally accept target models*: The collected feedback was incorporated in the target models. Afterwards, the formal acceptance by the nominated stakeholders and the steering committee was achieved.

The entire project was accompanied by continuous communication and training. Achieved results and planned activities were regularly communicated in a newsletter to all employees. The project's progress and required decisions were reported biweekly to the steering committee. Executive meetings with the top management were also held throughout the project. A multitude of presentations and training sessions were offered to all employees, which provided a general introduction to BPM as well as an overview of the BPM concepts that were customized for ME Telco. More detailed training sessions were conducted for those who had specific roles in the processes, such as the process owners, who received intensive one day training. Activities related to implementing the BPM department included staffing it, and detailed training for these new employees in BPM. A new BPM section was also launched on ME Telco's intranet for communicating the BPM methods, policies, and templates. The process framework and target process models, designed in Business Process Model and Notation (BPMN), were also published there as well as being stored in a central repository. An interface between the process-modeling tool and the intranet page was realized. Implementation of the target incident management process also included training the employees who executed the process on an operational level.

4 Results Achieved

Because of the project's broad scope, the results achieved are related to a variety of qualitative and quantitative criteria (Dumas et al. 2013). The establishment of a central BPM department and a company-wide process framework are related to the overall governance and cultural change, which can be described qualitatively, while improvements of the incident management process are directly related to quantitative criteria (e.g., resolution time).

From a *qualitative perspective* three primary results were achieved:

1. *A central BPM department was established*: The detailed design of the new BPM department included the organizational structure, roles and responsibilities, policies, and templates. All new positions were staffed, and detailed training sessions were conducted. All nominations of personnel were based on the process ownership model, and regular reports and committees (e.g., process owner meetings) were initiated. The executive board confirmed and communicated all results. At the end of the project, the new central BPM department has been started its daily operations.
2. *A company-wide process framework was established*: The new process framework was customized and detailed for all processes up to level 2, and ownership was defined for all of these processes. All results were accepted by the responsible process owners. Understanding of the new process framework was ensured through a broad variety of communication measures (e.g., website, training, official announcement). At the end of the project, the process framework has been implemented throughout the company.
3. *The incident management process was improved*: The detailed design of the incident management process was conducted according to the newly introduced structures of the BPM department, resulting in confirmation of these concepts in a pilot implementation. All responsible stakeholders accepted the operational changes. Implementation in the organization was realized through communications and training. The IT implementation was realized through changes in existing application systems. At the end of the project, the improved incident management process has been started its operation.

The involvement of employees, communication, and training was a core part of the project. The respective results are related to the people dimension (Rosemann and vom Brocke 2010). The following figures provide an indication of the achieved results:

- 18 stakeholder groups were identified and were involved in design workshops during the customization of the process framework.
- 170 employees received training on the new BPM department and process framework.
- 30 interviews and site visits were conducted during the as-is analysis of the incident management process.
- 120 employees received an operational training on the improved incident management process.
- 8 employees in the new BPM department received a detailed off-site BPM training.

The improvement of the incident management process resulted in measurable *quantitative* improvements in efficiency and effectiveness. Four indicators were used to measure performance:

- *Resolution time* is the total lead time (in days) from when a customer reports an incident to its closure. The indicator was calculated automatically by the ticketing system.
- *Reassignment rate* is the percentage of incident tickets that are assigned to different technical experts for their resolution, i.e., the assignment between call center and back office as well as back office and focal point is not counted as a reassignment. The number of reassignments was automatically counted by the ticketing system.
- *Working time* (in hours) of the employees who are working in this process during a defined period (e.g., per week). Working time was documented using the timekeeping system. Most employees worked full-time in incident management (e.g., incident group in the call center), so their working time was directly derived from the system. Work distribution was estimated for employees who worked part-time in the process (e.g., technical experts).
- *Number of incidents* is the total number of incidents reported in a defined period (e.g., per day). The number was counted automatically by the ticketing system.

These four indicators had been reported and documented before the process-improvement began. Figure 7 summarizes the effects of the improved incident management process. All figures are averages that were calculated based on performance for 2 months before and 2 months after implementation. For example, the resolution time averaged 13.0 days during the 2 months before implementation and 3.6 days during the 2 months after implementation. Because of the unclear responsibilities for incident tickets, the pre-implementation reassignment rate was 85% (i.e., 85% of incidents were reassigned after initial assignment). This high reassignment rate is related to the 13.0 days resolution time and 2976 working hours per week. The improved incident management process defined clear responsibilities through focal points for specific incident categories. The reassignment rate was reduced to 20%. This improvement of the reassignment rate resulted in a significant decrease of the resolution time (3.6 days) and working hours (1815 hours per week). In addition, the number of incidents declined by 23%, perhaps because of the elimination of the repeated reports of incidents that is typically related to long resolution times. However, this interrelation was not analyzed in detail. Although a positive effect of those performance improvements on customer churn can be assumed, a measurement of customer churn was not performed during the case study.

From a cost perspective, the project implementation can be structured into personnel expenses for the employees, costs for the external experts, and costs of adapting IT systems. The observed improvements were measured 6 months after the start of phase 2, during which time the internal project management team and core team were dedicated to the project full time. The employees from the line

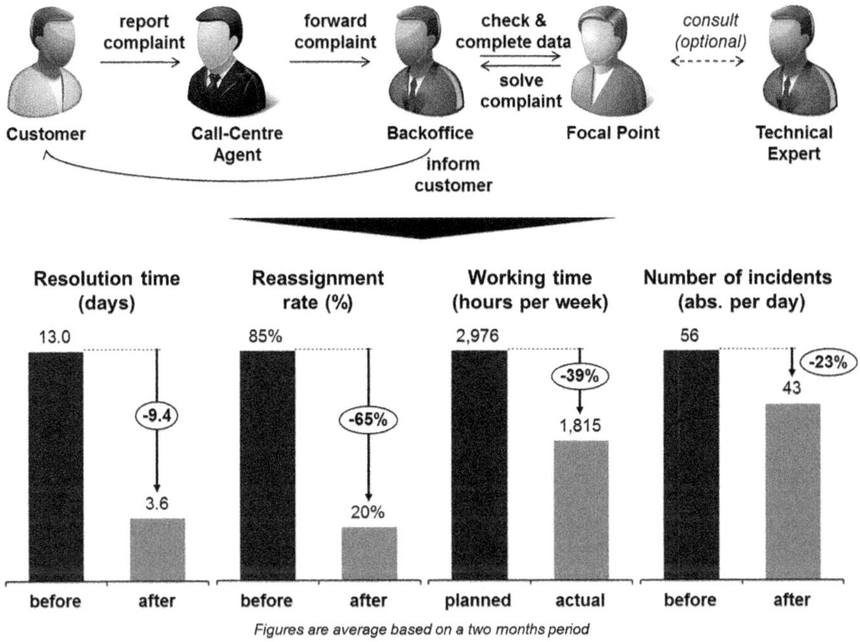

Fig. 7 Results of the improved incident management process

organization (e.g., process owners) supported the project with 30–40% of their working time. In addition, a team of eight external experts was involved. All process optimizations were realized through minor changes of existing IT systems, which was one of the initial project requirements.

The qualitative and quantitative results illustrated in Fig. 7 are based on the project scope described in Sect. 3. The project's objective was the overall enhancement of the process governance in order to improve customer satisfaction and operational efficiency. Both of these goals were shown by quantitative improvements on an operational level related to the pilot implementation of the incident management process. However, gaining the full benefits of the project would require application and extension to other processes. At the end of the project, this result was not finally evaluated. Four insights provide indications for future efforts:

- *Detailed implementation tasks were only partially finished.* A monitoring of all planned implementation tasks showed that 45% were realized during the project duration. The implementation of further 38% was started. And 17% were not started yet.
- *Planned changes of application systems were only partially finished.* 40% of these changes were realized during the project, while 60% require additional budget and decisions.

- *Continuous changes in organizational positions required ongoing re-nominations and additional training*. The results achieved in the implementation of process ownership and training of relevant stakeholders were jeopardized by parallel reorganization initiatives.
- *Alignment with future initiatives was not completely ensured*. Other transformational initiatives were launched during the project that were not completely aligned with the project. For example, a reorganization of the call center was started, which might influence the incident management process.

5 Lessons Learned

The case described here is an example of the establishment of a central BPM organization combined with a company-wide process framework, as well as the improvement of a selected process on an operational level. Figure 8 provides a classification of the project context based on criteria proposed by vom Brocke et al. (2015). In this section, the actions taken and results achieved are discussed ex post based on general BPM concepts and literature.

According to the BPM lifecycle model proposed by Dumas et al. (2013), the case describes one complete execution of this lifecycle. The process framework provided a high-level architecture for the identification and discovery steps. The

Contextual Factors	Case Characteristics
Goal dimension	
Focus	Exploitation (Improvement, Compliance)
Process dimension	
Value contribution	Core processes
Repetitiveness	Repetitive
Knowledge intensity	Medium knowledge intensity
Creativity	Medium creativity
Interdependence	High interdependence
Variability	Medium variability
Organizational dimension	
Scope	Intra-organizational process
Industry	Service industry
Size	Large organization
Culture	Culture medium supportive of BPM
Resources	Medium organizational resources
Environmental dimension	
Competitiveness	High competitive environment
Uncertainty	Medium environmental uncertainty

Fig. 8 Contextual factors of the project case

incident management process was selected for a detailed as-is-analysis, redesign, and implementation on the operational level. The results were monitored, and quantitative performance improvements were identified.

The case illustrates concrete artifacts of the BPM dimensions (Rosemann and vom Brocke 2010). The diagnostics study provided strategic alignment through the identification of gaps and planning of improvements measures, both of which were aligned with the overall strategic objectives. From the governance perspective, process-related standards, roles, responsibilities, and management decisions were centralized in a new BPM department. Methods for design, implementation, monitoring, and improvement were also defined and supported by information technology, for example, through a central repository for process models.

The people dimension was addressed through continuous involvement of all stakeholders and various communication and training measures. A prerequisite of the project was identification of relevant stakeholders and their informational needs. Both were supported by the process ownership model and the specific process framework. Consideration of the organizational hierarchies and a fact-based allocation of responsibilities were important aspects of the project. Especially during the process design, a balance between the incorporation of specific requirements and standardization according to reference models was essential. Therefore, a transparent procedure for decision-making was defined and communicated at the beginning of the project. The incident management process was improved by executing the developed process governance and methods.

On an operational level, the process implementation was supported by changes in application systems. Monitoring the performance improvements provided a link between the strategic improvement planning and the process execution on an operational level.

In summary, from the general BPM perspective, five primary lessons learned are derived from the case:

1. *Process content is an important success factor in a BPM implementation.* A major part of the project was the establishment of general BPM governance and methods. Even in an early stage of the project the knowledge of specific processes—related in this case to the telecommunications industry—was important. This process content was provided by the industry-specific reference process model eTOM. The process framework based on eTOM combined the general methods with the specific situation. For example, the nomination of process owners for the detailed design required an understanding of the specific processes. During the BPM diagnostics, eTOM was also used in evaluating the existing situation.
2. *Process ownership requires consideration of the various BPM elements.* The mapping between the processes and the organizational structure was an important result of the project. This mapping should support the analysis, design, implementation, and execution. It should provide a balance between a cross-functional view and operational details. Furthermore, the general governance should be differentiated from the topical responsibility for specific processes.

The case provides an example of a process ownership model that defines detailed roles and responsibilities. The process ownership model was mapped to the concrete organizational positions using the specific process framework.
3. *Early involvement of stakeholders from top management to the operational level is essential for successful implementation.* The successful implementation resulted in various changes in the current situation. For example, changes in governance were related to the overall corporate management, while operational improvements impacted the daily work that was supported by application systems. Already during the planning and design, the involvement of relevant stakeholders was essential. Consensus and acceptance were in most cases a prerequisite for an implementation. Early communication and the opportunity to give feedback helped to avoid resistance to the planned changes.
4. *Customization of reference models requires a transparent approach to decision making.* The detailed design included various decisions about specific requirements that differed from the reference model. However, a benefit of reusing a reference model is standardization according to general recommendations. A balance between deviation and standardization was important. Therefore, a clear approach to fact-based decision making was defined, where responsibilities were based on the process ownership model. The official agreement and communication of this approach before the start of the detailed design was also important.
5. *General BPM governance and methods are important for an operational process improvement.* The improvement of the incident management process resulted in proven, documented performance enhancements. This improvement was a pilot implementation of the general governance structures and methods defined in the central BPM department. Hence, this case provides an example for operational improvements that were strongly supported by prior establishment of BPM. Furthermore, this case illustrates the interrelation between BPM and operational improvements.

The transformational needs of the telecommunications industry are intensively discussed by researchers and practitioners (e.g., Grover and Saeed 2003; Picot 2006; Czarnecki et al. 2010; Bub et al. 2011). In this context, the case provides an example of transforming the processes of a historically grown operator to address the typical requirements of more customer orientation and cross-functional alignment (e.g., Bruce et al. 2008). An example of the reuse and customization of the well-recognized reference process model eTOM (Kelly 2003; Czarnecki et al. 2013) is also provided. Hence, the case can be used as a reference for planning transformational projects in the telecommunications industry.

References

Bruce, G., Naughton, B., Trew, D., et al. (2008). Streamlining the telco production line. *Journal of Telecommunications Management, 1*, 15–32.

Bub, U., Picot, A., & Krcmar, H. (2011). The future of telecommunications. *Business and Information Systems Engineering, 3*, 265–267. doi:10.1007/s12599-011-0178-0.
Czarnecki, C., & Dietze, C. (2017). *Reference architecture for the telecommunications industry: Transformation of strategy, organization, processes, data, and applications*. Berlin: Springer.
Czarnecki, C., Winkelmann, A., & Spiliopoulou, M. (2010). Services in electronic telecommunication markets: A framework for planning the virtualization of processes. *Electronic Markets, 20*, 197–207.
Czarnecki, C., Winkelmann, A., & Spiliopoulou, M. (2012). Transformation in telecommunication – Analyse und clustering von real-life Projekten. In D. C. Mattfeld & S. Robra-Bissantz (Eds.), *Multi-Konferenz Wirtschaftsinformatik 2012* (pp. 985–998). Braunschweig: GITO.
Czarnecki, C., Winkelmann, A., & Spiliopoulou, M. (2013). Reference process flows for telecommunication companies: An extension of the eTOM model. *Business and Information Systems Engineering, 5*, 83–96. doi:10.1007/s12599-013-0250-z.
Dumas, M., La Rosa, M., Mendling, J., & Reijers, H. A. (2013). *Fundamentals of business process management*. Berlin: Springer.
Grover, V., & Saeed, K. (2003). The telecommunication industry revisited. *Communications of the ACM, 46*, 119–125. doi:10.1145/792704.792709.
Hammer, M. (2007). The process audit. *Harvard Business Review, 85*, 111–123.
Hammer, M. (2010). What is business process management? In J. vom Brocke & M. Rosemann (Eds.), *Handbook on business process management* (Vol. 1, pp. 3–16). Berlin: Springer.
Hevner, A. R., March, S. T., Park, J., & Ram, S. (2004). Design science in information systems research. *MIS Quarterly, 28*, 75–105.
Kelly, M. B. (2003). The TeleManagement forum's enhanced telecom operations map (eTOM). *Journal of Network and Systems Management, 11*, 109–119.
Picot, A. (Ed.). (2006). *The future of telecommunications industries*. Berlin: Springer.
Pousttchi, K., & Hufenbach, Y. (2011). Value creation in the mobile market: A reference model for the role(s) of the future mobile network operator. *Business and Information Systems Engineering, 3*, 299–311. doi:10.1007/s12599-011-0175-3.
Rosemann, M., & vom Brocke, J. (2010). The six core elements of business process management. In J. von Brocke & M. Rosemann (Eds.), *Handbook on business process management* (Vol. 1, pp. 107–122). Berlin: Springer.
Schermann, M., Prilla, M., Krcmar, H., & Herrmann, T. (2008). *Bringing life into references process models: A participatory approach for identifying, discussing, and resolving model adaptations*. Multikonferenz Wirtschaftsinformatik.
vom Brocke, J., Zelt, S., & Schmiedel, T. (2015). Considering context in business process management: The BPM context framework. *BPTrends Class Notes*, 1–15.
Wulf, J., & Zarnekow, R. (2011). Cross-sector competition in telecommunications: An empirical analysis of diversification activities. *Business and Information Systems Engineering, 3*, 289–298. doi:10.1007/s12599-011-0177-1.

Christian Czarnecki is Professor of Information Systems at the *Hochschule für Telekommunikation Leipzig*, Germany. He received his Doctor of Engineering from the University of Magdeburg. He has extensive practical experience in different consulting companies and has managed numerous transformation projects in Europe, North Africa, and the Middle East. His research includes process management, reference models, and enterprise architectures with a focus on the telecommunications industry. In the industry organization TM Forum he is involved in the further development of the reference model *enhanced Telecom Operations Map* (eTOM). He has authored various publications including articles in *Business and Information Systems Engineering* (BISE) and *Electronic Markets* (EM) as well as a book about a *Reference Architecture for the Telecommunications Industry.*

BPM Adoption and Business Transformation at Snaga, a Public Company: Critical Success Factors for Five Stages of BPM

Andrej Kovačič, Gregor Hauc, Brina Buh, and Mojca Indihar Štemberger

Abstract

(a) **Situation faced**: Snaga is a Slovenian public company that provides a series of waste treatment services for 368,000 citizens of the Municipality of Ljubljana and ten other municipalities. In 2006, prior to adopting BPM and implementing a new information system, the company had obsolete and non-integrated IT solutions that did not provide sufficient support to the business operations. The existing business processes were not well organized, resulting in unnecessary duplication of work and excessive delays. The company also faced new challenges in waste management and new legislation that dictated the development of waste-processing technologies.

(b) **Action taken**: The company's executives were aware that the company's way of doing business was inadequate and that changes were necessary if the company was to improve its business operations and maintain its competitive advantage. The company comprehensively transformed its business operations and adopted BPM in order to undertake the critical examination, rethinking, and then redesigning of current business processes, practices, and rules. The BPM project was conducted in three phases: (1) planning for strategic business transformation, (2) business process restructuring and information architecture development, and (3) information system development and implementation in six interdependent projects.

A. Kovačič • B. Buh • M.I. Štemberger (✉)
Faculty of Economics, University of Ljubljana, Ljubljana, Slovenia
e-mail: andrej.kovacic@ef.uni-lj.si; brina.buh@ef.uni-lj.si; mojca.stemberger@ef.uni-lj.si

G. Hauc
Snaga Public Company Ljubljana, Ljubljana, Slovenia
e-mail: gregor.hauc@snaga.si

J. vom Brocke, J. Mendling (eds.), *Business Process Management Cases*,
Management for Professionals, DOI 10.1007/978-3-319-58307-5_5

(c) **Results achieved**: Adopting BPM brought considerable benefits to the company. A key change brought by the BPM adoption was the transition from a functional to a more process-oriented organization with an increased customer focus. The company implemented an ERP solution to support the redesigned business processes, established process ownership and a BPM office, and introduced KPIs to measure the performance and efficiency of processes and business operations using a business intelligence solution. BPM became a way of life at Snaga, and the company has undergone considerable transformation in the last decade, evolving from a traditional, functionally organised and managed company in 2005 to a process-oriented company in 2010. Today it is one of the most effective and efficient municipal utility companies in Europe. In the past 2 years, the company also transformed itself from focusing on waste collection and delivery to separate waste collection, waste processing and promoting a zero-waste society. The company's operating results improved significantly from 2012 to 2015, and in the 10 years ending in 2015 increased the waste it processed after collected separately from 16 to 145 kg per user, which ranked the company at the top of the industry in Europe.

(d) **Lessons learned**: The involvement—rather than just support—of top management is one of the most important critical success factors in all phases of BPM adoption. The role of the chief process officer, who was enthusiastic and encouraging during all stages of the project, and business drivers were particularly important, and the chief process officer's communication approach contributed to the employees' openness to change, which was essential for success. The professional guidance of external consultants was also helpful. Identifying key performance indicators and persons responsible for their achievement was the most important critical success factor I the production phase. The company also integrated the BPM philosophy with ISO 9001:2015 into a strong management system.

1 Introduction

The adoption of BPM is a complex and time-consuming process that requires considerable effort, time, resources, and discipline. Bandara et al. (2009) observed that many organizations have tried to change their businesses to comply with a process orientation, yet only a few have managed to completely integrate their business functions into end-to-end processes.

Snaga, a Slovenian public company that adopted BPM successfully, provides a series of services for a third of the Slovenian population, including the collection and processing of waste, the removal and disposal of municipal waste (which accounts for only 4.5% of total waste), cleaning of public areas, restroom management, placarding, and overhaul. Snaga is part of Public Holding Ljubljana, which provides services to ensure efficient, economical, and user-oriented mandatory public utility services in the Ljubljana Green Capital of Europe 2016 (EU 2015). In 2016 the company employed 500 workers and collected more than 130,000 tons of waste, of which 95% is processed, while the rest is disposed of.

In 2005 Snaga's executives recognised that the company's way of doing business was inadequate and changes were necessary. The company comprehensively transformed its business operations and adopted BPM by conducting several consecutive and interdependent projects over the next 7 years. Adopting BPM brought considerable benefits to the company and enabled it to maintain its competitive advantage. This chapter discusses how the organization transformed into a process-oriented organization.

2 Situation Faced

Prior to adopting BPM and implementing a new information system (IS), the company had obsolete and non-integrated information technology (IT) solutions provided insufficient support to its business operations. Data acquisition for employees was time-consuming, and many business transaction records and other data were held manually in Microsoft Excel and Word. The existing business processes were not well organized, resulting in the unnecessary duplication of work and excessive delays.

In addition, the company faced new challenges in waste management and new legislation that dictated the development of waste-processing technologies. In the future, Snaga will have to process as much waste as possible into secondary raw material and burn only the residue without disposing of it, so the company was granted resources from the EU Cohesion Fund to develop a regional centre for processing waste, the RCERO project, which started in 2003 with project planning and finished at the end of 2016 (RCERO 2015). The regional centre entered trial operations in November 2015.

The company's executives were aware that the company's way of doing business was inadequate and that changes were necessary if the company were to improve its business operations and maintain its competitive advantage. Therefore, they decided to completely redesign the existing business processes and to adopt other BPM practices.

Snaga's main objectives in adopting BPM were to improve the effectiveness and efficiency of its business operations, thereby reducing the costs and time spent providing the services, increasing productivity, making the transition from functional to process organization, and increasing the service quality. In addition, the company's executives anticipated that adopting BPM and optimizing the business processes would enable them to select and implement the appropriate enterprise resource planning (ERP) solution and business intelligence (BI) system to support business processes in the company. Moreover, adopting BPM would enable the implementation of CRM, SCM, and HRM and help the company to maintain its quality certificates (ISO standards).

3 Action Taken

Snaga comprehensively transformed its business operations and adopted BPM by means of several consecutive and interdependent projects. The company used the business transformation approach (BTA) methodology and the professional guidance of external consultants.

BTA is an iterative methodological framework that focuses on business processes, business rules, and data in a system from which all knowledge of the business derives. It incorporates the best practices of more than 20 business transformation projects and certain fundamental principles that are already known in business system planning, BPR, and the IS development environment: business rules and the business activity meta-model, iterative development, and prototyping (O'Regan and Ghobadian 2002; Perkins 2002; Kovacic 2004).

BTA planning, development, and implementation can be divided into several iterative development phases (Fig. 1):

- Strategic business transformation planning
- Business process restructuring and information architecture (IA) development
- Information system (IS) development and implementation

Strategic business transformation planning implies an attempt to alter a company's strength relative to that of its competitors in the most efficient and effective way possible. This kind of planning focuses on the organization's direction and the actions that are necessary to improve its performance (O'Regan and Ghobadian

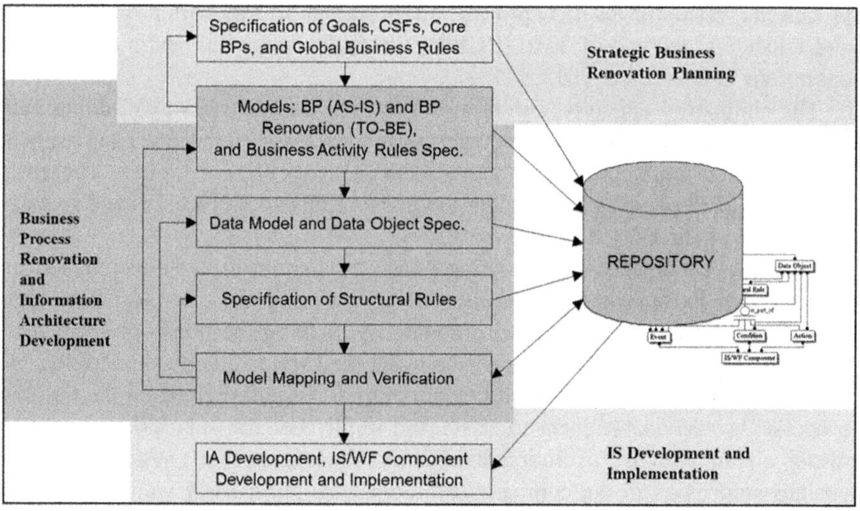

Fig. 1 Business transformation approach: phases and results. Source: adopted from Kovacic (2004)

2002). All of these results are captured in the rule repository and used in the next phases of the business transformation process.

In the business process transformation phase, the company undertakes the critical examination, rethinking, and then redesigning of current business processes, practices, and rules. The as-is model is developed in several iterations, in each of which the model is validated against the actual process for process flow by performing several executions of the process executions and for performance by comparing the times obtained in the simulations to average times measured for the entire process and its segments. The final as-is model is reasonably close to the actual process, with some minor discrepancies resulting because not all real situations can be anticipated and modelled. Finally, the to-be model is developed and its efficiency is analysed.

During this phase of BTA the IA is also defined. IA is the planning, designing, and constructing of an information blueprint that covers the business process rules on the activity level and satisfies the informational needs of business processes and decision-making. It is derived from the to-be business process model and the strategic business process transformation plan that is developed in the strategic planning phase. IA calls for full recognition of the importance of business rules and data in the design and development of an IS from the perspective of a balance between processes and data.

The results of the business transformation and IA development phase are the organization's to-be business process model (Process Architecture), a global data model (Data Architecture), and technological/organizational foundations. Determination of the global data model or data architecture is the next step in IA development. The global data model is presented as an entity-relational model that contains the company's major data entities and business rules. It reflects the company's global information needs.

In the IS development and implementation phase, we presume that the organization's to-be business process model and global data model that were developed in the previous stage contain the models' major business rules and information needs and are a suitable foundation for further development activities. In the case of a proprietary development, the activities are concerned with conceptual data modelling and logical database design. The final results of this stage are a database and application solutions developed for the particular application area or business process selected.

Service-oriented architecture (SOA), ERP application solutions, and other modern software packages are emerging process-oriented tools that can enable and implement business transformation in this phase. In this context, we recognize our to-be business process model and business-rule model as the starting points of the ERP implementation process.

Snaga's adoption of BPM is discussed later using Rosemann's (2010) framework, so the BPM adoption process at Snaga is presented in Fig. 2.

The first step in Snaga's adoption of BPM was the awareness that there were problems with the organization's processes and opportunities to improve them. Snaga's executives were aware of the future challenges and the need to change their

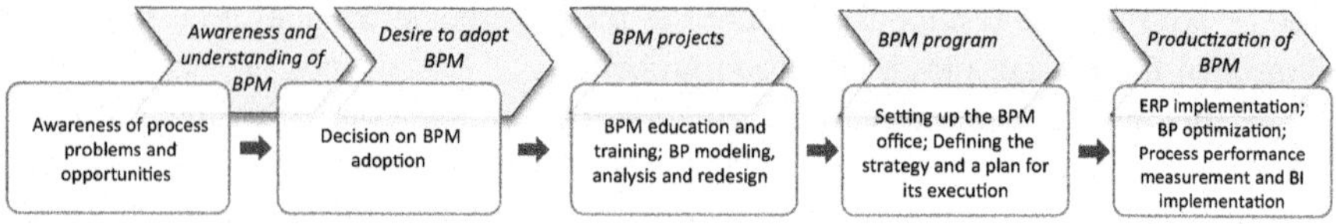

Fig. 2 Stages of BPM adoption at Snaga. Source: Snaga's internal documentation; Rosemann (2010)

business operations, so they decided to adopt BPM because, as the CEO said, they believed "that BPM would bring Snaga greater competitiveness, better management of business processes and long-term success." A precondition of this decision, which represents the second stage of Snaga's BPM adoption, was the awareness and understanding of BPM, which led to the desire to adopt it.

The initiator of the BPM adoption was the company's chief information officer (CIO), who worked closely with external consultants and garnered the support of top management. External consultants were hired to supervise the projects' implementation and advise the company when the projects deviated from the main objectives of the BPM adoption.

At the beginning of the third stage of BPM adoption, the CEO appointed the project team, which consisted of employees who had the knowledge and experience to contribute to the successful adoption of BPM, including executives, heads of departments, and key users. The first project they conducted was business process modelling, analysis, and redesign. External consultants modelled and analysed several existing business processes using a BTA methodology that had been verified in interviews with employees involved in the process and the available documentation. Even during the modelling and description of the processes many uncertainties were resolved, and the employees' understanding of BPM and business process orientation increased.

Next, the consultants and Snaga's managers proposed several process improvements in line with the adopted strategy and other employees: process optimization, introduction of process ownership, and setting up a BPM office. During the project a number of workshops were conducted to encourage the 'process' way of thinking in the company. The company accelerated its training of employees to raise their competence. The biggest challenge in redesigning the company's existing processes lay in changing the mentality of the people in the processes. At the end of this stage, Snaga introduced some of the important concepts of process orientation, such as process ownership for core end-to-end processes.

The fourth stage of the BPM adoption at Snaga involved the establishment of the BPM office, which is managed by chief process officer (CPO), who was once the CIO. The company's executives and BPM office redefined the company's development strategy, including the vision, mission, and strategic objectives, and identified strategic projects to achieve them using a strategy and a roadmap for BPM adoption (a BPM program). As the CPO said, "The company paid a lot of attention to ensure proper communication, both vertically (top to bottom and vice versa) and horizontally (within the business processes) among the various sectors and departments." By encouraging communication they hoped to ensure that all employees understood the objectives of the BPM adoption and that a suitable organizational culture would emerge.

In the last stage of the BPM adoption, Snaga implemented a new ERP solution to support the redesigned business processes. Best practices from ERP solutions were studied prior to the implementation and taken into account in redesigning processes.

Other projects (Fig. 3) conducted during this stage by several project teams with some help from external consultants included implementation of a Balanced ScoreCard (BSC) system and standards and criteria for measuring the business processes' effectiveness and efficiency. Snaga developed key performance indicators (KPIs) for every core business process and implemented a BI solution that allows it to measure efficiency and performance across all core business processes. With the new BI solution's support, the process owners monitor KPIs

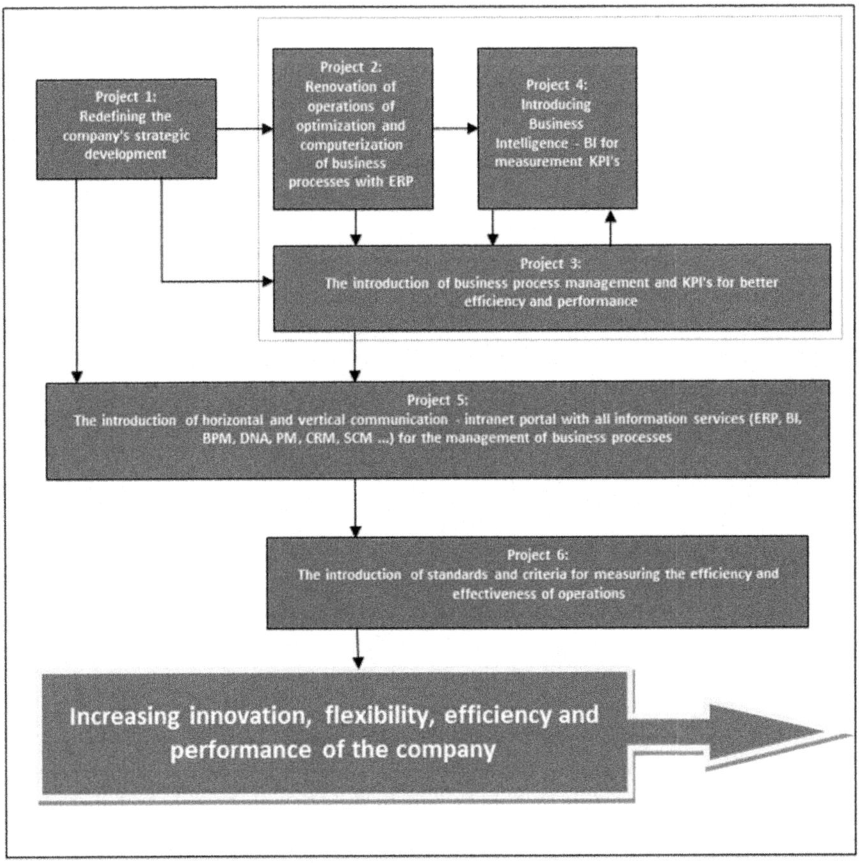

Fig. 3 BPM projects at Snaga. Source: Hauc (2016)

daily and often find ideas for improvement in the results. Snaga also re-certified the ISO 9001:2015 quality system through which it manages and improves its business operations.

The CEO, who was actively involved in the projects, proposed improvements and encouraged employees to accept changes. The CPO and other members of the BPM office cooperate with the process owners and suggest further improvements of business processes. The BPM office is responsible for maintaining the process models and informing employees about ongoing events via the intranet. The CPO also writes ongoing news about the BPM adoption, which is published in the in-house newsletter *Snagec* and is accessible to all employees.

4 Results Achieved

To determine whether Snaga's BPM adoption was successful, we chose two out of ten BPM maturity models identified by Röglinger et al. (2012): Process Performance Index (PPI) from the Rummler-Brache Group (2004) and the BPO maturity model from McCormack and Johnson (2001). Both models have been validated empirically, both are generic (i.e., they are used for business processes in general), both produce quantitative data (i.e., they can be statistically analysed and compared easily, independent of the assessors' interpretations), and both take into account all business processes in the organizations involved. In addition, the assessment does not take a lot of time, and the assessment questions and corresponding calculations are fully known and publicly available without charge.

Snaga's PPI index is 47, so the company is in the third stage of process management maturity, called "process management mastery." For organizations in this final stage of process maturity, BPM is a way of life and process management is fully integrated into the organization's planning and overall performance evaluations (Rummler-Brache Group 2004). The BPO maturity questionnaire gives Snaga a score of 4.6, the highest level of BPO maturity, defined as "integrated." This level is characterized by process-based organizational structures and jobs and process measures and management systems that are deeply imbedded in the organization (McCormack and Johnson 2001).

Adopting BPM has brought considerable benefits to the company. A key change brought about by the BPM adoption was the transition from a functional to a more process-oriented organization with an increased customer focus. The company introduced process ownership, established a BPM office, and incorporated KPIs to measure the performance and efficiency of processes and business operations. In addition to process owners, the company introduced administrators of business processes whose job it is to connect core and support business processes and, in cooperation with the process owners, search for opportunities for improving business processes.

The BPM office plays an important role in the company and is at the executive level. It is responsible for assigning tasks to the process owners and other employees in the company and for motivating and training them to work in accordance with the new (process) ways of working. The process owners are responsible for ensuring that business processes are clearly determined and have well-defined CSFs and KPIs.

Business processes are managed with the support of Snaga's BI system, where each process owner monitors the KPIs for his or her own process and can measure the process's efficiency and effectiveness on the company level.

A process-oriented culture at Snaga, which was established by educating the employees and encouraging the 'process' way of thinking, is maintained by means of continuous employee training, presentations and analyses of results of business operations, and appropriate actions. Top-down, bottom-up, and especially horizontal communication has been improved. Every year, the CPO, in cooperation with the process owners, process administrators, and key users, reviews the CSFs, objectives, measures, and indicators for each process, including the suitability of process models and descriptions of process activities. To ensure realization of the company's strategy, they consider three critical factors for the company's efficiency and success: human resources, processes, and technology.

Employees accepted BPM as a permanent activity that is carried out in an organised and standardised manner. At least once a year the company performs internal audits of the management system in accordance with the requirements of ISO9001:2015, ISO18001:2009, and ISO14001:2004. Employees who are internal auditors are invited to look for emerging gaps and opportunities for improvement.

The adoption of BPM has yielded significant positive results for the company and its business operations. The company gained a good overview of its business processes and the deficiencies of the processes were exposed and eliminated, which contributed to an increase in customer and employee satisfaction, a 50% reduction in complaints, increased price competitiveness, and the company's improved business value.

5 Lessons Learned

Based on our experience from the project and on additional interviews with Snaga's CEO and process owners, CSFs for Snaga's BPM adoption were identified for each stage of the adoption process, as presented in Table 1.

In the first stage of Snaga's BPM adoption, the empowerment of employees was important because of the company's increased customer focus. When the company put its customers in first place, top management became aware of process-related problems and the need for their improvement. Another important factor identified was openness to changes, which was critical in the company's ability to advance to the second stage of BPM adoption.

In the second stage top management support and a project champion were important success factors, together with business drivers. Business drivers (a sense of urgency) and champions are required if the desire to adopt BPM is to be triggered (Rosemann 2010). The business drivers for the BPM adoption at Snaga can be summarized as (1) new challenges in waste management and new legislation that dictates the development of waste-processing technologies, as waste disposal without processing will not be possible in the future; (2) the need to replace outdated and inadequate IT solutions and systems; and (3) the need to establish technical and quality control over business operations in order to enhance customer satisfaction

Table 1 Critical success factors at five stages of the BPM adoption at Snaga

BPM adoption stage	Critical success factors
Awareness and understanding of BPM	• Empowerment of employees • Customer focus • Openness to change
Desire to adopt BPM	• Involvement and full support of top management • Project champion • Business drivers (a sense of urgency)
BPM projects	• Well-communicated and clearly defined objectives, purpose, and plan for the BPM project • Professional guidance of external consultants • People who are willing and motivated to change
BPM program	• Involvement and full support of top management • Vertical and horizontal communication • Professional guidance of external consultants • Communication
Productization of BPM	• Involvement and full support of top management • Professional guidance of external consultants • Identification of key performance indicators and persons responsible for their achievement • Educated, trained and motivated employees • Synergy between BPM and ISO9001:2015

through faster and cheaper provision of services. At Snaga, the project champion was the company's CPO, who was responsible for building support among the company's executives and other employees by actively promoting the BPM projects and spreading information about their progress. Special attention to promoting the BPM adoption is necessary to create a positive atmosphere in an organization.

In the third stage of BPM adoption, the well-communicated and clearly defined objectives, purpose, and plan of the BPM project were essential. For a successful business process modelling, analysis, and redesign project an organization has to clearly define the project objectives and its purpose and communicate them to all participants before the project starts (Indihar Štemberger and Jaklič 2007). The project at Snaga was led by the company's CPO, who is an expert in project management and who paid considerable attention to communicating the project's clearly defined objectives, purpose, and plan, which enabled the participants to recognize the expected benefits of the project. In addition, as the CEO and other Snaga employees claimed, the help of external consultants who provided appropriate methodology and professional assistance significantly contributed to the project's success. Thus, the organization avoided many problems during the project, such as inadequately described and evaluated existing business processes, employee resistance, and unwillingness to participate in the project because of fear of redundancies and changes that would degrade employees' positions.

Since the success of any project largely depends on the organization's people and their willingness and desire to change, communication among all employees in the organization is important. The experience of two consultants who participated in our case study indicated that all participants in the project have to cooperate fully and understand the purpose of adopting BPM. Employees must be appropriately educated, and motivated to understand and adopt the necessary changes in the company. At Snaga, the communication among employees was ensured through the intranet, meetings, and interviews, and the education was promoted by means of several workshops.

The CSFs of the fourth stage of BPM adoption were top management support (especially the support and involvement of the CPO and the CEO), the professional guidance of external consultants, and good communication skills. As one consultant said, "It is essential that top management not only provides support, but is also actively involved." The strategy, objectives, and implementation plan should be specified, and the organizational culture must be open to change.

In the last stage, the people (top management support, guidance from external consultants, and knowledgeable employees), the identification of KPIs, and assigning individuals to be responsible for their achievement were important. The CEO set the objectives at the company level and the employees set the indicators for achieving these objectives at the process level.

References

Bandara, W., Alibabaei, A., & Aghdasi, M. (2009). Means of achieving business process management success factors. In P. Ein-Dor, A. Poulymenakou, & M. Amami (Eds.), *Proceedings of the 4th Mediterranean Conference on Information Systems*, 25–27 September 2009, Athens University of Economics and Business, Athens.

European Commission. (2015). *Environment European Green Capital.* Finding on web site http://ec.europa.eu/environment/european greencapital/winning-cities/2016-ljubljana/

Hauc, G. (2016). *The methodological approach for the holistic business renovation and its Support* (pp. 242). PhD thesis, Faculty of Economics Ljubljana.

Indihar Štemberger, M., & Jaklič, J. (2007). Towards E-government by business process change—A methodology for public sector. *International Journal of Information Management, 27*(4), 221–232.

Kovacic, A. (2004). Business renovation: Business rules (still) the missing link. *Business Process Management Journal, 10*(2), 158–170.

McCormack, K. P., & Johnson, W. C. (2001). *Business process orientation: Gaining the e-business competitive advantage*. Boca Raton, FL: St. Lucie Press.

O'Regan, N., & Ghobadian, A. (2002). Formal strategic planning: Key to effective business process management. *Business Process Management Journal, 8*(5), 416–429.

Perkins, A. (2002). Business rules are meta data. *Business Rules Journal, 3*(1).

RCERO. (2015). *The upgrade of the Regional Waste Management Centre RCERO Ljubljana.* Finding on web site http://www.ljubljana.si/en/living-in-ljubljana/focus/100619/detail.html

Röglinger, M., Pöppelbuß, J., & Becker, J. (2012). Maturity models in business process management. *Business Process Management Journal, 18*(2), 328–346.

Rosemann, M. (2010). The service portfolio of a BPM center of excellence. In J. vom Brocke & M. Rosemann (Eds.), *Handbook on business process management, International handbooks on information systems* (Vol. 2, pp. 267–284). Berlin: Springer.

Rummler-Brache Group. (2004). *Business process management in U.S. firms today*. Accessed June 23, 2012, from http://r.ummler-brache.com/upload/files/PPI_Research_Results.pdf

Andrej Kovačič is a retired full professor of information management at the Faculty of Economics, University of Ljubljana, Slovenia. He is the head of the Business Informatics Institute at Faculty of Economics. Between 2010 and 2014 he was a Vice Rector at the University of Ljubljana. His main research areas are business process management and information systems development. He has published several scientific and professional papers and was engaged as a consultant and project manager on several Business Process Reengineering and Information System development projects. He is an expert on Management Consulting and IT, Management Consultant (Certificate PHARE-Cegos) and EDP (Information Systems) auditor. He is the founder of Slovene Business Process Management conference and ex Chair and member of the editorial board of the Slovene journal for business informatics Uporabna informatika, and member of Slovene Society of Informatics.

Gregor Hauc is assistant director in public company Snaga L.t.d. in Ljubljana, which offers services for waste collected and waste recycling to more than 760,000 inhabitants of Slovenia region. He is responsible for business process management, quality system management (ISO9001:2015, ISO14001:2015 and ISO18001:2007), information technology (ERP, BI, GIS), process oriented organization and corporate facility services. In September 2016 he successfully defended his doctoral thesis at Faculty of Economics, University of Ljubljana, in which he highlighted in particular the methodological approach "Comprehensive redesign and digitalization of business processes" through six interconnected and dependent projects. He also works as consultant in area of BPM and IT.

Brina Buh is a Risk Analyst at Nova Ljubljanska Banka, d.d., Ljubljana. She completed her PhD at the Faculty of Economics, University of Ljubljana, Slovenia, where she was employed as a Young Researcher. Her research interests include Business Process Management and its connection to Organizational Culture. She presented her work at several international and domestic scientific conferences and published her work in Economic Research, Baltic Journal of Management, and Economic and Business Review. She also worked on consulting projects in the area of business process renovation. She is a member of Beta Gamma Sigma society, which is the international honour society recognizing business excellence.

Mojca Indihar Štemberger is a Full Professor of Business Informatics and a Chair of Academic Unit for Business Informatics and Logistics at Faculty of Economics, University of Ljubljana, Slovenia. Her main research areas are business process management and information systems management. She published her work in International Journal of Information Management, International Journal of Production Economics, Business Process Management Journal and others. She is also active in consulting and applied research, and was involved in several BPM and IS management projects.

Enabling Flexibility of Business Processes Using Compliance Rules: The Case of Mobiliar

Thanh Tran Thi Kim, Erhard Weiss, Christoph Ruhsam, Christoph Czepa, Huy Tran, and Uwe Zdun

Abstract

(a) **Situation faced**: Insurance case work can follow established procedures only to a certain degree, as the work depends upon experienced knowledge workers who decide the best solutions for their clients. To produce quality documents in such a knowledge-intensive environment, business users of Die Mobiliar, the oldest private insurance company in Switzerland, were guided by a wizard application that enabled them to compose insurance documents from predefined building blocks in a series of pre-defined steps. As these steps were hardcoded into the wizard application, the processes could not adapt quickly enough to accommodate new insurance products and associated documentation. Rapidly changing insurance markets produce new types of documents daily, so business users must react flexibly to client requests. Although fully automated processes can be defined when sufficient process knowledge exists, they seriously hinder the innovation and business agility that is critical in insurance markets.

(b) **Action taken**: To overcome this problem, Die Mobiliar uses the Papyrus Communication and Process Platform (http://www.isis-papyrus.com/e15/pages/software/platform-concept.html) as the basis for its customized "Mobiliar Korrespondenz System" (MKS, Mobiliar Correspondence System), with full functionality for online interactive business document production (ISIS Papyrus). Our approach combines automatically executed

T.T.T. Kim • E. Weiss • C. Ruhsam (✉)
ISIS Papyrus Europe AG, Maria Enzersdorf, Austria
e-mail: thanh.tran@isis-papyrus.com; erhard.weiss@isis-papyrus.com; christoph.ruhsam@isis-papyrus.com

C. Czepa • H. Tran • U. Zdun
Research Group Software Architecture, University of Vienna, Vienna, Austria
e-mail: christoph.czepa@univie.ac.at; huy.tran@univie.ac.at; uwe.zdun@univie.ac.at

J. vom Brocke, J. Mendling (eds.), *Business Process Management Cases*,
Management for Professionals, DOI 10.1007/978-3-319-58307-5_6

business compliance rules with process redesign to provide the flexibility that is essential for insurance processes. The original processes are split into reusable sub-processes, accompanied by a set of ad hoc tasks that the business users can activate at runtime to meet clients' emergent requirements. A set of compliance rules guarantees that the process conforms to corporate and regulatory standards.

(c) **Results achieved**: The business compliance rule approach has two primary benefits: (i) company management has a process that is well-documented and provably compliant, and (ii) the business users can respond flexibly to their clients' needs within the boundaries of defined compliance rules, thus improving the customer experience. The flexibility achieved by this approach allows business users to adapt their insurance processes, an advantage from which the whole insurance industry can benefit. The redesigned process with few reusable core elements, combination with a set of ad hoc tasks, decreases the number of process templates (wizard processes) that are required to handle unpredictable situations. A smaller template library also reduces maintenance efforts for business administrators.

(d) **Lessons learned**: Rigid process modeling is not suitable for highly dynamic business domains, like the insurance industry, that are moving into the digital era. Instead, a hybrid of declarative and imperative modeling is best suited to such domains. Our approach provides a maximum of flexibility within mandated constraints, enabling businesses to adapt to changing market requirements with minimal involvement by IT departments. In order to set expectations properly, the use of the two modeling types should be transparent to business users. The adoption of the new approach happens gradually to cope with business considerations like the integration of compliance checking into Die Mobiliar's production system.

1 Introduction

The Swiss insurance company Die Mobiliar is the oldest private insurance organization in Switzerland. As a multiline insurer that offers a full range of insurance and pension products and services, Die Mobiliar handles a large number of documents, which are exchanged with approximately 1.7 million customers (Mobiliar: Die Mobiliar Versicherungen und Vorsorge). An insurance document issued by Die Mobiliar is not only a piece of paper; it serves as a business card, representing the company to its customers. Moreover, Die Mobiliar considers well-designed documents that are rich in content as an opportunity to communicate and build a strong relationship with its customers.

Die Mobiliar uses the Papyrus Communication and Process Platform[1] as the basis for its customized "Mobiliar Korrespondenz System" (MKS), with full

[1]http://www.isis-papyrus.com/e15/pages/software/platform-concept.html

functionality for online interactive business document production (ISIS Papyrus). MKS uses wizard processes to assist several thousand business users in handling various types of documents related to insurance cases. A wizard contains steps that guide business users through the document-generation process. Therefore, the wizard resembles a dedicated imperative process modelled in BPMN (BPMN Specification) for guiding users through a sequence of activities. To be effective in generating high-quality documents, these processes must be well-prepared and suitable for such a large and complex work environment. They must also comply with requirements involving laws, contracts with business partners, general standards, best practices, and civil and corporate regulations. A rigid process configuration ensures that the process execution remains controlled and satisfies these compliance requirements; however, it does not consider the workers' tacit business knowledge, which is usually an underestimated source of compliance with regulations (Governatori and Rotolo 2010). To be able to react quickly to changing business needs, modern business systems must be under the control of business departments that depend only minimally on IT departments. Process changes and introductions of new applications must be accomplished in days or weeks, not months or years. Rigid wizard processes that are predefined in the design process and executed sequentially at runtime cannot meet such modern requirements. The rapidly changing insurance markets generate requirements for new types of documents daily, obliging business users to react quickly to client requests. A case that requires insurance documents to be generated can follow established procedures only to a certain extent, as the task usually depends on knowledge workers' finding the best solutions for their clients. In our insurance context, knowledge work is performed by insurance clerks, thus we will use the term clerks to represent knowledge workers through our paper. This purpose is what Adaptive Case Management (ACM) (Tran Thi Kim et al. 2013) is designed for: customer-oriented work driven by goals contained in a case that allows the clerks to choose the appropriate actions from a context-sensitive set of ad hoc tasks with needed data and content to fulfill the related goal.

In this paper, we show how to simplify the wizard design and enhance the flexibility of its execution using a compliance-rule-and-consistency-checking system embedded in an ACM system (Tran Thi Kim et al. 2015). Instead of mapping the entire process into predefined task sequences, the system offers a selection of up-coming tasks at runtime, which are governed by compliance rules defined by business administrators at design time. Clerk must adhere to the loosely interrelated task sequences defined by these rules but can decide which tasks will be executed based on the workers' ad hoc assessment of the situation. Thus, a case evolves gradually instead of being predefined by business administrators who cannot predict all knowledge-intensive scenarios.

As a consequence, this approach guides both business users at runtime when they select from ad hoc task templates and business administrators at design time when they define new or amend existing sub-processes. The consistency-checking system consists of a model checker (Czepa et al. 2015) that supports process administrators at design time, and an on-the-fly compliance checker (Czepa et al.

2016a) that observes clerks' behavior at runtime to ensure that both activities comply with company regulations. We restructure the wizard process and combine it with compliance rules in order to provide optimal flexibility for business users during process execution. The resulting approach can be applied to any knowledge-intensive domain and is not specific to the insurance industry.

2 Situation Faced

MKS is built on the ACM and Correspondence Solution of the Papyrus platform. While the Correspondence Solution handles the design and content of documents, the ACM solution's process modeling and execution capabilities manage the processes involved in document generation.

MKS enables clerks to generate documents interactively based on wizard process templates and to retrieve data dynamically from various business systems. The wizard is an ACM case that defines processes comprised of interactive user steps to be executed by the clerks, as well as service tasks, such as web services, that the system executes automatically for data retrieval. A document template that is composed of text-building block templates with embedded data, variables, and/or logic is used as artifact for steps in the wizard process. Forms, as integral parts of the wizard definition, request that the clerks enter the document data as variable values, populating the document in a step-by-step approach. Figure 1[2] shows a typical wizard input form and the preview of the corresponding document at a certain stage of the document generation process. The entered data are imported directly to the document.

As shown in Fig. 2, the wizard steps executed by clerks at runtime are prepared by business administrators as templates and stored in a template library at design time. The processes are defined with an editor that has full functionality to edit, visualize, and simulate the execution of wizards before they are released into production. Transitions connect the steps, and each step defines actions that select and add text building blocks to the document.

The motivation for this paper is to support unpredictable or unlikely situations that could explode the number of process variants. Suppose that a clerk recognizes during wizard execution that the customer's address is incorrect and must be updated in the external system that was queried by the service task. In this case, the clerk should be able to edit the address right in the wizard form and notify the data's owner about the change. The clerk, who is engaged in a strict wizard process, would benefit from the ability to perform ad hoc actions in this situation. In order to support flexibility at runtime, we address this challenge by applying consistency-checking methods in combination with compliance rules, as discussed in the next section.

[2]This figure and others show original screenshots from Mobiliar's business application. Relevant items in German are translated as needed.

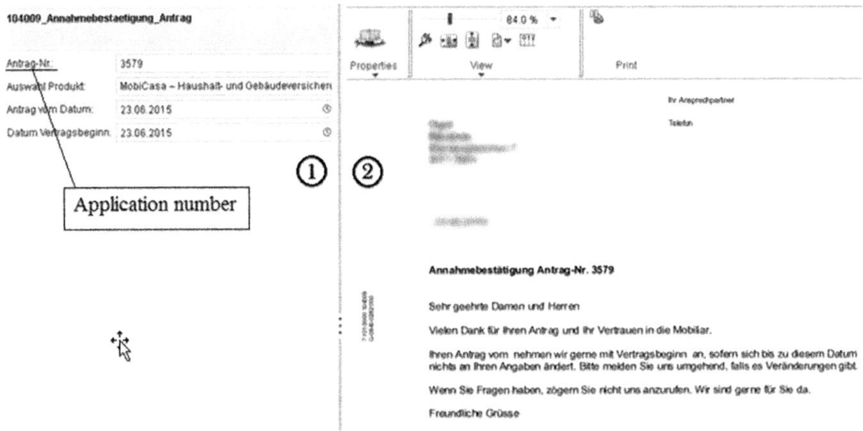

Fig. 1 Wizard step with data form (1) and document preview (2). The value "3579" for application number is entered in the form on the *left side* and simultaneously displayed in the document preview of the related building block on the *right*

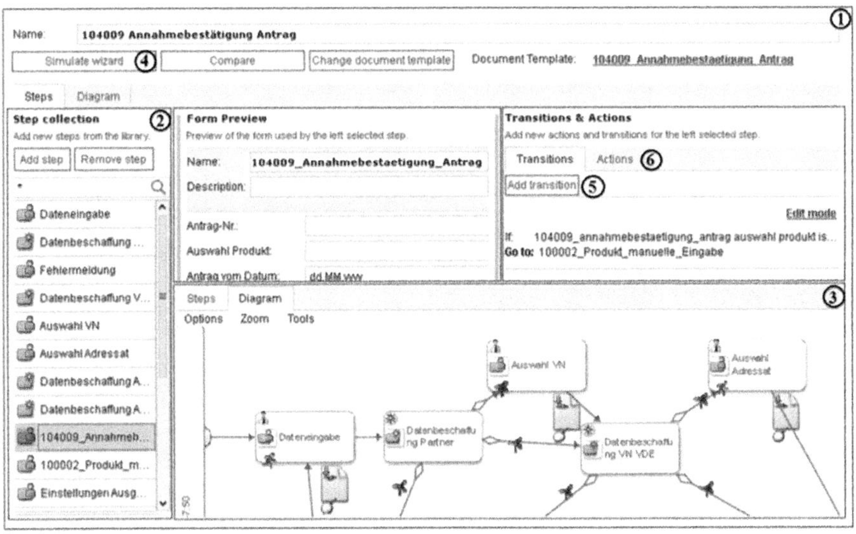

Fig. 2 Wizard template composition editor (1) with functionality to edit (2), visualize (3) and simulate (4) the execution of a wizard containing steps that are connected by transitions (5) and defined with actions (6)

3 Action Taken

Our approach introduces a generically applicable consistency-checking method to enable a more flexible execution of document-creation wizards. The following subsections outline the approach, describe our extension of the wizards with ad hoc tasks, and explain how to guarantee these flexible processes' compliance through a set of managed compliance rules. In the original operating principle of MKS, shown in Fig. 3a, business administrators defined a wizard process template at design time, which was instantiated by clerks for execution at runtime. Clerks strictly followed the steps predefined in the wizard to create a document, but because the system did not allow clerks to adapt the process at runtime, they could not react to unforeseen situations within an insurance case.

The overview of MKS extended by the consistency-checking system is provided in Fig. 3b. In this approach, a wizard ACM case template (Tran Thi Kim et al. 2013) is assembled at design time from goals that are achieved through predefined sub-processes and/or individual ad hoc tasks. Each sub-process is attached to the goal and combines the necessary tasks in a particular sequence. The quality of case templates is ensured by means of model-checking (Czepa et al. 2015) before the templates are released. At runtime, the set of compliance rules assigned to the case checks the execution of case elements—goal instances, process instances, task instances, and ad hoc actions—on the fly (Czepa et al. 2016a). Clerks can follow the steps defined in the templates while performing ad hoc actions to adapt to new situations. A goal is reached when all its tasks are completed and the attendant data

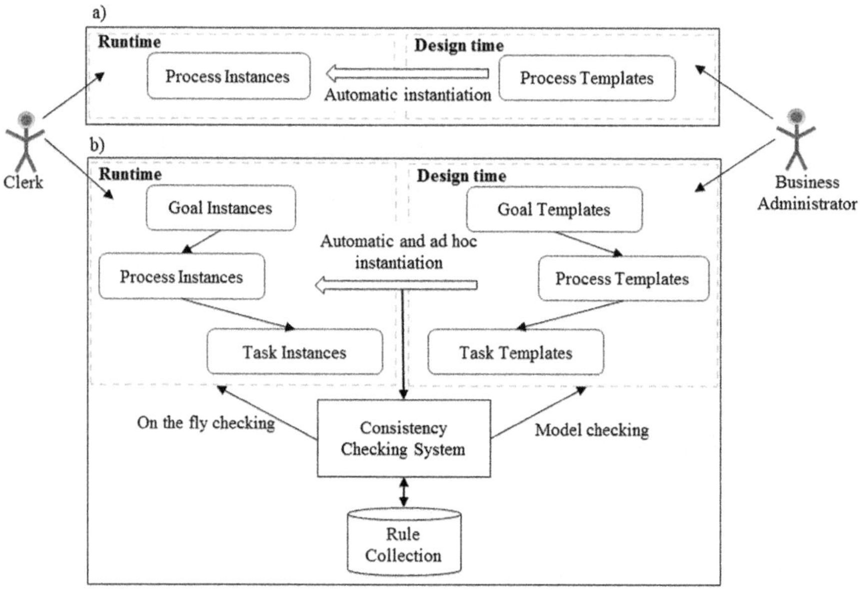

Fig. 3 (**a**) MKS operating principle and (**b**) MKS with consistency checking

are acquired. Consequently, a document is finished when all goals of a wizard are reached.

3.1 Design of Compliance-Rules-Enabled Wizards

Figure 4a shows the original MKS wizard process, which can be divided into beginning, middle, and end parts of the process. The beginning part of the process retrieves the client's personal data and selects an insurance product. The end part defines the document-delivery channel, while the middle part is comprised of the steps that are necessary for the specific insurance case. The system's analysis of the original wizard processes led to the simplified model in Fig. 4b. Numerous processes share the same beginning and ending parts, but the middle part of each process is distinct from the others, although they might have tasks in common.

In our approach, the original wizard processes are transformed into flexible processes with a goal-driven structure. The beginning and ending parts are modeled as predefined sub-processes that can be reused in various cases. The middle part is split into several individual ad hoc tasks. A case that uses the restructured processes

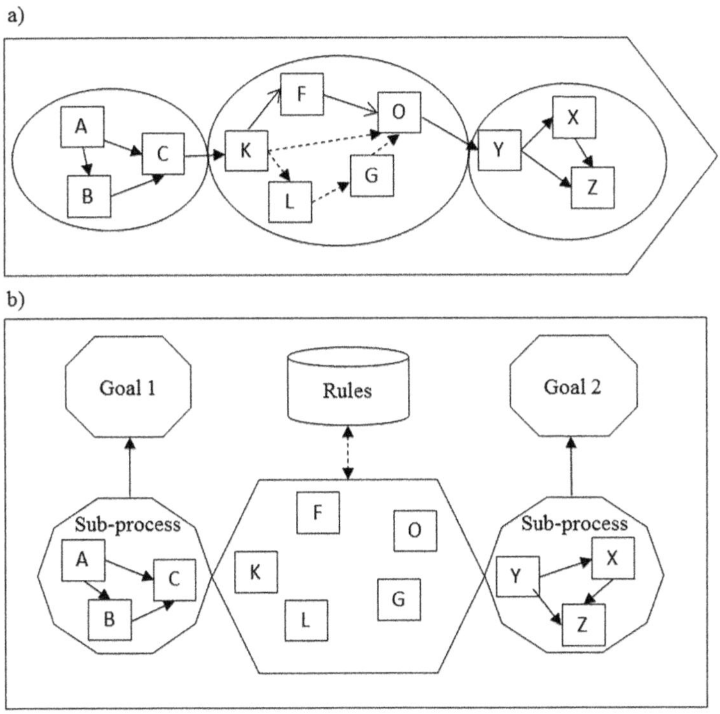

Fig. 4 (**a**) Typical MKS processes and (**b**) Flexible MKS processes. The tasks in this figure are anonymized as *squares* with capital letters and grouped. *Arrows* indicate the direction of process execution, and *dashed lines* represent alternative workflows of the middle part

is driven by two goals: *Goal 1*, defining the beginning sub-process, and *Goal 2*, defining the ending sub-process. The tasks of the middle part are either related to *Goal 1* or *Goal 2* or could be assigned by the clerks to newly defined goals. If the tasks of the middle part must follow a certain execution sequence, they are monitored by associated compliance rules. In other words, the rules define the boundaries of the middle part without rigidly predefining the processes. The consistency-checking system enables clerks to maintain compliance by highlighting tasks that do not comply with one or more rules. If certain tasks are optional and do not have to follow any specific sequence, the business users can add them as needed. Because the same rules are active when business administrators define process templates, the rules enforce compliance at design time as well.

3.2 Constraint Definitions Using Compliance Rules

In order to govern the middle part of a wizard process, we use state-based and data-based rules. State-based rules define the sequences of tasks based on their states, such as "started," "finished," and "running." For example, a sequence from Task K to Task F can be described by the rule, "Task F can be started only after Task K is finished." This rule is expressed in the constraint language as.

```
Constraint No1 for MobiliarCase{
K.finished leads to F.started }
```

In this example the states of tasks *K* and *F* are *finished* and *started*, respectively. The temporal pattern of type precedence is defined by the keywords *leads to.*

To define the temporal patterns in our system, we adapt temporal expressions from the patterns defined by Dwyer et al. (1999):

- Existence: K.finished *occurs*
- Absence: K.finished *never occurs*
- Response: K.finished *leads to* F.started. In other words, only if K.finished happens, can F.started happen.
- Precedence: K.finished *precedes* F.started. In other words, F.started can happen only if K.finished has happened.

Data-based rules enable business users to define task dependencies that are related to data conditions. State-based and data-based rules can be combined to express a compliance requirement. For example, Task F can be started only when Task K is finished and the value of a certain data attribute meets a certain requirement, such as the customer's birth year is greater than or equal to 1981.

```
Constraint No2 for MobiliarCase{
(K.finished and CustomerBirthyear >= 1981) leads to F.started
}
```

In unforeseen circumstances, the underlying data models might not provide access to critical data. In order to support flexibility in such situations without the need for explicit data definitions by IT, business users can check conditions manually using voting tasks that are guarded by compliance rules. Let us assume a voting task called "*Inquire additional customer interests*" must be concluded before the final pricing can be finished:

```
Constraint No3 for MobiliarCase{
InquireInterest.approved leads to Pricing.finished
}
```

Voting tasks like *InquireInterest* can be employed quickly to adapt to new situations. The business administrator can create the task template without the support of database experts or IT people and can specify with checklists which items must be verified with the customer. Alternatively, the business user can define the checklist at runtime to adapt even more dynamically to the current situation. Unstructured data is popular in real-life systems since data definitions cannot be amended quickly in IT systems with bureaucratic change-management cycles. In a car insurance case, for example, the result of an investigation into whether the car was damaged intentionally or accidentally can be reported by means of a simple voting task decided by a clerk.

Since MKS is based on the ISIS Papyrus ACM framework, processes and tasks are reusable components of the ACM system to be shared with other goals and cases. The sequence of the tasks in the sub-processes is modeled with transitions and gateways following BPMN standards (BPMN). The tasks of the middle part are ad hoc tasks selected by the clerks at runtime. Each of these tasks can be added to the case when the clerk sees the need to do so based on the case's content or context. The tasks' order of execution is not predetermined but is constrained by rules. A User Trained Agent (UTA) implemented in the Papyrus ACM system further assists the clerk in new situations by suggesting best next actions that were learned earlier from similar situations faced by other users (Tran et al. 2014). Thus, knowledge acquisition and sharing becomes an integral part of the business application, enabled by the business intelligence component, UTA.

To demonstrate the results achieved in applying our approach, we used the original wizard case *Acknowledgement of Application* (Fig. 5). Before the redesign, an ACM wizard case was completely driven by a predefined process that contained all of the steps of the wizard. In this insurance case, a clerk created a document that confirmed the successful submission of an insurance application. First, the clerk entered some identification numbers, such as the insurance ID, customer ID, or case ID, into the system. The customer's data was retrieved by the predefined process through web service tasks from various sources based on the entered data. Then the clerk selected the matching insurance holder and address and inserted specific information for the particular insurance case. A document confirming the

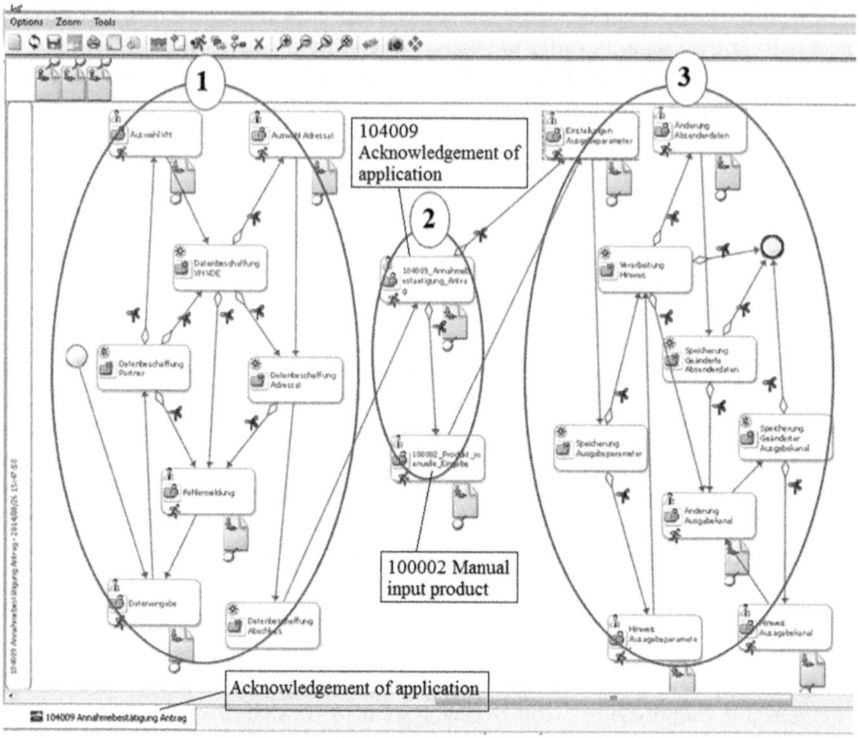

Fig. 5 Process model before redesign analyzed into three parts

acceptance of the insurance application was generated and sent to the customer based on the output channel determined by the clerk at the end of the process.

An ACM wizard case is not driven by predetermined steps, but by goals that are fulfilled by the clerk. The redesigned wizard process of the *Acknowledgement of Application* case is divided into three parts, as illustrated in Fig. 4. The first and last parts require no flexibility and are linked to the goals of predefined processes. The clerk can freely add the flexible part's tasks at runtime, and their sequence is determined, if necessary, by the compliance rules introduced in our approach.

Like any other ACM case, the redesigned *Acknowledgement of Application* ACM case has associated goals, processes, and tasks. The *First Core Goal* holds the beginning part of the process, which is configured as a sub-process for retrieving insurance customer data from the database. The *Last Core Goal* contains the ending part of the wizard process for choosing the channel by which the document will be delivered to the customer. The tasks of the middle part are not predefined in the wizard template but are added by the business user as necessary at runtime to address the specific customer situation. In this specific case, the ad hoc task templates are prepared as *manual input product* and *acknowledgement of application*.

The task execution of the middle part is controlled by three compliance rules, defined by business administrators. For example, rule *R0* may express that the task *acknowledgement of application* must be present at least one time, while *R1* defines the dependency of task *acknowledgement of application* on task *manual input product* when the *selection product* is *manual input*, and Rule *R2* expresses the dependency of task *acknowledgement of application* on task *selection output channel* when the *selection product* is not *manual input.*

```
Constraint R0 for MobiliarCase{
acknowledgement_of_application.started occurs at least 1x
}
Constraint R1 for MobiliarCase{
 (acknowledgement_of_application.finished  and  selection_product
equal to "manual_input") leads to manual_input_product.started
}
Constraint R2 for MobiliarCase{
 (acknowledgment_of_application.finished and selection_product not
equal to "manual_input") leads to selection_output_channel.started
}
```

The two data-based rules *R1* and *R2* can be visually simplified by an alternative expression using a voting task to check whether the *selection product* is *manualinput*. The voting task is named *check_selection_product_manual_input.*

```
Constraint R3 for MobiliarCase{
      (acknowledgment_of_application.finished       leads      to
check_selection_product_manual_input.started
}
Constraint R4 for MobiliarCase{
    check_selection_product_manual_input.approved    leads     to
manual_input_product.started
}
Constraint R5 for MobiliarCase{
     check_selection_product_manual_input.denied     leads     to
selection_output_channel.started
}
```

Compliance rules are composed in natural language by business administrators using the Papyrus rule editor, as shown in Fig. 6. To facilitate that activity, the editor offers a selection of elements from a list of items using business terminology. Thus, the language of business is used to define the rule with auto-completion features as the user types.

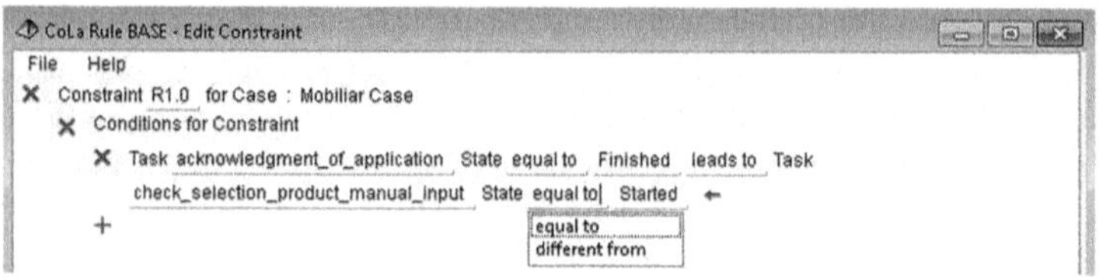

Fig. 6 Compliance rule editor

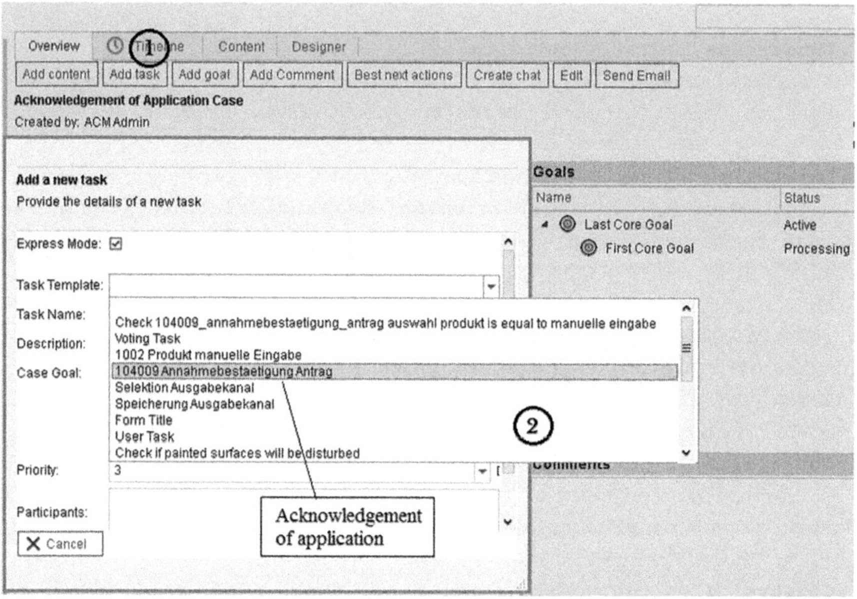

Fig. 7 Add an ad hoc task at runtime by the function Add task (1) with a list of task templates (2)

At runtime, when a clerk creates a confirmation for a customer who has submitted an application, an instance of the *acknowledgement of application* case is created upon the clerk's selection of that template.

During processing of the *First Core Goal*, the clerk is presented with a form to enter the insurance ID, customer ID, or case ID. When all of the first core goal's predefined tasks are finished, the clerk adds task *acknowledgement of application*, as suggested by the consistency-checking system, which is used to create a confirmation of an application. Figure 7 demonstrates the use of function *Add task* with a dialog showing a list of task templates that are provided to the clerk for adding an ad hoc task on the fly.

Although the task *acknowledgement of application* is suggested to the clerk because Constraint *R0* was temporarily violated, the clerk can do other tasks as well. However, as soon as an ad hoc task related to the compliance rule constraint is added, it will be controlled by the consistency-checking system. The constraint that defines the occurrence of tasks is used to ensure the presence of the task that initiates the variable middle parts, like the task *acknowledgement of application*. Therefore, to complete a case successfully, the clerk must eventually execute that task.

When task *acknowledgement of application* is finished, the constraints *R1* and *R2* are investigated by the consistency-checking system. Since task *acknowledgement of application* is finished, and if the *selection product* is chosen as *manual input*, the consistency-checking system suggests the task *manual input product* to the clerk. If *selection product* is not chosen as *manual input,* task *selection output channel* is suggested to the clerk. Thus, the execution of the ad hoc tasks is controlled by the consistency-checking system so the clerk does not overlook any tasks that would violate the case's compliance with the rules. The user can also consult the experience of other users who have been in the same situation by asking the UTA for best next actions. When there are no more suggestions, the clerk can continue the steps defined in the *Last Core Goal*. When the goal is reached, a confirmation document for the application is generated and the case is closed.

In summary, compliance rules can control ad hoc tasks added at runtime when business compliance requirements demand it. Some of these tasks must be executed in a certain order and/or depend on the availability of certain data, which is defined by a set of compliance rules. Other tasks that do not require such control can be added at the clerk's discretion, such as when the clerk institutes an *add additional information* task when the document is lacking required information. Therefore, our approach enables clerks to add ad hoc tasks—tasks that may not have been foreseen when the wizard was initially designed—at runtime under the control of the compliance rule system based on the current context.

4 Results Achieved

The ACM technology used to build the wizard processes supports the definition of tasks to be performed by business staff at design time and their selective application by knowledge workers at runtime so Die Mobiliar can react quickly to new business requirements without involving IT. Instead of defining rigid process models that IT must implement with lengthy change-management and rollout cycles, the processes can be defined directly by Die Mobiliar's business administrators using a process editor built on the Papyrus platform.

MKS's ability to edit wizard templates at any time enables Die Mobiliar to define new document and wizard templates within the boundaries imposed by the predefined processes. The process management in ACM is highly flexible, as it supports both automatic and ad hoc actions (Tran Thi Kim et al. 2013). Although fully automated processes can be defined for well-behaved and predictable domains, they hinder the innovation and business agility that is critical in insurance markets. The clerks who come face-to-face with insurance situations should have the flexibility to adapt the case at runtime.

The enhanced structure of the ACM wizard gives clerks immediate flexibility while staying within the boundaries imposed by compliance rules. Clerks can institute goal and task templates manually using the predefined wizard case for adding new actions at runtime. A set of compliance rules in a constraint-specification language examines the consistency of the tasks performed and verifies process compliance (Czepa et al. 2016b).

Compliance rules are also enforced at design time through model-checking (Clarke 2008; Czepa et al. 2015, 2016a) when business administrators develop sub-process templates. Model-checking verifies the structural consistency of the predefined sub-processes. By observing compliance rules at design time as well as at runtime, business administrators and clerks are prevented from violating compliance requirements, and dynamically assembled sequences of tasks are guaranteed to meet the same structural criteria that are applied to predefined wizard processes. Thus, the boundaries defined by the rule system ensure the compliance of the overall case execution. This approach confers a significant benefit during the change-management and release process by reducing tests and error-correction efforts.

With MKS's redesigned structure, the goal, process, and task templates can be reused in various wizard cases, so the number of predefined process templates in the library can be reduced considerably. Based on the subset of wizard process templates from Die Mobiliar that we could use for our study, we estimated a 40–90% reduction, depending on the degree of the core process templates' standardization and their efficient reuse. To that end, goals and related sub-processes that appear in several wizards can be predefined in the wizard case at design time. The reuse of shared items will improve the quality and consistency of related cases and avoid redundancies, which are always a source of inconsistency, especially in large-scale and continuously evolving systems. Clerks can process the variable tasks between the predefined processes at runtime, and ad hoc tasks instituted from task templates can be added to adapt to unforeseen situations that require new documents. By defining a case partially at design time and completing it with variable and ad hoc tasks at runtime, Die Mobiliar can avoid inordinately complex wizard cases.

5 Lessons Learned

The trade-off between comprehensibility and flexibility in business process modeling has been addressed by both academia and industry (De Smedt et al. 2016), and declarative and imperative models have been studied to improve the flexibility of process models (Fahland et al. 2009, 2010; Haisjackl et al. 2016; Prescher et al. 2014). To address this challenge, we introduced a theoretical approach and its successful application in the hybrid declarative-imperative modeling and enactment of a business process. We learned lessons from this practical application and case study.

A rapidly changing industry like insurance presents a plethora of unpredictable business situations. By attempting to cover all business cases up front, rigid process modeling of such markets produces bloated process template libraries that hinder an organization's ability to respond to emergent requirements. The construction and maintenance of such systems consume significant effort and resources (ISIS Papyrus).

No specific discovery methodology was applied in this case study; the discovery for the process redesign was based on the designers' experience. The shared portions of hundreds of process templates were discovered and manually extracted as sub-processes. In the resulting approach, the tasks in the variable, transitional part of the process—that is, the middle part—are loosely connected by constraints. Depending on the designers, the relationships between two tasks are defined either declaratively by constraints or imperatively in a sub-process. The hybrid model can be evolved gradually through multiple iterations to improve the enterprise's productive system.

The inherent flexibility of declarative models makes them suitable to the goal-oriented approach of ACM in providing an adaptive and flexible system to deal with unpredictable business events. Our case study employs an ACM framework that supports the application of imperative models to reusable sub-processes and of declarative models to ad hoc actions within a case structure. The duality of modeling is hidden from business users, as the associated steps can be instituted automatically, making case execution transparent.

The conversion between imperative and declarative models has been addressed by various studies (De Smedt et al. 2016; Prescher et al. 2014), which focus on how to obtain a set of declarative constraints from an imperative model or vice versa, or even how to combine them into a hybrid model. Our case study is unique in that regard, as it does not consolidate the two model types into a hybrid model at design time but incorporates them separately into the process instances, which are manipulated by knowledge workers at runtime without explicit modeling. The compliance-checking employed by our approach ensures the consistency of the execution by suggesting activities and preventing user mistakes within the boundaries described by the applied compliance rules. We kill two birds with one stone: compliance rules maintain compliance automatically, and they provide business users the freedom to decide which tasks will best achieve their business goals based on their own experience.

Lessons were also learned from a practical perspective. Die Mobiliar appreciated the benefits of this approach, which enables a customer-oriented business strategy that focuses on service quality and the customer's experience. In the midterm Die Mobiliar will look into changing several of its predefined process models into flexibly managed workflows. However, such a change would involve a paradigm change, and its adoption will occur gradually, as the company must also address considerations like the installation of new business user responsibilities for the integration and maintenance of the consistency-checking solution in the production system.

Acknowledgement This work was supported by the FFG project CACAO, no. 843461 and the Wiener Wissenschafts, Forschungs, and Technologie funds (WWTF), Grant No. ICT12-001.

References

BPMN. *Specification—Business process model and notation*. Accessed July 14, 2016, from http://www.bpmn.org/

Clarke, E. M. (2008). The birth of model checking. In O. Grumberg & H. Veith (Eds.), *25 years of model checking: History, achievements, perspectives* (pp. 1–26). Berlin: Springer.

Czepa, C., Tran, H., Zdun, U., Rinderle-Ma, S., Tran Thi Kim, T., Weiss, E., & Ruhsam, C. (2015). Supporting structural consistency checking in adaptive case management. In *International Conference on Cooperative Information Systems (CoopIS)* (pp. 311–319).

Czepa, C., Tran, H., Zdun, U., Tran Thi Kim, T., Weiss, E., & Ruhsam, C. (2016a). Towards a compliance support framework for adaptive case management. In *5th International Workshop on Adaptive Case Management and other Non-workflow Approaches to BPM (AdaptiveCM 16), 20th IEEE International Enterprise Computing Workshops (EDOCW 2016)*.

Czepa, C., Tran, H., Zdun, U., Tran Thi Kim, T., Weiss, E., & Ruhsam, C. (2016b). Ontology-based behavioral constraint authoring. In *2nd International Workshop on Compliance, Evolution and Security in intra- and Cross-Organizational Processes (CeSCoP 2016), 20th IEEE International Enterprise Computing Workshops (EDOCW 2016)*.

De Smedt, J., De Weerdt, J., Vanthienen, J., & Poels, G. (2016). Mixed-paradigm process modeling with intertwined state spaces. *Business Information System Engineering, 58*, 19–29.

Dwyer, M. B., Avrunin, G. S., & Corbett, J. C. (1999). Patterns in property specifications for finite-state verification. In *Proceedings of the 21st International Conference on Software Engineering* (pp. 411–420). New York: ACM.

Fahland, D., Lübke, D., Mendling, J., Reijers, H., Weber, B., Weidlich, M., & Zugal, S. (2009). Declarative versus imperative process modeling languages: The issue of understandability. In T. Halpin, J. Krogstie, S. Nurcan, E. Proper, R. Schmidt, P. Soffer, & R. Ukor (Eds.), *Enterprise, business-process and information systems modeling: 10th International Workshop*, BPMDS 2009, and *14th International Conference*, EMMSAD 2009, held at CAiSE 2009, Amsterdam, June 8–9, 2009. Proceedings (pp. 353–366). Berlin: Springer.

Fahland, D., Mendling, J., Reijers, H. A., Weber, B., Weidlich, M., & Zugal, S. (2010). Declarative versus imperative process modeling languages: The issue of maintainability. In S. Rinderle-Ma, S. Sadiq, & F. Leymann (Eds.), *Business Process Management Workshops: BPM 2009 International Workshops*, Ulm, September 7, 2009. Revised Papers (pp. 477–488). Berlin: Springer.

Governatori, G., & Rotolo, A. (2010). Norm compliance in business process modeling. In *Semantic Web Rules—International Symposium, RuleML 2010*, Washington, DC, October 21–23, 2010. Proceedings (pp. 194–209).

Haisjackl, C., Barba, I., Zugal, S., Soffer, P., Hadar, I., Reichert, M., Pinggera, J., & Weber, B. (2016). Understanding declare models: Strategies, pitfalls, empirical results. *Software and System Modeling, 15*, 325–352.

ISIS Papyrus. *ISIS Papyrus solution catalog – Swiss Mobiliar*. Accessed March 11, 2016, from http://www.isis-papyrus.com/e15/pages/solutions-catalog/solutions-catalog-mobiliar-wizard.html

ISIS Papyrus. *ISIS Papyrus Press Release*. Accessed August 18, 2016, from https://www.isis-papyrus.com/e15/pages/press/PR20151208-WfMC-Award.html

Mobiliar: Die Mobiliar Versicherungen und Vorsorge. Accessed March, 11, 2016, from https://www.mobi.ch/.

Prescher, J., Di Ciccio, C., & Mendling, J. (2014). From declarative processes to imperative models. In Accorsi, R., Ceravolo, P., & Russo, B. (Eds.), *Proceedings of the 4th International Symposium on Data-driven Process Discovery and Analysis* {(SIMPDA} 2014), Milan, November 19–21, 2014. pp. 162–173. CEUR-WS.org

Tran Thi Kim, T., Pucher, M. J., Mendling, J., & Ruhsam, C. (2013). Setup and maintenance factors of ACM systems. Lecture Notes in Computer Science (including Subser. Lecture Notes in Artificial Intelligence Lecture Notes in Bioinformatics). 8186 LNCS (pp. 172–177).

Tran Thi Kim, T., Weiss, E., Ruhsam, C., Czepa, C., Tran, H., & Zdun, U. (2015). Embracing process compliance and flexibility through behavioral consistency checking in ACM – A Repair Service Management Case. BPM 2015 4th Work. ACM Other Non-Workflow Approaches to BPM (pp. 1–12).

Tran, T., Ruhsam, C., Pucher, M. J., Kobler, M., & Mendling, J. (2014). Towards a pattern recognition approach for transferring knowledge in ACM. In *18th IEEE International Enterprise Distributed Object Computing Conference Workshops and Demonstrations*, EDOCW 2014 (pp. 134–138). doi:10.1109/EDOCW.2014.28.

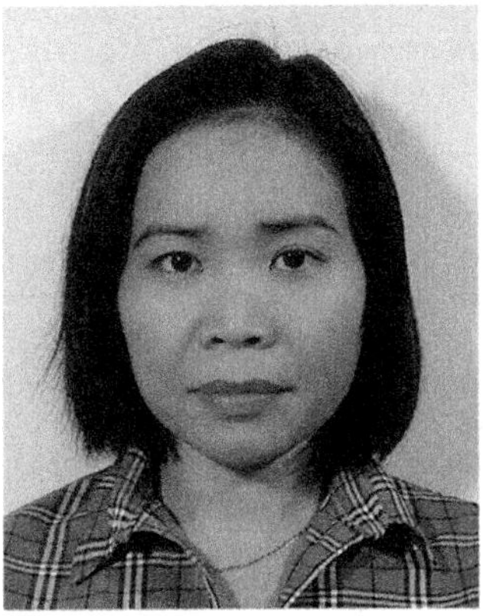

Thanh Tran Thi Kim is an application researcher working at the Academy Department, ISIS Papyrus Europe AG. She received her doctoral degree in Computer Science at Vienna University of Technology, Austria in December 2012. Her research focuses on adaptive case management, flexibility in process-aware information system, compliance verification. Besides supporting research and development, she participates in cooperation projects between ISIS Papyrus Europe AG and universities. Her main publications are in international conferences, workshops and book chapters for industry cases and best practices of process-aware information systems.

Erhard Weiss is Academy member at ISIS Papyrus Europe AG. He received a bachelor's degree in CIT and a master's degree in Business Process Management and Engineering. His research focuses on Adaptive Case Management.

Christoph Ruhsam is Senior Manager at ISIS Papyrus. He is head of the ISIS Papyrus Academy focusing on applied application research and coordinates scientific projects with external partners. The Academy has a dedicated group for user interface and usability concepts. Another group produces all Papyrus software related documentation and delivers education programs including the ISIS Papyrus Certification. He studied at Vienna University of Technology Communications Engineering and received his doctoral degree in 1994 on digital signal processing of biomedical signals. Since 1995 he works at ISIS Papyrus in a variety of management positions and established in 2003 a dedicated project supervision team (Project-QA), caring for ISIS Papyrus large scale installation projects. In 2012 he started the ISIS Papyrus Academy to stimulate scientific research projects like CACAO in cooperation with the University of Vienna.

Christoph Czepa is a researcher at the Faculty of Computer Science, University of Vienna, Austria. His research areas include Business Process Management (BPM), Adaptive Case Management (ACM), Domain-Specific Languages (DSLs), software architecture, software engineering, compliance/consistency and the application of machine learning and formal verification methods in the aforementioned domains. He has received a master degree in computer science in December 2013 (with distinction). Currently, he is pursuing a PhD in computer science. Christoph is the (co-)author of more than 15 peer reviewed scientific articles and papers, and he participated in two research projects, namely the CACMTV (Content-Aware Coding for Mobile TV) project and CACAO (Consistency Checking, Recommendations, And Visual Modeling For Ad Hoc Changes By Knowledge Workers In Adaptive Case Management) project.

Huy Tran is a senior postdoc working at the Research Group Software Architecture (SWA), Faculty of Computer Science, University of Vienna, Austria. Before that Huy received his doctoral degree in December 2009 and worked as a postdoc at Vienna University of Technology, Austria. He has published some 40 articles and papers in peer-reviewed journals, conferences, book chapters, and workshops. He has also taken part in several European and domestic R&D projects since 2008. His current research interests are in the field of software engineering including software architecture, view-based architecture, model-driven engineering, service-oriented computing, distributed event-based software systems, business process management, business process compliance, and applied formal methods in software engineering.

Uwe Zdun is a full professor for software architecture at the Faculty of Computer Science, University of Vienna. Before that, he worked as assistant professor at the Vienna University of Technology and the Vienna University of Economics respectively. He received his doctoral degree from the University of Essen in 2002. His research focuses on software design and architecture, empirical software engineering, distributed systems engineering (service-based, cloud, mobile, and process-driven systems), software patterns, domain-specific languages, and model-driven development. Uwe has published more than 210 articles in peer-reviewed journals, conferences, book chapters, and workshops, and is co-author of the books "Remoting Patterns", "Process-Driven", and "Software-Architektur." He has participated in 26 R&D projects. Uwe is editor of the journal *Transactions* on Pattern Languages of Programming (TPLoP) published by Springer, Associate Editor of the Computing journal published by Springer, and Associate Editor-in-Chief for design and architecture for the IEEE Software magazine.

Comprehensive Business Process Management at Siemens: Implementing Business Process Excellence

Bartosz Woliński and Saimir Bala

Abstract

(a) **Situation faced**: Siemens is a complex organization with offices worldwide. Through many years of development, it grew into a set of businesses, each with a substantial degree of autonomy, supported by central departments. This autonomy gives the departments the flexibility needed to achieve customer intimacy, which requires different process flows in different businesses. When the global initiative concerning the implementation of standard business process management was introduced and enacted, businesses were bundled into four sectors. Every sector in the Siemens organization, including that in Poland, was managing its processes according to the local business specifics and needs, which made the comprehensive process management approach challenging. The processes were disconnected and stored in multiple conventions. Corporate initiatives that were intended to address the effectiveness and efficiency of business processes were not supported.

(b) **Action taken**: Siemens strengthened its process-wise approach and worldwide process standardization by implementing a formalized process policy. As a first step, the Business Process Excellence (BPE) regulation (also referred to as BPE policy) was introduced. It formulated the Siemens Processes for Excellence (SIPEX) process standards, which replaced the previous processes base, referred to as Reference Process House (RPH). At the same time, process roles (sponsor, owner, and manager) and corporate

B. Woliński (✉)
Siemens sp. z o.o, Warszawa, Poland
e-mail: bartosz.wolinski@siemens.com

S. Bala
Wirtschaftsunivesität Wien, Vienna, Austria
e-mail: saimir.bala@wu.ac.at

J. vom Brocke, J. Mendling (eds.), *Business Process Management Cases*,
Management for Professionals, DOI 10.1007/978-3-319-58307-5_7

tools with which to visualize the processes, such as ARIS, were introduced. In the Polish organization, the program was formulated as a vehicle with which to implement the process organization. The goal of the initiative, which was referred to internally as "Streamlining business processes," included chief financial officers (CFOs) as process sponsors and the head of the business process management team as the program manager.

(c) **Results achieved**: At present, on the corporate level Business Excellence is a core element of Siemens—Vision 2020. It is embedded into the Corporate Technology structure, which enables it be the part of innovative products and management standards. It is also a key lever that empowers the company's lasting business success and strengthens its competitiveness in the market.

(d) **Lessons learned**: From the implementation of the program we learned four primary lessons:
- Complexity in many dimensions (number of processes, number of roles, and number of formal documents and circulars) is not supportive of effective process management.
- Having a strong, dedicated sponsor is one of the most important keys to success.
- Not everyone in the organization will appreciate the effort at first, but they will if an attempt is made to understand their businesses and support their efforts.
- Be flexible: without putting one's best effort into implementing the corporate recommendations and without alignment with the business, no appreciation or cooperation should be expected.

1 Introduction

Siemens is a global powerhouse that focuses on the areas of electrification, automation and digitization. With a presence in 190 countries, roughly 413,000 employees working at 1640 locations around the globe and 176 R&D facilities, it is one of the world's largest producers of energy-efficient and resource-saving technologies. Its solutions span along the electrification value chain, from power generation, transmission and distribution to smart-grid solutions and the efficient application of electrical energy, and to the areas of medical imaging and laboratory diagnostics. Numerous goals, such as those related to Power and Gas, Wind Power, Power Generation, Energy Management, Building Technologies, Mobility, Digital Factory, Process Industries and Drives and Financial Services are pursued by the company.

Such a complex structure could easily result in the misalignment of knowledge about the overall business process and consequent difficulties in managing the department-specific processes. Departments were allowed a certain degree of freedom in pursuing their goals without centralized control. This approach reduced inter-departmental coordination and created differing views and specializations of the overall meta-process on the company level. As a result, the various entities had differing levels of awareness of their processes, ranging from "islands" that already used business process management (BPM) in a mature way, to areas that were completely process-unaware and behaved only according to short-term goals.

The company's top management made a first step toward increasing the synergy among the units by focusing on improving three areas: (1) the effectiveness of structures and processes in the organization itself, (2) the change management culture and proactivity, and (3) collaboration among the businesses using best practices on sharing and innovation, process transparency (i.e., processes that are well defined, well communicated, and measured), and BPM competencies that are centralized, not scattered throughout the company.

The implementation of such strategic alignment comes with a number of practical challenges, one of which is making employees aware of the process in which they are involved and aware that this process belongs to a comprehensive meta-process in the company. This challenge triggered the need for a BPM initiative on an organizational level, which was conducted through workshops that educated the employees about BPM.

This paper describes a case in which a global BPM policy was applied throughout a large company. Section 2 explains the problem setting and points out the problems before the BPM initiative was enacted. Section 3 describes the action taken, the practical challenges, and the methods used to implement the BPM policy. Section 4 describes the results achieved from the policy, and Sect. 5 concludes with the lessons learned from the case.

2 Situation Faced

At Siemens Poland, as well as in the global Siemens organization, the number of divisions changed from four sectors (energy, industry, infrastructure and cities, and healthcare) to the nine current divisions: Power and Gas, Wind Power, Power Generation, Energy Management, Building Technologies, Mobility, Process Industries and Drives, Digital Factory and Financial Services). This change decentralized expertise and created misalignment in how the departments pursued their goals. In order to address this change, Siemens introduced a global BPM policy for all of its affiliated companies to follow. The goal of the new BPM policy was to increase effectiveness and efficiency across all of the company's business processes while standardizing them and aligning them with its goals. From a practical point of view, this effort required that the processes be defined and their performance measured and improved incrementally. Another aspect of the effort was that the reworked processes had to draw from the company's previous performance results and strategic goals in order to minimize resource leaks and performance issues. Adoption of a centralized framework addresses these issues by facilitating the improvement and alignment of the processes.

Prior to the introduction of the centralized BPM policy, the company was divided between two levels of BPM awareness: (1) sectors that already used BPM and were fully aware of the overall business process, and (2) sectors that were BPM unaware. The unaware sectors used sets of tools to handle their tasks that differed from those of the BPM-aware sectors, including non-standardized business process schemata and other graphic representations of workflows. In contrast, the process-aware sectors used process modeling tools like ARIS and automatic support for executing their processes.

In order to manage the processes of its complex organizational structure, the company used the so-called Reference Process House (RPH) process corporate framework (Fig. 1). RPH provides a high-level picture of how the company should organize its processes and enables the company to configure its business processes, including product, system, project, and service activities. RPH consists of three main kinds of processes: management processes, business processes, and support processes. The management processes control the goals and the quality of the core processes defined in the business processes layer, so the core processes must adhere to specified standards and requirements defined by the management processes. The business processes, which are the core processes of the company, typically aim at producing a concrete product. These core processes were divided

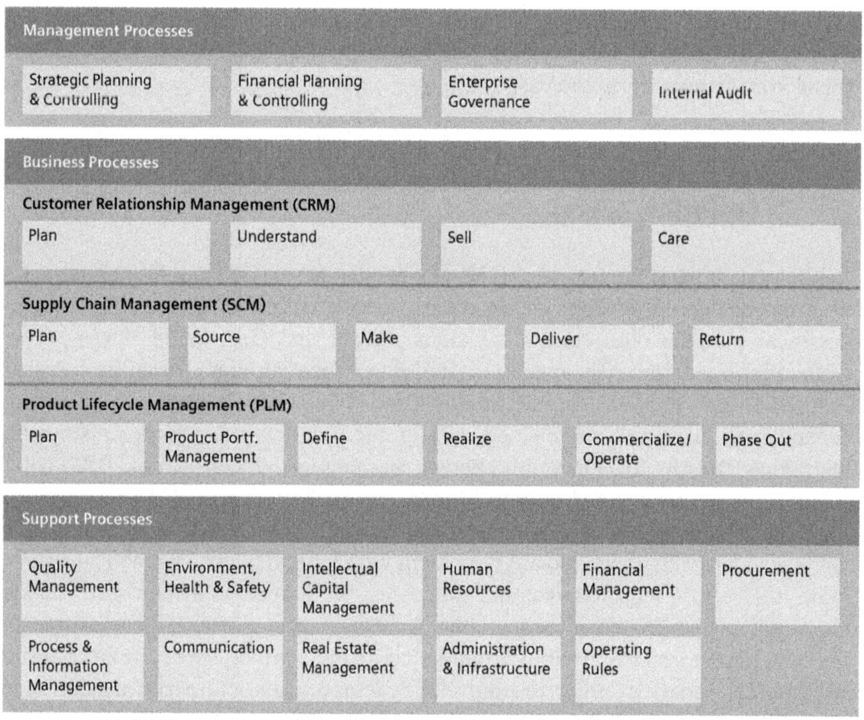

Fig. 1 Siemens' reference process house

into three core processes: customer relationship management (CRM), supply chain management (SCM), and product life-cycle management (PLM). The support processes support the execution of the core processes by providing additional input or managing the resources the core processes need for successful execution.

Although RPH worked in some sectors, it was not sufficiently useful in the context of Siemens, as RPH provided only a high-level picture of how the overall process should look and how the processes should be named. In such a huge and dispersed organization, the role of RPH was only to provide a generic guideline, leaving out many important aspects of implementation. As a result, every sector was managing its processes according to the local business's specifications and needs, which made the comprehensive process management approach challenging. In addition, the processes were stored in various conventions and were disconnected, and RPH did not support the BPM initiative on addressing efficiency and effectiveness issues. As a consequence, employees were still using various conventions to communicate their processes, and the company was characterized by process-aware "islands" that were surrounded by organizational structures that had no vision of the processes in which they were involved.

Consider, for example, two core processes, *sales* and *process execution*. The *sales* process is in close contact with the customer, and its focus is on delivering in the most effective and efficient way. Process execution, on the other hand, takes care of making the processes execute properly, which requires organizing and managing the resources needed to accomplish the goal. In this case, the *sales* processes was not modeled, and *sales* workers operated in an ad-hoc manner in order to be able to react to changes. At the same time, the *process execution* was already using BPM to manage the complexity of processes and resources. This misalignment in BPM maturity led to obstacles in the interactions between the sales and process execution processes, as there was no way to communicate the results, performance, or bottlenecks of the sales processes in such a way that the execution process could provide support.

Hence, the goal of the BPM initiative was to make the employees aware that they were part of a process; to evaluate and improve the performance of the processes; to improve process transparency, compliance, cooperation; and to identify areas where the processes could be automated.

3 Action Taken

This section explains the goals of the solution and the methodology used. We divide the section into three main parts: First, we observe the requirements of the newly introduced BPM policy. Next, we outline the steps taken toward its implementation at Siemens. Then, as we used best practices that were supported by existing excellence policies at Siemens (i.e., SIPEX), we describe the tools and technologies that were adopted to obtain compliance with the BPM policy.

3.1 Requirements of the BPM Policy

The BPM policy, referred to as BPM@Siemens, was developed from the previous Siemens Process Framework (SPF), which used RPH as a model. However, how SPF could address the efficiency and effectiveness requirements (Rohloff 2009) was not sufficient to the newly defined worldwide BPM requirements. To close this gap, Siemens strengthened the process-wise approach and process standardization for its companies worldwide by implementing a formalized process policy based on three principles:

- Simplification—reducing organizational complexity for process management.
- Usability—improving the structure of available data.
- Transparency—well-defined and well-executed processes.

The policy applies to all Siemens organizational units worldwide and sets a company-wide framework for BPM at Siemens as a minimum standard. This regulation is binding for all of Siemens' units. The policy covers seven general topics:

- Elements and terms of Siemens' BPM.
- BPM organization, roles, and responsibilities.
- Process structure and process cascading.
- Process harmonization and standardization.
- Continuous process improvement.
- Methods and tools.
- Governance via regulations and processes.

The new BPM policy focused on aligning processes on the business, operational, management, and support process levels in order to meet the needs of customers, employees, and suppliers. To create value for customers, employees, and business partners the focus was on:

- Excellent quality.
- Short development cycle (time to market).
- Low non-conformance costs.
- Effective communication.
- Efficient deployment of employees.
- A culture of continuous improvement.

The standardization of processes is an important success factor. An example of a company-wide standardized process and consistency in interactions with customers is PM@Siemens, the implementation of which has led to significant improvements in project execution. The policy's goal was to improve flow through the whole value chain, creating a system of a transparent flow. More specifically, PM@Siemens aimed to:

- Design processes as a system (i.e., processes must be organized and interconnected),
- Use Siemens AG conventions (i.e., processes must be standardized),
- Indicate connections (i.e., processes must be transparent),
- Continuously improve processes (i.e., processes must be iteratively refined).

PM@Siemens was implemented using two timeframes:

- On the corporate level within 12 months of publication.
- In lower-level organizational units (e.g., business units) within 24 months of publication.

These goals were summarized to require that f existing process management systems are changed significantly, the regulations defined (in PM@Siemens) are to be used or the tools used are to be changed to the defined standard. This requirement also imposed significant changes to the existing tool landscape, requiring major upgrades, introduction of a new tool landscape, or adjustment of the functionality in existing tools.

Taking into account business needs and costs, migration to the newly defined standard was scheduled for the medium term. In the interim, the initiative had to build an awareness of process management, so the training on the concept of process management at RC Poland had to be completed within 24 months. Standardized frameworks, such as the Business Process Excellence regulation (BPE policy) also had to be adopted. The BPE policy formulates the process standards SIPEX, which replaces the previous referential processes base RPH. Process roles, including the roles of process sponsor, process owner, and process manager, had to be defined. Tool support for processes design and visualization had to be adopted [The corporate process tool is ARIS (Scheer and Nüttgens 2000)].

In the Polish organization, the program, named "Streamlining Business Processes," was formulated as a vehicle with which to implement the process organization. A chief financial officer (CFO) was the sponsor, and the head of the BPM team was the program manager. The program scope was divided into three areas:

- Streamlining and improving all supporting processes (cf. Fig. 1: SCM, HR, FA, IT, etc.).
- Adjusting the core business process as much as possible with respect to the BPE corporate policy (standards, roles, corporate tool) while extending the scope to every business process in use in the Polish organization during the program realization because of growing demand from the business leaders.
- Conducting the appropriate training on process management policy.

The program team consisted of members of the BPM team, and although the initial schedule spanned more than 2 years, it was soon extended and is now maintained as an ongoing business since the formalized process management approach has become an established part of the organizational culture.

The processes were supposed to support the implementation of the company's strategy, so the first activity of the program was to focus on the processes prioritization from the strategy perspective. This activity involved categorizing the existing processes into groups and assessing every process in terms of its importance and its influence on the business results. For instance, if the execution of any activity in the process could impact the business results (e.g., income, customer or vendor relationships), the whole process was assigned to the high-priority group.

Based on that decision, every high-priority process was assigned a process sponsor, an owner, and a dedicated project team of business representatives and a process consultant. The project had a clearly defined goal, a scope, and a timeline that was aligned with the master BPE implementation program schedule. Therefore, the scope of the whole program was based on the list of high-priority processes, an approach that helped avoid scope creep. The approach also helped to keep the BPE schedule on the agreed timeline. After the scope was agreed upon, the processes were set in a sequence that supported a business logic (sales, realization, and service). This logic was deployed in each business by streamlining the detailed processes several times so almost the whole company was covered by process maps and process excellence.

3.2 Implementing the BPM Initiative

The purpose of the BPM initiative was to improve the quality of the company's processes, so quality standards for processes and projects were fundamental. Quality standards can be met only by adopting standardized processes that all employees can use while still providing transparency and relatedness across projects. Standardization also facilitates the synergies by using continuously refined best practices, so a standardization initiative was enacted.

However, before the standardization could take place, processes had to be identified. To address this task, Siemens took the BPM lifecycle model as a reference (Dumas et al. 2013). The BPM lifecycle consists of an initial phase of process identification, where the process boundaries are defined, and then iterates the process through five activities in a loop that iteratively improves the process (cf. Fig. 2). The actions taken fit into the first four activities of the BPM lifecycle: process identification, process discovery, process analysis, and process redesign.

These activities of the BPM life-cycle were conducted through workshops and tutorials that involved the organization's hierarchy. The adopted approach to implementing the BPM policy are described in Fig. 3 as a five-step process.

Step 1. Identify Business Process Owners

Several meetings were organized with the business process owners (typically the managers of the divisions) to discuss the advantages of adopting BPM by comparing current performance indicators with possible values after adopting BPM.

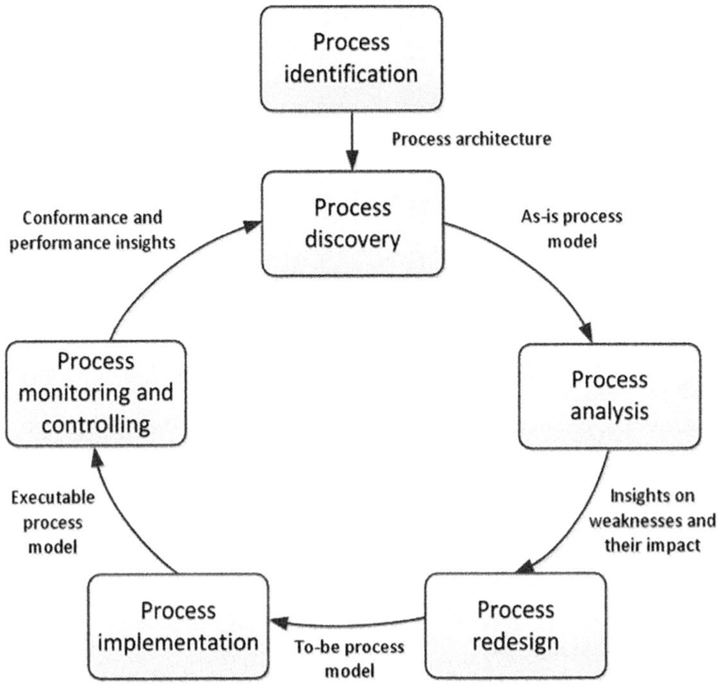

Fig. 2 The BPM lifecylce (Dumas et al. 2013)

Fig. 3 A five-step process for implementing the BPM policy

Step 2. Nominate Process Sponsors

Process sponsors were nominated to be responsible for about 20 business processes. Their task was to facilitate and drive the management of these processes.

Step 3. Assign Process Owners

The process sponsors nominated process owners to be responsible for one or two processes.

Step 4. Conduct Workshops

Process owners, project managers, and the employees (domain experts) who were involved in the processes were invited to workshops in which process identification (from whiteboards to as-is processes) took place.

Step 5. Systematically Refine the Process
At the first stage, workshops were held throughout the company every 2 days. Then their frequency became weekly or monthly based on the progress of the identification phase and the affected employees' learning curve. The project was expanded to a period of 3 years, so it is still ongoing in a continuous-refinement fashion, with around 300 people participating.

Applying the methodology came with the need for some practical changes:

- **Involving the project managers**: Project managers had often been give unrealistic goals that made them unaware of the real process or caused them to misunderstand the relevancy of the work. The main reason for this issue was that there were no processes defined. Project managers would seek higher production goals, allocated by process-unaware sectors. Under these circumstances, project managers were unable to fulfill their contracts.
- **Involving the financial controllers**: Prior to the initiative, financial controllers were not involved in processes. Involving financial controllers in the workshops meant designing the processes taking the accounting, budget, audit, and other finance-related perspectives on the process into account.
- **Involving the buyers**: Buyers had not been involved in the processes, but involving them was helpful in aligning the process goals and identifying non-value adding activities.
- **Acceptance of the change**: Many employees were experts in their domains but were unaware of the business process that affected them. As a consequence, resistance to changing their habits and adopting new tools was encountered. Although, the resistance to technology was not particularly high, the ARIS process modeling tools found some obstacles in adoption.

3.3 Methods and Tools for Business Process Excellence

Once the processes were defined, designed, improved, and documented, we used existing proprietary tools and frameworks to implement our solution.

Project Business@Siemens Professional project management was a key success factor for Siemens because nearly half of its revenue comes from "project business," that is, business that requires implementing a project. Siemens' customers expect that their projects will be handled professionally and responsibly. In the future, Project Business@Siemens will support the comprehensive and continuous improvement of all Siemens units that are active in the project business. The aim is to add value to the worldwide operations and processes of the divisions and lead countries by supporting them in reducing the risks associated with project business and achieving operational excellence.

Quality Management Siemens delivers excellent quality by following its quality strategy: implementing the mandatory elements of Siemens' quality management and continuously improving the quality of the personnel, the processes, and the products.

Operational Excellence The Operational Excellence department offers methods and processes that address function-specific areas like engineering, product management, and production, as well as the business areas of software and services. The businesses can make measurable and sustainable improvements by applying these methods and processes.

Operational Excellence also assists the business units as a partner and a service provider by supporting them in continuously improving their processes (e.g., in engineering, product management, and production). The department, which is comprised of benchmarking and productivity management, encompasses top+, 3i,[1] and other important approaches to increasing competitiveness. Lean is addressed in Operational Excellence's various departments.

An ongoing exchange of knowledge among the business areas is ensured by close collaboration with the divisions and business units.

Process and Production Consulting Internal process and production consultancy strengthen the competitiveness of Siemens' businesses along the global value chain. Consulting services draw on extensive expertise in the areas of innovation, research and development, engineering, procurement, supply chain logistics, manufacturing, services, and project and crisis management. Process and production consulting enables Siemens units to implement world-class processes successfully and sustainably.

top+ top+ provides the framework for business excellence and supports our businesses in cutting costs, increasing revenue, and optimizing assets. Key elements are the top+ approach (transparency, clear goals, concrete actions, definite consequences); the top+ Toolbox, which provides proven Business Excellence methodologies; and sharing of best practices. The main tool for top+ is business benchmarking, which assesses qualitatively and quantitatively market position, sets targets based on best practices, acquires outside learning and external knowledge, and undertakes continuous process improvement. The top+ Business Benchmarking Process consists of hypothesis generation, data collection, analysis and gap calculation, scenario-based simulation, definition of actions, and implementation.

Business Process Analysis and Optimization Siemens uses standard tools for process documentation, modeling, and publication. The process owner for BPM on the corporate level is responsible for specifying the standard tools and related services. The standard tools for Siemens' BPM are ARIS and the internal tool Dynamic ProcessWorld (DPW). These software tools provide a framework that supports users from process definition to process execution. These software tools

[1] 3i, which stands for ideas, impulses, and initiatives, is the idea-management program at Siemens and is an element of continuous improvement.

are embedded into a software architecture that takes into account KPIs (e.g., number of offers, hit rate, average order value per sales channel) and supports execution. Analysis and optimization can be done by analyzing the process execution logs to identify the as-is process and compare it to the designed process.

4 Results Achieved

Three areas were improved by implementing the corporate BPM policy.

Simplification The corporate process structure benefitted in terms of simplification, which entails increased flexibility, reduced manual conventions, and reduced number of processes. Flexibility increased because process changes can be easily modeled, executed, and shared among the divisions. New manual conventions were reduced by more than 60%, leaving space for standardized processes. The number of resource roles was reduced from eight to three: process sponsor, process owner, and process manager.

The process sponsor, typically the CEO of the organizational unit or a person from the top management level appointed by CEO, is in charge of defining the process portfolio, appointing the process owner, and promoting the process management topic. The process owner is responsible for handling a process in terms of planning, budgeting, implementation, communication, monitoring, interfaces, and target-setting. The process manager, selected by the process owner as an expert in the process, supports the process owner in the operational implementation, suggests improvements, and is the primary contact for process users.

Usability Usability was improved in terms of visualization of the processes and increases in the supporting tools' ease of use. Such is particularly the case with the process-unaware divisions, which moved from managing large spreadsheets to enhanced process visualization and graphical navigation provided by the ARIS tool. Moreover, the improved process structure helps to clarify and retrieve information about the process.

Clarity The new BPM program brought improvements in terms of clarity. The standardization of processes on the firm level reduced the number of regulating circulars from three to one and the number of regulating control requirements from three to two. Moreover, the program clearly defined the process owners and their responsibilities and introduced a new policy as an overarching framework.

Business Process Excellence (BPE) is currently adopted on the corporate level and has become a fundamental element of BPM at Siemens, in line with the Vision 2020 project. It is embedded into the Corporate Technology structure, so it is part of innovative products and management standards. BPE is also a key lever that facilitates the company's lasting business success and strengthens its competitiveness. One of BPE's objectives is to optimize the entire value chain across all business types: product, project, and service businesses. The foundation of BPE is a culture of continuous improvement, openness, and trust that is anchored Siemens-wide and is "lived" by all employees in their daily work.

Another goal achieved was the establishment of a knowledge center that bundles all the essential tools for the businesses' operational improvement, such as top+, Quality Management, PM@Siemens, and 3i, and helps to make knowledge at Siemens usable for the company as a whole in the form of a corporate memory.

By using top+, Project Business@Siemens, Quality Management, and Operational Excellence, the Business Excellence department, the Quality Management department, and the top+ department bundle all of the corporate resources, essential improvement tools, and expertise needed to achieve business excellence. The implementation of the tools in practice is also supported by the Process and Production Consulting unit.

5 Lessons Learned

Four primary lessons were learned from the program at Siemens:

- Complexity in many dimensions (number of processes, number of roles, number of formal documents, and circulars) is not supportive of effective process management.
- Having a strong, dedicated process sponsor is one of the most important keys to success.
- The entire organization will not appreciate the work at the beginning, but they will if one does her or his best to understand their businesses and support their efforts.
- Be flexible: Failure to align the businesses with the corporate recommendations will lead to lack of appreciation and cooperation.

References

BPM Modeling Manual, *Siemens internal documentation.*

Dumas, M., La Rosa, M., Mendling, J., & Reijers, H. A. (2013). Fundamentals of business process management. *Quantitative Process Analysis.* doi:10.1007/978-3-642-33143-5.

Rohloff, M. (2009). Case study and maturity model for business process management implementation. *LNCS, 5701*, 128–142. doi:10.1007/978-3-642-03848-8_10.

Scheer, A.-W., & Nüttgens, M. (2000). ARIS architecture and reference models for business process management. In *Business process management* (pp. 376–389). Berlin: Springer.

SIPEX, Siemens Process for Excellence. Siemens internal documentation (Circular 188—Policy of Siemens Business Process Management).

The Policy of BPM@Siemens. Siemens internal documentation (Circular 188—Policy of Siemens Business Process Management).

Bartosz Woliński within his professional career focuses on project management and operations management. His Ph.D. dissertation contributed to research efforts on Chinese economical transformation.

He's been working as project manager or head of department for international corporations including Dassault System, Philips and currently Siemens—mostly in IT (SAP) and SSC/BPO business and previously Business Process Excellence Program Manager.

Bartosz published several articles in-line with his professional and academic interests—project management and operations management. He also carries the lectures at the universities and technical universities in Poland (including Technical University of Warsaw and Warsaw School of Economics) which provides expertise mainly in service excellence (digital transformation and processes): Business Process Management, Robotics Process Automation and Digital Enterprise—Industry 4.0.

Saimir Bala is a Project Staff Member and Ph.D. student at the WU (Vienna University of Economics and Business) since 2014. He obtained his master degree in Distributed Systems at Sapienza University of Rome. His master thesis dealt with the implementation of a fault tolerant web-service orchestrator for the GreenerBuildings EU project. Currently he is part of the Safety-critical Human- and dAta-centric Process management in Engineering projects (SHAPE) funded by the Austrian Research Promotion Agency (FFG) under grant 845638 (SHAPE). Saimir's research focuses on mining project using the data generated from the various project management tools and version control systems. His research interests include mining software repositories, process mining and text mining.

People-Centric, ICT-Enabled Process Innovations via Community, Public and Private Sector Partnership, and e-Leadership: The Case of the Dompe eHospital in Sri Lanka

Wasana Bandara, Rehan Syed, Bandula Ranathunga, and K.B. Sampath Kulathilaka

Abstract

(a) **Situation faced**: This case study is a unique example of a people-centric ICT-enabled BPM effort that overcame many challenges through steady championship fuelled by a multi-sectorial support network (local community, government agencies, private sector and institutes of higher education). Driven by a desire to make a difference, a weakly reputed regional hospital in Sri Lanka with chaotic, mundane, manual processes became a landmark success in its service efficiency and effectiveness via staged-continuous improvements, collaborative ideation, creative resource utilization, and effective management of its "people" aspects.

(b) **Action taken**: The project took a multi-staged people-centric approach. Major attitudinal change efforts with staff helped to build a unified internal workforce that was empowered to understand the patients' needs. The hospital's physical environment was transformed into a peaceful, pleasant atmosphere that was free of chaos. The entire patient-care-process was mapped, analyzed, and transformed with IT enabled process improvements. A new patient records management system and a mobile-channeling system was implemented to eliminate long queues and increase the quality of

W. Bandara (✉) • R. Syed
Queensland University of Technology (QUT), Brisbane, QLD, Australia
e-mail: w.bandara@qut.edu.au; syedrehan.abbaszaidi@qut.edu.au

B. Ranathunga
Information Communication and Technology Agency (ICTA), Colombo, Sri Lanka
e-mail: bandular@icta.lk

K.B. Sampath Kulathilaka
District Hospital Dompe, Medalanda, Sri Lanka
e-mail: ehosp.gp@healthdept.wp.gov.lk

J. vom Brocke, J. Mendling (eds.), *Business Process Management Cases*,
Management for Professionals, DOI 10.1007/978-3-319-58307-5_8

patient care. Continued reviews and improvements are key in this case, as the vision to make a difference does not end with a single initiative.

(c) **Results achieved**: The case illustrates how an ordinary government regional hospital's patient-care process was transformed with the collective efforts of multi-stakeholder power. The reforms have enabled the hospital to increase the quality of patient care, enhance staff satisfaction, gain deep support, and get buy-in from higher authorities and the community. These process reform efforts enabled not only a one-off improvement initiative but a sustained success story that has received national and international attention.

(d) **Lessons learned**: A key takeaway is how all of the enabling elements (championship, community, and executive support), lined up, each making its own significant contribution. The absence or misaligned timing of any one of these elements could have caused the effort to stall or fail. The e-champion and his supporters selected and managed the people-centric resources and opportunities in a highly resource-constrained environment while balancing and strengthening the ongoing stakeholder relationships. These efforts served as the foundation for the success and sustainability of this case.

1 Introduction

Health sector reforms, especially technology-supported process improvements in developing nations, are known to be a challenge because of resistance that emerges from such issues as lack of required capabilities resulting from technology phobia among key stakeholders (e.g., doctors, nurses, and hospital administrators), fear of losing control, and even fear of job loss (Anwar et al. 2011; Cline and Luiz 2013; Khan et al. 2012). Even the ICT-enabled process improvements that do take place are often not sustained; they break down after a while because of lack of resources, poor leadership, or the system's inability to cater to the institution's real (and continuously evolving) needs.

There are many stories of healthcare reform, both successful and failed driven by top-down initiatives, where influential institutions like Health Ministries, WHO, and other governmental agencies or funding bodies sponsor and push for the reforms. This case is different, as the call for improvement came from within the hospital, and it continued because of a collection of critical factors, all lining up, each making its own significant contribution. The absence or the misaligned timing of any one of these elements could have led the effort to stall or fail.

The case takes place at Dompe Hospital, in Sri Lanka (Daily FT 2015). Sri Lanka's public health care is free and open to all Sri Lankan citizens. Sri Lanka has had considerable success in health care delivery, both in terms of development indicators and relative ranking in South Asia (UNDP 2015). Though there has been significant investment in the sector in terms of capital, technology, and manpower, the hospital sector as a whole has failed to evolve as customer-centric service providers. In hospitals, the patient experience is rarely considered, perhaps because of the sheer number of cases (patients) who come through the system, but it is also influenced by weak management practices and poor staff attitude. Long queues, confusing instructions, and unfriendly staff are common and accepted features in almost all public hospitals. Little attention has been paid to improving patient welfare or to making service delivery simple and efficient. It was against this backdrop that this case emerged (Kulathilaka 2013).

Dompe Hospital is located in the Western Province of Sri Lanka, in the Gampaha district. The only district hospital within a 25-km radius, Dompe is a designated export-processing zone and is reputed to be an isolated, unattractive location, far away from anything of much interest. There are idioms in the Sinhala language, the main dialect in Sri Lanka, about "going to Dompe" that reflect this view.

This case is the story of how Dompe changed that image and became an example of patient-centric public health service provisioning in Sri Lanka. This change was achieved through a multi-stakeholder-engaged reform effort that resulted in improvements in the use of physical and personnel resources and ICT-enabled process improvements. The rest of this chapter describes the background to the reform work, the then *as-is* situation, and the actions taken, concluding with a summary of the results achieved and a set of lessons learned.

2 Situation Faced

Dompe Hospital consists of five wards and 102 beds and is headed by a District Medical Officer (DMO), who reports to the Regional Director of Health Services (RDHS), Gampaha (NIHS 2008). A long-standing hospital in the area, it was upgraded to the status of District Hospital in 1970. It provides curative and preventive health care services for more than 500,000 beneficiaries, including the local residents and the 20,000+ employees of the more than 60 industrial organizations in the region.

One of Dompe's strengths is a strong community presence, which equates to a capability if it is appropriately channeled. As the closest public hospital for a large area, Dompe Hospital has always been an important asset of the local community, and collaborative efforts have taken place with the hospital and local community welfare groups. Intense dengue[1] awareness and eradication programs run in 2009 in collaboration with the hospital staff, the local temple, and community welfare groups connected the hospital staff closely with enthusiastic local community members, a connection that later became a key asset in the BPM initiatives described here.

The industrial organizations in the region had formed strong alliances with the hospital, developed in conjunction with the employee health and safety programs,

[1]See details at the National Dengue Control unit at http://www.dengue.health.gov.lk/ for details about dengue in Sri Lanka (last accessed June 14, 2016).

mandated by regulatory requirements, to which Dompe Hospital staff contributed. These organizations provided a continuous trickle of monetary donations to support the hospital maintenance costs as part of their corporate social responsibility (CSR) agendas. These funds, often deployed to meet ad hoc needs, represent another asset if managed and used differently.

The RDHS, Gampaha and the acting director of the hospital were keen to change the hospital's status but lacked the resources to do so. Like many government hospitals in developing countries, Dompe was a disorganized, overcrowded hospital where little attention was given to the overall patient experience and where unempathetic, discourteous health care providers and long delays were an accepted norm.

It was the championship of a doctor who had recently been transferred to work in the role of medical-officer-in-charge that ignited and sustained the reforms. He became the glue that brought all the other "assets" and enablers together and brought the *digital revolution* to the hospital.

The desire and willingness to improve how things were done at Dompe Hospital emerged collectively from all these sources: the champion himself, the senior hospital staff, and the resident and industrial community formed a group of program leaders, an unofficial group tasked with thought leadership for the efforts. Their vision was "happy and content patients," and they sought to achieve that vision incrementally, using all resources available to overcome any roadblocks that arose.

The reforms were designed and executed with a clear focus on patient well-being and were supported and directed by a situational analysis and research on best/better practices. The outcomes were a much more comfortable and conducive physical environment for patients while they were receiving medical services, transformation of the problematic manual systems towards an ICT-enabled patient-centric medical service delivery model, and incorporation of an online appointment system for m-Channeling.[2] Staff training and empowerment, which was a key focus (and challenge) throughout this initiative, and the development of steady and strong leadership, especially for the ICT aspects of the initiative (hereafter referred to as e-leadership), are important results of this case.

The initial support from government bodies was minimal, but the results produced by the early stages of the efforts provided the evidence needed to manage and communicate upward at later stages in order to gain the buy-in and support required to sustain the initiative. The program leaders' network which had excellent rapport with senior members in the public health sector, access to ICTA,[3] and community connections) was a primary factor in achieving this goal.

---

[2]'m-Channeling' is short for 'mobile-channeling', which is an Interactive Voice Response method (IVR)-based patient appointment system.

[3]ICTA, the Information Communication and Technology Agency, leads and supports IT innovations and implementations in Sri Lanka's public sector. See https://www.icta.lk/ for details (last accessed June 24, 2016).

The initiative was a success due to the partnerships among the public sector, the community (with support from professionals in the community), the private business sector (large and small), and academia. This case demonstrates the feasibility and success of a new service model that can be emulated and adapted broadly. Cases like this bring a paradigm shift to public sector management in developing nations by pointing to new management models that bring together a public-private-community tripartite to overcome critical resource challenges.

The initial step, a situational analysis, commenced early in 2011 and lasted approximately 3 months. The goal of the analysis was to determine the current service standards and derive a vision and mission. The analysis was done through an informal survey of the nursing and reception desk staff based on their observations at both peak and off-peak times and by talking with other staff, patients, and other stakeholders. The focus was on patients' waiting time and their experiences during that time. These techniques served to get the staff engaged in the discussions and to "break the ice," thereby empowering the staff to be active stakeholders in the project and helping to ensure that rich insights were obtained across the board. These techniques also created a *need within* for improvements, which resulted in an environment in which staff were encouraged to raise areas of concern and exchange ideas for improvements.

One critical bottleneck (and opportunity) in the hospital's process concerned how its physical space was used and managed. For example, there was only one narrow entrance gate to the hospital and one six-foot-wide corridor at the entrance (Fig. 1). This corridor was:

- The main access to the emergency, OPD, pharmacy, and injections and dressings areas;

Fig. 1 The congestion observed at the hospital entrance

- Where patients queued to collect their 'tickets',[4] so it also held a line of chairs for patients who were waiting for their tickets;
- Where visitors gained access to the wards to visit loved ones during visiting hours; and
- Where external institutional transfers occurred in the hospital.

Surely no further explanation is needed to depict the chaos in this single hospital corridor alone!

Medical records are paramount in a good health system. In most public hospitals in Sri Lanka, these records are paper-based and are kept manually, as was the case in Dompe Hospital as well. The records were stored in a separate records room and were often disorganized (Fig. 2).

For each visit to the hospital, patients registered, queued, and waited to get a number before being seen by a doctor. Patients with previous records and prescriptions went to the records room and queued again to retrieve their medical history and records. The number-issuing counter opened at 7:30 a.m. daily, and patients began lining up as early as 6:00 a.m., sometimes leaving home at dawn to reach the hospital on time to be ahead in the queue. Some previously registered patients registered as new patients, lying about their medical history, in the hope of avoiding the records queue and getting faster service. This practice created duplicate and incomplete records for the same patient and interfered with the doctors' ability to perform accurate diagnoses and holistic treatments. Even when a doctor

Fig. 2 A shelf from the old records room

[4]'A ticket' is a term commonly used in the Sri Lankan health system to refer to the piece of paper that denotes the patient's number and relevant service for the waiting queue.

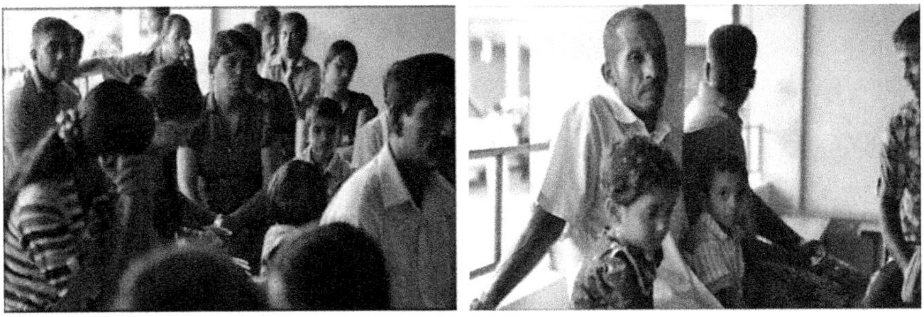

Fig. 3 Long waiting times and patients left in discomfort

asked patients about their medical history, such patients would not mention the medications they had taken earlier for fear of being caught as a previous patient. When doctors cannot see a patient's history, allergies, and so on, they cannot guarantee the correct diagnosis nor the prescription of the most suitable medication, as they can see only a small fragment of the patient's medical situation.

In addition, since out-patients at Sri Lankan public hospitals cannot choose the doctors they see, when such patients were not allocated their preferred doctors, they sometimes discarded medications and advice received from visits with other doctors and visited repeatedly until they were allocated their preferred doctors, creating an unwarranted capacity issue in the hospital. Patients waited an average of 1 h 41 min, with a minimum waiting time of 1 h 15 min and a maximum waiting time of 2 h 30 min (Fig. 3).

All work was done in silos, such that a patient's *overall* experience at any given visit was never considered. The patient's experience was always a fragment of activities, where they were sent from one place to another. For example, if a returning patient was not reminded to collect his or her medical records and went in to see a doctor, he or she would have to go back, stand in the queue to get the medical records, and then stand in queue again with the records to see a doctor. What's more, if the numbers for retrieving prior medical records were already issued or if it was later in the day, the patient would have to come back the next day and start over.

The need for a change was clear. United with the local community and supporting authorities, Dompe hospital executives, commenced work with the motto: *We need to fix this!*

3 Action Taken

The Sri Lankan public sector is governed by strict regulations and compliance requirements. In addition to the provincial and ministerial health authorities, the employee unions (e.g., for doctors, nurses, and minor staff) also have a say, especially in regard to changes in work practices and duties. Any changes must be reported and approved through multiple channels prior to enactment, and there is little tolerance for any "trial and error" with any initiative (because of legitimate concerns about the risks). Such approvals took a long time and sometimes were unobtainable. This aspect of the problem was not easy to manage.

One key success factor was the support from Dompe Hospital's executives, particularly the DMO, who embraced the opportunity to make a change and vested trust in the people driving it: the champion, the supportive resident and business community, staff, and patients. The executives were willing to take the risk of proceeding without seeking approval from the provincial or ministerial level, which could have delayed and blocked the initiative.

The recommendations were proposed and planned as incremental steps. Change management was a core pillar and was started immediately (and it continues to date as an ongoing dynamic). The incremental process improvements started with input from the situational analysis, which studied six processes: patient registration, out-patient management, pharmacy and drug management, clinic management, in-patient management, and emergency patient management.

The initial focus was on the first three processes with the goal of having "happy and contented patients" through three targeted areas of work: creating a comfortable and hassle-free physical environment for patient welfare and care, designing and implementing requisite changes to the existing manual system in pursuit of a patient-centric medical service delivery on an ICT-based solution platform, and incorporating an Interactive Voice Response method (IVR)-based patient appointment system, referred to as "m-Channeling".[5]

How these three goals were achieved is described below.

3.1 Changes in the Physical Environmental

The end-to-end process models were documented along with a map of the hospital's physical spaces. The hospital floors were reorganized to minimize the spatial disruptions to the patient-care process. Rearrangement and upgrading of main service points, such as Admission, Emergency Treatment Unit (ETU), Dispensary, Laboratory, Consultation, Dressing, Injection, and the Out-Patient Department (OPD), took place along with upgrades common utility areas like internal roads, staff restrooms, and the Health Education Room. The overall changes made to improve the hospital's physical space included simple things like building a new (second) gate for the hospital and routing all visitors through that gate to improve flow, creating an opening in one of the ward walls to ease access from this new gate,

[5]m-Channeling refers to "mobile channelling service" an option that allows patients to make their appointments using Interactive Voice Response (IVR). IVR is a voice-activated system for easy human-system interaction (For more information, see https://www.techopedia.com/definition/1525/interactive-voice-response-ivr; last accessed Sept 19, 2016).

and organizing the spaces so what each section was doing was clearly communicated, helping the patients to navigate within the hospital premises.

The mapping invented a new flow system for services at the hospital and provided the blueprint for all of the physical infrastructure's layout and human skills needed. It also showed how the proposed new physical layout and staff allocations were aligned with the proposed revised process flows and IT system.

The costs for these physical changes were paid from the local industrial organization donations mentioned earlier. Additional donations were sought through community involvement and hospital staff networks. In return, donors were recognized through signage placed in these spaces and through other social marketing strategies (see Appendix). This incentive encouraged individuals and companies to sponsor the improvements in the physical infrastructure. The ongoing relationships between the hospital staff and resident community members played a key role in winning these sponsorships.

3.2 Patient-Centric ICT-Enabled Processes for Delivery of Medical Services

The patient records management process was a clear candidate for an ICT-enabled solution. An environmental scan/market research was conducted to identify the best solution, and the Hospital Health Information Management System (HHIMS) was chosen. The HHIMS was introduced in Sri Lanka during the 2004 tsunami-recovery period to support patient records management, and the software was licensed for open-source use in the Sri Lankan public sector health organizations (formalized by ICTA through their e-government programs[6]), but had rarely been used since.

ICTA's support was sought at this stage in order to gain access to the licensed software. The program leaders also applied for ICTA's e-society grant scheme and received LKR 4.15 million through the grant, which paid the costs of the IT components' wired networking and computer hardware and software. The grant's funds were managed through the Gampaha District Director of Health, as Dompe Hospital was not qualified to handle funds. The District Director of Health set up the required governance for the funds and the program management. The networking services were obtained through Sri Lanka Telecom, the project leaders managed the overall project internally as a joint effort, and costs were reduced where possible with additional community contributions.

Site visits to where the HHIMS had already been installed (but had failed in overall implementation and adoption) were conducted to study the system functionality and identify the system requirements. These site visits confirmed that massive customization was required if the system was to be implemented at Dompe Hospital, and they triggered a series of in-depth discussions and negotiations with the vendor that resulted in a revised system: HHIMS V 1.3.

[6] See http://www.hhims.org/ for additional details.

The IT budget remained a challenge. The community contributed man-hours to arrange the physical environment so it was ready to implement the technology. This work included a thorough clean-up of the hospital premises and other efforts, such as excavation for the installation of the fiber-optic network cable.

The use of the HHIMS has significantly improved the hospital's patient life cycle management process. Patients' details are added to the system when the patients arrive at the hospital for the required treatment. The process starts with the patient's arrival at the OPD, when the system generates a unique barcode for the patient that is then used to generate a patient identification number and a barcoded patient heath card. The barcoded card contains the required personal and health-related details of the patient. For each visit, a "Today's Token" is issued using the Electronic Queue Management Centre. The token guides the patient to the relevant service queue and doctor, reducing the chance of incorrect diagnosis and service delivery.

At the Electronic Queue Management Centre, a doctor, equipped with a laptop and a barcode scanner, can access a patient's medical history with a simple swipe of the patient's health card and update to the HHIMS the patient's diagnosis details, drug prescriptions, and required medical procedures or tests. Patients are then transferred to the required hospital unit for the prescribed treatment, drugs, or medical tests (i.e., dispensary, dressing room, injection room, emergency ward, or sample-collection center).

The staff at each unit can also retrieve the patient treatment details by swiping the patient's health card from the central database. The consulting doctor receives updates as soon as a unit updates the details of prescribed treatment in the system. The medical records of patients who are admitted to a ward are updated, and a system-generated diagnosis card is issued at the time of discharge.

The system can also use email to notify the relevant staff on the nature of diseases treated at each clinic in the hospital. Independent clinics (i.e., the medical clinic, the family clinic, and the screening clinic for non-communicable diseases) are also linked with the centralized system. The DMO can monitor the hospital's performance online.

All operational reports (e.g., the OPD register, drugs dispensed) are now generated by the system. Sensitive patient-health data is stored in encrypted form in the in-house server as a secure location instead of on individual computers. System access is maintained by usernames and passwords, with a pre-defined user-access policy.

A three-layered disaster-recovery strategy is in place to minimize data losses that are due to system failures. An automatic online system backup that is maintained at the DMO's offices (in a remote location) is scheduled at three times each day (mid-day, evening, and midnight). Data is also stored on a CD every day (off-line), and printed copies of the OPD register and drugs dispensed are maintained in the medical records room under the custody of the chief pharmacist for reference and auditing requirements.

The system has other built-in security features to ensure security of sensitive patient data. The server is kept in a secure place under the direct supervision of the doctor on call. Every user is given an individual user name and password. To prevent unauthorized access, each user data-access level is predefined.

3.3 m-Channeling

Subsequent to making the physical improvements and putting an improved patient records management system in place, the m-Channeling system was brought in. this system was not used previously in Sri Lankan public hospitals. Equipped with growing support from the staff and the community, an online consultation appointment system was launched on 5 November 2013.

The m-Channeling system is an automated consultation appointment system that uses the IVR method and allows patients to book appointments using their mobile phones. The service is offered to the public through a hotline (+94711370370). The system, which allows patients the convenience of selecting the required medical services, is designed to be tri-lingual, using Sinhala, Tamil, and English, the main languages used in Sri Lanka, although it currently uses only Sinhala. Upon dialing the hotline, the user will be prompted to select the language (when all three languages are available) and the hospital.

Once the hospital is selected, the system prompts the user to select the required date and OPD session time. (The user can book two consultation slots at a time.) The system generates a confirmation SMS with appointment details and send it to the user. At the time of the appointment, the patient presents the confirmation SMS to the reception staff, who then guide the patient to the doctor appointed to m-Channeling patients. Patients collect the prescription drugs from a dedicated drug counter.

Administrative staff update the appointment schedule using a web-based hospital administration portal. The doctor appointed to deliver m-Channeling services receives the appointment details by SMS and email. The administration also has access to incident reports and a visual display of reservations.

3.4 People Factors: Supporting the Change

> People are at the heart of processes. (Jeston and Nelis 2010, p. 5)

Employees play a major role in the success of health sector reforms, especially in an e-health context. The engagement of Dompe Hospital's staff commenced at the situation-analysis stage, when the staff at all levels were given a voice in what was going well and what was not.

Lack of appropriate technology skills is a common issue in ICT-enabled improvement initiatives, and such was the case here as well. The training of the system's users (60 of the 102 staff members) was done systematically through input

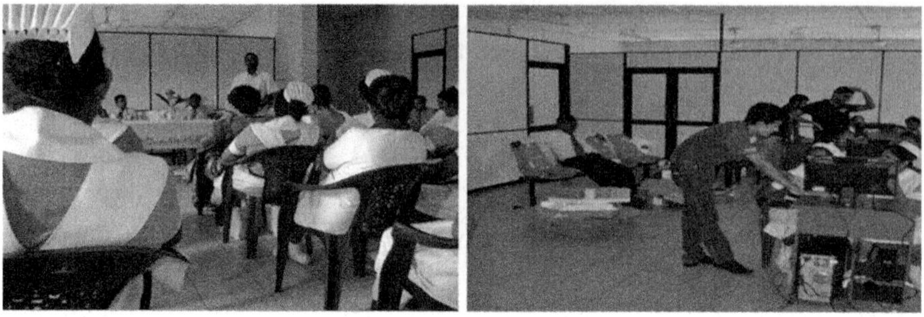

Fig. 4 Staff ICT training

from the HHIMS vendor, Lunar Technologies.[7] In order to avoid creating a barrier between those who knew IT and those who did not, a detrimental obstacle to employee buy-in and team spirit in many other e-health initiatives (Kimaro and Twaakyondo 2005), the opportunity for general IT training was offered to all staff, including janitors. This effort helped to maximize support from all staff by making them feel that they were part of the reform and members of the team. The aim was not to have all staff use the system but to increase the staff's overall technology literacy and keep the team's unity intact. Resourcing such a massive effort to increase skills was a challenge, as a series of hands-on workshops was required. (See Fig. 4 for a visualization of how these workshops were conducted.) Getting all staff members to commit to attending the sessions was a challenge as well, and a carrot-and-stick approach was used as needed. For example, staff were given a day off to attend the trainings and were sometimes rewarded with things like an internet dongle (sponsored by the industry network). The few who did not oblige were called upon for explanation by the senior hospital staff and required to attend. No one was exempt.

A thirst for basic IT knowledge and the desire to attend was created by positioning the workshops as a mechanism through which to gain essential life skills. The workshops were often held at times and settings when not only the staff but sometimes their family members could attend, and the trainings were positioned as a community effort to improve technology skills, driven by the IT-skilled community members who supported the initiative.

The head of the University of Moratuwa's[8] IT Department provided university students as trainers. The design, conduct, and evaluation of these workshops were done as a student project. The students were hosted on Dompe Hospital's premises as residential trainers for 2 weeks, using vacant staff quarters.

The workplace organization method 5S (Brandao de Souza 2009; Young 2014) was also integrated into the project as part of the organizational culture

[7]See http://www.lunartechnologies.net/ for details about the vendor; last accessed June 28, 2016.

[8]University of Moratuwa is the leading technology university in Sri Lanka. See https://www.mrt.ac.lk for details.

Fig. 5 5S principals applied at the doctors' diagnostics tables

development to help create a professional workplace that supports productivity. The method was taught to staff at all levels and encouraged not only as a workplace practice but also as a home-productivity practice so the concepts would be firmly instilled in each employee. The 5S principals have enabled the staff to know where things are and how things are used. 5S was also used in the implementation of technology solutions. Figure 5 shows an example of where a clear demarcation for all of the technology equipment at a doctor's desk was made. The minor staff's roles were enlarged to include handling IT equipment so they could set things up for daily use. They knew exactly how to do this as an outcome of the 5S approach and the generic IT training.

The program leaders conducted internal training programs as well as Outbound training for staff at all levels (Fig. 6). The Outbound training took the staff away from the hospital premises and were designed to enhance mindset/attitudinal changes, create an environment that helps to build trust, and convince the staff of the importance of addressing the challenges the hospital faced. This training also helped to build a sense of ownership in that such challenges must be addressed collectively, as each person's role (no matter how senior or junior) made a difference in the patients' experience. Some of the funds from local industry were used for outbound training, and a senior executive from one local industry donated his personal funds to support this important task of culture-building. The Outbound training groups were selected to enable and enhance the staff interactions in the hospital, and each group consisted of hospital staff across levels. This choice was important for team-building purposes to break down the wall between the staff groups (i.e., doctors, nurses, and minor staff). This approach had a positive effect on the overall change-management effort, as it developed and sustained a team spirit among the hospital staff and encouraged the "we are all from one unit—Dompe Hospital" attitude. The segregation of the staff groups in the Sri Lankan health sector has been a barrier in many reform attempts, but it was carefully managed

Fig. 6 Outbound training for staff at all levels. (**a**) Moments from outbound training. (**b**) Team-building across multiple staff levels. (**c**) Making a group pledge to commit to positive change. (**d**) Building trust in the teams

here. The training and workshops had an inclusive agenda, where a mix of staff minimized segregation and ice-breaking team-building activities were embedded to support the overall change-management efforts in the long term.

A range of activities/programs are in place to sustain and develop the team-spirited culture created during the program's implementation. An annual staff trip is held to help maintain the relationships formed, and a "best worker of the year" competition encourages staff to initiate and lead improvements as a way to instill a continuous-improvement mindset. Ongoing events, such as *pirith* ceremonies,[9] in partnership with the hospital staff and the community, are organized to sustain the valuable community network and their contributions.

Celebrating success is an important aspect of a positive organizational culture. Each year, on 27 December, the go-live date of the new patient record system, the hospital celebrates its success and the ongoing achievements in enhanced patient care and recognizes the contributors' efforts. These celebrations tend to be ceremonies in which hospital staff cut a "birthday cake" for the project, and plaques of recognition are presented to key contributors (hospital staff, resident community leaders, and industry sponsors) as further encouragement for continuous support (Figs. 7 and 8).

[9]"*Pirith* (or *paritta*) is a collective term designating a set of protective chants or runes sanctioned by the Buddha for the use of both laymen and bhikkhus" (Kariyawasam 1995, p. 22). Pirith-chanting is a popular ceremony among the Buddhists of Sri Lanka.

Fig. 7 Celebrating success annually with all staff

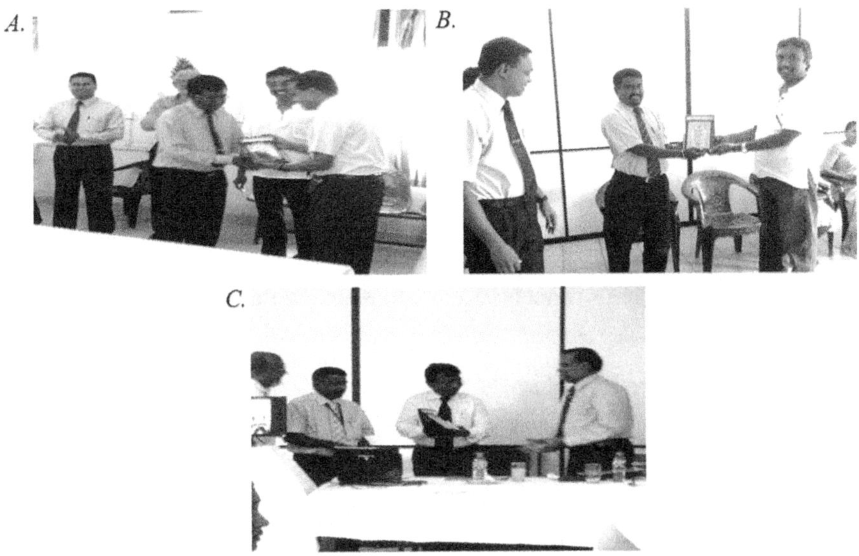

Fig. 8 Formal recognition of community leaders for their ongoing support. (**a**) Recognition of staff leaders. (**b**) Recognition of resident community leaders. (**c**) Recognition of individual donors' support of the initiative

Educating the patient community on the upcoming changes was an important aspect of the project for which the resident community leaders played a central role. They took the message of the changes to the patient care processes to the village community via workshops (i.e., at community gatherings in the local temple), mini road trips in the community, and one-to-one discussions. Listening to the details from a Dompe community member helped the patients believe that the changes were for their own benefit. The hospital staff was also trained to assist the patients in the transition process, so the patients were educated and supported as they came in for services after the new implementations. Senior hospital staff used invitations to address the industrial worker community and present how and why Dompe Hospital was different as a result of the new processes. The project champion spent many hours of his personal time interacting with patients to build a rapport, educate them one-to-one, and to understand remaining challenges from the patients' perspective. The patients' experiences with the reformed Dompe Hospital and their word-of-mouth advocacy related to how positively different Dompe Hospital is now were the most powerful methods in getting other patients' buy-in.

The program's success depended heavily on the champion, especially because of his transformational leadership skills, IT expertise, and passion to make a difference. As he is a central pillar of the community and force behind the initiative, the sustainability of the project would be at risk if he left. A core team of seven—two doctors, a head sister, and four nurses and a secondary team of five nurses was put in place to address this risk. They meet formally once a month and informally daily; the champion visits the operational "in-production" sites with the team and engages in the conceptualization and implementation of ongoing improvement efforts. These team members are in training, shadowing the champion and developing both transformational and IT leadership skills to create sustained leadership at Dompe Hospital.

4 Results Achieved

The physical space improvements were completed within 3 months of the situational analysis. The ICTA e-society grant was received by August 2011, and the initial system implementation for the ICT-enabled patient care process was completed on Dec 27, 2011. These improvements enabled patients to access the services they needed easily and effectively.

Multiple entry points introduced in place of the single entry eased congestion and created space for the staff to perform their duties effectively and efficiently. Patient waiting time was reduced, and patient feedback that "Dompe Hospital is a better place now" began to emerge. The hospital became a pleasant place to visit instead of a chaotic one, with the inward rush reduced and people knowing where to go and what to do.[10]

[10]This YouTube video clip demonstrates the changes in the environment that have resulted from the reform efforts: https://www.youtube.com/watch?v=-YqujXDfHHQ; last accessed June 14, 2016.

The bigger impacts took place with the implementation of the digitized health management information system (HHIMS V1.3) on 27 December, 2011. The system-supported process improvements have benefitted multiple stakeholders in multiple ways:

- Introducing the electronic queue management system made management of patients' waiting time more efficient, and generation of daily reports improved OPD staff's productivity.
- Doctors have real-time access to patients' medical history and demographic details, the availability of drugs in the stores, and lab reports. The availability of this vital information has helped to improve the doctors' efficiency and accuracy in making diagnoses. Access to the stock reports help doctors to manage the ordering and monitoring of inventories in line with the procedures. Doctors can also analyze their own performance by accessing performance reports.
- The efficiency and productivity of nursing staff have improved as a result of them having easy access to treatment instructions from doctors. Access to the patient treatment information has helped the nursing staff improve their ward planning and scheduling activities.
- The pharmacy staff has access to legible prescriptions and automation of the required quantities of prescribed drugs for patients. The automation of stock counts and inventory processes has significantly reduced the staff workload.
- Appropriately labelled lab samples that are now delivered to the lab technicians have improved the accuracy of the lab analysis reports and reduced human error.
- Administrative staff can easily monitor operational performance and make effective decisions by analyzing the required statistical data.
- The ultimate beneficiaries are the patients, whose healthcare services have improved as a result of the improvements in the processes and culture of Dompe Hospital.

The OPD now manages the records of those who make appointments through the m-Channeling system, which not only eliminates wasted time by patients but also reduces congestion in the hospital premises.

Several positive outcomes have been achieved;

- Patient information management and drugs information management, which had been run manually, are now IT-based.
- Changing negative public opinion to one that is positive has resulted in more people seeking hospital services and consultations. Walk-in OPD patients get service within an average of 40 min, as opposed to ~2 h previously. Patients who use m- Channeling are served in a 15–30 min from arrival to exit.

Fig. 9 Award from the nation's president in recognition of enhanced productivity at Dompe Hospital

- Changing the staff's mindset to being patient-centric and helping them to realize who their real customer is have resulted in doctors' having more time to make better diagnoses through the use of the IT-based health information system and ready assistance from the support staff.
- The information gathered through the systems enables the decision-makers to make more timely and more informed decisions.

Dompe Hospital has become a landmark success story in Sri Lanka's ICT-enabled government process-transformation efforts. The initiative received a national productivity award[11] from the Sri Lankan Presidential Secretariat (Fig. 9) and an *e-Swabhimani*[12] award in recognition of its ICT-enabled transformations, making Dompe Hospital an example for future government initiatives in Asia.[13] The Ministry of Health, Sri Lanka and ICTA are driving an effort to take the lessons learned from Dompe Hospital, particularly with regard to electronic records management, to other public hospitals in Sri Lanka. A national program is in place that will help 300 of the 1084 public hospitals in Sri Lanka to implement the process and

[11]See details of Dompe Hospital receipt of a national productivity award at http://www.ft.lk/article/414253/ICTA-project-Dompe-e-hospital-wins-prestigious-National-Productivity-Award; last accessed June 14, 2016.

[12]e-Swabhimani, an initiative of the Information Communication Technology Agency (ICTA) of Sri Lanka, recognizes excellence in digital content creation. See http://www.eswabhimani.lk/ for additional details; last accessed June 14, 2016.

[13]See http://drdigible.com/2013/12/02/ehospital-dompe-in-the-international-spotlight/, which positions Dompe Hospital in the spotlight of future government initiatives in Asia; last accessed June 14, 2016.

systems changes deployed at Dompe Hospital. The goal is to create electronic patient records that can be accessed nationally for 80% of the country's population by 2018. The champion of Dompe Hospital, who is a senior consultant for these efforts, has been building on and sharing Dompe Hospital's experiences nationally and internationally.

5 Lessons Learned

This story of Dompe Hospital is unique in terms of its stakeholders, its resource mobilization, and its management. This case study brings a number of lessons, especially in relation to the culture and "people" facets of BPM, which Rosemann and vom Brocke (2010, 2015) describe as two core pillars of BPM. Rosemann and vom Brocke (2010, p. 113) describe the "people" factor as "individuals and groups who continually enhance and apply their process and process management skills and knowledge in order to improve business performance," and explain that this factor should be seen in the light of an organization's human capital and its ecosystem. This case study demonstrates how wide that ecosystem of human capital can be. The collaboration between public and private sectors and the community in this case shows that the set of stakeholders who can have a positive impact on BPM initiatives is much broader than the narrow stakeholder analysis typically done within BPM projects indicates. A typical stakeholder analysis is often limited to those who are within the current process or organization's boundaries, but social networks' ability to expand these boundaries is rarely considered. Formal and informal social networks (physical and virtual) can play an important role across the BPM life cycle (Dumas et al. 2013) in the identification, discovery, analysis, redesign, implementation, monitoring, and controlling of processes. The case also provides insights into the mechanisms of tapping into these social networks. The project is also evidence of the essential role of a champion, particularly an e-leader in the case of ICT-driven process change. The e-leader does not have to be a top-level executive; in the Dompe case, the champion was a humble middle manager with IT expertise and a passion for having a meaningful impact. He maximized the technology's affordance to optimize and streamline the processes. The case demonstrates that an e-leader must have strong interpersonal skills to be able bind everything and everyone together.

Rosemann and vom Brocke (2010, p. 113) describe the culture factor as one that "incorporates the collective values and beliefs in regards to the process-centred organization." Culture and change management play a vital role in all process-reform work (De Bruin 2009), especially in the sustainability of these initiatives. The desire to make meaningful changes has to be instilled into employees, and the ability to do so provisioned for staff at *all* levels. The overall change-management efforts here were creatively integrated by presenting the initiative to the staff as an essential life-skills learning opportunity, through which the phobia about technology and process changes was overcome. The optimistic "can-do" attitudinal changes were the energizing catalyst that kept the important "people" aspect of the project intact and in harmony. The case also demonstrates that support from senior management can be challenging to obtain but can be obtained when evidence-based initial outcomes are presented. The support of the Health Ministry was non-existent at the start of this case but was gained with the demonstration of positive outcomes. This strategy is a powerful one for BPM professionals who are managing and communicating upward. A takeaway message is to commence with what you can and show results, and the required support will follow. The need to "sell" BPM efforts with impactful, evidence-based success stories is well established (Taylor 2012) but is not often practiced. (Denning 2005) "story-telling guidelines" are a useful resource in this effort.

This narrative also presents creative means of resource identification and utilization, especially in a highly resource-constrained environment. Constraints can sometimes lead to innovative practices (Johnson 2013; Stokes 2014). As in many developing countries, funding was a key inhibitor to getting started in this case. The initiative succeeded because of the partnerships among the public sector, the community, the private business sector (large and small), and academia. While the business community undertook the expenses for the physical changes, the local community provided funding support at times and manpower on a voluntary basis, with support from able professionals in the community. ICTA paid for the IT equipment, and the university sector contributed the resources required for the IT training for the whole staff. These partnerships formed an unprecedented new multi-sector service delivery model in the hospital. The project champion tapped into the resources, orchestrated them, and built them into the initiative's overall project planning.

This case can inspire individuals and communities to see what they can do to address key challenges and improve their surroundings and their services. BPM program leaders should see powerful multi-sector and community-driven or supported initiatives as a valued capacity and tap into them.

We leave the reader with four primary thoughts to consider in their own BPM efforts:

- What are the physical and virtual social networks in the targeted BPM context that can play a role in creating impactful, innovative, and sustained process-improvement initiatives, and how can they be tapped?
- When resource constraints exist, can other options (e.g., open-source systems, grant schemes, people's talents and skills beyond their normal job roles, collaboration with local institutions) be used creatively?
- What change management efforts are in place to continue, succeed, and sustain the outcomes?
- How can a project champion identify and orchestrate the use of available resources?

Process-reform work is a complex undertaking, and one needs to be proactive and creative in identifying and deploying all resources available. There are many idle assets, human and otherwise, that can be tapped to support such initiatives

(Rosemann 2013; Skurkova et al. 2013) Constraints will always exist, but instead of being discouraged, project champions should embrace such limitations to support creative problem-solving (Euchner and Henderson 2011; Garriga et al. 2013; Stokes 2014). Championing these efforts and deploying the right change-management practices that fit the context best may be more of an art than a science, but they certainly get better with each attempt, so the keys are persistence, a thirst for positive change, and an open mind that invites opportunities in.

Acknowledgements We acknowledge the help of several friends and counselors in our documentation of the Dompe Hospital case.

– Mr. Chandana Rodrigo, former Secretariat of Health, Western Province; Dr. A. L. A. L. Padmasiri, RDHS, Gampaha; and Dr. Hajitha Piyantha Kumara, Medical Officer and Acting Director of the Hospital, who trusted the initiative's vision and goal and supported the proposed changes from the beginning.

– Ms. Chitrangani Mubarak, Chairperson, ICTA; Mr. Shriyananda Rathnayaka, Program Manager; and Mr. Wasantha Deshapriya, Secretary, Ministry of Digital Infrastructure and IT/Former Director-Reengineering Program of the ICTA, who provided support for the grant obtained through the ICTA e-society initiative.

– The local industry and individual donors who supported the infrastructure changes, particularly Mr. Dhanajaya Rajapakse of Brandix Sri Lanka, who sponsored the outbound training.

– The Dompe resident community, particularly the welfare group "Ape- Raane," who supported the initiative by volunteering many hours of their time and for supporting the social marketing campaign,

– Dr. Chandana Gamage of the University of Moratuwa and his IT students, who supported the organization-wide IT training efforts.

– Most important, Dompe Hospital's staff members at all levels, who operationalized the initiative and made it a success.

Appendix: Further Details About the Physical Changes Done in Support of the Patient Care Process

Fig. 10 Signage around the hospital directing patients where to go. The *picture* on the *left* acknowledges a local industry sponsor, and the *picture* on the *right* acknowledges a local resident donor

References

Anwar, F., Shamim, A., & Khan, S. (2011). Barriers in adoption of health information technology in developing societies. *International Journal of Advanced Computer Science and Applications, 2*(8), 40–45.

Brandao de Souza, L. (2009). Trends and approaches in lean healthcare. *Leadership in Health Services, 22*(2), 121–139.

Cline, G. B., & Luiz, J. M. (2013). Information technology systems in public sector health facilities in developing countries: The case of South Africa. *BMC Medical Informatics and Decision Making, 13*(1), 1–12. doi:10.1186/1472-6947-13-13.

Daily FT. (2015). ICTA project Dompe e-hospital wins prestigious National Productivity Award. *Daily FT*. Retrieved from http://www.ft.lk/article/414253/ICTA-project-Dompe-e-hospital-wins-prestigious-National-Productivity-Award#sthash.tezIUOgd.dpuf

De Bruin, T. (2009). *Theory on progression and maturity*. Brisbane: Queensland University of Technology.

Denning, S. (2005). Mastering the discipline of business narrative. In *An advance copy of a forthcoming article in strategy and leadership*.

Dumas, M., La Rosa, M., Mendling, J., & Rejers, H. (2013). *Fundamentals of business process management*. New York: Springer.

Euchner, J., & Henderson, A. (2011). The practice of innovation: Innovation as the management of constraints. *Research Technology Management, 54*(2), 47–54. doi:10.5437/08953608X5402009.

Garriga, H., von Krogh, G., & Spaeth, S. (2013). How constraints and knowledge impact open innovation. *Strategic Management Journal, 34*, (9), 1134–1144. doi:10.1002/smj.2049.

Jeston, J., & Nelis, J. (2010, April). Down under: 10 impediments to achieving process excellence. *BP Trends*.

Johnson, W. (2013). Why innovators love constraints. *Harvard Business Review*.

Kariyawasam, A. (1995). *Buddhist ceremonies and rituals of Sri Lanka*. Kandy: Sri Lanka Buddhist Publication Society Kandy.

Khan, S. Z., Shahid, Z., Hedstrom, K., & Andersson, A. (2012). Hopes and fears in implementation of electronic health records in Bangladesh. *The Electronic Journal of Information Systems in Developing Countries, 54*.

Kimaro, H. C., & Twaakyondo, H. (2005). Analysing the hindrance to the use of information and technology for improving efficiency of health care delivery system in Tanzania. *Tanzania Journal of Health Research, 7*(3), 189–197.

Kulathilaka, S. (2013). "eHospital-Dompe" project—The story of the transformation of a district hospital in Sri Lanka. *Sri Lanka Journal of Bio-Medical Informatics, 4*(2).

NIHS. (2008). *Health institutions & Bed strength by district*. Colombo: National Institute of Health Sciences. Retrieved from http://203.94.76.60/nihs/BEDS/western.pdf

Rosemann, M. (2013). The internet of things: New digital capital in the hands of customers. *Business Transformation Journal, 2013*(9), 6–15.

Skurkova, K. L., Szander, N., & Bajor, P. (2013). *Beergame reference scenarios for balanced scorecard evaluation, highlighting internal perspective*. In Paper Presented at the 13th International Scientific Conference Business Logistics in Modern Management, October 17.

Stokes, P. D. (2014). Crossing disciplines: A constraint-based model of the creative/innovative process: Crossing disciplines. *Journal of Product Innovation Management, 31*(2), 247–258. doi:10.1111/jpim.12093.

Taylor, C. (2012). *Selling BPM – Three things that make the difference*. Retrieved September 18, 2016, from http://www.successfulworkplace.org/2012/01/17/selling-bpm-three-things-that-make-the-difference/

UNDP. (2015). *Human development report 2015: Work for human development*. New York: United Nations Development Programme.

Young, F. Y. (2014). The use of 5S in healthcare services: A literature review. *International Journal of Business and Social Science, 5*(10).

Wasana Bandara is a tenured Senior Lecturer at the Information Systems (IS) School, Science and Engineering Faculty, Queensland University of Technology, Brisbane Australia. She has researched in a broad range of topics such as Process Modelling, Enterprise Systems, Shared Services, IS/BPM education. More recently her research is focused on Human Centric BPM and BPM in the developing country context. In addition to research in her discipline areas of IS and BPM, she has a passion for scholarly investigation into and the teaching of research methods. She has published over 90 refereed articles in leading IS and BPM outlets and has received institutional, national and international awards in recognition for her academic excellence (for both research and teaching).

Rehan Syed is currently pursuing his Ph.D. on 'BPM leadership' at QUT. Syed has taken substantive management and leadership roles in the tertiary education sector before moving to Australia to pursue his Ph.D. He has held the post of Director Local Technical Secretariat of the prestigious 'Improving Relevance and Quality of Undergraduate Education' (IRQUE) Project (Sponsored by the World Bank). He also acted as the reviewer of Higher Education for Twenty-First Century Project (HETC) World Bank Grant for State Universities in Sri Lanka. Syed specialises in project management for large-scale and complex IS projects. His professional work, consultancies and projects focus on BPM, business analysis, software development in medium to large scale organisations, e-government, and educational institutions. His research and publications are in the areas of Business Process Management and Leadership in developing countries. He has published and presented his research work in reputed conferences and professional forums.

Bandula Ranathunga is a Program Specialist of Information and Communication Technology Agency (ICTA) of Sri Lanka. He plays an active role in a number of Sri Lankan Government process reform initiatives, where he is responsible to ensure that government business processes are enabled with sound and innovative ICT solutions and implemented properly. He is also a member of a number of ICT policy committees.

Before he joined ICTA, he was the CIO of the Ministry of Local Government and Provincial Councils and held various roles in the context of Business Process Re-engineering within the government sector.

He holds a diploma in Information Technology from Sri Lanka Institute of Development Administration (SLIDA), an Advanced Diploma in Local Government from Sri Lanka Institute of Local Government (SLILG), a post graduate diploma in eGovernment from Postgraduate Institute of Management of University of Sri Jayewardenepura (PIM-USJ) and a Master of Public Administration from PIM-USJ.

Sampath Kulathilaka is an M.B.B.S qualified Medical Doctor with a passion to digitize medical services. He initiated and lead the "eHospital Dompe" project, to date, the most successful ICT deployment in a Government Hospital in Sri Lanka, and was the winner of the National Award for Science and Technology Achievements (2014) for this work. He also initiated and lead the first automated appointment system for a Government Hospital in Sri Lanka (called "mChannelling") and received the prestigious presidential award 'eSwabhimani' in recognition of his excellence and dedication. Dr. Kulathilaka is trained in e-Health, Change Management, and Knowledge Management and has applied his medical and ICT expertise in a range of e-Health initiatives. He has presented his work in International eHealth conferences and events as an invited speaker, published his expert insights in specialized outlets, and also promoted e-Health, nationally through mass media.

Fast Fish Eat Slow Fish: Business Transformation at Autogrill

Stijn Viaene and Joachim Van den Bergh

Abstract

(a) **Situation faced**: Autogrill Belgium, part of the world's largest provider of catering services to travellers, drifted into a worrisome position in 2006. The company had just gone through a merger, was experiencing financial difficulties, and appeared unable to respond adequately to a changing market context.

(b) **Action taken**: The case addresses Autogrill's approach to aligning its staff with the company's vision and strategy, and increasing internal communication and cooperation between functions and departments using a business process perspective as part of a holistic approach to business transformation that led to organisational survival in adverse conditions.

(c) **Results achieved**: The main outcomes of the business transformation were the establishment of an internal customer orientation, increased decision-making speed and the organisational resilience required to thrive under adverse market conditions.

(d) **Lessons learned**: The Autogrill case study provides a valuable example of and insights into how business transformation can be managed successfully. The story triggers critical thinking about major pitfalls and success factors and how the business process perspective can add value to a holistic approach to business transformation.

S. Viaene
Vlerick Business School, Ghent, Belgium

KU Leuven, Leuven, Belgium
e-mail: Stijn.viaene@vlerick.com

J. Van den Bergh (✉)
Vlerick Business School, Ghent, Belgium
e-mail: Joachim.vandenbergh@vlerick.com

J. vom Brocke, J. Mendling (eds.), *Business Process Management Cases*,
Management for Professionals, DOI 10.1007/978-3-319-58307-5_9

1 Introduction

Autogrill Belgium, part of the world's largest provider of catering services to travellers, drifted into a worrisome position in 2006. The company had just gone through a merger, was experiencing financial difficulties, and appeared unable to respond adequately to a changing market context. This case follows Chief Operating Officer (COO) Mario Orinx and Chief Sales and Operations Officer (CSOO) Stan Monheim over a period of 8 years as they led the company through an enterprise-wide business transformation that expanded from Belgium to the Netherlands and France. The story touches upon Autogrill's approach to aligning its staff with the company's vision and strategy and increasing internal communication and cooperation between functions and departments using a business process perspective as part of a holistic approach to business transformation that led to organisational survival.

In early 2014, Orinx and Monheim were still guiding the region through an organizational transformation, as they had been since 2008, helping the company increase its internal customer orientation, decision-making speed and resilience. They had started their transformation journey in Belgium, expanded to the Netherlands, and then went on to France. The transformation was far from over, but the approach they had adopted seemed to be working so well, that they were intent on promoting it throughout the rest of Autogrill, as their approach had caught the attention of Autogrill's headquarters in Milan.

Monheim and Orinx agree that they have come a long way since they first took charge of Autogrill Belgium. Autogrill Belgium was in tight financial spot, and the way the company was run and how it managed its employees were miles away from the current situation. In hindsight, they say that, if they had not changed the company's way of working, it would have been bankrupt or acquired by a competing company by now. Today, the company is in calmer waters, and Monheim and Orinx are contemplating how to explain and pitch their business transformation approach to their colleagues in the company's headquarters. This case focuses on that business transformation approach and its implications in the period between 2006 and 2014.

2 Situation Faced

Autogrill, with corporate headquarters in Milan, Italy, is the world's leading provider of catering services for travellers. Operating mainly through concessions along motorways and in airports, the company offers a wide selection of products and concepts, including proprietary brands like Ciao, Bistro and Beaudevin and third-party brands like Starbucks and Burger King. Its 55,000 employees offer food and beverage services to 900 million customers each year, bringing in revenues of 4.3€ billion in 2015.

The company began in 1977, when Italian state-owned conglomerate IRI acquired and merged three Italian restaurant groups. Autogrill was privatized in

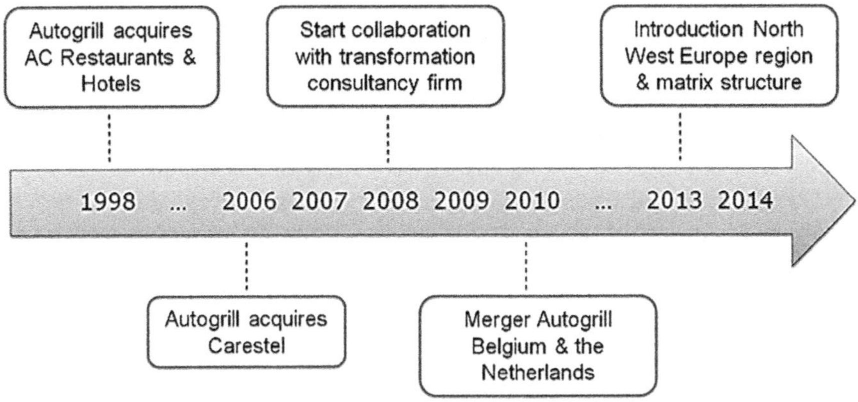

Fig. 1 Timeline for Autogrill's history in Belgium

1995 and listed on the Milan stock exchange 2 years later, marking the start of enormous expansion, including takeovers in North America, South America, Africa, the Middle East and Asia, as well as in France, Belgium, the Netherlands and the rest of Europe. Autogrill first entered the Belgian market in 1998. Figure 1 provides a timeline for Autogrill's history in Belgium.

In Belgium's travellers' catering services market, two companies had dominated: AC Restaurants and Hotels, a company that started out as part of the Albert Heijn Dutch supermarket chain in 1963 as a continuation of The American Lunchroom; and Carestel, which was founded in 1977 by the Van Milders family with restaurants along motorways and in airports and which quickly became the biggest motorway catering group in Belgium.

In 1998, Autogrill acquired AC Restaurants and Hotels, establishing a solid market share in Belgium's motorway catering services market. Eight years later, in 2006, Autogrill took over Carestel too, becoming the largest provider of catering services to travellers along motorways in Belgium and establishing a foothold in the Brussels Airport catering business. This action merged two companies that had been the two largest competitors in the Belgian travel catering market.

Acquiring Carestel meant merging two fierce competitors and taking over a company that had been dangling on the edge of bankruptcy for 2 years. Once Carestel became the biggest motorway catering group in Belgium, the Van Milders family decided to expand internationally and go public, but it soon became clear that the company wasn't financially prepared for its expansions in France, the UK and Scandinavia. To save the company, management decided to sell most of its business units. When Autogrill acquired Carestel in 2006, Carestel had refocused on its core business of food and beverage along motorways and at airports, and had managed to save itself financially.

Things did not go well after the 2006 merger, especially with the former Carestel and AC Restaurants management teams. After following their own strategies for decades, they had a difficult time communicating, let alone collaborating. Autogrill

Belgium's CEO engaged a transformation consultancy organization, which invited Autogrill's management team to a 2-day workshop on strategy and communication.

The workshop, held in 2008, started out in a defensive mood. As soon as the small group of directors from marketing, finance, operations and other departments walked in, the consultants started firing questions at them. Did they have a vision for the company? How many employees were aware of this vision?

The directors' first reaction was to dismiss the question: "Of course we have a vision like every other company. We even have framed vision statements on the walls of every restaurant and shop we own, so obviously all of our employees are aware of it!"

But the consultants' questions kept on coming and became more complex: What was the added value of their products for their customers? Who were the customers they were targeting, and how often did they communicate with them? How were they dealing with the changing market? Opinions differed, sometimes widely, especially between the former AC Restaurants and Carestel employees. Some of the questions were left unanswered.

The workshop ended in silence, as the participants paused to understand what had just happened. There was a rapidly growing awareness that something needed to change fundamentally in order to create strategic clarity and achieve alignment between departments and hierarchical layers.

The workshop acted as a wake-up call for Autogrill's management team in Belgium. For the past 2 years—(between 2006 and 2008)—they had done their work as usual, operating in a near-monopoly environment and once in a while opening new sites or introducing new concepts that they thought would appeal to their customers.

But outside the company, things had been changing:

- The need for restaurants near motorways was declining, as cars could drive much greater distances than before, and the current models had air conditioning and the amenities to store and cool food and drinks.
- Petrol stations and shops were becoming competitors, selling food and beverages and offering a range of products to motorway travellers that was broader and cheaper than Autogrill's.
- Customer preferences were changing, as people were increasingly interested in particular concepts or brands that Autogrill could only sell under licensing agreements, which meant sharing margins with the brand owner.
- Changing customer preferences were also reflected in the lifecycles of catering concepts. In the old days, catering concepts would last 20 years; now the lifecycle was down to about 5 years.
- Economic circumstances like rising prices for raw materials and energy were pushing Autogrill Belgium into an increasingly difficult financial situation, with declining margins and decreasing returns on investments.

The workshop made clear that Autogrill was having trouble getting everyone on board in order to work through these turbulent times, and they had some homework to do: The consultants suggested that they create a dream image of their 'to be' company and then perform a gap analysis with the 'as is': What should Autogrill look like? To what extent did that image differ from the company they knew today?

After a few weeks, the team reconvened to agree upon and show their commitment to a vision "to be seen as the market leader in multi-brand food and beverage operations by offering an 'A-star' experience for people on the move" and the key areas on which to work toward it. This was the start of what would grow to become an enterprise-wide transformation programme aimed at changing Autogrill's way of working, engaging, and making decisions. The consultants would be there to help along the way.

But first Orinx and Monheim had to ensure that the rest of Autogrill's managers would embrace the new vision so they could execute the vision as a unified team.

3 Action Taken

"Getting everyone involved in how we saw Autogrill's future was not easy," Orinx explained.

> Our whole culture was like a restaurant's kitchen: Every kitchen has a chef, and he or she is called 'chef' for a reason. People were not used to asking questions of their supervisors. You simply did what you were told to do. For example, when we needed a new marketing plan, the marketing department devised one based solely on their own ideas and expertise. When it was finished, they just forwarded the plan to the operational managers, who were left to figure out how to perform their new tasks.

Autogrill's lower management echelons weren't used to being involved in strategic issues, as they focused primarily on carrying out the work that was given to them, but Orinx and Monheim were convinced that involving them in discussions about implementing the company's vision was indispensable to getting everyone on board and motivated to turn the company around. The company organized several workshops for its top and middle management to discuss the company's vision and make sense of it from their points of view: Why was transformation necessary? How would they be involved? How would their unit be impacted? What was in it for them?

The 10–20% of the workforce that these managers represented was then expected to cascade the vision down through the organization. To help them do so, the company offered 2-day coaching sessions in which managers were trained on coaching employees, critically reviewing their management style, adapting to the maturity of employees, and providing continuous feedback. They were also urged to visit the restaurants and shops themselves and to talk to the staff who performed the customer-contact work and observe for themselves how things were done. They were stimulated to engage with every other staff member in the company, regardless of their roles or functions.

Monheim and Orinx hosted breakfast meetings to engage with their managers. There was no formal agenda: They listened, asked questions, ensured that everyone understood what was going to happen, and invited everyone to express their concerns without holding back. The attendees were expected to replicate these meetings to get their own people involved and even received a scenario with detailed instructions for preparing for and hosting such meetings.

The intended effect of these initiatives was to quicken decision-making across the organization and to improve directors' and managers' understanding of the company's strategy so they could align their decisions with it and to help everyone see the decisions positively by understanding them in light of Autogrill's vision.

A significant challenge was how to move the employees from habitually following their old routines to making time to attend workshops and focus on change. As Monheim explained,

> Long-term change should be driven by the employees, but a company has to support this expectation by providing training and a context in which employees can focus on change. The trick is to bring people together at an external location where they can forget about their day-to-day jobs for the duration of the training session. And a leader has to push the short-term change to bring people together; after that, the momentum for change can come from the people themselves.

3.1 Internal Customers

As Orinx explained,

> Involving our managers in strategic and high-level discussions and decision-making wasn't the only thing that we needed to achieve. People simply weren't used to talking, let alone collaborating, with colleagues from other departments. More often than not, you would have to rework an assignment because your colleague would deliver something completely different from what you had expected them to deliver.

To overcome this issue and make people more aware of for whom they were working, the concept of internal customers was introduced such that every manager was an internal supplier of products or services to an internal-customer colleague. All of the tasks that a manager performed were framed from this perspective.

To facilitate this process, a framework was provided that consisted of nine elements of a customer-supplier relationship. The nine elements are relate to; no action is involved. Formulating answers to nine questions, or asking your customers questions regarding these nine elements structures the managers' thinking (and that of his or her internal customers) into nine key elements, shown in Fig. 2.

These 9-elements framework served as a guide for managers to get a clear and holistic view of aspects of the project that were important in achieving a sound customer-supplier relationship. Among other questions, managers had to ask themselves who their customers were and what expected from them, what they could deliver, how they were going to communicate with their customers, and how much time they were going to spend on the assignment.

Element 1: Market.

For whom do you work? To whom do you deliver added value? What do you need to know about your clients in order to deliver the promise of added value? Note that there is a difference between customers outside the organisation (external) and inside the organisation (internal).

Element 2: Product.

What 'pure' product or service do you offer to your customers? What are the advantages of this product for your customer? How do you organise the preparation, project management, quality management and care of your product?

Element 3: External Communication.

How do you want to communicate with your customers? How often do you want to communicate with them? What 'spark' do you want your customers to feel when they use your products?

Element 4: Process.

An organisation can be divided into six main processes or functional departments: identification, development, launch, sales, delivery and care. In which activities or processes are you involved? About which processes do you want to be informed?

Element 5: Internal Communication.

Internal communication is talking to peers or experts who are working within the same scope. This communication takes place in policy, operational and managerial meetings. Whom would you like to have as your peers? When do you want to meet them? How often? What do you want to talk about?

Element 6: Resource Allocation.

How do you want to distribute your time over the processes or activities for which you are responsible (as defined by the Process element)? For which activities will your resources create the most value?

Element 7: KPIs.

How do you want to measure your success? Do you talk about achieving your goals and why you achieved them? Which KPIs are important in your company?

Element 8: Suppliers.

Suppliers can help you deliver added value. Who are your suppliers? Whose input do you need in order to deliver the promise? What do you expect from your suppliers? How do you want to communicate with them? How often?

Element 9: Me/Team.

Do you fit within the company's vision? Do you have a positive attitude toward your colleagues, your job, the organisation? What is your strongest competence? What is your biggest accomplishment? What do you want to learn?

Fig. 2 The 9-elements framework, developed by ViCre, the transformation consultant firm that guided Autogrill's transformation process

To help identify their internal customers, managers were introduced to the company's value chains to see where their own roles were situated and who would use their output in the next step of the value chain. Once the managers had a version of the 9-element framework adapted to their individual situation, they drafted an agreement called 'the 6 points' with each of their internal customers that specified what and how they would deliver to their internal customers. Figure 3 summarizes the 6-points framework.

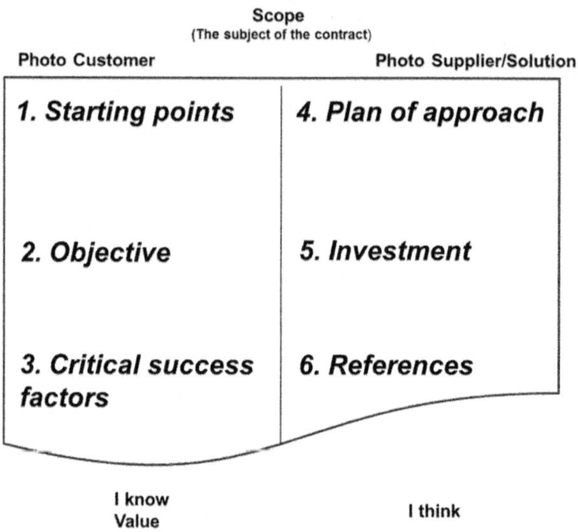

By drafting agreements with your (internal or external) customers, you show commitment and set expectations. You promise something, and you agree to keep your promises. The left side of the 6 points framework deals with understanding the customer (the 'photo' of the customer), and the right side deals with the solution (the 'photo' of the supplier or the solution).

First, you must understand your customer, as only then can the customer understand you. An agreement contains the following points:

- Starting points: What is the customer's present situation?
- Objective: What is the objective, the goal, the desired result?
- Critical success factors: What are the minimum demands for both parties to ensure a successful result? These conditions are necessary but not sufficient.
- Plan of approach (solution): Who is going to do what? When will it be delivered?
- Investment/Budget: What purpose does the investment serve and how much resources are needed?
- References: Has the supplier executed a similar project with successful results?

Fig. 3 The 6 points, developed and implemented by ViCre, the transformation consulting firm that guided Autogrill's transformation process

3.2 The 9 s and 6 s

The 6-points agreement serves as a personal business plan for every manager and aids them in delivering the promise, that is, delivering the service or product to their internal customers as they agreed in their 6-point agreement. The agreement was made official only when they had discussed and agreed upon it with their internal customers.

For example, unlike the past, when Marketing would use its own expertise and ideas to generate the marketing plan, they first sit down with all of their internal customers (e.g., the CSOO and colleagues from operations) to devise a marketing plan based on their combined input, supplemented by input from site landlords and feedback received through social media channels. Autogrill's increased focus on internal customers also impacted its relationship with external customers. For example, the concession contract with Brussels Airport was renewed partly because of a new way of engaging with the landlord.

The staff's increasing awareness of the variety of internal customers with whom they were engaging helped them to 'connect the dots' for end-to-end customer value creation and motivated them to take charge of their parts in the process, creasing the atmosphere of bottom-up empowerment and improvement that Monheim and Orinx had hoped for when they started their transformation journey. For example, some employees set up an internal message board on which anyone could post a request for help on any kind of task, and people from all over the organization responded and offered their help.

Once a month, each manager discussed his or her 6-point agreements with his or her supervisor, a natural opportunity to review the manager's objectives and tasks, verify their alignment with the company's strategy, and discuss how he would contribute to the strategy.

At the end of 2014, the challenge for Autogrill was to determine how to make the 9-element and 6-point frameworks work for all employees—even waiters and kitchen personnel. While Autogrill's management was grappling with this issue, the 9 s and 6 s became a standard management frame for all who had been exposed to it. Orinx and Monheim made sure to carry the torch by consistently using the framework and its terminology in management meetings and whenever projects were proposed or re-viewed.

3.3 Managing 100 Years of Experience

Frank Vandillewijn, Autogrill's Continuous Improvement Manager, explained how the company's core business pro-cesses lacked disciplined design and careful execution, fundamental problem:

> Now we were all sailing in the same boat, heading in one direction, which was a very important achievement. But we were still launching new products without in-depth market research and opening new establishments from scratch, acting on our gut feelings rather

than involving knowledge from previous efforts. It was striking that a company that owned restaurants that were over 100 years old didn't feel and act like a company that had over 100 years of experience.

New product-market combinations were introduced in ad hoc ways, and new stores were opened without using carefully conceived, standardised scenarios. There was process documentation, but it was simply not used. As a result, products and concepts that might have been good in their own right were targeted at the wrong customers or introduced in the wrong places. What's more, there had been little knowledge management at Autogrill over the years.

To help establish best practices and knowledge-sharing, the company introduced a system of micro-communities that focused on fixing these broken business capabilities. Each community consisted of a mix of profiles who worked together to improve a set of business processes. Monheim and Orinx kicked off the work of each micro-community by inviting a selection of staff members to join them for a 'vision creation' workshop. Then the micro-community selected a few smaller business process redesign projects to promote business process orientation. It was important for Autogrill to have these small success stories at the start to get people accustomed to a new way of working that emphasized process discipline and knowledge-sharing, but as the community and the organization became more proficient at improving business processes, more complex process redesign projects could be tackled.

Annual employee surveys helped to identify effective interventions. The use of employee surveys was not new at Autogrill, but there had never been a standard practice for using the survey results effectively. In an attempt to make better use of the surveys, the company sent a team of HR and operations managers to an off-site location for 2 days to come up with a process for following up and acting on the survey results. This process was institutionalized to inform the yearly planning for process cultivation and redesign projects.

"Mapping and improving processes still scares people," Frank Vandillewijn said. "This has improved over the past 2 years, but people still have trouble seeing the long-term benefits. It's something that takes a lot of time and effort to get people accustomed to, so we have to keep investing time and money in it."

3.4 The Master Plan

Year after year, the management team agreed on an objective or target state for the next year's transformation (Table 1), which was then translated into the support initiatives that comprised a maturity growth master plan. The plan included five types of projects that together enabled the organization to mature in a progressive and balanced way over time: vision creation projects, vision focus projects, knowledge management projects, personal contribution projects, and progress management projects.

Table 1 Transformation initiatives timeline

	Vision creation	Vision focus	Knowledge management	Personal contribution	Progress management	Objective
2008	0	0, 1	2	1	0	Vision alignment board of directors
2009	0	0, 1, 2	0	1, 2	0	One language, one method
2010		1, 2, 3	1	1, 2	0	Vision implementation
2011	0, 1	0, 1, 2, 3	0, 1	0, 1, 2	0	Collaboration HQ and operations
2012	0, 1	0, 1, 2, 3, 4	0, 1, 2	0, 1, 2, 3	0	Focus on cash flow
2013	0, 1	0, 1, 2, 3	0, 1, 2	0, 1	0, 1	Integration BeNeFra
2014	0, 1	0, 1, 2, 3, 4	0, 1, 2	0, 2, 2	0, 1, 2	Integration NW and corporate

Note: the numbers indicate which layers of the organization were involved: 0 = COO and CSOO; 1 = board of directors; 2 = managers; 3 = restaurant managers; 4 = restaurant personnel

1. Vision Creation Projects

   The purpose of vision creation was to introduce mechanisms that helped management create focus and ensure strategic targets were set accordingly. These projects included organizing sessions with the heads of the region and board of directors.
2. Vision Focus Projects

   Initiatives in the vision focus category sought to create buy-in to the vision and pursuing targets with the employees. Management breakfast meetings fell into this category. Over time, vision focus initiatives were cascaded down through the organization so an increasing number of employees were exposed to the vision and became oriented toward its execution.
3. Knowledge Management Projects

   Initiatives to increase business process orientation and internal customer orientation were catalogued under knowledge management.
4. Personal Contribution Projects

   Personal contribution initiatives introduced routines that helped individual employees commit to vision execution by, for example, discussing the 6-point agreements with their supervisors.
5. Progress Management Projects

   Progress management projects introduced mechanisms that exposed and allowed employees to discuss the transformation's progress, to exchange experiences and best practices among the department managers, and to address commonly occurring hurdles collaboratively.

All of the initiatives in the master plan were tracked monthly to ensure follow-up, continuity and balance in the transformation approach. Over the years, as more employees across Belgium, the Netherlands and France were exposed to the new ways of working, consultancy guidance intensified.

4 Results Achieved

> They used to say that big fish eat small fish, but now I would rather say that fast fish eat slow fish, and we were steadily becoming one of those faster fish. We were gradually evolving from a rusty and static organization to an adaptable company that wasn't afraid of the changes yet to come.—Stan Monheim

Throughout the long transformation effort, yearly objectives had been set (Table 1) and consistently met. In the initial years, Monheim and Orinx focused the company's objectives largely on its internal functioning in the belief that doing so would lead to survival first and better performance in the long term.

Orinx and Monheim successfully merged Autogrill Belgium with Autogrill in the Netherlands in 2010. Thanks to the new way of working, employees knew how to deal with change and what was expected of them in the merger. Orinx and Monheim were in the process of establishing a North West Europe Region organization that spanned operations in Belgium, the Netherlands and France. Business development, finance and IT were centralized at the corporate level and reported directly to headquarters. The creation of North West Europe was a pilot project to see whether and how Autogrill could improve bottom-line results and returns on investments by mutualizing costs and investments on a regional basis.

In principle, this next step would not cause any major upheaval in how the transformation was supported, as Orinx and Monheim had introduced a transformation maturity framework in 2008 that, in their view, could support this next stage of the transformation perfectly.

Although the creation of the North West Europe region made financial sense, with several departments now reporting directly to headquarters, the regional managers faced another cultural challenge: Their new bosses were not familiar with the 9 s and the 6 s, which by that time had become a standard engagement routine in the region.

Perhaps the biggest achievement was the transformation of a financially unstable, old-fashioned regional organization into a stable, change-ready and flexible body that was ready to realize growth, adopt structural changes and withstand external market shocks. Some of Autogrill's regional financial results had improved over the years. For example, Autogrill in the Netherlands regained positive store cash flows after years of financial distress, and in Belgium, the company had reinforced its financial position, in part because of a licensing contract with Starbucks, a new partner.

Therefore, Orinx and Monheim felt that headquarters could benefit from replicating the approach across the group, which would also solve the communication issue that had emerged from the centralization of certain functions. Orinx and Monheim were convinced of the value of their transformation approach and decided to convince the Milan headquarters to subscribe to the new way of working. It was the right time to tell the tale of the last 8 years. Several former North West Europe managers who then held positions at headquarters joined in the meeting with the company's top management as a sign of their support for the proposal.

5 Lessons Learned

Business transformation has been described as the orchestrated redesign of a corporation's genetic architecture (Gouillart and Kelly 1995). It is a way of systematically altering the basic elements that make up an organisation's DNA, that is, its structure, processes, strategy and so on. It is also a term that is hyped in management practice as companies experience ever-increasing turbulence as a result of global economic shifts, changes in governmental regulations, mergers, competitive threats, performance crises, and more. Therefore, we believe that the ability to conduct a successful business transformation has become a condition for business continuity and long-term success.

The case study provides a valuable example of and insights into how business transformation can be managed in practice. The story triggers critical thinking about major pitfalls and success factors and how a business process perspective can add value in a holistic approach to business transformation. The most important lesson here is that every aspect of the organisation must be incorporated into the transformation approach, so every element of Galbraith's Star Model should be paid attention to: strategy, structure, processes, people and rewards (Galbraith 1973). The case triggers questions related to whether the transformation approach is holistic, some aspects of transformation are missing and what the company should have done differently and why. To dive more deeply into the transformation approach, another question concerns why the approach worked. The following sections explain some of the lessons learned from this case, making use of existing BPM frameworks. Three elements and theories of leadership also come to mind as reasons for the transformation approach's having worked: leadership style, culture change and psychological contract theory.

5.1 BPM Reference Frameworks

First of all Autogrill had a burning platform, the transformation was led and supported by top management, and they actively involved employees in the transformation. These would be common success factors in any BPM initiative and is generally included in BPM reference frameworks such as the Rosemann and vom Brocke (2015) framework. For example, the 'leadership attention to process management' variable probes for the leadership's commitment to process management practices. After the acceptance that the organisation needed to be fixed, Autogrill's leadership has shown true commitment towards the transformation, the approach and the process management practices that it entailed. Employee involvement, largely covered by the 'Culture' and 'People' dimensions in Rosemann and vom Brocke (2015), was included as a central element in the approach from the start, with initiatives such as the breakfast meetings and project teams around several process improvement trajectories. The more formal dimensions of the framework, such as process documentation and methods, were less present in the Autogrill approach.

Furthermore we can relate the success of the Autogrill approach to the BPM context framework by vom Brocke et al. (2016), which advocates a context-sensitive BPM implementation, instead of a one-size-fits-all. The transformation approach has been worked in such a way that it fitted the Autogrill environment as much as possible. That does not mean it has been without friction, as the case mentions, but still they managed to avoid fatal showstoppers. The tools that were used, have been adapted to a language and tone of voice that is recognisable and acceptable for Autogrill employees. Technical BPM lingo and concepts were purposely avoided, as the transformation leaders and consultants felt that this would risk being perceived as too engineering-like, too complex, or overhead, rather than useful improvement methodologies. Moreover, the approach has been adapted over time as it expanded to other geographical regions and lower tiers in the organisation.

5.2 Leadership Style

The leadership style exerted by Monheim and Orinx and why it was successful in leading and supporting the transformation is particularly interesting. We like to propose two frameworks here: Transformational Leadership (Avolio et al. 1991) and Instrumental Leadership (Antonakis and House 2002). In essence, Transformational Leadership is a process of building commitment to an organisation's vision and objectives and then empowering followers to accomplish those objectives. In contrast to focusing on where the organisation is today, transformational leaders look at where the organisation should be heading. A transformational leader does this by using four types of behaviour:

- Inspirational Motivation: devising and communicating a vision that is inspiring to followers.

  Example from the case: organising workshops to inform managers about the company's vision.
- Idealised Influence: acting as a role model for followers.

  Example from the case: Orinx and Monheim use the '9 and 6' language and tools for every project and every meeting.
- Individualised Consideration: attending to each follower's needs and actively coaching them. This also stimulates the individual contribution that each follower can make to the team or the company.

Example from the case: breakfast meetings with Monheim, and individual coaching sessions.

- Intellectual Stimulation: encouraging followers to be innovative and creative.
  Example from the case: involving managers in strategic and process workshops.

When looking at Transformational Leadership, the question remains: How can we incorporate this vision and leadership behaviour into the DNA of our organisation and make these things less dependent on particular people? And how do we not only clarify the vision but also translate it into a strategy and make sure people can reach that vision and the goals we set for them? This is where Instrumental Leadership comes in, which also consists of four types of behaviour:

- Strategy formulation and implementation: when leaders formulate an inspiring vision, like the Inspirational Motivation behaviour from the Transformational Leadership framework, they have to design a strategy to achieve this vision and implement it with specific objectives and policies for employees.
  Example from the case: using the '9 and 6' to align employee behaviour with the vision.
- Environmental monitoring: leaders also need to be able to scan the environment for opportunities and threats and incorporate them in the company's vision.
  Example from the case: changing customer preferences (threat) and a new licensing contract with Starbucks (opportunity).
- Path-goal facilitation and outcome monitoring: providing followers with the necessary resources and feedback to attain their goals.
  Example from the case: supervisors following up and giving feedback on the managers' 6 point agreements.

5.3 Culture Change

To discuss why Autogrill's 9 elements and 6 point agreements worked well to increase internal customer orientation, we focus on the cultural change framework and on the concept of psychological contract. For cultural change, we refer to the organisational culture model of Schein (1992) and later additions by Shook (2010). Autogrill's 6 point agreements may carry the risk of acting as a straitjacket instead of leading to a real change in culture (promoting networking in the organisation). Nevertheless, this can actually lead to culture change in the long run, according to Schein's and Shook's models of culture. According to Edgar Schein, an organisation's culture consists of three layers: basic assumptions, values and attitudes, and artefacts:

- Artefacts are the physical representations of a company's culture and consist mostly of signs and symbols. This layer can most easily be recognised by people outside the culture.

- Values and Attitudes contain the company values, attitudes and behavioural rules. This is what people usually talk about when describing their company's culture.
- Basic Assumptions—the core layer of organisational culture—are the unconscious beliefs and unspoken assumptions in a company that everyone accepts. This is the culture layer that we would want to ultimately change. The difficulty is that this layer is hard to observe and we don't have direct access to it.

Schein's original model suggests taking the difficult route of changing culture by influencing the basic assumptions that will, in their turn, influence the values, attitudes and artefacts. Recent work by Shook (2010) suggests starting by changing artefacts (behaviour and symbols) and values (the way people talk in and about the company culture) and be consistent in this until the basic assumptions change over time as well. For this to succeed, a lot of time, consistency and patience is required. The latter approach to changing culture is exactly the one Autogrill adopted by installing the language of the '9 and 6'. Instead of trying to directly influence people's basic assumptions about internal customer orientation, they installed physical representations of internal customer orientation—like the 6 point agreements—to change people's behaviour and, in the long run, influence basic assumptions.

5.4 Psychological Contract Theory

Another way to frame Autogrill's 6 point agreements is with psychological contract theory. A psychological contract is a mental representation of the unspoken mutual beliefs, perceptions, and informal obligations between an employer and an employee (Rousseau 1989). It contains beliefs regarding the exchange arrangement outside the formal written employment contract. This concept of a psychological contract can also be applied to the exchange relationship between employees. Psychological contract theory suggests that adherence to the contract, assuming the expectations match, results in better employee performance and satisfaction levels (Turnley et al. 2003). The strength of the 6 point agreement at Autogrill is that it has operationalised part of this psychological contract between employer and employees, as well as between employees, and made it explicit. In the pre-transformation phase, employees and supervisors did not seem to have a mutual understanding of the company vision and how it impacted their personal tasks and objectives. In fact, the psychological contract seemed missing or broken. In contrast, the transformation has resulted in clear communication and mutual agreement about expectations, restoring the psychological contract between employees. Moreover, instead of just assuming that employees would be internally customer-oriented, Autogrill made this explicit and traceable by installing the 6 point agreements.

5.5 Advocating a Business Transformation Approach

Finally, the case inspires to consider how transformation leaders can leverage their efforts by positioning their approach as a repeatable process. In the Autogrill case, it comes down to the regional management readying themselves to convince the corporate headquarters in Milan. Why would corporate Autogrill even need this approach? Would this approach work if corporate Autogrill's original situation was different from the one Belgium was in? Which results could they use to build their arguments on? How would you deal with a lack of hard numbers to support the approach? To what extent is the transformation approach repeatable? Was Autogrill successful in setting up a repeatable transformational routine—so that they're ready for future changes by being able to transform over and over? Or, did they merely go through a one-off business transformation?

Because they successfully imposed the introduction of the regional and matrix structure, one thing that corporate Autogrill is already aware of is the fact that North West Europe is now quick to adapt to change. To make a strong case to convince the stakeholders, they would also need financial results and measurements of specific transformational capabilities, which are harder to come by. However, hard numbers might not be needed after all, as long as there is strong belief in the approach within the organisation that is conveyed by a strong group of influencers.

Acknowledgments We thank Mario Orinx, Stan Monheim, Fred Hegt, Frank van Dillewijn, Patrice Fievet, Steven Govaerts and their colleagues at Autogrill for their contributions. We also thank Eddy Helsen and Annelies Helsen of ViCre for providing additional input and funding.

References

Antonakis, J., & House, R. J. (2002). The full-range leadership theory: The way forward. In B. Avolio & F. Yammarino (Eds.), *Transformational and charismatic leadership: The road ahead* (pp. 3–34). Amsterdam: JAI.

Avolio, B. J., Walderman, D. A., & Yanimarina, F. J. (1991). Leading in the 1990s: The four is of transformational leadership. *Journal of European Industrial Training, 15*, 9–16.

Galbraith, J. R. (1973). *Designing complex organizations*. Boston: Addison-Wesley.

Gouillart, F. J., & Kelly, J. N. (1995). *Transforming the organisation*. New York: McGraw-Hill.

Rosemann, M., & vom Brocke, J. (2015). Six core elements of business process management. In J. vom Brocke & M. Rosemann (Eds.), *Handbook on business process management: Introduction, methods, and information systems (International handbooks on information systems)* (Vol. 1, 2nd ed., pp. 105–122). Berlin: Springer.

Rousseau, D. (1989). Psychological and implied contracts in organizations. *Employee Responsibilities and Rights Journal, 2*, 121–139.

Schein, E. (1992). *Organizational culture and leadership*. San Francisco, CA: Jossey-Bass.

Shook, J. (2010, January 1). *How to change a culture: Lessons from NUMMI*. Retrieved December 2, 2014, from http://sloanreview.mit.edu/article/how-to-change-a-culture-lessons-from-nummi/

Turnley, W. H., Bolino, M. C., Lester, S. W., & Bloodgood, J. M. (2003). The impact of psychological contract fulfillment on the performance of in-role and organizational citizenship behaviors. *Journal of Management, 29*(2), 187–206.

vom Brocke, J., Zelt, S., & Schmiedel, T. (2016). On the role of context in business process management. *International Journal of Information Management, 36*(3), 486–495.

Stijn Viaene is a Full Professor and Partner at Vlerick Business School in Belgium, where he heads the Information Systems Management cluster and sponsors the Digital Transformation and Innovation spearhead. He is also a Professor in the Department Decision Sciences and Information Management at KU Leuven. At the university he holds the VDAB Research Chair of "Digital business innovation in public services". His research and teaching focus on information systems management (ISM) issues in three primary areas: (1) digital innovation and transformation, (2) business and IT alignment, and (3) business process management (BPM). Stijn teaches in Vlerick Business School's full-time and part-time MBA programmes. His work has been published in research for business outlets such as MIT Sloan Management Review, Communications of the ACM, Information and Management, Journal of Information Technology, and Business Process Management Journal.

Joachim Van den Bergh is a senior research associate at Vlerick Business School in the Technology and Operations Management Area. His main research and teaching interests are focused on digital transformation and innovation, smart cities, e-Government, and business process management. In short: customer and citizen value creation through people, processes and technology. Joachim has been managing the Centre for Excellence in Business Process Management and the Centre for Excellence in Business Transformation, working together closely with the industry to develop thought leading insights and applied research in BPM. Currently he manages Vlerick Business School's strategic focus area, Digital Transformation. Joachim's research has been published in academic journals such as Business and Information Systems Engineering (BISE) and BPM Journal.

Part II

Methods

The NESTT: Rapid Process Redesign at Queensland University of Technology

Michael Rosemann

Abstract

(a) **Situation faced**: The higher education sector faces like most information-intensive industries an opportunity-rich, digital future. Nowadays, students demand contemporary, multi-channel learning experiences and fast evolving digital affordances provide universities with a growing design space for their future processes. Legislative changes, a globalizing market of learners and educational providers, and the emergence of new technology-based business models (EduTech) are further features of the current situation in this sector. In order to prepare for and to capitalize on this changing environment the Queensland University of Technology (QUT), like any university, needs to ensure operational inefficiencies are addressed as part of the required organisational transformation. However, traditional BPM approaches are often time-consuming, exclusively focused on pain points and not tailored to immediate process transformation, meaning a new, dedicated and agile approach for QUT was needed.

(b) **Action taken**: A rapid process redesign methodology called the NESTT was developed by QUT, facilitating accelerated process improvement in the four stages of 'navigate', 'expand', 'strengthen' and 'tune/takeoff'. An integral and defining feature of the NESTT is the way physical space is used as part of the methodology. Each of the four walls and the floor of the workshop space carry specific meaning leading to a new process design experience. Two such NESTT rooms have been established at Queensland University of Technology and a number of processes have been redesigned based on this methodology. Further, the involvement of QUT's human

M. Rosemann (✉)
Queensland University of Technology, Brisbane, QLD, Australia
e-mail: m.rosemann@qut.edu.au

J. vom Brocke, J. Mendling (eds.), *Business Process Management Cases*,
Management for Professionals, DOI 10.1007/978-3-319-58307-5_10

resource experts ensured that the NESTT experience is embedded into QUT's capability building framework.

(c) **Results achieved**: The NESTT led to three tangible outcomes for QUT. First, the performance of the processes, which were redesigned using the NESTT, has been significantly improved. Many of the ideas were implemented within a 20 days timeframe and proposals for 20 months and by the year 2020 now guide QUT process implementation teams. Second, the NESTT, as a methodology, a dedicated physical space and with its growing team of trained facilitators has provided the organisation with a much valued, business-as-usual redesign capability and capacity. Third, participation in the NESTT has been an important up-skilling for the QUT staff involved (across a broad range of designations) and has had a positive impact on the organisational culture and attitude towards change.

(d) **Lessons learned**: It is proven possible to rigorously redesign complex business processes in 20 days. However, a number of success factors needs to be addressed including (1) a sound methodology with short term milestones and well articulated and monitored intentions for each stage, (2) participants who are intellectually agile, collaborative and have a positive attitude towards emerging design options and the changes required to today's process, (3) facilitators who are able to guide conversations under time pressure on multiple levels of conceptualization, from vision to individual idea assessment, (4) a decisive attitude among the NESTT team and the judging panel, and (5) a smart utilisation of the spatial affordances, in particular the ability to articulate the right level of information and to ensure an always correct, relevant and easy to use display of information across all dimensions of the NESTT space.

1 Introduction

The digital age has triggered a shift from an economy centered around corporations to an ecomomy of people. As a consequence new customer engagement channels, business models, revenue streams, sourcing strategies and pricing models have emerged in many information-intensive sectors. Higher education is no exception and universities around the globe are exposed to a rich design space promising new value propositions while at the same time existentiell disruptive forces emerge (Coaldrake and Stedman 2016).

Queensland University of Technology (QUT) in Brisbane, Australia, proactively engaged in this context by establishing the REAL Difference project. With more than 46,000 students, QUT is an established, but still young university with a focus on transdiscplinary research and a contemporary under-graduate and post-graduate curriculum grounded in a strong focus on the real-world requirements of today and tomorrow.

Motivated by the possibilities of the digital economy, students who are expecting personalised service delivery and driven by legislative changes to the economic model of higher education in Australia, the REAL Difference project is dedicated to creating both new and unlocking hidden value across the entire university.

A subset of this initiative has been the requirement to develop the capability and capacity for rapid process improvements in order to quickly secure operational efficiency gains for essential decision making processes. However, current Business Process Management methods and tools are not designed for fast process change. They tend to be either selective in their scope (e.g., resolution of problems via lean management) and are analysis-intensive making them a time-consuming undertaking. Thus, the QUT team needed to design and implement an entire new approach that was not just dealing with short-term fixes, but also catered for new digital opportunities.

This approach was named the NESTT, an abbreviation capturing the main four stages navigate-expand-strengthen-tune and take-off. This chapter will outline its unique methodology including the way spatial affordances are used, reflect on QUT's experiences and elaborate on the perceived success factors. The article is grounded in the higher eduction sector, but the methodology and findings are so geneneric that the NESTT will be of interest for organisations in all types of industry sectors.

2 Situation Faced

In the context of the REAL Difference initiative, QUT desired to establish a rapid process redesign capacity and capability for the following reasons

- Identify and benefit from quick wins for operational gains within selected, high volume decision making processes,
- Contribute to a culture of positivity with regards to the changes required,
- Create a capacity that accelerates design activities in other, significant REAL Difference projects such as travel management and
- Upskill QUT staff in the areas of process analysis and design.

It was important that the new methodology aligned with the endorsed design principles of the REAL Difference project such as user-centred design, manage by exception, standardise where possible or simple and sustainable.

The opportunity to create an entire new process redesign methodology was facilitated by the fact that QUT is home to one of the largest and most influential Business Process Management Disciplines in the world. The availability of unique intellectual property in the area of systemic ideation (Recker and Rosemann 2015) allowed the accelerated development of the NESTT methodology and ensured availability of qualified facilitators. The ambitious goal was *to redesign one decision-intensive process every month.*

3 Action Taken

Based on the need to develop a fast and engaging process improvement methodology, the NESTT approach was developed. The acronym NESTT stands for navigate-expand-strengthen-tune/take-off, i.e. the four main stages of its methodology. Inspirations for the NESTT came from a number of areas including

- Business Process Management (Hammer 2015; Rosemann and vom Brocke 2015), in particular simple process visualisations, issue identification and resolution and process design principles,
- Design Thinking (Brown 2008), in particular, customer and employee journey mapping, customer/employee empathy, acting out of process scenarios and the use of space as part of the redesign and
- Agile methodologies and sprint approaches in terms of speed and decisiveness of the process, but also in terms of the use of visualisations (Larman and Vodde 2004; Knapp 2016).

The NESTT consists essentially of a space with five viewpoints, a methodology and a number of teams, i.e. the innovation team, the panel, the facilitators and the implementation team.

3.1 The NESTT Space

It is a unique characteristic of the NESTT that it takes full advantage of the spatial affordances of a dedicated room. The room needs to be able to cater for a group between 8 and 10 people and should allow the use of all four walls and the floor. Each wall and the floor itself depict a different viewpoint on the process. This design was loosely inspired by the IGOE approach (Long 2012) where a process integrates the four areas input, guidelines, enablers and output.

3.1.1 The Future

The most important wall within the NESTT is *'The Future'*. This wall describes the ambition for the future process and is broken down into the three columns *20 days, 20 months and 2020*. Each of these columns (drawn on the wall) is a place to capture related ideas as they emerge during the NESTT. With the intention of the NESTT to be a rapid redesign capability, it is not surprising that a core focus of the work in the NESTT is on 20 days improvements.

The heading above these three columns is the *process vision*. A process vision is a motivational, simple statement articulating the ambition and future state of the process. Examples for a vision are 'The zero-touch claim process', 'One-click shopping' or 'Every applicant gets a job'. In particular, the process vision helps to channel the subsequent ideation. For example, calling an insurance customer regarding the status of a claim submitted is not a design option, if the vision is a zero-touch claim process.

In the ideal case, it is be possible to define a vision that captures the demand for a streamlined process as well as possible new design opportunites. An example is the vision, *'Minimum effort, maximum impact'*, the process vision that was derived as part of QUT's NESTT on travel management. Here, minimum effort captures the idea of a friction-less, self-service process, and maximum impact is related to the opportunity of capitalising on the consolidated years QUT staff is spending every year overseas as part of their travel. These two parts of the vision can then be used for each of the three timeframes (20 days, 20 months, 2020) and help to cluster the emerging ideas.

Articulating the right process vision is one of the most important, but also most difficult activities within the NESTT. It is desired to have the process vision and the unconditional commitment of the team to this vision early on in the process. However, often the vision will be the result of an iterative process and only shapes up in its final form in the second part of the NESTT.

3.1.2 The Now

The wall opposite to *The Future* is called *The Now*. This is essentially the as-is model of today. This wall is used to:

- Capture the core value chain of the process. It is recommended to break down this value chain into three to four stages to derive a simple point of reference. These will be often a sort of apply/request, use or produce and consume or other post-usage activities.
- Model a detailed, swimlane visualisation of the process describing the main activities in each of the value chain phases. Where possible, the process should be modelled with not more than five stakeholders involved (swimlanes) and not more than 15 activities. These constraints help to make discussions about the process intuitive. It also channels the team to the right level of conversation, i.e. ideas should have, where possible, an impact on these activities, and not be simple micro-improvements to single activites only.
- Describe the emotional state along the process in the form of three states (happy, indifferent, disappointed). These states are modelled above each activity and follow the idea of customer journey mapping. Depending on the customer, this is an internal and/or an external customer. Capturing the employee journey can be helpful in identifying gaps between customer and employee experiences.
- Capture issues along the process leading to a so-called 'pain wall'. Issues will be written down on post-it notes in individual colors depicting specific types of issues, e.g., these could be the seven types of waste as per the lean management approach or policy/system/people issues.
- Capture any further information about the process, e.g. number of instances, processing time, probabilities or areas that are supported by systems.

Depending on the context of the specific NESTT project, different aspects of the NOW will be more important than others. For example, if the focus is on reducing processing time, this would get more attention than creating new customer experiences.

3.1.3 The Resources

The third wall captures all the resources involved in the current and in the future process. Again, this wall graphically displays three vertical sections called (1) systems, (2) people and (3) documents. Each of these sections is further differentiated into the Now and the Future sections.

1. The systems section consolidates all the IT artefacts involved in this process. These could be enterprise systems, apps, databases or specific hardware. Screenshots and identified issues with any of these systems will also be captured on this wall.
2. The people section summarises all human resources involved. This could include relevant organsational charts, job descriptions, roles, external stakeholders such as vendors or customers or interaction diagrams.
3. Finally, the document section is the place where the paper or digital forms used within the process are visualised.

3.1.4 The Policies and Procedures

The wall opposite the *Resources* wall has the purpose to capture all existing internal and external policies and procedures that guide and often constraint the process. Depending on the comprehensiveness of the related policies and procedures, this means the relevant documents will be attached to the wall. Like the pain wall in the Now, this could lead to a *visually dramatic* display of the comprehensiveness or variety of policies and procedures. Color coding helps to differentiate between policies that can be changed and policies that cannot. Like the resources wall, this wall is seperated into the two sections The Now and the Future.

3.1.5 The Ambition

Finally, the floor is used to articulate the ambidextrous ambition of the NESTT (Rosemann 2014) and is differentiated via a line in the middle of the room into problem resolution and opportunity deployment.

Problem resolution is the half of the room closest to the Now wall. Improvements as part of the problem resolution are initiated by the current state and the reactive analysis and overcoming of identified issues. They can be characterised as 'pain relief' and most of the solutions generated in this half of the room are result of a 'reactive ideation'. Such ideas tend to be predictable and constraint-driven. Typical BPM methods and approaches such as root cause analysis and weakness-focused approaches such as lean management and Six Sigma are typically used here.

The room half closest to the Future wall is called *Opportunity deployment*. Working in this half of the room requires much more design than analysis, 'proactive ideation' and a strong sense for what (else) is possible (as opposed to what is broken). Working and thinking in this part of the room is driven by the process

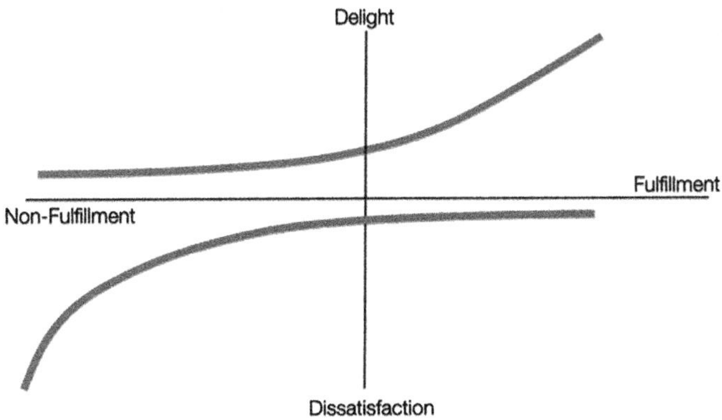

Fig. 1 The ambidextrous NESTT: Working above and below the line

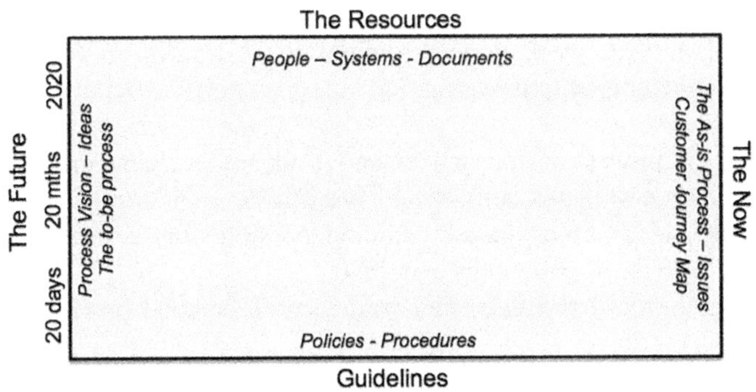

Fig. 2 The use of the four walls in the NESTT

vision, i.e. the future state. In this space, there is a scarcity of tools and finding appropriate methods and capable facilitators for this second half of the NESTT is a significant challenge. Additionally the vocabulary used in this space is positive and future-focused, discouraging of certain language and unrestrained by known constraints typical of the Now sector.

The figure below captures these two halves of the room using the common Kano model (Kano et al. 1984). Problem resolution is depicted as the bottom curve and characterizes that this has largely become a hygiene factor. Opportunity deployment is visualized by the curve above the line (Rosemann 2014) (Fig. 1).

The populated walls and the ambidextrous ambition of the NESTT are a defining feature and make the act of process redesign tangible. In fact, when QUT staff talked about the NESTT they often meant first of all the actual room. The following figures visualises the use of the four walls in the NESTT (Fig. 2).

3.2 The NESTT Methodology

The physical space comes to life with the NESTT methodology. Overall, the NESTT consists of three main stages over a period of 3 months. The first 4 weeks are dedicated to scoping the initiative, defining expectations, constraints and forming the team. The second stage, the focus of this article, is concentrated on the actual redesign of the process. The final stage then takes the NESTT ideas and implements these where possible within a 20 day timeframe and under the leadership of an implementation champion (Fig. 3).

According to QUT's intention of 'one process change every month', stage 2 of the methodology (Innovate) had to be constrained to a roughly 20 working day period. The 20 days are split into the first 10 days being dedicated to divergent thinking followed by the second 10 day period dedicated to convergent thinking. Each of the 4 weeks will be outlined in the following.

3.2.1 Week 1: Navigate

The focus of the first week is on the initial population of all four walls of the NESTT. This includes activities such as

- Deriving the process vision and essential attributes characterising the vision (e.g., agile, free of paper, self-service, one click),
- Collecting and grouping ideas regarding possible future states for the three timeframes 20 days, 20 months and 2020,
- Modelling the current value chain and a more detailed process in swimlane notation,
- Capturing emotional states, KPIs, efforts and issues along the process (customer/employee journey mapping) and
- Capturing information regarding the Now of the resources (systems, people, documents) and policies and procedures.

In addition to these activities, the first week is spent on activities such as agreeing on the overall objective of the NESTT project, defining its scope, i.e. the unit of analysis and also team bonding.

3.2.2 Week 2: Expand

Based on the process contextualisation as the main outcome of week 1, week 2 is exclusively focused on the *'The Future'* wall. The activities in this week are dedicated to rapidly broadening the design space and to derive a comprehensive set of ideas with a focus on the 20 days period. The main methods used here are derived from QUT's systemic ideation methodology (Recker and Rosemann 2015). Thus, selected days are concentrating on

- *Enhancing* the existing process using improvement patterns such as elimination, resequencing, integrating or specialisation and reactively generating ideas based on addressing the issues as depicted in the 'pain wall',

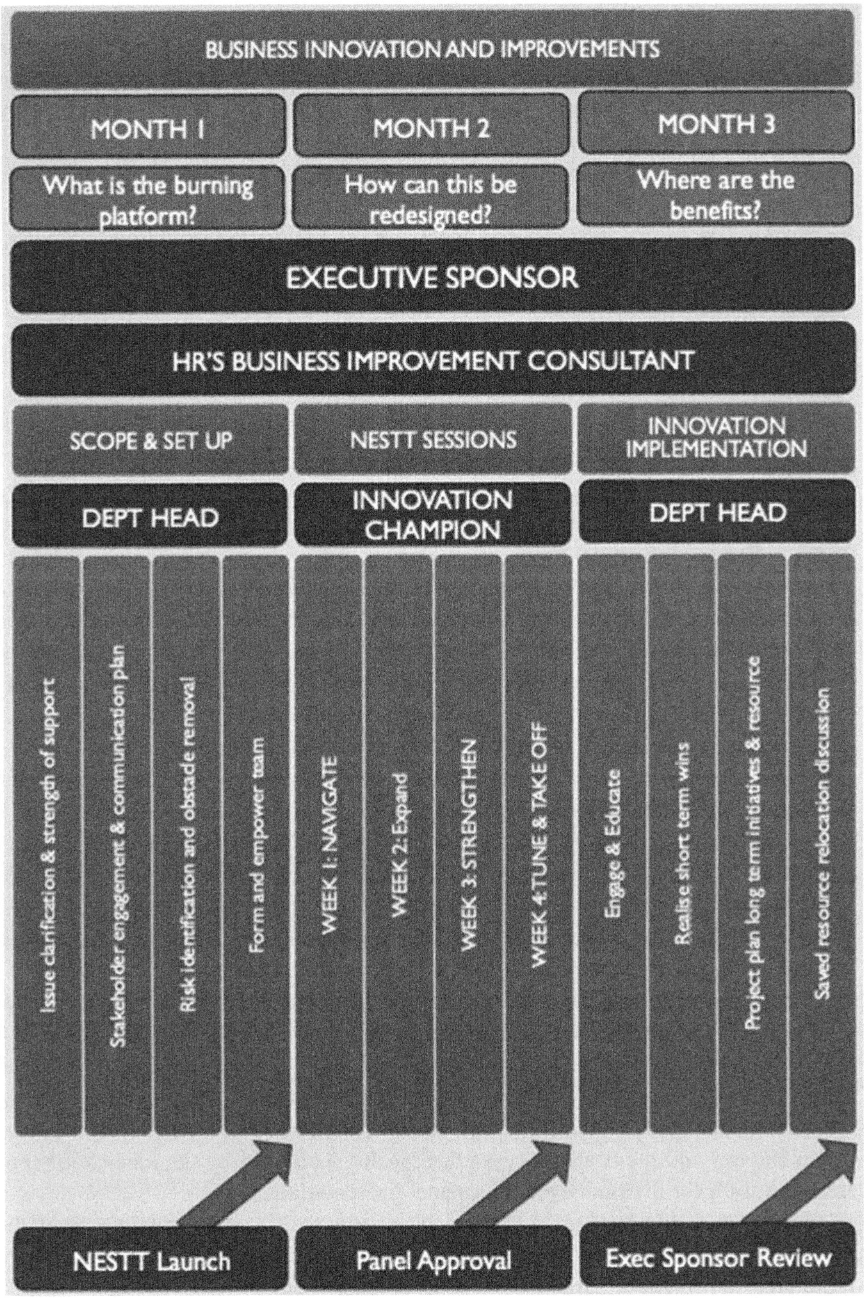

Fig. 3 The NESTT methodology

- *Deriving* ideas from different industries either in the form of general industry patterns (e.g. dynamic pricing/airlines; pockets of creativity/film production; intelligent triage/emergency department) or via learning from specific organisations. The latter means inviting representatives from these organisations to selected sessions into the NESTT,
- *Utilising* idle assets which could be systems, (big) data, employees, customers, physical assets, etc.,
- *Desiging* new experiences based on design-led innovation techniques. A particular feature of the NESTT is a session in which a drama teacher faciliates acting out current and future process experiences leading to much deeper, authentic insights into the emotional states along the process than what could be derived via whiteboarding or process modelling.

At the end of the second week the possible design space, i.e. a comprehensive set of clustered, interrelated and numbered ideas should be defined.

3.2.3 Week 3: Strengthen

The third week starts with the allocation of idea champions to each of the identified ideas. Based on individual expertise, passion and closeness to the required data and users, each member of the NESTT team will take ownership for one or more ideas.

The essential document during this week is called *'Idea on a Page'*. It is literally a one page document capturing the essence of each idea and it is the main working document for each idea champion.

In this document, each idea is profiled in terms of its timeframe (20 days, 20 months, 2020) and the relevant stage in the value chain. The idea champion is named and the idea is briefly described. The next two sections are used to quantify current and future efforts (e.g., costs of execution, time required) or experiences (e.g., net promoter score) leading to a defined impact statement. Depending on the process and the data available this will require making assumptions. This work is similar to the develoment of a brief business case (for each idea).

In addition to the analysis-intensive work of writing these mini business cases, user validations are required. Here, and in line with design thinking principles, selected ideas are presented by the idea champions to and discussed with user groups allowing early feedback and important input to the further development of each idea. In QUT's NESTT, such user validations are attended by approx. 30 colleagues and the draft process changes are socialised by the idea champions in preperation for the final executive panel presentation.

Finally, and this requires a dedicated session with a representative from the internal risk management team, each idea needs to be risk assessed and where required risk mitigation strategies need to be described.

A successful third week leads to completed, validated and risk-assessed ideas-on-a-page documents and idea champions who are excited about and proud of their achievements. It is to be expected that after the validations in this week a number of the initial ideas as derived in week 2 will be excluded from further consideration.

3.2.4 Week 4: Tune and Take-off

The fourth and final week in the NESTT is all about the 20 days ideas and getting these ready for the 'take-off'. The ideas-on-a-page documents are the key input and complemented with further artefacts needed for their implementation.

The week starts with developing a framework consolidating and interrelating all ideas-on-one-page, i.e. an investigation into any cause-effect relationships among these ideas. This could, for example, mean aligning the ideas along the value chain. This framework will also be used to calculate the total impact of the NESTT project on this process.

Tuning every idea involves activities such as developing revised policies and procedures, crafting new forms as required by the new process or a detailed assessment of the compliance of an idea with external requirements. Job descriptions might need to be revised requiring HR involvement or minor IT changes need to be discussed with the IT department.

A highly interactive session during this week is about the pitching of the idea as ultimately each idea champion will have to 'sell his/her idea' to the panel.

The most important milestone of the entire NESTT is the presentation to the panel, i.e. a group of senior stakeholders who judge the ideas. A *'Decisions-on-a-page'* document lists all ideas per row and the panel will be asked to endorse, or reject, each idea. The panel receives all ideas-on-a-page documents in advance and might fast track some obvious ideas while question other ideas in more detail. Ideally, a decision can be made for each idea by the panel in this assessment session. The decisions need to be documented and provide the go-ahead for the idea implementation, i.e. the take-off.

A seperate implementation team will work on the accelerated idea implementation. Selected members of the innovation team might be members of the implementation team to ensure the design intentions are considered. In many cases implementation might entail an incubation phase where an idea is further tested in one area (e.g. a school in the context of a university) before the company wide roll out (take-off) of the (revised) idea.

3.2.5 Process Selection

In order to select the most relevant business processes for the QUT NESTT three focus groups involving more than 40 senior leaders (Head of Schools, Directors and Faculty Admin Managers) have been conducted. In these focus groups particpants were introduced to the overall intentions and high level methodology of the NESTT. Each participant was given the opportunity to propose business processes that should be considered for upcoming NESTTs. These processes needed to be decision-intensive, repetitive, involving a number of stakeholders and be of medium complexity. Each process was discussed in smaller groups and the improvement potential for each process was captured. All processes were then depicted in a two-dimensional framework covering impact of change and likelihood of success. Processes rated as high in both dimensions were shortlisted. The REAL Difference project steering committee selected finally the first three processes, i.e. corporate card, web page approval and travel management.

3.3 The NESTT Teams

The NESTT consists of four teams, the innovation team, the facilitators, the panel and the implementation team.

3.3.1 The Innovation Team

The innovation team is made up of approx. 8 stakeholders from across the organisation and consists of the following roles.

1. The *innovation champion* is the inspirational, positive, consolidating leader and external interface of the team assembled for the process. The innovation champion has to be carefully selected as this person needs to have the right authority, respect, mindset, ambition and network. As the core node, the innovation champion has to manage the dynamics of the internal team, liaise regularly with and provide feedback to the facilitators and be the spokesperson to the outside world. Communicating updates about the NESTT at QUT included activities such as a NESTT-Open-Day or regular updates via the social enterprise solution Yammer. In the context of QUT's redesign, the innovation champion is typically a Faculty Admin Manager, a Director or a Head of School.
2. Two *intensive users* ensure the ongoing inclusion of customer viewpoints and understanding of and empathy with the user requirements. The users involved should be diverse (e.g., an academic and a professional staff) and should have a consumption view on the process, i.e. they do not need to be aware of the technical details behind the line of visibility.
3. The *service/process owner* will have a vested interest in improving this process. However, it is essential that the NESTT is not perceived as an opportunity to push pre-formulated ideas and concepts to accelerated implementation.
4. Two *service providers* ensure that access to substantial end-to-end process experience, but also expertise with all process-related viewpoints, e.g. policies, systems or job descriptions is available. These stakeholders will often be tasked to provide relevant figures such as transaction volumes or probabilities.
5. The *process expert* is the team member closest to the process. This role represents the micro-expertise needed to discuss every single step and will be invaluable for detailed feasibility assessments.

3.3.2 The Panel

The panel ultimately judges, and in this capacity endorses, the ideas proposed by the innovation team. As such, the panel needs to have the authority and the competence to assess the proposed process changes. The panel will meet the innovation team shortly after the 20 days period when all ideas are consolidated into a 'Decisions-on-a-page' document leading to simple go-or-stop decisions.

Ideally, the head of the panel is the most senior executive available. In the context of QUT, the NESTT panel was regularly made up of the Vice Chancellor (head of the panel), the relevant Deputy Vice Chancellor, a senior service owner (e.g., director of marketing), an intensive user, an outside challenger (e.g., a partner of a consulting company) and a member of the REAL Difference Project Leadership Group.

3.3.3 The Facilitators

A number of facilitating roles are needed to ensure the success of each NESTT initiative. Besides the senior facilitator who takes care of the entire management of the initiative including methodology, facilities, team composition and communication, other facilitators contribute as moderators of sessions, analysts, ideators or coaches for pitching, business cases, etc. As the NESTT captures the entire process lifecycle from process vision to detailed idea implementation, faciliators need to have a broad, comprehensive skillset not just of typical BPM methods, but also design, communication, conflict management, team work, project management and motivation skills.

A specific feature of QUT's NESTT is a drama facilitator, i.e. a facilitator trained in helping stakeholders to uncover experiences, emotions and improvement ideas by acting out current or future process scenarios. In our case, this has been a drama teacher from QUT's Creative Industries faculty.

3.3.4 The Implementation Team

Once the ideas have been presented and endorsed, an implementation team takes over. It is of importance to keep up the momentum and aim towards rapid implementation and communication of the change. In many cases, this might first involve further discussions of detailed concerns with selected stakeholders as the panel might not have been able to go to this level in their assessment. At QUT, we conducted road shows at both campuses to communicate the changes as resulting from the NESTT project.

In addition to the innovation team, the panel, the facilitators and the implementation team, a number of *other stakeholders* are involved in ad-hoc engagements within the NESTT, including vendors (of current systems or new vendors showcasing future development pathways of their systems), selected benchmark organisations (ideally from outside the sector) for the ideate-via-derivation exercise, internal HR, IT, legal or policy advisor as needed as well as internal risk managers.

3.3.5 The Processes in the NESTT

As the time of writing this article, QUT had engaged in four NESTT initiatives covering the following processes, corporate card, web page approval, travel management and research grants. As an example, we will elaboate on the corporate card process in more detail.

A complex, costly corporate card process becomes a roadblock to the wider rollout of corporate cards and the related benefits, as the administrative costs-to-serve are higher than the benefits gained from card payments. At QUT, approx. 500 staff used the corporate card in more than 20,000 transactions annually leading to approx 5,000 monthly statements. Besides addressing the immediate process issues within the corporate card process, an improved corporate card experience also facilitates significant improvements in other substantial processes such as procurement or travel management.

The NESTT innovation team working on corporate card was headed by a Faculty Admin Manager and included representatives from finance, selected intensive users (e.g., alumni manager, academic) and experts on the different aspects of the process.

The vision created in the NESTT for this process was *'Enabling business, anytime, anywhere'*. 2020 ideas related to near field communication (NFC) and cardless payments were generated, but the core focus was on immediate 20 days improvements. The process was broken down into the stages issue card, use card and reconcile expenses. It became clear that the act of issusing a card was approval intensive (up to seven signatures), paper-intensive (up to ten documents) and as a consequence time consuming and costly to facilitate. Furthermore, the reconcilation was constrained by system limitations leading to time-consuming coding and approval processes.

In summary, it became obvious in the navigation stage (week 1) of this NESTT initiative that this process had significant potential for improvement.

3.4 Results Achieved

The NESTT innovation team worked for 4 weeks on the corporate card process following the four staged methodology and using the NESTT room. The ideation stage involved acting out future corporate card scenarios and in fact being the corporate card (!). Vendors from large Australian banks were invited to elaborate on the features of their related future services.

In total, ten significant ideas were developed ranging from streamlined, self-training and single approval arrangements as part of the issuing of the card over to an increased use of credit cards replacing purchase orders and reimbursements to digital receipts and declarations (instead of time-consuming state declarations). Revised, streamlined procedures complemented these process-centred ideas.

The ideas were presented to a panel consisting of QUT's Vice Chancellor, the CFO and further senior stakeholders where the majority of the ideas were approved. In follow-up meetings, details of the implementation (e.g., risk assessment, policy implications) were discussed with relevant stakeholders leading to a dedicated roadshow a few weeks after the presentation to the panel. During this roadshow the new process was communicated to the wider QUT community. In summary, these ideas eliminated the administrative efforts per corporate card process by more than 50% and eliminated the majority of approval steps and documents involved.

In addition to these tangible process performance improvements, the NESTT had a substantial impact on the mindset and design capabilities of everyone involved. Staff involved in the NESTT appreciated the insights into design-centred process improvement, the positive, constructive and decisive energy and the satisfaction of the fast idea-to-implementation cycle. As a consequence, other colleagues expressed an interest in being involved in future NESTTs.

3.5 Lessons Learned

The experiences with the NESTT have demonstrated that rigorous process change can be done quickly and that conducting such change can be a highly enjoyable experience for everyone involved. As such the NESTT adds a new capability to the BPM framework and provides in particular new approaches for governance, methodology and people as part of the six elements of BPM framework (Rosemann and vom Brocke 2015). Consequently, the three essential lessons learnt affiliated with the NESTT are in the areas of governance, participants (people) and facilitation (methodology).

Decisive Governance
It is essential to embed the rapid NESTT approach into an equally rapid governance structure. Otherwise, the NESTT loses its momentum and the desired accelerated idea-to-implementation is impossible to achive. At QUT, this was addressed by fast tracking the implementation in the form of an endorsing, decisive panel immediately after the NESTT work was finalised. Furthermore, a senior executive (Deputy Vice Chancellor) was the named executive sponsor overseeing the work of the innovation champion and the implementation champion.

Intellectually Agile Participants
The NESTT relies heavily on the creativity, energy, mindset, competence and attitude of the participants. Over a period of 4 weeks, the team will see each other on a daily base 1–2 h per day and working constructively as a team is essential. This will be often challenging, in particular when there is no aggreement regarding controversial ideas, but the constrained NESTT timeframe requires quick decision making processes. Participants may also arrive opionated at the NESTT. However, being stuck to past ideas and being reluctant to consider design alternatives will become a roadblock to progression.

Our experiences show that working in the problem resolution part of the NESTT comes easy to most participants, but that the second half of the room is at least initially a challenge as most participants, including trained BPM professionals, will not be used to this sort of thinking and ideation.

Finally, participants need to be receptive to the guidance of the facilitator. In particular, it is crucial to channel conversations into the right sessions, i.e. to decouple, for example, conversations regarding the current state from their weaknesses and possible solutions.

Comprehensive Facilitators
The core of the BPM body of knowledge abstracts from the role of the facilitator. In fact, most BPM methods and techniques are people-agnostic and ignore the impact of the facilitator on the quality of the outcomes.

The NESTT is the opposite and the role of the faciliator is propobably the most critical success factor (Rosemann et al. 2011). NESTT facilitators are not expected to be domain experts, but they must have the following characteristics

- Being able to work in the second half of the room, i.e. strong design capabilities and an ability to develop shared stories of compelling future process scenarios,
- Strong conceptualisation and system thinking skills, for example the ability to quickly 'see' essential process triage opportunities or clusters of ideas,
- Being decisive and being able to guide conversations in a limited timeframe towards the desired outcomes and
- Being able to work with stakeholders who are diverse in terms of seniority and attitude towards change.

A common mistake of the facilitators has been to be too enthusiastic with collecting lots of information. In the spirit of the moment, it is exciting to see the flood of input and a significant amount of post-it notes are seen as the outcome of 'a great session'. However, it is important that each wall at any point in time will be intuitive, concise, relevant and simply 'beautiful'. Thus, it is required to continuously reflect on the content of each wall and redesign, synergise and literally clean up a wall before beginning the next session. This could mean rewriting post-it notes to ensure they are consistent and actually can be read.

Ultimate future *success* with the NESTT will come in three ways. First, the NESTT has significantly improved the performance of a number of essential, decision-intensive processes at QUT. Only tangible success provides credibility—now there is a long queue of processes lined up for future NESTT sessions. Second, the NESTT is exposed to an over-supply of staff members who like to be part, contribute and benefit from this rapid redesign methodology. Third, and ultimately, success will mean the NESTT has become a widely used verb, i.e. when staff are exposed to a process problem they propose *'to nestt'* it.

Beyond our very own organisation, success would materialise in other organisations, across industries and regions, replicating NESTT-like initiatives and making these a successful part of their business-as-usual operating model.

Acknowledgements The NESTT approach has emerged from collaborative work with many colleagues at Queensland University of Technology. In particular, I like to thank Mr Paul Mathiesen from QUT's BPM Discipline who piloted many concepts as a co-facilitator, Dr Michelle Vickers from QUT's HR Organisational Development who made significant contributions to the three stage model of the NESTT and to Matthew Brown and Jamie Ford from Ernst & Young who were as reflective facilitators involved in the conceptualisation and design of the NESTT.

References

Brown, T. (2008). Design thinking. *Harvard Business Review, 86*(6), 84–92.

Coaldrake, P., & Stedman, L. (2016). *Raising the stakes: Gambling with the future of Universities* (2nd ed.). Brisbane: University of Queensland Press.

Hammer, M. (2015). What is business process management? In J. vom Brocke & M. Rosemann (Eds.), *Handbook on business process management: Introduction, methods and information systems* (Vol. 1, 2nd ed., pp. 3–16). Berlin: Springer.

Kano, N., Nobuhiku, S., Takahashi, F., & Tsuji, S. (1984). Attractive quality and must-be quality. *Journal of the Japanese Society for Quality Control (in Japanese), 14*(2), 39–48.
Knapp, J. (2016). *Sprint: How to solve big problems and test new ideas in just five days*. New York: Simon & Schuster.
Larman, C., & Vodde, B. (2004). *Agile and iterative development: A manager's guide*. Boston: Addison-Wesley.
Long, K. A. (2012). What is an IGOE? *Business Rules Journal, 13*(1), 10–22.
Recker, J., & Rosemann, M. (2015). Systemic ideation: A playbook for creating innovative ideas more consciously. *The Business Transformation Journal, 13*, 34–45.
Rosemann, M. (2014). Proposals for future BPM research directions. *Proceedings of the 2nd Asia Pacific Business Process Management Conference, Brisbane*, pp. 1–15.
Rosemann, R., Hjalmarsson, A., Lind, M., & Recker, J. (2011). Four facets of a process modeling facilitator. In D. Galletta & T.-P. Liang (Eds.), *Proceedings of the 32nd International Conference on Information Systems. Association for Information Systems, Shanghai, China.*
Rosemann, M., & vom Brocke, J. (2015). The six core elements of business process management. In J. vom Brocke & M. Rosemann (Eds.), *Handbook on business process management: Introduction, methods and information systems* (Vol. 1, 2nd ed., pp. 105–122). Berlin: Springer.

Michael Rosemann is the Executive Director, Corporate Engagement, and Professor in Information Systems at the Queensland University of Technology and the Honorary Consul for the Federal Republic of Germany in South Queensland. Michael has published more than 250 refereed papers, including publications in renowned outlets, including *MIS Quarterly (MISQ), European Journal of Information Systems (EJIS)* and *Information Systems*. His books are available in five languages and he has conducted invited keynotes at international, academic and professional BPM conferences. Michael provides regular advice to executives on revenue resilience, innovation systems and process design.

Kiss the Documents! How the City of Ghent Digitizes Its Service Processes

Amy Van Looy and Sabine Rotthier

Abstract

(a) **Situation faced**: The case focuses on the digitization of service processes in the City of Ghent. Front-office e-services are integrated into the corporate website and into the back office thanks to digitization of the internal way of working in value chains. Before 2014, the City's digital services were limited primarily to web forms offered by three departments for taxes, mobility and parking affairs, and citizens' affairs in a non-integrated way, as the departments used different applications and a considerable amount of manual work in the back office. Other departments focused primarily on downloadable forms that were available on the corporate website. Customers could also create profiles for some services, resulting in multiple user names and passwords to be managed for the same customer. Because of this silo mentality, the digital investments did not pay off, and a more integrated approach was needed to make the digital service processes more efficient in terms of return on investment (ROI) and customer-oriented.

(b) **Action taken**: The City of Ghent formulated a digitization vision based on fifteen reusable building blocks, including that facilitate the use of an authentication platform, a single customer profile, a digital signature platform, and a service-oriented architecture. These building blocks guide projects that digitize the total value chains or business processes. To stimulate reuse, the building blocks were built as generic components

A. Van Looy (✉)
Faculty of Economics and Business Administration, Ghent University, Ghent, Belgium
e-mail: Amy.VanLooy@UGent.be

S. Rotthier
Faculty of Economics and Business Administration, Ghent University, Ghent, Belgium

City of Ghent, Ghent, Belgium
e-mail: Sabine.Rotthier@stad.gent; Sabine.Rotthier@UGent.be

J. vom Brocke, J. Mendling (eds.), *Business Process Management Cases*,
Management for Professionals, DOI 10.1007/978-3-319-58307-5_11

or process activities that e-services typically contain (e.g., "create profile," "pay electronically"). The generic components were first translated to the digitization of three pilot chains regarding taxes, environment-related subsidies, and citizens' affairs. The pilots were chosen based on their having volunteered to participate and their opportunities to take advantage of digitization.

(c) **Results achieved**: Although the pilot for citizens' affairs is still running, the results of the pilots for digital tax submissions and environment-related subsidies are already positively perceived. All environment-related subsidy requests are now digitally processed in the back office, with a digital alternative in place for the process steps of receiving and responding to the subsidy requests in the front office since 2015. The number of digital tax submissions increased to a third of all submissions in 2016, compared to only five percentage in 2014, while the number of input forms was cut in half in favor of prefilled tax proposals. Besides being generalized to apply to all services in the City of Ghent, the digitization approach with building blocks and building projects will also be applied in other business processes and future projects such as a participation platform or intranet, so it is not exclusive to e-services. The main idea is to develop once and then to reuse it maximally.

(d) **Lessons learned**: The case concludes with five lessons learned, from which other public and private organizations may benefit. First, from the perspective of reuse and inter-organizational collaboration, data about products or services should align semantically with external partners. The City of Ghent used linked open data for this purpose. Two lessons learned promote a pragmatic approach to achieving success by concretizing initial principles and temporary workarounds to achieve quick wins. The fourth lesson was the need for assistance by an internal support office or competence center. Finally, the demonstrated advantages arise from working with a single profile per customer, rather than working in silos.

1 Introduction

The case of the City of Ghent ("the City"), a Belgian public-sector organization, contributes to the broader discussions of e-government, e-citizenship, digital identities, and smart cities. Belgium has closely followed international e-government trends (Rotthier 2004) and is one the first countries to require (since 2003) a mandatory electronic identity card (eID) for all citizens of age twelve and older, which facilitates authentication efforts and creates new opportunities for e-services.

The case fits within a master plan called "LEO" to make all services delivered by the City more customer-oriented and more closely driven by the demands of local citizens, organizations, and associations. The master plan seeks to optimize the City's physical and digital services, with digital service delivery taking the lead in

Table 1 vom Brocke et al. (2016) contextual factors applied to the City of Ghent

Dimension	Contextual factor	Characteristics of the City of Ghent
Goal	Focus	Exploration (innovation)
Process	Value contribution	Core processes
	Repetitiveness	Repetitive
	Knowledge intensity	Medium knowledge intensity
	Creativity	Low to medium creativity
	Interdependence	Low, medium, and high interdependence
	Variability	Low to medium variability
Organization	Scope	Intra- and inter-organizational processes
	Industry	Service industry
	Size	Large organization
	Culture	Medium supportive to not supportive of BPM
	Resources	Medium organizational resources
Environment	Competitiveness	Low competitive environment
	Uncertainty	Low environmental uncertainty

the long term based on the concept of "do it yourself" (DIY). In terms of the contextual factors of vom Brocke et al. (2016), the case thus concerns the innovation of core processes, which tend to be repetitive in nature and not highly creative or variable (Table 1). LEO's future vision is described as follows:

> The administrative services in the City of Ghent maximally run through digital channels. The products delivered by the City of Ghent are offered in an efficient and customer-friendly manner through the digital channels. Citizens are maximally aware of the digitally offered products. (Translated from Stad Gent 2014, p. 3)

Ghent is the second largest city in the Flemish community of the federal state of Belgium. According to Stad Gent (2016), the City as a local government in Belgium (Western Europe) has approximately 250,000 citizens, plus 65,000 residential students registered in another town, and about 3000 employers. The City itself employs about 5000 civil servants. The City has multiple physical locations, including an administrative center and local community centers. Intergovernmental relations are required, mainly with the Flemish government, but the City also collaborates closely with the Public Welfare Center of Ghent and with Digipolis, an organization that offers technical support to the local administrations, Public Welfare Centers, and police of the cities of Ghent and Antwerp (i.e. the largest city in Flanders).

The environment in which the City operates is less competitive and more certain than the average organization (Table 1), which explains to some degree why the departments are accustomed to working in silos, rather than in the multidisciplinary, customer-oriented culture that typifies Business Process Management (BPM) and Business Process Orientation (BPO) (Van Looy et al. 2014). Nonetheless, recent budget savings due to the need to cut down on expenses force people to better handle the workload more efficiently and effectively.

The contextual factors in the City are summarized in Table 1.

2 Situation Faced

The departments in the City are accustomed to working in silos. For instance, before 2014, three departments offered web forms for taxes, mobility and parking affairs, and for citizens' affairs. All of these web forms were developed by the same IT supplier, who also took care of the back office applications in which the forms were processed. However, the usage figures for these web forms were disappointing (e.g., only forty digital tax submissions per year); not all web forms were browser-independent, resulting in customer complaints; and the back-office processing of web forms was not always fully digital. Some services worked with loose e-forms developed in various technologies, and numerous forms could be downloaded (i.e., in MS Word and PDF) that customers had to fill out, print, and post or deliver physically.

In 2014, the corporate website (https://stad.gent/) was renewed to feature a more intuitive structure and advanced search functionalities so customers could easily find the information they were looking for. For instance, customers can now launch a search query based on a keyword or filter their results based on themes. The new corporate website is also based on Search Engine Optimization (SEO), because most website visitors arrive at a webpage directly by means of a search engine like Google instead of navigating to the homepage and browsing it. In addition, an increasing number of unique visitors use the corporate website, providing evidence for the value of more investment in e-services.

Inspired by the digital evolution in society, the City wants to take another leap into digitization.

2.1 Needs

- A more customer-oriented way of working
- A more uniform way of working
- Higher ROI from IT projects, especially lower costs to conduct and maintain IT projects
- Increased reuse of digital investments (e.g., by means of a common IT architecture and moving away from a silo mentality)

2.2 Constraints

As a public organization, the City faces some specific constraints:

- High privacy concerns (higher than those in an average company)
- Limited budget because of the need to cut down on expenses (budget savings) and because of customer expectations about an efficient use of tax money
- Monopoly on most services, which requires service delivery through multiple channels instead of relying only on digitization

- Services largely specified by legislation and politics, resulting in limited degrees of freedom
- Large set of heterogeneous services (i.e., about 300 products)
- Large set of heterogeneous customers (i.e., citizens, students, organizations, and associations)
- If in-house development is not possible, an official call for outsourcing should always be launched publicly
- Historical evolution of working in silos (more than an average company), resulting in a large number of applications

2.3 Incidents

Three departments offered digital services for taxes, for mobility and parking affairs, and for citizens' affairs before 2014. Customers had to log on for each digital service separately, such as, for citizens, using their eID or token or, for enterprises, using an "Isabel" card. In addition to these initial digitization efforts, several other departments started with a specific profile per process (e.g., to apply for a job as local civil servant, for internships, for the library), so the same customer had to cope with multiple user names and passwords. Moreover, the various web forms were often complex, and the use of some were limited to specific browsers. Therefore, only a few customers used the digital services, and customer complaints were rising. These incidents also illustrate a silo mentality, which was the main reason that the early digital investments did not pay off.

The City provides about 300 services, each of which required considerable manual intervention in the back office. For instance, in 2015 the City processed about 3000 tax submissions, 851 environment-related subsidy requests, and 68,850 citizens' affairs certificates in 2015, most of which required manual effort on the part of the citizen and the City. Digitizing such business processes would provide a significant gain in efficiency.

2.4 Objectives

The City's goal was to digitize more and to digitize better. The City's digitization effort not only targets its direct contact with customers on the corporate website (front office) but also its internal way of working (back office). In 2010, the City decided to go beyond the digitization of downloadable forms into e-forms, which would be little more than window-dressing. While the initial focus was on simplifying the administrative forms, the emphasis expanded to including the simplified forms in optimized and automated business processes in 2014. In other words, business processes would be translated into digital chains that build as much as possible on generic components to facilitate reuse for both the front office and the back office. Possible examples of reuse across value chains (and, thus, across departments) include a standardized way to authenticate users (i.e., employees and customers), to sign a document electronically, and to pay for an online service. Information and forms regarding e-services should be available on any browser and on any device.

3 Action Taken

With respect to the typical stage models of e-government (Lee 2010), the case organization can be positioned as having had a web presence for many years and as moving from interactions to more transactions with ideally a fully digitized front office and back office. The "LEO" master plan focuses on all physical and digital service delivery, including vertical integration with external partners and horizontal integration across the City's departments. The case differs from other e-government stages related to digital democracy or political participation and is thus closely linked to the domain of BPM.

This section starts with a brief description of the actions taken by linking them to the process literature. The measures regarding process innovation are situated throughout the entire lifecycle of a business process (Dumas et al. 2013; Van Looy et al. 2014). The core business processes were modeled using the standard BPMN process language for process identification, discovery, and analysis (OMG 2011), albeit with different modeling tools in each department (e.g., ARIS and MS Visio). The process-redesign phase was driven primarily by the optimization approach or philosophy of Lean Thinking (Ohno 1988; Womack and Jones 2003), which seeks to minimize (or even eliminate) waste and to maximize customer value by means of logical reasoning in order to do more with less. Next, for process deployment and implementation, a service-oriented architecture (SOA) was chosen to reuse service components and to create a common architecture (Rosen et al. 2012). For each digitization project, the process lifecycle phases are managed by two project managers, a business project manager and an IT project manager, who collaborate closely. The IT project manager typically coordinates the public tender procedure: After inviting tenders or deciding on an in-house development, the IT project manager acts as the single point of contact for the IT suppliers chosen or internal developers. The IT project manager is also responsible for timing the development, roll-out, and testing and for coordinating feedback during the testing phase. The business project manager is responsible for the overall planning (including communications) of the project, modifications to the employees' way of working, and the overall impact on the workplace. The business project manager also manages the testers and is one of the active business testers. The business project manager typically plays a unifying role between the departments and Digipolis, and takes into account the interest of the entire organization in order to counter any silo effect. After a project is deployed and implemented, process ownership remains on the business side, and the IT project manager focuses on another process or value chains to be digitized. Since the digitization projects consider chains within departments, the role of a process owner (or process manager) has been departmental rather than cross-functional so far (Müller et al. 2016; Van Looy et al. 2014).

The case can be linked to Rosemann and vom Brocke's (2015) six core elements of BPM: methods, information technology, strategic alignment, governance, people, and culture. The City follows the typical process lifecycle, as well as BPM's core elements of methods and information technology The core element of strategic alignment is covered by starting with a digitization vision, the LEO master plan, that focuses on more efficient and customer-friendly services based on top-down coordination and planning. Until now, the focus had been more on these first three core elements and less on the others. For instance, the governance element is restricted to the notion of process ownership, while the people and culture elements are supported primarily by process-management leaders and leadership attention, given the top-down approach taken. The City is relatively weak in terms of being a process-oriented organization, focusing instead on a project-based BPM approach. By starting from a story of digital chains in which employees participate actively, the realization of BPM is also pragmatic. Although the corporate culture is still strongly based on a silo mentality, the need for budget savings caused a change in the employees' perceptions: While IT was initially perceived as job-threatening, employees now increasingly believe that IT may help to make their workloads easier to handle. Moreover, resistance against the LEO master plan is also countered to some extent because a physical alternative for service delivery will remain for the customers.

Thus, the six core elements of BPM are all covered by the City, albeit to differing degrees. The City conducted a BPM maturity assessment based on similar elements almost eight years ago, inspired by the need for work transparency and to avoid knowledge losses. Its use was discontinued later because of high costs and because the maturity model's focus was more on BPO or the entire process portfolio instead of specific processes or projects (Van Looy et al. 2013). With the current digitization vision, the City intends to relaunch the idea of a process-oriented way of working.

The remainder of this section provides details about the case. In particular, the digitization vision in the City builds on fifteen principles called "building blocks," shown in Fig. 1. The principles were drawn from the maximum of what a public service may include and what is required for such a maximal service. For this purpose, existing service processes were compared to obtain an overview of possible process steps.

The two general principles shown at the bottom of Fig. 1 are the fundamentals from which to start: *corporate identity* and "*KISS the documents*." All e-services should comply with the corporate identity of the City (e.g., using the same colors, fonts, logos). The acronym in "KISS the documents" stands for "King," "Individualized"/"Immediate," and "Simple"/"Stupid." In other words:

- The customer is king.
- Services are immediate and individualized without corrective actions needed and without requesting the same information multiple times (e.g., a customer's address and phone number).
- Keep it simple (and stupid), for instance to be easily usable for an heterogeneous audience of users and customers from across the society.

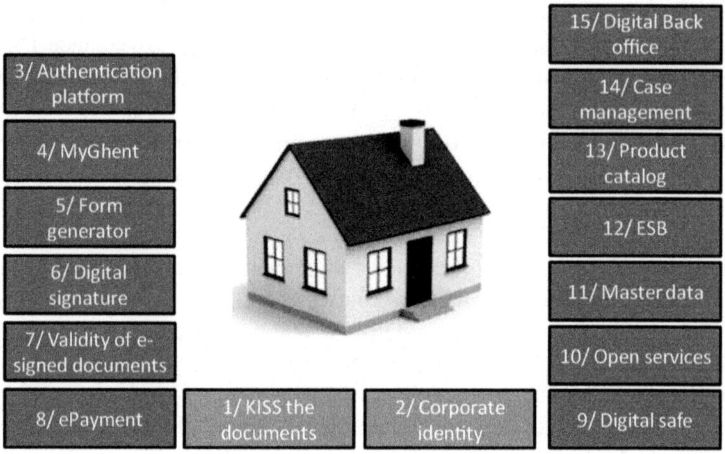

Fig. 1 Digitization principles (building blocks) in the City of Ghent, translated from (Stad Gent 2014)

The principle of "KISS the documents" should avoid translating downloadable forms directly into a web form; it should digitize, not just automate. Which information is required for each service should be verified, along with in which sequence this information should be acquired, and the degree to which the questions in the web form can be dynamic (i.e., questions to be added or removed depending on previous answers in the form). From the perspective of administrative simplification, the processing of web forms in the back office will also be reconsidered in order to be optimized. This principle is important since the City offers about 250 products that must be requested by means of a form.

The other digitization principles in Fig. 1 are more technology-oriented. As a third principle (or building block), the City should have an *authentication platform* that is based on the type of authentication. For instance, when strong authentication is needed, the eID platform can be used, and when a weaker authentication suffices, the *MyGhent* authentication platform, which is based on a user name and password, can be used. MyGhent requires a single profile per customer and can be used for purposes other than only authentication. For instance, it allows customers to check the history of service requests, to subscribe to newsletters, or to add profile data themselves (e.g., a personal e-mail address, mobile phone number, the names and birth dates of their children, and their interests in events, such as sports or youth events). As such, citizens can specify and modify their data themselves, which is in line with the more global trend of digital identity management and citizens providing their own data (Sullivan 2016). Although the authentication platform and MyGhent, the third and fourth principles, are closely related, the authentication platform is a separate building block because it is not limited to MyGhent, and it facilitates the log-in using strong digital keys (e.g., concerning an eID or token) offered by the federal government. Nonetheless, the City intends to create a coupled profile with the eID in the long run.

As for the fifth building block, the City intends to use a single *form generator* to create any form in a uniform way. A citizen who logs on using MyGhent should be able to see his/her personal data prefilled in the digital form. If the forms were built using different technologies, an additional link would be needed per technology. This fifth building block requires only the development of a single technological link for MyGhent and the chosen form generator. As for the sixth and seventh principles, both customers and employees should be able to *sign documents electronically*, including a *check of the signature's validity* to verify whether the document the customer receives fully corresponds with the document sent by the City (i.e., that the document was not changed meanwhile). Signature verification is particularly important for certificates (e.g., regarding birth, family composition or an extract of criminal records) that the City delivers to its citizens and other parties (e.g., an employer). The system also supports an eighth principle, *electronic payment* for services by means of the e-payment service provider Ingenico (formerly Ogone). The ninth principle refers to a *digital safe* to store (signed) documents and share them both internally and externally. Reuse by external parties can be realized by means of the tenth and eleventh principles, *open services* and *master data*. For example, energy-saving measures may also be relevant for use in forums or websites in the construction sector. Master data should also facilitate maximal reuse of what the City already knows. One example is a dropdown that includes a list of all official street names from which the user can choose when filling out a form (e.g., when requesting a car-free street). Reuse is also enabled by means of the twelfth principle, an *Enterprise Service Bus* supported by Digipolis. The City also targets an interdisciplinary *product catalog* with record cards for each product that contain all product information. The product catalog is currently designed as linked open data (i.e., Open Data Protocol) and is aligned with the catalog of the Flemish government as a semantic web. Such an ontology-based approach with open standards, data dictionaries, and a central data front office across governments can be created on the long run. Finally, the fourteenth building block of *case management*, which ensures that requests will be followed up, or the 15th principle, of a *customized digital back office*, relate to each other in an "either-or" way, as either a generic case-management system will be used when a back office application is not yet in place or should be changed (e.g., when work is still based on MS Excel or MS Access), or an (existing) service-specific back office application can remain (e.g., the customized software for taxes called "Unibel"). In any case, the City intends to replace the customized back office applications with a generic case-management system to the degree possible.

Using these fifteen principles, the City identified generic components shared across business processes in order to encourage reuse. The analysis shows that a service in the City typically contains the generic components shown in Fig. 2 (multiple generic components per service, but not necessarily all of them). Figure 2 also presents the links between the principles or building blocks and the generic components in a digital chain.

Next, the generic service components were translated to the digitization of three pilot chains (Table 2) before generalizing the approach to all services and translating all business processes into digital chains. The use of pilots is commonly seen as a conversion strategy with relatively low risks, medium costs, and medium time required (Tegarden et al. 2013).

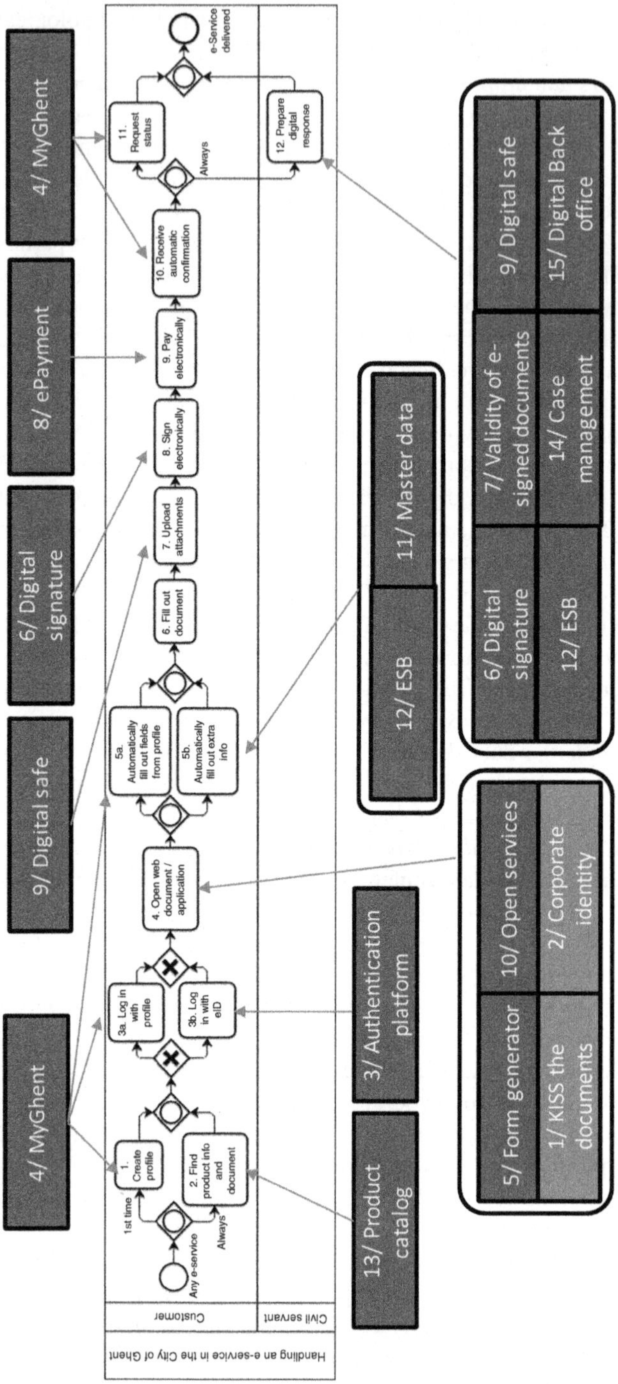

Fig. 2 Generic e-service components in the City of Ghent, based on (Stad Gent 2014)

Table 2 Overview of the digital chains that serve as pilots

Digital chain	Functionalities
Taxes	Submitting taxes
Environment	Requesting and handling an energy-saving subsidy (5 types)
Citizens' affairs	Requesting and delivering a certificate (11 types)

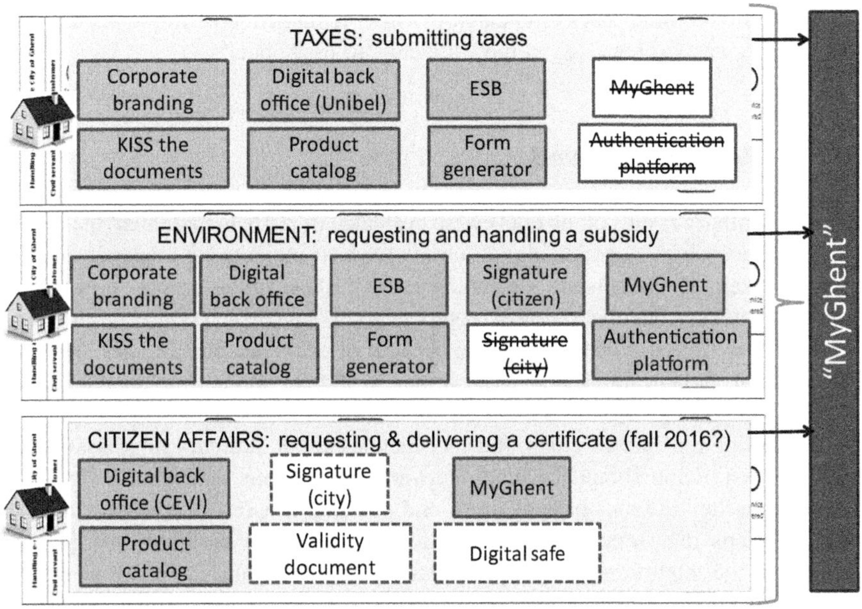

Fig. 3 The degree of reusability in the pilot digital chains

The City selected these three pilot chains for several reasons. The "taxes" chain was chosen because of the disappointing results for the existing web form and because of political aspirations of the elected representatives. Regarding the "environment" chain, the department itself asked to participate in the pilot, as it saw digitization as the next logical step after having made its subsidies uniform. The citizens' affairs chain was targeted because of political aspirations of the elected representatives, because other Belgian cities had digitized their citizens' affairs, and because of the high workload related to citizens' affairs, so digitization would ensure a positive and quick ROI. Since the citizens' affairs department handles more forms than other departments in the City do, it is likely to have the most to gain from e-services.

More specifically, the business processes related to taxes, environment, and citizens' affairs were considered in identifying the generic service components shown in Fig. 2, in line with the principles shown in Fig. 1. The initial translation, presented in Fig. 3, indicates the high degree of reusability in the pilot digital chains.

Some of the digitization principles in Fig. 3 refer to building blocks that became chain-dependent (e.g., in the chain for taxes) or could be eliminated because of administrative simplification (e.g., in the "environment" chain). Since the pilot chain for taxes still uses a service-dependent or customized back office application, not all of the intended generic components were adopted in this pilot. Nonetheless, unlike a front office application, a back office application does not necessarily have reuse as an ultimate goal. Instead, the City could choose between a specific back office application (the fifteenth building block) or a generic case management system (the fourteenth building block, which was not yet available). Some of the building blocks indicated in Fig. 3 remained to be implemented when this article was written (e.g., in the "citizens' affairs" chain).

4 Results Achieved

The preliminary results of the pilots were evaluated in 2016. In particular, the number of digital tax submissions and digital subsidy requests increased immediately after the actions taken. The results are thanks in part to the realization of most principles or building blocks, but the reusable component of MyGhent (single profiles) was realized only for citizens and students; because of some practical hurdles, the single profiles for organizations and associations will take more time than expected. Tables 3, 4 and Fig. 4 present the preliminary results for each pilot.

Regarding the "taxes" chain, the City handles about 3000 tax submissions each year. A distinction should be made between input forms that require significant input from the customer-organizations and prefilled proposals to which customer-organizations must react only if they do not accept the prefilled data. Table 3 compares the total number of tax submissions in 2014 using the previous e-forms to 2016 using the newly developed e-forms linked to the back office application. The number of input forms was almost halved, and the percentage of digital tax submissions for both the forms and the proposals increased from 5.5% to 28.9% of

Table 3 Changes in performance measures for the "taxes" chain

Chain	Performance measures	Before	After
Taxes	Number of submissions	Total (2014): 2952 • Forms: 1,579 (of which 5.5% are digital) • Proposals: 1373 (of which 2.6% are digital)	Total (2016): 3136 • Forms: 808 (of which 28.9% are digital) • Proposals: 2328 (of which 35.5% are digital)

Table 4 Changes in performance measures for the "citizens' affairs" chain

Chain	Performance measures	Before	After
Citizens' affairs	Number of certificates	Total (2015): 68,850 • E-forms: 8552 • E-mails: 17,104 • Physical: 43,194	Unavailable

Total	851	926
Energy-saving measures	572	690
Green roofs	63	35
Reusable diapers	61	99
Environment-friendly mobility	149	95
Climate projects	6	7

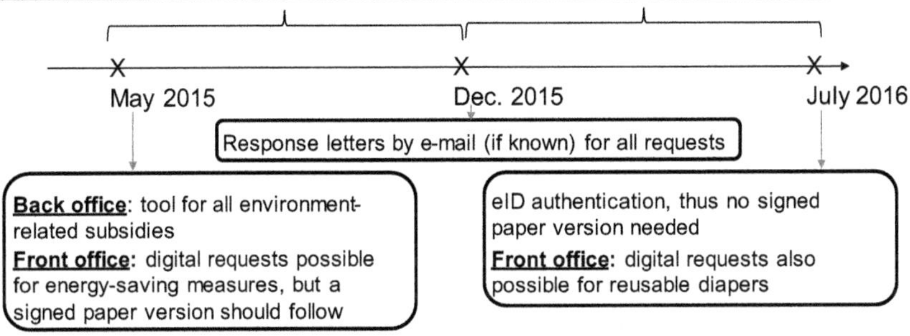

Fig. 4 Changes in performance measures for the "environment" chain

the total tax submissions. These digital performance measures are expected to increase as customers become more acquainted with the new forms.

In the second pilot, shown in Fig. 4, the "environment" chain has to cope with several types of subsidy requests (e.g., for energy-saving measures, for green roofs, for reusable diapers, for environment-friendly mobility, for climate projects). A response letter should be sent for each subsidy request. The back office has been fully digitized for all these environment-related types of subsidies since May 2015, while the front office had already offered the possibility of an e-form on for the energy-saving measures. However, a signed paper-based version was still required due to the lack of a strong authentication until July 2016. The roll-out of the e-form for reusable diapers took place in July 2016. Based on this experience, the other types of subsidies will follow soon.

The response letters were still paper-based for all environment-related subsidy requests until December 2015, but they required only scanned (instead of real) signatures. Optimizations in line with Lean Thinking allowed further streamlining of the "environment" digital chain by eliminating an initial component. In particular, it turned out that a digital signature suffices for requesting an energy-saving subsidy, and a digital signature of a civil servant or a political representative on the response letter was not required. A City employee describes the early benefits as follows.

> Thanks to the elimination of an additional digital signature, we are now working with scanned signatures included in the template. This decision meant that we did NOT have to go to the alderman and the city secretary to sign the response letter about 850 times in the past six months. Consequently, we also gain time, and the customers will know more quickly whether they get the requested subsidy or not.

Since December 2015, these response letters have been sent by e-mail if the electronic mail address of the requester is known, even for paper-based requests. Therefore, the subsidy requests are now digitally processed in the back office, and customers are offered a digital alternative, whereas all subsidy requests were still paper-based before. This second pilot also illustrates the need for a step-by-step approach and for taking small steps at a time. For instance, approximately a third of all requests for energy-saving measures are already made via the new e-form. If the City had waited to go live until the eID authentication in July 2016, hundreds of requests would have had to be retyped in the back office. An additional advantage of working with the tool is access to figures for management reporting, which may result in useful insights that support management decisions in the long run.

The digital chain for "citizens' affairs" involves certificates like certificates of residence (with or without history of addresses), family composition, legal cohabitation, birth, marriage, life, death, the method of interment, nationality, and criminal records. This third pilot is not yet live because of the time needed to create a generic digital signature platform and because the legal department in the City prefers sending signed documents with a link to a digital safe rather than as an e-mail attachment. Therefore, this digital chain cannot be fully evaluated (Table 4). Nonetheless, the numbers may act as a future point of comparison and provide insights into the opportunities and ROI that already exists since this department handles the largest number of forms in the City. While the large numbers in Table 4 give evidence for the central role of citizens' affairs in the City, the current digital alternatives (i.e., e-forms and e-mails) illustrate an interruption between a digitized front office and a manual back office. After the pilot, this interruption will be eliminated by also digitizing the back office. For instance, a citizen might receive a link to the personalized certificate electronically only a few moments after requesting for it. The massive number of physical visits is also expected to be significantly reduced.

Based on the promising pilot results, the City will continue investing in the digitization of its services with reusable components in digital chains. Since the approach of using building blocks is not exclusive to e-services, the goal is to reuse the digitization principles in future projects and other business processes. For example, the authentication platform and the digital signature platform could also be used to develop a participation platform or to improve the intranet. The idea is to develop something once and then to reuse it maximally. In other words, e-services can be seen as the first realization of a larger digitization vision in the City. From this perspective, master data serve as a source of information and facilitate reuse of information for other applications.

5 Lessons Learned

Other organizations may benefit from the lessons learned in this case. The most important (and most surprising) lesson from this case is that departments that are accustomed to working in silos can be convinced to work from an organization-wide vision instead as long they understand "why" and the potential benefits. Firms should also work toward their final objective with small steps at a time. In particular, the City's departments are aware of the overall vision because the story of building blocks and digital chains was explained in person using a strong visual representation. Therefore, employees acknowledged the benefits of working with generic components and started thinking along those lines. For instance, the strong organization-wide way of thinking in the pilot of the "environment" chain encouraged employees to reflect on how to digitize the subsidies in other departments as well. What the City would do differently is to start the difficult phases of the projects soon after a new legislature so there is no short deadline for elections and more margin for time-intensive decisions that fit the overall vision.

Overall, there were five main lessons learned.

5.1 Align with External Partners Semantically

The product catalog is aligned semantically with an external business partner in the chain, the Flemish government. This strategic choice created the availability of open data and will eventually lead to a shared catalog for public services. This shared catalog may be a new open-data source for contact information that will allow customers and governments to find an up-to-date catalog of services and serve the customers beyond governmental borders. Currently, linked open data already allows information to be reused in the product catalog.

Other (public or private) organizations may profit from open standards and from using ontologies to increase semantic interoperability and optimize data sharing. For instance, supply chains are only one example beyond the city council context of the need for close collaboration with external partners. In particular, the case emphasized the importance of data dictionaries and a central data front office.

5.2 Be Pragmatic Instead of Dogmatic

The initial idea was to use a single tool to generate all forms, but streamlining documents of simple documents turned out to be difficult. For instance, the procedure became burdensome for an online feedback sheet concerning a simple question like: "Did you find what you searched for?" As a result, the City decided to define different types of documents (e.g., registration forms, evaluation forms, and administration forms), each with a specific procedure. As such, a uniform procedure was established, albeit per document type.

In other words, sometimes taking a more pragmatic and "lean" view on an initial idea can avoid new types of waste. This lesson is applicable to any project, even outside the context of process innovations.

5.3 Assist Departments

Although the principle of "KISS the documents" is useful, the departments lacked experience in BPM and were unable (or uncomfortable) to reconsider their routines. Therefore, they were assisted by Organization and Development, a centralized competence center in administrative simplification. Employees perceived this assistance as positive, resulting in high scores in an employee satisfaction survey.

In sum, one way to overcome resistance is by giving centralized assistance to the departments (e.g., by means of a support office or competence center with experts or internal consultants) in order to undertake the endeavor together. Since change management is key for any innovation project, this lessons is not limited to the context of a city council.

5.4 Be Open to Temporary Workarounds to Achieve Quick Wins

Since the digitization vision in the City requires generic components, the implementation was more complex than merely providing the functionality required for a single chain. For instance, signing documents in Belgium can be realized by means of an electronic identity card (eID), but the City decided to make the component for signing documents more generic by means of a digital signature platform. Since this decision had a tremendous impact on the timing of the pilots, a pragmatic view was taken to release a first version with a more simple eID signature as a temporary workaround.

Thus, the quest for generic components may affect the timing of related IT projects. Although reuse is beneficial in the long run, quick wins (and less resistance) can be achieved by means of a pragmatic approach with temporary workarounds. Workarounds are common practice in many IT projects and are not limited to e-government projects, so they may support change management since early success stories are critical to convincing employees to undertake a new way of thinking.

5.5 Switch from Silos to a Single Profile per Customer

The switch from customer profiles per department to a single profile per customer suits the high expectations of customers. For instance, customers frequently send messages to inform the City about a changed telephone number or e-mail address. With multiple profiles across departments, either the customer remembers to change only one, leaving some departments with incorrect data, or he or she has to repeat the process several times. Another problem solved by single profiles concerns the multiple user names and passwords customers had to remember for multiple services.

Customer expectations can be met more appropriately by means of a single profile. Although this lesson seems especially relevant to multilayered governments, the message of creating a single point of contact for customers is also relevant to private organizations. This final lesson is also closely linked to the idea of a (social) Customer Relationship Management (CRM) system, which is frequently present in private organizations.

References

Dumas, M., La Rosa, M., Mendling, J., & Reijers, H. (2013). *Fundamentals of business process management*. Berlin: Springer.

Lee, J. (2010). 10 year retrospect on stage models of e-Government: A qualitative meta-synthesis. *Government Information Quarterly, 27*(3), 220–230.

Müller, O., Schmiedel, T., Gorbacheva, E., & vom Brocke, J. (2016). Toward a typology of business process management professionals: Identifying patterns of competences through latent semantic analysis. *Enterprise Information Systems, 10*(1), 50–80.

Ohno, T. (1988). *Toyota production system beyong large-sclae production*. New York: Productivity Press.

OMG. (2011). *Business process model and notation (version 2.0)*. Retrieved March, 2016, from http://www.omg.org/spec/BPMN/2.0/PDF/

Rosemann, M., & vom Brocke, J. (2015). The six core elements of business process management. In J. vom Brocke & M. Rosemann (Eds.), *Handbook on business process management. Introduction, methods and information systems* (Vol. 1, 2nd ed., pp. 105–122). Berlin: Springer.

Rosen, M., Lublinsky, B., Smith, K. T., & Balcer, M. J. (2012). *Applied SOA: Service-oriented architecture and design strategies*. Indianapolis: John Wiley Publishing.

Rotthier, S. (2004). e-Government policies, strategies and implementation: e-Government in the federal country Belgium. In R. Traunmüller (Ed.), *Electronic Government, EGOV proceedings* (LNCS 3183, pp. 549–551). Berlin: Springer.

Stad Gent. (2014). *Stuurgroep eDienstverlening 14 okt 2014*. Retreived February, 2016, from https://stad.gent/

Stad Gent. (2016). *Ghent in statistics*. Retrieved March, 2016, from https://visit.gent.be/en/

Sullivan, C. (2016). Digital citizenship and the right to digital identity under international law. *Computer Law and Security Review, 32*(3), 474–481.

Tegarden, D., Dennis, A., & Wixom, B. H. (2013). *Systems analysis and design with UML*. Singapore: John Wiley & Sons.

Van Looy, A., De Backer, M., & Poels, G. (2014). A conceptual framework and classification of capability areas for business process maturity. *Enterprise Information Systems, 8*(2), 188–224.

Van Looy, A., De Backer, M., Poels, G., & Snoeck, M. (2013). Choosing the right business process maturity model. *Information and Management, 50*(7), 466–488.

vom Brocke, J., Zelt, S., & Schmiedel, T. (2016). On the role of context in business process management. *International Journal of Information Management*. doi:10.1016/j.ijinfomgt.2015.10.002.

Womack, J. P., & Jones, D. T. (2003). *Lean thinking. Banish waste and create wealth in your corporation*. London: Simon & Schuster.

Amy Van Looy holds a Ph.D. in applied economics. She is Assistant Professor at the Faculty of Economics and Business Administration of Ghent University (Belgium). Before entering academia, Amy worked as an IT consultant for e-government projects. She is passionate about the adoption and evolution of a process-oriented approach, including organizational capabilities and the impact on culture, people, governance, strategy, and structure, the contextual factors affecting process realizations, and digital innovation. Her research is published in scientific outlets such as Total Quality Management & Business Excellence, Enterprise Information Systems, Information & Management, Business & Information Systems Engineering and Journal for the Association of Information Systems. She obtained the "Highest Award for Achievement" at the Dale Carnegie Consulting Program (2007) and the "Award for Best Contribution" at the OnTheMove Academy (2010). Additionally, Amy was nominated in the top-10 for "Young ICT Lady of the year 2014" by the Belgian magazine DataNews.

Sabine Rotthier holds a Ph.D. in political sciences (2011). After ten years of working in academia (2001–2011), she decided to use her expertise to strengthen the department for organizational development in the City of Ghent. Since then, she has been the senior project leader for eGovernment in the City of Ghent. Additionally, Sabine is a guest professor at the Faculty of Economics and Business Administration of Ghent University (Belgium), where she teaches among others a course on governmental digitization.

Application of the Design Thinking Approach to Process Redesign at an Insurance Company in Brazil

José Ricardo Cereja, Flavia Maria Santoro, Elena Gorbacheva, and Martin Matzner

Abstract

(a) **Situation faced**: During the review of an information system for medical material purchasing at a Brazilian insurance company, it became clear that part of the process supported by this system was done informally and there was no consensus among the employees about some of the related fundamental concepts and procedures.

(b) **Action taken**: A consulting firm hired by the insurance company to find a solution to these challenges proposed to use the Design Thinking approach to process redesign, by aligning the Design Thinking stages with the phases of the Business Process Management (BPM) lifecycle. A series of workshops that applied various Design Thinking tools was conducted with representatives from all of the company's departments that deal with the purchasing process, as well as a team of information technology (IT) professionals.

(c) **Results achieved**: The Design Thinking approach facilitated the following outcomes: (1) formalization of the employees' perceptions regarding the existing purchasing process, (2) design of a *to-be process* for material purchasing, which was approved by all stakeholders, and (3) formalization of requirements for the new information system for managing the material-purchasing process.

J.R. Cereja • F.M. Santoro (✉)
Federal University of the State of Rio de Janeiro (UNIRIO), Rio de Janeiro, Brazil
e-mail: ricardo.cereja@uniriotec.br; flavia.santoro@uniriotec.br

E. Gorbacheva • M. Matzner
University of Muenster, European Research Center for Information Systems (ERCIS), Münster, Germany
e-mail: elena.gorbacheva@ercis.uni-muenster.de; martin.matzner@ercis.uni-muenster.de

J. vom Brocke, J. Mendling (eds.), *Business Process Management Cases*, Management for Professionals, DOI 10.1007/978-3-319-58307-5_12

(d) **Lessons learned**: The case demonstrated the value of applying the Design Thinking approach to process redesign and improvement, adding useful instruments for BPM analysis. The BPM lifecycle phases correspond well with the Design Thinking stages, and Design Thinking techniques match BPM's social-construction viewpoint well.

1 Introduction

The insurance market in Brazil is dominated by a few large companies that operate in various segments and offer insurance services ranging from protection of property and assets to securing events (e.g., funerals) and covering health issues. In an insurance company, each of these segments functions as an individual business or division with its own budget, rules, and value chain, so business processes can differ substantially from division to division. Each of the divisions has its own information system to support its routines related to services (e.g., hospital services, cargo transportation) and products (e.g., cars, computers).

The company described in this case study ("the Insurer" hereafter) is the largest independent insurance company in Brazil. Founded more than 100 years ago, the Insurer currently employs more than 5000 people. In 2014, the company generated R$16.9 billion of revenue (around US$4.2 billion), obtaining a profit of R$548.7 million (US$138 million) and serving about seven million customers.

The health insurance market in Brazil has seen significant changes recently, especially in the process of purchasing raw materials for medical treatments. In responding to these changes, the Insurer reviewed its health insurance information system (a proprietary system developed internally called "Sourcing Saúde") to determine whether it (1) could support great demand from hospitals quickly and adequately, and (2) could help to control the entire purchasing process, from purchase authorization, to acquisition, delivery, and payment to suppliers.

When the Insurer reviewed the features of its health insurance information system, it was clear that part of the material-purchasing process was done informally instead of being implemented through the system. Moreover, there was no consensus among the stakeholders about some of the process's fundamental concepts and procedures that the system must support. These challenges occurred partially because of the absence of a common understanding of which materials did not require authorization—the "Authorization Not Required" (ANR) materials—and the process for purchasing such materials. Therefore, the Insurer employed ADDTECH (http://www.addtech.com.br/en/), a business consultancy that specializes in the areas of business, management, and technology. ADDTECH suggested using Design Thinking techniques to collect requirements for the new information system's features and designing a new process model for material purchasing. This chapter reports on the actions taken and the results achieved.

The chapter is divided into five sections. The initial situation faced by the Insurer is described in Sect. 2. The action taken and the details of the Design Thinking approach application are detailed in Sect. 3. The results achieved in the series of

Design Thinking workshops are discussed in Sect. 4. Finally, lessons learned are presented in Sect. 5.

2 Situation Faced

The insurance market for health services in Brazil is facing many changes. Earlier, the material procurement procedure was implemented when the request for material was created by a doctor, who then forwarded it to a brokerage company, which executed the material purchase and delivery. Each request was marked as either regular for periodic treatments or immediate in case of emergency. An application for authorization of the purchase was sent to an insurance company, and after analyzing required quantities and material prices, the company authorized (or not) the clinical procedure and payment of related expenses.

However, this process allowed issues that insurance companies wanted to avoid. In particular, doctors and hospitals often received commissions from producers of medical equipment and pharmaceutical companies for giving preference (often unjustified) to their products, which resulted in more expensive and, even worse, suboptimal treatment. Insurance companies' decision to take control of this procurement process launched significant changes onto the market. As a result, hospitals are now obligated to send the material requests directly to insurance companies, who are responsible for quotation, selection, approval, and delivery of materials, significantly reducing costs. In addition to initial resistance from doctors and hospitals, who no longer had the decision power on purchasing, the insurance companies, had to create new, robust structures for the purchasing process and develop appropriate information systems to manage and control this process.

Because the Insurer had to restructure its purchasing process, it acquired a new information system for research, quoting, and selection of the most appropriate material. However, the existing internal purchasing process came into conflict with the new system, so the Insurer tried to create a "supra-system" (as part of the internally created "Sourcing Saúde" system) to control the information system and perform operations related to materials analysis, approval, purchase, and payment. However, the initiative was again not entirely successful. The Insurer used the term "supra-system" to reflect that it was a superior information system that incorporated the previous one. However, there was a huge overlap of information stored in the two systems' databases because they belonged to different vendors (Orizon http://www.orizonbrasil.com.br/ and GSMi http://www.gsmi.med.br/) and were not integrated. In other words, there were two information systems in operation, automating two different parts of the same process.

The root problem, though, was that some items that doctors and hospitals requested that were classified as "basic" for certain procedures were released immediately for purchase without being registered in the information system. The entry of these ANR materials was not considered a priority because of the ease of evaluation and approval. However, over time, four major problems emerged:

- ANR materials did not have a standard definition, so deciding a material was an ANR material was subject to the individual interpretation of the professional in charge.
- The share of ANR items increased to 40% of all ordered materials, but because they were not considered relevant to be registered, they were ignored during the development of the "supra-system."
- ANR materials were purchased outside the information system using a manual process and using phone and email for communication and decision-making.
- The number of frauds involving ANR materials increased.

Therefore, the Insurer assigned to its information technology (IT) team the task of collecting the requirements necessary for the development of an updated, improved, unified information system that could fulfill two primary objectives:

- Make the material purchase process efficient and consistent, excluding the intermediate information system.
- Include management of ANR materials in the information system in order to eliminate manual and uncontrolled actions.

The IT team first used traditional procedures, such as meetings and interviews, to elicit the information necessary to meet these objectives. More than 100 meetings were held over nine months with representatives of all departments involved in the purchasing process (e.g., the departments responsible for material analysis, authorization, and payment). These meetings failed to result in a satisfactory outcome, because people could not communicate their problems and needs in a clear and effective way. Therefore, the Insurer decided to hire the ADDTECH consultancy to help in gathering requirements for the development of information system functionality, encompassing the needs of all departments involved in the purchasing process.

ADDTECH proposed using the Design Thinking approach (Meinel and Leifer 2011) to address the problem. To make participants active in designing the desired purchasing process, a series of workshops were held. At that time, the ADDTECH team incorrectly assumed that the issues related to the definition of ANR materials and their incorporation into the purchasing process had already been resolved internally.

3 Action Taken

ADDTECH proposed applying the Design Thinking approach to gather requirements for the information system that would manage the redesigned purchasing process of materials, particularly ANR materials (Meinel and Leifer 2011; Fig. 1). Design Thinking focuses on finding creative and innovative responses to specific demands (e.g., Brown and Rowe 2008); in this case, it was used to improve the purchasing process through process discovery, analysis, and redesign. The

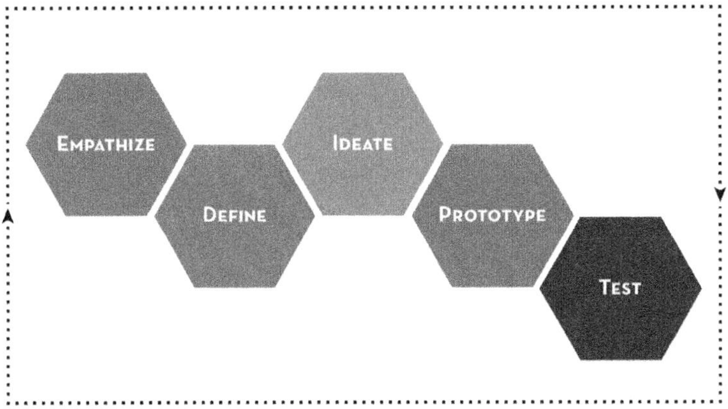

Fig. 1 Design thinking stages (Source: Stanford Design School, http://dschool.stanford.edu/; Brown and Rowe 2008)

Design Thinking approach was followed in several phases of the Business Process Management (BPM) lifecycle (Dumas et al. 2013).

The Design Thinking approach, which brings together a set of practices to address challenges and develop projects or even new businesses, has been characterized as encouraging innovative thinking and leading to an accumulation of distinct ideas about an issue (Brown and Rowe 2008). Collaboration is essential in this process, where members of a multidisciplinary team are stimulated to open their minds to insights and to provide input about their perceptions of the problem and possible solutions. According to Brown and Rowe (2008), the Design Thinking approach can comprise five iterative stages: *empathize*, *define*, *ideate*, *prototype*, and *test* (Fig. 1). The *empathize* stage seeks understanding about the target audience (end users, customers, or clients) for the action. The *define* stage focuses on identification of root causes of a problem to be addressed. Solutions to the problem are developed in the *ideate* stage. The selected solution is then implemented in the *prototype* stage and, finally, assessed in the *test* stage. However, the Design Thinking stages are not linear, but iterative and dynamic, which supports creativity and innovation (Brown and Katz 2011; Dorst 2011; Liedtka 2015; Lydon and Garcia 2015; Rowe 1987; Simon 1969).

The Design Thinking stages can be mapped onto the five phases of the BPM lifecycle suggested by Dumas et al. (2013): The *empathize* stage is related to process discovery, the *define* stage to process analysis, the *ideate* stage to process redesign, the *prototype* stage to process implementation, and the *test* stage to process monitoring and controlling. Figure 2 visualizes and Table 1 describes the mapping of the Design Thinking stages to the BPM lifecycle phases.

The ADDTECH consultancy proposed forming three multidisciplinary working groups (WGs) of members of each of the eight areas that deal with the Insurer's purchasing process. In addition, a project team (PT) of eight members of the IT

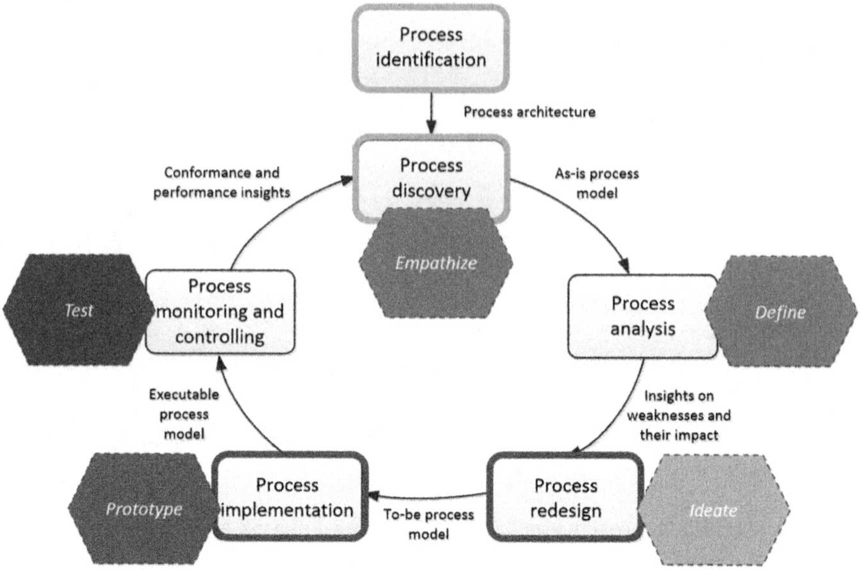

Fig. 2 Correspondence of the design thinking stages (Brown and Rowe 2008) to the BPM lifecycle phases (Dumas et al. 2013)

Table 1 Comparison of the design thinking stages (Brown and Rowe 2008) with the BPM lifecycle phases (Dumas et al. 2013)

Design thinking stage	BPM lifecycle phase	Comparison
Empathize	Process discovery	The *empathize* stage stimulates the discovery of contextual elements that might clarify a process
Define	Process analysis	The *define* stage provides the problem analysis that supports the design of an *as-is* process model
Ideate	Process redesign	The *ideate* stage supports finding creative and implementable solutions to be reflected in the *to-be* process
Prototype	Process implementation	The *prototype* stage comprises execution of the *to-be* process
Test	Process monitoring and controlling	The *test* stage keeps the solution running, acquiring insights into how it could be improved

department responsible for the improvement of existing information system was organized. As a result, the project involved four groups and thirty-two people. Each group participated in a series of Design Thinking workshops (the Sessions) in September 2015. Table 2 summarizes who participated in each workshop and how many meetings took place.

Table 2 Summary of workshops conducted and participants

Workshop	Participants	Number of meetings
Kick-off	All participants	1 meeting
Immersion	PT	3 meetings and 1 visit to the organization
	WG representatives	1 meeting
	WGs	3 meetings (1 for each WG)
Material definition	WG representatives	1 meeting
Process design	WG representatives	2 meetings
Business model	PT and WG representatives	1 meeting
Stories and requirements	WGs	1 meeting with 3 WGs simultaneously
Prioritization	PT and WG representatives	2 meetings
Functionality refinement	All participants	2 meetings
Development planning	All participants	1 meeting

Figure 3 presents the workshops that took place in each Design Thinking stage and the tools applied at each workshop. These tools were inspired by Osterwalder's studies (e.g., Osterwalder and Pigneur 2010), which proposed, among other tools, the Business Model Canvas (Fig. 10), a visual chart template divided into blocks that supports the development of new or documents existing business models. Its elements usually describe a company's or a product's value proposition, infrastructure, customers, and finances. Based on practical needs, ADDTECH extended the Business Model Canvas for a variety of purposes. The canvasses used in this case study, presented and described in Appendix 1 (Figs. 7, 8, 9, 10, 11, 12 and 13), were used to extract and organize the participants' thoughts, leading to the solution development.

Nine collaborative Sessions took place and all followed a similar structure. First, the Session facilitator, an ADDTECH representative, created empathy among the participants by clarifying what results the Session was intended to achieved and using what tools. The main idea and goal of each canvas was explained and the tasks to be performed were clarified. For each task, a strictly defined period of time was set and controlled by the facilitator, an approach called timeboxing. The goal of timeboxing is to speed the work and encourage the participants' cognitive processes. Then the facilitator described the brainswarming technique, which elicits ideas about ways to achieve a goal or address a problem, taking into consideration the available company resources. Members freely expressed their thoughts by writing them on sticky notes, which were then placed on part of a canvas. Next, the facilitator guided the participants in selecting, organizing, and synthesizing the ideas placed on the canvas. The solution that came up was adjusted until a consensus among all Session participants was achieved. Additional information about the workshops conducted and the tools applied is provided in Appendix 1.

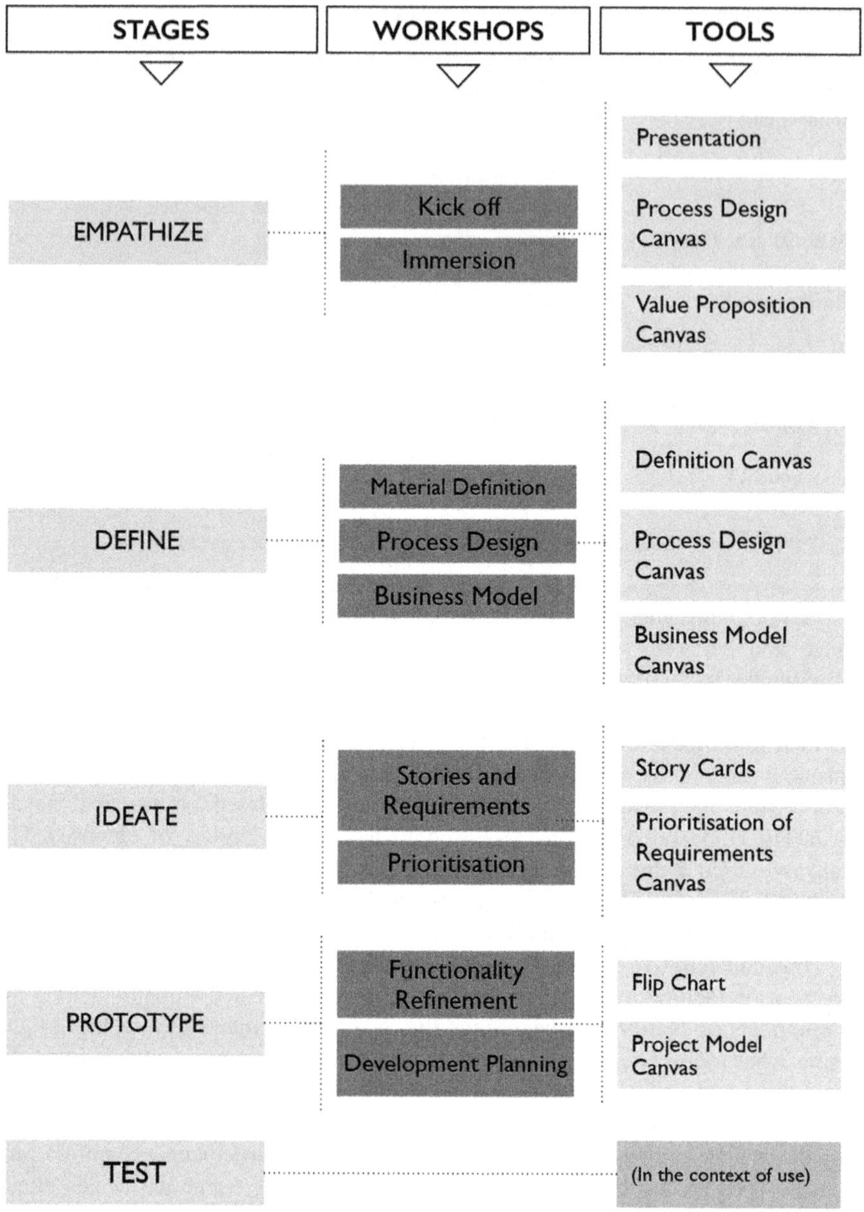

Fig. 3 Workshops and tools applied at each design thinking stage

3.1 Action Taken During the *Empathize* Stage

The actions performed during the *empathize* stage correspond to the BPM lifecycle's process discovery phase. According to Dumas et al. (2013), it is necessary first to understand how a business process operates in order to represent it in a model properly. Therefore, multiple stakeholders with differing but complementary skills might collaborate on this task, which typically involves communication and information-gathering.

In this case, the *empathize* stage was intended to establish a consensus on the issue the Sessions were to address. It was important to understand not only the wishes and needs of the *clients* (members of the three WGs), but also issues other than those presented a priori. In order to clarify the problem, the *immersion* workshop was conducted after the *kick-off* workshop. (See sub-section "Workshops Conducted and Tools Applied During the *Empathize* Stage" in Appendix 1 for additional details.)

3.2 Action Taken During the *Define* Stage

The actions performed during the *define* stage correspond to the BPM lifecycle's process analysis phase. According to Dumas et al. (2013), the identification and assessment of the opportunities for process improvement take place during the process analysis phase. In the *define* stage the information acquired in the *empathize* stage is analyzed and synthesized, and the participants generate insights and patterns that help to define the problem context.

At the beginning of the *define* stage, the groups agreed that the purchasing process of ANR materials (the ANR process) was critical enough to be incorporated into the purchasing information system. Since this process was not contemplated in the as-is process model designed during the previous stage (Fig. 4), the Session schedule was adjusted to include the activities related to the ANR process design and its incorporation into the purchasing process, supported by the information system. As a result, three workshops were performed during the *define* stage: the material definition workshop, the (desired) process design workshop, and the business model workshop (Fig. 3). (See sub-section "Workshops Conducted and Tools Applied During the *Define* Stage" in Appendix 1 for additional details.)

3.3 Action Taken During the *Ideate* Stage

The actions performed during the *ideate* stage correspond to the BPM lifecycle's process redesign phase, which is typically informed by the ideas and directions elicited during the process analysis phase. Process redesign is not always conducted in a systematic way but is instead a creative activity (Dumas et al. 2013). Similarly, the *ideate* stage is the most creative stage of the Design Thinking process.

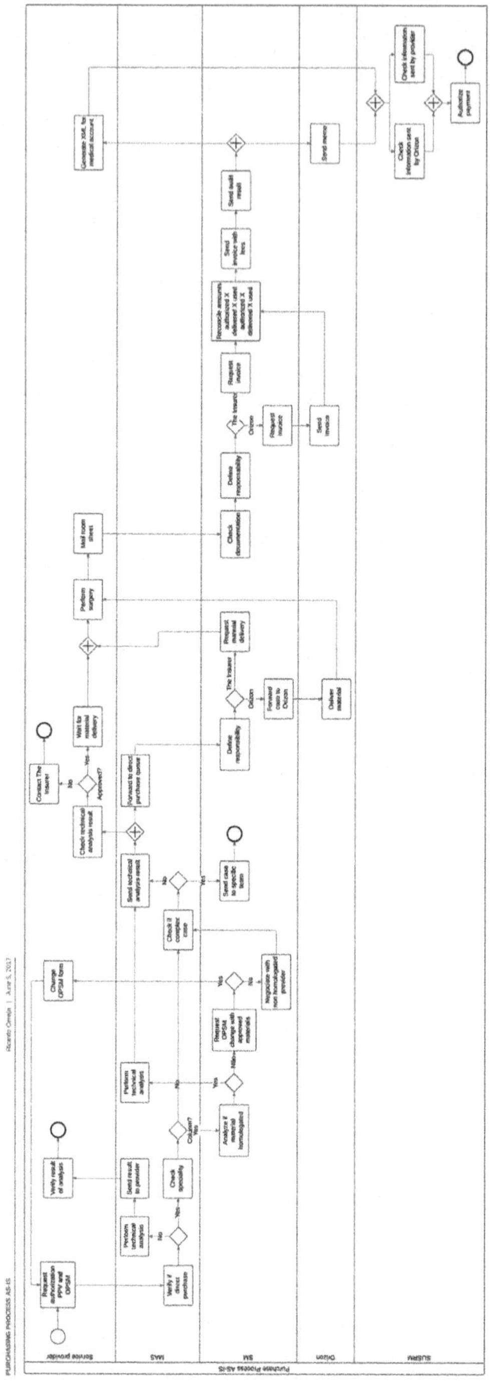

Fig. 4 "*As-is*" purchasing process

After the collection, organization, analysis, and synthesis of all relevant information, as well as the immersion into the context and root causes of existing issues, creative solutions that address the clients' needs and desires emerge. The Stories and Requirements workshop and the Prioritization workshop were conducted during this stage. (See sub-section "Workshops Conducted and Tools Applied During the *Ideate* Stage" in Appendix 1 for additional details.)

3.4 Action Taken During the *Prototype* Stage

The actions performed during the *prototype* stage correspond to the BPM Lifecycle's process implementation phase. According to Dumas et al. (2013), the process implementation phase comprises the execution of the to-be process by bringing into practice the necessary changes in how the work is done (organizational change management) and in the IT systems (process automation).

During the *prototype* stage, WG representatives validated and brought into force the outcomes of the previous Sessions. Together with the PT, during the Functionality Refinement workshop and the Development Planning workshop they discussed the final list of the features (with priorities) to be implemented by the information system. (See sub-section "Workshops Conducted and Tools Applied During the *Prototype* Stage" in Appendix 1 for additional details.)

3.5 Action Taken During the *Test* Stage

The actions currently being performed during the *test* stage correspond to the BPM Lifecycle's process monitoring and controlling phase. This stage closes the "cycle" and serves as a basis for the new loop of Design Thinking. Once the implementation is completed, continuous monitoring and controlling of the process execution is required in order to determine whether any adjustments are needed (Dumas et al. 2013).

In the Insurer's case, the *test* stage is still underway. Many of the main features have been implemented and validated, but comprehensive results of implementing and monitoring the redesigned purchasing process are yet to be reported.

4 Results Achieved

This section summarizes the outcomes of the workshops that were related to each Design Thinking stage (*empathize*, *define*, *ideate*, and *prototype*), as well as those of the overall case.

4.1 Outcomes of Applying the Design Thinking Approach

In the *empathize* stage, applying the Process Design Canvas (Fig. 7) resulted in the as-is process model of the existing purchasing process (Fig. 4). Table 3 in Appendix 2 lists the acronyms used in the model. As a next step toward the to-be process, the Value Proposition Canvas (Fig. 8) generated 133 requirements to be met by the new information system.

During the *define* stage, the Definition Canvas (Fig. 9) was used to facilitate the inclusion of the participants' perceptions and opinions about ANR materials, resulting in a common definition: "ANR is a specific concept for materials that facilitates the provision of the services that streamline the authorization process." Then a task force was assigned to identify all the materials covered by this definition in order to add them to a single ANR database.

Members of WGs could then formulate the desired purchasing process's characteristics by again using the Process Design Canvas (Fig. 7). As a result, the to-be purchasing process (Fig. 5) and the sub-process for procurement of ANR materials (Fig. 6) could be modelled. The to-be process improved the as-is process in three primary ways: It included the formalized model of the process flow for procurement of ANR materials, the process was optimized by identifying and eliminating unnecessary activities, and the to-be process anticipated the automation of parts of its flow, which ensured the new workflow's quality and security.

Finally, in order to determine the value of the information system to its users, future users, and the company as a whole, value propositions (requirements), direct customers, aspects of user support service, key activities and features, and key partners were formalized using the Business model Canvas (Fig. 10).

During the *ideate* stage, the requirements and associated features to be implemented in the information system were further structured and prioritized. With the help of the Story Cards tool (Fig. 11), the initial set of 133 requirements that was revealed during the *empathize* stage was reduced to 43 key requirements. Table 4 in Appendix 2 presents the final list of requirements. In order to decide what requirements should be implemented, the related features were ranked using the Prioritization of Requirements Canvas (Fig. 12). The ranking was done based on the value a feature brought to the overall improvement of the information system, as well as the levels of difficulty and effort required for its implementation.

In the *prototype* stage, the PT discussed the features to be implemented with the representatives of the working teams. As a result, all participants had a shared understanding of the system's desired functionality. The PT then used the Project Model Canvas (Fig. 13) to visualize the elements required to manage the software implementation project. Finally, the prototypes of the new features that corresponded to the to-be process were developed.

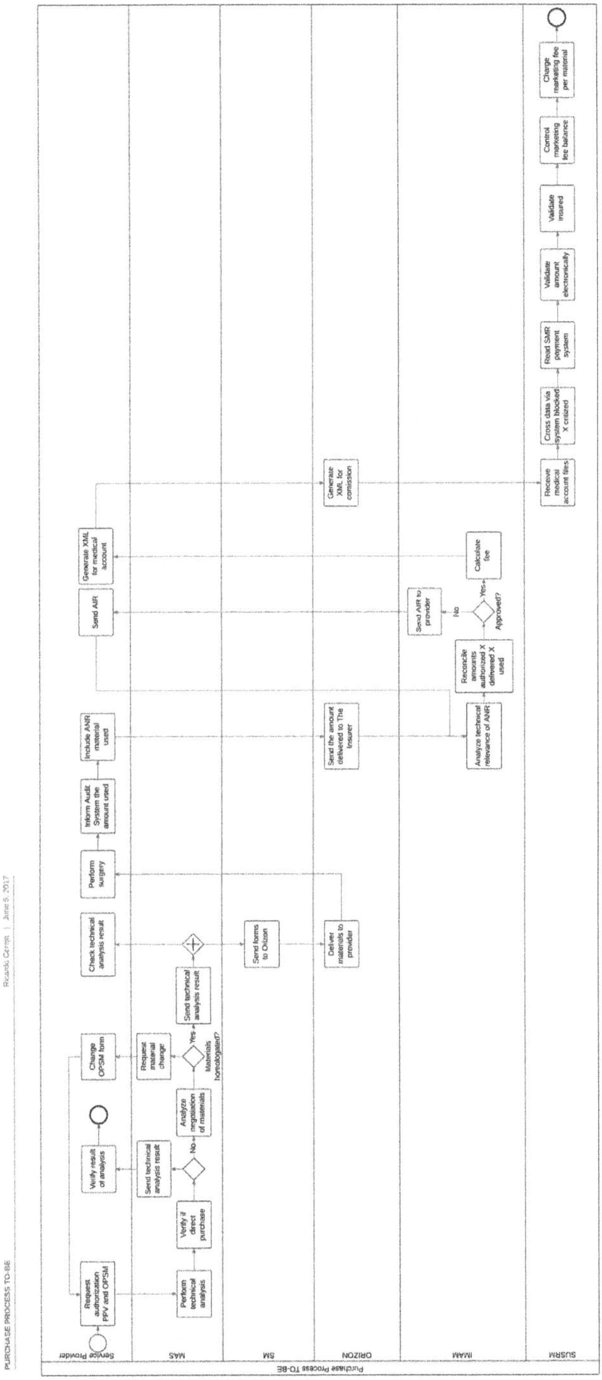

Fig. 5 *"To-be"* purchasing process

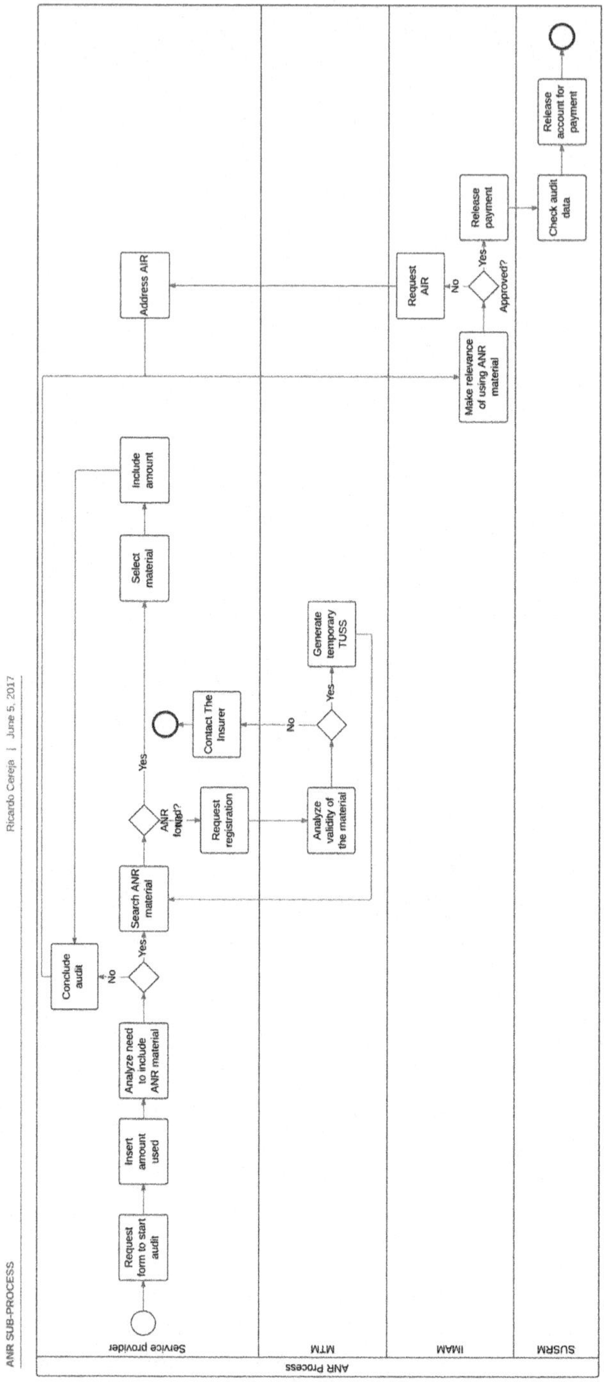

Fig. 6 Process flow for procurement of ANR materials

4.2 Contributions of Applying the Design Thinking Approach

The results achieved during the Sessions addressed the gaps between existing and desired features of the information system in managing the purchasing process and sub-processes. In particular, during one of the first workshops, the absence of a common understanding of what materials should be classified as ANR materials was revealed. Therefore, reaching a common definition of such materials and streamlining the related sub-process for their procurement was accomplished during the Sessions.

The Design Thinking approach that the Sessions followed facilitated the attainment of a considerable amount of useful information for the company. The two major outcomes were formalizing the clients' perceptions regarding the existing purchasing process and the designed to-be process, which was simpler and more objective than the as-is process and included significantly fewer steps to be performed.

The Sessions were initiated after unsuccessful attempts to collect requirements for the improved information system. After more than 100 meetings conducted over more than nine months, neither a definition of ANR materials nor sub-processes for their procurement was specified. The Design Thinking approach made accomplishing this task within a single working day (8 h) possible. The approach supported simultaneous and non-linear actions throughout the Sessions. Analyzing at each step the previous step's resulting information allowed the outcomes of previous steps to be validated and reworked where necessary. Consequently, a robust, co-created solution could be developed with a high chance of successful implementation and adoption.

The requirements and desired features of the new information system that resulted from the Sessions were organized and delivered in a feature-specification document that reflected the wishes and needs of the clients from all of the departments involved in the purchasing process. The clients' recognition of the improvements in the purchasing process is an important result of the Sessions.

The redesigned purchasing process is still being implemented so, although we can report the desired approach's preliminary success by referring to the attained results, we cannot yet draw conclusions on the overall project's outcomes and success. The consulting team from ADDTEC is still following the case and keeping in contact with the IT team that is performing the process implementation. Once the overall project is completed, we will analyze the information system's operation and the employees' reaction to and feedback about using the new procurement process. We will report on the results of this analysis in a future publication.

5 Lessons Learned

This chapter discussed a real-world BPM case of a Brazilian insurance company, the Insurer, which applied the Design Thinking approach to redesign its medical material-purchasing process and derive requirements for further development of its related enterprise information systems. This case provides organizations with general insights on how to apply Design Thinking to process redesign. Based on the lessons learned from the practical application of the innovative Design Thinking techniques, we can report on three important observations that reflect the overall case:

1. Design Thinking added useful instruments to BPM analysts' tool set, as the case demonstrated the successful application of Design Thinking for process redesign and improvement. The BPM lifecycle phases correspond well with the stages of Design Thinking. Details of the Design Thinking techniques applied in the case are summarized in Appendix 1.

   The initial series of conventional workshops, which required tremendous effort by the Insurer, were unsuccessful in achieving the required change of processes and systems, so the company requested the assistance of the ADDTECH consultancy. The consultants faced a tricky situation, but their novel techniques opened up the company's perspective and allowed it to create innovative and unconventional solutions. While the traditional workshops failed, the Design-Thinking-fueled workshops made a difference and achieved the desired goal.

   A possible cause for the success of Design Thinking techniques is that they are geared toward achieving a consensus in multidisciplinary groups that have been tasked with finding a solution to a design problem. The techniques encourage and facilitate the group members' joint and interactive acquisition of knowledge about the design problem by establishing the feeling that the group can collectively construct a solution.

   These characteristics of Design Thinking techniques match the social-construction viewpoint of BPM, where the design of business processes is understood as a social process that connects actors who jointly envision potential process designs and then negotiate the roles and responsibilities for each sub-process and activity (Smeds and Alvesalo 2003). Such a social-construction perspective requires the people involved to co-operate "despite possible conflicting interests, dispersed knowledge, [and] differing management strategies" (Becker et al. 2013, p. 41). Design Thinking techniques provide ways to promote co-operation, so a particularly promising phenomenon to be investigated in future research is the question concerning why Design Thinking techniques could address two design goals at the same time: finding a novel solution and achieving agreement through the group.
2. The case described here is likely to render a methodological contribution to the Design Thinking approach. Contrary to the common procedure, ADDTECH consultants implemented a "pre-immersion" stage at the project outset, preceding the Design Thinking *empathy* stage. It is likely that this decision was central to the project's success. This stage was created with the intention to extract the domain knowledge that was required to validate the requirements regarding the project's scope and process up front. Thus, the time spent in the later *empathy*

stage was significantly reduced, as that the project work was grounded in maximum objectivity and focus had been assured.

This additional "pre-immersion" stage included activities of three types. First, the consultants performed additional work that focused on clarifying the Insurer's needs and motivation in undertaking the process. Second, they put in place instruments to organize the project's processes and stages. Third, they organized the physical space for the process innovation and design project. A meeting room was exclusively reserved for the interviews and workshops, where the materials produced by the groups were constantly available to be accessed by the participants. The "pre-immersion" stage consisted of conducting interviews and required the physical presence of the facilitator during collaborative workshops. The facilitator socialized with the representatives of all the departments and IT professionals involved in the project and acquired the required information by asking questions in order to understand the operation of the existing information system. While implementation of the "pre-immersion" stage was useful in the reported case, the specific circumstances under which the application of this stage is beneficial and the contribution of this stage to the project success call for a detailed investigation in the future.

3. A final observation relates to the flexibility of Design Thinking techniques in making adjustments to their procedure. The case included examples of such modifications after the *empathize* stage, when the understanding, validation, and development of solutions were executed repeatedly until the users' needs were met to a sufficient degree.

Appendix 1

Workshops Conducted and Tools Applied During the *Empathize* Stage

Workshops Conducted During the *Empathize* Stage

Kick-off Workshop

During the kick-off workshop, a facilitator from ADDTECH clarified all aspects of the planned Sessions to the members of all four groups involved. The facilitator presented and discussed the work proposal, reached a consensus about the activities to be performed, and emphasized that participation and engagement in the Sessions was vital for their success. All participants then collaboratively defined the procedures and rules during the Sessions, and the facilitator answered the participants' questions.

Some participants (mostly supervisors and managers) tried to divert the workshop focus to activities with which they were more familiar. As a result, the facilitator had to stop the workshop occasionally to explain again the stages of work and improve cooperation among the participants.

Immersion Workshop

The purpose of the *immersion* workshop was to clarify the problem and its characteristics from the client perspective. Resulting customer requirements could then guide the development of the services to be offered by the information system. During this workshop, it became clear that the WGs had no common understanding of ANR materials, as the participants disagreed on what should and should not be considered ANR materials and how such materials could be registered in the information system. ADDTECH also saw that the existing information system had been developed without a comprehensive understanding of the processes it was intended to support, so it was necessary to review the planned Sessions and work steps to address both the definition and the procurement process for ANR materials.

Tools Applied During the *Empathize* Stage

Process Design Canvas

The goal of the Process Design Canvas (Fig. 7) was to compare the existing information system's features with those the users (clients) wanted. In order to understand the existing process (the as-is process), representatives of each WG described (a) the course of the process, (b) results of the process, (c) resources required to perform the process, and (d) existing obstacles to performing the process. Figure 4 depicts the resulting as-is process model.

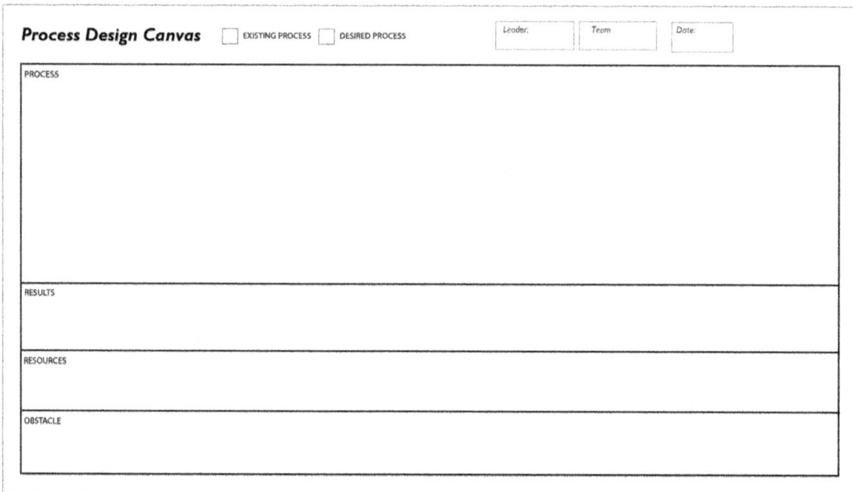

Fig. 7 Process design canvas (designed by José Ricardo Cereja)

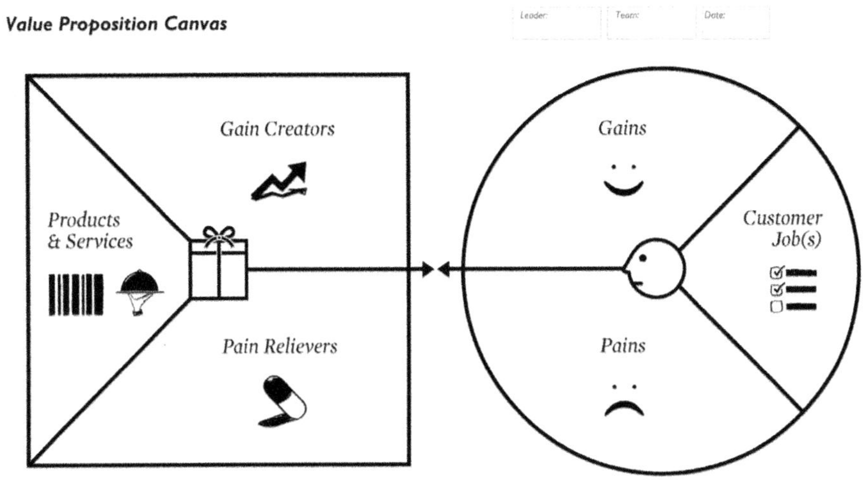

Fig. 8 Value proposition canvas (Osterwalder and Pigneur 2010)

Value Proposition Canvas

The goal of the Value Proposition Canvas (Fig. 8) was to set the path from the as-is process to the to-be process by following the concept that each product or service must deliver value to the customer/user. Members of all WGs participated in the canvas development. First, each participant described (a) current "pains" (difficulties) related to the use of the procurement system and (b) the "gains" they would obtain (or expect to obtain) if the system works optimally. Then the participants described (a) what products or services correspond to customer/user activities specified, (b) what "pain relievers" could address the existing difficulties, and (c) what "gain creators" could support achieving the potential gains specified.

In the next step, the participants used the same procedure to select, cluster, and synthesize the information from all Value Proposition Canvasses. These syntheses were then compared, generating 133 requirements for the desired information system that reflected the users' needs and expectations (called "value propositions"). Information about these value propositions formed part of the Business Model Canvas built in the next stage.

As a result of the previous step, the participants learned the as-is process, agreed on its authenticity, and recognized the need to review the activities and tasks. They also tried to analyze the process's system use, but no one could explain why the system was built as it was and why it had the identified gaps. The use of Value Proposition Canvas revealed (a) the global quality issues that should be addressed by the system, such as agility, accuracy, and reliability, and (b) the features necessary to implement improvements.

The participants faced problems in understanding how to apply this tool. The Value Proposition Canvas should be filled in the following order: (1) user activities, "pains," and "gains" and (2) what products and services can meet the users' activities, what solutions address the "pains," and what generates the "gains." It was difficult for the participants to distinguish these aspects of the issue, so their responses were analyzed and revised in an iterative way. The confusing responses were clarified and rewritten, and similar responses were grouped.

Workshops Conducted and Tools Applied During the *Define* Stage

Workshops Conducted During the *Define* Stage

Material Definition Workshop

The Material Definition workshop involving WG representatives was not planned initially but was added once ADDTECH realized that there was no shared understanding of ANR materials. These materials had been ordered by email or phone with no prior analysis, authorization or registration in the information system. The aim of the workshop was to reach a consensus among the WGs on the definition of ANR materials.

Process Design Workshop

The goal of the Process Design Workshop involving WG representatives was to design the to-be process, where the information system would be employed to manage the procurement process of all company materials (including ANR materials). Prior to designing the to-be process, participants had reached a common definition of ANR materials and a common understanding of how the procurement process (particularly purchasing of ANR materials) had been performed. The participants could then define the target purchasing process and the features the new information system should have.

Business Model Workshop

The subsequent Business Model workshop involving PT members determined the value that the updated information system was to bring its users, future users, and the company as a whole. Based on this knowledge, the PT could then determine how this value could be delivered in the most efficient way and the associated costs.

Tools Applied During the *Define* Stage

Definition Canvas

The goal of the Definition Canvas (Fig. 9) was to support finding a common definition of ANR materials. For that, WG representatives specified, why ANR materials need to be there. Participants used sticky notes to express their ideas, and then each participant went through and considered all the points made by the whole group and proposed a list of features that might define an ANR material. Finally, WG representatives agreed on a common definition of an ANR material (presented in the Sect. 4).

This work was first attempted through an open discussion in an effort to include individual perspectives, but it was soon apparent that brainswarming was required. The applied Product Definition Canvas gave the participants the opportunity to present their perceptions and understanding about what ANRs are and what they should be.

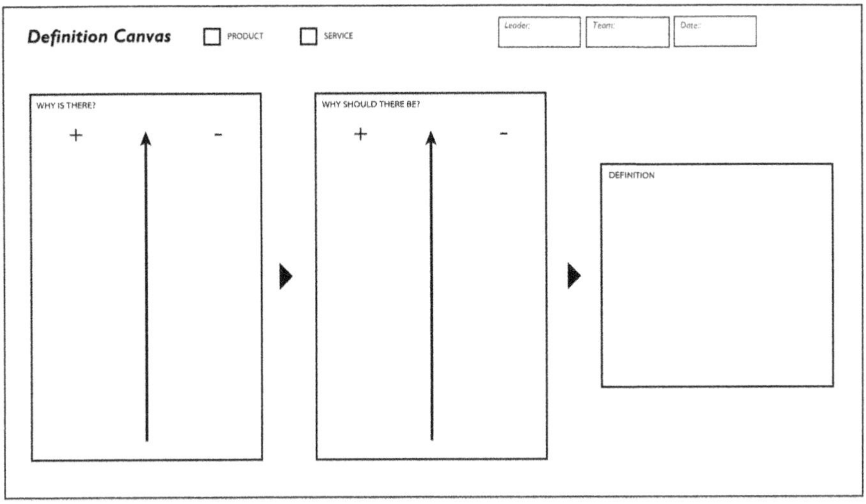

Fig. 9 Definition canvas (designed by the ADDTECH Team)

Process Design Canvas

The goal of the Process Design Canvas (Fig. 7) at this stage was to support the design of the desired material-purchasing process ("to-be process"), with the procurement of ANR materials as one of its sub-processes. Application of the Process Design Canvas followed the same steps as were followed during the *empathize* stage for the as-is process model design. The resulting to-be process and the ANR sub-process are presented in Figs. 5 and 6, respectively.

Business Model Canvas

The goal of the Business Model Canvas (Fig. 10) was to formalize (a) the requirements of the information system, derived from the resulting Value Proposition Canvas developed during the Immersion sessions, (b) the customers who receive direct benefits from using the information system, (c) how user support should be organized, (d) the information system's key activities and the key features required, and (e) partners who would be key to ensuring the system worked properly.

Workshops Conducted and Tools Applied During the *Ideate* Stage

Workshops Conducted During the *Ideate* Stage

Stories and Requirements Workshop

During this workshop, the participants of all three WGs gathered to describe as stories each of 133 requirements that they generated through the Value Proposition Canvas during the *empathize* stage. Each story focused on describing a service that

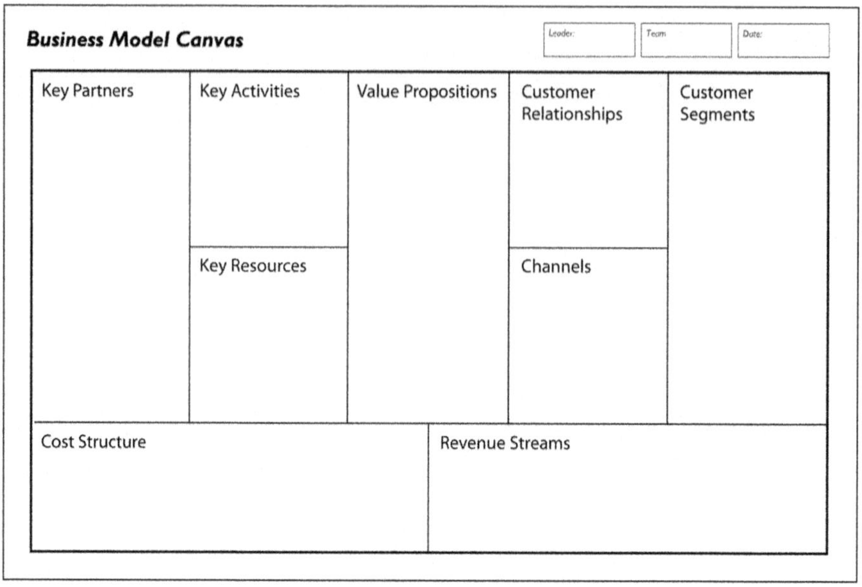

Fig. 10 Business model canvas (Osterwalder and Pigneur 2010)

fulfilled a client need or desire. As a result, duplicate or similar requirements were identified and merged, and the requirements were reviewed and rearranged, resulting in 43 requirements that were fundamental to improving the information system.

Prioritization Workshop

During the subsequent Prioritization workshop, the participants of all three WGs met to analyze the 43 final requirements that had been extracted, grouped, and ranked during the Stories and Requirements workshop. The goal was to identify the most important features that should be prototyped and implemented.

Tools Applied During the *Ideate* Stage

Story Cards

The goal of the Story Cards tool (Fig. 11) was to translate the clients' requirements to the features to be implemented in the information system. Each of the three WGs received about a third of the 133 value propositions identified during the *empathize* stage. The task was to describe the service behind each requirement. The interdisciplinary nature of each WG and the opportunity to communicate with the members of the other WGs facilitated the discussion of the nature of each requirement and ensured consideration of diverse opinions. The check for duplicate or similar value propositions reduced their number from 133 to 80. The stories written for the remaining 80 value propositions contained customer identification (department, position), the requirement's level of importance to the customer, and the perceived benefit from incorporating this requirement in the information system. In the next step, the PT analyzed and classified the 80 Story Cards and concluded that, in many cases, one solution could address more than one requirement. As a result, the PT defined 43 features that addressed all 80 requirements.

Participants could describe easily who would benefit from implementation of a certain feature but often faced difficulties in formalizing the motivation for implementing this functionality. Although the initial plan was to write individual stories by each participant, in the course of the workshop the participants organized themselves into groups that interacted with each other. This collaborative process accelerated the stories' construction, which were beneficial in understanding the required system features.

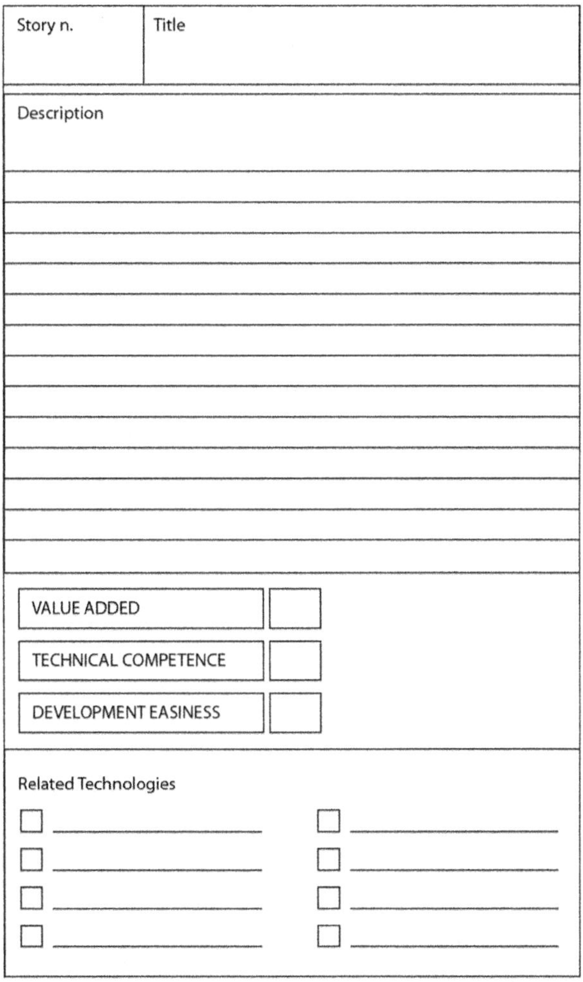

Fig. 11 Story card (designed by the ADDTECH Team)

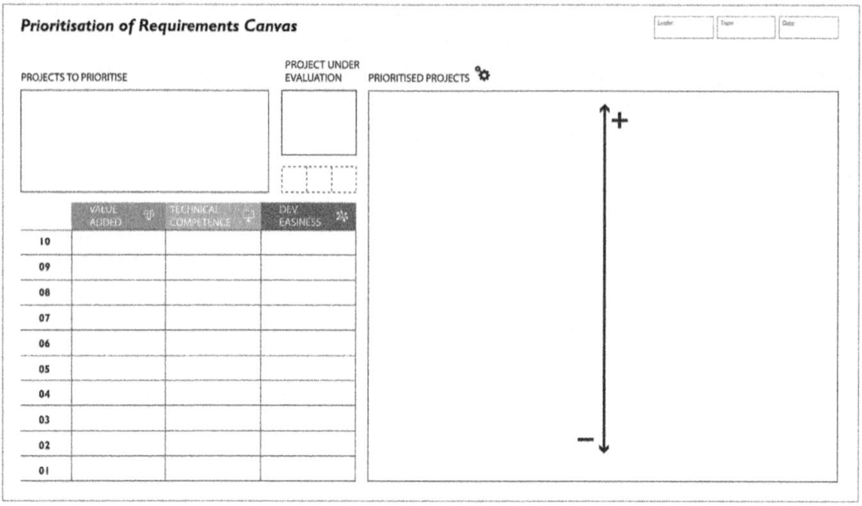

Fig. 12 Prioritization of requirements canvas (designed by the ADDTECH Team)

Prioritization of Requirements Canvas

The goal of the Prioritization of Requirements Canvas (Fig. 12) was to support ranking of the features to be implemented in the information system, based on three criteria:

Added value: the extent to which the functionality a requirement generated improved the overall service the information system delivered.

Technical competence: the level of expertise required from the development team to implement a requirement.

Development easiness: the level of effort (time) required of the development team to implement a requirement.

Workshops Conducted and Tools Applied During the *Prototype* Stage

Workshops Conducted During the *Prototype* Stage

Functionality Requirement Workshop and Development Planning Workshop

Based on the input from the Prioritization Workshop, during the Functionality Refinement workshop WG representatives and the PT jointly categorized each feature's importance as large, average, or small. All participants then discussed and elaborated on the plan for implementing the feature during the Development Planning Workshop.

Tools Applied During the *Prototype* Stage

Flip Chart

The goal of the Flip Chart was to encourage the participants to express their thoughts on detailing, adjusting, and ratifying the features to be developed and implemented.

Project Model Canvas

The goal of the Project Model Canvas (Fig. 13) was to assist the participants in elaborating on the project plan for implementing the improved information system. The participants placed on the canvas the important attributes to be considered when managing any project, including the work to be done, the timeline, and the effort required. The plan was designed following the agile software-development methodology, where the tasks are accomplished in iterations (sprints).

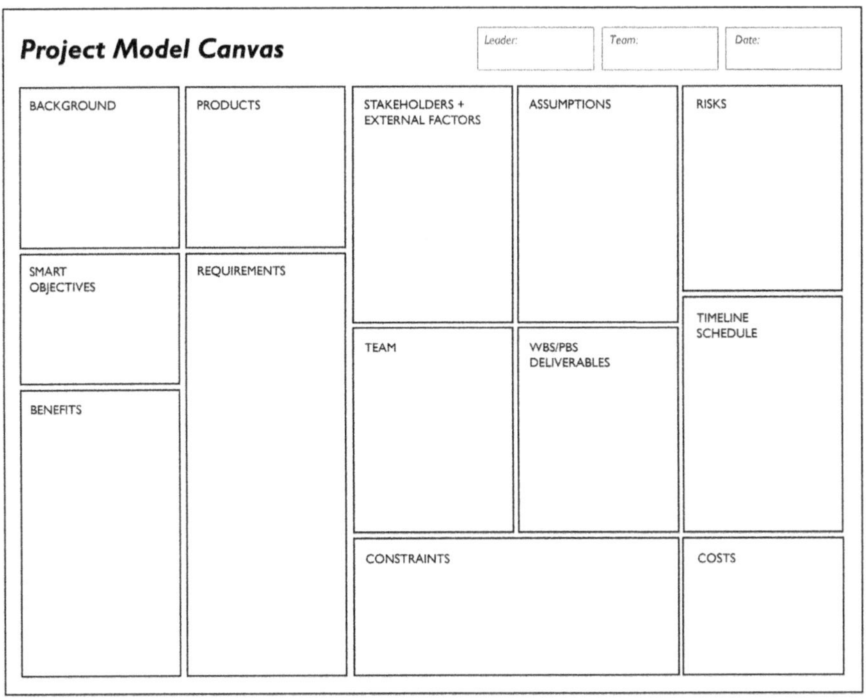

Fig. 13 Project model canvas (Finocchio 2013)

Appendix 2

Table 3 List of abbreviations

PPV: Prior Procedure Verification
SMR: Special Material Request
OPSM: Orthosis, Prosthesis, and Special Material
MTM: Materials Technical Management
SM: Sourcing Management
MMAM: Material and Medicine Analysis Management
IMAM: Internal Medical Audit Management
MAS: Medical Authorization Supervisory
SUSRM: SUS Reimbursement Management
AIR: Additional Information Request
SLA: Service Level Agreement
SHUT: Supplementary Healthcare Unified Terminology
ABC curve: The diagram used to control material types (A is the most valuable material, 20% of the amount; B is intermediate value material, 30% of the amount; and C is less valuable material, 50% of the amount)
ENR: Electronic Note Resource

Table 4 List of final requirements

Register marketing fee
Assign the cases negotiated by analyst
Calculate marketing fee
Register the supplier/negotiate with the suppliers that are not in Orizon
Register reversed prioritized requests
Request ANR materials
Queue requests already negotiated for technical analysis
Monitor based on the analyst case
Cancel SMR
Include ANR materials by provider
Register material
Visualize marketing fee
Register SLA
Check material charged x-audit system
Control values per supplier
Control marketing fee
Receive electronic billing
Reopen PPV
List materials of "direct purchase"
Choose providers of "direct purchase"
Communicate between areas
Visualize unified table with information for electronic validation
Code SHUT

(continued)

Table 4 (continued)

Provide report of material per ABC curve
Audit ANR not registered
Provide reports of inconsistencies between supplier and provider
Alert cases that have not been paid to Orizon
Block sending undocumented attachment
Register previous ANR materials
Calculate costs
Send message of divergence to the provider
Provide management reports
Provide saved values with performance of complex cases
Distribute ANR for analysis
Provide payment statement
Identify direct purchase process
Sort complex cases, CD SAS, CD Orizon
Monitor pending cases
Interface with supplier/audit opinion
Input hospitals with direct purchase right
Communicate with suppliers and providers
Generate complements
Enable disallowance via ENR

References

Becker, J., Beverungen, D., Knackstedt, R., Matzner, M., Müller, O., & Pöppelbuß, J. (2013). Designing interaction routines in service networks. *Scandinavian Journal of Information Systems, 25*(1), 37–68.

Brown, T., & Katz, B. (2011). Change by design. *Journal of Product Innovation Management, 28* (3), 381–383.

Brown, T., & Rowe, P. G. (2008). Design thinking. *Harvard Business Review, 86*(6), 252. doi:10.5437/08956308X5503003.

Dorst, K. (2011). The core of "design thinking"and its application. *Design Studies, 32*(6), 521–532. Retrieved from http://www.sciencedirect.com/science/article/pii/S0142694X11000603

Dumas, M., La Rosa, M., Mendling, J., & Reijers, H. (2013). *Fundamentals of business process management*. Berlin: Springer.

Finocchio, J. Jr. (2013). *Project model canvas: Gerenciamento de Projetos sem Burocracia*. Editora Campus.

Liedtka, J. (2015). Perspective: Linking design thinking with innovation outcomes through cognitive bias reduction. *Journal of Product Innovation Management, 32*(6), 925–938.

Lydon, M., & Garcia, A. (2015). *Tactical urbanism*. Washington, DC: Island Press/Center for Resource Economics.

Meinel, C., & Leifer, L. (2011). *Design thinking research. Design thinking: Understand, improve, apply*. Heidelberg: Springer.

Osterwalder, A., & Pigneur, Y. (2010). Business model generation: A handbook for visionaries, game changers, and challengers. In T. Clark (Ed.), *A handbook for visionaries, game changers, and challengers*. Hoboken: John Wiley and Sons.

Rowe, P. G. (1987). Design thinking. *Havard Business Review*. Retrieved from http://www.icsid.org/smallbox4/file.php?sb4bdef72141c99

Simon, H. (1969). *The sciences of the artificial*. Cambridge, MA, *1*(3rd), 123. Retrieved from http://scholar.google.com/scholar?hl=en&btnG=Search&q=intitle:The+Sciences+of+the+Artificial#0

Smeds, R., & Alvesalo, J. (2003). Global business process development in a virtual community of practice. *Production Planning and Control, 14*(4), 361–371.

José Ricardo Cereja is Professor at Applied Informatics Department in the Federal University of the State of Rio de Janeiro, Brazil. He's got his D.Sc. in Production Engineering from Federal University of Rio de Janeiro (COPPE/UFRJ) and his M.Sc. in Design from Catholic Pontifical University (PUC/Rio). His research has a multidisciplinary approach involving: Innovation, Design Thinking, Business Process Management, Entrepreneurship and Information Technology. He has been collaborating with research projects, consulting and workshops about these subjects along his academic and professional career.

Flavia Maria Santoro is Associate Professor at Applied Informatics Department of the Federal University of the State of Rio de Janeiro, Brazil. She received her Ph.D. and M.Sc. degrees in Computer Science from Federal University of Rio de Janeiro (COPPE-UFRJ). Her research focuses on Information Systems, especially on the following subjects: Business Process Management, Knowledge Management, Computer-Supported Cooperative Work and Computer-Supported Collaborative Learning. She participated in international research projects and has experience in organizing workshops and conferences. She has joint the *Université Pierre et Marie Curie*—Paris VI, France, and the *Queensland University of Technology*, Australia, in sabbatical research projects. Flavia has also worked as advisor on BPM on big organizations in Brazil.

Elena Gorbacheva completed her PhD in 2016 at the University of Muenster (Muenster, Germany). Elena holds BSc and MSc degrees in Business Informatics (both with honours) from the State University—Higher School of Economics (Moscow, Russia) and a MSc degree in Information Systems (IS) from the University of Muenster. In her Ph.D. thesis Elena addressed the existing challenges in the Business Process Management (BPM) workforce, focusing on the BPM competence gap, the under-representation of women in the field, as well as under-theorization and immaturity of gender and BPM research. Her research was published in the *Business and Information Systems Engineering journal, Enterprise Information Systems Journal, Australasian Journal of Information Systems, Communications of the Association for Information Systems*, and several IS conferences. Elena was awarded the Leoni Warne Prize for Outstanding Publication in the Area of Women and IT in 2014 and the AIS (Association of Information Systems) Doctoral Student Service Award in 2015.

Martin Matzner is Professor of Information Systems and the Chair of Digital Industrial Service Systems at Friedrich-Alexander-Universität Erlangen-Nürnberg (FAU Erlangen-Nuremberg), Germany. In 2012, he received a Ph.D. degree in Information Systems from the University of Münster for his work on the management of networked service business processes. His research areas include business process management, business process analytics, as well as service engineering and service management. In these areas, he concluded and currently manages a number of research projects funded by the European Union, by the German Federal Government and by industry. He has published more than 70 research papers and articles, among others in MIS Quarterly and IEEE Transactions on Engineering Management. He is editor of the Journal of Service Management Research.

Collaborative BPM for Business Transformations in Telecommunications: The Case of "3"

Thomas Karle and Kurt Teichenthaler

Abstract

Many business changes in the telecommunications sector are initiated by mergers and acquisitions, and the fast pace of this sector requires that businesses adjust or extend business processes in a minimum of time. "3," the mobile communication brand of CK Hutchison Holdings, whose headquarters are in Hong Kong, is a leading global mobile telecommunications, data services operator, and pioneer of mobile broad-band technology. Therefore, "3" constantly faces the challenges associated with take-overs and mergers. To master these challenges a comprehensive social BPM environment with predefined process structures was developed to master these challenges within given time restrictions. Corresponding process structures support the merging of telecommunication processes during a merger and can be used for collaborative drafting of business processes across organizations. The key task in these projects is to use the knowledge and experience of all parties involved efficiently and in a short amount of time in order to carry out process consolidations or to build comprehensive processes. Therefore, support for collaborative work was implemented on all project phases, from requirements specifications for designing, implementing, and testing the respective software components to launching the new processes and providing training.

T. Karle (✉)
Horus software GmbH, Ettlingen, Germany
e-mail: thomas.karle@horus.biz

K. Teichenthaler
Hutchison Drei Austria GmbH, Wien, Austria
e-mail: kurt.teichenthaler@drei.com

J. vom Brocke, J. Mendling (eds.), *Business Process Management Cases*,
Management for Professionals, DOI 10.1007/978-3-319-58307-5_13

(a) **Situation faced**: Many business changes in the telecommunications sector are initiated by mergers and acquisitions, and the fast pace of this sector requires that businesses adjust or extend business processes in a minimum of time. "3," the mobile communication brand of CK Hutchison Holdings, whose headquarters are in Hong Kong, is a leading global mobile telecommunications company, data services operator, and pioneer of mobile broadband technology. Therefore, "3" constantly faces the challenges associated with take-overs and mergers.

(b) **Action taken**: A comprehensive social BPM environment with predefined process structures was developed to master these challenges within given time restrictions. Corresponding process structures support the merging of telecommunication processes during a merger and can be used for collaborative drafting of business processes across organizations. The key task in these projects is to use the knowledge and experience of all parties involved efficiently and in a short amount of time in order to carry out process consolidations or to build comprehensive processes. Therefore, support for collaborative work was implemented on all project phases, from requirements specifications for designing, implementing, and testing the respective software components to launching the new processes and providing training.

(c) **Results achieved**: A business process repository with predefined process and function documentation was built, and a collaborative BPM environment, embedded self-service training components, and integrated test management system were established to provide the basis for conducting projects during acquisitions, mergers, and other businesses transformations.

(d) **Lessons learned**: Four lessons learned were identified: (a) Successful implementation of BPM in a company requires combining it with other fields of operation, such as testing and training; (b) interconnecting a variety of model types helps to manage the increasing demands regarding speed of change and complexity of both business and IT; (c) embedding BPM in a collaborative environment also supports active knowledge management; and (d) business transformations require that management provides the necessary strategic control.

1 Introduction

"3" is the mobile communication brand of the Asian corporation CK Hutchison Holdings (CK Hutchison), whose headquarters are in Hong Kong. CK Hutchison is a conglomerate with five core businesses—ports and related services, retail, energy, infrastructure, and telecommunications. In 2015 it had a turnover of 36.8 billion euros and 278,000 employees in more than fifty countries. The company's success is founded on a commitment to innovation and leading-edge mobile technology. Because of the brand's commitment to innovation and leading-edge mobile technology, mergers and acquisitions have to be managed in as little time as possible. What's more, changes in business processes, which occur regularly in this fast-paced segment, must be implemented both technically and organizationally on short notice. "3" relies on a global single instance (GSI), which is based on a global ERP instance, to implement its processes in the areas of finance and logistics (Karle and Teichenthaler 2015).

To meet the challenges, "3" wanted to build an extended social BPM environment for the GSI. To build such an environment, the company pursued a strategy for enriching the GSI using a BPM repository, collaboration functions, integration of a test management system, and integration of self-service training components.

The GSI's core are the processes and functions implemented with an ERP standard software (Oracle E-Business Suite). In addition, a BPM repository with all the documentation of the processes implemented was created that contains both organizational processes and technical-detailed processes. In building this repository, the company implemented a process hierarchy based on the organization's processes, with the activities and the respective business roles on the upper levels and the technical, detailed processes and concrete user instructions on the lower levels. A collaboration platform was implemented on top of this BPM repository that allows a joint design of GSI processes both organizationally and technically. The foundation for this collaboration was laid by providing a synchronous interface between the BPM repository and a wiki-environment.

In addition, a test management system was integrated technically through a corresponding interface and methodically with an integrated BPM approach. Thus, the detailed processes in the process hierarchy down to the ERP software user instructions are automatically transferred to the test management system and are tested there, partly automatically and partly manually.

The BPM repository also contains self-service training components for the business users. Here, the micro-processes of the system-handling for each possible business transaction were recorded with an appropriate tool. The components can be used in various training modes and are provided in the BPM portal's process model descriptions.

The extended collaborative BPM environment that was realized provides an adequate base for fast analysis, design, and implementation of the requirements during mergers, acquisitions, and other business transformations in a global context. The detailed process documentation supports comparison of processes between two companies. New global requirements can be evaluated quickly based on available process variants for different countries, and rollouts can be done efficiently based on predefined processes, including documentation, test cases, and self-service training components. Collaboration functions and connections between different model types and artefacts help to manage complexity and knowledge.

2 Situation Faced

2.1 Problem

“3” conducts acquisitions and mergers in Europe, requiring numerous adjustments in processes across organizations because of, for example, changes in partners in the supply chain. These adjustments lead to many business transformations that must be managed. When businesses are merged, the challenges can include consolidating divergent business processes and joining implementations that often have different system components. Whenever processes across organizations are changed, they must be managed well, especially concerning procedures related to technical details, system components, required integration, and organizational business processes. The “3” Group Europe pursues the GSI concept, which requires a centralized ERP system with consolidated business processes for every associated operating company (Karle and Teichenthaler 2015). The concept is shown in Fig. 1. This centralized ERP instance, which is physically located in Vienna, Austria, provides common and country-specific ERP processes and functions that the company uses also in other local operating companies in the “3” Group Europe (Ireland, the United Kingdom, and Italy).

The GSI consists of the standard ERP system Oracle E-Business Suite (EBS) and the so-called Belt Systems. Modules for nine areas are used within the scope of the standard ERP system (Karle and Teichenthaler 2015):

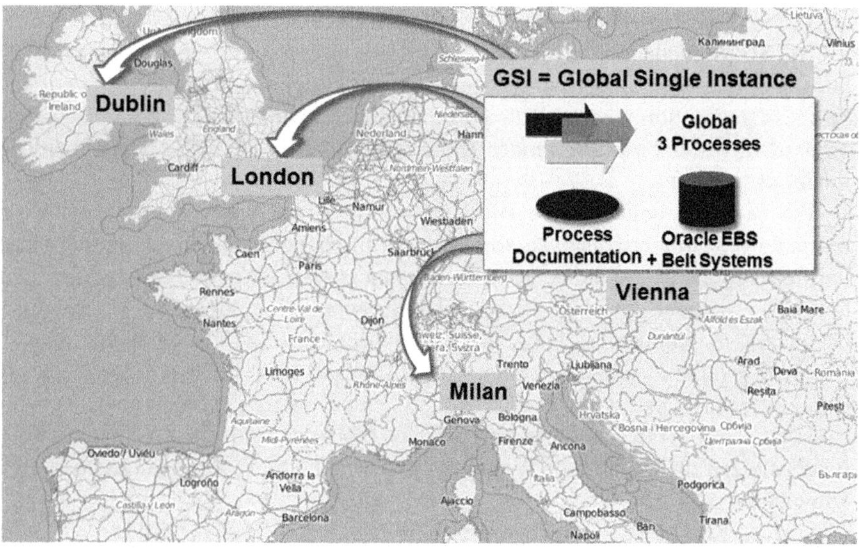

Fig. 1 Global single instance (Karle and Teichenthaler 2015; Map from OpenStreetMap)

- Order management
- Inventory management
- Manufacturing
- Purchasing
- Receivables
- Payables
- Assets
- Cash management
- General ledger

The Belt Systems, custom-developed systems that are integrated into the ERP standard software (Karle and Teichenthaler 2015), are connected via standard interfaces and are also an element of the GSI. Individual components of the Belt Systems are usually developed based on a database and specific development tools. One of the biggest GSI Belt Systems at the moment is the SCM Hub, which covers the specific logistical telecommunication requirements in an individually realized component.

The current solution, based on configurable business software and the global business processes it supports, has reached such a high level of complexity that it is barely manageable.

2.2 Needs

A BPM solution had to be implemented for the GSI that met nine requirements:

- Support the implementation of new or adapted processes and functions of the global ERP instance.
- Provide an extensive documentation of processes, functions, and the corresponding IT implementation.
- Ensure efficient management of mergers and acquisitions—that is, alignment and adjustment of processes and functions.
- Establish an environment for and an approach to a global requirements management system.
- Support execution of rollouts of the centrally administered ERP system.
- Harmonize global business processes and local particularities.
- Provide an integrated test management system; that is, use the defined business processes to create corresponding test cases in a semi-automatic way.
- Establish knowledge management for all parties involved (e.g., business, IT, management).
- Ensure that the approach and environment can manage the complexity of the global ERP instance, including process variants, the IT systems to be integrated, and so on.

After building an adequate BPM environment, the ERP solution of the GSI must be documented with models for the business processes, business objects, and the corresponding GSI solution functions and components (Karle and Teichenthaler 2015). These models should be used for changing and merging businesses. The essential processes had to be predefined for the global solution to be aligned and possibly extended according to new business requirements. Mergers and business process implementations across organizations should be supported based on an extension for collaborative business process management that includes all phases, from requirement analysis to training. The content provided should be used as a knowledge base for the rollout of ERP processes in order to minimize the risks of such extensive ERP projects.

2.3 Objectives

3 Group Europe wanted to build such an environment for the implementation and extension of business processes across organizations within the frame of differently sized ERP projects (Karle and Teichenthaler 2015). During this BPM case, the business processes that had already been implemented in the GSI were initially provided as models in a centralized repository and were subsequently extended and adapted collaboratively by all parties involved. In order to do so, the environment had to support the alignment and definition of country-specific variants for particular operating companies, as well as corporation-wide business processes across organizations, such as corporation reporting.

3 Action Taken

This section describes the decisions made and actions taken to create a social BPM and knowledge management environment for the corporation. Social BPM combines the classic BPM with a collaboration that includes a corresponding integrated environment and a specific approach (Erol et al. 2009; Swenson 2011). The case covers all phases of the typical process lifecycle: identification, discovery, analysis, design, implementation, and monitoring and controlling (Dumas et al. 2013). The corresponding ERP implementation projects were done based on a phased approach, and an agile approach for implementing new projects is in evaluation. There is no focus on a specific area of BPM capabilities; the objective is to build capabilities in strategic alignment, governance, methods, information technology, people, and culture in all areas (Rosemann and vom Brocke 2015).

In a first step, a BPM repository for the GSI processes was created, the BPM environment was extended by means of collaborative functions, and a corresponding approach was established at the company. Based on this approach, the divergent business processes of different business entities were coordinated and the technical integration between relevant system components was aligned. Finally, the

BPM environment was integrated with the test management system to provide a generation of test cases based on the business process models.

3.1 Creation of a Business Process Repository for the GSI

"3" conducts projects for the realization of business processes across organizations on the basis of predefined reference processes that depict the current state of the global solution (Karle and Teichenthaler 2015). The purpose of these reference process models is to describe business processes (e.g., procurement process, order process), business objects (e.g., order, customer, item), functions (e.g., order entry, order approval), and their relationship to each other in order to depict and communicate the possibilities for realizing business processes using already existing GSI system components (Karle and Teichenthaler 2014). The management of the operative business and the further development of such complex solutions is supported by the separation of business process descriptions on several levels, each with a particular amount of detail. The process descriptions are based on the assumption of generally intelligible business processes on the highest abstracted level, which are specified on the lower detailed layers through a realization that is predefined by the GSI solution. In addition, more models that deal with process descriptions are provided that support the implementation of business software like business object structures, organization structures, and work instructions for the system's use in particular business transactions. Furthermore, a link between the business transactions and procedures to respective test cases can be executed automatically. The models and other artifacts in the repository are linked to each other, enabling an extensive view on the business processes. The GSI reference processes are generally structured like the business's core processes—that is, Order2Cash, Procure2Pay, Work Orders and Manage Stock, and so on. Figure 2 shows an overview of the core processes of the applied GSI reference model.

Figure 3 shows the GSI repository's general process structure, including the process hierarchy and the types of process models and levels that are currently being used. The rough, top-level business services and the detailed procedures of the underlying levels are described. Business transactions are depicted by business use cases (BUCs), which describe cases of the daily business from the specific business department's point of view. BUCs are assigned to the individual process steps, so they are depicted in the GSI processes and functions. On the lower function level, the standard functions and detailed procedures of the available GSI are provided, and predefined integration components in the form of main integration processes (MIPs) are documented. A MIP describes the technical process within the integration of involved systems. It is common that user interaction is needed when processes are based on standard ERP functions or special telecommunication-specific extensions of the underlying ERP software. In the GSI repository, this need for interaction is documented using correspondent instructions, also called user instructions. These instructions are micro-procedures that describe the GSI handling. On this level self-service training components are

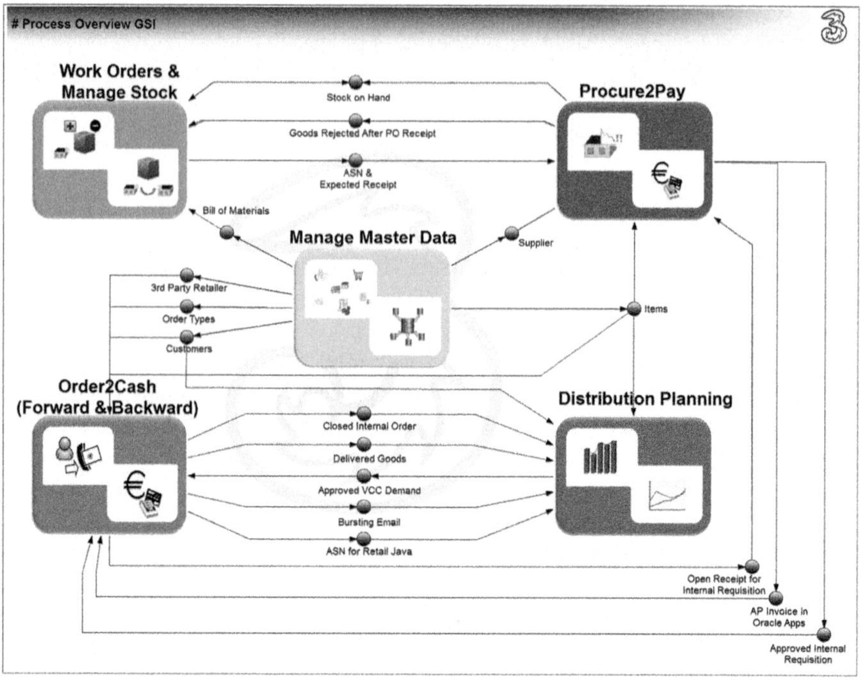

Fig. 2 Core processes of GSI reference model (Karle and Teichenthaler 2014)

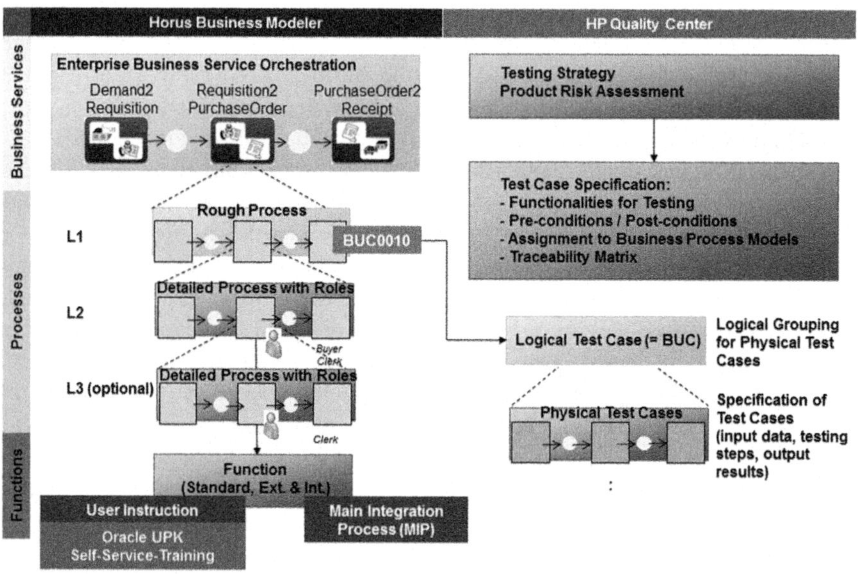

Fig. 3 Core processes of GSI reference model (cf. Herfurth et al. 2008)

also provided that offer exemplary handling records for the particular procedure while also offering the possibility for the user to document and practice interactively. In addition, the link to the test management system is shown, for which BUCs are carried over as logical test cases. They stand for basic, subject-specific groups of individual physical test cases on the test management system's environment side.

The BPM repository for the GSI consists of three main components, as shown in Fig. 3 (Karle and Teichenthaler 2015):

- Horus Business Modeler: Hierarchical business process and business transaction descriptions
- Oracle User Productivity Kit: Additional self-service training components on the functional level of the business process hierarchy
- HP Quality Center: Test cases that are linked to the particular business transactions (BUCs)

3.2 Implementation of a Collaborative BPM Approach

In order to use the knowledge of all parties involved in the projects effectively, the design and the implementation of business processes is supported by an extension of the BPM environment for social media to provide a collaborative environment (cf. Erol et al. 2009). Process experts and IT can simultaneously adapt the models needed for realization of the new business processes in the modeling tool (Karle and Teichenthaler 2014). The key users from the departments use wikis that contain the self-service training components for the business users, made possible by using a wiki environment that is linked to the business process modeling tool with a bidirectional synchronization mechanism. The processes that IT must implement technically are deposited in the IT view and linked to the subject-specific business processes. As a result, all three views of a business process (business, process, and IT) can be created, as shown in Fig. 4.

Figure 5 shows the wiki access for the department in which key users can submit textual changes easily (Karle and Teichenthaler 2014). They can also share comments on necessary diagram modifications that are then handled by business process modelers. Figure 5 also shows the synchronization between subject-specific input from the wiki and the changes in the business process model made by the process modeler. Here, modifications can be aligned and conflicts can be resolved when modifications have been made on both sides.

3.3 Coordination of Business Processes Based on Environment and Approach

The alignment of the future business processes of merged businesses or other business transformations usually starts with mapping the business transactions in

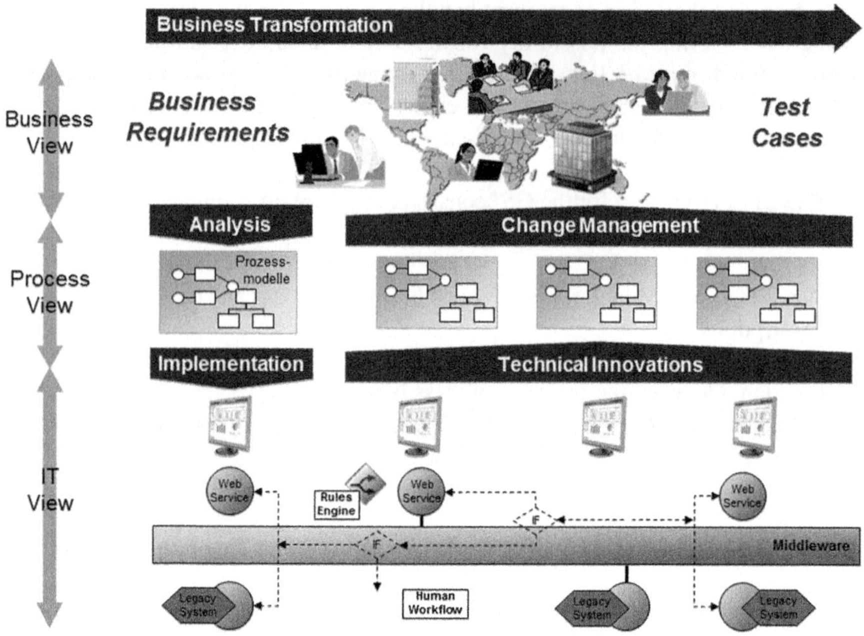

Fig. 4 Views of business processes for adaptation (Schönthaler et al. 2012)

the form of BUCs (Karle and Teichenthaler 2015). Then the essential process level must be discussed and adapted to the appropriate level. First, the GSI must be analyzed based on the predefined procedure, looking for modifications of the global process that need to be made. If there are modifications or extensions identified during the analysis, they are highlighted in the particular process. In this context, some activities in processes are covered by GSI standard functions, and no modifications are needed, while some activities must be modified or existing functions must be extended. Some process steps represent integration steps between systems are additionally, and some are extensions—that is, additional developments that accompany the standard software.

These technical components are part of the parallel processed system architecture, which is described in the same tool with special system architecture models. As a result, the allocation of individual modules of the ERP software or technical components like additional development packages or interfaces is possible. Since the system architecture models are constructed hierarchically, the process models' abstraction levels can be used with the respective levels of the system architecture. Individual extensions and interfaces are provided on the lower levels of the system architecture.

Figure 6 shows an exemplary process for creating new sales orders. Sales orders have to be imported from web shops or distributor systems via interfaces within the scope of predefined business transactions, but it must also be possible for sales orders to be manually created in the ERP system. All recorded and imported

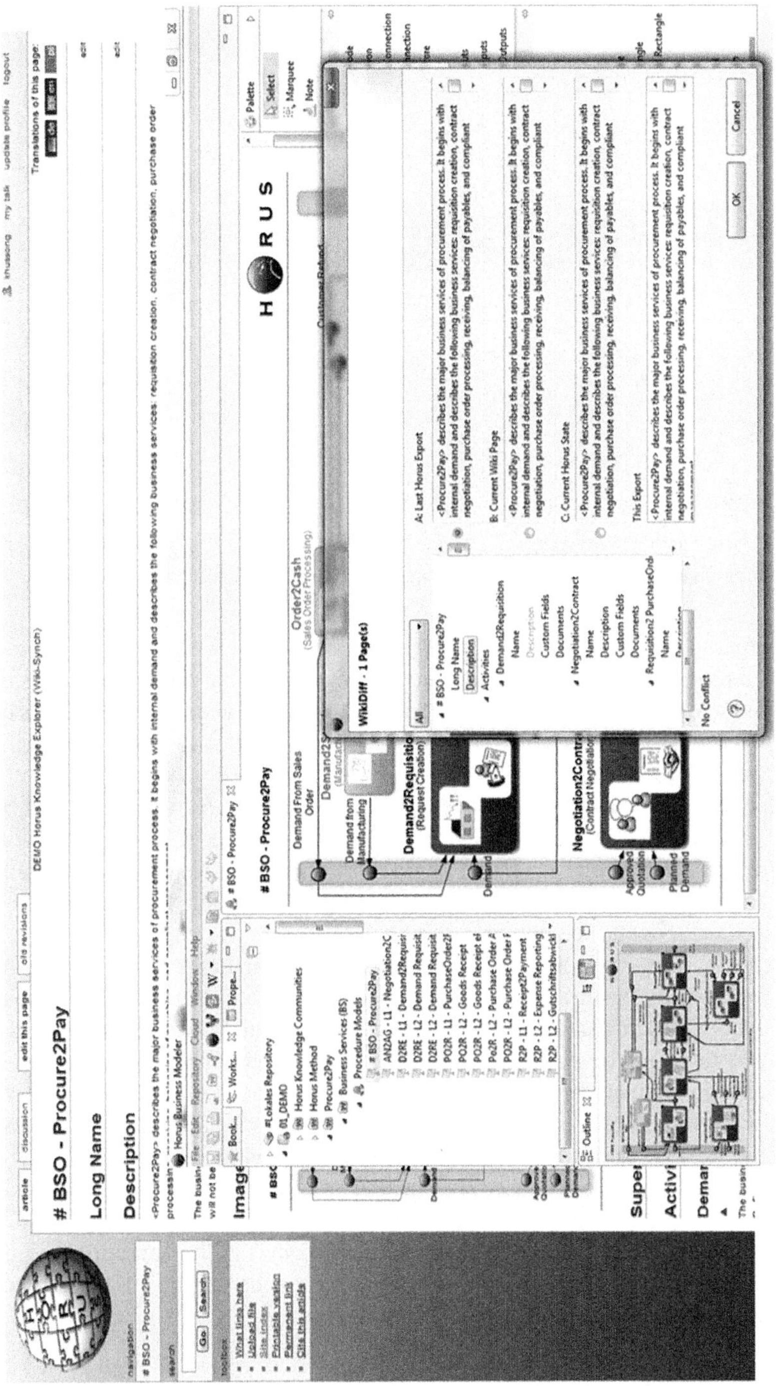

Fig. 5 Wiki for key users and synchronization by process expert (Karle and Teichenthaler 2014)

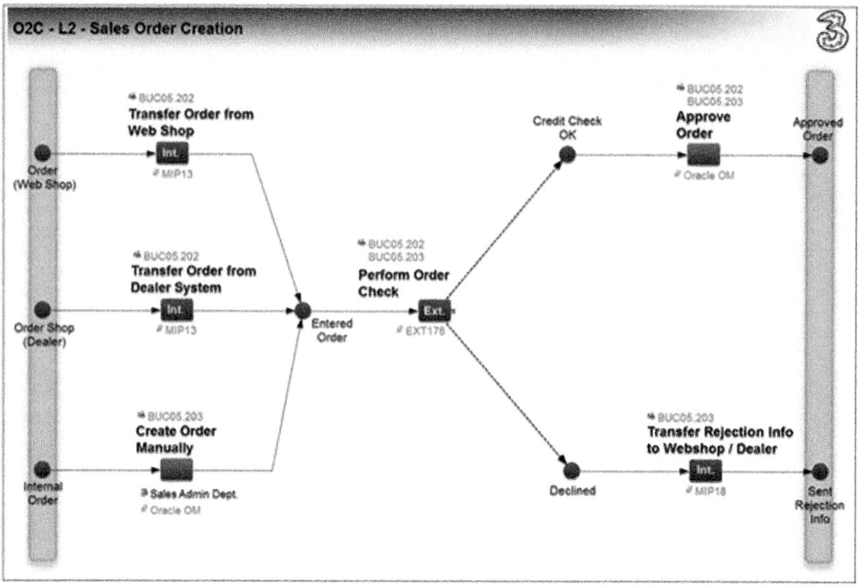

Fig. 6 Definition and alignment of detailed processes (Karle and Teichenthaler 2015)

sales orders must be checked and approved. For each process step, one or several business transactions (e.g., BUCs), the department responsible for the execution of manual tasks, and the necessary system components are assigned to the activities of the detailed processes. Assigned system components can either be MIPs needed for integration or an extensions that have to be developed.

In the example at hand, both the integration and the checking of orders must be changed and extended within the project scope. Such changes often occur in these kinds of projects based on systems to be integrated, or other distribution channels must be taken into consideration. Even the process of checking sales orders often differs from one country to another.

The Oracle User Productivity Kit (UPK) (Oracle User Productivity Kit 2016) records handling by business users, which records can be used to attune business process details. Descriptions of detailed processes on the user instruction level can also support this task. Here, procedures related to handling of individual business transactions are documented in the scope of GSI documentation with UPK. Users can then work with them in several modes, including a mode called “See It,” which exemplarily demonstrates a particular business transaction or another mode called “Try It,” which enables the user to practice treating the respective business transactions with the implemented GSI solution functions. The special handling knowledge is deposited with the business process models at the appropriate steps and is provided by the wiki environment, creating a coherent model and artifact knowledge base that broadly describes the whole system.

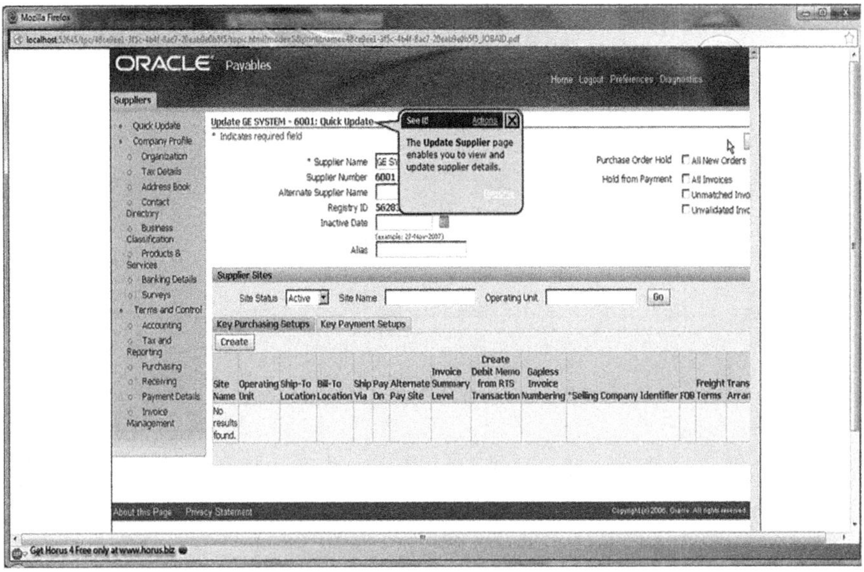

Fig. 7 "See It" mode for self-service training (Oracle User Productivity Kit 2016)

Figure 7 shows the "See It" mode for handling the ERP software. Here, the user is shown step by step how to create a supplier for the Procure2Pay process in the system (Karle and Teichenthaler 2015). The user is guided through the system and gets handling tips every step of the way. These tips, short texts that are shown in the corresponding forms, explain how the particular fields or other system controls should be handled. The systems' micro-procedures, which match the detailed procedures on the level of the business process hierarchy function, are executed in the "See It" mode based on example data. Analogously, the user can practice a procedure in the "Try It" mode, where the user's entries are validated according to the rules that have been set.

3.4 Alignment of the Technical Integration

Communication among all included parties' IT experts on a technical level is needed to align the technical integration (Karle and Teichenthaler 2015), so technical detailed procedures and data structures from the previously covered process level must be clarified for every step. Figure 8 shows the technical procedure for transferring and importing sales orders in a particular MIP. The starting point for the technical process is the ERP standard software, after which it is controlled by the middleware Qorus. PL/SQL programs are called up and executed depending on the process. The data is automatically transferred through preparation steps, loaded into staging tables, and then imported by the order management module via the order interface. Many of these technical integration processes must be checked and extended by IT experts in the scope of mergers of businesses or ERP rollouts, but it

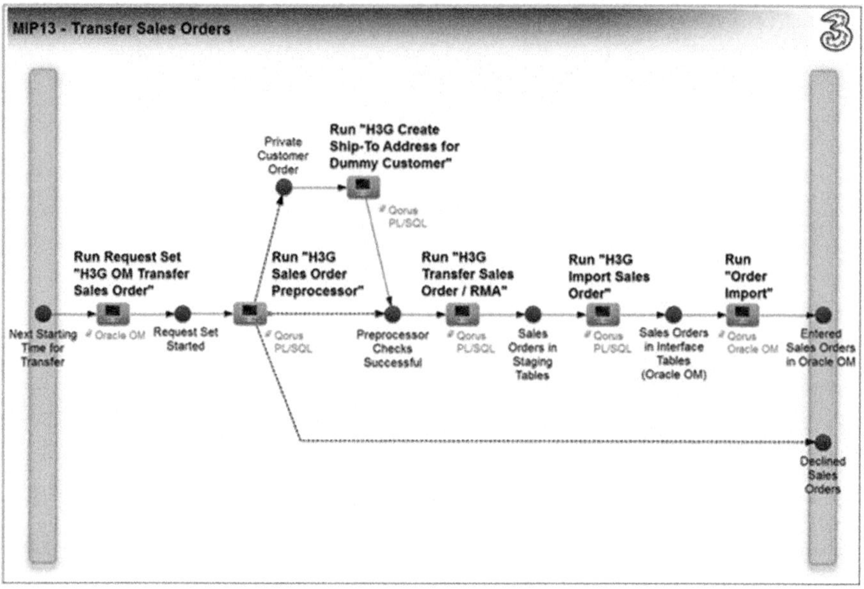

Fig. 8 Definition and alignment of technical integration (Karle and Teichenthaler 2015)

is often sufficient to adapt the individual components in terms of the particularities of the data structures that need to be handled. The according data structures are also a part of the BPM documentation of the GSI.

3.5 Integration of BPM and Test Management

The test management system was integrated into the BPM repository to realize adapted business processes and their IT-technical implementation by implementing an interface that delivers each detailed step of the micro-processes such that all possible runs of the ERP system's handling on the lower level of the process hierarchy are forwarded to the test management system (Karle and Teichenthaler 2015).

When respective tagging of possible runs in the micro-processes are created, all known outcome possibilities are marked within the process model. The allocation of the BUCs on higher levels allows for an automated inquiry of all underlying process models down to detailed levels. Consequently, all defined possibilities of micro-processes for a BUC can be established and delivered to the test management system as single steps, as shown in Fig. 9. This requirement is essential for further preparation of the test cases because of the test cases' structuring in the test management system. Here, each physical test case is summarized into a container, where one logical container exactly corresponds to one BUC and holds all physical test cases that are necessary for the functional test of the BUC. The single test execution is maintained in the test management system, while some tests are also automated in the test management system. If required they can be executed by the system itself.

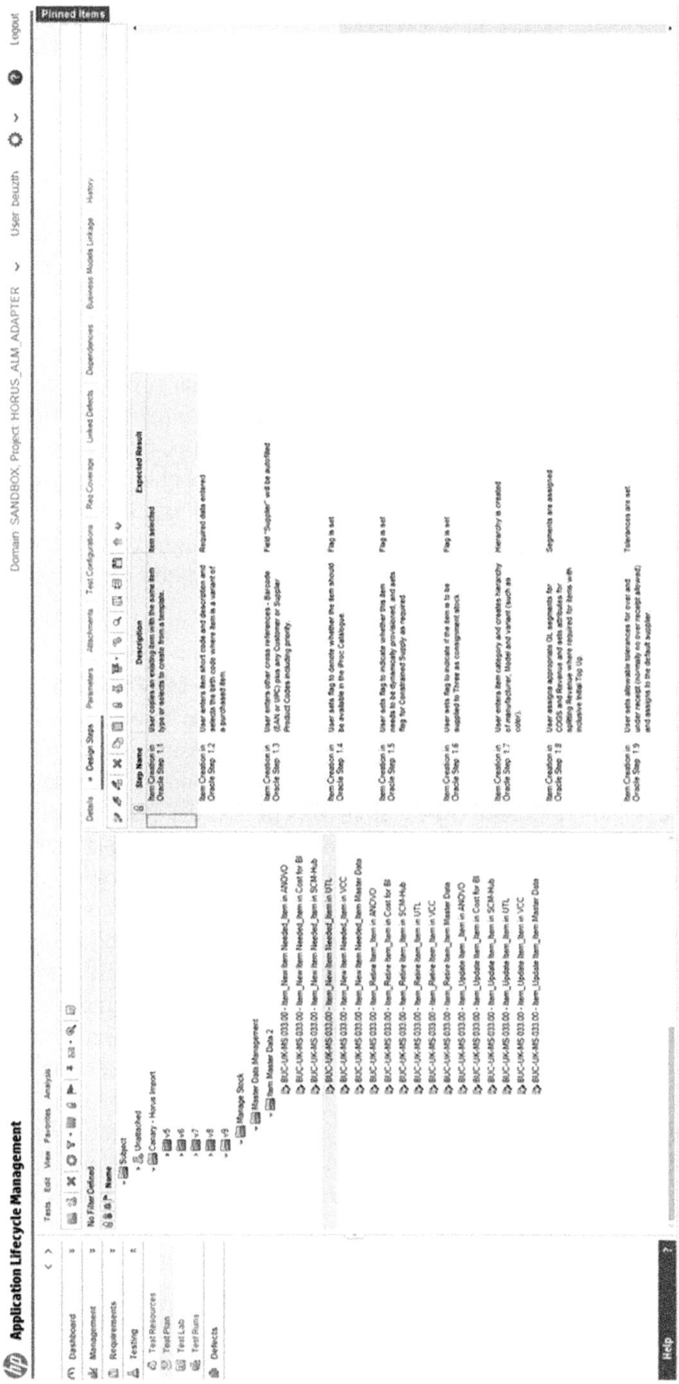

Fig. 9 Generated and transferred test cases (HP Quality Center 2016)

4 Results Achieved

Based on the realized BPM environment and the developed approach, many positive effects resulted from the actions taken.

4.1 Deliverables

4.1.1 Collaborative Global BPM Environment

In addition to the implementation of logistics and finance processes on a global instance, the main result is documentation of the entire global business process for the corporation on three levels: business services, rough business processes, and detailed business processes with assigned roles and system components. This documentation considers common processes and local, country-specific process variants. The corresponding technical processes are also documented in detail.

A collaborative environment supporting communication and cooperative work on business processes was also established. The new possibilities of collaboration based on social media were used for efficient access to experience-based knowledge, creative solution management, and implementations of best practices. Social BPM was realized by combining the procedures and technologies of social media with BPM methods.

4.1.2 Establishment of a Social BPM Approach for Projects

A corresponding approach for the projects was established based on the social BPM environment. Socialization in the projects starts with business requirements engineering, where the business members of involved companies and organizations are granted access to the social BPM environment for the purpose of modeling, analysis, design, and evaluation of the business processes to be discussed. In the social network, the requirements of the involved parties can be exchanged and BUCs, process models, and other artifacts can be defined for a common solution. An important improvement is the ability to collaborate to produce designs that are to be implemented based on previously defined requirements, such as the design of process consolidations and cross-organizational processes. The implemented environment supports this collaborative design by connecting the experts from different organizations and domains (business and IT). The processes are monitored after they are implemented, for which the functional key figures and the execution of the technical process instances and the social BPM environment are used. A general benefit of the combined use of social media and BPM was that the employees at CK Hutchison had fun at work and the motivation of the team that was working on a common solution increased.

A specific approach to managing mergers and acquisitions was created, starting with the existing GSI reference models in the BPM repository to compare processes between companies and to identify required adaptions. The alignment and design of consolidated processes are based on this documentation.

The BPM environment and the approach are also used for a global requirements management. New requirements from a country can be evaluated in terms of potential benefits for other companies operating in the corporation and in terms of these requirements' dependencies with particular implementations for other countries, based on implemented and documented process variants.

The use of social BPM also enables a much more effective alternative of global coordination and collaboration compared to the doing so through many face-to-face-meetings. On the basis of a repository that contains the respective GSI reference models, the reconciliation is accomplished in a social network using functionalities like context-related chat, forums, wikis, and collaborative modeling in combination with BPM in an integrated environment.

4.1.3 Active Knowledge Management

Another important result was creation of a knowledge net based on types of models that are connected with each other (e.g., process models, object models, organization models, system architecture models). This net provides information about the dependencies of business processes and their technical realization. The net helps to identify efforts and license costs for changes or rollouts to the corporation's other operating companies and, since it is provided in the collaboration functions of the social BPM environment, all involved parties (e.g., business, IT, management) can use it. In combination with the collaboration functions, the knowledge net supports active knowledge management.

4.1.4 Support of Process-Based Testing

The predefined test cases linked with the corresponding process models support a fast rollout of business processes in newly acquired operating companies. Test cases for new business processes can be created semi-automatically out of the process models based on the process descriptions on the detailed levels (e.g., user instructions and technical process executions). To create the tests, the business analyst who is responsible for implementing a set of requirements defines possible testing paths and outputs with the testing team, tags these paths in the process models, and transfers them to the test management system as physical test cases. An interface between the BPM system and the test management system generates the individual steps of the test, each of which contains the required information, such as the description of the activity, the system component used, and the expected output. The relationship between process models and test cases is also used during the test execution to clarify the testers' current test task by showing it in context of the process. A recording of an automatic test execution is done in the test management system for some of the test cases, as changes in these processes cause the test cases to be adapted and recorded for automatic execution. This recording can be identified by the links between process models and corresponding test cases. The self-service training components integrated into the BPM environment's process documentation support the objective of efficient rollouts. Involvement in the test management and in the training provide "living" process models that are permanently in use.

4.1.5 Management of Increased Complexity

The combination of predefined GSI reference process models and social BPM has proved to be helpful in managing the existing complexity. The predefined processes, functions, business objects, and system components define a basis on which the communication regarding cross-company processes between parties involved (e.g., in supply chains) can be coordinated. When a merger or an acquisition of companies occurs in this sector, using the described approach to identify and consolidate differences and similarities provides a substantial advantage. The key to managing the complexity is the associations built between the different types of models and between models and other artifacts, such as test cases and self-service training components. These associations provide transparency about the as-is state, allow navigation through the knowledge net, and help to identify deltas to estimate the effort required for changes and to support design, implementation, documentation, education, and testing.

4.2 Business Outcomes

The collaborative BPM environment and the established approach provide fast implementations of ERP projects; for example, a rollout of the finance modules was accomplished in 3 months. Regarding the collaborative work based on this social BPM approach, there is currently almost no staff turnover among the people working in this area.

5 Lessons Learned

This section describes the four lessons learned from the HK Hutchison case.

5.1 BPM Must Be Combined with Other Fields

BPM must be combined with other fields of activity to provide “living” process models. Considered only by themselves, process models are often created and used only in certain phases of projects, such as analysis and design, and tucked away after the projects are finished, never to be used again. If the process models are connected with related areas like test management or training, they become “living” process models. “3” has a large software-testing team, and connecting the BPM environment with the test management system improves the collaborative work between the business analysts and the testing team. A second field of activity that is combined with BPM at “3” is education. In addition to documentation, the self-service training components were integrated in the process portal of the BPM environment to make the training units available in the process context. That is, employees to be trained navigate in the process models to get to self-service training components for the ERP software in order to use training modes like

"See It" and "Try It." This combination helps employees become permanently aware of the processes and improves their understanding of their processes' dependencies on other departments involved in the entire business process.

5.2 Complexity Management Requires Linking Artifacts

Management of complexity in global environments can be managed only by linking model types with each other or with other artifacts. Separate models offer only limited help in managing complex systems for global processes and their implementation. The associations between model types are necessary to provide the required information in the corresponding business transformations. The affected processes should be directly visible or retrievable in the BPM environment, as one must determine which system components are used in the processes in order to identify the consequences of a change and know which process variants are implemented in the corporation for different countries. If business objects need to be extended, the dependencies to the assigned processes that use these objects should be retrievable. All process activities of a specific role of the organization model have to be identified for staff analysis and changes. Furthermore, associations with more strategic model types, such as objective models, strategy models, SWOT models, and key performance models, help to define the right priorities during a project. Business processes can be discussed in a more concrete way by also going through predefined test cases or showing the integrated use of the system by integrated training components.

5.3 Social BPM Increases the Effectiveness of International Work

Social BPM helps to connect people in an international environment to enable effective collaborative work. The combined use of a BPM environment and social media provides a framework for working together efficiently in a global context. People are accustomed to acting in social communities in their private lives, so building a community for specific BPM cases via social BPM is more cost-efficient than face-to-face-meetings in an international project. Social BPM also helps to limit work to specific artifacts instead of sending one e-mail after another.

5.4 Business Transformations Require the Involvement of Management

Embedding the steering of business transformations into the corporation's mechanisms for governance, risk, and compliance (GRC) is an important success factor. Business transformations are strategic projects, and they need the awareness and support of top management. Such projects can change the corporation's business model (cf. Schönthaler 2014) and can affect the business architecture by affecting the products, services, and corresponding business processes such that the software, hardware, and other technical infrastructure have to be changed. Many decisions must be made, and the best way to make them efficiently is to include the business transformations in the corporation's GRC mechanism. The governance aspect provides the corporation objectives, strategies, and the global corporate culture, while the compliance aspect deals with rules, laws, norms, and standards, and the risk aspect covers the corporation's risk management. Business transformations must have support, and they have the best chance to be successful when they are included in this corporate management mechanism.

References

Dumas, M., La Rosa, M., Mendling, J., & Reijers, H. (2013). *Fundamentals of business process management*. Berlin: Springer-Verlag.

Erol, S., Granitzer, M., Happ, S., Jantunen, S., Jennings, B., Koschmider, A., Nurcan, S., Rossi, D., & Schmidt, R. (2009). *Combining BPM and social software: Contradiction or chance? Software process: Improvement and practice journal* (Special Issue on BPM 2008 Selected Workshop Papers).

Herfurth, M., Karle, T., & Schönthaler, F. (2008). Reference model for service-oriented business software based on web service nets. In *Proceedings of 3rd EuroSIGSAND Symposium 2008*, Marburg/Lahn, GI-LNI P-129 (pp. 55–69). Koellen-Verlag.

HP Quality Center. (2016). Accessed October 2016, from http://www8.hp.com/de/de/software-solutions/quality-center-quality-management/

Karle, T., & Teichenthaler, K. (2014). Collaborative cross-organizational BPM – Case study Hutchison 3G. In *IEEE Conference on Business Informatics*, Geneva.

Karle, T., & Teichenthaler, K. (2015). Kollaborative Geschäftsprozessumsetzung bei Unternehmensfusionen und ERP-Rollouts. *DOAG Business News*, Ausgabe 02-2015.

Oracle User Productivity Kit. (2016). Accessed October 2016, from http://www.oracle.com/us/products/applications/user-productivity-kit/

Rosemann, M., & vom Brocke, J. (2015). Six core elements of business process management. In J. vom Brocke & M. Rosemann (Eds.), *Handbook on business process management: Introduction, methods, and information systems (International handbooks on information systems)* (Vol. 1, 2nd ed., pp. 105–122). Berlin: Springer.

Schönthaler, F. (2014). *BPM is not for programmers – It's a business tool and makes your business processes more excellent*, Collaborate 14, Las Vegas.

Schönthaler, F., Vossen, G., Oberweis, A., & Karle, T. (2012). *Business processes for business communities: Modeling languages, methods, tools*. Berlin: Springer-Verlag.

Swenson, K. (2011). *Social BPM: Work, planning, and collaboration under the impact of social technology*. Future Strategies Incorporated.

Thomas Karle studied Computer Science at the University Karlsruhe (TH)—nowadays called Karlsruhe Institute of Technology (KIT)—and earned his doctorate at the Institute for Applied Informatics and Formal Description Methods. As a Senior Consultant and Project Manager he has been working in the area of web portals, integration workflow solutions and implementation of ERP systems since 1990. In 2000 he was appointed into the Management Board of the PROMATIS Group and is currently responsible for the division Enterprise Architecture, dealing with business process oriented implementations of complex solutions containing standard business software and customized components. He is advising customers on the subjects of strategy and business process management. Since 2013 he is COO and Executive Consultant of Horus software GmbH, the product company of the PROMATIS Group, providing a method and according software tools for holistic business modeling and for the execution of business transformations featuring Social BPM mechanisms.

Kurt Teichenthaler has been working within various IT Management positions for more than 20 years. Since 2013 he is the Senior Head of IT at Hutchison Drei Austria GmbH. Over the past 5 years Kurt consolidated the IT stack in course of M&A projects. He also integrated various companies on a single ERP Instance and owns the ERP development and operations for them. Within this transformation programs he introduced centralized documentation of implemented business processes to support test automation and high quality deliveries. Further on he supported stakeholders in order to successfully automate and manage their process landscape.

Process Management in Construction: Expansion of the Bolzano Hospital

Elisa Marengo, Patrick Dallasega, Marco Montali, Werner Nutt, and Michael Reifer

Abstract

(a) **Situation faced**: Frener and Reifer (F&R) is a leader in engineering, fabricating, and installing facades with non-standard designs. The company was looking for comprehensive, domain-specific approaches to improve the company's control over facade processes, from design to execution and monitoring. What makes process management particularly challenging in this setting are some peculiarities of the domain, such as high levels of variability, unpredictability, and inter-organizational synchronization (vom Brocke et al., BPM Trends, 1, 2015), as well as the non-standard and non-repetitive nature of the designs, which complicates the ability to formulate reliable estimates. Indeed, in many cases the installation department exceeded the number of hours that were initially estimated.

(b) **Action taken**: A group of researchers developed a domain-specific methodology, called PRECISE, that provides methods with which to support the process lifecycle (Dumas et al., *Fundamentals of business process management*. Springer, 2013) in construction. F&R applied the methodology to construction of the hospital in Bolzano, Italy, by implementing three steps: (i) collaborative process design, with the main figures taking part in the construction project (e..g the project manager, the architect and the foreman on site); (ii) process implementation, which involves defining short-term (i.e., daily or weekly) schedules for tasks based on actual data

E. Marengo (✉) • P. Dallasega • M. Montali • W. Nutt
Free University of Bozen-Bolzano, Bolzano, Italy
e-mail: elisa.marengo@unibz.it; patrick.dallasega@unibz.it; marco.montali@unibz.it; werner.nutt@unibz.it

M. Reifer
FRENER & REIFER Metallbau GmbH/Srl, Bressanone, Italy
e-mail: m.reifer@frener-reifer.com

J. vom Brocke, J. Mendling (eds.), *Business Process Management Cases*, Management for Professionals, DOI 10.1007/978-3-319-58307-5_14

on the progress of the work; and (iii) continuous monitoring and measurement of the progress of the work on site.

(c) **Results achieved**: By applying the methodology, which supports a detailed modelling and monitoring of the activities, F&R could perform reliable estimates of progress on tasks and expected cost to completion. For instance, F&R recognized that the budget it had initially estimated was too tight. By analyzing the up-to-date data on the progress of the work and consulting with the workers on the construction site, the company could identify problems and sources of delay promptly and act to mitigate their effects. During the application of PRECISE, F&R recorded an increase in productivity that was estimated to have saved 400 man hours.

(d) **Lessons learned**: Application of the methodology singled out some aspects of the process that should be addressed to improve process management. Flexibility, which is required in dealing with the domain variability, is achieved by defining a process model and a short-term schedule, while the availability of reliable and up-to-date data on the progress of the work is obtained by applying continuous, detailed process monitoring. Engagement of the workers in the process management allows the project to benefit from their expertise (Rosemann and vom Brocke, *Handbook on business process management, introduction, methods, and information systems.* Springer, 2015), which is the basis of the collaborative approach. However, better IT support for the methodology is needed (Rosemann and vom Brocke, *Handbook on business process management, introduction, methods, and information systems.* Springer, 2015; Dumas et al., *Fundamentals of business process management.* Springer, 2013).

1 Introduction

Frener and Reifer (F&R) (2016), a medium-sized enterprise, is a leader in engineering, fabricating, and installing facades with non-standard designs. The context in which the company works is characterized by non-repetitive processes that have a high level of originality (vom Brocke et al. 2015). As a consequence, management of the façade-realization process cannot be standardized and can rely only partially on experience gained from other projects. Among the main challenges are (1) the engineering and construction of non-standard components; (2) their fabrication; (3) the need for specialized manpower for all of the phases, from engineering to physical installation; and (4) the need for on-site training of the installation workers. These issues make the overall project management challenging for the company, complicating aspects of the project like the estimation of the resources required. Additional challenges come from peculiarities of the construction sector, including high variability (vom Brocke et al. 2015) because of customers' changing requirements and unavoidable, unpredictable events, such as bad weather conditions that preclude installation. In addition, multiple trades must be on site simultaneously, which requires that they synchronize their activities.

It is important for the company to make an accurate budget estimate and to respect it while executing the process. While the budget should be sufficient to carry out the project, the company has to make appealing offers that beat its competitors, so it usually designs tight budgets for which the process must be efficient and planned carefully.

In this setting, F&R had a problem with lack of control over the project's execution. When the company's installation department exceeded the estimated man hours needed to perform the work on site, the company could not identify the causes of the delay or predict them in advance in order to mitigate them. Traditionally, the execution plan is not defined in detail but only identifies the main milestones to be achieved. It is then refined on a daily basis by the foreperson on site, who has inadequate IT support and no way to analyze the project's overall progress. As a consequence, a delay is discovered only when the established deadline is not met.

With the aim of improving the project management, F&R collaborated with the Faculties of Science and Technology and the Faculty of Computer Science at the Free University of Bozen–Bolzano and with the Fraunhofer Italia Research Center in the context of the research project *build4future* (Build4Future 2014). During that project a methodology called PRECISE was defined (Dallasega et al. 2013) that the company applied to the Bolzano hospital project. The methodology provides methods that support the construction process (Rosemann and vom Brocke 2015; Dumas et al. 2013) by focusing on (1) *process design*, supporting the definition of a process model; (2) *process implementation*, defining a short-term and detailed scheduling of the activities; and (3) a continuous *process monitoring and controlling*.

2 Situation Faced

In 1998, the province of Bolzano issued a call for refurbishing and then expanding its hospital by building a new clinic composed of three wings and a new entrance area. The work started in 2008 and was estimated to end in 2015 with an overall budget of 480 million Euros, later updated to 610 million Euros. F&R was responsible for the design, engineering, fabrication and installation of the facades of the three wings of the new clinic, which were planned for completion by the end of 2016.

F&R proposed a solution that was tailored to the project. For instance, the company designed large, high glazing instead of single windows to improve both the internal lighting and the view of the landscape. To guarantee optimal illumination, several customized solutions were designed for the facades based on their orientation to the sun. Sliding sun-protection elements were also built that could operate both individually and via the building automation system. The single semi-finished components for the facades were delivered separately to the site and then integrated into it.

A number of issues made the management of this project challenging for F&R. Specifically, the process is non-repetitive and requires a high level of creativity (vom Brocke et al. 2015), as the components for each part of the facade differ. The company had to ensure that the components were available when needed and that they were unloaded at the right place on site. In addition, to avoid delays, F&R had to synchronize its activities with those of the other companies that were working on site. For instance, the installation of the high glazing required the use of the tower crane that is shared among the companies working on the site, so F&R had to agree on a plan with the other companies regarding its use. This need emerged only when the project had already begun, and since the companies did not define a usage plan up front, the crane was not available for F&R when it was needed for facade installation. F&R also had to synchronize plans with the company that installed the building's automation system, which had to be connected with the sun-protection elements installed by F&R. Synchronization among the companies is needed also to avoid that two companies work at the same time in the same area. This in order to avoid interferences among them.

Overall, F&R wanted to improve different aspects of the process management, to improve its control over the execution process. With the traditional approach, the company compared the costs incurred with the planned costs to determine whether a process was running on time, although these two values rarely coincided, and F&R wanted to understand the causes for the discrepancy. The company also wanted to know about potential delays sufficiently in advance to implement recovery plans that would prevent or to limit them. In short, the company wanted to improve the process design, implementation, and monitoring phases of their process management lifecycle (Dumas et al. 2013).

Process Design: Lack of a Detailed Process Model The aims of a process model are to communicate with the customer and to synchronize at a high level the work of multiple companies. Traditional process models rely on Gantt charts or similar, but because of strict budgets and few resources, such process models often contain few details, thus providing only an abstract idea of the process execution. Moreover, these models typically focus on the long term without accounting for the actual progress of the work or the performance estimate, so they are rarely used as guides in the process execution. A more detailed process model could support the early discovery of potential problems or inconsistencies in the process, thus allowing the company to define more feasible milestones and more effective plans to achieve them. Such a model could also be used as a basis for synchronizing the work of multiple companies.

Process Design: Difficult Synchronization Among the Company's Departments F&R not only installs facades but also engineers and fabricates the facade components. However, the company's departments work with tasks at differing levels of granularity: the engineering department focuses on elaborating floor drawings, the fabrication department focuses on producing components, and the installation department focuses on performing all of the required tasks on site. This misalignment among the departments complicates the internal synchronization and the alignment with the construction site. One way to achieve the desired coordination was to rely on a common process model according to which the three departments could synchronize their activities.

Process Implementation: Lack of Support for Detailed Scheduling In most cases, detailed scheduling of the activities to be performed on site is left to the foreperson, who has inadequate IT support so must rely on oral communication with the workers and on pen and paper to define a daily schedule. F&R could rely on experienced forepersons who can manage complex processes, but this approach introduces risks because it is prone to error and binds the success of the project closely to the abilities of one person. For instance, if a foreperson leaves the company mid-project, fundamental knowledge about the project leaves with her.

Process Monitoring: Unreliable Measuring of the Project's Progress In general, the progress of the work on site is measured in terms of expenses incurred rather than in terms of the work performed. This approach has two main consequences for the project management: First, delays are discovered only when a task that should be finished is not, but by then it is often too late to identify the causes and define repair mechanisms, so the delay typically delays the end of the project. Second, aligning the production of components with the progress of the work on site is difficult, although it would allow F&R to avoid both the expenses of storing the produced components and interruptions in the process when components are not ready when they are needed. Such alignment is possible only when the company has a reliable way to monitor the process.

3 Action Taken

In the context of the project *build4future*, the research partners and 12 small and medium-sized enterprises (SMEs) from the Bolzano province, developed a methodology called PRECISE (Dallasega et al. 2013), the purpose of which was to support and improve the phases of the construction process-management lifecycle (Dumas et al. 2013). The PRECISE methodology supports primarily three interconnected project phases: (1) *process design*, by supporting collaborative process modelling; (2) *process implementation*, by supporting detailed short-term *scheduling* of the activities; and (3) *process monitoring*, by supporting short-term monitoring and measurement of the construction progress.

3.1 Development of the PRECISE Methodology

Process Design The first phase of the methodology is the process design, which consists of defining a process model that captures the set of tasks to be executed on site and the temporal dependencies among them. The aim of a process model is

twofold: to synchronize the activities of the various companies involved and to synchronize the activities of one company's departments.
To achieve a reliable process model that organizes the work to improve the final result, the methodology suggests the involvement of experts from the various companies involved (Rosemann and vom Brocke 2015). They define the model in a collaborative way based on the methodology, organizing collaborative workshops in the project's early stages, once the overall design of the building is clear and when the participating companies are established. The workshops are orchestrated by a neutral moderator who has no economic interest in the project.
As a first step, starting from the approval and the shop floor drawings, the companies define an abstract representation of the building by identifying precisely the *locations* in which the tasks are performed (Dallasega et al. 2015). For instance, a building can be organized in sectors (identifying the different parts of the building like wings), each of which is organized in levels (floors) and sections (identifying the technological content of an area), which are then enumerated with unit numbers. Based on this definition, a location would be identified by a sector (e.g., sector A), a level (e.g., level one), a section (e.g., room), and a unit (e.g., unit 4).
As a second step, the companies discuss the main *tasks* to be performed based on which their activities are synchronized. Each task is defined by (1) the specification of the job's content, (2) the responsible trade and the skills required to execute it, (3) the (shared) resources needed, (4) the location(s) where it must be executed, and (5) the expected productivity, i.e. the amount of work that should be completed in a certain period of time. To represent the expected productivity, the methodology introduces the concept of *pitch* (Dallasega 2016) which defines the number of locations in which work has to be performed by what kind of crew and its size (e.g., three locations with a crew of two plumbers) during a specific period (e.g., 1 day).
The final step of the process modelling concerns the definition of the temporal *dependencies* among the tasks on which the companies involved have to agree. The dependencies are conceived as a set of mandatory constraints that rule the temporal execution of the tasks—for example, the floor has to be installed before the window in each location—but they do not define a strict sequence according to which other tasks should be performed—that is, other tasks can be performed between the floor and the window installation. All that is not specified by a process model, such as when a task should start, is left to the companies.
To support the collaborative nature of the approach, PRECISE defines a graphic representation of the process models (Marengo et al. 2016). Figure 1 reports the representation of a task. A temporal dependency among two tasks is defined by drawing an arrow between them to indicate that one should be performed before the other.

Process Implementation The second phase is the process implementation, which, starting from a process model, details it with additional information. The result is a *short-term schedule* that specifies (1) at what points in time work on tasks is to commence and (2) how many workers are needed per day, including who is to work on individual tasks or groups of tasks, which determines the duration of the tasks.

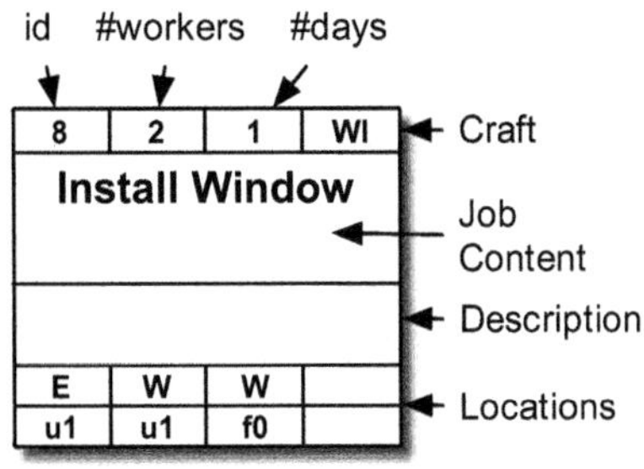

Fig. 1 Task representation

In addition, decisions are made concerning when to make resources like cranes and materials available.

Information about the tasks, such as the job content, the locations where they are performed, the required skills, and the expected productivities (pitch), is specified in the process model. However, collaborative models usually specify only the main tasks among which synchronization problems among the companies involved may arise. When schedules are set, it might be necessary to refine the tasks by specifying them in terms of subtasks, with their corresponding expected productivities and dependencies.

To specify a schedule, the foreperson defines: (1) the period of *time* (a specific day or week), (2) *which* activities to perform in that period, (3) by *whom* they should be performed, and (4) *where* to perform them. The foreperson also considers the temporal dependencies from the process model in order to schedule tasks in such a way as to satisfy them.

The PRECISE methodology defines certain criteria to support the schedules' reliability. In particular, in order for a schedule to be reliable, it must cover only a short period of time and be based on actual data from the site, such as information about the tasks that have been completed. Long-term schedules rely heavily on forecasts of the progress of the work and are inevitably less detailed since less information is available to the foreperson at scheduling time. Accordingly, the methodology suggests defining daily or weekly activity scheduling such that a weekly schedule best suits the initial phases of a construction process, when there are fewer interactions among the companies and the tasks' execution takes longer (e.g., excavating or pouring concrete). In the subsequent phases of the process execution, more companies have to work in the same locations (such as when companies work on the facade and the interior), and the tasks usually require less time to be completed. In this case, a daily activity schedule is more reliable and is better for task synchronization among companies.

When making a schedule, the foreperson also defines the crews of workers and assigns them to the tasks. To facilitate this activity, the methodology suggests a *presence list*—that is, a list of workers who are expected to be present on site on that particular day/week.

Monitoring the Construction Process The aim of monitoring is to collect data on the progress of the work on site. The methodology suggests using this data as a starting point for scheduling so the scheduler has updated information on the tasks that are not yet completed. For instance, if the schedule for the following week is defined at the end of the current week, then it must be based on the data from monitoring the current week. Relying on the information on the schedule rather than on the monitoring may lead to incorrect assumptions about the progress of the work and to a schedule that is not feasible. It is often the case that unpredictable events like bad weather conditions introduce significant delays, in which case, the scheduled activities may progress more slowly than foreseen or be postponed in favor of other activities.

The data from the monitoring is also used to update the expected productivity for the tasks in the process model. The expected productivity is initially estimated in the collaborative workshops by defining the pitch for each task. It is continually refined based on current data and considering the learning curve effect when multiple instances of the same task are performed by the same crew, and thus the task is performed faster.

The companies can take advantage of the monitoring data by performing various kinds of analysis to evaluate the project's overall progress. Among other kinds of analyses, they can determine whether the project is progressing on time and within the estimated budget by comparing the budgeted hours with the number of completed locations, the resources used, and hours consumed. Based on this information, they can forecast the amount of work yet to completed in a detailed and reliable way.

3.2 Application of the Methodology

This section presents how the PRECISE methodology was applied in the Bolzano hospital project.

Bolzano Hospital Process Design The PRECISE methodology was developed in the context of the build4future project. As one of the participating companies, F&R decided to apply the methodology to its Bolzano hospital project. However, since none of the other companies that were working on the hospital project was also taking part in build4future, they did not participate in the collaborative process modelling phase.

Before F&R executed the process on site, the Free University of Bozen-Bolzano and the Fraunhofer Italia Research Center, as scientific partners of the project, organized a collaborative workshop involving the project manager and the foreperson. The workshop participants first agreed on how to represent the locations by identifying four elements as characterizing the building's locations (Dallasega et al. 2015): (a) *level*: four levels, identified as 1–4, from the ground floor to the fourth floor; (b) *wing*: three wings, identified as A, B, and C; (c) *orientation*: four facades, identified as north, east, south, and west facades based on their orientation to the sun; and (d) *units*: small parts of similar size, where the space between the two main axes of the building was used as a reference to define the units.

After this phase, the main tasks were identified in keeping with the seven main phases of facade installation: substructure, frame assembly, inner connection, sealing and insulation, glazing and installation of panels, paneling, and final assembly. The tasks were represented as in Fig. 1. The information on the tasks (e.g., location, productivity) was specified, along with the dependencies among the tasks, as shown in Fig. 2.

When modelling the dependencies among the tasks, the participants found that the modelling language lacked some details needed to capture the nature of a dependency. In particular, only one kind of temporal relationship was provided in the language. As a result, the language was extended to define three kinds of dependencies: *workflow*, which captures a temporal dependency on the execution of two tasks; *information flow*, which captures whether tasks need specific information, such as detailed measurements, in order to be performed; and *material flow*, which captures whether tasks need specific components in order to be performed. Magnetic white-boards were used as a support for the definition of the process model. At the end of the workshop, the process model was copied and transformed into a digital document.

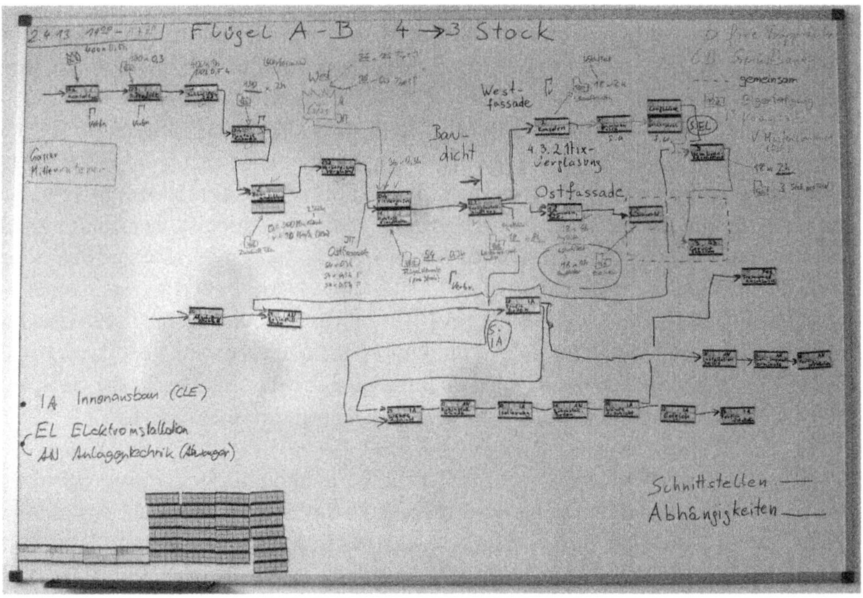

Fig. 2 Excerpt of the Bolzano hospital process model defined on a magnetic board

Scheduling of the Tasks Once the process model was defined, it provided a significant amount of detailed information on the tasks (e.g., the locations where a task needs to be performed, the resources needed to execute them). The next step was to plan the tasks' execution based on the process model and the dependencies among the tasks. When the process model defined no strict temporal constraints on a task, the company could decide when to schedule the task according to internal priorities and preferences.

When the methodology was applied, there was no specific IT support, so the scientific partners provided the foreperson with tables like the one shown in Fig. 3 to support scheduling. The tables were generated ad hoc, relying on the information from the process model and using Microsoft Excel. Each table concerns a specific period of time according to which a schedule had to be specified. In line with the methodology, short-term (weekly or daily) schedules were required. By filling in these tables, the foreperson could schedule the activities to be executed in that period, the locations where they would be executed, and the crews assigned to them. In particular, a table obtains from the process model the list of tasks, the expected productivity, and the possible locations.

The foreperson could schedule a task to be completed at a location by filling in the cell at the intersection of the row corresponding to the task and the column corresponding to the location. If the cell is not empty, the task cannot be scheduled there.

After defining the tasks to be performed, the foreperson defines the presence list—that is, the list of workers who are expected to be present on site at that particular time—and the number of hours they are expected to work. Then, the foreperson forms the crews by assigning workers to the scheduled tasks.

The foreperson usually defined the schedules on Friday afternoon for the upcoming week using Microsoft Excel, filling in the tables that were prepared by a researcher from the scientific partners. Excel allowed the foreperson to visualize the *saturation* of the workers, which was generated automatically, as a chart plotted a comparison between the number of hours a worker was available and the hours spent on tasks he or she was assigned. The tables were linked to each other so scheduling information could be propagated to the subsequent periods. For instance, a task scheduled for 1 day could not be scheduled for the next day as well.

On Monday morning, the foreperson hung the scheduling tables at the construction site, where workers could see to which tasks they were assigned.

Monitoring of the Work on Site In line with the methodology, the progress of the work was monitored daily and at the end of each day's work hours, the installation teams met to record the tasks performed, the hours spent, and the completed construction units. When the productivity for a task was lower than that which had been estimated, the reason was noted. Tables similar to those used for the scheduling (Fig. 3) were used for this purpose, and every Friday afternoon a researcher from the scientific partners collected the data and copied it into Excel spreadsheets. The information on the (un)completed tasks was automatically propagated to the tables so the foreperson could plan the activities for the next week using the most current information. Then the tables for the next week's scheduling and monitoring were printed and hung.

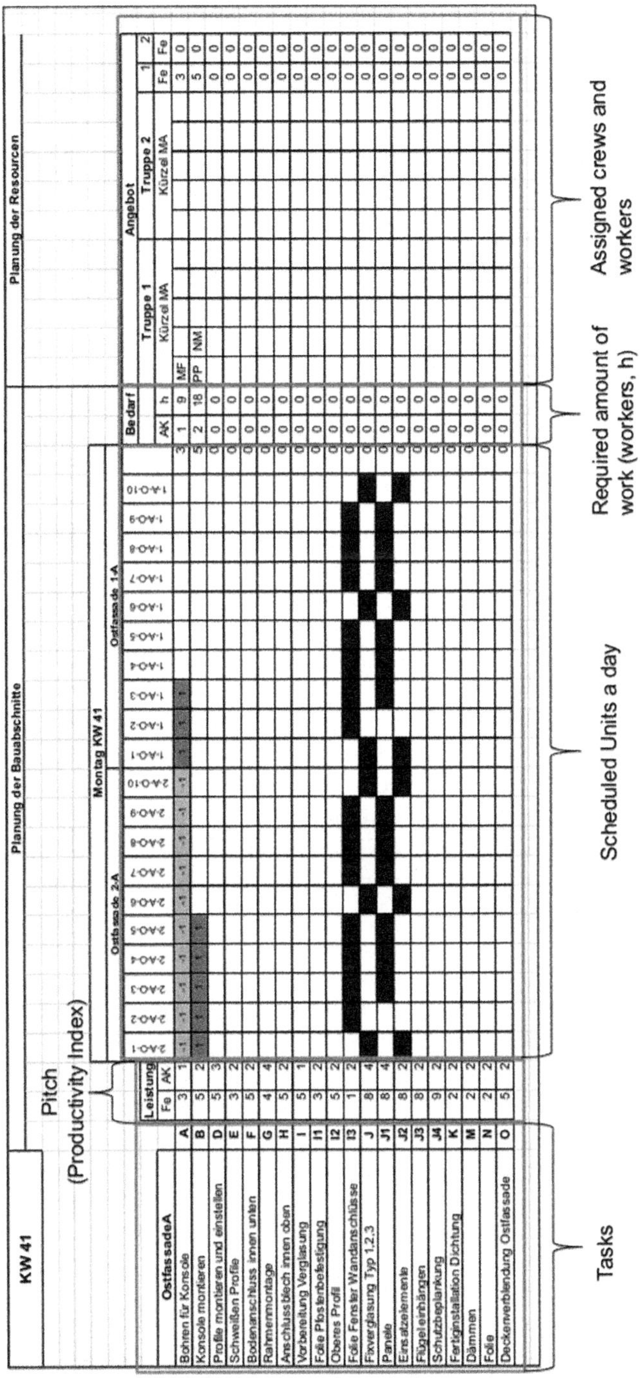

Fig. 3 Excel spreadsheet used to support F&R's daily schedule

The Excel spreadsheets allowed the monitoring data to be elaborated in order to support analysis of the project's overall progress. In particular, the data was used to compare the actual progress of the work with the initial project forecasts; to plot the number of hours consumed and the estimates to completion for each location; to compare the hours that should have been consumed on the completed tasks with the number of hours actually consumed; and to plot the difference between the estimated and the effective hours. A positive difference corresponded to an increase in productivity.

All of these charts were hung at the construction site so every worker had an overview of the project's progress.

Continuous Improvement Workshop on Site Four "continuous improvement workshops" were held to analyze the data collected from the construction site and the charts produced from it. During these meetings, the project director, the project manager, the construction foreperson, and the vice-foreperson discussed the general overview of the construction performance, focusing on the most recent 4 weeks. Causes of problems and delays were discussed to avoid their recurrence and estimated productivity for the tasks (pitch) was adapted to the actual conditions on site.

4 Results Achieved

F&R's employees were initially skeptical about using the new methodology, but after the initial phase they saw that it did not require significant time expenditure in addition to their other activities, nor was it used to control them. On the contrary, it was used so the workers could have *more* control over the process management. F&R was satisfied with the results it obtained and has already applied it to other projects (e.g., the construction of a new library, research center, and archive for St. Antony's College in Oxford).

By applying the methodology, F&R was able to see that its estimated budget had been too tight, although the approach was applied to the Bolzano hospital project when an initial budget estimate for cost and time had already been made. However, when implementing the collaborative planning phase, the foreperson could provide cost and time estimates at the task level, based on which the estimated budget for the overall project could be computed and compared to the initial one. Of course, the tasks' level of productivity provided by the foreperson was an estimate, so it could also have led to wrong conclusions, but by monitoring the actual progress on site, it was possible to refine the estimated productivity to make it increasingly close to the real conditions on site. Without the monitoring, F&R could rely only on the budget estimate, and the only way to determine its reliability would have been to wait until the end of the project or, in the best case, to check the progress at predefined milestones that occurred approximately every 6 months. This kind of infrequent monitoring would have limited the possibilities for intervention in the process execution or for adjusting the budget.

Another important result was an *increase in the productivity* as a result of improved scheduling of the activities, monitoring the progress of the work, and holding the continuous improvement workshops, where problems and solutions were discussed collaboratively. During the 4 months in which these workshops took place, indeed, there was an increase in the productivity on site, estimated as saving 400 man hours (Dallasega 2016). Once the workshops were halted, productivity began to decrease.

Our analysis could not quantify how much of the savings in man hours were thanks to the application of the methodology and how much was applicable to other factors (e.g., good weather conditions, greater availability of the resources). However, improved control over the process and schedules that covered short time periods allowed the company to react promptly to problems that arose during the process execution. For instance, the company discovered a decrease in productivity that was attributable to the lack of synchronization with the other companies for the use of the crane, which was sometimes unavailability for relatively long periods of time. The problem affected several tasks since materials to be installed could not be unloaded from the trucks. After a synchronization plan was established with the other companies, productivity began increasing again.

Applying the methodology allowed F&R to identify one of the main causes of variation in productivity, as the company concluded that the *learning curve effect* had an impact on individual tasks. The company compared the productivity when the same crew performed a task several times with the productivity when a new crew was assigned to the same task for the first time. Using an experienced crew may result in performing activities faster, but it could also cause a misalignment between the production line and the construction site when productivity for a task increases too much. By monitoring the progress of the work, the company discovered several such possibilities in advance and increased the production of certain components or scheduled different tasks according to the resource availability. The effect of the learning curve is an important aspect of the process that should be investigated by the company and its scientific partners.

The methodology also improved the synchronization among F&R's departments. Each task was labelled with the components required, and thanks to the process model and the detailed scheduling of the activities, it was possible to relate the engineering department's drawings, the components to be produced by the fabrication department, and the tasks for the installation department and to synchronize the scheduling with the production line (e.g., to start the production early enough to supply the necessary material for a scheduled task, or to prevent the scheduling of tasks for which the components were not ready).

Another effect of applying the methodology was improved transparency of the process's execution. Information was consistently available on the planning board, where the daily schedule, the tables for monitoring the progress, the charts on the overall process, and the issues identified to that point were posted and accessible by every worker. This kind of approach improved the working environment, as the workers felt engaged and like important contributors to the project's success, rather than just like executors of tasks (Rosemann and vom Brocke 2015).

5 Lessons Learned

One of the main characteristics of the methodology is its *collaborative* nature, which support the active involvement of the main figures that take part in the project. This collaboration was done in the course of the Bolzano hospital project by involving the main figures from F&R in the process modelling and in the continuous improvement workshops. Ideally, the methodology also fosters collaboration across companies. One of the advantages of this approach is that each worker all of the companies are experts in their own areas of competence. By involving them in the process management, F&R could take advantage of their expertise and put them in the position of agreeing on a strategy that benefits both the project and the companies themselves (Rosemann and vom Brocke 2015). Collaboration supports inter- and intra-organizational synchronization (vom Brocke et al. 2015), as the methodology supplies a way for companies to discuss how they want to execute the process and find an agreement that suits all of them while still guaranteeing the quality of the final result. A company can also discuss the process model internally in order to identify possible problems in advance and implement ways to overcome them.

Another important aspect of the methodology is that the process management must be *flexible* in order to address the variability of the processes that are part of construction projects (vom Brocke et al. 2015). Given the number of unpredictable events that often occur on site and that are often responsible for delays, if the process is flexible, such delays can be reduced more easily by defining a process model that, by capturing only the main dependencies among the tasks, can be changed easily if needed. The methodology also foresees the need for defining short-term, detailed schedules. Traditional approaches usually use long-term schedules for bidding purposes or for communicating with the customer, who is probably not interested in the details of how the process will be carried out, but these schedules are less precise than are schedules with shorter terms, so when a problem occurs, how to address its cause to limit delays is often unclear.

A *reliable measurement* of the progress of the work on site is a prerequisite for making reliable schedules. If these schedules are based on forecasts of the construction project's progress, they are likely to become inapplicable soon. Reliable measurement of progress also allows a company to identify and limit possible sources of delays, thanks to the approach's flexibility. Finally, reliable measurement makes multiple kinds of analysis possible that can suggest how to improve the process, how to redistribute or acquire new resources, whether the deadlines are going to be met, and so on.

Workers' *empowerment* is an aspect of the methodology that is seldom considered to be important. However, such empowerment can improve the process's overall execution (Rosemann and vom Brocke 2015). Giving people responsibility and helping them to feel actively involved in the process creates a working environment in which workers are motivated and feel like important elements in the project's success. Empowerment in the Bolzano hospital project was achieved by implementing the collaborative approach and transparency of the process execution. At any time, workers could access the planning board on site to see the schedule for the week, the daily progress reports, the charts that plotted the productivity analysis, and so on.

The application of the methodology also showed that good systems for process management are lacking, so *IT support* needs work (Rosemann and vom Brocke 2015). An IT system must be easy to use and non-intrusive if it is to be adopted by employees. The workers in the Bolzano hospital project expressed some skepticism when the new approach was introduced because they perceived that it would require additional work. The non-intrusiveness of the methodology and its ease of use helped to overcome this resistance: The process modelling was performed with the support of a graphic and intuitive language, which allowed the process designers to use it with little additional effort, and the scheduling and monitoring were realized by means of Excel. Thus, workers were asked to work with tools with which they were already familiar.

The Excel spreadsheets were developed in an ad-hoc way for the project, but the approach can be generalized to any construction project and automated with the support of suitable technologies (Dumas et al. 2013; Rosemann and vom Brocke 2015). In particular, we are developing a software prototype (Dallasega et al. 2015; Marengo et al. 2016) that will generalize the concepts of the PRECISE methodology; support the graphic process modelling; generalize the Excel spreadsheets by automatically gathering the data from the process model to configure the scheduling and the monitoring; implement some automatic checks, such as a check on the process model's feasibility and the schedule's compliance of a schedule with the model; suggest schedules that are optimal with regard to desired criteria; and generate charts and reports for the productivity and progress analyses as soon as data from the monitoring is inserted in the system.

The prototype is designed to be used with digital touch boards that reproduce the planning boards that are currently used on site so the workers will have concepts and tools with which they are already familiar. The prototype will have fewer functionalities than commercial tools like ConstructSim Planner (2016), Sitesimeditor (2016), and Vico Software (2016), but these commercial tools are often complicated to use and require specific competencies. From this perspective, the approach that we will adopt is less intrusive since it will not require specific training for its adoption nor long configuration procedures in order to start working on a project. For this reason, we believe that this solution will better suit SMEs, which often lack the resources to invest in expensive products (vom Brocke et al. 2015).

Acknowledgement This work was done within the auspices of the research projects MoMaPC and KENDO, which were financed by the Free University of Bozen-Bolzano.

References

Bentley. (2016). *ConstructSim Planner*. Last accessed April 2016, from https://www.bentley.com/en/products/product-line/constructionsoftware/constructsim

Build4Future. (2014). Last accessed April 2016, from http://www.fraunhofer.it/en/focus/projects/build4future.html

Dallasega, P. (2016). *A method and IT-framework for on-demand delivery in make-to-order construction supply chain*. PhD thesis, Submitted to the University of Stuttgart, Germany.

Dallasega, P., Matt, D. T., & Krause, D. (2013). *Design of the building execution process in SME construction networks*. In 2nd International Workshop on Design in Civil and Environmental Engineering.

Dallasega, P., Marengo, E., Nutt, W., Rescic, L., Matt, D. T., & Rauch, E. (2015). *Design of a framework for supporting the execution management of small and medium sized projects in the AEC-industry*. In 4th International Workshop on Design in Civil and Environmental Engineering.

Dumas, M., La Rosa, M., Mendling, J., & Reijers, H. A. (2013). *Fundamentals of business process management*. Berlin: Springer.

Frener&Reifer. (2016). Last accessed April 2016, from http://www.frener-reifer.com/home-en/

Marengo, E., Dallasega, P., Montali, M., & Nutt, W. (2016). Towards a graphical language for process modelling in construction. In *CAiSE Forum*.

Rosemann, M., & vom Brocke, J. (2015). The six core elements of business process management. In J. vom Brocke & M. Rosemann (Eds.), *Handbook on business process management, introduction, methods, and information systems* (Vol. 1, 2nd ed., pp. 105–122). Berlin: Springer.

Sitesimeditor. (2016). Last accessed April 2016, from https://www.inf.bi.ruhr-uni-bochum.de/index.php?lang=de&Itemid=361

Vico Software. (2016). Last accessed April 2016, from http://www.vicosoftware.com/

vom Brocke, J., Zelt, S., & Schmiedel, T. (2015). Considering context in business process management: The BPM context framework. *BPM Trends, 1*.

Elisa Marengo is Research Assistant with the KRDB Research Centre on Knowledge and Data, Faculty of Computer Science, Free University of Bozen-Bolzano, Italy. Her main research interests concern business processes, with a particular emphasis on business process management, modelling and manipulation of data. She is also interested in data quality aspects, such as data completeness, and interaction protocols for multiagent systems. She is serving as a reviewer for several international journals and conferences.

Patrick Dallasega is Assistant Professor at the Free University of Bolzano in the field of Industrial Engineering. He teaches Industrial Installations in the Bachelor degree and Project Management in the Master degree. His research interests are in the field of Industry 4.0, Supply Chain Management, Lean Construction, and Lean Management for Make-to-Order (MTO) manufacturing companies.

Marco Montali is a Senior Researcher with the KRDB Research Centre on Knowledge and Data, Faculty of Computer Science, Free University of Bozen-Bolzano, Italy. He devises techniques grounded in artificial intelligence, formal methods, knowledge representation and reasoning, for the intelligent management of dynamic systems operating over data, with particular emphasis on business processes and multi-agent systems. On these topics, he authored more than 130 papers, appeared in top-tier, international journals, conferences, and workshops, such as ACM Transactions on Intelligent Systems and Technology, ACM Transactions on the Web, Journal of Artificial Intelligence, Information Systems. His Ph.D. thesis received the "Marco Cadoli" 2007–2009 Prize from the Italian Association for Logic Programming, as outstanding thesis in computational logic. In 2015, he received the "Marco Somalvico" 2015 Prize from the Italian Association for Artificial Intelligence, as the best under 35 Italian researcher who autonomously contributed to advance the state-of-the-art in artificial intelligence.

Werner Nutt is a full professor of Computer Science at the Free University of Bozen-Bolzano. Prior to this appointment, he held positions at Heriot-Watt University, Edinburgh, The Hebrew University in Jerusalem, and the German Reserach Center for Artificial Intelligence, Saarbrücken, Germany. He worked on automated theorem proving, logic programming, knowledge representation and reasoning, management of incomplete information, and business processes. He has published more than 100 international papers on these topics. He is currently leading an interdisciplinary project with the aim to develop techniques and tools for modelling, organizing and monitoring construction processes.

Michael Reifer Since 2014 he is employed as Head of Innovation and TQM at FRENER & REIFER GmbH/ Srl (www.frener-reifer.com), a well-known, leading manufacturer of customized innovative building envelope solutions, founded by Georg Frener and Franz Reifer on the 15th October 1974 and located in Brixen-South Tyrol-Italy. After his diploma at the Faculty of Civil Engineering at "Leopold-Franzens" University, Innsbruck-Austria Michael Reifer started full time activities within the department of structural engineering as technical project developer and project manager. In 2007 he started innovation projects in the fields of Freeform Architecture, Light Wight Structures, Sustainable Facades, Adaptive Facades and Lean Construction. Since 2014 he is responsible for Integrated Business Model Innovation and Total Quality Management. Further important missions are the work as president of an innovative cooperation platform for sustainable alpine construction technologies (www.kab-net.com) and as member of the regional entrepreneurship association.

Exposing Impediments to Insurance Claims Processing

Compulsory Third Party Insurance in Queensland

Robert Andrews, Moe Wynn, Arthur H.M ter Hofstede, Jingxin Xu, Kylie Horton, Paul Taylor, and Sue Plunkett-Cole

Abstract

(a) **Situation faced**: Processing injury-compensation claims, such as compulsory third party (CTP) claims, is complex, as it involves negotiations among multiple parties (e.g., claimants, insurers, law firms, health providers). Queensland's CTP program is regulated by the Motor Accident Insurance Commission (MAIC). The Nominal Defendant, an arm of MAIC, determines liability for claims when the vehicle "at fault" is unregistered or unidentified and manages such claims from injured persons. While the relevant legislation mandates milestones for claims processing, the Nominal Defendant sees significant behavioral and performance variations in CTP claims processing, affecting the costs and durations of claims. The reasons for these variations are poorly understood.

(b) **Action taken**: The BPM initiative took a process-mining approach that focused on the process identification, discovery, and analysis phases of the BPM Lifecycle. We undertook automated process discovery and comparative performance analysis with the aim of identifying where claims processing across cohorts of interest to the Nominal Defendant differed. In parallel, we conducted a context analysis with the aim of identifying the context factors that affect claim duration and cost. The personal injury

R. Andrews (✉) • M. Wynn • A.H.M ter Hofstede • J. Xu • S. Plunkett-Cole
Queensland University of Technology, Brisbane, QLD, Australia
e-mail: r.andrews@qut.edu.au; m.wynn@qut.edu.au; a.terhofstede@qut.edu.au; j15.xu@qut.edu.au; sue.plunkettcole@qut.edu.au

K. Horton • P. Taylor
Motor Accident Insurance Commission, Brisbane, QLD, Australia
e-mail: kylie.horton@maic.qld.gov.au; paul.taylor@maic.qld.gov.au

J. vom Brocke, J. Mendling (eds.), *Business Process Management Cases*, Management for Professionals, DOI 10.1007/978-3-319-58307-5_15

literature and interviews with representative Nominal Defendant staff informed our selection of data attributes.

(c) **Results achieved**: Process models were developed to facilitate comparative visualization of processes. The Nominal Defendant was particularly interested in differences in the processes for specific cohorts of claims: (i) overall claims, (ii) claims involving unregistered vehicles versus unidentified vehicles, and (iii) direct claims versus legally represented claims. The model facilitated identification of aspects of claims processing where there were significant differences between cohorts. Data mining/feature selection techniques identified a set of process-related context factors affecting claim duration and cost. Models utilizing these context factors were able to distinguish between cases with short and long durations with 68% accuracy and between low-cost and high-cost claims with 83% accuracy.

(d) **Lessons learned**: This multi-faceted process-mining study presented many challenges and opportunities for refining our process-mining methodology and toolset. Data-related challenges arose because of the replacement of claims-management software during the study. Legislative changes, changes to key personnel, and the semi-structured nature of CTP claims-processing introduced issues related to concept drift. Each of these issues affected process discovery, but close collaboration with the stakeholders proved valuable in addressing these issues. Novel visualization techniques were developed to support delivery of insights gained through comparative analysis that will guide process improvement. Consideration of context considerably broadens the scope of process mining and facilitates reasoning about process specifics.

1 Introduction

Processing injury-compensation claims, such as compulsory third party (CTP) claims, is complex, as it involves negotiations among multiple parties (e.g., claimants, insurers, law firms, health providers). In Queensland, Australia, CTP insurance operates as a fault-based system that provides motor vehicle owners, drivers, passengers, and other insured persons an unlimited liability policy for personal injury caused through the use of the insured vehicle in incidents to which the Motor Accident Insurance Act 1994 applies. For an injured third party, the CTP scheme provides common-law rights that allow the injured person to seek compensation from the person at fault for the injury and other related losses. Since it is a fault-based system, a valid claim requires the injured party to prove liability—that is, to establish the presence of negligence—against an owner or driver of a motor vehicle.

The Queensland CTP scheme is governed by the MAI Act 1994 ("the Act") and is underwritten by four licensed, commercial insurers who accept applications for insurance and manage claims on behalf of their policyholders. CTP premiums, collected as a component of vehicle registration, contribute to the insurers' premium pool and are used to pay compensation to accident victims. The Nominal Defendant (ND), a statutory body established under the Act, manages claims when the vehicle at fault is unregistered or unidentified (i.e., not covered by CTP insurance so not within the ambit of the participating licensed commercial insurers). The ND is considered a licensed insurer under the Act and is funded by a levy within the CTP insurance premium. The CTP program is regulated and monitored by the Motor Accident Insurance Commission (MAIC), and the ND is an arm of that commission.

During the project, the ND had ten staff members, eight of whom had claims portfolios to manage. Over the most recent three fiscal years, the ND received an average of 230 claims per year, which were distributed across the claims officers based on the claims' characteristics and the claims officers' experience.

2 Situation Faced

The legislation governing the CTP scheme—that is, the Act—includes certain provisions for the establishment of a claim by an injured person with a CTP insurer (i.e., the ND when the vehicle at fault is either unregistered or unidentified). The provisions prescribe the time that may elapse between when the injured person's notifying the insurer of his or her intention to claim compensation by lodging a Notification of Accident Claim (NOAC) form following the occurrence of an accident involving a motor vehicle and when the insurer receives the claimant's NOAC form and determines whether (1) the claim complies with the legislation, (2) the insurer will meet the injured person's rehabilitation expenses, and (3) the insurer is liable for the claim.

The Act also requires that the insurer, as soon as practicable after receiving the claimant's NOAC form, make a fair and reasonable estimate of the damages to which the claimant is entitled in an action against the insurer, and make a written offer of settlement, or invite the claimant to do so. A party who has received an offer must indicate acceptance or rejection of the offer within 3 months. Under the Act, failure to respond provides the party that made the offer the option of making application to the court.

Once the claim has been established—that is, compliance with the Act and liability has been determined—the time required to reach settlement is generally driven by (1) the claimant's willingness to settle the claim, and/or (2) the claimant's reaching a point of medical stability such that further recovery is not likely. The Act provides several modes by which the cost of attaining expert medical opinion as to the extent of medical impairment may be met or shared by the claimant and the insurer. The Act also makes provisions for various forms of settlement negotiations, including informal agreement, mediation, a formal compulsory conference, and litigation. (See Fig. 1 for an overview of the general claims-management process.)

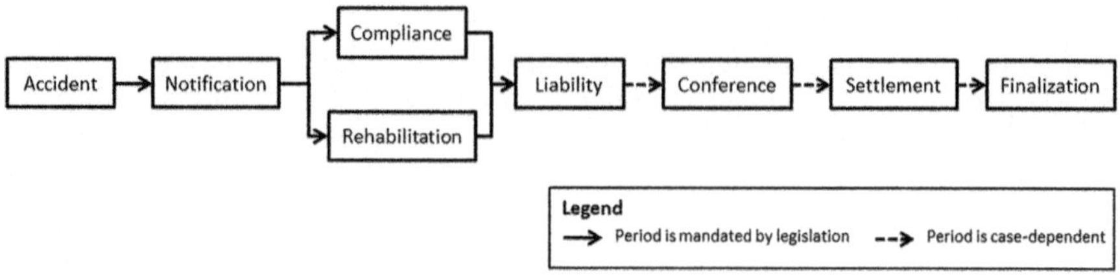

Fig. 1 Schematic of the general CTP claims-management process

CTP claims processing involves interactions between many organizations (e.g., the insurer, ambulance and police services, hospitals, law firms, independent medical experts, investigators, social welfare bodies like Centrelink and Workers Compensation, rehabilitation services providers). CTP claims processing is also affected by factors like the size of the claims portfolio managed by the insurer, the insurer's internal claims management process (and supporting information system), the claims-management personnel's experience and skills, the level of resourcing, and so on.

Despite the legislation's mandating certain milestones for claims processing and providing for various pathways for the claim to be progressed and finalized, the ND (and other CTP insurers) see significant behavioral and performance variations in CTP claims processing and variations in the costs and durations of claims. For instance, of the 306 settled cases in the study's dataset in which the injury severity was rated "minimal," the duration from notification to settlement ranged from a minimum of 0 months to a maximum of 171 months, and the administrative and settlement costs ranged from AU$0 to AU$864,300.[1] Grant et al.'s (2014) study of recovery outcomes for traffic accident-related personal injury compensation claimants concluded that process-related stressors like claimants' ability to understand the process and the duration of the process affected claimants negatively, leading them to suffer from high rates of disability, anxiety, and depression.

While the Act provides the overarching framework that governs the general processing of CTP claims, the individual parties' behavior–that is, the context in which the process is executed—has a bearing on how any individual claim progresses. Dey (2001) defined context as "any information that can be used to characterize the situation of an entity." Here, we define context as the set of internal and extrinsic properties that affect the execution of a business process. Rosemann et al. (2008) argued that understanding of the effects of context on process execution indicates the ability to anticipate "relevant changes in the business environment [in order to] trigger the timely adaptation of business procedures, [leading to] increased process flexibility, decreased reaction time and improved risk management." Similarly, van der Aalst and Dustdar (2012) contended that context data

[1]The median settlement figure for "minimally" severe injuries was AU$50,000, and the average settlement figure was AU$77,000. In this particular case, the claimant had a history of prior CTP and Workers Compensation claims.

(especially process, social, and environmental context) plays a pivotal role in understanding the differences in process behaviors and levels of performance.

The aims of the current study are to (1) identify process-related factors that affect claim duration at the ND, (2) investigate the differences in process behaviors for certain cohorts of claims that are of interest to the ND (i.e., context factors that ND sees as having an impact on claim outcomes), and (3) identify sets of previously unrecognized context variables that affect claim outcomes in terms of duration and cost.

3 Action Taken

Prior to the commencement of this study, the ND conceived a multi-pronged process-improvement strategy that was based partly on cultural changes related to adopting a more proactive approach to claims management and partly on certain claims-management initiatives. The modifications to the claims-management process included (1) changing how the ND engaged with its advising law firms by altering the fee basis of the engagement away from hourly rate to an agreed fee and encouraging a more collegial relationship in order to foster more in-house management of claims under advice from the supporting law firm, rather than outsourcing the management of entire claims to the law firm; and (2) encouraging claimants to manage their claims themselves, where appropriate, rather than engaging a legal representative. Further changes, particulary in the notification to liability decision phase of the claim, are envisioned for claims that involve unregistered vehicles.

The BPM initiative took a process-mining approach that focused on the process identification, discovery, and analysis phases of the BPM lifecycle (Dumas et al. 2013). We undertook a process discovery and comparative performance analysis for the ND with the aim of identifying differences in how claims were processed across cohorts of interest to the ND. The ND had instigated some changes in claims management for these particular cohorts of claims and was seeking an assessment of the changes' effects on claims processing. In parallel, we conducted a context analysis with the aim of identifying context factors the ND had not recognized but that affect claim duration and cost.

The study had seven phases:

1. *Domain familiarization (process identification)*—Researchers familiarized themselves with the domain, including the legislation that governs the CTP program, formal process models already in existence, informal process-support documentation (e.g., guidelines for assigning claims officers to cases), and electronic process data available from MAIC's and ND's information systems.
2. *Preparation of a set of context data*—Researchers determined candidates for process-related context attributes from the literature related to personal injury compensation (Cassidy et al. 2000; Glover et al. 2006; Kenardy et al. 2013; Murgatroyd et al. 2011; O'Donnell 2000; Roberts-Yates 2003; Yang et al. 2010) and from interviews conducted with key ND staff. The 49 resulting context

attributes were grouped into attributes that relate to the claimant, the claimant's history of personal-injury claims, the accident, the claim itself, the injury, legal representatives involved, damages and costs, third parties involved in the claim, and details of staff/teams involved in processing the claim. The candidate set was reviewed by key ND and MAIC staff and then amended according to what was possible to collect from available data (e.g., MAIC's Personal Injury Registry).

3. *Preparation of a claims data set*—The initial data extraction consisted of 4371 finalized claims records dating from December 2002 to March 2015, inclusive. After initial analysis and consultation with key ND and MAIC personnel, the study data were restricted to claims that were finalized between September 2012 and November 2015 or were been lodged since September 2012 but not yet finalized. This process resulted in a data set consisting of 1599 claims (1117 finalized claims and 482 open claims), which was reduced to 1523 claims (1049 finalized claims and 474 open claims) following data cleaning.
4. *Assessment of data quality and data cleaning*—The raw log data for both claims and context was scrutinized to determine its quality and suitability for the purposes of the study. We used the event log quality framework proposed by Bose et al. (2013) to classify the quality issues discovered in the raw logs.
5. *Process discovery*—Process models in the form of workflow nets were derived from the existing, formal process maps and the cleaned claims event log.
6. *Analysis of process performance*—Various performance measures were derived that relate to overall process performance and comparison of the process performance for cohorts of interest to the ND.
7. *Context analysis*—The context data set was analyzed using data mining techniques (supervised learning) to determine sets of context variables that can be used to distinguish between short- and long-duration claims (time between the liability decision and claim settlement) and between low- and high-cost claims.

A critical success factor in any data-driven analysis is the selection and preparation of the data. Data that is both aligned with the purpose of the analysis and of high quality ensures that the data itself is not an impediment to deriving meaningful insights from the analysis. We provide more detail on two of the phases of the study—preparation of the set of context data and assessment of data quality and data cleaning—that related to selecting, pre-processing, and formatting the data to be suitable for use in our process-mining analysis.

3.1 Preparation of a Set of Context Data

The context data selected for the study was grouped into attributes that relate to the accident in which the claimant was injured, the claimant himself or herself, the claimant's employment pre- and post-accident, the claimant's injury type and severity, and legal aspects (whether the claimant engaged a law firm, whether the

ND engaged a "panel" law firm, whether the claim was settled as a result of court proceedings).

Context variables that the literature indicated have a bearing on the outcome of personal injury compensation claims but which that could not be populated from available data sources were (1) variables related to the claimant's psycho-social background (history of mental illness, history of absenteeism, expectations regarding recovery, effect of the accident on mental health), socio-economic status, perception of the process (transparent or opaque), and willingness to settle); (2) variables related to the claims officer's individual work behavior (workload, rate, work ethic), relationship with team members, and manner of dealing with third parties (e.g., law firms, police, ambulance, hospitals, Centrelink, Work Cover) involved in the claim; and (3) variables related to third parties (internal processes for dealing with requests for information from ND, resourcing).

The context data used in the study was collected from information claimants provided when submitting their claims (i.e., information on the NOAC form) and from the ND's event logs. Neither of these sources included fields that directly recorded or facilitated calculation of the candidate variables.

The context data set used in the study consisted of data related to the claim status (finalized or open); the accident's location, time of day, vehicle class involved, and vehicle type (unregistered or unidentified); the claimant's gender, age at the time of the accident, marital status, home location; the claimant's employment (employment status and occupation at the time of the accident, whether and when the claimant returned to work, and the claimant's occupation at the time of settlement); medical data (whether an ambulance and/or hospitalization was required, injury severity, presence of whiplash, and treatment code); data related to legal issues (e.g., the number of Work Cover claims, the number of previous CTP claims, whether the claimant was legally represented, information about the claimant's solicitor (name, specialization, location, organization size), whether the claimant used ND's legal advice and the name of the panel law firm, whether an independent medical examination was required); claim-related costs (e.g., expenses incurred by the ND in meeting the costs of the investigation, independent medical examinations).

3.2 Assessment of Data Quality and Data Cleaning

The data-quality assessment and data cleaning aspect of the study revealed a number of quality issues in the event log. We discuss the major data quality issues from the event log—incorrect time stamps, incorrect activity names, irrelevant events, and concept drift—and use the data quality framework and naming conventions described by Bose et al. (2013) to categorize them.

Incorrect Timestamp Distinct sets of activities that had timestamp irregularities included (1) activities with only date values for the entirety of the period covered by the data extraction, so all of these activities ultimately had a time component of

"00:00:00" in the event log; (2) activities with a date value recorded in the source data only after a particular point in time (at or around 27 June 2005), prior to which the activities have a time component of "00:00:00"; (3) activities with "minute" values in the range of 1–12, indicating that the "month" values had inadvertently been written in the "minute" component of the event timestamp.

These timestamp-quality issues had the potential to affect negatively both the process discovery analysis and the process performance analysis by, for example, ordering activities incorrectly and providing incorrect durations of activities. Timestamp issues were addressed by requesting a second data extraction to resolve the month/minute transposition and then removing cases that included events recorded before 27 June 2005.

Incorrect Activity Name Sets of activities that displayed incorrect activity names manifested in the log as (1) activities that represented the same processing step but were recorded with different names for the activity because the event log contained data extracted from both the legacy system and the replacement Connect system, each of which had their own naming conventions; and (2) an unusually high number of activity labels in the source logs. The information systems from which the source logs were extracted were not "process-aware information systems" so they did not explicitly record events and activities. The activity labels were constructed as the concatenation of two (possibly) free-form text fields in the log that were derived from the values recorded in form fields of the underlying system. There were initially 3775 distinct pairs of the form fields in the log.

The *incorrect activity names* had the potential to create unnecessarily complex models, which would negatively affect the performance analysis. The activities in (1), above, were identified but retained in the final event log in order to distinguish claims handled in each of the systems. With reference to (2), above, using string matching and consultation with domain experts, we reduced the 3775 label pairs to a set of 85 consistent activity labels.

Irrelevant Events Irrelevant events manifested in the log as (1) activities that could be performed at any time in the process (e.g., setting of a diary note by the claims officer), so they were irrelevant to both process discovery and performance analysis; and (2)

1. Activities that occur multiple times in a claim, often on the same day (e.g., the recording of every offer and counter-offer made during a mediation/conference), as individual offers were irrelevant events from a process-discovery and performance-analysis point of view. We added a single record indicating the offer/counter-offer cycle.

These *irrelevant events* were removed from the log.

Concept Drift The changeover from a legacy claims-management system to the "Connect" claims-management system was revealed in the distribution of certain activities in the log (i.e., some activities occurred only prior to the change-over date and others occurred only after it) and the granularity of timestamp recordings in event log records (i.e., some activities that migrated from the legacy system had only a date component to the timestamp, so the time component defaulted to "00:00:00").

4 Results Achieved

The results achieved from the study are discussed in terms of the process-mining results achieved and the outcomes the ND derived from the study.

4.1 Process Discovery

A workflow net discovered from the event log was a "hybrid" in the sense that it consisted of activities drawn from both the legacy and the Connect claims-management systems. The initial model suffered from "underfitting," as it permitted behaviors that were not evident in the event log. The model was manually adjusted based on domain knowledge and verified by replaying the event log on the model to ensure that fitness remained high (approx. 80%). Achieving this level of fitness required the inclusion of many "silent" transitions that allowed activities to be skipped, including business steps that are not compulsory in all cases (e.g., conferences) and some transitions to deal with differences between the legacy system and the Connect system. For instance, the two systems use different activity names to represent the same business step, such as three names in the legacy system that refer to the operation of deciding liability ("accept liability," "reject liability," and "accept partial liability," but only one name ("approve liability decision") in the Connect system.

4.2 Process Performance Analysis

In this phase of the study, the discovered process models and event logs were analyzed to determine performance differences between the claim cohorts of interest to the ND. Because of the models' complex nature and the fact that processes are, by nature, knowledge-intensive and semi-structured, we used the average time taken for a claim to reach certain key processing steps relative to a fixed (starting) point in the process to measure performance (e.g., the occurrence of the "receive claim form" event, indicating that a claimant had lodged a NOAC form). Only "finalized" claims were considered.

Unregistered Versus Unidentified Vehicles Figure 2 highlights the 14 activities for which there was greater than 20% variation between cohorts in terms of the average time required to reach certain key events (and where there were more than

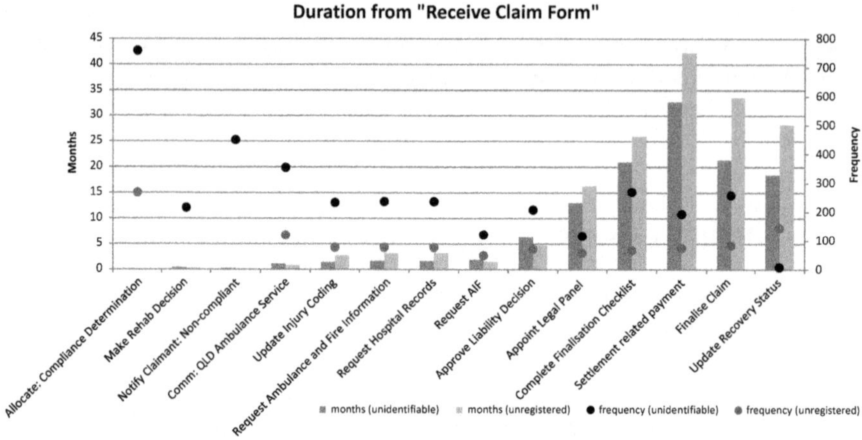

Fig. 2 Key activity differences—unregistered and unidentified vehicles

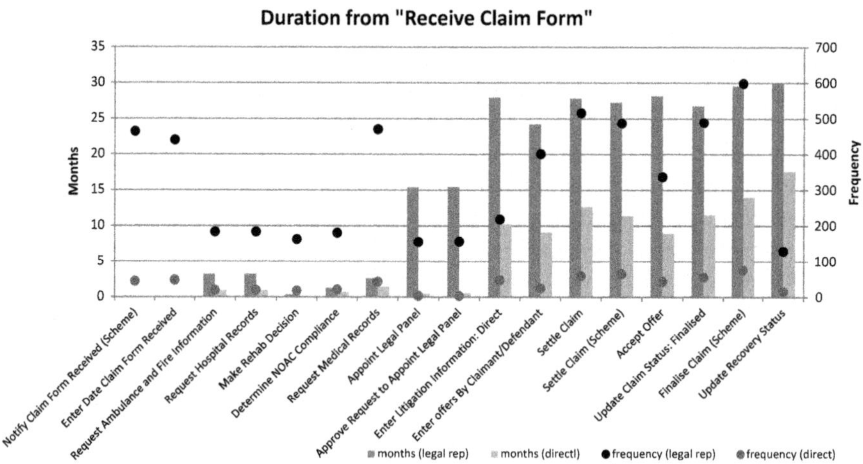

Fig. 3 Key activity differences—legally represented and direct claimants

ten cases in both cohorts that reached the key activity). The comparative performance analysis revealed that claims that involved an unregistered vehicle generally proceeded faster from notification through to making a liability decision than did claims that involved an unidentified vehicle. However, from this point on, the unidentified vehicle claims proceeded to finalization faster than the unregistered vehicle claims did, as the former were completed an average of 3.7 months faster than the latter.

Legally Represented Claimants Versus Direct Claimants Figure 3 highlights activities in which there was greater than 40% variation between cohorts in terms of the average time taken to reach certain key events (and where there were more than ten cases in both cohorts that reached the key activity).

As Fig. 3 shows, there are clear differences in the average time taken to reach key milestone events, as the cohort of direct-claimant claims take less time on average to reach the milestones than does the cohort of legally represented claims. This evidence indicates that the process changes that related to direct claimants had a positive effect on claims-management and process outcomes.

4.3 Context Data Analysis

Analysis of the context data was carried out using the RapidMiner[2] modelling tool. In one investigation, the aim was to identify a set of context variables that would be useful in predicting the duration of claims. The aim of a second investigation was to identify a set of context variables that would be useful in predicting the cost of claims. Figure 4 shows the major milestones in the claims process and where in the process values for the various sets of context variables become known.

Supervised learning (a decision tree) was used with the set of cases to undertake a binary classification of the cases as being "short" or "long" in the case duration investigation and "low" or "high" in the costs investigation. RapidMiner's "binning by frequency" operator was used to split the data into the two categories for each investigation. Binning by frequency results in each class having approximately the

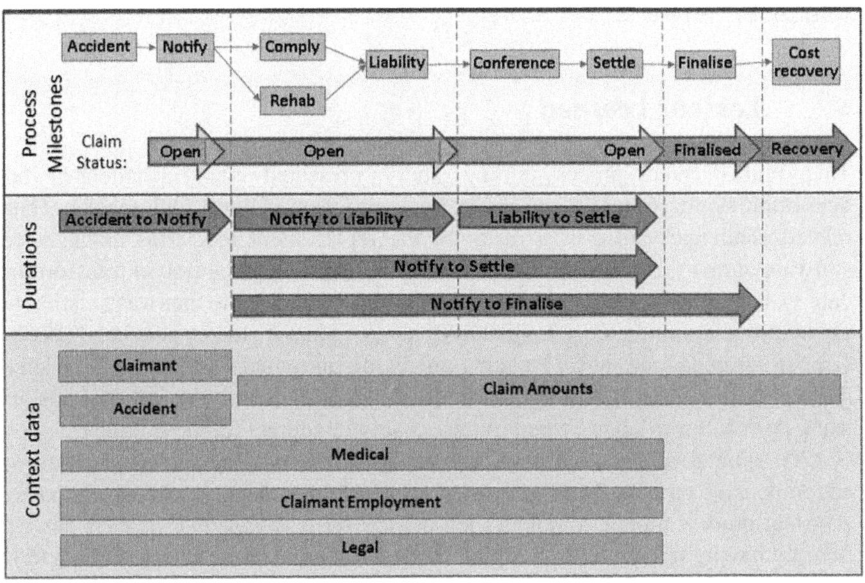

Fig. 4 Process milestones and availability of context data

[2]https://rapidminer.com/

same number of cases. In the duration investigation, "short" duration cases were those in which settlement was reached within 22.5 months of notification, and "long" cases were all others. In the costs investigation, "low-cost" cases were those in which the total (administrative plus settlement) cost of the claim was in the range of $45.00–$62,735.50, and "high-cost" cases were all others.

The decision tree algorithm achieved 68.21% accuracy, correctly predicting the class for 268 of 396 claims used in the claim-duration investigation. Analysis of the tree revealed that the ND's decision to appoint its own legal advisor was the key factor in differentiating between short- and long-duration cases. Other differentiating factors included the claimant's employment status, whether the claimant engaged legal representatives, whether the legal representative was a personal injury specialist, the severity of the injury (particularly whether the injury was whiplash), and whether the case involved an independent medical examination.

The decision tree algorithm achieved 83.15% accuracy, correctly classifying 592 of 712 claims used in the claim costs investigation. Analysis of the tree revealed that the requirement for an independent medical examination was the significant factor in differentiating between low-cost and high-cost cases. Other factors indicated by the model included the claim duration (period between insurer accepting liability and a settlement amount being accepted by the claimant), the claimant's age at the time of the accident, the severity of the injury, the claimant's pre-accident occupation, and whether the claimant's legal representative had a "no win, no fee" fee basis.

5 Lessons Learned

This multi-faceted process-mining study presented many challenges and opportunities for refining our process-mining methodology and toolset. Data-related challenges arose as a result of the replacement of claims management software during the period of the study and the largely manual task of transforming data extracted from source information systems into a log file that was suitable for use by process-mining tools. Legislative changes, changes to key personnel, and the semi-structured nature of CTP claims-processing introduced concept drift. Each of these issues impacted the study, but close collaboration with the stakeholders and using domain knowledge helped immeasurably in addressing these issues.

CTP claims management may best be described as a semi-structured, knowledge-intensive process. Semi-structured processes are characterized by not having a formal process model, although they usually have an informal process description; by having many points at which different continuations are possible, and by being driven largely by content status and human decision-making (Lakshmanan et al. 2011). The semi-structured nature of the CTP claims-management process posed its own difficulties in our ability to conduct performance analysis in terms of durations between key events. Analysis on a direct-follow and even an eventual-follow basis proved inconclusive. The best results were obtained by comparing cohorts based on the time they took to reach key milestones.

The comparative performance analysis showed, in the case of legally represented claims versus direct claimants, that there was a distinct difference in the performance of the two cohorts and indicated that the process-improvement initiatives that relate to direct claimants had resulted in overall shorter case durations.

The analysis of the cohorts of unidentified vehicles versus unregistered vehicles showed that significant differences related to investigations in the processing occur early in the claim process and differences related settlement and finalization occur toward the end of the claim process. These two areas are aspects of claims management where process-improvement initiatives could be targeted.

The context analysis resulted in a set of indicator variables that can be considered predictors of claim behavior. Of interest to the ND was a particular cohort of claims in which the injury is not severe, the injury type is whiplash, and the claimant is female and middle-aged. This cohort, as the context analysis revealed, had an unusually long claim duration compared to other low-severity whiplash claims. There is also some support for the presence of this phenomenon in the literature (Harder et al. 1998; Sterner et al. 2003), so this cohort may be a likely subject for targeted process-improvement initiatives.

Follow-up meetings with the key process stakeholders revealed that the project had delivered valuable insights to the stakeholders, raised additional questions for investigation, and generated opportunities for further collaborative research.

A key lesson learned from this case study was that there are particular deficiencies in the process-mining toolset for conducting process-performance comparisons across cohorts of claims. In particular, there was a requirement that we conduct performance analysis one cohort at a time and then manually combine the results to compare the cohorts. This one-cohort-at-a-time analysis involved a separate data preparation phase for each cohort, a performance-analysis phase, as well as a manual- comparison phase, all of which proved to be tedious and time-consuming. Therefore, we developed a multi-cohort, multi-perspective, comparative performance process-visualisation tool with automated support for defining cohorts.

Another lesson learned from the case study is that the consideration of context factors broadens the scope of process modelling beyond simply uncovering sequences and durations of events to facilitate reasoning about process specifics (e.g., differences in performance) and even predictions about process behavior.

Acknowledgements The research for this article was supported by a Queensland Government Accelerate Partnerships grant. We gratefully acknowledge the contributions made to this project by Neil Singleton (Insurance Commissioner) and Mark Allsopp.

References

Bose, J. C., Mans, R. S., & van der Aalst, W. M. P. (2013). Wanna improve process mining results? It's high time we consider data quality issues seriously. In *Proceedings of the IEEE Symposium on Computational Intelligence and Data Mining (CIDM)* (pp. 127–134). Singapore.

Cassidy, J. D., Carroll, L. J., Cote, P., Lemstra, M., Berglund, A., & Nygren, A. (2000). Effect of eliminating compensation for pain and suffering on the outcome of insurance claims for whiplash injury. *New England Journal of Medicine, 342*(16), 1179–1186.

Dey, A. K. (2001). Understanding and using context. *Personal and Ubiquitous Computing, 5*(1), 4–7.

Dumas, M., La Rosa, M., Mendling, J., & Reijers, H. (2013). *Fundamentals of business process management*. Heidelberg: Springer.

Glover, J., McDonald, S., Brombal, K., & Fisher, E. (2006). *A social health atlas of compensable injury in South Australia*. Public Health Information Development Unit.

Grant, G., O'Donnell, M. L., Spittal, M. J., Creamer, M., & Studdert, D. M. (2014). Relationship between stressfulness of claiming for injury compensation and long-term recovery – A prospective cohort study. *JAMA Psychiatry, 71*(4), 446–453. doi:10.1001/jamapsychiatry.2013.4023.

Harder, S., Veilleux, M., & Suissa, S. (1998). The effect of socio-demographic and crash-related factors on the prognosis of whiplash. *Journal of Clinical Epidemiology, 51*(5), 377–384.

Kenardy, J., Heron-Delaney, M., Lang, J., Brown, E., Hendrikz, J., Connelly, L., Sterling, M., & Bellamy, N. (2013). *Psychological and physical outcomes following a road traffic crash: 24 month follow-up*. In Presentation for the Actuaries Institute 2013 Injury Schemes Seminar, Gold Coast, Queensland.

Lakshmanan, G. T., Keyser, P. T., & Duan, S. (2011). *Detecting changes in a semi-structured business process through spectral graph analysis*. In IEEE 27th International Conference on Data Engineering Workshops (ICDEW) (pp. 255–260).

Murgatroyd, D. F., Cameron, I. D., & Harris, I. A. (2011). Understanding the effect of compensation on recovery from severe motor vehicle crash injuries: A qualitative study. *Injury Prevention, 17*(4), 222–227.

O'Donnell, C. (2000). Motor accident and workers' compensation insurance design for high-quality health outcomes and cost containment. *Disability and Rehabilitation, 22*(1–2), 88–96.

Roberts-Yates, C. (2003). The concerns and issues of injured workers in relation to claims/injury management and rehabilitation: The need for new operational frameworks. *Disability and Rehabilitation, 25*(16), 898–907.

Rosemann, M., Recker, J., & Flender, C. (2008). Contextualisation of business processes. *International Journal of Business Process Integration and Management, 3*(1), 47–60.

Sterner, Y., Toolanen, G., Gerdle, B., & Hildingsson, C. (2003). The incidence of whiplash trauma and the effects of different factors on recovery. *Journal of Spinal Disorders and Techniques, 16* (2), 195–199.

van der Aalst, W. M. P., & Dustdar, S. (2012). Process mining put into context. *IEEE Internet Computing, 16*(1), 82–86.

Yang, Z., Lowe, A. J., David, E., & Richardson, M. D. (2010). Factors that predict poor outcomes in patients with traumatic vertebral body fractures. *Injury, 41*(2), 226–230.

Robert Andrews is a Research Fellow within the Business Process Management discipline of the School of Information Systems at Queensland University of Technology. He obtained his PhD in 2003 from the Queensland University of Technology (QUT). Since 2015, after more than a decade in commercial practice, he has been involved in a number of research projects in the area of Business Process Management. His main research interests are in the area of process mining, machine learning and business intelligence.

Moe T. Wynn is a Senior Lecturer in the field of Business Process Management (BPM) within the School of Information Systems at Queensland University of Technology. Her research interests include process automation, process mining, data quality and comparative process analytics. She has published over 60 refereed research papers. Her work appeared in well-known journals in the field including Information Systems, Decision Support Systems, Information Sciences, Data and Knowledge Engineering, Information and Software technology, Formal Aspects of Computing, Journal of Computer and System Sciences, and Transactions on Petri Nets and Other Models of Concurrency.

Arthur ter Hofstede is a full Professor in the School of Information Systems of Queensland University of Technology in Brisbane, Australia. He has co-authored more than 80 journal articles, among others in Decision Support Systems, ACM Transactions on Software Engineering and Methodology, Information Systems, IEEE Transactions on Knowledge and Data Engineering, and Information Sciences. His main research interests are in business process automation and process mining.

Jingxin Xu received his bachelors degree in telecommunications engineering from Xidian University, Xian, China, in 2008, masters degree in information technology from the Queensland University of Technology (QUT), Brisbane, QLD, Australia, in 2010, and PhD degree in signal processing from QUT, in 2014. At the time of writing, Dr. Xu was a Postdoctoral Research Fellow with QUT, investigating process mining techniques for business process management.

Kylie Horton Appointed to MAIC in 2012, Kylie has held leadership positions in personal injury insurance across the public and private sectors for more than 15 years. Kylie is responsible for leading the Nominal Defendant, supervising licensed insurer claims management compliance and performance, and managing claims related legislated functions.

Paul Taylor is a Principal Business Intelligence analyst with the Motor Accident Insurance Commission (MAIC), Queensland, Australia. His Bachelor of Information Technology qualification has enhanced his ability to use new technologies and algorithms to drive change within MAIC. One of his roles is to connect, model and portray data using analytical tools to divulge practical insights used to drive strategic and legislative change for the Queensland Government. His work stretches from road trauma risk mitigation strategies to improving rehabilitation outcomes for those injured from road crashes.

Sue Plunkett-Cole is a Business Process Management consultant and data professional in Brisbane, Australia. She obtained her Master of Information Technology degree from Queensland University of Technology (QUT) in 2016. In the course of her higher degree studies, her report on data mining context variables to discover novel and useful predictive knowledge about business process outcomes gained her a faculty award from QUT in 2016.

Mining the Usability of Process-Oriented Business Software: The Case of the ARIS Designer of Software AG

Tom Thaler, Sabine Norek, Vittorio De Angelis, Dirk Maurer, Peter Fettke, and Peter Loos

Abstract

(a) **Situation faced**: The quality of the technical support of business processes plays an important role in the selection of corresponding software products. Against that background, software producers invest considerable capital and manpower in improving their business software's usability with regard to customers' needs and process-related requirements. However, existing approaches from the field of usability engineering generally require laboratory environments, which do not cover the real user behavior without limitations. Therefore, the case described here seeks to improve a user-centric UX approach based on the idea of automatic identification of real customer needs.

(b) **Action taken**: For that purpose, the German Research Center for Artificial Intelligence (DFKI) and Software AG analyzed the issues in the currently available UX process at Software AG. Research and practice were searched for additional approaches to the critical point of *understanding the user*. Finally, a four-step approach based on process mining, consisting of *user monitoring*, *trace clustering*, *usage model derivation*, and *usage model analysis* was conceptualized and evaluated in a user study.

(c) **Results achieved**: The application of the developed approach showed high flexibility and scalability in terms of the level of detail. Despite the small

T. Thaler (✉) • P. Fettke • P. Loos
Institute for Information Systems (IWi) at the German Research Center for Artificial Intelligence (DFKI), Saarbrücken, Germany

Saarland University, Saarbrücken, Germany
e-mail: tom.thaler@iwi.dfki.de; peter.fettke@iwi.dfki.de; peter.loos@iwi.dfki.de

S. Norek • V. De Angelis • D. Maurer
Software AG, Darmstadt, Germany
e-mail: sabine.norek@softwareag.com; vittorio.deangelis@softwareag.com; dirk.maurer@softwareag.com

J. vom Brocke, J. Mendling (eds.), *Business Process Management Cases*, Management for Professionals, DOI 10.1007/978-3-319-58307-5_16

number of participants, it was possible to identify several process-related software issues and to reduce significantly needed resources (e.g., cost and time). Hence, a promising alternative to the existing techniques of *understanding* was found, leading to important improvements regarding a comprehensive and continuous lifecycle.

(d) **Lessons learned**: The adapted UX approach increases flexibility and a widens the spectrum to proceed to the development of a user-centric business software. Although the improved procedure had a promising performance for further application in production environments, there are some open questions, such as handling the possibly high amount of upcoming data or privacy aspects that must be addressed in the future. Independently and regarding the transferability to other application scenarios, promising potential were identified, such as a mechanism for controlling the software's evolution, the inductive development of usage reference models, and an approach to measuring the ease of learning a new business software.

1 Introduction

Software AG empowers customers to innovate, differentiate, and win in the digital world. Its products help companies combine their existing systems on their premises and in the cloud into a single platform to optimize and digitize their businesses. The combination of process management, data integration, and real-time analytics on one Digital Business Platform enables customers to drive operational efficiency, modernize their systems, and optimize processes for smarter decision-making. Building on over 45 years of customer-centric innovation, Software AG is ranked as a leader in many innovative IT categories. It has more than 4300 employees in 70 countries and in 2015 had total revenues of 873 million euros.

Business process models play an important role in the Digital Business Platform, from the analysis and design of business processes to their implementation, execution, monitoring, and controlling. Therefore, business process models are key artifacts in business process management. Traditionally, process models are generated by human modeling experts using modeling tools like the ARIS Designer, the market-leading BPM tool and one of Software AG's main products. Although ARIS has stood for professional business process design in more than 20 years in practice and research, many facets of the process of process modeling still need research.

Against that background, the Software AG has applied expert interviews, pre-release usability tests, and other established usability methods in order to improve the ARIS software. Therefore, a comprehensive user experience (UX) approach was established that understands the user as a key to identifying and defining existing usability issues and to designing and testing possible solutions. The user experience research for ARIS has covered 10 years of usability testing and interviews with more than 300 users all over the world, which led to over 400 h of recorded video sessions, thousands of person hours in usability sessions, and the evaluation of the recorded and collected data. Still, there are many aspects of the supported business processes to discover. The challenges in the users' daily work are often unknown or cannot be explicated easily, in part because of the mostly strong focus on particular functionalities or cuttings of the software.

Since we also understand business software as tools that support particular business processes, the aim of improving its usability requires not only analyzing the technical aspects of software that affect their operability, but also analyzing the supported processes for areas of improvement. In addition, since customers have the deepest insights into their processes, we see them as a key to that task. Hence, in the context of a research project, we were looking for new approaches that take user behavior in their real environments and in their daily work into account in order to improve the modeling tool based on actual, not yet identified customer needs. Therefore, the case at hand seeks to develop a method for analyzing the dimensions of usability whereby both the system design (in terms of a technical support of the process of process modeling) and the business process it supports are explicitly addressed. For that purpose, existing methods and techniques from the field of process mining are adapted and enhanced with basic ideas of usability engineering in order to improve the current UX approach.

The resulting approach was applied to a use case that focuses on the process of modeling business processes with the ARIS 9 Designer. Therefore, participants were asked to perform some generic modeling tasks with the software, and the recorded user behavior was then analyzed with regard to the issues mentioned above using the developed lifecycle approach. Finally, the approach covers several phases of the BPM Lifecycle (Dumas et al. 2013) and generally starts with recording the user behavior in order to reveal and continuously improve, implement, monitor, and control the supported processes. We were able to produce promising results and revealed several new improvements that support the process of process modeling.

Section 2 describes the current UX approach at Software AG and the initial situation regarding its issues. The basic ideas of improvement and the corresponding actions that focus on the parts of the UX approach that are lacking are presented in Sect. 3. Section 3 also presents the user study that supports the whole improvement process. The improved UX process is then demonstrated and explained in Sect. 4. Finally, Sect. 5 summarizes the lessons learned and outlines further potential for the proposed approach.

2 Situation Faced

In order to develop useful, efficient, and appealing products, Software AG defined a user-centric development process that is influenced by the ideas of design thinking, collaborative design, and lean UX. Embedded in an agile development

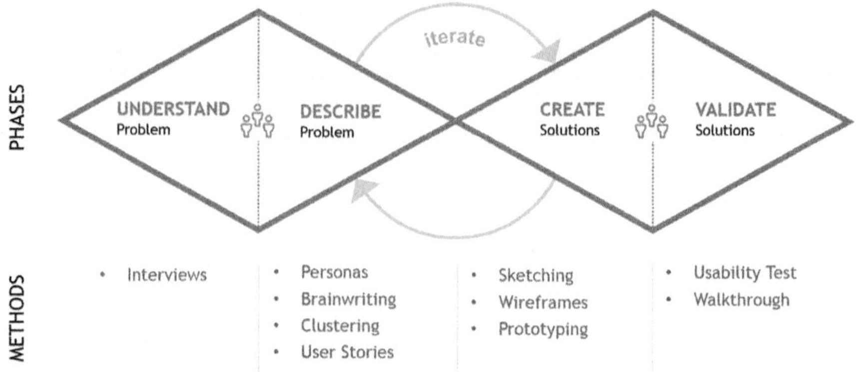

Fig. 1 The UX process at Software AG

environment, the process leans heavily on learning early and often. The basic phases and methods of this user experience process are illustrated in Fig. 1.

The process starts with understanding the users and their problems (*understand problem*). Methods like contextual interviews with members of the target group, surveys, and non-participatory observations are used to gather as much information as possible about the users' goals, tasks, and pain points. These methods also help the team to build empathy with the user and to keep the user in mind during the whole product-development process.

The first step generates many useful insights and considerable amounts of data. Therefore, the second step, *describe problem*, creates a common understanding about the most important pain points in the process. Methods like brainwriting, clustering, and voting help to facilitate this process, and instruments like personas and user stories are used to document the results.

Only when the problem is well-defined does the team start to ideate on possible solutions in the *create solutions* step. In addition to typical creativity techniques, sketches, wireframes and prototypes are used to visualize, communicate, and select ideas.

The last step, *validate solutions*, tests selected ideas with real users and real tasks by running local or remote usability tests or by doing internal walkthroughs of typical tasks.

If needed, this process runs in iterations. For example, a usability test conducted in the validation phase may reveal that the test participants are not able to pursue their goals. In this case, additional interviews are needed, which requires re-entering the understanding phase. In other cases, a series of usability tests may show that none of the tested ideas leads to satisfactory task completion rates or execution times. In these cases, the ideating phase, *create solutions*, must be re-entered.

While large projects like projects for creating new products or developing new components require the full set of methods, smaller projects like projects for implementing new features can get along with a subset or slight variations of the methods mentioned above.

For an existing application, the problem may be easiest to understand by conducting a combination of interviews and usability tests. Interviews focus on identifying typical tasks, which may be known to a certain extent, as they reveal users' opinions. Usability tests, which focus on identifying problems that occur when performing these tasks within the current solution, reveal users' behavior.

In a smaller project, defining the problem might mean agreeing about the most important problems found in a usability test. Creating solutions might be done by discussing a few hand-drawn ideas by hand, and then implementing the solution in the code itself. To validate this solution, the usability test may be repeated.

The basic process approach has been applied successfully in many development and customer co-innovation projects, and considerable effort is expended to improve the software. However, the investigations so far have been focused on particular functionalities and have often relied on (pre-release) tests, the statistical validity of which is limited. In addition, the costs of performing these tests and analyzing the results are high. For example, since it is necessary to talk to the test users during the test run(s), it is also necessary to have employees on site, which may lead to travelling or workshop expenses in addition to the costs of the user experience research's core activities.

Moreover, the functional focus and the essential laboratory environment hinder a holistic view of the software since the test users have the considered function in their minds. However, distorted results are generally expected in non-participatory observations of real-life scenarios. At the same time, a holistic view of the software is necessary to identify the customers' everyday challenges. There are also typical situations in which users cannot adequately explicate the problems they have with a particular functionality or the software as a whole. Hence, the main objective is to develop a comprehensive, methodical approach that facilitates the target-oriented further development of process-oriented business software, especially in order to improve the user experience. Therefore, it is necessary to observe the users in their daily work without spying on them or measuring their performance. In addition, the costs incurred should be as low as possible.

The general idea is to use established process-mining techniques to derive usage models automatically, which can then be enriched by data like GUI information (e.g., element positions) and random user, system, or context data (e.g., user experience). Therefore, a second objective is to extend and improve the current UX approach in a cost-efficient way by using the possibilities of automating that result from the application of process-mining techniques. This approach makes it possible to analyze real user behavior in order to improve the IT support of a business process, especially in terms of its usability. The term "business process usability" should be understood as referring to the extent to which a business software can be used for the effective, efficient, and satisfactory execution of business processes.

3 Action Taken

As a first step toward improving the existing UX approach in the intended way, alternative techniques for *understanding* and covering the state of the art are identified and analyzed in both business information systems engineering (especially process mining) and software engineering (especially human computer interaction and usability engineering). Adequate knowledge in all fields involved is required, as only then can the two disciplines be combined meaningfully. A broad analysis of relevant aspects in these fields was carried out in Thaler et al. (2015a). Approaches from the field of usability engineering and the resulting effort in terms of data analysis are expensive, and they usually require a laboratory environment. Although some work has already been done (Hilbert and Redmiles 2000; Siochi and Ehrich 1991) in deriving process models (petri-nets) and addressing some possibilities for usability analyses, the mining techniques that were used lean toward the rudimentary, as they do not take into consideration such aspects of process mining as dealing with noise and harmonizing the log data of multiple systems. Consideration of current methods and techniques from information systems research is also missing.

At the same time, current approaches, such as genetic algorithms (Alves de Medeiros 2006) and cluster techniques that handle noisy data or avoiding spaghetti-like models (van der Aalst 2011) could be helpful in making it possible to derive meaningful models or meta-information that enables practitioners and researchers to draw concrete conclusions about the usability of business software. Moreover, metrics from the various research disciplines may make it possible to quantify automatically some aspects of the quality, understandability, and usability of business processes and their application. However, a practical, integrated application of the concepts discussed in the context of usability has not yet been observed.

Hence, the identified methods and techniques from the fields of process mining and usability engineering were analyzed with respect to their applicability in the given case. The relevant methods and techniques were consolidated in a four-step approach to *understanding the user*. That approach is described in detail in what follows and is evaluated by means of a user study in the context of a Software AG product.

3.1 Design of the User Study

Several users were asked to work on tasks in the context of business process modeling using Software AG's ARIS Designer, Version 9. The objective was to evaluate whether the identified techniques could serve as an alternative to existing approaches to *understanding the user*. Hence, the focus is on an automatic identification of the problems the users have in performing the tasks. Thirteen students were asked to use the rich modeling client of Software AG's ARIS Designer, which is based on natural language text descriptions, to (1) model an organigram, (2) model an EPC, and (3) modify an EPC. The exercises cover basic actions of business process modeling and do not focus on particular functionalities. The study's objective was to learn how users act in reaching a solution, not to evaluate the correctness of the solution itself. Ten of the students had modeling experience, while the other three had not, so the exercises also revealed information about how users with no prior knowledge interacted with the software. The average time needed to execute the tasks was 47 min. In order to identify concrete usability issues from the analyses, the user screen was recorded by a screen-capturing software.

3.2 A Four-Step Approach to Understanding the User

For the design of an adequate approach with corresponding tool support, the idea of process mining was adapted with regard to the specific requirements of usability engineering. Referring to Thaler (2014) and Thaler et al. (2015b), the steps (Fig. 1) are *user monitoring*, *trace clustering*, *usage model derivation*, and *usage model analysis*. In contrast to previous approaches, the steps can be applied during live operation, so they take real user behavior into account and expensive laboratory experiments are not usually necessary (Fig. 2).

3.2.1 User Monitoring

Process execution data (instance data) is the basis for business process usability mining. Depending on the analysis's objectives, the requirements for log data differ. It is usually necessary to fulfill the traditional log data requirements of process mining (case, task, originator, timestamp) (van der Aalst 2008), and these data should then be extended with additional information depending on the context. When weak points in usability are identified, it might be helpful to log information like GUI information related to element positions and case-specific data. Collecting additional information may require the use of other data sources, such as an enterprise database, external services, or sensors. Since Software as a Service plays an increasing role in the business context, (web) server logs or error logs—which are not traditionally considered in the context of process mining—are possible sources as well. Against that background, one must design a logging strategy based on the

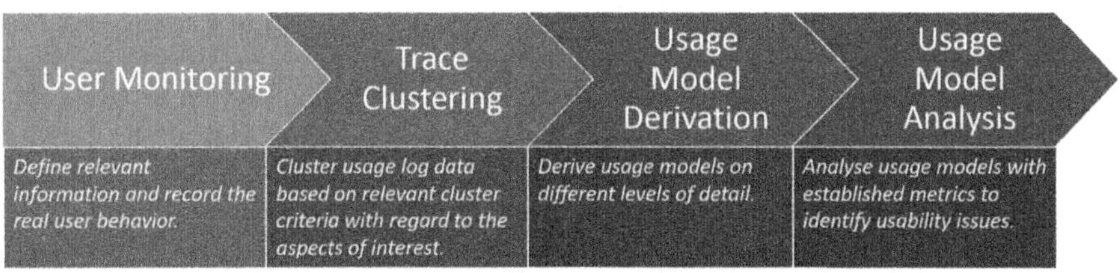

Fig. 2 Understand the user: a four-step approach

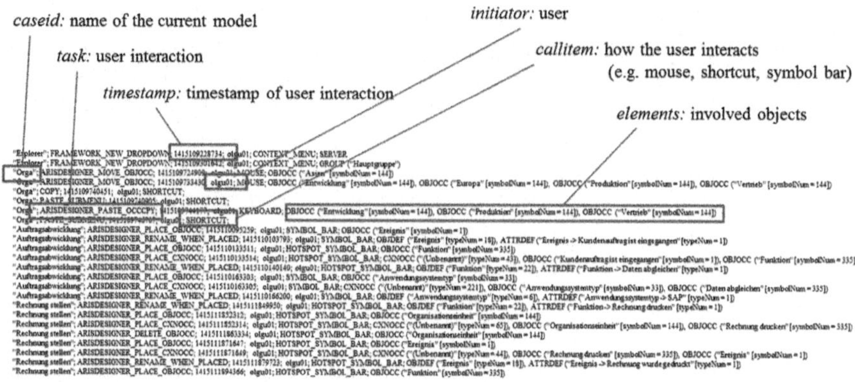

Fig. 3 Sample log file generated in the user monitoring phase

objectives of the analysis or the application scenario and implement it in the software being addressed. Consolidating the various data sources is also important.

Evaluation in User Study In addition to the traditional log information of process mining, he callitem, which describes how the user triggers particular actions (e.g. with a mouse, using a shortcut, using an item on the symbol bar), and the objects involved (e.g., the elements on the grid) are recorded as well. A sample log file generated by the ARIS 9 Designer in the user monitoring phase is presented in Fig. 3.

3.2.2 Trace Clustering

Trace clustering, the task of clustering traces within log data using a specific cluster criterion, is a traditional challenge in the context of process mining. As business software and BPM tools usually cover a multitude of business processes, a corresponding log file covers all of these processes too. Discovering a process model based on a non-clustered log file usually leads to highly complex models that cannot be read by humans (so-called spaghetti-like models), so processes or instance classes must be identified in order to generate less complex process models (e.g., Ekanayake et al. 2013; Jagadeesh and van der Aalst 2010). Therefore, the choice of a particular trace-clustering technique depends on the analysis's objectives (Thaler et al. 2015c). Trace clustering may have any of many criteria, including:

- Processes: variants, patterns, occurrence of loops or tasks, etc.
- Resources/performance: time, budget, hardware, load values, etc.
- Cases: value of a shopping cart, etc.
- Users: experience, age, groups, etc.
- Software: version, device, etc.

Therefore, the recorded log data can be interpreted as a multidimensional data cube whose dimensions are partially not known a priori. In fact, some dimensions are given by the log specification (the recorded attributes), while others, such as the actual recorded process, are unknown. Therefore, it is possible, at least in part, to apply slicing-and-dicing approaches from the area of data warehousing. However, especially in the context of business process usability analysis, the identification of new information and patterns related to the processes and variants, possibly depending on user profiles, is important. A good overview of existing trace-clustering techniques with their corresponding implementations and an evaluation of their applicability in various contexts is presented in Thaler et al. (2015c).

Evaluation in User Study Since the user study contains three exercises, in the trace-clustering phase we initially focused on separating the log file based on the processes that are equivalent to that exercise. Prior to the clustering, we knew that each of the exercises contained actions that are usually not performed in the other ones. Referring to Thaler et al. (2015c), we used the known causal dependencies (case-specific tasks) as a basis for separating the log file. Then we separated the log file based on the information concerning whether a user had experience working with ARIS.

3.2.3 Usage Model Derivation

Process mining distinguishes three fields of inquiry: process discovery, conformance checking, and enhancement (van der Aalst 2011). Process discovery seeks to derive a new process model based solely on log data, while conformance checking compares the as-is process to the to-be process. Enhancement focuses on the derivation of new information from log data in order to extend or improve an existing process model.

Against that background, all three of these fields of inquiry play important roles in business process usability mining in general and in the phase of usage model derivation in particular. In that phase, one derives a process model based on the clustered log data and enriches it with information like performance data, execution probabilities, correlation matrices, and additional (scenario-specific) data and metrics. Many process-mining techniques that produce output models with differing characteristics already exist; they differ in terms of the fitness and appropriateness of the resulting models to the underlying log files, such as in their simplicity, their abstraction level, and the resulting model type (e.g., petri-nets, EPC, FSM) (Thaler 2013), or in their approach to calculations. Therefore, a concrete algorithm should be selected based on the concrete objectives of the analysis (e.g. Alves de Medeiros 2006; van der Aalst et al. 2004; Weijters and Ribeiro 2011; Weijters et al. 2006). In contrast to discovery and enhancement, conformance checking should be seen as belonging to the phase of usage model analysis (phase 4), as it might be important to know whether the users use the software in the intended way.

Evaluation in User Study We applied the Heuristics Miner (Weijters and Ribeiro 2011) with default parameters to derive the usage models based on the clustered log

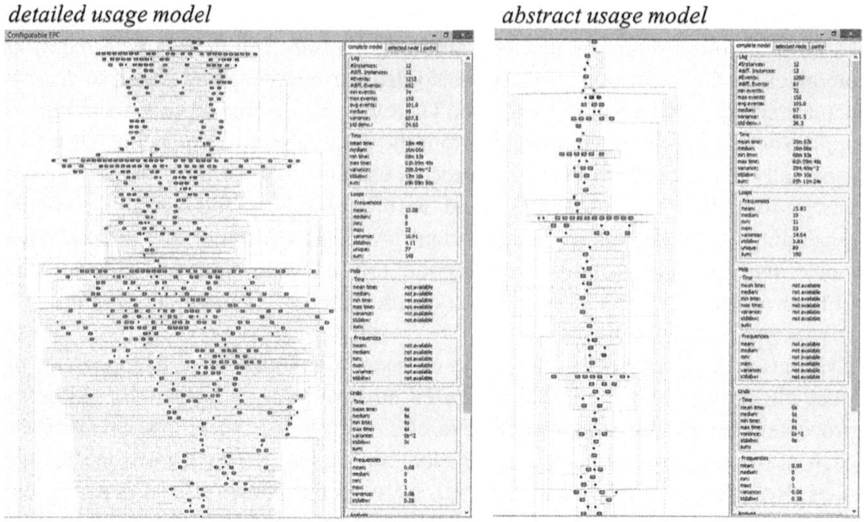

Fig. 4 Detailed vs. abstract usage model visualized with the RefMod-Miner

files. In so doing, we prepared the log files in two settings: (1) task, callitem, and elements are consolidated and use a task description like "place event 'Event' by HOTSPOT_SYMBOL_BAR," and (2) the task is used as it is recorded, such as "place event." Extracts of the resulting EPC models from the two settings are presented in Fig. 4, which shows that the models' complexity differs to a high degree, grounded in the fact that setting 1 produces much more detailed node labels and, thus, a significantly higher absolute number of nodes than setting 2. Hence, the degree of detail in the task description again depends on the analysis's objectives.

3.2.4 Usage Model Analysis

There are several possibilities for analyzing the usage model. Many metrics from a variety of research fields exist to characterize the model(s) and give first indications of weak points:

- Model metrics: complexity, extent, cross-connectivity, etc. (Melcher 2012; Mendling et al. 2012).
- Process metrics: execution count, execution time, error rates, cancellation rates, etc.
- Usability metrics: irrelevant actions, undo actions, using help function, etc.

These categories can be broken into subcategories, such as size and complexity in terms of model metrics or placement, and time aspects in terms of usability metrics. Other performance metrics may include:

- Achievement of objectives/conformance checking: In the context of business processes and their management, there are often objectives that should be achieved at process execution. These objectives could include the process's overall execution time and consumption of resources. Business rules that are obligatory at the process execution, such as legalities, might be important in determining conformance.
- Causal dependencies: Process models may contain causal dependencies between activities or process fragments that are not evident in the process model. A correlation matrix may reveal those dependencies.
- Core and exception fragments: Process models often contain activities or fragments that are executed in a high percentage of cases (core actions) or those that are seldom executed (exception actions). Knowledge about frequency helps in keeping the focus on the most important system points during development.
- Non-supported processes: Sometimes users use a system to execute processes that were not intended by the system's producer. Identifying these processes helps in the effort to improve a system in light of customer needs or to identify other business areas that can use the system.
- System avoidance: Users can avoid a software's particular functionalities, even though they are available, which may indicate a non-working or badly implemented functionality that needs analysis.

In short, simple statistical indicators might provide hints concerning process or software usability issues, although these indicators cannot be used to analyze these issues in detail. In most cases, further information on the process and its execution logs is needed based on input from human experts.

To calculate the metrics, we implemented a tool support in the research prototype RefMod-Miner.[1] An extract of the available metrics and statistical analysis techniques is illustrated in the screenshots presented in Fig. 5. It is also necessary for the tool to have functionalities that allow graphical navigation through the model, like the visualization of a node's predecessor and successor nodes or the highlighting of particular nodes (like help or undo calls). The application of these analysis techniques may provide concrete hints about weak points in the technical support of modeling and how to prevent them.

Evaluation in User Study Analyzing the models with the RefMod-Miner led to the identification of several aspects from which to view the models, ranging from a purely technical perspective to a professional one. Three of these perspectives are presented in Fig. 6.

The first example shows that users could not understand the toggled-edge mode. When the mode was activated, they expected an automatic connection of edges based on the element positions, which led to the effect that some modelers

[1]RefMod-Miner: http://refmod-miner.dfki.de

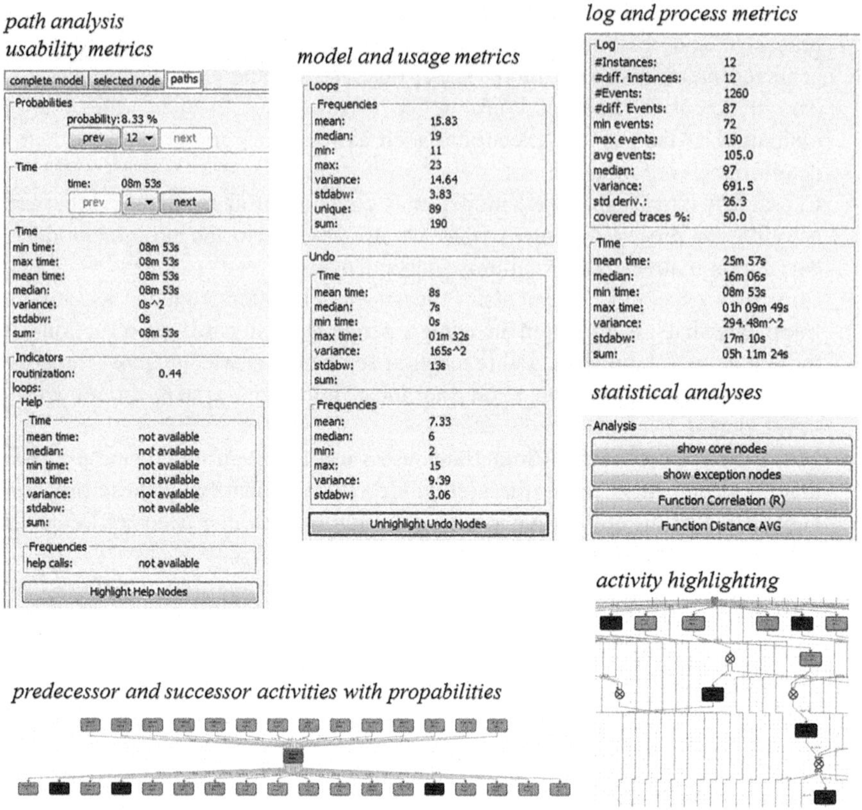

Fig. 5 Extract of metrics and analysis tools implemented in the RefMod-Miner

placed connectors over the edges that connected several nodes. In contrast to their expectations, the connector was not automatically connected.

The second case takes a more professional perspective. Some modelers placed organizational units on the grid and connected them to an activity. They expected the connecting edge to be undirected, but the system automatically produced a directed edge from the organizational unit to the activity. The only solution to the problem was to delete the edge direction manually for all corresponding edges. A similar case showed that it was not possible to modify the edge direction, and this limitation might be meaningful in many contexts.

The third case reveals other strategies in modeling. While some modelers placed the nodes and labeled them immediately, others added a set of nodes and labeled all of them afterwards, a strategy that consumes much more time.

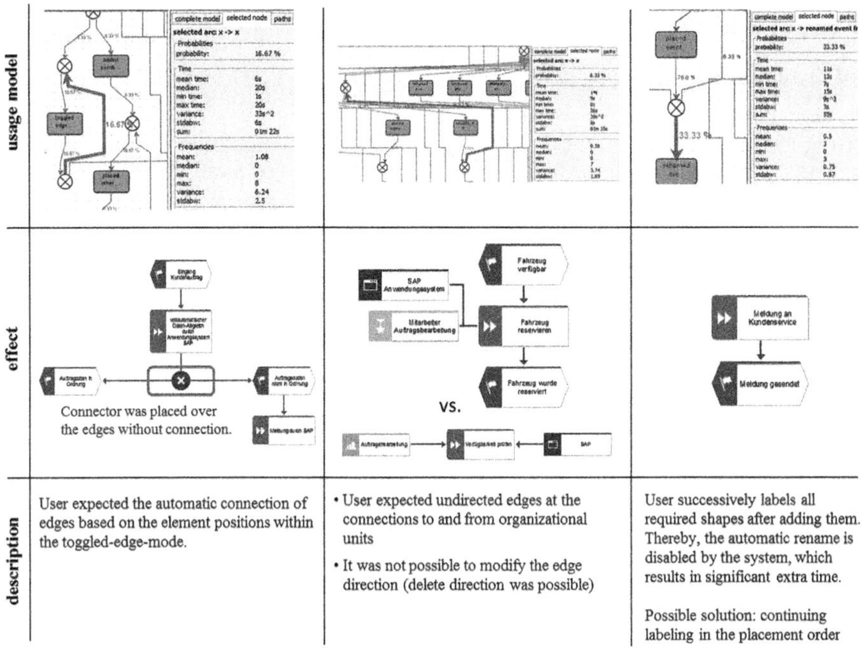

Fig. 6 Presentation of three identified issues

4 Results Achieved

In order to clarify whether the four-step usability-mining approach meets its objective, one must determine whether the subsequent phase of the overall UX approach, *describe problem*, can be processed based on the generated results. In other words, it should be possible to explicate the customers' needs in order to design improved IT support for their business processes.

The first identified issue results from users' inability to interpret the meaning of the "toggled-edge mode," a problem derived from the users' interaction with the software, where the corresponding button was clicked several times in sequence without the intended effect. Renaming the functionality might improve its understandability. The second issue is a bug that can be fixed by allowing the user to modify the edge directions. Since the third issue uncovers a user demand (a modeling strategy that had not yet been considered), a new functionality that supports that strategy is necessary. Continuous labeling in the placement order might be a meaningful feature in meeting that demand.

Hence, despite the early stage of studying and applying the approach in a real context and although the number of participants in the user study was small, we identified ten issues, ranging from minor bugs and general weak points to specific user demands. The derived information was also sufficiently detailed to be described in a professional way and to be addressed with concrete improvements, which are currently being implemented. Therefore, there is potential for application of the approach in a broader user study with pilot users and beyond.

The instantiation of the phases showed that the approach is highly flexible and scalable. Starting at the user monitoring phase, the log information could be enhanced with information like the heart rate of a user or parallel interaction with other cases or software tools. An analysis's level of detail can also be individually scaled, as shown in the usage model derivation phase. Moreover, the graphic representation of usage models enables human observers to easily conceive the human interactions in a broad context and, thus, to replay critical cases in order to detect issues and develop possible solutions.

Especially in a real business environment, the application requires additional thought and action on privacy. Since the procedure might enable employee monitoring, concepts for reliable anonymization are essential to ensure that the recorded information is not traceable to a particular employee or used to measuring the performance of departments. The end users must be able to decide whether they agree to the process of recording and transferring the resulting log data to the software-providing company.

In summary, the four-step usability-mining approach meets expectations. Since it can be applied in customers' production environment, a laboratory environment is not necessary (although it may be necessary in the case of user studies). Problem situations and their locations in software can be detected automatically based on metrics from the areas of usability engineering and business process models. Thus, much of the work that is traditionally performed by usability analysts is done by the analysis tool. Even so, it is not possible for these metrics to detect all issues, so analysts are still necessary; additional application of qualitative interviews in particular might be meaningful. At the same time, visualization of the usage models enables analysts to understand real user behavior and the issues that result from them more easily, more effectively and more quickly. Thus, the necessary resources in terms of costs and time can probably be reduced significantly, although concrete data is missing in the current state.

Finally, promising results led to an enhanced UX process that includes an additional *understand* approach and several effects on the overall UX process (see Fig. 7). In fact, the proposed usability-mining approach reveals a new way to understand the software users based on their real behavior in their daily work. Hence, an alternative was found to interviews in terms of both the procedure and the results. Interviews can provide both high-level deep-level insights on particular aspects of a process and are appropriate for discussing solutions that have not yet been designed or implemented. In contrast, usability mining focuses on the details with which users are confronted, facilitating a broad or overall evaluation of all user interactions with a software, which is not possible with interviews. However, interviews can also be an appropriate technique with which to analyze that quantitative results of usability mining in a qualitative way.

Since the necessary data for usability mining are acquired automatically, it is possible to redo the usability-mining steps on that data, as well as on new data.

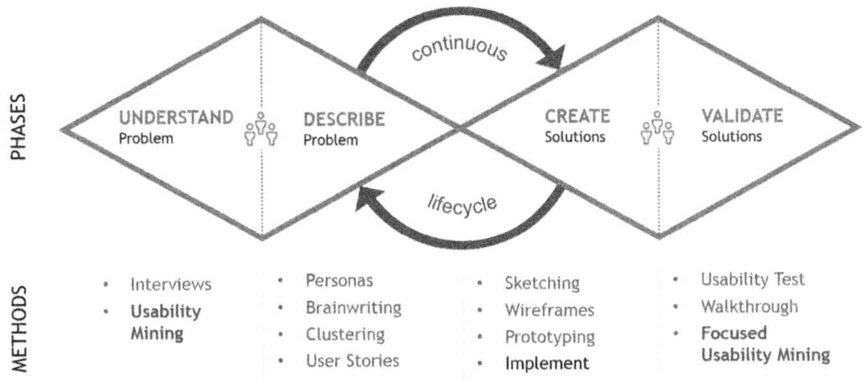

Fig. 7 The improved UX process

Hence, it is easy to determine whether a particular issue is fixed by recalling the corresponding usage data in the next software version. This process, *Focused Usability Mining*, has two important effects. First, comprehensive and perhaps expensive prototyping with a corresponding usability test walkthrough is not necessary before the general roll-out, as the effect of a fix can be measured with the upcoming version. As a consequence, the release cycle can be shortened so there are more resources for the further development of the software. Second, the UX process should not be considered a straightforward process with a fixed start and end and several iterations but as a lifecycle, which allows the continuous and target-oriented further development of a software. Hence, the borders between *validate* and *understand* are often blurred since *understand* in particular covers the users' understanding not only to identify unknown issues but also to verify the solution to known issues in a continuous way.

In summary, the developed method significantly enhances the capabilities of the UX work since it enables continuous screening of usability issues in a semi-automated way. At the same time, focused work is still important, especially in cases like those of developing new products or functionalities and redesigning existing ones.

5 Lessons Learned

Although the results are promising, there are still some aspects of the user study that remain to be discussed. First, the statistical relevance of the found issues and user demands to general user is currently unknown. Another study with more participants would have to use statistical tests, such as the p-Value to make this determination. Second, from a technical point of view, the amount of upcoming log data will require the use of methods that can handle it. Depending on the degree of detail of the log files (e.g., every click, every mouse movement), the number of monitored users, and their intensity of use, its processing will require considerable memory. Therefore, the content of these log files will become more complex and challenges like user tracking, clustering of the log files, and the potentially high complexity of resulting usage models, which are difficult for humans to interpret, will have to be met. First methods and techniques that address these challenges already exist (e.g., Ekanayake et al. 2013; Evermann and Assadipour 2014) and should be evaluated with regard to their applicability in this context.

Another challenge refers to the case of hidden tasks. Hidden tasks are user actions that cannot be recorded by the logging mechanism since they occur apart from the analyzed software, such as manual tasks or tasks done using another software. A typical example is asking a colleague about a functionality by telephone or in person.

One might also ask whether it is more expedient to improve the usability of software tools that support a particular business process than it is to train the end users. While adequate training might help the users to work more efficiently, effectively, and satisfactorily with a modeling tool, individual approaches to modeling business process models based on the end users' habits and preferences are equally important. Therefore, it is necessary to do both: train the end users and improve the software's usability based on the end users' needs. Whether user training or software improvement leads to more promising results in terms of business process usability—efficiency, effectiveness, satisfaction, and costs—must also be determined, as these are important factors, especially for small and medium-sized enterprises. The cost factor is a major strength of the method developed here.

The UX approach (Fig. 7) used here uses an interview technique for *understanding the user*, as usability mining does not replace it. Interviews may also be important in evaluating qualitatively the quantitative results from usability mining in terms of indications regarding particular usability issues. When one is developing new functionalities or software, it is also necessary to include the users in the design phase. Usability mining is not applicable here since the software is already rolled out. Nevertheless, it can meaningfully applied to validate generated solutions.

In addition the important improvements to the UX approach, as presented in Sect. 4, usability mining can deliver insights into the software usage that have not yet been addressed. Among others, several design-related questions can be answered as well:

- What are the core application scenarios on the user side? Which implemented processes or functionalities are not used?
- Are there observable user profiles other than user role and user experience? Are there significant differences in how users use a system?
- Are there observable case profiles for a process that influence its execution?
- Are there other functional requirements on the user side?
- Are there ways to improve the supported process (e.g., user- or case-sensitive processing, adding new functionalities, data preloading, reorganization of forms)?

With regard to the transferability of the developed method to other domains and applications, the analysis of the real user behavior can also be seen a basis for working in several application scenarios (Thaler 2014; Thaler et al. 2015b):

- *Controlling the Software Evolution.* Further development of a software is in the nature of a product's lifecycle, although it can be challenging to determine whether such a development leads to the desired effect and whether it is used as it is intended. This issue affects both new supported processes and existing ones. Since the developed method analyzes real user behavior, it is possible to follow the software evolution from the user side. This benefit can also be seen in Thaler et al. (2013).
- *Inductive Usage Reference Model Development.* Information about a process's performance, resource consumption, and other collected data facilitate the inductive development of reference models with a best-practice character. Based on the process instances, a process model could be derived that pursues objectives like minimizing costs or resources or optimizing output quality.
- *Ease of Learning.* One quality criterion of a business-process-supporting software is the effort required to learn to execute it. An analysis of users' usage models over time would visualize their learning effects and allow the derivation of individual learning curves.

In summary, the paper at hand presents a method for assessing the usability of process-supporting software tools based on process mining. It addresses important areas that must be investigated in order to gather insights about the further development of the software based on users' needs. While the phases of user monitoring, trace clustering, and usage model derivation have an established theoretical and technical foundation that can be adapted to apply to usability, a detailed analysis of the resulting data is challenging. Several ideas have been proffered to quantify the usability of a software system and process models, but these ideas are yet to be developed, conceptualized, implemented, and evaluated.

We showed that the developed method links the software-engineering view and the process-oriented view on business-process-supporting software, which suggests the potential for their design and further development. We also identified several promising scenarios for meaningful application of the method in other domains that will be addressed in future work.

Finally, the developed method has several advantages over extant approaches. It can be applied to processes already in production and in real environments, so it involves real user behavior. At the same time, it clarifies measurement results, which are usually problematic in direct observations. Moreover, the measurement and analysis of aspects of usability can, in many cases, be arranged automatically or with only a little input, so costs are lowered, making the method attractive for use by small and medium-sized enterprises. The approach also significantly improves the overall UX approach by considered it as a broad and continuous lifecycle instead of a focused process with fixed start and end points.

References

Alves de Medeiros, A. K. (2006). *Genetic process mining*. Dissertation. Eindhoven: CIP-Data Library Technische Universität Eindhoven.

Dumas, M., Rosa, M. L., Mendling, J., & Reijers, H. A. (2013). *Fundamentals of business process management*. Berlin: Springer.

Ekanayake, C. C., Dumas, M., García-Bañuelos, L., & La Rosa, M. (2013). Slice, mine and dice: Complexity-aware automated discovery of business process models. In F. Daniel, J. Wang, & B. Weber (Eds.), *Business process management, LNCS 8094* (pp. 49–64). Berlin: Springer.

Evermann, J., & Assadipour, G. (2014). Big data meets process mining: Implementing the alpha algorithm with map-reduce. In *Paper Presented at the Proceedings of the 29th Annual ACM Symposium on Applied Computing*, Gyeongju, Republic of Korea.

Hilbert, D. M., & Redmiles, D. F. (2000). Extracting usability information from user interface events. *ACM Computing Surveys, 32*(4), 384–421.

Jagadeesh, R. P., & van der Aalst, W. M. P. (2010). Trace alignment in process mining: Opportunities for process diagnostics. In *Paper Presented at the Proceedings of the 8th International Conference on Business Process Management*, Hoboken, NJ, USA.

Melcher, J. (2012). *Process measurement in business process management – Theoretical framework and analysis of several aspects*. Karlsruhe: KIT Scientific Publishing.

Mendling, J., Sánchez-González, L., García, F., & La Rosa, M. (2012). Thresholds for error probability measures of business process models. *The Journal of Systems and Software, 85*(5), 1188–1197.

Siochi, A. C., & Ehrich, R. W. (1991). Computer analysis of user interfaces based on repetition in transcripts of user sessions. *ACM Transactions on Information Systems, 9*(4), 309–335. doi:10.1145/119311.119312.

Thaler, T. (2013). *Entwicklung einer Methode zum Process Mining unter besonderer Berücksichtigung von Organisationswissen* (p. 121). Master thesis. Best Diploma Award 2012 – Semiramis Research and Service Unit (SeReS Unit), Institut für Wirtschaftsinformatik im Deutschen Forschungszentrum für Künstliche Intelligenz (DFKI) GmbH.

Thaler, T. (2014). *Towards usability mining*. In Paper Presented at the Lecture Notes in Informatics. Jahrestagung der Gesellschaft für Informatik, Stuttgart.

Thaler, T., Fettke, P., & Loos, P. (2013). Process mining – Fallstudie leginda.De. *HMD Praxis der Wirtschaftsinformatik, 50*(5), 56–65.

Thaler, T., Maurer, D., De Angelis, V., Fettke, P., & Loos, P. (2015a). *Mining the usability of business process modeling tools: Concept and case study*. In Paper Presented at the 13th International Conference on Business Process Management, Industry Track (BPM 2015), Innsbruck, Austria.

Thaler, T., Maurer, D., De Angelis, V., Fettke, P., & Loos, P. (2015b). Mining the usability of business process modeling tools: Concept and case study. In *Paper Presented at the Proceedings of the Industry Track at the 13th International Conference on Business Process Management 2015*. Business Process Management (BPM-15), Innsbruck.

Thaler, T., Ternis, S., Fettke, P., & Loos, P. (2015c). *A comparative analysis of process instance cluster techniques*. In Paper Presented at the 12th International Conference on Wirtschaftsinformatik, Osnabrück, Germany.

van der Aalst, W. M. P. (2008). Decision support based on process mining. In F. Burstein & C. W. Holsapple (Eds.), *Handbook on decision support systems 1. Basic themes* (pp. 637–657). Berlin: Springer.

van der Aalst, W. (2011). *Process mining: Discovery, conformance and enchancement of business processes*. Berlin: Springer.

van der Aalst, W., Weijters, T., & Maruster, L. (2004). Workflow mining: Discovering process models from event logs. *IEEE Transactions on Knowledge and Data Engineering, 16*(9), 1128–1142. doi:10.1109/TKDE.2004.47.

Weijters, A. J. M. M., & Ribeiro, J. T. S. (2011). *Flexible heuristics miner (FHM)*. In Paper Presented at the IEEE Symposium on Computational Intelligence and Data Mining, Paris.
Weijters, A. J. M. M., van der Aalst, W. M. P., & de Medeiros, A. K. A. (2006). *Process mining with the heuristics miner-algorithm* (BETA Working Paper Series, WP 166).

Tom Thaler is Product Manager at Software AG and responsible for Business Process Modeling and Analysis with ARIS. He received his master degree in information systems from Saarland University, where he graduated with honors and received the Best Diploma Award from SERES Unit. He worked at META-LEVEL Software AG as a Software Developer and at SAP as a Business Intelligence Consultant. In 2012, Tom started working at the German Research Center for Artificial Intelligence (DFKI). He managed and worked in various research projects. He received the Outstanding Matcher Award 2013 in Beijing for his work on process model matching and developed an outstanding performing approach in the Process Model Matching Contest 2015. His work has been published in leading scientific conferences such as BPM and WI. In parallel to his Product Management position, he finalized his doctoral thesis in the area of Business Process Management.

Sabine Norek is Director User Experience at Software AG, Germany. She holds a master's degree in information science from Saarland University with minors in business administration and psychology. She works as a UX professional since 20 years in the areas of software development, web design, online media and consulting. Her special interest areas are user research, design thinking and lean UX.

Vittorio De Angelis is a Senior Lead Software Engineer at Software AG, Germany. He holds a Master degree in computer science from HTW Saarland with a focus on Business Information Systems. Next to his Software Engineering position, he works as a UX professional since over 10 years in the area of business software development and user interface design. As a full stack web developer, he has a long time passion in developing cutting edge enterprise web solution.

Dirk Maurer is development manager for the ARIS Design Platform products at Software AG.He studied electrical engineering and started with the company (formerly IDS Scheer) in 1995 as part of the ARIS development team. Along with ARIS Toolset version 4 he took over first project responsibilities for several core components. Starting in year 2000 Dirk has been in charge for the Java migration of the ARIS products that are sold till this day as ARIS Architect/ARIS Designer. In parallel he took over product management responsibility for the ARIS BPA and EA solutions. In the framework of the acquisition of IDS Scheer by Software AG Dirk became Vice President ARIS R&D. Amongst others he got the lead for an innovation program in order to enable ARIS products for the cloud and provide a new set of fully HTML5 based user interfaces, resulting in the current ARIS Connect products.

Peter Fettke is Professor of Business Informatics at Saarland University and is a principal researcher and a Research Fellow at the German Research Center for Artificial Intelligence (DFKI GmbH), Saarbrücken, Germany. He heads the Business Process Management Group at DFKI. His research interests embrace all facets of socio-technical processes, including process management, process modelling and process mining. He uses a broad spectrum of research methods comprising engineering methods/ design science and empirical/experimental research approaches. His publications rank among the most-cited works of renowned journals of Business Informatics and he belongs to the top 10 of the most-cited researcher at DFKI. Furthermore, he is a highly-demanded reviewer for renowned conferences, journals and research institutions.

Peter Loos is director of the Institute for Information Systems (IWi) at the German Research Institute for Artificial Intelligence (DFKI) as well as full professor and head of the chair for Information Systems at Saarland University. His research activities include business process management, conceptual modeling and enterprise systems. During his earlier career, Peter had been professor at University of Mainz and at Chemnitz University of Technology. Furthermore, he had worked for 6 years as manager of the software development department at a software and consulting company. Peter has written several books and contributed to more than 50 books. He also published more than 30 journal articles and more than 300 articles in proceedings and papers.

Improving Patient Flows at St. Andrew's War Memorial Hospital's Emergency Department Through Process Mining

Robert Andrews, Suriadi Suriadi, Moe Wynn,
Arthur H.M. ter Hofstede, and Sean Rothwell

Abstract

(a) **Situation faced**: Improving Emergency Department (ED) patient flows in terms of processing time, resource use, costs, and patient outcomes is a priority for health service professionals and is vital to the delivery of safe, timely, and effective patient care. Poor patient flows manifest as overcrowding in the ED, prolonged length of stay (LoS), patients "boarding" in EDs and "access block" for admission to inpatient wards. Consequences include poor patient outcomes, reduced access for new patients who present at the ED, and negative effects on staff, including dissatisfaction and stress. Further motivation for improving patient flows in EDs arises because Commonwealth- and state-sponsored financial incentives for hospitals are tied to achieving targets for improved patient access to emergency services. One measure of such improved access is meeting nationally agreed targets for the percentage of patients who are physically discharged from the ED within 4 h of arrival.

(b) **Action taken**: A key challenge in deriving evidence-based improvements for patient flows is that of gaining insight into the process factors and context factors that affect patient flows. The case study reported here adopted the BPM Lifecycle reference framework to improve patient flows. In particular we focused on the process identification, discovery, and analysis phases of the BPM Lifecycle. Process-oriented data-mining

---

R. Andrews (✉) • S. Suriadi • M. Wynn • A.H.M. ter Hofstede
Queensland University of Technology, Brisbane, QLD, Australia
e-mail: r.andrews@qut.edu.au; s.suriadi@qut.edu.au; m.wynn@qut.edu.au; a.terhofstede@qut.edu.au

S. Rothwell
UnitingCare Health, Brisbane, QLD, Australia
e-mail: sean.rothwell@uchealth.com.au

J. vom Brocke, J. Mendling (eds.), *Business Process Management Cases*,
Management for Professionals, DOI 10.1007/978-3-319-58307-5_17

techniques were applied to real practices to discover models of current patient flows in the ED of St. Andrew's War Memorial Hospital (SAWMH) in Queensland, Australia. The discovered models were used to evaluate the effect on patient flows of certain context factors of interest to stakeholders. Case histories of 1473 chest pain presentations at SAWMH between September 2011 and March 2013 were analyzed to determine process differences between ED patients with short stays (<4 h) and those with long stays (>4 h).

(c) **Results achieved**: Process models were discovered for the hospital's ED patient flow. From a control-flow perspective, only minor differences were observed between short- and long-stay patients at SAWMH, although there were timing differences in reaching specific milestone events. Waiting time in the ED following a request for hospital admission added significantly to overall ED LoS.

(d) **Lessons learned**: This project demonstrated that process mining is applicable to complex, semi-structured processes like those found in the healthcare domain. Comparative process performance analysis yielded some insights into ED patient flows, including recognition of recurring data-quality issues in datasets extracted from hospital information systems. The templated recognition and resolution of such issues offers a research opportunity to develop a (semi-)automated data-cleaning approach that would alleviate the tedious manual effort required to produce high-quality logs. The project highlighted the importance of hospital information systems collecting both start and end times of activities for proper performance analysis (duration, wait time, bottlenecks). Additions to our process-mining toolset include novel comparative process-performance visualization techniques that highlight the similarities and differences among process cohorts.

1 Introduction

Improving Emergency Department (ED) patient flows in terms of processing time, resource use, costs, and patient outcomes is a priority for health service professionals and is vital to the delivery of safe, timely, and effective patient care. If patients are not moving through the system efficiently, other patients may experience delays in accessing care, with possible deleterious consequences. Inefficiencies in patient flow may also raise the cost of providing healthcare services through the failure to make the best use of available resources, such as the time of skilled staff (Liew and Kennedy 2003).

Recent years have seen an increasing demand for ED services in Australia's public hospitals (Australian Institute of Health and Welfare 2015) without a corresponding rise in inpatient beds. Table 1 highlights the steadily increasing

Table 1 ED presentations—Public Hospitals 2010–2011 to 2014–2015 (from the Australian Institute of Health and Welfare 2015, which cites the National Non-Admitted Patient Emergency Department Care Database as its data source)

		2010–2011	2011–2012	2012–2013	2013–2014	2014–2015	Avg. change since 2010–2011 (%)
# Hospitals Reporting ED Data	Major	140	143	144	144	146	1.1
	Other	46	60	60	145	144	42.9
	Total	186	203	204	289	290	12.9
Presentations		6,183,288	6,547,342	6,712,357	7,195,903	7,366,442	4.5

number of patient presentations at public hospitals' EDs. (The increase in the overall number of reporting hospitals is due to a large number of smaller hospitals' reporting patient presentations in their EDs, so interpretation of changes over time should take these changes of coverage into account.)

In July 2011, the *National Health Reform Agreement—National Partnership Agreement on Improving Public Hospital Service* was signed by all of Australia's states and territories. Under this agreement, financial incentives were established for public hospitals to meet targets. In particular, the *National Emergency Access Target* (NEAT) was created to improve patient access to public hospitals' EDs. Performance against the NEAT is measured as the percentage of patients who physically leave the ED within 4 h of their arrival. (The term "physically leave" includes patients who leave without treatment, are discharged from the ED, are admitted to another hospital unit (including the short-stay unit attached to the ED), or are transferred to another hospital). Incremental NEAT targets for Queensland were 70% in 2012, 77% in 2013, 83% in 204, and 90% in 2015.

Although no state or territory, including Queensland, has consistently achieved its NEAT, the initiative has seen a reduction in average Length of Stay (LoS) in Queensland's public hospitals' EDs from 280 min in July 2011 to 198 min in June 2014 (Queensland Audit Office 2015) and has motivated changes in EDs' and wider hospitals' procedures (Queensland Clinical Senate 2014). Two significant innovations have been the introduction of short-stay units attached to EDs, specifically for patients who require monitoring for up to 24 h, which allows patients to be discharged from EDs to short-stay unit, and the introduction of the Emergency Department Information System (EDIS), which is used by most major public hospitals to record real-time admission/discharge information. EDIS features a sort of traffic-light system that gives operators a visual indication of the current patient waiting time (Queensland Audit Office 2015).

Patient flows have been adopted as a management strategy to systematize the processing of patients from arrival at the ED to either discharge from the ED or admission to hospital. In March 2010 the Queensland Government launched its patient-flow strategy with the aim of reshaping Queensland Health's processes so the healthcare system could cope with increasing demands, deliver improved performance, reduce delays, increase access, and ensure best practice across the state (Queensland Health 2011). While patient flows alone cannot resolve all of the issues that affect equitable delivery of care to ED patients, improving patient flows has been shown to have a positive impact in terms of time, costs, and patient outcomes (Showell et al. 2012) and is one of the key priorities in the healthcare domain.

Evidence-based process improvement is an approach to process improvement in which the improvement initiatives are driven by the results of an empirical analysis of process-related data derived from the *as is* process. The analysis is designed to reveal process inefficiencies like bottlenecks, protracted activity durations, and rework loops. A key challenge in deriving evidence-based improvement to patient flows is that of gaining insight into the process factors and context factors that affect patient flows. This project involved a detailed analysis of patient flows in

St. Andrew's War Memorial Hospital's (SAWMH) ED using a process-mining methodology with the aim of providing insights into the *as is* processes in the ED, particularly as these processes apply to patients who present with chest pain. The project also sought opportunities for improvement in existing process-mining methodologies and tools (particularly in the areas of process comparison and visualization). St Andrew's Emergency Centre is a private ED that is not subject to the public EDs' NEAT-based financial incentives, but it does report the NEAT data publicly, and it is benchmarked against public EDs' NEAT performance. The project identified differences in patient flows between short LoS (<4 h) and long LoS (longer than 4 h). Process analysis quantified the effect of waiting time (the time between when it was determined that a patient required admission to hospital and the time of admission) had on overall ED LoS. While it was not possible to determine the root cause of these effects, they form the basis for potential process improvements that would have direct impact on achieving the NEAT. The project also drove the development of several novel visualization tools for comparing processes.

2 Situation Faced

Processes in healthcare settings, especially in hospital EDs, are often semi-structured. Semi-structured processes are characterized by their lack of a formal process model (although they usually have an informal process description), many points at which different continuation paths are possible, and being driven largely by context factors and human decision-making (Lakshmanan et al. 2011). In the ED, while specific treatment plans for each patient can be designed after a triage assessment, the delivery of the treatment requires flexibility and ad-hoc decision-making because of regular disruptions in patient flows (Catchpole et al. 2013). Disruptions to patient flows arise from such issues as those related to resources (e.g., lack of medical personnel and "access block"), teamwork (e.g., lack of communication that ensures smooth transition from one activity to another), and external interruptions (e.g., slow turnaround time for pathology tests) (Wiegmann et al. 2007) and manifest as long wait times, delays in administering/reporting on ordered tests, "boarding" of patients in the ED, ambulance ramping (ambulance arrives at ED and there is a delay in handing over the patient to ED staff requiring ambulance officers to continue administering care to the patient), and overcrowding in the ED. Overcrowding and prolonged LoS in the ED (for admitted patients) is associated with poor outcomes, including increased mortality rates (Richardson 2006; Sprivulis et al. 2006; Forero et al. 2010). The constant need to adjust patients' treatment plans likely contributes to a high level of variations in patient flows in hospital settings. This phenomenon is consistent with insights reported in Suriadi et al. (2014) and Partington et al. (2015).

To illustrate the complexity of healthcare processes and ED processes in particular, consider the BPMN process model/abstraction of Queensland Health's Possible Cardiac Chest Pain Clinical Pathway (Queensland Health 2015), shown in Fig. 1.

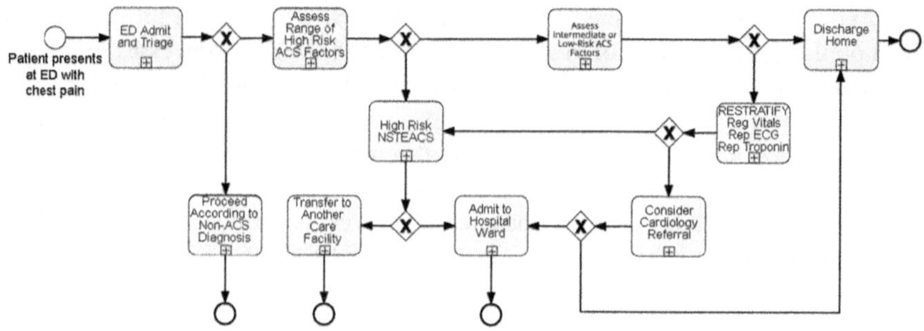

Fig. 1 Abstraction of Queensland Health's Cardiac Chest Pain Clinical Pathway

Clinical pathways are standardized, evidence-based, multidisciplinary management plans that identify an appropriate sequence of clinical interventions, timeframes, milestones, and expected outcomes for a homogenous patient group (Queensland Health Clinical Pathways Board definition 2002). Clinical Pathways are guidelines made available to all hospitals, while patient flows are generally hospital-specific and devised by each individual hospital. Each Clinical Pathway is published with the advice to clinicians that "clinical pathways never replace clinical judgement" and that " care outlined in [the] pathway must be altered if not clinically appropriate for the individual patient." Each step in the process model is itself a multi-step sub-process, with many of these steps being the performance of clinical tests. Decision points in the pathway are generally expressed in terms of "if any of the tests..." or "if none of the tests...." In the ED that was analyzed for this case study, the usual sequence of events is for a patient's arrival at the ED to be recorded and then the patient to be triaged and then later by a member of the medical staff (a doctor, a registered nurse, or both). To highlight the non-structured and patient-centric nature of patient flows, in accordance with the recommendation that clinical judgement take precedence, in 45% of the cases in our study of patients presenting with chest pain, the patient was seen by a doctor before being triaged, a flow that is not in accordance with the typical pathway shown in Fig. 1.

SAWMH was particularly interested in identifying the differences between patient flows for the cohort of chest-pain patients who spent <4 h in the ED from time of arrival to discharge from the ED and the cohort of chest-pain patients who spent longer than 4 h in the ED. Of further interest to SAWMH was the impact of its practice of routinely requesting blood tests and radiological imaging of patients who present with chest pain.

Devising an effective improvement plan for patient flow requires a baseline understanding of where variations in patient flow occur in the end-to-end treatment of patient cohorts and, most important, how the variations manifest. The study was expected to deliver an objective evaluation of SAWMH's treatment practices for chest-pain patients, including a performance analysis with particular emphasis on factors that influence LoS in the ED. The ultimate aim was to identify potential improvements to patient flows that could contribute to improvements in SAWMH's performance against the NEAT.

3 Action Taken

The focus of this project was the application of process-mining techniques to derive evidence-based insights about the behavior and performance of patient flows at SAWMH, from which comparisons of patient flows across patient cohorts could be made. We adopted the BPM Lifecycle reference framework, focusing on the process identification, discovery, and analysis phases. Table 2 shows the steps taken and the key challenges phased in each phase of the BPM Lifecycle.

In the next section, we discuss the key challenges faced in working through each of the project's phases.

3.1 Process Identification

Identify research questions that are relevant to SAWMH
The research questions identified were:

- What are the differences in the patient flows between patients who stayed in the ED for <4 h and those who stayed for more than 4 h?
- How much delay was introduced to the patient flows as a result of conducting routine clinical activities, including blood tests and X-ray imaging?
- What are the factors that influenced the patients' LoS?

Table 2 BPM lifecycle phases and key challenges

Steps in lifecycle phase	Key challenges
Process identification phase	
• Identify research questions that are relevant to SAWMH	With respect to the research questions of interest, define the aspects of ED and hospital patient flows to be investigated
• Extract process-related datasets from IT system(s), including data pre-processing	Identify relevant data from hospital information systems Identify and (if possible) resolve any data-quality issues evident in the extracted data so event logs that are aligned with the study's aims can be constructed
Process discovery phase	
• Discover *as is* process models that show dominant care paths	Deal with the highly variable, patient-centric flow to discover readable models that capture the dominant (most frequent) care paths
Process analysis phase	
• Extract performance-related information for each patient cohort and conduct comparative process-performance analysis	Extract comparative process-performance metrics Visualize comparative process-performance

Key challenge—With respect to the research questions of interest, define the relevant aspects of ED and hospital patient flows to be investigated
A key challenge was to limit the study's scope to patient-flow events in the ED and the hospital that affected the research questions. After consultation with ED clinicians from SAWMH, events related to ED arrival and discharge, clinical activities conducted as part of the patient's stay in the ED, blood and imaging tests ordered for the patient, and hospital admittance events were selected as being within the study's scope.

Key challenge—Identify relevant data from hospital information systems The case histories of all patients who presented with chest pain at the ED between September 2011 and March 2013 were identified as being relevant to the study. Four tables from four hospital information systems were identified as holding the relevant data:

- *Encounter table*: The Encounter table recorded the arrival and departure of patients from the ED using a unique "encounterID" value. As patients may present at the ED multiple times over time, a unique patient identifier (Medical Record Number) was associated with each patient and recorded in the Encounter table. Encounters were classified as either "emergency," indicating an ED presentation, or "hospital," indicating a hospital admission. The encounterID value was used as the common identifier in the remaining tables so records could be linked.
- *Emergency table*: The Emergency table recorded the key intra-ED patient flow milestone events, such as when a doctor was assigned to a patient, when the doctor first saw a patient, and when triage was started.
- *Clinical table*: The Clinical table recorded results of clinical observations of patients, including the initial assessment, ongoing nursing observations, periodic nursing, and medical notes.
- *Orders table*: The Orders table recorded orders for pathology tests, imaging tests, and other medical procedures requested for patients.

Key challenge—Identify and (if possible) resolve any data-quality issues evident in the extracted data so event logs aligned with the study's aims can be constructed
The most significant data-quality issues that affected the extracted data were issues related to correlation, diverse activities with the same timestamp, inadequate granularity of event names, duplicate events, references to the same event in multiple tables, irrelevant events, events that represented case attributes, and missing events.

- *Correlation*: The same patient (the same Medical Record Number) with multiple Encounter table records on the same day, where one was an "emergency" and one was a "hospital" encounter type. This represented a single case, so records from the four tables with either encounterID value were merged into a single case.

- *Multiple activities with the same timestamp*: Many events in the Clinical table were recorded with the same timestamp. This concurrency came about through the affected events being extracted from different fields in the same on-line form with the timestamp associated with each event being the time the form was "saved". Such events were assumed to be related to the same clinical activity, so clinical events were grouped by timestamp and a set of cleaning heuristics based on the occurrence of patterns of events in the groups were applied to reduce the group of events with the same timestamp to a single event (or sometimes a pair of events) that represented the actual clinical activity performed.
- *Inconsistent granularity of event names*: The Orders table recorded orders at a finer level of granularity than was required for the analysis. For instance, Orders table records that related to pathology tests listed the individual blood components to be tested for, and Orders table records that related to imaging used shorthand references like "xr" and "rad exam". We addressed these issues by aggregating multiple requests for individual blood tests into a single event named "Blood test" and replaced occurrences of "xr" and "rad exam" with "Radiology".
- *Duplicate events*: Some cases contained sequences of Clinical table and/or Order table events with only a few seconds' time difference. Where groups of events occurred with no more than 15 s' time difference between neighboring events, duplicated events in the group were removed. The duplication was deemed to be an artefact of system logging rather than an indication that the event actually occurred more than once.
- *References to the same event in multiple tables*: We found that certain process steps were recorded with different activity names in two tables. For example, the "Register_in_Emergency" event from the Encounter table coincided with the "Arrive_Start," "Arrive_Request," and "Arrive_Complete" events in the Emergency table. These events were replaced with a single "Arrive" event. Other instances were observed in the Orders table and Clinical table. Again, a single event was retained and the related events removed.
- *Irrelevant events*: After consultation with the domain expert, a set of events that were not relevant to the analysis, such as when all events happened after a patient had been admitted to a hospital ward, was identified and removed.
- *Events that represented case attributes*: For some events, it was more important to know that the event had occurred in the case than it was to know when it had occurred. For instance, the value associated with the "Glascow Coma Score" event is of more interest than was the time the score was determined. For such instances, the events were removed, a case attribute (named after the event) was added, and the value was recorded against the case attribute. In a similar vein, each of nine events associated with ED discharge indicated the discharge destination. A case attribute that represented the discharge destination was added, and the nine events were reduced to a single "ED Discharge" event. The final log contained 40 case attributes.
- *Missing process-related events*: A research question SAWMH proposed dealt with determining the impact of conducting routine tests (blood and imaging) on

chest-pain patients. While references to orders for such tests were present in the Orders table, no reference to either the performance of the test or the return of results was evident in the source data. Investigations into the recording of blood and medical imaging test results undertaken with SAWMH's data manager revealed that no medical imaging results and few blood test results were recorded electronically in such a way that they could be matched to the original order. For this reason, events associated with blood tests and medical imaging results were not included in the final event log.

3.2 Process Discovery

Key challenge—Deal with the highly variable, patient-centric flow data to discover readable models that capture the dominant (most frequent) care paths

After data cleaning, the event log contained 1473 cases, representing 1472 different execution paths—that is, only two cases followed exactly the same path—reflecting the semi-structured, patient-centric nature of ED patient flows. The initial discovered model reflected the "spaghetti"-like process. There were 30 separate activities in this version of the log. To discover readable models, the log was partitioned into four parts representing major milestone events of a patient's journey through the ED, the major clinical activities, cases in which ED LoS was <4 h, and cases in which ED LoS was longer than 4 h. Disco,[1] a commercial process-mining tool, was used to filter the log to abstract the relevant partitions from the log, from which readable but still meaningful process models were constructed.

3.3 Process Analysis

Key challenge—Extract comparative process performance

Extracting differences between cohorts' processes required manual inspection of models and manual compilation of observations. While doing so is possible, it is not an efficient way to discover and highlight variations in performance.

Key challenge—Visualize comparative process performance

Visualization, the depiction of non-visual data in visual form, provides an effective way to communicate, particularly where the raw data is large or complex. The visualization aspect of process comparison is still in an exploratory stage (Pini et al. 2015), so the challenge was to devise novel forms of visualization to highlight differences in process performance across multiple perspectives for the cohorts being compared.

[1] http://fluxicon.com

4 Results Achieved

In this section we detail the outcomes of the process discovery and analysis phases of the case study.

4.1 Process Discovery

The discovered process model shown in Fig. 2 represents the dominant (most frequent) pathways for the major milestone events in the patient flow for chest-pain patients. For example, there are 1473 cases with an "Arrive_Start" event, and the major milestones are arrival and departure from the ED (to either home or hospital), triage, and when the patient is first seen by medical personnel (a doctor, a registered nurse, or both).

The initially discovered process model for clinical activities was complex and unreadable. Events in the Clinical table are the main contributors to process variability (1263 different execution paths in 1471 cases). To discover a simpler process model for clinical activities (Fig. 3), the set of activities was reduced (in consultation with the process stakeholder) to include only key activities from the Clinical table: "Pre-Arrival Note," "Nursing Assessment," "Nursing—Primary Assessment," "Nursing Progress Notes," "Medical Note (final)," and "Discharge Letter." Figure 3 depicts the process model with the most frequent paths (those in the top 9% of process variants), although only 21% of the cases follow this process model.

To address SAWMH's research question about process differences between the cohort of patients with a LoS of <4 h (short LoS) and the cohort with a LoS of more than 4 h (long LoS), separate process models were discovered for each cohort. Figure 4 is the discovered model for short ED LoS, and Fig. 5 is the discovered model for long ED LoS.

An area of interest to SAWMH was the relationship between routinely requesting blood tests and imaging for patients presenting with chest pain and the patient's overall LoS. Do such practices introduce delays into the patient flows? Blood testing for SAWMH is carried out by a third party pathology laboratory, but the two organizations' information systems are not integrated to the point at which orders for tests can be sent directly from SAWMH to the laboratory. SAWMH records orders the tests in its own clinical IT system, however the pathology lab only becomes aware of the order when blood samples and printed test request physically arrives at the lab. On completion of the tests, the laboratory faxes test results to the ED, as this is the currently fastest method of returning test results to the treating physicians. Further, as the two organizations do not use a common patient identifier, it was almost impossible to match cases across the two systems. Because electronic records of imaging tests are not stored in the data sources that were available to the study, only a small sample of matching orders and results were obtained, which was too small for proper process discovery or analysis.

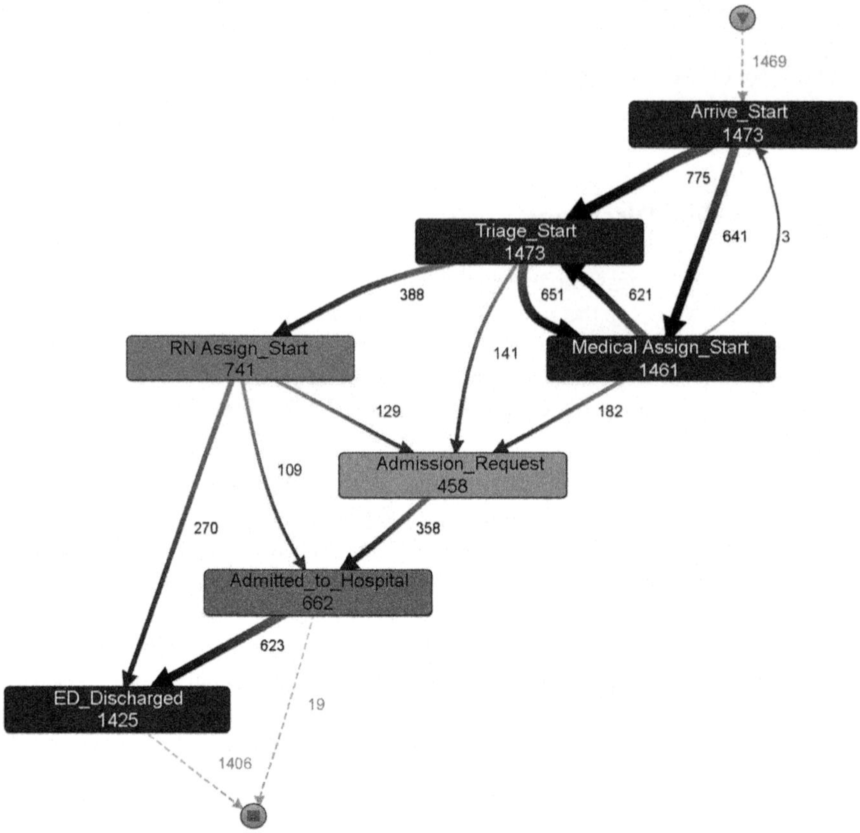

Fig. 2 Process model describing the main patient flow (major milestone events). In this model, each *rectangle* represents an activity, and the *color* density of the *rectangle* represents the frequency of the activity. *Arrows* represent transitions between activities, and the width of the *arrow* represents the frequency of the transition. The numbers on the *arrows* and in the *boxes* indicate the case frequency

4.2 Process Analysis

This section lists the main findings of process analysis as they relate to the discovered process models.

Four primary observations with respect to the general ED patient flow could be derived from the milestone events model (Fig. 2):

- There is a logical flow of activities to which most cases adhere.
- The Medical_Assign event can occur before the Triage event and even before the Arrive event.
- Fewer admission request events are recorded than the number of hospital admissions (i.e., 458 admission requests vs. 662 admission events).

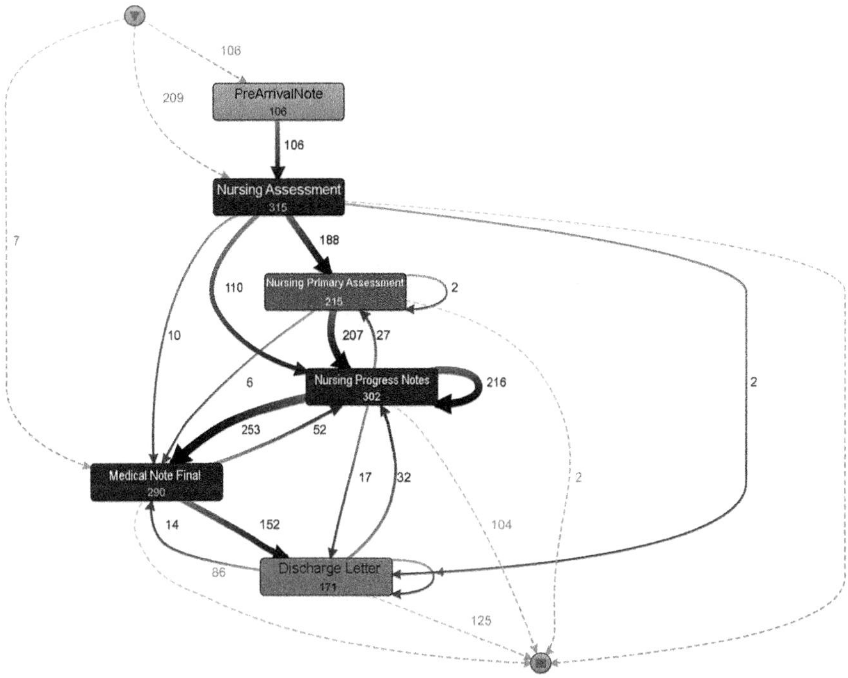

Fig. 3 Most frequent process paths for clinical activities. *Arrows* are annotated with case frequencies

- Patients in all but 48 of 1473 episodes were ultimately discharged home, while the remaining patients were discharged otherwise (e.g., they were discharged to a different hospital, they did not wait, or they died), so these 48 episodes are not captured by the model.

Three primary observations with respect to clinical activities could be derived from this model (Fig. 3):

- Nursing activities form the backbone of the clinical events—that is, the majority of activities/interactions with patients in the ED are carried out by nursing staff.
- Even though it represents only 9% of the variants, it is still a complex process model, so it shows that the treatment processes are highly patient-specific in terms of the fine-grained clinical activities and their registration.
- Simple process visualizations cannot provide significant insights.

The (control-flow) process models in Figs. 4 and 5 show "direct follow" activities and reveal some differences in patient flows between short-stay and long-stay patients:

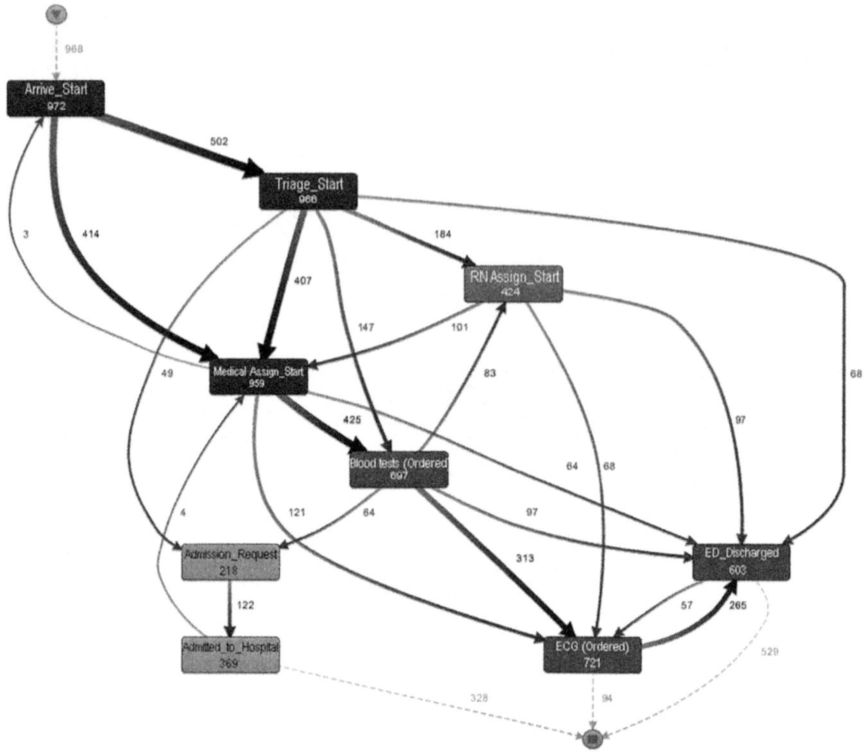

Fig. 4 Discovered process model for ED LoS up to 4 h

- Approximately 7% of short-stay patients proceed immediately from Triage to ED Discharge, but no long-stay patients do.
- The "Admission Request" event occurs in 48% of long-stay cases, compared to only 22% of short-stay cases.
- 58% of long-stay cases are ultimately "Admitted to Hospital," compared to only 39% of short-stay cases.

Extract performance-related information for each patient cohort and conduct comparative process-performance analysis (including visualizations)

LoS in the ED was calculated as the time between the "Arrive_Start" event and one of the two events—"ED_Discharged" and "Admitted_to_Hospital"—chosen as marker events representing the patient's physically leaving the ED. Under these conditions, 63% (972 of 1472) of cases completed the transit through the ED in <4 h (average transit time 2.9 h), and 37% (500 of 1472) of cases took more than 4 h to transit through the ED (average transit time 7.3 h).

The short- and long-LoS cohorts were also filtered to show the ED discharge destination. Table 3 shows the average time taken to reach certain key events.

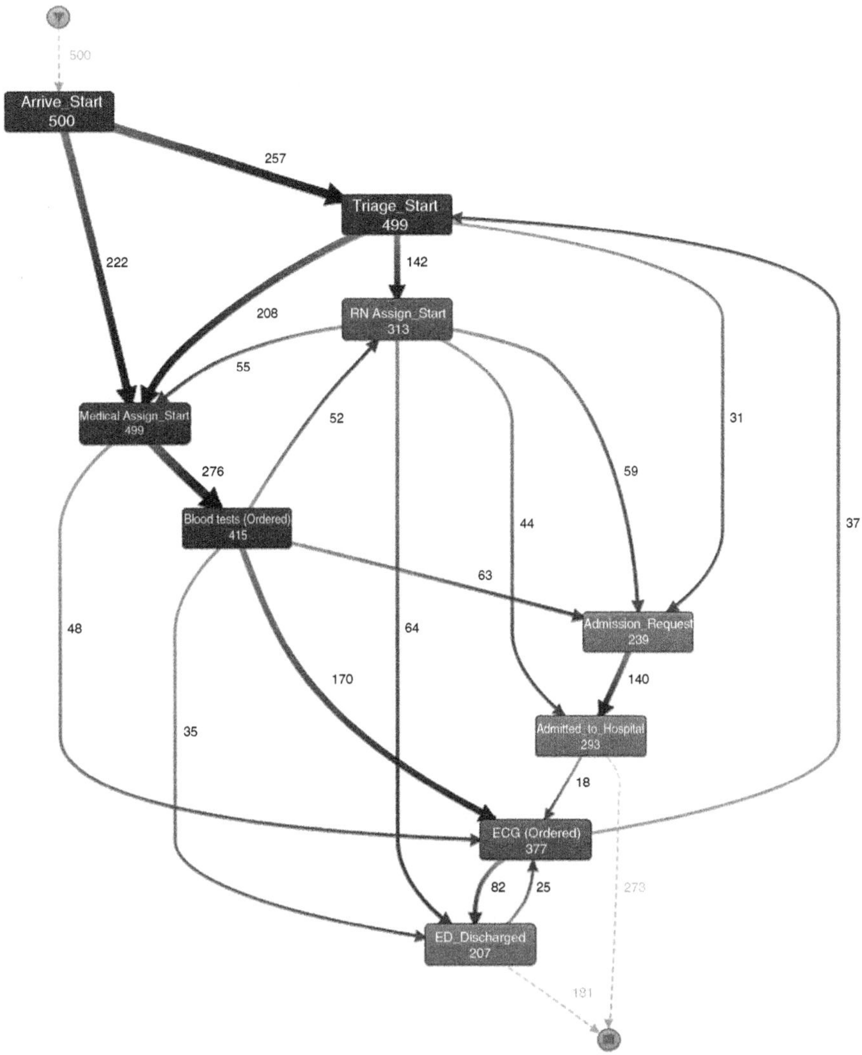

Fig. 5 Discovered process model for ED LoS longer than 4 h

It is clear that the event timing for the two cohorts is similar until blood tests are ordered. Differences in event timing are observable from the "RN Assign_Start" event. We could not determine the causes of this difference.

An even more stark contrast between the short- and long-stay cohorts is evident in the timing of the "Admission_Request" event, as shown in Fig. 6. The "Admission_Request" event occurs significantly earlier in the patient transit for short-stay patients than it does for long-stay patients. A similar discrepancy in the time from "Arrival_Start" to "ECG (Ordered)" is also observed. Again, we could not determine the cause of this observed difference.

Table 3 Times of milestone events (minutes after Arrive_Start event)

	Triage start	Medical assign start	Blood test (ordered)	RN assign start	Admission request	ECG (ordered)	Admitted to hospital	ED discharged
LoS > 4 h								
Admitted	16.3	20.6	29.5	96.3	173.3	239.5	364.0	N/A
Home	14.7	17.7	29.2	98.6	173.5	321.5	N/A	341.1
LoS ≤ 4 h								
Admitted	15.3	16.7	23.9	46.9	83.3	147.7	154.1	N/A
Home	12.4	17.5	26.0	41.9	91.4	106.5	N/A	141.9

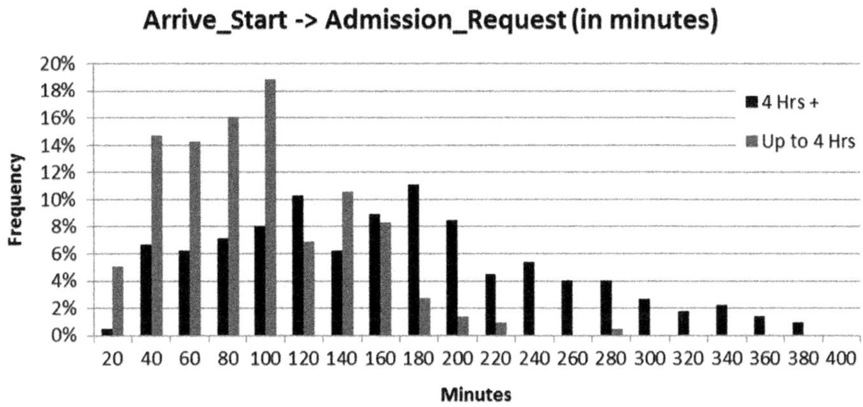

Fig. 6 Time from Arrive_Start to Admission_Request (ED LoS comparison)

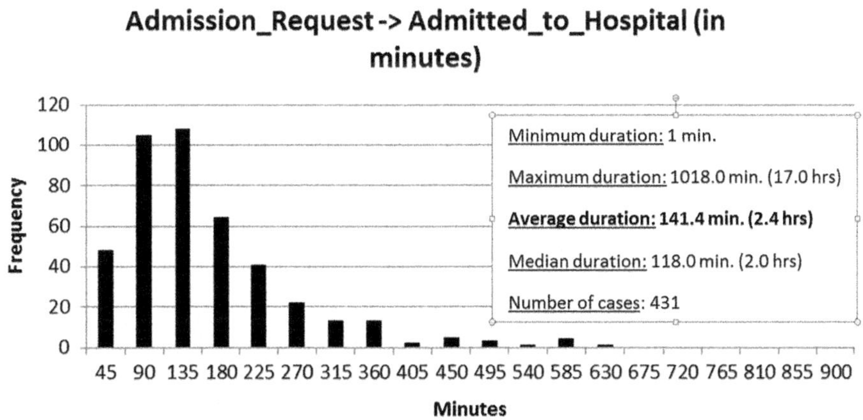

Fig. 7 Time from Admission_Request to Admitted_to_Hospital

Figure 7 shows the additional time spent in the ED between the time it was decided that hospital admission was necessary and the time the patient was actually admitted to hospital. It is clear that the waiting time in the ED following admission requests contributes significantly to overall LoS.

Visualize comparative process performance

This project highlighted the deficiencies in current approaches to comparative process-performance visualization. A parallel development of novel visualization approaches in Pini et al. (2015) resulted in three styles of visualizations, to which the authors referred as the *general model*, the *superimposed model*, and the *side-by-side comparison*. The general model shows the differences in performance (duration and frequency). The superimposed model compares the process flows of cohorts from the perspective of one of the cohorts such that correspondence of

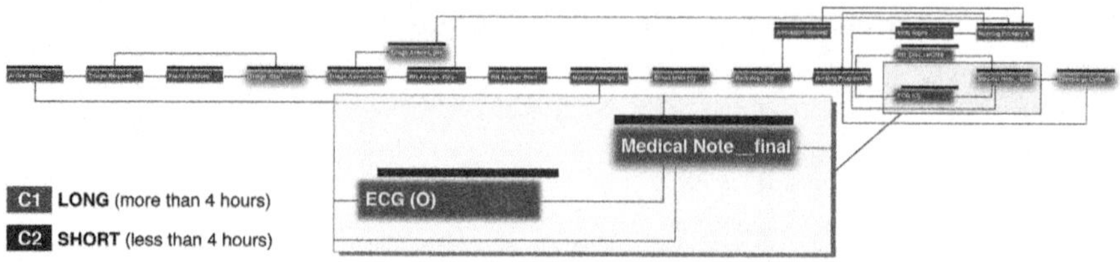

Fig. 8 Superimposed model of long-stay and short-stay cohorts (Pini et al. 2015). To illustrate how a superimposed model is used for comparative process performance visualization, two events are exploded out of the model to highlight their relative temporal ordering

activities is visualized through alignment and superposition of an activity element. The side-by-side comparison, which is specifically concerned with the time perspective, exploits the process model's logical flow to describe temporal dependencies between activities through predecessor and successor nodes of a directed graph. The superimposed model and side-by-side comparison were applied to aspects of the SAWMH case study, as shown in Figs. 8 and 9.

Figure 8 shows a superimposed model that compares the relative execution times of events between cohorts of long-stay and short-stay ED patients from the perspective of the long-stay cohort.

Figure 8 shows that the "ECG (O)" event occurs later in the process for short-stay patients than it does for long-stay patients, while the "Medical_Note_Final" event occurs at approximately the same point in the process for both cohorts.

The side-by-side comparison model (Fig. 9) shows the process difference (in terms of execution time) between the two cohorts. The side-by-side model is particularly useful in highlighting process delays. Considering the process fragments for the activities "Medical Note_final" and "Discharge Letter" in models for long-stay and short-stay patients makes clear that the individual activity durations and the waiting time between activities are significantly shorter for the short-stay cohort than they are for the long-stay cohort.

Through a combination of process discovery, analysis, and novel visualization techniques, we were able to detect differences in process behavior for cohorts of interest to SAWMH and obtain three important insights. First, there are fewer admission requests than actual hospital admissions. Second, significant differences in time spent in the ED between short-stay and long-stay patients become evident at the "RN Assign_Start" event and become more pronounced as the patients' journeys proceed. Third, there is evidence of patients "boarding" in the ED following the decision that the patient requires hospital admission, so the patient stayed in the ED waiting for a hospital bed to become available or to be transported to a ward. While we recognized these three points in the process where improvements can be made, we could not determine the causes of the differences. Nevertheless, these insights form a starting point for improvements in patient flow that would have direct impact on achieving the NEAT.

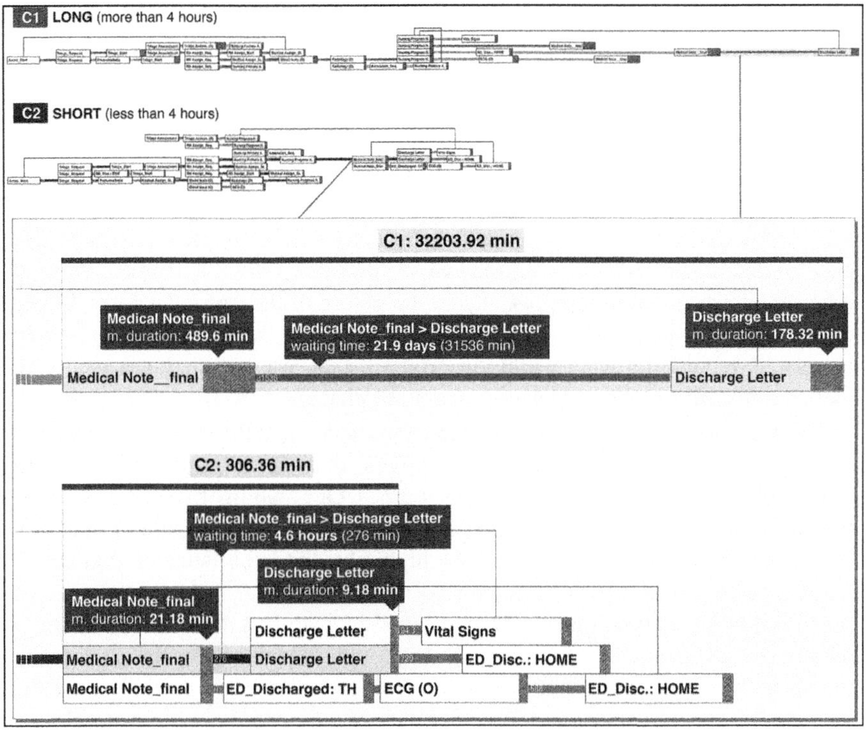

Fig. 9 Side-by-side comparison of long-stay and short-stay cohorts (Pini et al. 2015). The exploded sections of the models (*bottom* of the figure) represent the activity duration (width of the *colored rectangle* to the *right* of the activity name) and the waiting time between activities

5 Lessons Learned

From a clinical perspective, this project showed that process mining can be applied to a complex, semi-structured process like that found in a hospital ED. Through comparative process-performance analysis, we identified a point in the overall process at which variations between cohorts of interest (chest-pain patients who left the ED in <4 h and those whose LoS was longer than 4 h) became most apparent. The performance analysis also quantified the effect of waiting time (the time between its being determined that a patient required admission to hospital and the time of actual admission) on overall LoS in the ED. These two observations provide a starting point for patient-flow redesign and process-improvement initiatives.

From a data-quality perspective, this case study proved to be similar to other case studies with which we have been involved, in that the process of preparing event log/s suitable for process mining required considerable manual effort and benefited from the input of a domain expert in terms of attaching meaning and context to source data. A positive outcome was the identification of several recurring quality issues. For example, we found multiple instances of sets of events with exactly the same timestamp as a result of a forms-based information system's being used to record aspects of the patient's case. Users (e.g., doctors and nurses) click a "Save" button to record data captured on the form, with the effect of associating all data on the form with the same timestamp (the time the user clicked "Save"). Ignoring such an issue would have led to unnecessarily complex models, as all events with the same timestamp would have been modelled in parallel. The solution was to aggregate events with the same timestamp into a single event that represented the process step associated with the use of the particular form. Identification and resolution of the first instance of each such problem provided a templated recognition-and-resolution strategy that was applied repeatedly and that significantly sped up the data-preparation phase.

Another data-quality issue resulted in the project's inability to address one of the key questions from the project's stakeholders, that is, the impact of conducting routine clinical activities on patient transit times. Our inability to do so was because the data required to address the question was not stored in accessible format in the hospital information systems. This issue highlights the importance of aligning data with research questions (and research questions with data) if the prosecution of a process-mining analysis (or any form of analysis) is to be successful. We offer two recommendations to address this issue: improving hospital information recording practices through real-time, electronic recording of data, and introducing methods that allow hospital data to be correlated with related data held by external health services providers (e.g., pathology labs).

Finally, we found that there was no existing automated, intuitive way to perform process-performance comparison, particularly where multiple process models were involved. This issue led to the design initiative described in Pini et al. (2015) and to the development of static and animated multi-model and multi-cohort comparison techniques described in Conforti et al. (2015). These techniques are general enough to be applicable in a wider context, including to other hospital processes and to other domains.

Acknowledgements The research for this article was supported by an Australian Centre for Health Services Innovation (AusHSI) Stimulus Grant. We gratefully acknowledge the contributions to this project of Dr. Kelly Foster, Annette Bailey, Cath Voysey, Dr. Raffaele Conforti, Dr. Anastasiia Pika, and Huang Huy Nguyen.

References

Australian Institute of Health and Welfare. (2015). *Emergency Department Care 2013–14: Australian Hospital statistics*. Health Services Series (No. 65, Cat. No. HSE 168), Canberra, Australia. http://www.aihw.gov.au/WorkArea/DownloadAsset.aspx?id=60129553618

Catchpole, K. R., Gangi, A., Blocker, R. C., Ley, E. J., Blaha, J., Gewertz, B. L., & Wiegmann, D. A. (2013). Flow disruptions in trauma care handoffs. *Journal of Surgical Research, 184*(1), 586–591. http://www.sciencedirect.com/science/article/pii/S0022480413001157.

Conforti, R., Dumas, M., La Rosa, M., Maaradji, A., Nguyen, H. H., Ostovar, A., & Raboczi, S. (2015). *Analysis of business process variants in apromore*. http://eprints.qut.edu.au/86669/

Forero, R., Hillman, K., McCarthy, S., Fatovich, D., Joseph, A., & Richardson, D. W. (2010). Access block and emergency department overcrowding. *Emergency Medicine Australasia, 22*, 119–135.

Lakshmanan, G. T., Keyser, P. T., Duan, S. (2011). *Detecting changes in a semi-structured business process through spectral graph analysis*. In IEEE 27th International Conference on Data Engineering Workshops (ICDEW) (pp. 255–260).

Liew, D., & Kennedy, M. P. (2003). Emergency department length of stay independently predicts excess inpatient length of stay. *Medical Journal of Australia, 179*(10), 524–526.

Partington, A., Wynn, M., Suriadi, S., Ouyang, C., & Karnon, J. (2015). Process mining for clinical processes: A comparative analysis of four Australian Hospitals. *ACM Transactions on Management Information Systems (TMIS), 5*(4), 19.

Pini, A., Brown, R., & Wynn, M. T. (2015). Process visualization techniques for multi-perspective process comparisons. In *Asia Pacific Business Process Management: Third Asia Pacific Conference, AP-BPM 2015, Proceedings* (LNBIP, Vol. 219, pp. 183–197). Springer.

Queensland Audit Office. Emergency Department Performance Reporting. (2015). Report 3:2014–15. https://www.qao.qld.gov.au/files/file/Reports%20and%20publications/Reports%20to%20Parliament%202014-15/RtP3Emergencydepartmentperformancereporting.pdf

Queensland Clinical Senate. (2014). *27–28 March 2014 meeting – Report and recommendations*. Brisbane, Queensland. https://www.health.qld.gov.au/qldclinicalsenate/docs/fin-rep-mar2014.pdf

Queensland Health. (2011). *The State of Queensland (Queensland Health) annual report 2010–2011*. https://publications.qld.gov.au/storage/f/2014-06-10T04%3A57%3A03.689Z/annual-report-2010-11.pdf

Queensland Health. (2015). *Cardiac chest pain clinical pathway*. https://www.health.qld.gov.au/caru/pathways/docs/sw574-chest-pain-pathway.pdf

Richardson, D. B. (2006). Increase in patient mortality at 10 days associated with emergency department overcrowding. *Medical Journal of Australia, 184*, 213–216.

Showell, C., Ellis, L., Keen, E., Cummings, E., Georgiou, A., & Turner, P. (2012). *An evidence-based review and training resource on smooth patient flow*. eHealth Services Research Group, University of Tasmania, Australia (on behalf of the Ministry of Health, New South Wales Government).

Sprivulis, P. C., Da Silva, J. A., Jacobs, I. G., Frazer, A. R., & Jelinek, G. A. (2006). The association between hospital overcrowding and mortality among patients admitted via Western Australian emergency departments. *Medical Journal of Australia, 184*, 208–212.

Suriadi, S., Mans, R., Wynn, M., Partington, A., & Karnon, J. (2014). Measuring patient flow variations: A cross-organisational process mining approach. In *Asia Pacific business process management* (pp. 43–58). Cham: Springer.

Wiegmann, D., El Bardissi, A., Dearani, J., Daly, R., & Sundt III, T. (2007). Disruptions in surgical flow and their relationship to surgical errors: An exploratory investigation. *Surgery, 142*(5), 658–665.

Robert Andrews is a Research Fellow within the Business Process Management discipline of the School of Information Systems at Queensland University of Technology. He obtained his PhD in 2003 from the Queensland University of Technology (QUT). Since 2015, after more than a decade in commercial practice, he has been involved in a number of research projects in the area of Business Process Management. His main research interests are in the area of process mining, machine learning and business intelligence.

Suriadi Suriadi is a Senior Research Fellow at Queensland University of Technology. Before this, from 2014 to 2016, he was a Lecturer within the College of Sciences of Massey University, New Zealand. He obtained his PhD degree in the discipline of Information Security in late 2010 from the Queensland University of Technology (QUT). Since 2007, he has been involved in a number of research projects in the area of information security. From 2011 to late 2014, he was a Research Fellow within the Business Process Management discipline at Queensland University of Technology, Brisbane, Australia. He enjoys working in collaborative, cross-domain research projects that allow the application of research outcomes to address real-world problems. His main research interests are in the area of process mining and information security.

Moe T. Wynn is a Senior Lecturer in the field of Business Process Management (BPM) within the School of Information Systems at Queensland University of Technology. Her research interests include process automation, process mining, data quality and comparative process analytics. She has published over 60 refereed research papers. Her work appeared in well-known journals in the field including Information Systems, Decision Support Systems, Information Sciences, Data and Knowledge Engineering, Information and Software technology, Formal Aspects of Computing, Journal of Computer and System Sciences, and Transactions on Petri Nets and Other Models of Concurrency.

Arthur ter Hofstede is a full Professor in the School of Information Systems of Queensland University of Technology in Brisbane, Australia. He has co-authored more than 80 journal articles, among others in Decision Support Systems, ACM Transactions on Software Engineering and Methodology, Information Systems, IEEE Transactions on Knowledge and Data Engineering, and Information Sciences. His main research interests are in business process automation and process mining.

Sean Rothwell is a Fellow of the Australasian College for Emergency Medicine, an Associate Fellow of the Royal Australasian College of Medical Administrators and has a Masters in Health Management from the University of New South Wales. He is Director of Medical Services at Greenslopes Private Hospital and senior staff specialist at the Royal Brisbane and Women's Hospital. He has previously held positions of Director of Emergency Services for St Andrew's War Memorial Hospital and The Wesley Hospital and is Vice-Chair of the Australasian College for Emergency Medicine Private Practice Committee.

Part III

Information Technology

CrowdStrom: Analysis, Design, and Implementation of Processes for a Peer-to-Peer Service for Electric Vehicle Charging

Martin Matzner, Florian Plenter, Jan H. Betzing, Friedrich Chasin, Moritz von Hoffen, Matthias Löchte, Sarah Pütz, and Jörg Becker

Abstract

(a) **Situation faced**: An inadequate number of publicly available charging points is among the main reasons that consumers do not buy electric vehicles (EVs). To address this problem, we suggest a peer-to-peer (P2P) sharing approach for private charging infrastructures. We formed a joint consortium between academia and industry to design and implement a web platform and an underlying business model for an infrastructure of individually owned EV-charging stations for public use. Currently, there are no standardized processes for EV charging, so we had to look elsewhere for processes that could be adapted or partly adopted as a foundation for the proposed web platform.

(b) **Action taken**: We interviewed representatives of seven organizations that are already operating in the domain of EV charging about the relevant business processes. Applying the BPM lifecycle (Dumas et al., *Fundamentals of business process management*. Springer, 2013), we

M. Matzner • F. Plenter (✉) • J.H. Betzing • F. Chasin • M. von Hoffen • J. Becker
European Research Center for Information Systems (ERCIS), University of Münster, Münster, Germany
e-mail: martin.matzner@fau.de; florian.plenter@ercis.uni-muenster.de; jan.betzing@ercis.uni-muenster.de; friedrich.chasin@ercis.uni-muenster.de; moritz.von.hoffen@ercis.uni-muenster.de; joerg.becker@ercis.uni-muenster.de

M. Löchte
Stadtwerke Münster GmbH, IT-Management, Münster, Germany
e-mail: m.loechte@stadtwerke-muenster.de

S. Pütz
TÜV SÜD AG, Electromobility, Munich, Germany
e-mail: sarah.puetz@tuev-sued.de

J. vom Brocke, J. Mendling (eds.), *Business Process Management Cases*, Management for Professionals, DOI 10.1007/978-3-319-58307-5_18

analyzed the resulting as-is processes for best practices and redesigned them for the scenario of a P2P platform for EV charging.

(c) **Results achieved**: Sixteen to-be processes that comprised registration, authentication, charging, billing, and administration were modeled in BPMN and implemented in a software prototype. The prototype and associated processes are currently being evaluated to ensure their validity and effectiveness in the target environment while the partnering utility company prepares the solution's staged roll-out to operate their own charging stations and then open the system to other providers.

(d) **Lessons learned**: Analyzing and then designing business processes to reach a common goal has been a unifying factor in our joint research project, where partners from industry and academia have differing backgrounds, expectations, and individual goals. BPM practices enabled the project team to create an innovative business model and corresponding business processes that will have an impact in practice.

1 Introduction

In 2010, Germany's Federal Government announced the goal of one million registered electric vehicles (EVs) in Germany by 2020 (BMBF 2010). Although this goal might be too ambitious, increasing the number of EVs that are fueled by power from renewable sources is still a goal worth pursuing in the effort to reduce global carbon dioxide emissions.

Since EVs have a comparatively low range of distance, effective electric mobility must be built on an extensive network of charging points (Steinhilber et al. 2013). Currently, only 5800 public charging points at 2500 public charging stations are available in Germany (BDEW Bundesverband der Energie- und Wasserwirtschaft e.V. 2016) for the approximately 18,000 registered EVs and 100,000 registered hybrid vehicles in the country (Kraftfahrtbundesamt 2016).

Figure 1 compares the number of registered EVs to the number of publicly accessible charging points in Germany from 2006 to 2015. A sufficient network for the target of one million EVs requires, in addition to private charging points, roughly 110,000 charging points in semi-public spaces and 70,000 in public spaces (Nationale Plattform Elektromobilität 2014). Developing such an extensive charging infrastructure for EVs requires a substantial investment that would be rational only if demand increased well over its present level. So what should come first: demand with insufficient supply or supply with insufficient demand?

The joint academia-and-industry research project "CrowdStrom" addresses this "chicken-and-egg" problem. The local utility Stadtwerke Münster and the global testing and certification organization TÜV SÜD collaborated with researchers from the University of Münster's departments of Information Systems and Marketing and the University of Duisburg-Essen.

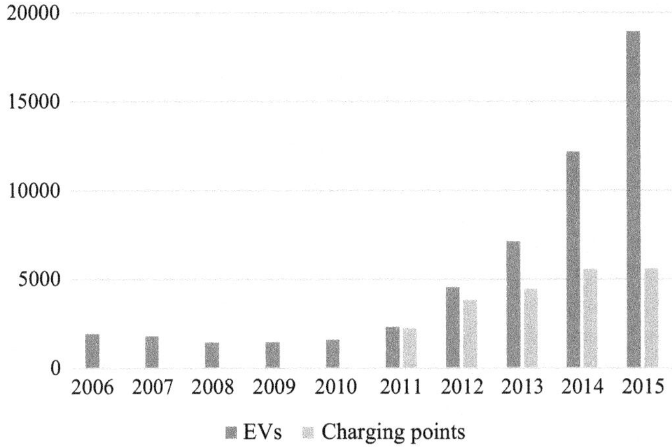

Fig. 1 Number of EVs and publicly accessible charging points in Germany from 2006 to 2015 (Nationale Plattform Elektromobilität 2015; Kraftfahrtbundesamt 2016)

The project's main goal is to support the establishment of a well-developed network of publicly accessible charging stations that can help to accelerate the diffusion of EVs. Our central tasks are to design, implement, and evaluate a business model, business processes, and the IT architecture of a peer-to-peer sharing service for charging EVs that networks individuals and small businesses and their charging stations with charging-service customers. A major obstacle in this endeavor is the absence of standards and best-practice processes for EV charging because of the novelty of and rapid technological developments in this field. The innovativeness of the proposed business model also requires additional processes that are new to either the field of EV charging or that of P2P sharing and so require modifications or even new development from scratch. Our review of the German market for EV charging identified seven organizations that participate in this market. We interviewed these players to capture and model their existing processes, scanned them for best practices, assessed these practices' applicability to the proposed business model, and remodeled them into to-be processes for the service. We are currently evaluating the resulting software prototype regarding the socio-technical aspects of the service and its viability for real-world application. Its roll-out in several stages into live operation is planned.

The remainder of this article is structured as follows: The next section delineates the current situation in more detail, focusing on the participating parties' motivation and existing obstacles. The third section describes the steps we took to derive to-be processes for CrowdStrom from several related organizations' as-is processes. The fourth section describes the analysis of the as-is processes and the resulting to-be processes in detail. The article concludes with a summary of the findings and lessons learned for future cases.

2 Situation Faced

An EV owner typically purchases a private charging point along with her or his EV in order to be able to charge the car more quickly than it is possible using a regular household outlet. Because there is usually only one user, these charging points tend to be underused. In the spirit of the sharing economy, the use rate and productivity of these charging points can be increased if they are rented to other people when the owners do not need them, an approach that would simultaneously increase the number of available charging points for other EV owners and make the purchase of an EV more practicable. This basic idea has been implemented in many peer-to-peer sharing and collaborative consumption (P2P SCC) business models, such as Airbnb (sharing of rooms) and Uber (sharing of cars).

The charging infrastructure landscape is fragmented, with many isolated small providers and little interoperability. These isolated solutions present a major obstacle for EV owners who travel long distances and must search for charging points along the way. Intercharge networks like *ladenetz.de* and *Hubject* approach this problem by interconnecting existing public charging providers. CrowdStrom follows this approach but expands it to include private providers to create an open charging infrastructure.

Sharing a charging point in return for monetary compensation requires the individual charging station to adopt the general P2P SCC paradigm, which poses challenges because of the nature of the resource that is shared. In addition, the whole process should be fully automated so the need for the provider's direct intervention is minimal or, at best, unnecessary. That the individual charging points are embedded in systems and have limited influence on their internal behavior adds another layer of complexity to the business processes because the processes have to be carried out within and across these systems, rather than by only one or a few application systems. In addition to the lack of knowledge about the required processes and how they should be implemented, the diversity of stakeholders' perspectives and expectations creates complexity. In a P2P SCC model, participants can take a variety of roles so service and monetary flows become bidirectional. Facing the absence of standards or reference models for many aspects of the service to be developed, we found the adoption of BPM practices like the BPM lifecycle appropriate for structuring and guiding our efforts. Our focus was not primarily on improving processes but on identifying best practices and their consequent adaptations for our project. In addition, Business Process Model and Notation 2.0 (BPMN 2.0) is a valid instrument for modeling the processes and communicating the various roles and tasks involved in service delivery in a way that every stakeholder can understand.

A crowdsourcing-based approach for the expansion of the charging infrastructure adds challenges concerning legal implications and the service's profitability. The proposed business model poses novel legal questions regarding network technology, laws for electricity-providers, and calibration and measurement techniques (Chasin et al. 2015). The service's profitability depends heavily on external factors like the prevalence of EVs and users' acceptance of the service, especially users who provide the charging infrastructure. Because of the approach's novelty and the general public's lack of involvement in the EV domain, many aspects of the service are not yet clearly defined. For example, the factors that motivate potential service providers to use CrowdStrom and how to incent them to participate remain unknown.

The project partners from industry provided important insights for the project's success. As a local utility, Stadtwerke Münster provides customers with electricity, heat, water, and public transportation and offers the PlusCard program, which enables their customers to do cashless payment for services provided by various partners. In the field of electric mobility, Stadtwerke Münster operates a local charging infrastructure for EVs. However, proper accounting is a major issue for the company, as customers of the utility currently charge their cars for free because of legal and technical restrictions. Consequently, Stadtwerke Münster's goal in participating in the project is the development of a profitable business model for its charging infrastructure that can be integrated into its current PlusCard service environment and accounting infrastructure.

TÜV SÜD is a German-based global certification and testing company with 24,000 employees in more than 60 countries. The company also provides consulting services in the EV mobility domain. Its focus in participating in the CrowdStrom project is on the development of data privacy, data security, and governance mechanisms in the business model and business processes.

3 Action Taken

The emerging domain of EV charging has brought organizations with a variety of business models and processes into the market. Therefore, instead of developing the necessary processes for the CrowdStrom web platform from scratch, we analyzed other organizations' existing processes for their suitability for CrowdStrom. The seven organizations whose processes for EV charging we analyzed are introduced next.

Stadtwerke Münster

The local utility Stadtwerke Münster introduced a radio frequency identification (RFID)-based customer card (PlusCard) for the authentication and payment of certain cashless services, including parking lots, taxis, and associated services. The experience of Stadtwerke Münster from the everyday use of the PlusCard system can inform the derivation of RFID-based customer processes for EV charging.

Ebee Smart Technologies

Ebee develops and distributes components for setting up and managing charging infrastructures to customers who provide infrastructure as a service. As a unique characteristic, Ebee's charging points are compact enough to be mounted on ordinary streetlights. The primary customer group consists of municipalities, municipal utilities, and electricity-supply companies. Ebee acts only as a hardware provider, not as the operator of charging points, and does not compete with the large number of charging-point operators. A similar business model with an extended focus on private providers is offered by PunktLaden.

Hubject
Hubject, founded in 2012 as a joint venture of car manufacturers and electric utilities, is an IT service provider in the domain of EV and charging infrastructure integration that serves all of Europe. The Hubject IT platform has been available since 2013, offering the possibility of eRoaming for charging-point infrastructures and enabling the independent use of charging points by connecting existing isolated solutions. While this roaming approach grants end users access to a large network of charging points, Hubject's core business area is in the B2B area. Primarily addressing end users is not part of the company's business model or processes.

ladenetz.de
Founded in 2010, ladenetz.de is a cooperation among municipal utilities with the goal of introducing, developing, and facilitating a well-developed charging infrastructure. Smartlab, ladenetz.de's parent company, was founded in 2010 as a subsidiary of Stadtwerke Aachen, Duisburg, and Osnabrück (municipal utilities of the cities of Aachen, Duisburg, and Osnabrück). These utilities focus on the development and distribution of innovative services, products, and concepts in the area of EVs, mainly directed at local energy utilities and municipal utilities.

RWE Effizienz
RWE Effizienz is a subsidiary of the large German electric utilities company RWE, which is primarily active in the domain of EV charging. The company offers the technical infrastructure and an extensive portfolio of services for the installation and operation of charging infrastructures. RWE Effizienz also manufactures charging points with two lines of its own charging points that are targeted to private and business customers, respectively.

The eLine products, which do not support any form of communication with backend systems, target primarily private users. The stations do not offer authentication methods, but RWE offers the possibility of regulating the access via locking systems in the context of private use.

eLine Smart offers several authentication methods, differentiated between local and remote authentication methods. The latter include requests to unlock the station via RWE's smartphone application and requests sent via text message. Local authentication methods are supported through intelligent charging cables with Powerline Communication and the use of RFID cards.

sms&charge
The research project sms&charge developed a simple authentication and accounting system for charging stations. Users write and send text messages to sms&charge, which then grants access to the charging point for a certain time

slot. Since virtually every potential user carries a mobile phone, this solution gives users non-discriminatory access to the public charging infrastructure. Services used are billed through the user's mobile service provider.

The New Motion

The New Motion, founded in 2009 in the Netherlands, offers charging infrastructure and services for EVs. The New Motion, which develops intelligent charging points and advanced charging services for EVs, is currently working on a comprehensive network of charging points. Since 2012, The New Motion has also been active in Belgium and Germany (The New Motion Deutschland). Its widely used charging network is the largest in Europe, with over 12,000 charging points. The New Motion provides services to both businesses and private customers. In addition to the distribution and installation of charging points, the company offers to operate the stations and to manage accounting of charging transactions.

Following Dumas et al.'s (2013) BPM lifecycle, our approach is comprised of the phases of *process identification*, *process discovery*, *redesign*, *process analysis*, *process implementation*, and *process monitoring and controlling*. In *process identification*, processes that are relevant to the problem are identified, their scope is delimited, and relationships between the processes are identified. *Process discovery* (or *process modeling*) describes the phase of documenting the process, as in *as-is process models*. *Process analysis* includes the identification and assessment of issues in the as-is processes. *Process redesign* addresses the issues identified in the previous phase and identifies and analyzes potential remedies that result in to-be process models. *Process implementation* performs the changes necessary to reach the to-be processes. Finally, during the *process monitoring and controlling* phase, relevant data is collected to identify necessary adjustments to the processes.

In the following, we describe the steps we undertook in applying the BPM lifecycle to our case. First, we conducted *process identification* by means of several workshops in which researchers, students, and company representatives who were involved in the project identified four process categories with regard to the proposed business model for an EV-charging service. In the *process discovery* phase, a comprehensive market analysis identified the aforementioned seven organizations that provide charging services. These organizations' processes were then elicited with regard to the processes category identified in the process identification phase, resulting in 23 as-is processes being modeled in BPMN 2.0. The as-is processes were then *analyzed* for best practices and their suitability for the CrowdStrom business model. Processes that indicated weaknesses during the analysis phase were *redesigned*. Eventually, a total of 16 to-be processes were derived and *implemented* in a software prototype that is currently being used in a field test in which two actual charging points are being operated. After the initial implementation of the to-be processes, an iterative improvement of the to-be processes began. It started with using the insights gathered during the first *process monitoring and controlling* phase to identify gaps in the processes landscape and to trigger the subsequent iterations of the BPM lifecycle. Continuous process improvement is important in the CrowdStrom case, as the developed software is scheduled to

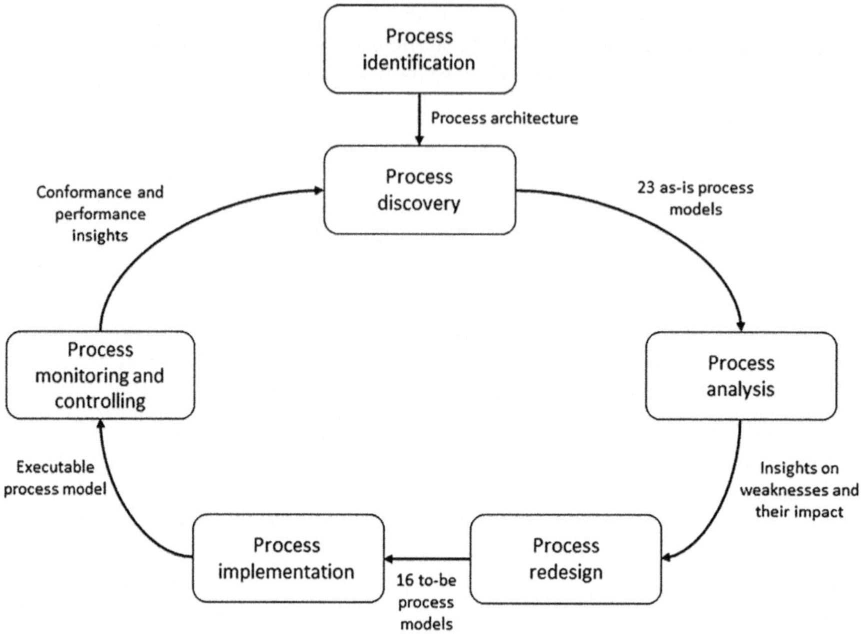

Fig. 2 Approach based on the BPM lifecycle (Dumas et al. 2013)

operate all of the project partner's charging points in the near future. Figure 2 visualizes the chosen approach according to the BPM lifecycle.

3.1 Process Identification

Since the focus of this assessment is on the operation of the charging service and all related processes, identifying all processes from authentication to billing of the charging service was required. Four process categories—registration, authentication, charging, and billing—were identified as particularly critical in this context.

Registration
The registration process is the basis for all user-oriented and provider-oriented processes. It collects all of the involved persons' relevant data and initiates the contractual relationship between the company and the users and providers of the service. All subsequent processes are designed based on the initial registration.

Authentication
The purpose of authentication is to ensure that only eligible persons are granted access to the service (in this case, the use of a charging point) so the provider is assured of receiving payment for the service. The legitimacy of use is evaluated through an identification measure determined by the provider. In most cases, the

identification measure is a customer-specific ID that can be read and compared to a list of authorized IDs (whitelist) and unauthorized IDs (blacklist). If the potential user does not have such an identification measure, or in case of authentication failure, he or she will not be granted access. If the authentication is successful, the person can use the service and be billed accordingly.

Charging

The charging process starts after successful authentication and continues until a stopping event—such as unlocking the charging cable on the vehicle side, cancelling the request via mobile application, or repeating the authentication at the charging point—occurs. The transaction data must be transmitted and saved throughout the charging process, as they are required for subsequent billing processes.

Billing

Billing is considered from two perspectives in the context of CrowdStrom: the user billing and the provider settlement. The user billing refers to the billing of services used by the user—that is, the consumption of electricity at a charging point after successful authentication. The transaction data gathered at each process step build the basis for the user billing and are used to create an invoice that is delivered to the user. The billing process is concluded after the invoice is paid.

The provider settlement refers to the payment for services that a charging-point provider delivered to a user. After each charging process, transaction data are transmitted from the charging point and allocated to a single, distinct charging point. They are then aggregated and the total costs calculated in order to pay the provider on a monthly basis.

3.2 Process Discovery

Since companies' processes are generally not public, we conducted interviews with business professionals from the organizations we identified. All of these organizations have been operating successfully for some time, so they are likely to have reliable processes in place. In the interest of capturing the processes in detail and observing their interactions, the interviewees we chose were all domain experts who were deeply involved in the processes or even the process owners or managers.

The project team drafted an extensive questionnaire with 85 questions on the topics of registration, authentication, charging, and billing to ensure comparability. The questions focused on the identification of a process's systematic series of actions, the actors involved, and the master data and documents that were relevant to the process. An interview guideline in the form of a checklist was created to provide guidance in preparing and conducting the interviews and modeling and documenting the processes. One interview was conducted in each organization, with two interviews taking place during personal meetings and the remaining five done via phone. Each interview lasted from 45 to 90 min, and each was tape-recorded, transcribed, and sent to the respective interviewee for audit and confirmation. We worked in groups of two, with one person responsible for tracking the questionnaire and the other guiding the interview.

3.3 Process Modeling

Based on the interviews, we modelled 23 as-is processes in BPMN 2.0. As expected, the organizations we interviewed handle their core processes differently, so we identified up to five variants per process category. Provider and user billing was identified and modeled only twice, as not all of the organizations had implemented these processes. The as-is processes were numerous and diverse, so they provide a good basis for identifying and deducing the to-be recommendations that take place during the *analysis* and *redesign* phases. Table 1 provides an overview of the processes we modeled and the organizations from which they were derived.

Table 1 Overview of as-is processes and corresponding organizations

Process category	Process identified	Organization
Registration	Registration	ladenetz.de
	Registration PlusCard	Stadtwerke Münster
	User registration	The New Motion
	Registration for customer portal	The New Motion
	Provider registration	The New Motion
Authentication	Authentication	Hubject
	Remote authentication	Hubject
	Authentication	ladenetz.de
	Authentication	sms&charge
	Authentication	Stadtwerke Münster
	Authentication	The New Motion
Charging	Start charging procedure	ladenetz.de
	End charging procedure	ladenetz.de
	Start charging procedure	sms&charge
	End charging procedure	sms&charge
	Service use and response	Stadtwerke Münster
	Charging procedure	The New Motion
Billing	Response	Hubject
	User billing	Stadtwerke Münster
	Provider billing	Stadtwerke Münster
	User billing	The New Motion
	Provider billing	The New Motion
Administration	Administration of customer account	Stadtwerke Münster

3.4 Process Analysis

The modeled as-is processes were subsequently analyzed and used as a foundation for the derivation of to-be processes. In the first step of the process analysis, we grouped the as-is process models according to the categories of registration, authentication, charging, billing, and administration. In the next step, we analyzed the as-is processes qualitatively. Traditional techniques for qualitative business process analysis, such as value-added analysis and root-cause analysis, were not applied because they would not have been expedient in our context. As our goal was to identify best practices and processes that were suitable to the proposed business model, we analyzed the modeled as-is processes for similarities, differences, and consistency with regard to their planned application. We selected three predefined process categories for later application: standard processes that were not specific to EV-charging (e.g., billing), large parts of which could be reused without modifications, especially when they included direct customer interaction; EV-related (but not EV-specific) processes that revealed new concepts and comprehensive best-practices for planned operations (e.g., a variety of options for authentication); and processes that were directly related to EV-charging, especially processes connected to communication between the backend system and charging stations using the Open Charge Point Protocol (OCPP), for which we treated the communication part as a black box that was implemented after the protocol's documentation. Additional information that the interviewees provided and that could not be fit into formal process models, such as Hubject's remote authentication procedure,[1] was taken into account. As a result, five best-practice process models out of nine core processes and additional details were derived from the information gathered on the elicited process models and the advantages and disadvantages of specific models. Since CrowdStrom's focus is on charging EVs, we did not classify administration processes as core processes.

3.5 Process Redesign

During the *process redesign* phase, we designed the to-be process models based on the identified best practices with regard to their applicability in the project context. The application of a P2P sharing approach to EV charging results in certain characteristics that differ from those of the established providers we interviewed. For example, the integration into the network of customers as peer-providers requires differentiating customers as peer-providers, peer-users, or both. Other issues included the processes' suitability for use with the future providers' existing

[1]A requirement for using Hubject's method is a backend system at the charging-point provider that can communicate with the Hubject backend system via the Open InterCharge Protocol. Such requirements were not modelled explicitly in BPMN but were considered informally in the accompanying textual descriptions.

processes as well as those of the local utility, and the partner concept that enables a third party (a partner) to offer participation in the CrowdStrom network and its corresponding services as a (white-label) service to the partner's own customers.

These issues required individual changes and additions to the identified best-practice processes and even whole processes to be conceptualized and modeled anew in order to obtain the desired to-be processes. In the end, we designed 16 processes, out of which we defined nine core processes. While five core processes were derived from best practices, the remaining 11 processes were designed from scratch to align with CrowdStrom's new concept. For example, registrations will be possible directly at CrowdStrom but also via contract partners like Stadtwerke Münster.

Applying the *Heuristic Process Redesign* methodology, we followed the three stages of *initiate*, *design*, and *evaluate* that Dumas et al. (2013) suggested. In the *initiate* stage, the project team gained a deep understanding of the targeted domain of EV charging by conducting the interviews and modeling the respective as-is processes. The goal of applying the BPM lifecycle was to devise suitable best-practice processes for the software prototype. Therefore, the primary focus in the application presented was not the traditional goals of process redesign, such as flexibility, time, cost, and quality (Dumas et al. 2013) but adapting and altering the existing processes so the resulting solutions comply with the proposed business model's technical and business requirements.

For the second stage, *design*, we considered Dumas et al.'s (2013) design heuristics; however, because of the project's special character, we deemed only the heuristics from three classes to be applicable: *customer heuristics*, *technology heuristics*, and *external environment heuristics*.

From the class of *customer* heuristics, we applied the heuristics *control relocation* and *integration* to the integration of peer providers into the processes by giving them access to the web platform, where they can add their charging stations and configure parameters like opening times and prices. We applied *contact reduction* to the process of customer registration, rejecting other alternatives in favor of online-only registration for direct customers in order to save administrative resources.

From the class of *technology heuristics* we applied the heuristics of *activity automation* and *integral technology*. We added new technology, such as that which enables user authentication via smartphone and offers users an integrated data analysis tool with a dashboard in the web platform, wherever possible. In order to increase the level of automation, we deliver bills only digitally, eliminating manual postal processes.

From the class of *external environment heuristics* we applied the *trusted party heuristic* by adding the partner concept, enabling third parties to add their customer bases to the CrowdStrom network and offer them participation in the network as a value-added service.

The project team and experts from our project partners, Stadtwerke Münster and TÜV SÜD, conducted the final stage of *evaluate*, after which we deemed the resulting to-be processes to be ready for implementation. After the processes were implemented in the software prototype, we conducted an extensive qualitative evaluation by means of several workshops with experts from Stadtwerke Münster, resulting in new insights and minor alterations to the prototype.

4 Results Achieved

Here we describe the resulting to-be processes sorted for each process category. For reasons of clarity, we do not describe all to-be processes in detail or show the respective process models. Instead, we provide four process models that illustrate our approach and the results.

Registration

The processes we captured differentiate between online and offline registration (service desk) procedures. The latter cannot be considered a best practice, as our goal is to provide fast, standardized process-handling. The installation of service desks also leads to additional cost and disproportionate effort. Since all of the providers we consulted offered online registration—with the offline option simply an optional addition—the online registration was determined the best practice. The online registration collects data on the customer's surname, first name, address, e-mail address, and payment method. (At present, only a bank account from which charges can be debited and to which payments can be deposited is allowed.)

The best-practice process identified was extended to include application for the CrowdStrom RFID card and the possibility of the customer's adding his or her own charging points and becoming a provider. The partner concept requires a special process with which to add a partner's customers to the CrowdStrom database. In this process, the partner transmits the customer's ID, a related RFID card number (if available), and existing charging points to be added to the CrowdStrom database. In return, CrowdStrom provides transaction data to the partner, who handles the billing of his or her customers.

Authentication

We captured authentication processes from six organizations that have only a few principal differences. The organizations can be categorized in terms of the authentication medium they apply, with the most common medium (five out of six providers) being the RFID card. Figure 3 depicts an extract of an as-is process using RFID technology that we observed during our interviews. The customer initiates the authentication by holding the RFID card in front of the charging station's card reader. The charging station requests authentication using the provider's information system, which looks up the transmitted contract ID and checks it for validity. If it's valid, authentication is successful, and the customer may continue.

Ebee, Hubject, and ladenetz.de provide the additional service of unlocking charging points via a smartphone app, although only sms&charge provides authentication via text message. When issues arise during the authentication procedure

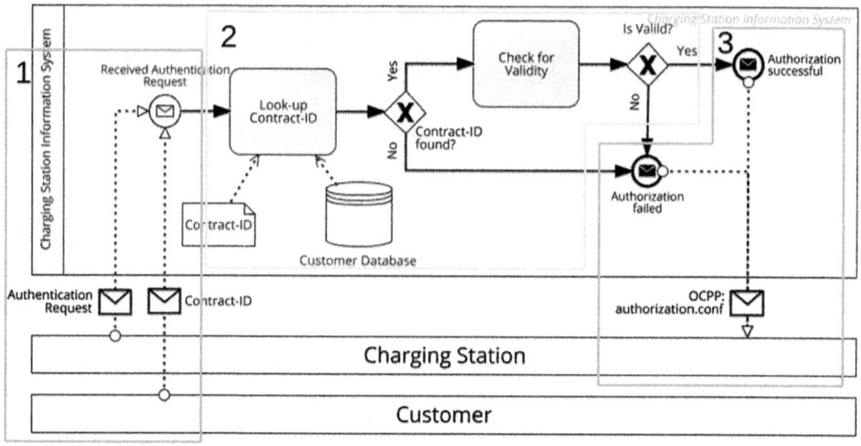

Fig. 3 Section of as-is authentication process

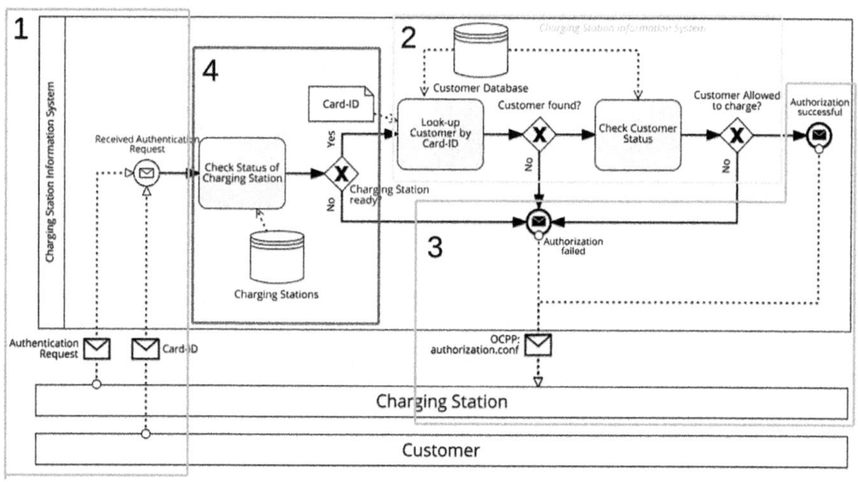

Fig. 4 Section of to-be authentication process with adaptations

because of unreadable cards, The New Motion offers authentication via phone call. The best-practice process in the context of CrowdStrom is the authentication via RFID card, as it is the most common variant, it corresponds to the recommendation of the project partner Stadtwerke Münster, and it was the method of choice in a survey that measured the preferences of potential customers (Matzner et al. 2015).

In the resulting to-be process, during the authentication process, the system automatically determines whether the current time falls within the opening hours the provider set. This feature was added for CrowdStrom since private charging-station owners should be able to define when others are allowed to charge at their stations. Figure 4 illustrates how we derived the to-be process from the as-is process represented in Fig. 3. While the tasks and messages covered by the green boxes (number 1 and 3) are directly derived from the as-is process, the parts within the yellow box (number 2) only differ in detail, but handle similar tasks. However, the contents within the red box (number 4) introduce our new approach of checking opening hours before continuing with authentication. The card ID should be compared with the customer data on the backend. A whitelist that is locally stored in the reading device supports the authentication services in case the Internet connection is temporarily interrupted, so charging points that are ready for CrowdStrom must support RFID and be able to store a whitelist locally. The alternative authentication via smartphone app (e.g., with a customer number and a PIN) should also be integrated. For this purpose, the charging point could be equipped with corresponding QR codes, which simplify transmitting the charging point's ID and speed up the unlocking process.

An optional smartphone app would enable authentication when users do not have their RFID cards, thereby enhancing the customer experience. (Reasons to decline an authentication also include non-readability of cards, a missing card ID in the customer data, and defective charging points—.) Such an app also has potential to offer additional services, such as searching for nearby charging points, navigating to the chosen one, and inspecting the most recent charging transactions and the corresponding costs or profits from the customer's or provider's point of view. An optional smartphone app was also reflected in the survey that measured user preferences (Matzner et al. 2015).

Charging

Processes that are related to the vehicle-charging procedure were elicited from Ebee, Hubject, ladenetz.de, sms&charge, and The New Motion. The analysis revealed that communication between charging points and the backend depends heavily on the charging point and the supported communication protocol. Most of the interviewees implement the OCPP 1.5 protocol[2] for initialization but use a variety of ways to cancel the charging process.

The user's authentication is required twice during the charging process: at the beginning to insert the charging cable into the charging station and start charging, and at the end to unlock the charging station and remove the charging cable from the station (or the vehicle). As authentication via RFID was identified as a best practice, it was implemented as the default solution to both start and terminate the charging process. With this approach, the RFID card's ID is transmitted from the charging point to the central charging station controller at the company's backend, which verifies whether the user is eligible to start/terminate the charging process. When the verification is successful, the charging process is started/terminated

[2]Open Charge Point Protocol (OCPP) is an open standard that was published in 2010 by the Dutch E-Laad Initiative. Its purpose is to create independence between the charging station and the backend or the control center. As a result, a charging station's provider can choose among all available electricity suppliers without being dependent on proprietary interfaces.

centrally by the backend, ensuring that only eligible users (i.e., registered customers for starting and users who initiated the charging process for terminating) can order the start/termination of the charging process. The entire communication uses the OCPP 1.5 protocol. Ebee, ladenetz.de, and The New Motion all use this approach.

Another possibility for initiating and terminating the charging process is direct communication with the backend. For example, text messages or a smartphone app can be used to communicate with the backend and to ensure proper authentication. The backend verifies whether either the phone number or the content of the text message (e.g., user ID) indicates the sender is eligible to use charging services. For maintenance and emergency service purposes, we implemented the ability to start or terminate a charging process remotely by a technician or service staff via the backend (Fig. 5).

The best-practice processes we identified include the application of the OCPP 1.5, with the data stored in a database at the company's backend and exported from there. Transaction data can also be stored locally in the charging point in case there are connection problems. The separate storage of customer data and transaction data can also be considered a best practice. No adjustments to the best practices identified had to be made for the CrowdStrom's to-be termination process.

Billing

In the CrowdStrom business model and its business processes, billing is considered from two perspectives: user billing, which is concerned with the settlement of all services provided (i.e., the power consumed at a charging point); and provider billing, which is concerned with monetary compensation for the services provided (i.e., the charging point, parking spot, and energy). The processes for user billing are the authentication and charging procedures discussed above, as they capture all relevant transaction data for the billing process.

We captured processes regarding end-user billing from Stadtwerke Münster and The New Motion, both of which conduct user billing monthly and send a personal invoice; the only major difference is that The New Motion sends the invoice via

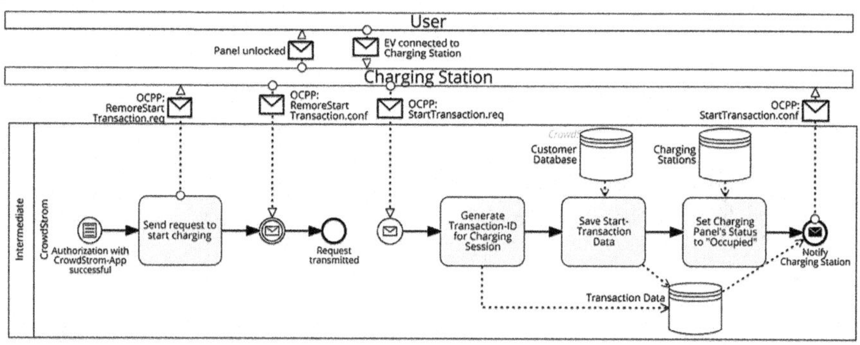

Fig. 5 Section of CrowdStrom's subsequent authorization and remote start-charging processes

e-mail, while Stadtwerke Münster uploads the invoice to its web portal. As for provider billing, both organizations bill monthly, calculating the amount payable using transaction data and the corresponding price models. They differ primarily in that The New Motion serves as an intermediary, collecting all data captured by the charging point and starting the billing process based on this data, while Stadtwerke Münster has service providers collect the data themselves and then send an invoice to Stadtwerke Münster.

The resulting to-be processes for billing consist of monthly billing for both users and providers via e-mail and within the web platform. The partner concept must also be considered in adapting these best practices for the CrowdStrom to-be processes. The user- and provider-billing of partner customers is not done directly via CrowdStrom but indirectly by the partner from whom the customers came. In another adaptation the peer providers are not charged for using their own charging points, and the difference between balances from the provision of charging points and from charging at other charging points is settled in the monthly billing. Invoices are created only when there have been transactions associated with the user—that is, when the user has charged at other charging stations or other users have used the user's charging station (Fig. 6).

Administration

In addition to the core processes, we designed to-be process models for administrative tasks that are concerned with actions that the user can perform on the online portal. Since the focus of the process analysis is on registration, authentication, charging, and billing, only one reference process was captured (from Stadtwerke Münster), and the remaining processes were designed from scratch. Required processes are concerned with registering a bank account, applying for (and possibly suspending) an authentication card, registering and removing charging points, changing opening hours, and eventually deactivating the user account.

Registering a bank account is essential for the CrowdStrom service, as at present customers can use the service only if they register a valid bank account. Customers can register a bank account in the customer portal, which is then validated by

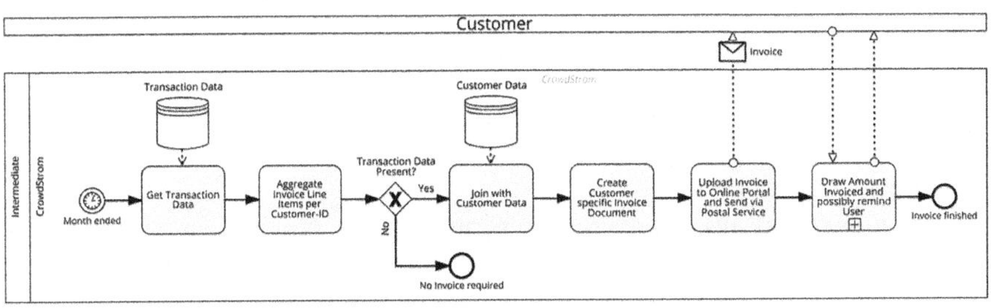

Fig. 6 Section of CrowdStrom's user billing process

CrowdStrom. If a registered bank account is invalid, the customer is informed via e-mail and asked to correct the details; otherwise, the customer is prompted to authorize a SEPA direct-debit mandate.

The CrowdStrom RFID card, which is required for customers to authenticate at the charging points of the CrowdStrom network, can be ordered via CrowdStrom's customer portal. The card is sent only if a valid bank account has been entered; otherwise, the customer is prompted via e-mail to enter a valid bank account. Only one active card is allowed per customer, so customers who request duplicate cards are informed that they can receive a new card only if the old one is suspended. When the card is sent, the card's ID is connected to the customer's user account. The card is sent by mail and is instantly operational.

If the card is lost or stolen, the customer can suspend the card via the customer portal. The request is transmitted to CrowdStrom, and if a card is linked to the requesting customer, the card's ID is removed from the customer data and stored in an archive with the customer ID, and the card can no longer be used for authentication.

Customers can register additional charging points on the user portal at any time by entering the required data into a form and transmitting it to CrowdStrom. CrowdStrom determines whether the customer has a valid bank account, assesses whether the charging point conforms to CrowdStrom's standards, and informs the customer of the result via e-mail. Then an external service provider connects the charging point to the CrowdStrom network, after which CrowdStrom determines whether the information entered conforms to the actual charging point and whether the station is connected to the power network correctly. Only after the station passes these tests is a corresponding record created in the database.

Active charging points can be removed from the network when a customer requests it on the customer portal. In such cases, the charging point's status is changed to "deactivated" in the database so users can no longer be authenticated and so the charging point is no longer displayed by the search function on the homepage.

Opening hours ensure that the owners of charging points can use their station exclusively at certain times. Opening hours are defined during the initial registration of a charging point but can also be changed on the customer portal. Changes take effect immediately, as long as the charging point is not in active use by a customer.

Customers can also disable their accounts via the customer portal. Deactivated customers cannot offer charging points or authenticate at the charging points within the CrowdStrom system.

Sorted by the respective process category, Table 2 provides an overview of all to-be processes for CrowdStrom that were the result of the *process analysis* and *process redesign* phases.

Table 2 Overview of to-be processes for CrowdStrom

Process category	To-be process
Registration	Registration
	Registration via contracting partner
Authentication	Authentication
Charging	Start charging procedure
	End charging procedure
Billing	User billing
	Provider billing
	Settlement contracting partner
	Response to contracting partner
Administration	Register bank account
	Apply for CrowdStrom card
	Suspend CrowdStrom card
	Register charging point
	Remove charging point
	Change opening hours
	Deactivate user account

5 Lessons Learned

After eliciting and analyzing as-is processes from organizations that are working in the EV-charging field for best practices and their applicability to CrowdStrom, we derived to-be processes tailored to CrowdStrom's requirements. Most of these to-be processes have already been implemented in a software prototype[3] that is currently used to gain insights into how well the processes perform in a real-world environment. In line with the *process monitoring and controlling* phase, the experience and feedback is being used to resolve issues and to adjust and improve the processes and the corresponding software.

Looking back at the approach chosen and the results achieved, we made several observations and derived corresponding lessons learned.

A joint research project with consortium members from industry and academia benefits all stakeholders but also poses challenges. Divergent interests and cultures must be combined and aligned in order to reach a common goal. In our case, analyzing and adapting the as-is processes to derive the to-be processes for CrowdStrom was the connecting and unifying element. Although the participants' understanding of and approaches to business process management differed initially because of their different backgrounds, discussing and deciding on final to-be

[3]A link to the prototype web portal can be found at the project's website, www.crowdstrom.de. The prototype is still under development and is subject to frequent changes. The online version is for testing and demonstration purposes only and is not connected to real charging stations or fed with real customer data. The project's website and the prototype web portal are available only in German.

processes provided all members with a joint basis for future activities regarding the further development of the project. Furthermore, joint research activities can have a real impact. We created real innovations regarding the business model and the corresponding business processes that Stadtwerke Münster plans to put into practical application.

Another observation concerns the nature of our case. Developing a P2P sharing platform for EV charging requires combining the technical aspects of EV charging with the allocative function of the Sharing Economy that connects supply and demand in a market. EV charging can be seen in the context of concepts like *Industrie 4.0* and *Cyber-physical systems*, where the goal is to develop a *smart service*. The P2P business models of the Sharing Economy focus on administrative processes that connect users and provide them with a comfortable customer experience. Although connecting these two domains poses a plethora of challenges, most of the fundamental problems can be solved by means of existing solutions that are either directly applicable to the case (administrative processes from the Sharing Economy) or adaptable to the requirements of the case (technical processes regarding the charging of an EV).

Based on the results from the application of the BPM lifecycle, CrowdStrom will advance in the near future into a mature solution operated by Stadtwerke Münster. Once the system has proven its functionality in the Stadtwerke Münster environment, the next step is to test the inclusion of peer providers in a local market. To this end, an extensive market analysis is underway to determine the number of potential customers (both providers and users) in the local market and the potential users' willingness to pay for such a charging service.

The BPM lifecycle provided the right tools for the problems we faced in our project—the absence of standards and reference models for the domain of EV charging—by providing a framework with which to elicit process models from organizations active in the field and to analyze, redesign, and implement them in a software prototype that is on the brink of live operation.

Acknowledgements This article was written in the context of the research project CrowdStrom. The project is funded by the German Federal Ministry of Education and Research (BMBF), promotion sign 01FE13019E. We thank the project management agency German Aerospace Center (PT-DLR).

References

BDEW Bundesverband der Energie- und Wasserwirtschaft e.V. (2016). *BDEW-Erhebung Elektromobilität*. https://www.bdew.de/internet.nsf/id/bdew-erhebung-elektromobilitaet-de

Bundesministerium für Bildung und Forschung. (2010). *Ideen. Innovation. Wachstum – Hightech-Strategie 2020 Für Deutschland*. Bonn.

Chasin, F., Matzner, M., Löchte, M., Wiget, V., & Becker, J. (2015). The law: The boon and bane of IT-enabled peer-to-peer sharing and collaborative consumption services peer-to-peer services. In *Proceedings of the 12th International Conference on Wirtschaftsinformatik (WI 2015)*. Osnabrück, Germany.

Dumas, M., La Rosa, M., Mendling, J., & Reijers, H. A. (2013). *Fundamentals of business process management*. Berlin: Springer.
Kraftfahrtbundesamt. (2016). *Bestand an Pkw in Den Jahren 2006 Bis 2015 Nach Ausgewählten Kraftstoffarten*. http://www.kba.de/DE/Statistik/Fahrzeuge/Bestand/Umwelt/b_umwelt_z.html?nn=663524
Matzner, M., Von Hoffen, M., Heide, T., Plenter, F., & Chasin, F. (2015). A method for measuring user preferences in information systems design choices. In *Proceedings of the European Conference on Information Systems (ECIS 2015)*. Münster, Germany.
Nationale Plattform Elektromobilität. (2014). *Fortschrittsbericht 2014 – Bilanz Der Marktvorbereitung*. Berlin.
Nationale Plattform Elektromobilität. (2015). *Ladeinfrastruktur Für Elektrofahrzeuge in Deutschland: Statusbericht Und Handlungsempfehlungen 2015* (p. 36).
Steinhilber, S., Wells, P., & Thankappan, S. (2013). Socio-technical inertia: Understanding the barriers to electric vehicles. *Energy Policy, 60*(0), 531–539.

Martin Matzner is Professor of Information Systems and the Chair of Digital Industrial Service Systems at Friedrich-Alexander-Universität Erlangen-Nürnberg (FAU Erlangen-Nuremberg), Germany. In 2012, he received a Ph.D. degree in Information Systems from the University of Münster for his work on the management of networked service business processes. His research areas include business process management, business process analytics, as well as service engineering and service management. In these areas, he concluded and currently manages a number of research projects funded by the European Union, by the German Federal Government and by industry. He has published more than 70 research papers and articles, among others in MIS Quarterly and IEEE Transactions on Engineering Management. He is editor of the Journal of Service Management Research.

Florian Plenter is a researcher and Ph.D. candidate at the European Research Center for Information Systems (ERCIS), University of Münster, Germany. He received a Master's degree in economics from the University of Münster. Florians' current research interests lie in the domain of the Sharing Economy and electric mobility. Amongst others, he is part of the CrowdStrom project (www.crowdstrom.de), which develops a peer-to-peer service for sharing electric vehicle charging stations. The project has recently won the Best Prototype Award at the 13th International Conference on Wirtschaftsinformatik (WI 2017).

Jan Betzing is a researcher and Ph.D. candidate at the European Research Center for Information Systems (ERCIS), University of Muenster, Germany. He holds a Master's Degree in Information Systems from the University of Muenster, Germany. His research interests comprise information systems engineering and service business model innovation. He is part of the CrowdStrom project (www.crowdstrom.de), which develops a peer-to-peer service for sharing electric vehicle charging stations. The project has recently won the Best Prototype Award at the 13th International Conference on Wirtschaftsinformatik (WI 2017). Jan currently researches, how smart devices and location-based, context-adaptive mobile services support digital transformation processes of SME retailers.

Friedrich Chasin is a research assistant at the European Research Center for Information Systems (ERCIS), University of Münster, Germany and private lecturer at the South Westphalia University and the Osnabrueck University of Applied Sciences. His research interests include green information systems, sustainability and peer-to-peer sharing. For the past two years, he has been studying the phenomenon of peer-to-peer sharing by studying corresponding businesses in Brazil, Germany and South Korea. His special focus is on the design-oriented research where he has been part of the CrowdStrom project. The prize-winning project is concerned with the development of peer-to-peer sharing services for the electric vehicle domain since 2013.

Moritz von Hoffen is a researcher and Ph.D. candidate at the European Research Center for Information Systems (ERCIS), University of Münster, Germany. He received a Master's degree in computer science from the Freie Universität in Berlin, Germany. Prior moving to Münster, he worked at the Technical University Berlin and Telekom Innovation Laboratories focusing on Context-aware Services. Moritz' current research interests lie in the domain of the Sharing Economy and electric mobility. He is part of the CrowdStrom project (www.crowdstrom.de), which develops a peer-to-peer service for sharing electric vehicle charging stations. The project has recently won the Best Prototype Award at the 13th International Conference on Wirtschaftsinformatik (WI 2017).

Matthias Löchte is IT Project Manager at the Stadtwerke Münster GmbH, Germany. He managed the Stadtwerke Münster part in the Joint Research Project CrowdStrom with partners from all over Germany. His main interests are Information Systems, employed to promote the Energy Transition, and the future design of the Energy Sector. His Thesis focused on the optimization of Combined Heat and Power Systems to adapt energy supply to demand in the heat and electricity sector (Power-To-Heat). The project CrowdStrom offered challenging opportunities to gain profound knowledge on the design and implementation of charging processes to support the usage of Electric Mobility. During the conceptual phase of the project, the Stadtwerke Münster employed their practical process knowledge for a scientific Business Process Model Survey. This knowledge was applied to design and implement a CrowdStrom prototype. The findings of the project team have contributed to several publications.

Sarah Pütz is a project-manager in the area of e-mobility at TÜV SÜD AG. She has a university law degree from Ludwig Maximilian University Munich and a degree in economics (majoring in Tourism (mobility and taxation) from University of Applied Science Munich. At TÜV SÜD AG she is responsible for European and national supported projects in the area of e-Mobility. Furthermore she represents the TÜV SÜD e-Mobility department at different national and international organizations and fairs.

Jorg Becker is head of the Department of Information Systems of the University of Münster and of the European Research Center for Information Systems (ERCIS). He is Professor of Information Systems and directs the Chair for Information Systems and Information Management. He holds an honorary professorship at the National Research University—Higher School of Economics (NRU-HSE) in Moscow and is member of the North Rhine-Westphalian Academy of Sciences, Humanities and the Arts. His research interests cover Information Modelling including Reference Modelling, Hybrid Value Creation, Business Process Management, E-Government, and Retail Information Systems. Jörg has published in renowned outlets, including *MIS Quarterly (MISQ)*, *European Journal of Information Systems (EJIS)*, *Business & Information Systems Engineering (BISE)*, *Information Systems Frontiers (ISF)*, *Information Systems Journal (ISJ)*, and *Business Process Management Journal (BPMJ)*. He has authored and edited numerous books, including *Retail Information Systems*, *Process Management*, *Modernizing Processes in Public Administrations*, and *Reference Modeling*.

Enabling Flexible Laboratory Processes: Designing the Laboratory Information System of the Future

Christoph Duelli, Robert Keller, Jonas Manderscheid, Andreas Manntz, Maximilian Röglinger, and Marco Schmidt

Abstract

(a) **Situation faced**: Recent developments in the medical and industrial laboratory market have increased the need for highly flexible laboratory processes. This pressure results from new requirements that have accompanied the internationalization of laboratories and the digitalization of paper-based, bureaucratic work practices. The execution of laboratory processes is supported by laboratory information systems (LISs), which handle the control and information flow of incoming orders end-to-end. State-of-the-art LISs do not feature sufficient flexibility-to-use and flexibility-to-change capabilities. To prepare medical and industrial laboratories for the challenges ahead, LISs require more advanced flexibility capabilities that meet the need for flexibility in complex laboratory processes.

(b) **Action taken**: To address the challenges of medical and industrial laboratories, MELOS, a leading German LIS provider, and the Project Group BISE of the Fraunhofer FIT conducted the *LIS4FUTURE* project. The project team compiled requirements on the flexibility of laboratory

C. Duelli • A. Manntz
MELOS GmbH, Franz-Beer-Str. 6, 86459 Gessertshausen, Germany
e-mail: duelli@melosgmbh.de; andreas.manntz@melosgmbh.de

R. Keller • M. Röglinger (✉)
Fraunhofer FIT, University of Bayreuth, Wittelsbacherring 10, 95444 Bayreuth, Germany
e-mail: robert.keller@fit.fraunhofer.de; maximilian.roeglinger@fit.fraunhofer.de

J. Manderscheid
FIM Research Center, University of Augsburg, Universitätsstr. 12, 86150 Augsburg, Germany
e-mail: jonas.manderscheid@fim-rc.de

M. Schmidt
Fraunhofer FIT, University of Augsburg, Universitätsstr. 12, 86150 Augsburg, Germany
e-mail: marco.schmidt@fit.fraunhofer.de

J. vom Brocke, J. Mendling (eds.), *Business Process Management Cases*, Management for Professionals, DOI 10.1007/978-3-319-58307-5_19

processes and derived corresponding requirements for the LIS's flexibility-to-use and flexibility-to-change. The lack of configuration capabilities and modularity across all layers of the software architecture was identified as a major inhibitor of flexible laboratory processes. Following an agile development process and grounded on extant knowledge, the project team developed the *LIS4FUTURE* demonstrator, a process-aware LIS with a modular architecture and a rule-based configuration mechanism.

(c) **Results achieved**: Based on identified requirements, the project team iteratively developed and evaluated the modular architecture and the rule-based configuration mechanism as part of the development of the *LIS4FUTURE* demonstrator. The modular architecture allows for the complete replacement of process steps at build time, while the rule-based configuration mechanism makes it possible to meet the ever-increasing demands for flexibility at runtime. The *LIS4FUTURE* demonstrator, which shows the applicability of the developed concepts in real-world scenarios, will help MELOS develop an innovative release of their LIS.

(d) **Lessons learned**: During the *LIS4FUTURE* project, the project team learned that: (1) advanced flexibility-to-use and flexibility-to-change IS capabilities are needed to prepare for flexibility demands on the process level; (2) radical redesign of existing processes and systems should be preferred over incremental improvement in order to tap the disruptive potential of innovation opportunities; (3) the LIS architecture must be aligned with the process paradigm if it is to be flexible; (4) discussions among academics and practitioners are more effective if they are based on running prototypes rather than on theoretical concepts; and (5) project results improve if project team members work a substantial fraction of their time at the same location.

1 Introduction

Flexibility has become an increasingly desirable corporate capability, particularly in the services industry, which is the largest and most rapidly growing business sector in many industrial nations (Fitzsimmons and Fitzsimmons 2013). In search of an optimal level of flexibility, insurance companies, for instance, must continually balance the benefits of automated and standardized and manual and flexible claims-handling processes.

In medical and industrial laboratories, daily operations may use a few highly individual samples or tens of thousands of standardized samples. A typical laboratory process starts with an order entry, such as one that uses a blood sample. The order requests that an examination, such as a hemogram, be performed on the sample. The examination results in a diagnostic interpretation, which must be validated by a physician before being sent back to the requesting physician. Finally, the process ends with accounting of and billing for the order. Despite this simple sequence, laboratory processes have considerable need for flexibility because of their content- and market-related complexity. From a content perspective, there are many process variations and exceptions (e.g., interdependencies of an examination or test within a single process instance or across multiple instances), as well as country-specific regulations that change regularly. From the market perspective, a high level of cost pressure leads to the laboratory market's increasing consolidation and globalization. Therefore, medical and industrial laboratories tend to expand their service offerings in order to realize economies of scale via, for example, mergers and acquisition. Laboratories also explore new market segments, offer new services (e.g., for human, veterinary, environmental, hygiene, or microbiological purposes), or follow the trend toward digitization (e.g., eHealth or mHealth) in providing advanced graphic diagnostics or keeping electronic health records. In short, the future of medical and industrial laboratories will be *connected, diverse, complex, and fast*, so laboratory processes need a highly flexible process-enactment infrastructure (van der Aalst 2013), commonly referred to as a laboratory information system (LIS).

In automating processes with a significant need for flexibility, a firm must consider business process flexibility and information systems (IS) flexibility jointly. Business process flexibility refers to volume and functional flexibility (Afflerbach et al. 2014), where volume flexibility, a partial abstract of installed capacity, helps a firm cope with risky demand, and functional flexibility helps the firm execute process variants and create even unplanned process output to satisfy customers' needs. While volume flexibility has been researched primarily from a capability and revenue-management perspective, functional flexibility has a rich tradition in business process management (BPM) (Schonenberg et al. 2008). One way to achieve functional process flexibility is to use flexible process-aware IS (Reichert and Weber 2012). IS flexibility can be split into flexibility-to-use and flexibility-to-change (Gebauer and Schober 2006), where flexibility-to-use refers to process requirements that can be supported without requiring major changes in the IS that underpins the process, and flexibility-to-change refers to the ability to extend IS to remain aligned with changing process requirements.

Against this background, LIS must evolve into flexible process-aware IS. In particular, there is a pressing need for an integrated and innovative approach that allows for the configuration and modularization of all software architecture layers, including data management, application logic, control flow management, and user interaction at both runtime (flexibility-to-use) and build time (flexibility-to-change). Because of extensive user-specific configurations and regulations, a LIS also requires capabilities related to efficient development and maintenance (flexibility-to-change).

To contribute to enhancing existing LISs so they are more flexible process-aware IS, collaboration in the research project Laboratory Information Systems for the Future (*LIS4FUTURE*) between September 2014 and October 2016 was undertaken by the Fraunhofer Institute for Applied Information Technology (FIT), a research institute that is experienced in the development of custom-tailored applications; its project group, Business and Information Systems Engineering (BISE), which specializes in BPM; and MELOS, a technological leader in the field of medical and industrial laboratory software solutions. Using the MELOS LIS as an example, the partners designed the *LIS4FUTURE*, a process-aware LIS with a modular architecture and a rule-based configuration mechanism that facilitates laboratory processes' functional flexibility. The *LIS4FUTURE* demonstrator exemplarily implements the design and architecture with respect to the accounting step of the laboratory process in order to verify the theoretical concepts' applicability and usefulness. The *LIS4FUTURE* project was funded by the Bavarian Ministry of Economic Affairs and Media, Energy and Technology's R&D program *Information and Communication Technology Bavaria*. The *LIS4FUTURE* project relates to the "process implementation and execution" capability area of the IT factor discussed in Rosemann and vom Brocke's (2015) six core elements of BPM.

2 Situation Faced

Before sketching the situation that leads to highly increased flexibility requirements for laboratory processes and LIS, we look at medical and industrial laboratories in terms of the laboratory process and the current market situation. We also provide information about the MELOS LIS that served as one of many reference points and as an example throughout the *LIS4FUTURE* project.

The laboratory process consists of all steps from order entry to accounting of the laboratory service (Fig. 1). After an order is made, the samples to be analyzed and the specification of the required examinations arrive at the laboratory. An order could request a hemogram involving a blood sample or an investigation for cancer in a tissue sample. Based on this information and enriched with customer-specific master data, the laboratory analyzes and tests the samples and summarizes all test results in a single report per order. A laboratory physician then validates the results, checks the report for plausibility, and adds further diagnostic information if needed before the laboratory transfers the validated results back to the customer. Finally, the laboratory charges for the services provided in line with current price lists and regulations.

Many content- and market-related factors affect the nature of the laboratory process. The BPM context framework from vom Brocke et al. (2016) offers guidance in characterizing relevant contextual factors, particularly the factors of repetitiveness, knowledge-intensity, interdependence, and variability.

Laboratories receive an average of about 20,000 samples per day, with three to four required examinations per sample. Because of the high number of orders and the standard examinations that are available, the laboratory process is generally characterized by *repetitiveness*. The processing of samples is highly standardized

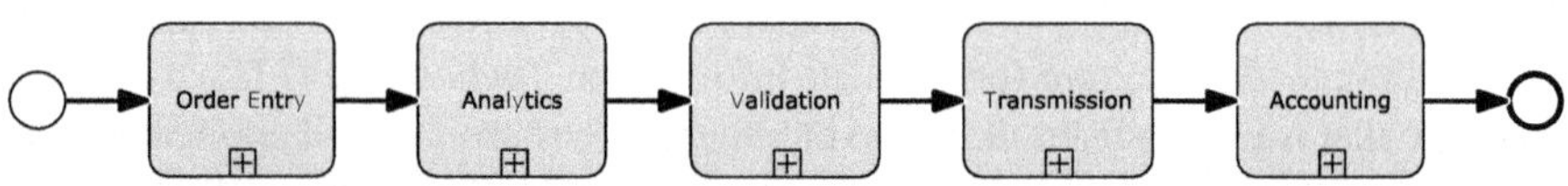

Fig. 1 Overview of the laboratory process

and automated. (E.g., laboratory devices analyze most samples automatically, sometimes leading to follow-up examinations based on pre-defined business rules.) The accounting of laboratory services also follows complex but strict guidelines, so there is little need for manual interaction and creativity. Pattern-detection mechanisms support or replace physicians' work in validating diagnoses. For common cases, physicians formulate rules that automate the process of checking plausibility, enabling them to spend more time on complex cases. Nevertheless, the diagnosis and device setup require domain-specific knowledge, so parts of the laboratory process are characterized by *knowledge-intensity*. As each order focuses on distinct samples, customers, and examinations, there is almost no *interdependence* on the process level. Cross-references need to be considered only for accounting purposes, when examinations are summarized on a quarterly basis and cumulative regulatory provisions apply.

Regarding *variability*, the laboratory process is a routine or runner/repeater process (Lillrank 2003; Johnston et al. 2012). The comparatively simple laboratory process includes an arbitrary but fixed number of variants and defined outputs. Variants of the laboratory process must be specified at design time so samples can be analyzed and orders can be billed. When orders are paper-based, the laboratory process includes an OCR scan, but whether a report is paper-based or not, urgent examination results can be reported immediately via fax or phone. In addition to industry-scale laboratories, specialized laboratories handle a small number of orders and place considerable effort into each order. Such laboratories run the risk that changes in routine or runner/repeater process instances become semi-structured or unstructured problems, referred to as non-routine or stranger instances (Johnston et al. 2012; Lillrank 2003). The processing of such instances requires functional process flexibility, as the following example ("the Example" hereafter) shows:

> A Spanish tourist in France is infected with Salmonella. She appears in person at the medical laboratory for blood sampling, as is usual in Southern Europe. Based on a cooperative arrangement with other laboratories, the French laboratory transfers the sample to a German laboratory close to the border for analytical and diagnostic purposes. However, since the sample was taken in France and it involves a Spanish tourist, both French and Spanish regulations and legal requirements apply. As a consequence, French regulations require that the German laboratory store detailed information on the blood sample (e.g., the place where the sample was taken and the distance from there to the laboratory), and Spanish regulations require that the German laboratory store the patient's health insurance data. In addition, the invoice is split among the patient, her employer, and her health insurances in Spain and France. In Germany, the accounting distinguishes only between private and legal insurance. If the patient were from Austria, the laboratory would also have been required to check the information stored on the patient's electronic healthcare card online.

The current situation in the medical and industrial laboratory market has pushed LIS providers to redesign their systems substantially in order to enable flexibility. For examples, with blurring national boundaries, as illustrated in the Example, medical and industrial laboratories must consider increasing numbers of country-specific regulations that increase complexity and their processes' need for flexibility. In addition, national authorities like *Kassenärztliche Bundesvereinigung* (National Association of Statutory Health Insurance Physicians) in Germany and the *Centre National de Dépôts et d'Agrément de l'Assurance Maladie* in France update price lists and thresholds for medical values at least once per quarter. This complication becomes even more complex with laboratory mergers that occur because of the competitive environment and cost pressures, as when a laboratory's subsidiaries are located in multiple countries, the LIS must comply with all national regulations. Further, the configuration mechanisms implemented in state-of-the-art LISs are geared primarily toward trained experts with strong backgrounds in computer science, but future demands will come from people with non-technical backgrounds (e.g., physicians) who are expected to use a laboratory's LIS. Therefore, among many other topics, future LISs will have to focus much more on convenient user interfaces and a transparent representation of configuration capabilities that non-technical people can understand. Despite the high number of variants in the laboratory process, most of these variants are substantially constant and require only one-time configuration. One notable exception is the price calculation in the accounting step of the laboratory process, which is subject to frequent changes. Future LISs must be able to implement changes in the laboratory process and changes that affect the accounting logic without touching the system's implementation, such as the system's database and software architecture. This capability can be achieved by leveraging metadata management, a modular architecture, and rule-based configuration mechanisms. These examples provide an impression of the overall need for improvement that LISs must implement in order to meet laboratory processes' need for flexibility.

From a technical perspective, LISs offer support for the control and information flow of laboratory orders end-to-end, so they must be aligned with the steps of the laboratory process. To cope with the high and varying number of orders per day, the order-processing must be highly industrialized, with a high level of automation and interfaces that enable automated communication with external IS and technical devices like CRM systems, medical devices, and specialist software. In response to laboratory processes' increasing flexibility demands, LISs must ingrain highly integrated flexibility-to-use and flexibility-to-change capabilities in all layers of the software architecture and in all software modules (Gebauer and Schober 2006) to enable functional flexibility of laboratory processes in both the short term and the long term. The foundations of flexibility-to-use and flexibility-to-change are rule-based configuration mechanisms, modular software architectures, and efficient development and maintenance concepts. A module is a self-contained unit that includes data, business, and processing rules and, in some cases, a user interface. Each module should be as independent from other modules as possible so it is configurable by a specific configuration mechanism that is based on rules stored as master data of the LIS. Laboratories should be able to customize these rules without having to recompile the LIS.

Although MELOS, with its current generation of LIS, is among the leading LIS providers in Germany, it has to prepare its LIS for a *connected, diverse, complex, and fast* business environment and the related flexibility demands. The MELOS LIS features powerful mechanisms for configuring and individualizing the IT support for complex laboratory processes. Its software architecture enables profound changes to the information and control flow and provides configurable interfaces for both users and technical equipment. However, these flexibility capabilities do not go far enough to meet the future flexibility demands on LISs.

Currently available LISs are too inflexible to cover laboratory processes' future demands for flexibility, so MELOS and the project group BISE of Fraunhofer FIT initiated their collaboration in the *LIS4FUTURE* project to develop a process-aware LIS with a modular software architecture and a rule-based configuration mechanism.

3 Action Taken

To enable functional flexibility of laboratory processes, the *LIS4FUTURE* project team designed and implemented a process-aware LIS into which are integrated a modular architecture and a rule-based configuration mechanism. The project team iteratively developed the *LIS4FUTURE* demonstrator following an agile software-development process in order to respond quickly to changes from newly identified requirements (Beck et al. 2001). The team used the *LIS4FUTURE* demonstrator to validate the developed concepts' applicability in real-world scenarios. The *LIS4FUTURE* project was comprised of four major phases: (1) requirements engineering, (2) design of the process-aware LIS with a modular architecture and a rule-based configuration mechanism, (3) implementation, and (4) validation of these concepts by evaluating the *LIS4FUTURE* demonstrator (Fig. 2). These phases were conducted iteratively and in an interleaving manner following the agile software development principles.

3.1 Phase 1: Engineering Requirements

In this phase of the project, the project team raised and structured requirements for the design of a process-aware LIS by analyzing the laboratory market, the state of the art in the related BPM and computer science literatures, and the architecture and components of the MELOS LIS. To take a comprehensive perspective, the project

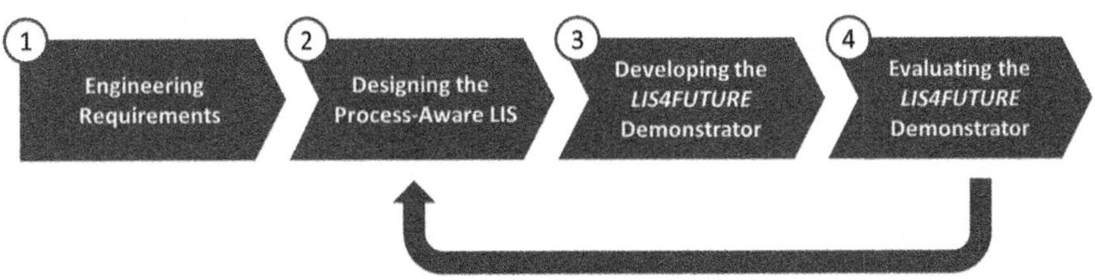

Fig. 2 Plan of the LIS4FUTURE project

team used a multi-method approach to gathering requirements: The team first conducted interviews with industry experts and examined the extant LIS-related scientific literature to collect external demands and ideas for solutions regarding flexibility-to-use and flexibility-to-change. The literature review included work on software architectures, modular data models, software configuration and customizing, rule processing, and declarative business process modelling. Then the team drew from the expertise of the MELOS software developers inside and outside of the project team in order to acquaint themselves with relevant design decisions and to identify the strengths and weaknesses of the MELOS LIS. A detailed analysis of LIS-related use cases identified during a series of workshops led to a broad coverage of possible process variants and process-related requirements. Next, the project team technically analyzed the inputs and outputs of the MELOS LIS, which yielded structural information about the system's functionality without the team's having to review the code itself, an endeavor that would have been much more complicated because of the dominant monolithic software architecture and code structure.

The insights gathered during these steps were aggregated to compile the relevant requirements regarding the modular software architecture and the rule-based configuration mechanism. Some external requirements emerged from the laboratory market and the laboratory process (discussed in Sect. 2), and some requirements emerged from system-internal—that is, functional and technological—boundary conditions of the current MELOS LIS, which already incorporated basic configuration capabilities. These requirements resulted from lessons learned during past efforts or from the technological continuity undertaken to reduce maintenance costs. Examples are the LIS-wide applicability of a single configuration mechanism and the protection of live data from user-defined configuration settings.

3.2 Phase 2: Designing the Process-Aware LIS

Given the requirements identified in the project's first phase, the *LIS4FUTURE* team designed a process-aware LIS that enables advanced flexibility-to-use and flexibility-to-change. The *LIS4FUTURE* team consolidated scientific literature and collected insights on their practical implementations in order to review existing approaches to flexibility-to-use and flexibility-to-change. We found the state of the art of process flexibility from the BPM domain and that related to software configuration in general to provide no ready-made solution that could be directly adapted to the case at hand. However, this review yielded promising approaches, such as the idea of modular software architectures (Sulivan et al. 2001) to enable flexibility-to-change and the use of domain-specific languages (Mernik et al. 2005) for implementing flexibility-to-use in terms of rule-based configuration.

Before flexibility-to-use can be considered, flexibility-to-change must build a solid core, enabling developers to adjust the laboratory of the future quickly to emerging requirements. The modular software architecture must implement flexibility-to-change capabilities, enabling developers to adjust the process sequence by easily reconfiguring existing interfaces and module interdependencies. With their own experiences in mind and influenced by the scientific approaches, the developers designed and refined a fundamental modular software architecture on which the future LIS can be based. A thorough analysis of the MELOS LIS's existing processes pointed to modules required in the *LIS4FUTURE* architecture. However, the concept of modular software architectures fundamentally differs from the MELOS LIS's monolithic structure, which is not process-aware. In general, modular software architectures are well established in computer science and are based on largely independent modules that operate on a determined set of input parameters and compile a predefined output. When modules call one another, a hierarchical or network-like structure emerges. By standardizing the communication among modules using contracts that define the information flow and reduce dependencies among modules, the project team boosted the modules' interchangeability.

This solid core paved the way for the integration of flexibility-to-use—that is, the independent configuration of single modules at runtime. Although this approach is not completely new to LISs, the targeted extent of configurability was unprecedented. Current configuration capabilities included various rule-based languages that are limited to single LIS modules. Each of these languages have a unique syntax and encompass over 1000 different operators that perform highly specific tasks within the respective domain. Because of limited rule-based configurability, the LIS also differentiates many special cases within the code base, a circumstance that hampers easy maintenance and code transparency. Discussions in the project team and with industry experts emphasized the need for a configuration mechanism that allows emerging flexibility demands to be implemented across module boundaries at runtime, facilitating the future daily use and the further development of the LIS.

The designed configuration mechanism builds on only two components: rules and plug-ins. Rules enable users to change and influence the fine-grained process flow of the laboratory process, while plug-ins can be provided only by developers, enabling the implementation of complex requirements that cannot be addressed by user-written rules. Rule-based configuration focuses on the demands of users who are working with the LIS on a daily basis and need to be able to adapt the LIS easily to their needs. A typical LIS contains more than 2000 rules, of which about 600 rules describe exceptions in the pricing process in the accounting module, such as: "A specific examination can be accounted only twice per quarter of the year for each patient," "The sum of the prices of several examinations is limited to a maximum threshold of, e.g., 20€ per patient and order," and "The accounting of an examination prohibits the accounting of another examination in the same order and for the same patient."

For some examinations, several rules may apply simultaneously, leading to dependencies among rules that can result in unforeseeable behavior. Therefore, the project team refined the configuration mechanism to support the writing of rules with verification capabilities that ensure correct rule-processing. Besides validating syntax and semantics, the verification detects and warns about possible conflicts and rule interdependencies by statically evaluating rules without the need to access real data. Consequently, this mechanism enables users to monitor flexibility-to-use in the *LIS4FUTURE* demonstrator and facilitates the identification of undesirable behavior in the module in advance.

The *LIS4FUTURE* project team operationalized the rule-based configuration by providing a central rule parsing and processing module that evaluates each rule syntactically and semantically before initiating it. To enable the ex-ante verification of rules, the syntax is based on imperative programming languages like JavaScript to capture the modification algorithmically instead of using individual operators for each task. We designed the functional modules to allow module-specific rule-execution routines to be integrated seamlessly, operating on a domain-specific data model that limits the rules' access to a distinct subset of readable and writable data and prevents the mechanism from altering live data.

Configuration demands that go beyond the rule mechanism's capabilities can be supplied to users as plug-ins written by developers upon request. These plug-ins can attach automatically to mounting points within or between modules. Since mounting plug-ins has been a concept in software development for years, we refrain from providing details here.

In sum, the developed concepts implemented in the *LIS4FUTURE* demonstrator enable flexibility-to-change through a modular software architecture so LIS developers can change the laboratory process if needed. In addition, flexibility-to-change is extended by the ability to write and mount plug-ins that can enhance the LIS's functionality based on customer requests. Flexibility-to-use is integrated by means of a verifiable, rule-based configuration mechanism, providing users with a straightforward rule language to adapt future LIS.

3.3 Phase 3 and 4: Developing and Evaluating the Demonstrator

The project team implemented and refined the *LIS4FUTURE* demonstrator in the course of an agile software development process. The *LIS4FUTURE* demonstrator focuses on implementing the essentials of the modular software architecture and those of the rule-based configuration mechanism while enabling the developed concepts' applicability to be validated based on real data. On the process level, the *LIS4FUTURE* demonstrator focused on the accounting step and on the accounting module's interplay with other modules. This focus was reasonable, as the accounting module is the most complex part of the LIS and it is subject to the most burdensome customer requests and flexibility demands. In fact, all identified requirements on flexibility-to-use and flexibility-to-change could be checked using the accounting module as example. However, the monolithic architecture and manifold interdependencies among existing modules aggravated the refactoring of the existing accounting module and the integration of the new concepts, so the *LIS4FUTURE* demonstrator was implemented from scratch, which allowed us to incorporate modern software engineering concepts, such as modules with clearly defined interfaces, dependency injection, and unit tests.

Once we familiarized the MELOS developers with these modern software engineering concepts, the development started in a Scrum-like agile development procedure that involved defining features that could be implemented during the next sprint, which we set to 2-week cycles. The wording of features' definitions, which are referred to as "user stories" in Scrum, emphasized the user-oriented benefit that comes with their attainment. The results of each sprint were reviewed at the end of each sprint, and adjustments to the backlog (i.e., the user stories to be processed) were discussed when planning the next sprint. This method facilitated the stepwise integration of the accounting module's functionality and the configuration mechanism's and modular software architecture's validation based on the use cases collected in the project's first phase.

The team frequently discussed the project's overall progress and the *LIS4FUTURE* demonstrator with project-external stakeholders like MELOS employees who were not involved in the project, laboratories that employed the MELOS LIS, and independent industry experts. Feedback from these stakeholders helped to improve the modular software architecture and the rule-based configuration mechanism in iterative cycles. Exemplary feedback was that LISs available on the market lack the ability to track the price calculations back to specific rules. This feature was not part of the initial backlog, but it was included after the preliminary *LIS4FUTURE* demonstrator was presented to external stakeholders for feedback. Thus, the project team extended the demonstrator with a price-tracing module that makes the price-calculation logic transparent to users. Although the price-tracer is currently limited to the accounting module, traceability and advanced logging of process executions can be applied easily to other parts of the process-aware LIS.

Figure 3 illustrates relevant parts of the modular software architecture's implementation of the accounting module in the *LIS4FUTURE* demonstrator, although the figure simplifies the architecture for communication purposes and abstracts from interfaces to other modules beyond the accounting domain, as well as from multiple rule-execution routines that are linked to one component. The core module is the *Quarterly Accounting* module, which calls the *Order Price Computation* module to account the order stack and initiates the price computation of single examinations (*Examination Price Computation*). Each of these steps provides additional *Rule Execution* modules, enabling the configuration of underlying processes. Each step also allows for the mounting of plug-ins, such as plug-ins to implement distance-dependent shipping costs. Finally, the customer is billed using the *Invoice Export* module. The architecture also includes the *Price Calculation Tracer* mentioned above.

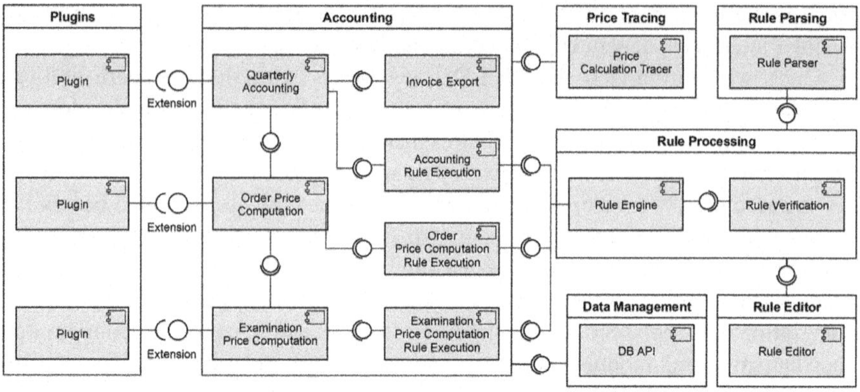

Fig. 3 Architecture of the LIS4FUTURE demonstrator's accounting module

4 Results Achieved

The actions taken in the *LIS4FUTURE* project resulted in the design of a process-aware LIS, prototypically realized in terms of the *LIS4FUTURE* demonstrator. As a preparatory task, we reviewed the need for flexibility in complex laboratory processes and extracted requirements for technological support by a process-aware LIS, considering content-related and market-related context factors. Then we focused on two major deliverables: (1) a modular and process-aware software architecture with largely independent modules and (2) a rule-based configuration mechanism that enables laboratory employees to customize by changing the LIS without recompilation and redeployment. The *LIS4FUTURE* demonstrator verified the developed concepts and confirmed their practical applicability.

4.1 Modular Architecture

To incorporate flexibility-to-change capabilities in future LIS, we designed a modular software architecture that facilitates the LIS provider's ability to add new functionality easily via modules. On the architectural level, modules can be added or replaced with significantly reduced effort. Although new modules still require the LIS to be partially recompiled, existing modules can be activated or deactivated during build time. The use of dependency injection as a software design pattern also helps to resolve dependencies between modules. As a result, the communication between two modules is managed by a third component (the *injector*). Modules need only a well-defined interface and a service level agreement that specify the communication and interaction standards, and other modules can use this interface to communicate with one another. In doing so, a nearly infinite combination of modules is possible to define new paths in the laboratory process.

For instance, referring to the Example, a French accounting module could easily replace or enhance German accounting functionalities.

We also modularized the LIS's support modules. In order to abstract data management from the real data source and to allow the data bases to be interchangeable, we added an intermediate data layer that provides defined interfaces for communication with databases and that can be adapted easily to new data sources. We also logically separated the module's configuration mechanism from the syntactical parsing and domain-specific processing of rules, which is enabled via a LIS-wide rule engine (Fig. 3). This measure also contributes to efficient further development and maintenance.

As a positive side effect, the modular software architecture is not restricted to the laboratory process but can be extended easily to other supportive LIS functionalities. For instance, we developed a rule-editor module to facilitate users' ability to configure the LIS directly in laboratories. In fact, this editor is an autonomous application, but it uses shared functionality in publishing syntactical keywords, which reduces future maintenance efforts.

4.2 Configuration Mechanism

We designed a rule-based configuration mechanism to support ongoing process adaption and LIS adaptation through flexibility-to-use capabilities. The configuration mechanism covers most of the laboratory process's flexibility requirements in terms of routing and calculation decisions, based inter alia on examination results and price lists. Consisting of rules and plug-ins, the configuration mechanism provides software developers and LIS users alike with a high level of customizability.

Rules enable LIS users to modify the process definition at runtime. Based on this foundation, all or selected currently running process instances can be migrated to a new process definition that is, for instance, requested by an external stakeholder. (E.g., physicians can ask for discounts or divergent processing in case of certain diagnostic findings.) Rules are clustered in collections based on the specific type of rule and can be enriched by metadata. In contrast to the existing rule languages, the new mechanism benefits from its own database that is built exclusively for the rule execution at runtime and that consolidates configuration capabilities across module boundaries.

We developed the rule-editor module to prevent the downside of user customization (e.g., higher risk of error). This module supports users using syntactical and semantical rule checks. As the probability that rules will interact increases with the number of rules in the LIS, we also integrated into the LIS a rule-checker that reduces the risk of unpredictable and unintended behavior that is due to disregarded sequence dependencies. This component enables the configuration of rules to be verified and controlled and ensures their compatibility. Overall, the measures taken significantly strengthen data security and increase the transparency of both process design and execution. The rule mechanism that is extended by the editing support reduces complexity and facilitates the refactoring of existing rule bases.

The configuration mechanism also includes plug-ins to add functionality that simple rules cannot cover. The plug-in concept replaces programs that have unpredictable effects when data is manipulated and that address highly complex, very specific, or seldom-used functionality that exceeds the LIS's core functionality (e.g., route optimization for sample collection by a laboratory's customers). The technical integration of plug-ins into the LIS is also based on well-defined interfaces and specific mounting points. Nevertheless, as plug-ins are not part of the LIS's core functionality, they add functionality without the need to recompile the entire LIS. Therefore, they are located at the intersection of flexibility-to-use and flexibility-to-change.

4.3 Summary

The modular software architecture and the rule-based configuration mechanism enable the future LIS generation to be highly customizable. Their practical application was confirmed by the *LIS4FUTURE* demonstrator. Whereas the modular architecture focuses on flexibility-to-change by allowing for the insertion or the replacement of modules, the configuration mechanism provides flexibility-to-use by enabling rules to be adapted and plug-ins to be added. Together, these two concepts help to address future requirements regarding the functional flexibility of laboratory processes by reducing the customization effort in daily business operations and facilitating procedural and technological innovation. Accordingly, LIS providers and laboratories can react to content-related and market-related context factors with a manageable level of effort.

5 Lessons Learned

To meet the upcoming flexibility requirements of laboratory processes, the project team developed and implemented the *LIS4FUTURE* demonstrator, a process-aware LIS with a modular architecture and a rule-based configuration mechanism. In so doing, the project team had first-hand experiences that can be classified into process-specific, architectural, and organizational lessons learned. We share the most important of these lessons from our perspective.

5.1 Lessons Learned from the Process Perspective

Lesson 1: Rely on both flexibility-to-use and flexibility-to-change IS capabilities to prepare for future flexibility requirements on the process level.

As illustrated in our laboratory market example in Sect. 2 (the Example), new requirements for process flexibility based on such conditions as new regulations, environmental changes, and other unforeseeable factors can pop up anytime and anywhere. In most cases, new requirements refer to process steps that are part of the extant configuration, but this assumption does not hold true in all cases, as the Example illustrates by highlighting the importance of multi-country support. Demanding requirements can even require inserting additional process steps or eliminating existing ones, a circumstance that usually requires significant changes in the underpinning information technology (IT) systems. We propose to implement flexibility-to-use and flexibility-to-change IS capabilities in order to enable the user to react easily to future changes and to consider flexibility at the time a process-aware LIS is designed.

Lesson 2: Incremental improvement is not always sufficient to achieve a target.

A well-known principle is that employees should question current work practices and refrain from excuses like "that's what we have always done." People are often hesitant to think in terms of radical process reengineering, getting lost instead in best practices, incremental improvements, and local optimization. The *LIS4FUTURE* project radically redesigned the software architecture and many modules of the MELOS LIS, particularly the accounting module. This radical redesign was rewarded with a significant increase in flexibility-to-use and flexibility-to-change as a result of replacing old, inefficient modules that have been grown historically and incrementally adapted to changing requirements. Radically rethinking existing modules and the architecture opened up completely new opportunities.

5.2 Lessons Learned from the Architecture Perspective

Lesson 3: The software architecture must be aligned with process thinking.

LISs that automate large parts of laboratory processes were once extremely complex. As we experienced in the *LIS4FUTURE* project, a significant part of this complexity stems from an inappropriate architecture. Following Stevenson and Pols' (2004), we dived deep into the MELOS LIS's software architecture to find a monolithic architecture that made even small adjustments highly complex. Therefore, we designed a modular and (in particular) process-aware architecture that substantially decreased the effort required in implementing changes and increased the potential of long-term-oriented flexibility-to-change, such as the replacement of entire modules (e.g., country-specific accounting mechanisms).

5.3 Lessons Learned from the Organizational Perspective

Lesson 4: Discussions among academics and practitioners are more effective if they build on running prototypes instead of theoretical concepts.

Although the MELOS management and employees supported the *LIS4FUTURE* project, experienced software developers and architects were skeptical about radically rethinking, based on the latest academic insights, previously made technological, architectural, and process-related design decisions. We explained this skepticism as being based on the recent rejection of some technologies and the well-known resistance-to-change phenomenon. Bad experiences, when changes that were due to novel requirements or developer initiatives led to enormously increased software complexity, intensified this resistance. There was also general uncertainty about whether academic insights can be useful in solving real-world problems like the design and implementation of a LIS. We learned that just talking about innovations like modularity and configurability on a conceptual level did not help to overcome the practitioners' skepticism. As a result, we switched to a discussion that was based on running code as an outcome of agile development sprints. This approach facilitated a much more constructive and effective discussion of essential ideas and targets. Moreover, theoretically promising but practicably infeasible solutions could be discarded much more quickly.

Lesson 5: If you want your team members to communicate, co-locate them.

In contrast to our initial plans, which intended team members to collaborate as a distributed team, the project team decided to work at the same location to foster informal communication among the academic and industrial team members. Since all MELOS developers worked at the same location anyway and were not familiar with distributed work environments, this measure significantly helped the project team get to know each other and to give feedback more directly and openly. The collaboration also improved in terms of the assessment of each other's strengths and weaknesses, which allowed us to anticipate realistically the outcome of work packages like sprints in our agile software development process. Based on our experience in the *LIS4FUTURE* project, we recommend that project teams share a common work location, at least during the project's setup phase.

References

Afflerbach, P., Kastner, G., Krause, F., & Röglinger, M. (2014). The business value of process flexibility – An optimization model and its application in the service sector. *Business & Information Systems Engineering, 6*(4), 203–214.

Beck, K., Beedle, M., van Bennekum, A., Cockburn, A., Cunningham, W., Fowler, M., Grenning, J., Highsmith, J., Hunt, A., Jeffries, R., Kern, J., Marick, B., Martin, R., Mellor, S., Schwaber, K., Sutherland J., & Thomas, D. (2001). *Manifesto for Agile software development.* Accessed July 23, 2016, from http://agilemanifesto.org/

Fitzsimmons, J., & Fitzsimmons, M. (2013). *Service management: Operations, strategy, information technology* (8th ed.). New York: McGraw-Hill.

Gebauer, J., & Schober, F. (2006). Information system flexibility and cost efficiency of business processes. *Journal of the Association for Information Systems, 7*(3), 122–147.

Johnston, R., Clark, G., & Shulver, M. (2012). *Service operations management.* Essex: Prentice Hall.

Lillrank, P. (2003). The quality of standard, routine and nonroutine processes. *Organization Studies, 24*(2), 215–233.

Mernik, M., Heering, J., & Sloane, A. (2005). When and how to develop domain-specific languages. *ACM Computing Surveys, 37*(4), 316–344.

Reichert, M., & Weber, B. (2012). *Enabling flexibility in process-aware information systems: Changes, methods, technologies.* Berlin: Springer.

Rosemann, M., & vom Brocke, J. (2015). The six core elements of business process management. In J. vom Bnrocke & M. Rosemann (Eds.), *Handbook on business process management. Introduction, methods and information systems* (Vol. 1, 2nd ed., pp. 105–122). Berlin: Springer.

Schonenberg, H., Mans, R., Russell, N., Mulyar, N., & van der Aalst, W. M. P. (2008). Process flexibility: A survey of contemporary approaches. In J. Dietz & A. Albani (Eds.), *Advances in enterprise engineering I* (pp. 16–30). Berlin: Springer.

Stevenson, C., & Pols, A. (2004). An agile approach to a legacy system. In J. Eckstein & H. Baumeister (Eds.), *Extreme programming and agile processes in software engineering* (pp. 123–129). Berlin: Springer.

Sulivan, K., Griswold, W., Cai, Y., & Hallen, B. (2001). The structure and value of modularity in software design. *ACM SIGSOFT Software Engineering Notes, 26*(5), 99–108.

van der Aalst, W. M. P. (2013). Business process management: A comprehensive survey. *ISRN Software Engineering*. doi:10.1155/2013/507984.

vom Brocke, J., Zelt, S., & Schmiedel, T. (2016). On the role of context in business process management. *International Journal of Information Management, 36*(3), 486–495.

Christoph Duelli is head of development and joint member of the management at MELOS GmbH in Gessertshausen, specializing in software for medical and industrial laboratories for over 25 years. He holds a diploma in computer science from the Ulm University and worked with Prof. Reif's KIV (Karlsruhe Interactive Verifier) team to develop provably correct software at the University of Augsburg. Apart from teaching duties, he published several papers on this topic and contributed to the KIV development.

Robert Keller is a Research Assistant at the University of Bayreuth. His research centers around Data Processing and Management Platforms. He publishes his work in renowned journals and at international conferences. Furthermore, he is project manager at the Project Group Business & Information Systems Engineering of the Fraunhofer FIT and leads several publicly funded research projects as well as consulting projects in the context of Data Management, Project Management and eHealth.

Jonas Manderscheid holds a doctorate in Business & Information Systems Engineering from the University of Augsburg. He formerly studied Business Informatics (B.A.) and Information Management (M.Sc.), while also serving as IT Consultant at Hamm Reno Group GmbH. From 2012 to 2016, Jonas has been a research associate at the Research Center Finance & Information Management and the Project Group Business & Information Systems Engineering of the Fraunhofer FIT, also engaged in applied research projects with companies like MLP AG and MELOS GmbH. Most of his work centers around business process management (BPM), focusing on the monitoring and improvement phases of the BPM lifecycle. He has published in journals such as Decision Support Systems, Information Systems Frontiers, and Business Process Management Journal and presented his research at relevant international conferences. Currently, Jonas serves as Project Manager for Internet of Things Product Lifecycle Management at Hilti Befestigungstechnik AG.

Andreas Manntz is Managing Director at the MELOS GmbH in Gessertshausen, one of the leading German providers for software for medical and industrial laboratories over the last 25 years. He holds a diploma in Business Administration from the University of Augsburg in connection with a trainee programme at the Siemens AG. He began his professional career at Siemens Nixdorf Informationssysteme AG as a Commercial Product Manager, responsible for product development, in 1990 and changed to Sortimo International GmbH in 1993. Seven years later he complemented his academic career with an MBA degree from the University of Augsburg and Katz Graduate Business School in Pittsburgh, before joining MELOS GmbH as Managing Director in 2003.

Maximilian Röglinger is Professor of Information Systems and Business Process Management at the University of Bayreuth. Maximilian also serves as Deputy Academic Director of the Research Center Finance & Information Management (FIM) and works with the Project Group Business & Information Systems Engineering of the Fraunhofer FIT. Maximilian's activities in research, teaching, and industry center around customers, processes, information technology, and digital transformation. Maximilian publishes in renowned journals such as Business & Information Systems Engineering, Decision Support Systems, Business Process Management Journal, Journal of Strategic Information Systems, and Journal of the Association for Information Systems. Maximilian is also strongly engaged in publicly and privately funded research projects, in which he contributes to the solution of relevant business problems. He already collaborated with companies such as Allianz, A.T. Kearney, Bayerische Bereitschaftspolizei, Deutsche Bahn, Deutsche Bank, HEINZ-GLAS, HILTI, Infineon Technologies, MELOS, Nord/LB, Radeberger, Siemens, and many more.

Marco Schmidt is a research assistant at the Research Center Finance & Information Management at the University of Augsburg and the Project Group Business & Information Systems Engineering of the Fraunhofer FIT. His research focusses on the Digitalized Life and Individual IS, i.e. the development of IS for individuals. Formerly, he studied Business Information Systems Engineering (B.Sc.) and Computer Science and Infonomics (M.Sc.) at the University of Augsburg. Marco engages in publicly and privately funded research projects in the context of BPM and IT Security with companies such as Hilti AG and MELOS GmbH.

Managing Environmental Protection Processes via BPM at Deutsche Bahn

FINK: The Information System for Nature Conservation and Compensation

Ingo Rau, Iris Rabener, Jürgen Neumann, and Svetlana Bloching

Abstract

(a) **Situation faced**: The law demands environmental compensation for interventions in nature and landscapes through the Federal Nature Conservation Act. Deutsche Bahn, one of the largest construction facilitators in Germany, encounters several hundred new such compensation obligations per year. Deutsche Bahn plans and develops compensation measures that usually require long-term maintenance. The Federal Railway Authority demands regular reports on the state of these obligations. Prior to the beginning of the case study described here, Deutsche Bahn had no IT system that could meet these requirements.

(b) **Action taken**: In order to create a comprehensive and legally compliant report, Deutsche Bahn initiated the project called *FINK*. Compensation obligations can last 30 years or more as they progress through various of Deutsche Bahn's business units. This life-cycle of a compensation obligation was initially modelled as a process using BPMN and, with the participation of stakeholders, an improved target process was developed. In order to control the transitions of responsibility within Deutsche Bahn and to ensure the quality of data, a web application based on Open Source components was developed, the core of which is a Business Process Management System (BPMS).

(c) **Results achieved**: The *FINK* project was initiated to engage intensively with the process of compensation obligations at multiple levels in Deutsche

I. Rau (✉) • I. Rabener • J. Neumann
econauten, Berlin, Germany
e-mail: ingo.rau@econauten.de; iris.rabener@econauten.de; juergen.neumann@econauten.de

S. Bloching
Deutsche Bahn, Berlin, Germany
e-mail: svetlana.bloching@deutschebahn.com

J. vom Brocke, J. Mendling (eds.), *Business Process Management Cases*,
Management for Professionals, DOI 10.1007/978-3-319-58307-5_20

Bahn. Today, committees at both the management level and the user level coordinate the processes across the business units. The result is a uniform understanding of what data needs to be stored for compensation obligations in order to ensure quality-controlled reporting. An interdisciplinary team of environmental experts, process experts, and software engineers developed *FINK* using agile methods. In the spring of 2016, the system was handed over to Deutsche Bahn and began regular operation. It is now used by a multitude of employees at Deutsche Bahn and by many external partners.

(d) **Lessons learned**: Successful BPM projects involve change. Business departments lacking sound competencies in process analysis, process design, and requirements management can build expertise gradually with the help of external experts. Mapping from quality requirements to business rules can largely automate the quality-assurance process, and the notation standards of BPMN and DMN integrate well. The use of a BPMS can also facilitate monitoring, documentation, and verification duties. Finally, a consistent Open Source approach using standard Java components was successful in the project presented here.

1 Introduction

Operating in 130 countries, Deutsche Bahn AG is one of the world's leading passenger and logistics companies. As part of the DB2020 strategy, Deutsche Bahn seeks to remain a profitable market leader and to become one of Germany's top ten employers and an eco-pioneer (Deutsche Bahn AG 2016a, b). One of its environmental goals is to improve nature and species conservation, so when it builds new lines or upgrades old ones, it avoids destroying or even interfering with natural habitat right from the beginning of the planning process. When interventions with landscape and nature cannot be avoided, it creates an acceptable alternative or replacement so natural habitats for endangered species are not lost (Deutsche Bahn AG 2016c).

The handling of these interventions in nature and landscape is regulated by the Federal Nature Conservation Act (Bundesministerium der Justiz und für Verbraucherschutz 2016), which results in that the entity responsible for any intervention is also responsible for the implementation of three phases of 'compensation obligations':

- **Planning**: Nature conservation specialists plan the compensation measure and seek official approval.
- **Implementation**: With the official approval, the compensation measure is established and developed, usually over several years.
- **Maintenance**: In most cases, after successful implementation, the measure must be maintained for up to 30 years.

The spectrum of issues related to such action is broad. Sometimes animals must be relocated to alternative habitats, and even then, construction may proceed only after the animals have settled in successfully at the new location. If the construction of a railway line impacts on the landscape or trees have to be cut down, new trees may have to be planted at a suitable alternative location, and the compensation obligation is fulfilled only if the trees actually grow and are still thriving several decades later.

The compensation obligation is not new, and the business units of Deutsche Bahn have taken responsibility for it for many years. The motivation for the case study presented here was an amendment to the Federal Nature Conservation Act in 2010, which stipulates that a competent authority must monitor the implementation and maintenance of compensation obligations and that the intervening party must provide a comprehensive report to that authority. The Federal Railway Authority, Deutsche Bahn's supervisory authority, requires an annual report on the state of all compensation obligations under Deutsche Bahn's control since 1st March, 2010. By the end of 2016, Deutsche Bahn had about 4000 such obligations, with several hundred being added every year. The number continues to grow, as many of these obligations must be maintained for up to 30 years.

This case study describes how Deutsche Bahn met these requirements as part of a Business Process Management (BPM) project and how, in the spring of 2016, the project culminated in the launch of the Information System for Nature Conservation and Compensation (***F****ach****in****formationssystem* ***N****aturschutz und* ***K****ompensation*), known as *FINK*. The core of this web-based application is a BPM System (BPMS).

2 Situation Faced

The requirements for quality-assured implementation and ongoing maintenance of compensation obligations and their annual reporting to the Federal Railway Authority led to the establishment of a new project that Deutsche Bahn called 'Compensation Obligations'. The members of its steering committee knew that the topic had to be anchored strategically within the organisation in order for the project to succeed. Even though they were not yet familiar with Dumas et al.'s (2013) Process Life-Cycle model, the steering committee started the *Process Identification* phase, as one work package was exclusively dedicated to the target process. Later in the project we took the stakeholders systematically through all phases of the model: the *Discovery*, *Analysis*, *Redesign*, *Implementation*, *Monitoring*, and *Controlling* of business processes.

At the time, there were few corporate compliance guidelines for compensation obligations. Each of Deutsche Bahn's business units was developing its own protocols, and processes were defined only for certain segments of work. No end-to-end process was described, from initial planning to ongoing maintenance in any of the business units involved, largely because Deutsche Bahn's responsibilities for any one compensation obligation change over time and many stakeholders are involved. We identified Deutsche Bahn's internal stakeholders as builders, planners, property agents, purchasers, property dealers, maintenance contractors, and nurturing partners, and its external stakeholders as regulatory authorities, nature conservation authorities, planners, landscape constructors, commercial real estate agents, eco-point vendors, landowners, and conservation partners.

As none of the Deutsche Bahn's business units had software to keep track of the company's obligations systematically, all documentation for planning, implementation, and maintenance of compensation obligations was paper-based. Environmental planning documents were not kept separate but were part of the technical files and were stored in filing cabinets after the project conclusion.

The specialist department for environmental issues in Deutsche Bahn, DB Environment, is the main contact for the Federal Railway Authority in terms of reporting, and it acts as the central interface with Deutsche Bahn's business units. Neither the Federal Nature Conservation Act nor any other German law specifies how to manage and report on environmental compensation obligations, so one of the first project tasks was to define the content and format of future reporting in conjunction with the Federal Railway Authority and the various Deutsche Bahn stakeholders. It became clear early in the process that an efficient software platform was needed to fulfil this reporting commitment.

In order to produce the initial report by the end of 2012, an interim solution based on Microsoft Access was introduced. DB Environment distributed the application on CDs and consolidated the collected data in a central database, which took several months. Reports were created as PDFs and Excel files and delivered to the Federal Railway Authority, but the final results were not satisfactory to any of the parties involved. The data acquisition process was time-consuming, expensive, and error-prone, and the Federal Railway Authority could not use much of it because of the quantity and the data structure's complexity. From this process, we learned several important lessons:

- All data collected regarding compensation obligations must be recorded digitally from the start. While information was being collected for the first report, many of the associated projects were already completed, and not all of the various parties involved were available any longer. As a consequence, accessing information on particular compensation obligations and their ongoing changes during planning and construction was cumbersome and laborious.
- External planners must be able to enter data without discontinuity of media. In construction projects, environmental planning is usually assigned to external planners, who also provide the bulk of the data needed for the first report. Since these external partners usually have no access to the Deutsche Bahn intranet, a solution had to be found whereby they could contribute data easily.
- Before being given to the Federal Railway Authority, the report must undergo an internal data-quality check and gain the approval of the responsible Deutsche Bahn business units.

3 Action Taken

In view of the situation faced, Deutsche Bahn decided on an action plan with three project phases:

- Creation of a preliminary study (econauten 2016) to provide recommendations for process redesign, a suitable IT-infrastructure, and key requirements of the IT system.
- Development of a proof-of-concept to demonstrate the chosen system architecture's feasibility.
- Development and rollout of the productive system.

3.1 Preliminary Study: First Half of 2013

To be able to define the target process across the company, Deutsche Bahn's participating business units had to develop a common understanding of the tasks necessary to fulfil compensation obligations. The econauten, a team of external experts who specialise in digitising business processes, led the effort to improve the status quo (*process discovery*) and the search for weaknesses and potential remedies (*process analysis*).

In the initial workshop with stakeholders from all Deutsche Bahn business units involved, the econauten developed a BPMN 2.0 model (Object Management Group 2011) of the current end-to-end process. BPMN proved to be suitable for visualising the various stakeholders' perspectives such that who does what in the process was clear to all through the model. The stakeholders' roles were reflected in the model's swim lanes, which also captured communication flows, decisions, documents, and the systems involved. The standardised and formalised presentation of the process helped workshop participants to comprehend which processes were unique for particular departments and which were essentially the same activities with different titles. The modelling work motivated the departments to agree on a common language and a standardised process.

In a second workshop, large-format prints of the current process formed the basis for a qualitative process analysis. Reporting to the Federal Railway Authority required analysing when and from where the required data was produced and in what quantitative distribution, which led to a redesign of the target process. We noticed that much of the data had to be recorded (on paper at that stage) when planning the measure and submitting the approval documentation to the Federal Railway Authority. Not much more data had to be added later in the process, during implementation and maintenance. Visualising the overall process made where else this data would be needed apparent.

The modelling also made clear that the compensation obligation process is a long-term process. From initial planning to actual implementation, a compensation measure can take years. An external planning office usually does the planning, and a public authority is responsible for the approval. These measures must often be maintained over several decades. As part of an analysis, participants evaluated the individual process steps and used User Stories (Cohn 2010) to highlight data-quality assurance and legal-related procedures, including regulatory approval and acceptance and transitions of responsibility between the business units, as critical to business value. Knowing that the measures are based on validated data proved to be an important requirement for the target process and a prerequisite for legally compliant reports to the Federal Railway Authority.

Inter-organisational processes were also clarified. An open and constructive dialogue began with the Federal Railway Authority, one of the key external stakeholders, on how best to fulfil the reporting requirements for both parties. Over several meetings, misunderstandings were clarified and participants described the difficulties they had experienced in the review and verification of the first report. As this first report was delivered in paper form and as an Excel spreadsheet, a systematic review was all but impossible. Therefore, the Federal Railway Authority decided to build its own IT system for storage and analysis of the data. On econauten's recommendation that all of the report data be defined as stipulated in an XSD schema, both Deutsche Bahn and the Federal Railway Authority familiarised themselves with XML, a data-exchange format that is understandable to both humans and machines.

Several key requirements for the IT system were derived from specialist workshops in conjunction with evaluation by Deutsche Bahn's legal department:

- Compliant, legally secure recording, storage, and provision of all necessary environmental data.
- A role-based access concept that enables Deutsche Bahn's internal and external users to access the system.
- Direct mapping of identified target processes in the system, where possible.
- Highly flexible and changeable processes that can be changed (preferably) by the department itself.
- Automatic monitoring of data quality.
- Quality checks with approvals by authorised process participants.
- Clear delegation of tasks and automated alerts.
- Automatic reporting to the Federal Railway Authority directly from within the system.
- Good price-to-performance ratio.

Such an application was not available at the time of the preliminary study either in the software pool of DB Systel GmbH (the IT subsidiary of Deutsche Bahn) or on the free market of environment specialist IT systems. A completely new IT system had to be developed from the ground up with three primary characteristics:

- **Web-based.** Nearly all professional applications run by Deutsche Bahn operate exclusively inside the company's own network. A Deutsche Bahn computer is usually necessary to access these applications, but external consultant are contracted for the majority of environmental planning at Deutsche Bahn. Access to the new system had to be made available to these planners without providing everyone with a Deutsche Bahn computer, so the new system had to be designed with a web interface that required a user to have only a modern web browser to gain access. The application would then be available to external users via a proxy server with a suitable firewall in place.

- **Open Source**. To develop an IT system within the available budget, the preliminary study recommended reliance on Open Source components as much as possible. Deutsche Bahn already had a Java standard operating environment based on Linux that contained the Open Source portal *Liferay* as the standard user interface. The company chose the JSF Library *Prime Faces* to provide a richer user experience.
- **Process Automation**. Because of the requirements' obvious process nature, it made sense to use a BPMS, which made operating asynchronously and handling processes in the background possible. Users can enter data into the system without waiting for further processing or delegation, and the BPMS automatically manages and forwards tasks to the user via a task list. Because a number of processes had already been modelled in BPMN, closer attention was paid to systems that could execute native BPMN 2.0. The decision was made to use *Camunda BPM*, which promised to be highly flexible and developer-friendly. To complete the software stack, *Drools* was selected for executing business rules.

3.2 Proof-of-Concept: September 2013 Until July 2014

After the preliminary study, it was necessary to set up the IT project to address the requirements. DB Systel GmbH, which would later operate the system, took over the project management. Although analysis and a preliminary study had already delivered important insights into how the future application should be designed, many of the requirements were still too vague for technical implementation. It was clear that some requested details would be able to be described accurately only weeks or months ahead. An in-house decision committee was created to manage coordination of important decisions with all business units.

As the next report to the Federal Railway Authority was due, we could not delay the project any longer, even though not all requirements had been fully defined. Therefore, DB Systel opted for an iterative approach based on the agile method Scrum (Pichler 2008). Using *Sprints*, which are fixed-term (often fortnightly) working periods, a defined number of functions are implemented and (ideally) presented in a working order. This method produces in advance no comprehensive specification sheet that defines all functions.

Organisational and technical prerequisites were established in order to apply Scrum in a practical manner. The participants met at a kick-off event in Berlin, where the typical Scrum project roles were discussed and assigned as follows:

- **Product Owner**—Product owners represent the business side of the system and define its functional properties. DB Environment took over this role, representing the involved DB business units. Two employees from DB Environment were allocated to focus specifically on this project.

- **Scrum Team**—The Scrum Team is made up of software developers and architects. Ancud IT, a company that specialises in Open Source and Java projects, was commissioned to do the software development. Over the course of the project, the size of the team varied from one to three software developers, plus additional resources for project management.
- **Scrum Master**—Scrum Masters monitor compliance with the method and ensure that the Scrum Team is supplied with a sufficient number of clearly defined functional descriptions for each Sprint. These specifications are described in Scrum as User Stories. A project leader from DB Systel GmbH took the role of Scrum Master.
- **Product Owner 'Proxy'**—The role of product owner 'proxy' is not explicitly described in Scrum, but in this case it linked the environmentally competent Product Owner and the IT-technically competent Scrum Team by specifying the requirements in such a way that the Scrum Team could implemented them consistently. This role was occupied by the econauten, a team of three specialists who had chaired the requirement workshops and developed the preliminary study.

The preparations for the technical project included the installation of a number of project management tools. Of particular interest were a ticket system in which the to-be-converted User Stories were described and managed in a scrum board, and a project wiki in which detailed conceptual notes and mock-ups of individual functions were recorded. Because the team would be working from a variety of geographic locations, the entire project infrastructure had to be available securely via the web.

After the kick-off in Berlin, all of the parties to the Scrum project started their work. The preliminary study had supplied a rough outline of the system architecture that had been refined, and the Scrum Team then began building this architecture. A web application based on *Liferay* was developed, and custom-designed input forms allowed users to input data regarding compensation obligations. This information was stored in a database in the background. In the next step, the BPMS Camunda was connected to the portal.

Meanwhile DB Environment and the econauten concentrated on clarifying the requirements. In a new round of workshops, representatives from all of the business units involved were asked to write User Stories in which they stated in which role they needed a specific feature and how they would benefit from it.

Over the following weeks, the new IT system was developed in 2-week sprints. After the end of each sprint, the Product Owner examined the implemented functions and processes via a test system. To collect feedback from future users as quickly as possible, selected users were able to enter test data using the first release on an additional proof-of-concept system after only a few weeks. Release 1.0 was presented to the decision committee with the following results:

- All data collected in 2012 via MS Access could be imported into the new system.
- The technical path adopted was effective, and a base system was set up in a relatively short time for users to log on and enter data via a web-interface.
- The key business process, collecting data and submitting an annual report in XML format to the Federal Railway Authority, had been automated.

3.3 System Development: September 2014 Until Spring 2016

After seeing the proof of concept, the decision committee approved the further development of the system. User Stories were written, prioritised, and implemented by the development team, and pilot users' experiences were used to improve the reporting process, masks, and the data model itself. Based on the User Stories and the high-level target process developed earlier, five additional processes were identified for automation in the new IT system:

- Managing requests for DB owned property on which a compensation measure is possible.
- Generating the *Maßnahmenblatt* (obligation fact sheet) exclusively via the system to summarise the data on which the project gains approval from the authority.
- Controlling the transition from the planning phase to the implementation phase, based on regulatory approval.
- Planning and documenting nature conservation approvals.
- Coordinating transitions of responsibility for a compensation obligation from establishment and development to maintenance.

Before the roll-out of the productive system in the spring of 2016, the project team and future users tested the system. Today the Information System for Nature Conservation and Compensation (***F****ach**in**formationssystem* ***N****aturschutz und* ***K****ompensation*, or *FINK*) is available to all who deal with nature conservation and compensation obligations at Deutsche Bahn.

4 Results Achieved

Looking back at the initial situation, the most important goal was to create an IT system that could submit compliant data on compensation obligations to the Federal Railway Authority. In order to meet this goal, it was necessary to manage compensation obligations in this IT system consistently throughout the DB Group in Germany. With the launch of *FINK*, the original goal was achieved and some expectations were even surpassed.

FINK is a hybrid of a BPM system and a web-based data application. Internal staff from all of the DB business units that are responsible for compensation obligations now have full access to *FINK*, as do their external consultants. The implementation of a roles and rights concept ensures that users can access only the system functions that are specific to their entitlements. DB Environment stipulated that the user management be based largely in the business units themselves. Today, segment administrators manage all accounts within their business units, setting up new users and assigning appropriate roles.

The demand for an IT system was the starting point for the project. While this demand could have been satisfied with classic software development, the experts opted for a software architecture in which a BPMS runs as the core application. The key concept of a BPMS is to execute logic described in business process models that can be changed easily, so system behaviour can be changed whenever business processes change, whether the system is in development or in operation. The model was improved with every iteration of the report process, and the application in operation reflected these changes soon after. All of these steps led toward an effective target process. Analysis of the most recent version of the report process and the effort to get there made clear that fewer resources were required as time went on; by that stage, the processes' inherent flexibility had paid off because knowledge was represented in the models instead of being hidden in software code.

Today the report process is started by the individual nature conservation experts whose job it is to submit data on compensation obligations to the Federal Railway Authority. The process invokes a rule set that compares the data entered in the system with predetermined quality rules. The results are immediately displayed via the user interface, where each test result highlights the exact data mask on which the quality problem was found. Thus, users can gradually correct the data until the desired quality is reached. The process then delegates the task of approving the pre-validated data to the task list of the person responsible for releasing the report to the Federal Railway Authority.

Only after this person has approved the data can the process engine initiate the conversion of the data in XML format. This procedure is run through all of the Deutsche Bahn business units involved. Then, in a final step, the process renders the actual report, including the XML input from all business units, which is then sent to the Federal Railway Authority.

FINK can do more than generate reports on compensation obligations. What users particularly like about *FINK* is that it supports their specific work contexts. For example, the system helps them to coordinate the transition of responsibility between the business units involved. They appreciate that processes guide them through their tasks over several masks on which all important contextual information is readily available. *FINK* is an expert system; the goal was not to automate everything with the BPMS but to use *FINK* to help expert users deploy their knowledge in the best possible way via intelligent processes and business rules. Human knowledge and interaction will continue to be significant when it comes to dealing with compensation obligations.

The BPM project initiated a more holistic approach with regards to compensation obligation processes throughout the DB Group in Germany. The visualisation of the processes, roles, and decisions involved, as well as the underlying data, message flows, and systems involved were all central to a consistent perspective on the status quo for all stakeholders. BPMN has proved its worth as a notation standard. Even people with little experience in analysing and visualising business processes found the diagrams easy to understand, as long as they were created with a limited number of modelling elements (Freund and Rücker 2012) One participant on the steering committee wrote: "Compared to the mapping of processes in other software, I find the representation in swim lanes much easier to understand." In this project, the BPMN model of the target process became the basis for a new corporate guideline at Deutsche Bahn.

With BPMN it was easy to model who participated in a process, in which particular role they acted, what decisions were necessary, and what tasks had to be completed. However the data on which these decisions were based and how this information had to be displayed on the user interface was not part of the BPMN model. The complex behaviour of the user interface had to be described in other ways through additional text and mockups. Also additional programming was necessary, as this was the only way to deliver an easy-to-use, dynamic interface on which users could manipulate large amounts of data in one process step.

Many of the ideas to improve the system that arose during the iterative development not only touched the process model of the application but also the user interface behaviour and the underlying data model. It was at this point that the customers' expectations regarding easy modification of the system could not be met. A project participant at DB Environment described the situation thus: "I had expected more flexibility, especially when setting up new processes. I had seen prototypes in other projects where it seemed easier to design and change processes. To me, this is very important when further developing the system."

BPM projects usually require an approach that differs from one that is suitable for classical software development projects. Many BPM projects aim to give the specialist departments increased ability to customise the IT systems to their requirements. As such, greater configurability through the departments should be implemented wherever possible, but the additional effort necessary must be balanced with the option of implementing other relevant features.

In the future, and with little extra effort required, the revision of quality rules could be transferred entirely to the specialist departments, which now define the criteria for data quality and document these rules in Excel spreadsheets. These spreadsheets form the basis of the rule definition in DRL, the domain-specific Drools Rules Language. These rules can be documented even better with the relatively new OMG standard DMN for decisions (Object Management Group 2015; Debevoise and Taylor 2016). Like BPMN, this notation is based on an XML scheme that can be executed by suitable systems (i.e., the current version of Camunda BPM). Following the DMN standard, decision tables can be built and filled with rules directly by specialist departments, and the BPMS calls these rules out of a process and executes them. Switching to DMN is planned for a future release of *FINK*.

5 Lessons Learned

For BPM projects to be successful, specialist departments must have sufficient expertise

Specialist departments are typically faced with challenging demands with respect to IT projects, especially BPM projects, as the responsibility for their success lies increasingly with the departments themselves. In order for these specialist departments to work as equal partners with the IT department, they must couple their professional expertise with other kinds of expertise. For example, in addition to having a common understanding of processes in general, the recording and reading of process diagrams requires knowing a modelling language—in this case, BPMN. Although the notation is easy for most people to understand, creating process diagrams, even if only a few modelling elements are used, requires some practice. Competency in process analysis and re-design is also necessary.

Department representatives (in this case, environmental protection and nature conservation representative) must contribute their expert and practical knowledge to completing software requirements. Especially with agile products, considerable responsibility rests on the Product Owners, who represent the business side. The Product Owner is responsible for specification and final acceptance of the various features and their prioritisation and is involved in release planning and cost and risk analysis. If the Product Owner is not sufficiently available or qualified, the whole project can be delayed.

In this particular case, the Product Owner's capacity and knowledge were not equal even at the initial stage to managing this complex IT project. Therefore, an external team supported the environmental experts and ensured the continued availability of a strong Product Owner throughout the development. Expertise was gradually transferred to the department, enabling further independent development in-house.

The success of BPM projects also depends on effective communication and cooperation between specialist departments and IT experts. All too often there is a lack of understanding of the other side's tasks and responsibilities. Technical vocabulary can be misinterpreted, and misunderstandings, fears, and prejudices can lead to conflicts.

The parties involved recognise the benefits of BPM only when the depicted processes are relevant to them

In order for an organisation's BPM initiative to fall on fertile ground, the first process to be implemented should be chosen wisely. Those who have had little experience with BPM may not immediately see the benefit in such projects, as much of it can sound abstract and can even be daunting. Immediate attention is paid to such an initiative if it addresses significant issues of those involved. In the present case, the first process to be implemented was the group-wide, quality-assured establishment of a standardised report on compensation obligations to the Federal Railway Authority. Before the introduction of the BPM application, this report process was highly complex, so the prospect of its creation being supported by IT

and obtaining a higher quality report at a lower cost was motivating for the participants.
The chosen process must be relevant to the organisation, but it cannot be too complex or it will quickly overload the participants. Ideally, a large process previously described in BPMN should have sub-processes identified for possible automation, but it is not as useful to specify them to the last detail as it is to deliver still 'raw' but ready to run to the subsequent users. In dealing with processes directly in the BPM system, users can quickly identify where further specification is needed, and the fine-tuning is then based on previously implemented processes. This approach saves both time and resources and establishes an iterative working method right from the beginning. The specialist departments and IT experts concluded that requirements face continuous refinement, and BPM was the right choice for that dynamic environment.

Adding systematic quality checks to processes can easily be achieved using DMN
How can those responsible at Deutsche Bahn ensure that their reports to the Federal Railway Authority conform with agreed quality standards? The two most important answers are:

- Quality must be contextually defined in rules.
- Compliance with these rules must be systematically and automatically checked.

In this example, the goal was achieved by combining processes with decision logic in a Rules Engine. A relatively simple process guides the user through the masks of the automated quality inspection. As per Rules Task, a set of rules is called upon from within the process, against which the collected data is checked. The user sees the identified quality problems prepared in a table and eliminates them one by one until the desired level of quality is reached.
The automatic quality inspection can also be invoked as a sub-process from other processes. Depending on the context, a particular rule set is used, but the basic structure of the inspection process remains the same. Without this approach, the quality assurance in the complex area of nature conservation would not have been possible.

The fulfilment of monitoring, documentation and reporting compensation obligations is significantly simplified with a BMPS
In the context of compensation obligations, the Federal Railway Authority are not the only body to which Deutsche Bahn must report. DB Legal Department requires specific documentation of relevant process steps as well, and Deutsche Bahn itself has employee representation guidelines and monitoring and compliance requirements. Some of these guidelines were initially non-specific but were recognised by the stakeholders as important non-functional requirements. Expectations behind these requirements could be anticipated and translated into concrete functional requirements for the system.

The target process's required procedures and responsibilities were mapped directly into roles, rights, and business rules. Adopting this approach made it easy to extract relevant information automatically for documenting and verifying obligations directly from the BPMS. Proof required in the form of journal entries that document, for example, the results of a completed process instance could be developed cost-effectively.
Another important component of the BPMS in this context is the integrated process monitoring. Each initiated process instance can be traced step by step so bottlenecks and problems that arise during its execution can be identified easily. With an increasing load on the system and a growing number of processes passing through it, patterns and vulnerabilities can be identified and methods continuously improved.

The standard compliant JAVA Process Engine and Portal Solution are good choices in the development and deployment process
The components of the new system were entirely implemented in Java and fitted seamlessly into the standard deployment and operating environment of DB Systel, Deutsche Bahn's IT subsidiary. Development and operation of this BPM application is no different from that of other Java enterprise applications, so the risk of unexpected side effects is predictably low. This prerequisite was important in meeting DB Systel's requirements and competing against the well-established solutions of major manufacturers and their heavyweight components. Easy embedding of the system into the heterogeneous IT landscape was a given, and other well-established technologies of the Java EE standards, such as reporting, monitoring, and logging components, could also be integrated easily into the system, all in addition to the pure operating environment. Since all of the components are Open Source, the risk of a software vendor lock-in was reduced and access to the large Open Source developer community was possible.

Successful BPM initiatives are anchored in the organisation as change projects
BPMS projects are equal parts organisational and IT projects, but IT is no longer necessarily the dominant partner, as it is seen to be on equal footing with other organisational areas. In this project, the necessity of standardising processes across business-unit boundaries was recognised early, and the steering committee assumed responsibility for the strategic implementation of this standardisation across the organisation.
The steering committee also established successful cooperation between the various departments and assisted the BPM development team throughout the project. The business units involved were well aware that they had to provide resources and make decisions over the long term, but the steering committee's and the decision committee's support for the successful implementation of the BPMS project contributed significantly to the project's success.
The steering committee coordinated feeding the results from the BPM project back into the business units and entrenching them. Heavy users of *FINK* regularly exchange ideas at top-user meetings, discussing aspects of the system and the various processes and flagging potential improvements. They share their knowledge of processes and how to work efficiently with *FINK* with users both inside and outside

the DB Group. The ongoing establishment of *FINK* in the DB Group ensures that the processes represented in the IT system stay in sync with the organisation.

References

Bundesministerium der Justiz und für Verbraucherschutz. (2016, May 10). *Gesetz über Naturschutz und Landschaftspflege (Bundesnaturschutzgesetz – BNatSchG).* https://www.gesetze-im-internet.de/bnatschg_2009/BJNR254210009.html

Cohn, M. (2010). *Userstories. für die agile Software-Entwicklung mit Scrum, XP u.a.* (1. Auflage). Heidelberg: MITP.

Debevoise, T., & Taylor, J. (2016). *Prozess- und Entscheidungsmodellierung in BPMN/DMN* (1. Auflage). Eine Kurzanleitung.

Deutsche Bahn AG. (2016a, May 10). *Facts and figures 2015.* http://www.deutschebahn.com/en/group/ataglance/facts_figures.html

Deutsche Bahn AG. (2016b, May 10). *Pioneering role in environmental protection.* http://www.deutschebahn.com/en/sustainability/environmental_pioneer/db_and_environmental_protection.html

Deutsche Bahn AG. (2016c, May 10). *Preserving our natural environment.* http://www.deutschebahn.com/en/sustainability/environmental_pioneer/db_and_nature_conservation.html

Dumas, M., La Rosa, M., Mendling, J., & Reijers, H. (2013). *Fundamentals of business process management.* Berlin: Springer.

econauten. (2016, May 10). *Zukunftsfähige IT-Systeme im Umweltschutz.* http://www.econauten.de/de/referenzen/deutsche-bahn/

Freund, J., & Rücker, B. (2012). *Praxishandbuch BPMN 2.0* (3. Auflage). München: Carl Hanser Verlag.

Object Management Group. (2011). *Documents associated with business process model and notation (BPMN), version 2.0.* May 15, 2016, from http://www.omg.org/spec/BPMN/2.0/

Object Management Group. (2015). *Documents associated with decision model and notation (DMN), version 1.0.* May 15, 2016, from http://www.omg.org/spec/DMN/1.0/

Pichler, R. (2008). *SRUM. Agiles Projektmanagement erfolgreich einsetzen* (1. Auflage). Heidelberg: dpunkt.verlag GmbH.

Ingo Rau is co-founder and Managing Director with econauten—a Berlin based consultancy, guiding companies on their journey of digital transformation. He has previously worked as creative planner with Kabel New Media. He was also co-founder and member of the board of directors with a German based property management firm. Ingo holds a diploma in media consultancy from Technical University Berlin. As senior consultant, Ingo coaches business departments and technical experts through complex IT projects. He specialises in business process analysis, the modelling of business processes (BPMN), decisions (DMN) and cases (CMMN). As a speaker, Ingo gives talks on Business Process Management (BPM)—primarily in service industries—for both IT and non-IT conferences.

Iris Rabener is co-founder and Managing Director with econauten—a Berlin based consultancy, guiding companies on their journey of digital transformation. She holds a diploma in media consultancy from Technical University Berlin. As senior consultant she coaches specialist departments in digitizing their business processes to make them faster, more efficient and more customer-orientated. During the last 12 years Iris has advised clients across a broad range of industries, specialising in process analysis, requirements engineering and agile methods. For many years she has been involved with women in leadership and, since 2012, been a board member of the Friends of the EAF Berlin.

Jürgen Neumann is co-founder and Managing Director with econauten—a Berlin based consultancy, guiding companies on their journey of digital transformation. Since 1990 Jürgen has founded and acted as CEO with several companies in the IT industry. Specialising in IT strategies and IT implementation, Jürgen has worked for a number of commercial and not-for-profit organisations. He is an expert in the area of free and open-source hardware and software and is also involved with the analysis of the impacts of IT on society. Jürgen is co-intitator of OHANDA, the European open spectrum alliance and also of freifunk.net. In 2013 he was nominanted as an Independent Expert by the European Commission.

Svetlana Bloching is a consultant for IT systems and environmental management in the environmental department at Deutsche Bahn AG. The focus of her activities is currently the administration of a web application, the core of which is a Business Process Management System (BPMS). During the past three years she has worked as part of a project team modelling the life-cycle of a compensation obligation in the nature protection area as a process using BPMN 2.0, implementing this process into an executable application. Svetlana received her Master's degree in Industrial Environmental Informatics from the University of Applied Sciences in Berlin. Her masters thesis dealt with the topic of the Life Cycle Assessment (LCA) for a solar module, a process conducted via the use of environmental management information systems (EMIS) and represented a material flow analysis. The thesis won her the Umberto Student Award.

Hybrid Process Technologies in the Financial Sector: The Case of BRFkredit

Søren Debois, Thomas Hildebrandt, Morten Marquard, and Tijs Slaats

Abstract

(a) **Situation faced**: Exformatics, a Danish adaptive case-management vendor, wanted to leverage declarative process tools to support the flexible processes found at BRFkredit. However, switching from the more common flow-based notations to a declarative notation brought new challenges in terms of understandability. We undertook the project described in this chapter to investigate and address these challenges.

(b) **Action taken**: We started our investigation by having several full-day and half-day meetings to discuss BRFkredit's requirements. Based on these requirements, we proposed and developed a prototype hybrid process-modelling approach with which models are defined declaratively, but the possible behavior of the model can be viewed and investigated using flow-based notions. The prototype was then presented to BRFkredit for feedback.

(c) **Results achieved**: Our investigation helped to clarify the requirements for making declarative process models understandable to end users at BRFkredit and showed how a hybrid approach could be used to satisfy these requirements. Based on these insights, we developed tools to enhance our existing declarative modelling framework with flow-based visualizations.

S. Debois (✉)
Exformatics/IT University of Copenhagen, Copenhagen, Denmark
e-mail: debois@exformatics.com

T. Hildebrandt • T. Slaats
IT University of Copenhagen, Copenhagen, Denmark
e-mail: hilde@itu.dk; tslaats@itu.dk

M. Marquard
Exformatics A/S, Copenhagen, Denmark
e-mail: mmq@exformatics.com

J. vom Brocke, J. Mendling (eds.), *Business Process Management Cases*,
Management for Professionals, DOI 10.1007/978-3-319-58307-5_21

(d) **Lessons learned:** Different stakeholders have different needs and preferred levels of abstraction when process models are used as tools for communication. However, one model that seems to fit most situations is a simple no-branches sequential swimlane diagram that was extracted automatically from a more detailed declarative model. These observations enabled Exformatics to enhance its declarative modelling framework to make it more attractive to end-users.

1 Introduction

This chapter describes an investigation by Exformatics A/S, a Danish vendor of adaptive case-management (ACM) solutions, into the feasibility of applying its declarative workflow modelling and execution engine in the financial sector. This investigation was carried out in collaboration with the Process and System Models Group of the IT University of Copenhagen and BRFkredit, a Danish mortgage credit institution.

In order to accommodate the diverse requirements of BRFkredit's process models, Exformatics extended its declarative modelling tools to derive from any model representative traces and other relevant flow-based visualizations. Through this extension, the tools now support a hybrid modelling approach in which processes are modelled declaratively based on their underlying business rules, but the behavior supported by the model can be visualized in more familiar flow-based notations, both in full and as representative traces. The new hybrid's features and the broader perspectives of the technology were well received by BRFkredit, but a more thorough evaluation with more users and case studies is needed before any firm conclusions on their use in practice can be drawn.

Exformatics A/S has a customer base of approximately forty organizations, both Danish and international and both private and public. Exformatics' core product is a case-handling system for knowledge workers like lawyers who work with intellectual property protection or real estate management, engineers and project managers who design and construct large power plants, marketing employees who plan campaigns for broadcasting, and case workers in areas like human resources, political hearings, and workforce-related political issues.

Exformatics believes in the need for formal workflow modelling notation as a way to

- strengthen communication of requirements from client organizations
- strengthen communication within client organizations post-deployment
- expedite development
- enable run-time system updates

However, for its current clientele of knowledge workers, Exformatics has found flow-based modelling notations insufficiently flexible. The cases Exformatics' clients handle are in some ways uniform, yet never actually equal. They typically follow a common set of rules, but the details of each individual case invariably differs a great deal. Hence, Exformatics co-developed and adopted a declarative workflow modelling notation, DCR Graphs, originally conceived at the Process and Systems Models Group of the IT University of Copenhagen, which is headed by Thomas Hildebrandt.

Exformatics has invested considerable resources into bringing DCR Graphs from an academic vision to a practical, marketable product in the form of a process-Execution Engine and Workflow-Modelling Toolkit (Marquard et al. 2015). The former has been deployed in Exformatics' solutions, most notably with a complete model of the workflow of the Danish foundation, Dreyers Fond (Debois et al. 2014).

However, the use of formal workflow modelling has, from the perspective of the customer, been an implementation detail, a technical "trick" Exformatics uses to speed implementation. Exformatics' vision is that (suitably authorized) expert end users should be able to update or even create models themselves, with the Exformatics Process-Execution Engine automatically reflecting such updates. With that vision in mind, Exformatics has been looking for a mature process-intensive, knowledge-worker–heavy company, preferably in the financial sector, with which to experiment with the possible future directions of Exformatics' Workflow-Modelling Toolkit.

Such a company was found in Danish mortgage credit institution BRFkredit. In late 2014, a formal collaboration was established among Exformatics A/S, IT University of Copenhagen, BRFkredit, and Visuel IT within the purview of and financially supported by the Copenhagen Fintech Innovation and Research Network (CFIR).

BRFkredit is a Danish mortgage credit institution that lends against collateral on owner-occupied homes, commercial properties, and subsidized housing. On the Danish housing market, mortgage loans are not typically taken out from a bank but from specialized credit institutions like BRFkredit, that issue mortgage bonds that pool together many borrowers and investors, thereby spreading the associated risk.

BRFkredit's loans for residential purposes account for the majority of its lending while corporate lending is done for office and business properties, private rentals, and cooperative housing. BRFkredit finances its current lending by continuously issuing covered bonds and mortgage bonds, that is, as tap issues.

BRFkredit A/S is owned by Jyske Bank A/S through the holding company BRFholding A/S. BRFkredit's market share of the total Danish mortgage market is approximately 8%. Jyske Bank/BRFkredit is Denmark's fourth-largest financial institution. BRFkredit has lending of around DKK 213 billion (approx. EUR 28 billion) distributed on around 120,000 mortgage loans that are managed by just over 750 full-time employees.[1]

[1]BRFkredit in Brief. Accessed August 2015 at http://www.brf.dk/Investors/About-BRFkredit/Additional-information/BRFkredit-in-brief

2 Situation Faced

Exformatics adopted a declarative notation because of a strong belief in their clients' need for flexibility. Knowledge-worker end users are the experts and should be inhibited in their possible actions only if required by law or business rules. As the academic literature often claims (Pesic and Schonenberg 2007), Exformatics contends that declarative notations are better suited for describing such laws and business rules than imperative or flow-based notations are.

However, declarative notations have been shown to be more challenging for end users to understand than are more common flow-based notations, such as BPMN (Zugal et al. 2014). Hence, the primary objective of the investigation for Exformatics was to determine how the DCR Graph process modelling can be made more accessible to expert end users. A secondary objective was to determine the motivation for and role of manual process modelling in financial institutions and the applicability of DCR Graphs to the same. Another secondary objective was to carry out a practical (yet anecdotal) test of the hypothesis that potentially collaborative simulation can be a useful tool for expert end users' work with process models. Exformatics places a high priority on support for simulation in its tool offerings (Marquard et al. 2015), contending that the ability to simulate and "play through" a process will help users understand the ramifications of a particular declarative model.

2.1 The Context of BPM in BRFkredit

Viewed in terms of the BPM Context Framework (Brocke et al. 2016) the focus of BPM initiatives at BRFkredit has been on *exploitation*, that is, using process models primarily to help case workers determine how to handle their cases while remaining compliant.

Both *core processes* and *support processes* are modelled. Examples are process descriptions of loans' lifecycles and models the customer service department use to determine how to respond to customer inquiries. As BRFkredit targets regular consumers with standardized loan options, most processes are highly *repetitive*. Processes are typically *highly knowledge-intensive*, and the case workers are required to have a deep understanding of the mortgage products offered. A *medium level of creativity* is required of the workers: The options for a particular loan can be highly diverse and can depend on a customer's unique situation, but unique cases also tend to be outliers, and many customers fall into common classes for which the best solution has been determined and little creative thought is required. There is a *medium level of interdependence* at play: Many of the processes interact on some level; for example, customer-service processes typically depend on the status of the customer's loan process. The processes at BRFkredit are *highly variable*: Not only is there a significant amount of variability in the products (loans) offered, but the case workers also have considerable flexibility in how they support customers, leading to a high degree of variability how activities are ordered and how they occur.

Most of the processes at BRFkredit are *inter-organizational* in the sense that each department has its own organizational structure, and most processes span many departments. As a mortgage institution, BRFkredit is a *large organization* that falls mostly within the *service industry*, as while the loans can be seen as products, they are not physical products. The culture at BRFkredit is *highly supportive* of BPM practices, with BPM diagrams of important processes adorning the hallways around the case workers' offices, so a *significant amount of the organization's resources* is dedicated to creating and maintaining these diagrams. Finally, the BPM activities at BRFkredit are performed in a *medium-level competitive environment* with a *medium level of uncertainty*.

2.2 Related Work

The direction taken in this project relates closely to the recently initiated work on hybrid business process modelling notations and technologies that seeks to combine the strengths of the flow- and constraint-based process modelling paradigms (Reijers et al. 2013). A common approach in this field is to provide hybrid modelling notations that combine both flow- and constraint-based elements (De Giacomo et al. 2015; Sadiq et al. 2001; van der Aalst et al. 2009; Westergaard and Slaats 2013). Our approach, on the other hand, uses the two paradigms separately: a constraint-based notation is used to model the process, whereas a flow-based notation is used to gain insight into the behavior supported by the models. This approach relates closely to recent work (De Smedt et al. 2015; Prescher et al. 2014) on mapping from the declarative Declare (Pesic and Schonenberg 2007) notation to Petri nets; however, contrary to the work presented here, these techniques are not being used in commercial tools or being applied to industrial case studies.

3 Action Taken

The investigation took the form of a sequence of full- and half-day meetings in early spring 2015 in which BRFkredit's needs for process modelling and the required extensions to the DCR Graphs tools to meet those needs were discussed. The present case study reports only on the conclusion of these discussions.

The objective of process modelling at BRFkredit is to communicate within the company. The constructed models are then used by stakeholders that include the IT department, which uses process descriptions as partial requirements specifications for IT systems that support new and updated financial products; caseworkers, who use process models as roadmaps for their daily work; and management (at multiple levels), who use process models as abstracted views of "what goes on in the company."

For BRFkredit, process modelling has enough value as a communication tool alone to merit allocating resources to its construction and maintenance. However, BRFkredit reported that its use of such models faces two major challenges:

Different stakeholders use different process-model notations, and the level of abstraction that is appropriate for a model depends on the stakeholder who uses it.

We treat each of these challenges in turn.

3.1 Different Stakeholders Use Different Notations

Attempts to introduce a small subset of BPMN as a standard modelling notation used everywhere in BRFkredit have not been successful. Most departments, including IT, find that notation unhelpful, not because those stakeholders are adverse to process modelling but because some departments have produced their own extensive and comprehensive models of their processes for internal consumption.

These models appear to have two primary commonalities across departments[2]: First, the models are trace models—that is, each model describes a single "happy-path"—the most common variant of a particular process—of the process in question—and typically include little or no possibility to choose between activities or reordering them. Second, the models heavily emphasize roles, whether occupied by humans or IT systems. Diagrams are invariably some form of swim-lane diagrams that are typically produced in PowerPoint.

The emphasis on single traces over branching models is in line with recent research on the understandability of process models (Haisjackl et al. 2013; Zugal et al. 2011). It appears that, for the majority of stakeholders, understandability far outweighs precision or generality when it comes to models' usefulness as tools for communication. For discussion and communication, a representation of a single "happy path" is far more helpful than a branching model like BPMN, as the greater precision afforded by the branching model sours discussion by bringing in irrelevant detail.

Where detail is required—when process models are used as requirements-specification for IT or when process model are used as roadmaps for caseworkers—BRFkredit simply produces more single-trace models. For example, the processes for granting various kinds of mortgages have grown to more than a thousand. BRFkredit mentions that this approach is burdensome when internal processes change, such as in response to changes in business requirements or the regulatory climate. It is likely that the large number of processes can profitably be represented as minor variations on a small number of core processes.

In a large company like BRFkredit, difficulties in agreeing on notation go beyond process notation. For example, a seemingly simple and precise notion like "client" means different things to different departments: For the sales department, the client is a person who might be interested in obtaining a mortgage, while for the Loan Monitoring department, the client is someone who has an active loan with BRFkredit, and so forth.

The differences in (ad hoc) model notations and terminology have the unfortunate consequence that two diagrams, one depicting a process as seen by IT and one

[2]For confidentiality reasons, we cannot include actual examples of the various customized models.

as seen by sales, may result in the observer's failing to realize that the two diagrams depict aspects of the same process.

3.2 The Level of Abstraction Appropriate for a Model Depends on the Stakeholder Who Uses It

This challenge is most easily explained by example. For instance:

- Caseworkers need process descriptions that show only the process variant on which they are working on and need not know details about the underlying IT processes.
- Sometimes managers need process descriptions that are precise about interactions between departments but do not contain details about what goes on inside departments.
- At other times managers need process descriptions that describe only the part of processes that pertain to particular (financial) products or product lines.
- IT needs process descriptions that contain every possible process variant and full detail on the process's interaction with IT systems, but IT does not care at all about human interactions (e.g., prospective client meetings).

Reconciling differences in terminology in a large organization is a problem beyond the scope of process modelling, so we focus on notation.

3.3 Regarding Differences in Notations

We contend that the differences in the process notations employed at BRFkredit do not arise from any inherent difference in the preference for modelling notations but from the absence of a single notation that is suitable for all stakeholders. BPMN is apparently not it, not for want of flexibility but simply because of its plethora of symbols and less than intuitive semantics.

Recall the observation that most of the ad-hoc diagrams with which we have been presented present only a single trace with precise distinction between roles. That notation is, then, apparently the appropriate notation for the majority of stakeholders. As such, we envision a mechanism for presenting process models in terms of a small number of representative traces. This idea fits well with the idea of declarative or constraint-based process modelling: A declarative model is a concise representation of a typically large number of admissible traces with semantics that allow us to compute efficiently whether a trace is admissible (Pesic and Schonenberg 2007). If BRFkredit's processes were represented as a single or, more realistically, a small number of general processes, one could extract from these models representative traces that "represent" the process in internal communications.

This idea begets the question: Which traces? Among all the possible traces admitted by our hypothesized general model, how do we find an appropriate set of representative traces?

We contend that, in a given process model, we can name activities whose execution is the objective of the process. In the case of BRFkredit, the objective of, say, an instance of a mortgage application process is the evaluation of that application. Variants of that process arise as different opportunities present themselves for reaching that goal. For instance, in one variant the value of the property that secures the mortgage can be appraised statistically, without a visual inspection. Another variant arises when the property is in an insufficiently uniform neighborhood, so the process model's constraints forbid the statistical appraisal.

In summary, at least in this instance, the process's objective can be defined as the execution of a particular activity (e.g., "assess loan application"), and the process's variants can be identified by which activities are executed in pursuit of that objective (e.g., "statistical appraisal" or "on-site appraisal").

This approach yields a method for identifying relevant traces: Domain experts, who must be consulted anyway when one is constructing the model, help to figure out which activities characterize the process's objective and the key activities that identify (collections of) process variants.

3.4 Regarding Differences in the Appropriateness of Abstractions

For the single-trace model representatives suggested above, determining the appropriateness of an abstraction is simply a matter of projecting the trace in question, that is, leaving out activities that are unwarranted at the desired level of abstraction.

Example 1 Caseworkers need process descriptions that show only the process variant on which they are working and need not know details about the underlying IT processes. Proposed solution: Given a complete trace, remove all activities that do not directly involve the caseworker.

Example 2 Sometimes managers need process descriptions that are precise about the interactions between departments but do not contain details about what goes on inside departments. Proposed solution: Given a complete trace, remove all activities that are not adjacent to an activity of a different department.

Example 3 At other times managers need process descriptions that describe only the part of the processes that pertain to particular (financial) products or product lines. Proposed solution: Look for a trace that concludes in, say, "assess additional loan application" to fulfil this requirement in part.

Example 4 IT needs process descriptions that contain every possible process variant and full detail on interactions with IT systems but does not care at all about human interactions (e.g., prospective client meetings). Proposed solution: In this case, where we do need branching structure, the picture is less clear. For IT, process descriptions often play a role as part of a requirements specification, so the process model must describe all of (and only) the desired system's behavior. However, we may assume minimal sophistication with formal models and so use the general DCR model as the appropriate model.

For DCR graphs, the possibilities for semantically well-founded projection has been well studied, so getting rid of "human interactions" in amounts to employing one of the known sound projection methods (Hildebrandt et al. 2011).

4 Results Achieved

To present the ideas of Sect. 3 to BRFkredit staff, Exformatics extended its existing workflow modelling tool with a proof-of-concept analysis tool that (a) presents projected traces and (b) generates minimal traces that are executing or not executing given activities.

The tool presupposes a single DCR Graph-based process model that encompasses a family of processes, including a particular class of mortgage loan application processes. For confidentiality reasons, we cannot report on an actual model here, but we constructed a fictional and somewhat simplified process that is heavily inspired by the actual processes at BRFkredit. This DCR Graph model is presented in Fig. 1 and can be found as a public graph (BPM 2015 BRF Example) at http://dcrgraphs.net. *Boxes* indicate activities and *arrows* indicate constraints.

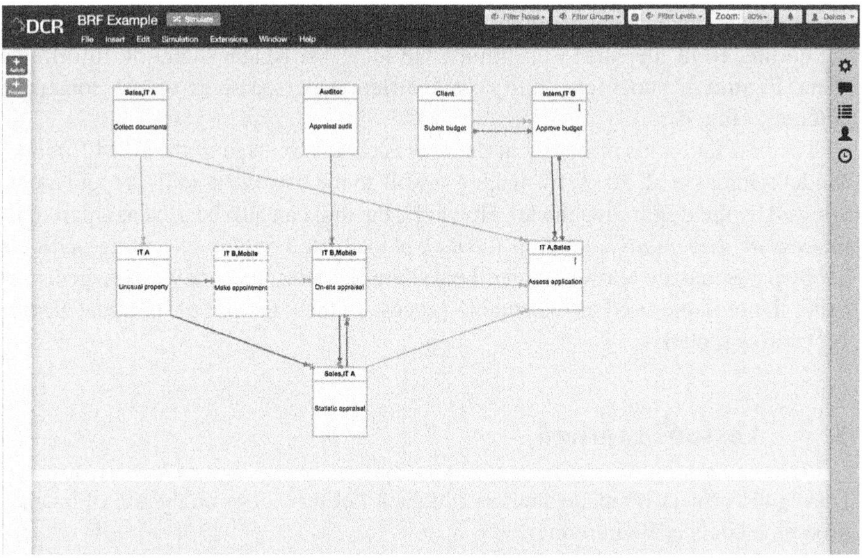

Fig. 1 DCR Graph model of a (simplified) mortgage loan application process.

Each *box* is labelled (in the *middle*) with the name of the activity and (at the *top*) with the roles that participate in the activity. The *arrows* with a *bullet* in the end (*yellow* in the tool) indicate conditions, so we cannot "Assess application" before we have executed, among other processes, "Collect documents." *Arrows* with a *bullet* at the beginning (*blue* in the tool) indicate required responses, so whenever "Submit budget" is executed—that is, whenever the prospective client updates his or her budget—"Approve budget" must be executed again. The graphic notation for conditions and responses is consistent with the notation for precedence and response constraints used in DECLARE (Pesic and Schonenberg 2007). The *arrows* with % and + at the end (and *red* and *green* in the tool) indicate exclusion and inclusion, respectively; *arrows* with *diamonds* at the end (*purple* in the tool) represent "milestones"; however, it is not necessary to understand these in detail to read the remainder of this report, so we omit further details and refer the reader to previous papers on DCR Graphs [e.g. (Debois et al. 2014; Hildebrandt and Mukkamala 2010)] for more details.

This model is only potentially suitable for the IT stakeholders as a requirements specification for implementation purposes. Accordingly, using Exformatics Workflow Editing Tool's plug-in infrastructure, we constructed a plug-in that provides perspectives on this model to be used by the other stakeholders (case-worker and management). One such perspective is the full state-space of the DCR Graph model in a flow-graph notation; this representation provides the full detail of the model, including branching structure (decision points), so it can be helpful for implementors, but it is generally far too detailed. The example in Fig. 2 shows the complete (but somewhat overwhelming) picture.

For stakeholders who are interested in representative traces, the prototype tool has a panel for specifying such, as illustrated in Fig. 3.

Figures 4 and 5 show examples of input constraints and the resulting trace.

Starting from the same constraints, we may restrict our attention to different roles. Figures 5 and 6 exemplify such different perspectives of the constraints entered in Fig. 4.

The new tool aims primarily at the *process analysis* stage of the BPM Lifecycle Model (Dumas et al. 2013) by making visible to the user what paths are and are not allowed by the declarative model. However, the tool can also be used as a part of the *process implementation* stage: If the user is interested only in executing particular happy paths that are allowed under the declarative rules, then they can be generated using the tool and used as executable process models instead of the more flexible declarative model.

5 Lessons Learned

During the project we made a number of useful observations on the use of business process models at BRFkredit:

1. BRFkredit uses process modelling primarily as an internal communication tool.

Fig. 2 Flow-graph representation of the model in Fig. 1

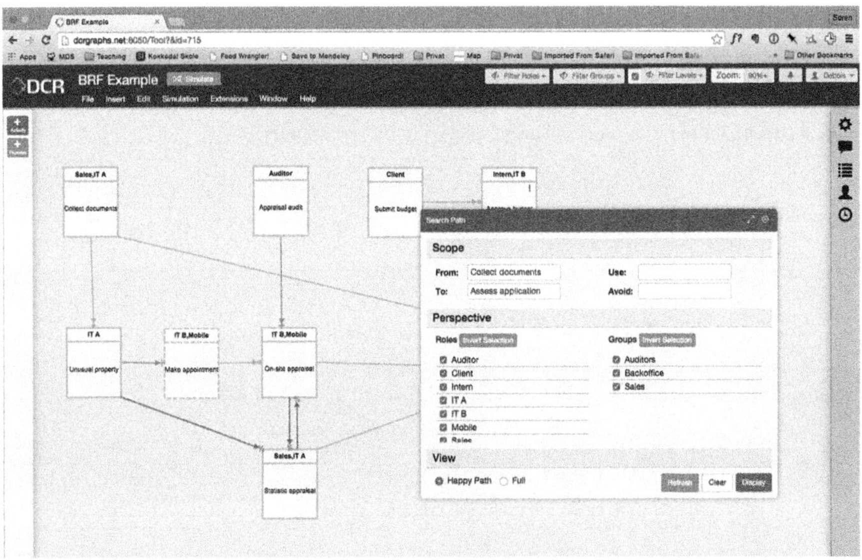

Fig. 3 Pop-up panel for specifying single-trace parameters. One specifies under "Scope" the activity that should be the starting point of the trace, the ending point, and optional activities that must or cannot occur along the way. Under "Perspective," one may indicate a projection onto specific roles or groups. The tool will then find the shortest trace that satisfies the given constraints (e.g., variants of the loan application process in which the property in question needs an on-site appraisal) by searching through the transition graph

2. Different stakeholders have radically different uses for the resulting process models.
3. Different stakeholders prefer somewhat different process notations.
4. Many stakeholders are content with representing processes as "representative traces."

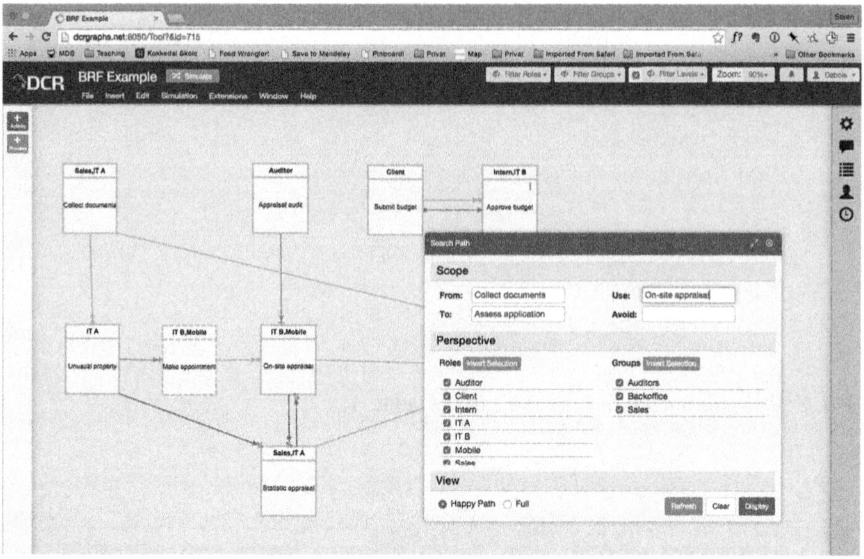

Fig. 4 Specification of a process variant requiring on-site appraisal

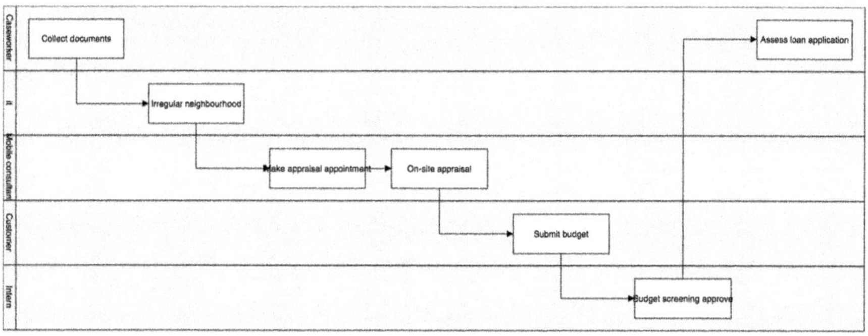

Fig. 5 Trace resulting from the parameters entered in Fig. 4

5. Such representative traces should contain only activities that are relevant to the business case at hand.

We speculate that many of these lessons can be observed at other large organizations as well, particularly in the financial sector.

Driven by these observations, Exformatics A/S extended the plug-in architecture for its Workflow Editing Tool to encompass the proof-of-concept technology reported here as an APP and evolved the proof-of-concept to an important feature of its current offering.

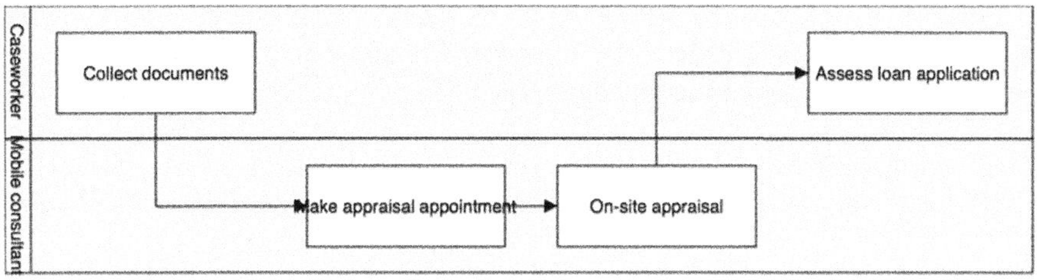

Fig. 6 Trace resulting from the parameters entered in Fig. 4, but keeping only the "Mobile Consultant" and "Caseworker" roles

In conclusion, this case demonstrates anecdotally a clear need for different visualization of processes for different stakeholders. In addition, the proof-of-concept implementation of the semi-automatic generation of "representative traces" was well received by BRFkredit. Both of these points are likely independent of the concrete case presented here and the notation used, although it is also likely that the possibility of producing the projections depends on the use of a formal declarative model like DCR Graphs. The solution is available at http://www.dcrgraphs.net.

Based on these observations we propose that there is a clear opportunity for hybrid process modelling approaches that provide different views of the same process to the various stakeholders of a process. Exformatics has made a first step in this direction by incorporating functionality for the semi-automatic generation of "representative traces" in their declarative modeling tool, but there are many opportunities for improvements, both in terms of tool-development and research.

First of all, the proposed approach needs to be tested on a larger audience, following a rigid experimental methodology, to determine if the hybrid approach taken by Exformatics truly benefits the understandability of declarative models.

Secondly, more encompassing hybrid approaches could be tried: instead of only using flow-based models for the visualization of relevant traces, one could also combine modeling notations directly and produce truly hybrid models. Alternatively, one could adopt a methodology where a flow-based notation is used to capture specific instances of a process that are interesting to individual stakeholders and then use these models to verify the correctness of a general declarative model that captures all possible behaviors, which would be of greater interest to e.g. a programmer who is tasked with developing software that can support all potential uses cases of the process.

It is not clear yet if the notations chosen by Exformatics are those best suited to the hybrid approach. For example, by using purely sequential swimlane diagrams, they extremely limit the local behavior that can be presented to a stakeholder in a single diagram. It would be interesting to experiment with a larger subset of BPMN that also supports constructs such as choice and parallelism.

Finally, it would be interesting to investigate the possible application of hybrid models to other parts of the BPM lifecycle (Dumas et al. 2013), such as process implementation, monitoring and discovery.

Acknowledgement The authors gratefully acknowledge the substantial resources set aside by BRFkredit to support this study, in particular the personal commitment of Thomas Bo Nielsen and Younes Nielsen.

References

Brocke, J. v., Zelt, S., & Schmiedel, T. (2016). On the role of context in business process management. *International Journal of Information Management, 36*(3), 486–495.

De Giacomo, G., Dumas, M., Maggi, F. M., & Montali, M. (2015). Declarative process modeling in BPMN. In *Proceedings of the 27th International Conference on Advanced Information Systems Engineering (CAiSE 2015).*

De Smedt, J., Vanden Broucke, S. K. L. M., De Weerdt, J., & Vanthienen, J. (2015). *A full R/I-net construct lexicon for declare constraints.* SSRN 2572869.

Debois, S, Hildebrandt, T., Marquard, M., & Slaats, T. (2014). A case for declarative process modelling: Agile development of a grant application system. In *International Workshop on adaptive case management and other non-workflow approaches to BPM.*

Dumas, M., La Rosa, M., Mendling, J., & Reijers, H. A. (2013). *Fundamentals of business process management.* Berlin: Springer.

Haisjackl, C., Zugal, S., Soffer, P., Hadar, I., Reichert, M., Pinggera, J., & Weber, B. (2013). Making sense of declarative process models: Common strategies and typical pitfalls. In S. Nurcan, H. A. Proper, P. Soffer, J. Krogstie, R. Schmidt, T. Halpin, & I. Bider (Eds.), *BMMDS/EMMSAD, volume 147 of Lecture Notes in Business Information Processing* (pp. 2–17). Berlin: Springer.

Hildebrandt, T., & Mukkamala, R. R. (2010). Declarative event-based workflow as distributed dynamic condition response graphs. In *Post-proceedings of PLACES 2010.*

Hildebrandt, T., Mukkamala, R. R., & Slaats, T. (2011). Safe distribution of declarative processes. In *Proceedings of the 9th International conference on Software Engineering and Formal Methods*, SEFM'11 (pp. 237–252). Berlin: Springer.

Marquard, M., Shahzad, M., & Slaats, T. (2015). Web-based modelling and collaborative simulation of declarative processes. In *Proceedings of 13th International Conference on Business Process Management (BPM 2015).*

Pesic, M., Schonenberg, H., & van der W. M. P. Aalst (2007). DECLARE: Full support for loosely-structured processes. In *Proceedings of the 11th IEEE International enterprise distributed object computing conference.* IEEE Computer Society.

Prescher, J., Di Ciccio, C., & Mendling, J. (2014, November 19–21). From declarative processes to imperative models. In *Proceedings of the 4th International Symposium on Data-driven Process Discovery and Analysis (SIMPDA 2014)*, Milan, Italy, pp. 162–173.

Reijers, H. A., Slaats, T., & Stahl, C. (2013). Declarative modeling—An academic dream or the future for BPM? In F. Daniel, J. Wang, & B. Weber (Eds.), *Proceedings of 11th International Conference on Business Process Management (BPM 2013), volume 8094 of Lecture Notes in Computer Science* (pp. 307–322). Berlin: Springer.

Sadiq, S., Sadiq, W., & Orlowska, M. (2001). Pockets of flexibility in workflow specification. In H. S. Kunii, S. Jajodia, & A. Sølvberg (Eds.), *Conceptual modeling—ER 2001, volume 2224 of Lecture Notes in Computer Science* (pp. 513–526). Berlin: Springer.

van der Aalst, W. M. P., Adams, M., ter Hofstede, A. H. M., Pesic, M., & Schonenberg, H. (2009). Flexibility as a service. In *Database systems for advanced applications, volume 5667 of Lecture Notes in Computer Science* (pp. 319–333). Berlin: Springer.

Westergaard, M., & Slaats, T.. (2013, August 26–30). Mixing paradigms for more comprehensible models. In *Business Process Management—11th International Conference, BPM 2013*, Proceedings. Beijing, China, pp. 283–290.
Zugal, S., Pinggera, J., Weber, B., Mendling, J., & Reijers, H. A.(2011). Assessing the impact of hierarchy on model—a cognitive perspective. In *EESSMod.*
Zugal, S., Soffer, P., Haisjackl, C., Pinggera, J., Reichert, M., & Weber, B. (2014). Investigating expressiveness and understandability of hierarchy in declarative business process models. *Software & Systems Modeling, 14*, 1081.

Søren Debois is an Associate Professor in the Models group at the IT University of Copenhagen. His current research focuses on concise representations of complex processes, specifically business processes, with an emphasis on the application of tenets of concurrency theory and fundamentals of IT security to business process modelling. Søren is a principal author on the DCR declarative process modelling notation and the architect of the DCR Academic Workbench (http://dcr.tools). He routinely participates both in academic conferences on formal methods in concurrency and industry-oriented knowledge networks on applications of business process management. His research is currently partly funded by Exformatics A/S, a Danish vendor of adaptive case-management systems.

Thomas Hildebrandt has a PhD in concurrency theory and computer science from Aarhus University. He is currently associate professor and head of the Process Intelligence, Models and Optimisation (PRIMO) research group at IT University of Copenhagen. Thomas has headed strategic research projects in collaboration with industry and public organisations during the last 10 years, focussing on the application of formal process models to the analysis and implementation flexible and secure business and workflow management systems. The research has lead to the invention and commercial adoption of the declarative Dynamic Condition Response (DCR) Graphs process technology developed jointly with Exformatics.

Morten Marquard is CEO of Exformatics, a Danish software company, developing software solutions to help knowledge worker increase their productivity. More than 40 Danish and international companies benefit from their Adaptive Case Management Solution (ACM) platform that can be configured to meet unique customer requirements. Business processes is supported through Dynamic Condition Response Graphs, DCR Graphs, which can be modelled on the portal http://dcrgraphs.net, and executed in Exformatics ACM, as well as in other ACM systems. Morten Marquard has unique working experience from strategic sales and marketing, and expertise from knowledge-based industries from previous positions at Commerce One, Netscape and Accenture. Morten Marquard holds a master degree in computer science from University of Copenhagen. Over the last 4 years Morten has authored and co-authored several peer-reviewed articles on BPM and DCR graphs. Morten works close with IT University of Copenhagen and has supervised an industrial Ph.D.

Tijs Slaats is a tenure-track assistant professor in the Department of Computer Science at the University of Copenhagen. His research interests include declarative and hybrid process technologies, the application of formal methods to business process management, process mining and information systems development. He is currently working on the Hybrid Business Process Management Technologies project, funded by a personal grant from the Danish Council for Independent Research. Tijs has published in various high-ranking international conferences and journals in the fields of formal methods, business process management and software engineering. As an industrial PhD student, he both played a fundamental role in the development of the theoretical foundations of the declarative DCR Graphs process modelling notation, and was the principal architect behind the DCR Portal (http://www.dcrgraphs.net/), the first web-based and commercially available declarative process modelling tool.

Business Process Management in the Manufacturing Industry: ERP Replacement and ISO 9001 Recertification Supported by the icebricks Method

Jörg Becker, Nico Clever, Justus Holler, and Maria Neumann

Abstract

(a) **Situation faced**: A family-owned manufacturing company recently went through the transfer of management from the older to the younger family generation. A number of problems were uncovered during this process, such as prevalence of tacit knowledge, an inefficient decision-making process, outdated IT system support, and an urgent need for certification of production processes according to quality-assurance standards (ISO 9001). Each of these problems required thorough documentation of the as-is business processes in the organization to guide their improvement.

(b) **Action taken**: To ensure that the created process models serve as a valid communication medium, the company's process landscape was created during an initial workshop between the executives and external BPM consultants. Then the information on processes in the company's various departments was gleaned from semi-structured interviews with the department employees. At the same time, process weaknesses and potential improvements were derived and discussed with the functions' management. The succeeding depiction of the to-be process framework was achieved with the help of the icebricks modeling method and the corresponding software tool, which is a lightweight, standardized approach to ensure high quality of process models.

J. Becker • N. Clever (✉) • M. Neumann
University of Münster—European Research Center for Information Systems (ERCIS), Münster, Germany
e-mail: joerg.becker@ercis.uni-muenster.de; nico.clever@ercis.uni-muenster.de; maria.neumann@ercis.uni-muenster.de

J. Holler
Prof. Becker GmbH, Altenberge, Germany
e-mail: justus.holler@prof-becker.de

J. vom Brocke, J. Mendling (eds.), *Business Process Management Cases*, Management for Professionals, DOI 10.1007/978-3-319-58307-5_22

(c) **Results achieved**: During the modeling phase of the project, external BPM consultants documented the process landscape, thereby explicating the company's knowledge and good-practice processes. The process landscape served as basis for well-informed decisions regarding the implementation options of a new ERP system, which was introduced on time and on budget in the second phase of the project. The ISO 9001 recertification of production processes was achieved in the third project phase with the help of the process documentation that had been created.

(d) **Lessons learned**: Simply deploying process models on the company's intranet platform does not necessarily lead to their desired comprehension and use. All employees have to be trained that process models are a means of communication and are never finalized, a notion that also applies to continuous process improvement. Process owners must be defined so they take responsibility for adjustments to the process environment beyond the project's lifecycle, but such responsibility is not solely that of a project manager. Furthermore, the project demonstrated the appropriateness of the icebricks modeling method for the manufacturing domain, although it was originally designed for the retail industry.

1 Introduction

The founder of a medium-sized family-owned manufacturing company retired, and his children took over the company's management. The takeover process uncovered certain deficiencies in the company's organization that had to be addressed as quickly as possible in order to maintain the company's leading position in the market. The company's original specialization was in assembling trucks' rear doors with rubber seals, but the production portfolio grew to include a wide range of products and services in the area of computer numeric control (CNC) production, machining, assembly, and coating. Currently, the company has about 200 employees and a 20,000-m^2 site in northwest Germany. The company acts primarily on the B2B market; it has about 23,000 customers and more than 90,000 production orders per year.

The dynamic market environment and increasing competition required the company to optimize its production processes in terms of time and costs and to prove compliance with modern quality standards. The new management wanted to improve the company's production processes and safety record. Moreover, since the company was highly dependent on its existing customer base, which at the time of the ownership transfer consisted of several large automotive producers, management wanted to empower the development of new products and services in order to enter new markets and become more independent and diversified.

Overwhelmed with these far-reaching change initiatives, the new owners needed support in structuring and organizing the modernization activities. Identification and documentation of the organization's existing business processes was seen as the most appropriate approach to managing the complexity of these activities. Invited consultants spent 6 months documenting the internal as-is processes, discussing them with the management and representatives of functional departments, deriving optimized to-be processes, and putting them to use by introducing a new ERP system, conducting ISO 9001 certification of the production processes, and laying the basis for the introduction of continuous management of process knowledge in the company. This paper focuses on the process-modelling phase of the project and highlights the rationales for the modeling technique that was applied.

The case is structured as follows. Section 2 provides details about the situation the company faced before the process modeling began. Section 3 discusses the chosen approach for the process-modeling project and the actions taken to address the company's problems. Section 4 presents the results of all three of the project's phases. We conclude with a discussion of the lessons learned from the case study.

2 Situation Faced

Lack of Process Documentation

Since its foundation in 1981, the company has been a family-owned organization with an autocratic management style. It was an effective organizational form at the early days of the firm, but with the growth of the organization, the effectiveness and efficiency of this management style decreased. The founder's management style and the concentration of decision-making power at top made the growth and further development of the organization problematic. According to the company's new CEO, "What was functioning well 30 years ago no longer satisfies the needs of an organization with 200 employees." The single decision point—the founder—slowed the management process, and in some cases, the founder changed decisions that had been made proactively at lower management levels. This situation demotivated the employees and produced a negative image of the company among them.

The autocratic management style also hindered the creation of a knowledge-sharing culture in the organization. Since the tacit knowledge of single process managers was seldom exchanged, there was no comprehensive overview of the existing processes in the organization. Even the CEO lost the "big picture" once the organization increased in size. Tacit knowledge was also prevalent at the lower organizational levels. Therefore, it was apparent that the missing process documentation was a major shortcoming and a barrier to effective knowledge management. When the new generation took control, they understood that everyone in a management position had to know the core company functions and to have at least a general understanding of the processes in the organization's various departments. This idea led to the decision to start a process-modeling project for the documentation of as-is processes. The main requirements for the documented processes were comprehensibility and completeness. Since the managers were not specialists in conceptual modeling, the modeling notation used for the project had to be as simple as possible, but it also had to allow for the depiction of a variety of elements in the organization. The company wanted each documented process to capture the process owners, to offer textual process descriptions, and to be accompanied by known weaknesses and potential for improvement. Besides representing the chronological order of activities, the process descriptions had to incorporate the IT systems' and organizational support's perspectives (Berente et al. 2009).

Outdated Information System Support

Outdated information system support added to the necessity for internal business process documentation (Berente et al. 2009). The existing ERP software had been introduced in the company in the year 2000 and suffered from a wide range of functional and usability problems. The company admitted that the ERP system lacked certain functionalities, such as efficient material requirements planning and reporting modules, which led to inefficient and ineffective decision-making and management. Because of the absence of an integrated reporting module, the company had to purchase ad-hoc reports from an external data analytics company, which was costly and time-consuming. For example, a single query cost about 500 € and 2–4 weeks of processing time. Moreover, since the most communication with the company's large customers was performed through the ERP system interface, the system had to function flawlessly, which was not the case with the existing ERP software. The company's employees often complained about the incorrect price listings or erroneous calculations performed by the CRM module.
The new owners wanted to replace the outdated software, but before starting the process of selecting and implementing a new ERP system, they had to know which processes had to be automated and to what extent. Moreover, it was sensible to perform at least some process improvement before the introduction of new ERP software, since automation of inefficient or superficial processes brings no benefits to the organization (Becker 1997).

Outdated Quality Assurance

Finally, the market and, in particular, the company's most important customer had demanded that the organization continuously demonstrate its compliance with the latest standards of production processes in terms of quality and safety at the workplace. Most of the company's competitors have undergone this certification, and while the company had once done so as well, the certificate was outdated and had be renewed as soon as possible. One of the most important certification standards was the ISO 9001, which demands well-documented production and quality-assurance processes.
Table 1 summarizes the problems faced by the company and their respective project goals.

Table 1 Problems faced and resulting project goals

Problem faced	Resulting project goal
Lack of process documentation with regard to knowledge management	Comprehensive documentation of as-is and to-be company processes
Ineffective decision-making and management because of outdated information systems support	Replacement of outdated ERP system
Outdated quality assurance because of missing recertification	ISO 9001 recertification through production and quality-assurance process documentation

3 Action Taken

The BPM project described in this case was carried out according to the procedures proposed in the frameworks of Becker et al. (2011) and Dumas et al. (2013). According to Becker et al. (2011), the first step in any BPM project should be the preparation of the modeling endeavor, which includes defining the overall modeling goal and selecting a modeling method with specific rules for syntax and semantics, along with a modeling software tool that supports the selected modeling method.

Preparation for Process Modeling

The BPM project described in the current case had three major goals: (a) creation of clean and resilient business process documentation that the company's management and employees could understand and use, (b) implementation of the new SAP Business One ERP system with follow-up end-user training, and (c) recertification of the company's production processes according to the ISO 9001 quality standard. The first goal is covered by the process identification and discovery steps of Dumas et al. (2013) framework. The latter two goals are highly dependent on the business process documentation created and can be seen as parts of the process analysis, redesign, and implementation steps of the same framework.

In preparing for process modeling, the choice of a suitable process-modeling method depends on factors like the BPM project's goal, the structure of the modeling team, and the model users' level of BPM knowledge. The current case required a process-modeling language that was easy to use and understand, but the company did not want to use textual descriptions in Microsoft Word or generic drawing tools like Microsoft Visio since these tools do not have the features that are necessary for BPM projects, such as management of the collection of process models, model analysis, or model creation by a distributed modeling team.

In the end, the icebricks modeling method and tool were chosen for the simple syntax and structure of its modeling language, predefined layers of abstraction, a semantic standardization approach using domain-specific glossary, and the use of attributes for storing related process information, particularly attributes of a hierarchical nature (Fig. 1). icebricks' corresponding web-based modeling tool has a central process repository, provides the user with a convenient way to create a

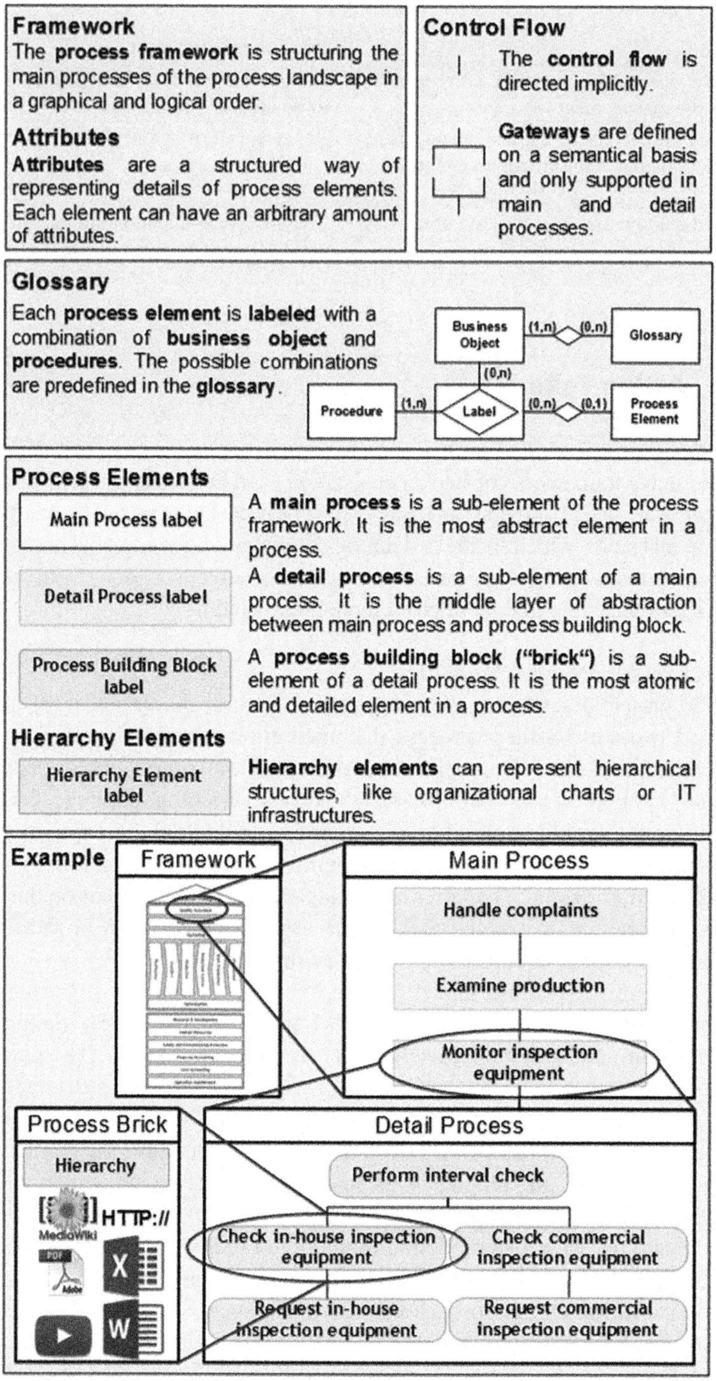

Fig. 1 Characteristics of the icebricks modeling method

standardized domain glossary, and allows model creation at different levels of abstraction by a distributed team of process modelers (Becker et al. 2013b).

Framework Construction

The new management required a comprehensive overview of all the processes in their company, but before starting the process identification cycle with detailed process analysis and redesign, it was necessary to reach agreement regarding the company's main processes and present them in the form of a process framework.

For this purpose, external consultants who had been invited to conduct the modeling and analysis part of the project organized and moderated two half-day workshops with the new owners and the relevant management representatives of the company departments. The revealed processes were organized graphically in a logical order, forming a company-specific process framework. The definition and acceptance of the process framework has significant influence on the overall modeling project's chances of success, as it provides structure and orientation for the modeling team and helps the model users to navigate efficiently through the process landscape (Meise 2001; Becker et al. 2011). In order to ease the process of defining the final form of the framework, the external consultants moderated the workshops, highlighted the important aspects of the framework, and provided examples of best-practice frameworks for the company's domain, such as the Y-CIM model (Scheer 1997). The company's strategic direction must also be taken into account when defining the process framework, so all of the high-level processes that had been identified were classified into management, support, and core processes (Porter and Millar 1985).

The icebricks modeling tool was easily applied to the creation of the framework. Its modeling language is based on the principle of abstraction, which is an inherent characteristic of every model-creation process (Stachowiak 1973). icebricks uses four layers of abstraction, which guide the modeler in creating a model. The first layer, the *process framework*, provides a high-level overview of the organization as a whole in the form of a process landscape. Under the process framework is the second layer, which consists of *main processes*, and here the various functional areas to be covered in a modeling effort are specified. The third layer consists of *detailed processes*, which specify the main processes on a more detailed level. In the fourth layer, the detailed processes are broken into *process bricks*, the most atomic process elements. These four layers, the result of long consultancy experience in the area of BPM and process-modeling projects, are depicted in Fig. 1.

After the external consultants reconciled the workshops results, the management agreed on the framework with 17 main processes, as depicted in Fig. 2.

As-Is Modeling

The next step of the BPM project, in compliance with Becker et al. (2011) and Dumas et al. (2013), was to record the detailed as-is process information regarding each of the 17 main processes. To accomplish this phase within 4 weeks, the consultants conducted semi-structured interviews with knowledgeable

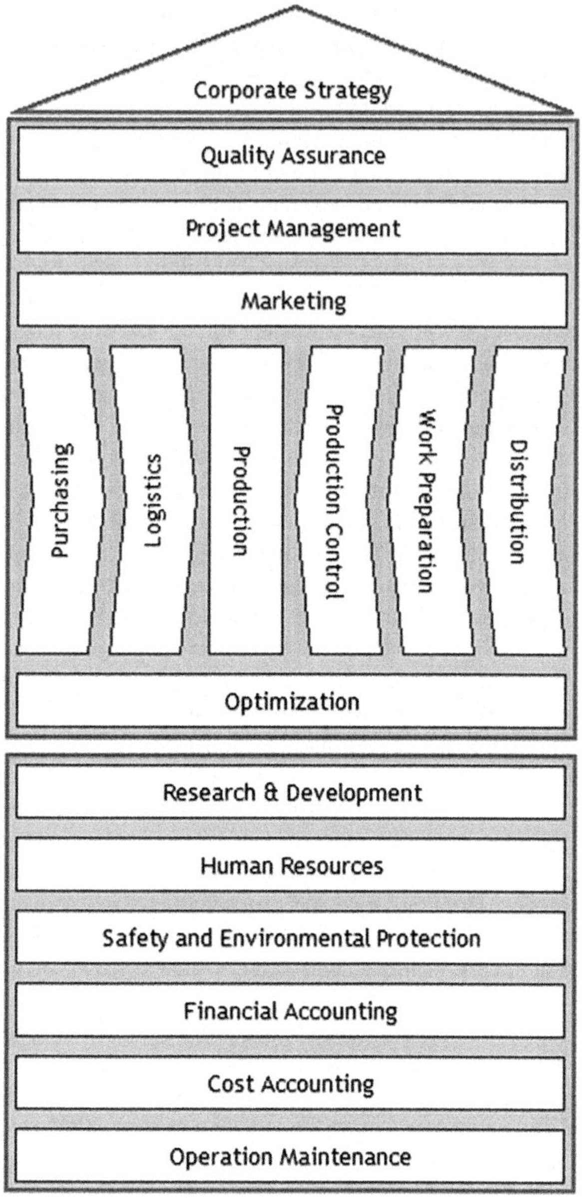

Fig. 2 Process framework (anonymized and trimmed screenshot)

representatives of each department. The as-is processes had to be optimized with respect to efficiency and strategic fit before they could be used as templates for the ERP implementation. Therefore, possible improvements were identified by investigating the recorded process information and including the domain knowledge and practical experience of the employees, who were encouraged to discuss weaknesses in and possible improvements for the processes during the interviews. Finally, the interview information was transferred from the consultants' notes into a form that was easily accessible by the modeling team in order to allow for continuous process improvement during the project and by the company afterward.

The modeling team consisted of eight invited BPM consultants, each of whom was responsible for the creation of a particular functional department's process models. Comparability of each modeler's modeling results was ensure so single models could be merged into a uniform process landscape at the end of the distributed modeling phase (Mendling et al. 2010b; Schütte and Rotthowe 1998).

In order to achieve such comparability, the element labels were standardized to a certain extent (Mendling et al. 2010a). The icebricks semantic standardization approach builds on the guidelines for labeling process elements from Rosemann (1996), Kugeler (2000), and Delfmann et al. (2009). Simple verb-object phrase structures are the most comprehensible (Mendling et al. 2010a), so every process element in icebricks is labeled in the form "<verb, imperative>" (<noun, singular> OR <noun, plural>)—for example, "pay invoice." Semantic comparability of icebricks process models is ensured through the use of a *domain glossary*, which consists of *business objects* (nouns) and *procedures* (verbs) that can be carried out on these business objects (Becker and Kahn 2011).

In the current project, the domain-specific glossary had to be created before the modeling activities began. The Retail-H reference model was used as a basis for the glossary (Becker et al. 2013b; Becker 1997), but the glossary was constantly expanded and adapted to the manufacturing sector during the creation of the as-is process models, so in the end it consisted of 305 business objects, 218 procedures, and 659 <business object, procedure> combinations. The modelers were restricted to using only these combinations of business objects and procedures in labeling the process elements. The use of these phrase structure conventions and the domain glossary allowed the creation of unambiguous and semantically standardized as-is process models that were comparable and could be directly used for (semi-) automatic analysis.

One of the most important requirements to the as-is process models was their simplicity so they could be understood easily. An excessively large set of modeling elements in a modeling language often leads to their erroneous use and to process models that their intended audiences cannot comprehend (Chen and Scheer 1994; Dehnert and Rittgen 2001; Kindler 2006; Langner et al. 1998; Leymann and Altenhuber 1994; Nüttgens and Rump 2002; van der Aalst 1999; van der Aalst and ter Hofstede 2005; Wynn et al. 2005). Unlike general-purpose modeling languages like the Business Process Model and Notation (BPMN) and the Event-driven Process Chain (EPC), the icebricks method uses just two modeling elements: *activities* and a *control flow*. Since these elements are used in all other modeling notations, the icebricks method uses a subset of existing and empirically approved language elements, rather than introducing new ones. The control flow in the icebricks method refrains from complex branching mechanisms and connectors, allowing only for simple, single-level branching with an arbitrary number of successor elements.

Use of this simple element set resulted in clear and understandable process models on both the main processes and the detailed processes. The largest main process contained 11 detailed process elements, and only two main processes included branching logic. The longest detailed process consisted of 13 process bricks. Because of their more specific nature, almost all of the detailed processes were created using branches to depict either parallel or alternative execution logic.

To increase the process models' simplicity and comprehensibility and reduce unnecessary branching, the concept of *process variants,* introduced in the icebricks method, was used in the creation of as-is process models. It is often observed in practice that the result of a process can be achieved in multiple ways (Becker et al. 2013a; Hallerbach et al. 2008), and the processes in the current project were no exception. Without using the variants, all of the alternatives to achieving a process's desired result must be represented in the same graphical model, which often leads to additional process elements to cover every circumstance and, in the end, to complex process models (Hallerbach et al. 2008, 2009). In the current project, nine additional non-standard main process variants and ten additional non-standard detailed process variants were created. The variants overlapped as little as possible. The rule of thumb regarding when to create a new variant is to do so whenever the input and output of a process match but at least one process step differs fundamentally from the steps in the standard execution. This rule of thumb was applied in the current project.

Process models can contain a great deal of information. Especially when the goal of the project is implementation of an ERP system, the detailed processes must be defined precisely in order to be translated correctly into the system workflow logic. In general-purpose process modeling notations, this information is included directly in the graphic process models by using additional model elements like data objects, aspects of the organization, or textual annotations. However, doing so increases the model's size and makes it more difficult to read and interpret, which contradicts with the principle of simplicity. Therefore, icebricks introduces *attributes* to store additional process information. The icebricks method provides a variety of attribute types, including simple textual attributes, numerical attributes for enhanced analyses, and more complex attributes like HTML pages, color annotations, and combination attributes, which allow attributes to be stored in various predefined combinations (Holler 2015). In the current project, such attributes as textual description, average execution time, number of executions per day, external reference, and attachments with relevant documentation were used in creating the process models. icebricks also provides the possibility of annotating a process's elements with hierarchical structures. The current project used this feature to annotate particular process steps with information about organizational responsibilities (elements of the company's organizational structure) and IT system support (elements of the company's IT architecture diagram).

Figure 1 summarizes and gives examples of the main aspects of the icebricks process modeling method.

Process Analysis and Improvement

After the creation of the as-is process models, the information about weaknesses and improvement potentials that was extracted from the semi-structured interviews and information from the literature and experiences of the involved consultants were used to develop improved to-be process models. The focus of these to-be models was on all three of the projects' goals: preparation for implementation of the new SAP Business One ERP system, ISO 9001 recertification, and rigorous documentation of the complete process landscape. The results achieved with the process documentation are presented in the next section.

4 Results Achieved

The company achieved all three of the project's goals: documentation of the process landscape, implementation of the SAP Business One ERP system, and recertification of the company according to the ISO 9001 quality standard.

Process Documentation

The outcomes of the first phase of the project, which is the focus of this case, fully satisfied the company's and the consultants' expectations. After the consultants formally handed over the process descriptions to the company, the new management had a complete and optimized process documentation at their fingertips. Figure 2 depicts the final process framework, which provided the company with structure and orientation in its process landscape. The printed version of the processes' documentation, in which all of the depicted processes and their attributes are described, has 238 pages. The process landscape consists of 17 main processes and 135 detailed processes, for a total of 372 process building blocks, not including the elements of the nine non-standard variants on the main process level and the 11 non-standard variants on the detailed process level. Besides these processes on icebricks' four layers of abstraction, IT infrastructure and organizational charts complemented the process landscape with the help of icebricks' attribution functionality.

From this point on, the manufacturing company's IT department could use the web-based modeling environment for continuous process improvement. The simplicity of the icebricks method facilitated employees' participation in the investigation of the process models, identification of potential improvements, and maintenance of the defined attributes for the process steps. Therefore, the outcome was simple, with mostly linear process models, but expressive enough and full of annotated attributes as a basis for the next two phases of the project: ISO certification and ERP implementation.

Always current process documentation improved new employees' on-the-job training. During periods of high workload the company hires additional workers, who need a quick overview of the processes that are relevant to their tasks. Depending on the terms of employment, new employees receive either a printed version of the relevant processes, including the annotated attributions, or a user account with read-only access to the web-based tool so they have continuous access to the models. The line managers, who are also process owners, are provided with user accounts with "read and write" access so they can suggest and directly implement changes to the models of the processes for which they are responsibility.

ERP Replacement

The SAP consultants in the EPR-implementation phase of the project relied on the harmonized to-be processes that were directly accessible in the web-based environment to align the ERP system to the desired behavior. This affordance reduced the communication effort with respect to workshops and interviews between the SAP consultants and the company's employees. Hence, the SAP consultants were able to present a system prototype with the expected system behavior in less time than they anticipated, based on their project experience with less-documented companies. This accomplishment was a main driver in introducing the SAP Business One solution within budget and with satisfactory quality in only 1 year. In particular, the company's management appreciated the increased functional range provided by the new system in perfect alignment to the processes. Because the new ERP system was capable of supporting the functional areas and the defined processes directed the system behavior, it was possible to incorporate end-to-end processes. Furthermore, issues regarding non-working material resource planning in combination with new orders because of missing inclusion of bill-of-material logic are now resolved. Another issue that hindered efficient production was the expensive (and all but impossible) adjustments that were needed for the old ERP software. With the new SAP system, the company can adjust the system's behavior more easily through simple customization. The same applies to information demands through ad hoc reports. With the SAP system there is no need for external suppliers to perform ad hoc reports since the SAP system's integrated query functionality allows the IT department to satisfy the departments' information demands, saving time and reducing costs. Finally, end-users' training materials can be built based on the documented processes, aligned with the ERP system functionality.

ISO 9001 Re-certification

The ISO certification had some challenges in terms of the necessary adjustments of the mostly optimized production processes. After overcoming these challenges, the improved and documented to-be processes fully satisfied the requirements of the ISO 9001 quality standard, with some minor remarks for further improvements in on-the-job safety. The ability to view and export the process documentation easily using the icebricks modeling tool eased the certification process. The certifier was given read-only access to the process models in the icebricks web-based modeling tool. Moreover, with the icebricks tool, the certifier could access the most recent documentation within minutes using the integrated Microsoft Word export functionality.

Continuous Process Management

After the project's successful conclusion, a work group made of representatives of the company's middle managers was established to discuss the company's processes regularly and to identify the additional improvements and adjustments necessary for the company to keep pace with its dynamic market. This form of continuous process management is probably the most valuable result of the overall modeling endeavor, and it fits well with the process monitoring and controlling phase of Dumas et al. (2013) BPM lifecycle model.

5 Lessons Learned

The BPM project at hand produced several lessons. From a general, methodological point of view, the selection of a web-based, lightweight modeling tool and a method with a high degree of pre-structuring helped to save time and budget. In particular, it made discussions about the level of model abstraction, naming conventions, and model layout obsolete. This time efficiency is likely also to be achieved in larger companies and in other industries. Nevertheless, certain difficulties arose during each of the project's phases, which are discussed in the next paragraphs. Several lessons can be derived from the ISO certification phase of the project. Since only a continuously recertified company can compete in the market, the conclusion of one successful certification project must mark the beginning of the next one. The certifier's input must be used as a basis for future process adjustments and the continuous process-improvement cycle. The potential of a easily comprehensible and used modeling method like icebricks must be exploited by creating pre- and post-certification versions of the processes. Thus, the certifier's suggestions can be presented transparently in the next certification process, and the company does not endanger its recertification.

Another lesson learned is the need to take full advantage of the web-based modeling and presentation environment. The company's quality-management employee was not accustomed to working with the digital versions of process models and so depended heavily on the print-outs. Although a print-out can be handy in meetings, the advantages of digitally reachable process models in a central repository must be communicated to non-digital naives. In the dynamic setting of the three phases of the project, there was a danger that people would be working with outdated print-outs. In the modeling phase of the project, the models changed regularly, particularly during the first weeks of modeling, so only the models in the central repository were sufficiently resilient for discussions and planning. This issue also applied in the two subsequent phases of the project, although the processes had reached a mostly stable state by that time and were adjusted only for further optimization or for alignment with the ERP system implementation.

Regarding the new ERP system, the implementation of any modern system would have improved the overall situation, but the rigorous selection process was time well invested. Although the external SAP consultants claimed the full budget because of some unforeseen adjustments, the selection of the system that fit best with respect to functional coverage, interfaces, and customization effort was a main driver of the project's staying on time and on budget with the required quality. Two main areas of improvement from introducing the ERP system were the end-user training and system testing. Because of missing test data and the line managers' commitment to providing test cases, the project manager was too involved in gathering the necessary data and even conducted some of the tests himself. Hence, the system was not tested to the desired extent, which led to some issues in the first 2 weeks after the new ERP system was introduced. The second issue regarding the implementation phase of the project was insufficient end-user training. Since the training was not mandatory before the introduction and offered only for interested employees, some of untrained employees had difficulty understanding the new system when they had to. A mandatory training plan during working hours would have had a clear advantage over training on voluntary basis.

The business process modeling itself had some challenges to overcome regarding the big team of consultants that conducted the interviews and consolidated the information into the final model. In particular, the icebricks modeling tool had no versioning functionality, hindering efficient collaborative modeling. Distinct versions of the models had to be created so information recorded by another consultant was not endangered. Although the diverse alternative solutions for version management worked out for the consultants, a specific versioning approach would have increased clarity and working efficiency. A positive lesson the predefined set of attributes that had to be filled for each activity in the process model, which allowed the IT systems and organizational structures that supported the processes to be compared and managed in a structured and, therefore, easy reporting style.

The use of the employees' knowledge about possible improvements was valuable input for the optimization of the as-is and construction of the to-be processes. This value demonstrated that it is not necessary to apply sophisticated and time-intensive means, such as process simulation or process mining, to perform process improvement. In general, it is enough to ask the subject matter experts *what is the longest action in this process* and *where do errors usually occur*. The year-long experience of the department workers and use of appropriate facilitation techniques in to-be process construction workshops often bring results similar to those of complex analysis techniques but with fewer resources invested.

Overall, the advantages of the web-based process model documentation must be actively introduced in the company and understood by all employees. Only then can possibilities like end-user training support and preparation for certification preparation be exploited to their full extent.

References

Becker, J. (1997). Handelsinformationssysteme und Handelscontrolling – ein methodenorientierter Ansatz. In D. Ahlert & R. Olbrich (Eds.), *Integrierte Warenwirtschaftssysteme und Handelscontrolling: konzeptionelle Grundlagen und Umsetzung in der Handelspraxis* (pp. 173–210). Stuttgart: Schäffer-Poeschel.

Becker, J., & Kahn, D. (2011). The process in focus. In J. Becker, M. Kugeler, & M. Rosemann (Eds.), *Process management: A guide for the design of business processes* (pp. 3–13). Berlin: Springer.

Becker, J., Kugeler, M., & Rosemann, M. (2011). *Process management: A guide for the design of business processes* (2nd ed.). Berlin: Springer.

Becker, J., Clever, N., Holler, J., Püster, J., et al. (2013a). Semantically standardized and transparent process model collections via process building blocks. In *Proceedings of the The Fifth International Conference on Information, Process, and Knowledge Management – eKNOW 2013*, Nice (pp. 172–177).

Becker, J., Clever, N., Holler, J., & Shitkova, M. (2013b). icebricks – Business process modeling on the basis of semantic standardization. In *Proceedings of the Design Science Research in Information Systems and Technologies (DESRIST) 2013*, Helsinki.

Berente, N., Vandenbosch, B., & Aubert, B. (2009). Information flows and business process integration. *Business Process Management Journal, 15*(1), 119–141.

Chen, R., & Scheer, A.-W. (1994). *Modellierung von Prozessketten mittels Petri-Netz-Theorie*. Saarbrücken.

Dehnert, J., & Rittgen, P. (2001). Relaxed soundness of business processes. In K. R. Dittrich, A. Geppert, & M. C. Norrie (Eds.), *Advanced Information Systems Engineering. 13th International Conference, CAiSE 2001 Interlaken, Switzerland, June 4–8, 2001 Proceedings* (pp. 157–170).

Delfmann, P., Herwig, S., & Lis, L. (2009). Unified enterprise knowledge representation with conceptual models – Capturing corporate language in naming conventions. In *30th International Conference on Information Systems (ICIS 2009)*. Phoenix, AZ.

Dumas, M., et al. (2013). *Fundamentals of business process management*. Heidelberg: Springer.

Hallerbach, A., Bauer, T., & Reichert, M. (2008). Modellierung und Darstellung von Prozessvarianten in PROVOP. In *Modellierung'08 Conference* (pp. 41–56).

Hallerbach, A., Bauer, T., & Reichert, M. (2009). Issues in modeling process variants with provop. In *BPM 2008 International Workshops* (pp. 56–67).

Holler, J. (2015). *Tool support for consultants in business process modeling projects. Design and evaluation of the business process modeling tool icebricks.*

Kindler, E. (2006). On the semantics of EPCs: Resolving the vicious circle. *Data and Knowledge Engineering, 56*(1), 23–40.

Kugeler, M. (2000). *Informationsmodellbasierte Organisationsgestaltung: Modellierungskonventionen und Referenzvorgehensmodell zur prozessorientierten Reorganisation*. Berlin: Logos-Verlag.

Langner, P., Schneider, C., & Wehler, J. (1998). Petri net based certification of event-driven process chains. In *19th International Conference on Application and Theory of Petri Nets and Other Models of Concurrency (ICATPN 2001)* (pp. 286–305).

Leymann, F., & Altenhuber, W. (1994). Managing business processes as an information resource. *IBM Systems Journal, 33*(2), 326–348.

Meise, V. (2001). *Ordnungsrahmen zur prozessorientierten Organisationsgestaltung. Modelle für das Management komplexer Reorganisationsprojekte*. Hamburg: University of Münster.

Mendling, J., Reijers, H. A., & Recker, J. (2010a). Activity labeling in process modeling: Empirical insights and recommendations. *Information Systems, 35*(4), 467–482.

Mendling, J., Reijers, H. A., & van der Aalst, W. M. P. (2010b). Seven process modeling guidelines (7PMG). *Information and Software Technology, 52*(2), 127–136.

Nüttgens, M., & Rump, F. J. (2002). Syntax und Semantik Ereignisgesteuerter Prozessketten (EPK). *Prozessorientierte Methoden und Werkzeuge für die Entwicklung von Informationssystemen, P-21*(6), 64–77.

Porter, M. E., & Millar, V. E. (1985). How information gives you competitive advantage. *Harvard Business Review, 63*(4), 149.

Rosemann, M. (1996). *Komplexitätsmanagement in Prozessmodellen: methodenspezifische Gestaltungsempfehlungen für die Informationsmodellierung* (p. 297). Wiesbaden: Gabler Verlag.

Scheer, A.-W. (1997). *Wirtschaftsinformatik – Referenzmodelle für industrielle Geschäftsprozesse* (7th ed.). Berlin: Springer.
Schütte, R., & Rotthowe, T. (1998). The guidelines of modeling – An approach to enhance the quality in information models. In T. W. Ling, S. Ram, & M.-L. Lee (Eds.), *Proceedings of the 17th International Conference on Conceptual Modeling* (pp. 240–254). Singapore: Springer.
Stachowiak, H. (1973). *Allgemeine Modelltheorie*. Wien: Springer.
van der Aalst, W. M. P. (1999). Formalization and verification of event-driven process chains. *Information and Software Technology, 41*(10), 639–650.
van der Aalst, W. M. P., & ter Hofstede, A. H. M. (2005). YAWL: Yet another workflow language. *Information Systems, 30*(4), 245–275.
Wynn, M. T., et al. (2005). Achieving a general, formal and decidable approach to the OR-join in workflow using reset nets. In G. Ciardo & P. Darondeau (Eds.), *Proceedings of the 26th International Conference on Application and Theory of Petri Nets and Other Models of Concurrency (ICATPN 2005)* (pp. 423–443). Berlin: Springer.

Jörg Becker is head of the Department of Information Systems of the University of Münster and of the European Research Center for Information Systems (ERCIS). He is Professor of Information Systems and directs the Chair for Information Systems and Information Management. He holds an honorary professorship at the National Research University—Higher School of Economics (NRU-HSE) in Moscow and is member of the North Rhine-Westphalian Academy of Sciences, Humanities and the Arts. His research interests cover Information Modelling including Reference Modelling, Hybrid Value Creation, Business Process Management, E-Government, and Retail Information Systems. Jörg has published in renowned outlets, including MIS Quarterly (MISQ), European Journal of Information Systems (EJIS), Business & Information Systems Engineering (BISE), Information Systems Frontiers (ISF), Information Systems Journal (ISJ), and Business Process Management Journal (BPMJ). He has authored and edited numerous books, including Retail Information Systems, Process Management, Modernizing Processes in Public Administrations, and Reference Modeling.

Nico Clever is a postdoctoral research assistant at the Chair for Information Systems and Information Management at the Department of Information Systems of the University of Münster. He received his Master's degree in Information Systems from the University of Münster. In his Ph.D. thesis, Nico covered the holistic design and application of the process modelling tool icebricks which is actively utilized in a number of practical consulting projects as well as further developed on an academic basis and applied in his teaching. Additional research interests lie in the areas of Compliance Management, Data Management, Business Intelligence, Software Engineering, and Test Management. Nico has presented and published his work at renowned conferences, including the European Conference on Information Systems (ECIS), Design Science Research in Information Systems and Technologies (DESRIST), and IEEE Conference on Business Informatics (CBI).

Justus Tillmann Holler is part of the European Research Institute for Information Systems (ERCIS) at the University of Muenster and consultant at the Prof. Becker GmbH with a focus on Business Process Management, Business Intelligence and ERP Implementation. Justus has conducted diverse studies in the area of BPM and ERP with extensive implementation and evaluation studies of web-based business process modelling tools in manufacturing and retail industry companies. He published in renowned conferences and books including the European Conference for Information Systems (ECIS).

Maria Neumann is a postdoctoral research assistant at the Chair for Information Systems and Information Management at the Department of Information Systems of the University of Münster and got her Ph.D. in the area of Business Process Management. Her research interests span a broad range of topics focusing largely on the design and development of business process modelling tools through application of usability engineering methods. Maria has scientific publications in international outlets and conference proceedings, including the European Conference on Information Systems (ECIS), Design Science Research in Information Systems and Technologies (DESRIST), and IEEE Conference on Business Informatics (CBI).

Why Are Process Variants Important in Process Monitoring? The Case of Zalando SE

Matthias Schrepfer, Matthias Kunze, Gunnar Obst, and Juliane Siegeris

Abstract

(a) **Situation faced**: Business process models serve various purposes. As precise documentations of an implemented business processes, they provide inputs with which to configure process monitoring systems, enabling the specification of monitoring points and metrics. However, complex business processes have a quantity of variants that can impede the activation of process monitoring. To mitigate this issue, we seek to reduce the number of process variants by performing behavioral analyses.

(b) **Action taken**: Variants of a business process originate from points in the process model where the control flow might diverge, such as at decision gateways and racing events. We systematically identify the underlying semantics to choose from a set of alternative paths and characterize the resulting variants. This effort offers the opportunity to reduce the variability in business processes that is due to modeling errors, inconsistent labeling, and duplicate or redundant configurations of these points.

(c) **Results achieved**: For a sub-process of an order-to-cash process from the e-commerce industry, we discovered 59,244 variants, of which only 360 variants lead to a successful continuation of the process. The remaining variants cover exception handling and customer interaction. While these variants do not lead to a successful outcome and might not qualify for the "happy path" of this process, they are crucial in terms of customer satisfaction and must be monitored and controlled. Using a set of methods (actions taken),

M. Schrepfer (✉) • M. Kunze • G. Obst
Zalando SE, Mollstr. 1, 10178 Berlin, Germany
e-mail: matthias.schrepfer@zalando.de; matthias.kunze@zalando.de; gunnar.obst@zalando.de

J. Siegeris
HTW Berlin University of Applied Sciences, Berlin, Germany
e-mail: juliane.siegeris@htw-berlin.de

J. vom Brocke, J. Mendling (eds.), *Business Process Management Cases*,
Management for Professionals, DOI 10.1007/978-3-319-58307-5_23

we reduced the number of variants to 11,000. These actions reduced overhead in the process and normalized decision labels, thereby significantly increasing the process model's quality.

(d) **Lessons learned**: We elaborate on the impact of variants on the configuration of a process monitoring system, and show how the number of model variants can be significantly reduced. Our analysis shows that the semantic quality of the process model increases as a result. This reduction effort involves a structured approach that considers all variants of a business process, rather than focusing only on the most frequent or most important cases.

1 Introduction

Business process management is an established discipline that is widely used in industry. Many companies focus on established methods to design, analyze, control, and optimize their business processes and to ensure high levels of customer satisfaction and close alignment with IT systems (cf. Hammer 2010). Rapidly growing multinational companies in the e-commerce sector in particular must overcome challenges in business process management in order to scale up their businesses and reach ambitious business goals, so business processes in this sector are largely automated. Setting up consistent and scalable process monitoring and process controlling helps firms to detect problems, derive remediating actions and to address these problems quickly.

1.1 Business Process Management at Zalando

Business process management found its entrance into Zalando in 2012, when the company set out to document its core processes in a structured way. Because of the company's rapid growth, we decided to develop and tailor to our needs our own ERP system, Zalando E-Commerce Operating System (ZEOS). For the requirements specification of this system and to ensure proper alignment between the business and IT, all departments involved contributed to the precise documentation of the relevant business processes using BPMN. Over time, increasing numbers of processes in Zalando's value chain were documented and integrated into the company's process landscape.

One year later, we began to use the documented business processes for operational tasks. We experimented with a self-developed process engine to automate our core order processes, which led eventually to the integration of an open source BPM engine and the first fully automated business process's going live early in 2014. Since then, we have continuously increased the automation of our processes.

We also found significant value in detecting anomalies in the execution of our processes, including non-automated and hard-coded behavior. We devised an approach that enables business processes to be monitored using real-time event data that are provided from all IT systems involved. Using a highly scalable architecture, we can monitor hundreds of thousands of orders per day and provide early warnings and near real-time detection of anomalies for our end-to-end core processes. The data created remains available for ex-post analysis and as a basis for continuous improvement.

BPM has become one of the driving forces and key factors of success in Zalando's endeavor to become a widely used platform that connects people with fashion beyond its core business.

1.2 The Role of Process Monitoring

Enabling process monitoring requires that process models contain all of the business logic required by underlying business scenarios and that they consider processes across the IT landscape and organizational boundaries. Doing so typically results in a large number of detailed and complex process models that capture all possible cases. While the creation of models of high syntactic and semantic quality is challenging in practice, it is required for process monitoring and it bridges the gap between business and IT, so it builds the basis for process execution, compliance checking, and continuous improvement.

Effective process monitoring ensures that business goals are met by continuously checking the state of and performance of business processes (Dumas et al. 2013). This monitoring includes detecting process problems and raising warnings and alarms when there are problems or deviations. While this monitoring may sound straightforward given detailed process models, it is subject to several constraints in practice. What makes process monitoring so complicated?

To detect and resolve problems with a business process rapidly, all process instances must be monitored. In the e-commerce setting of a large organization, where core processes are highly automated and executed many times, the number of process instances quickly rises beyond 100,000 in 24 h. It is critical that the productive and efficient operation of every one of this instances persists in a highly competitive environment, which is already a technical challenge in terms of the scalability of the monitoring system.

Furthermore, the more complex the process, the more complex the process monitoring because all process variants must be treated separately. Here, the term *process variant* refers to all possible paths in a process model that must be monitored (Dumas et al. 2013). Different process paths are triggered by parameters like the shipping or payment method chosen. Each parameter yields an individual process flow in such a way that individual values, such as those for payment methods like credit card and invoice, are handled properly. Business and IT users must know whether all of these flows are executed properly in order to ensure conformance with the process. However, each variant that is monitored should be treated separately, which results in the need for an enormous effort to set up the monitoring system.

The lower the number of process variants in a process, the easier its activation. In this chapter, we present approaches to analyzing the parameters that trigger process variants in an effort to reduce the number of process variants. By analyzing process variants, we also show opportunities to increase the quality of process models from a semantic point of view. Our goal is to reduce the effort in and increase the efficiency of activating process monitoring.

2 Situation Faced

We illustrate our approach using part of an order-to-cash process, a real-world example depicted in Fig. 1. The part of the process we investigate starts with the placement of a customer order and ends with the decision concerning to which warehouse the shipment of the ordered goods is assigned. The business process,

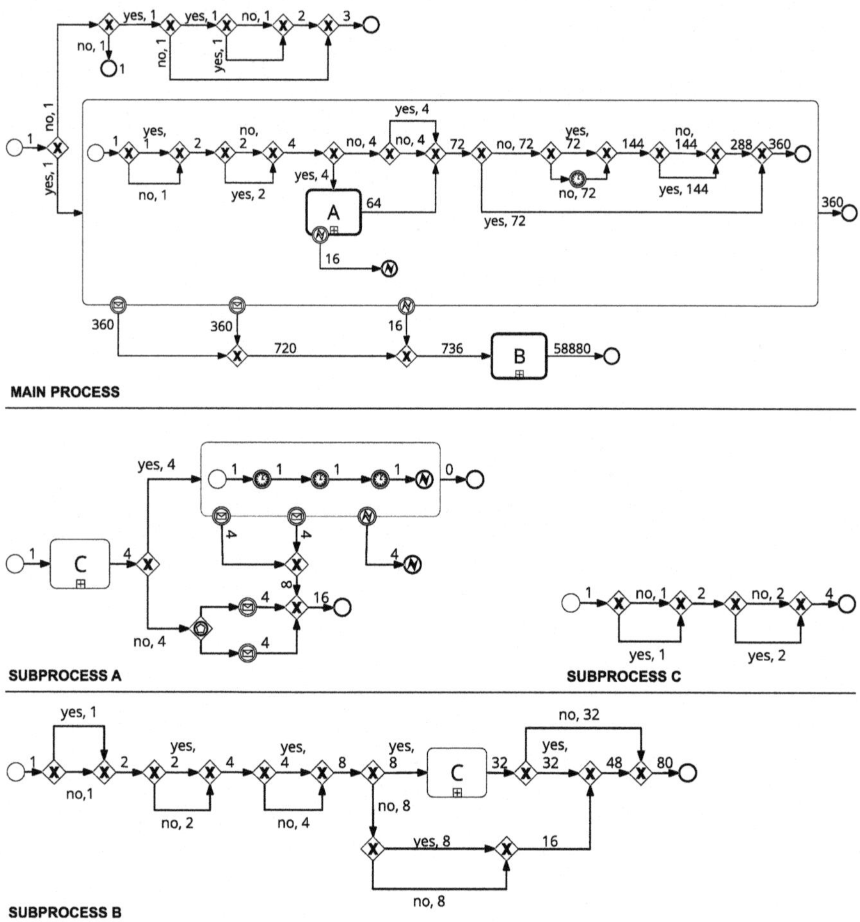

Fig. 1 Order-to-cash main process and subprocesses: The process model shows only the branching structure for our order-to-cash process, as we removed activities and labels. We annotated control flow edges with the number of variants that can pass through these points in the process model

modeled using BPMN, consists of one parent process and three subprocesses. The original models consist of 20–100 elements and contain both basic and advanced process modeling structures, such as error-handling, process hierarchy, and attached boundary events. In our case, all process steps are executed sequentially; that is, the business process contains no concurrency.

In Sect. 3.2, we discuss in greater detail how the number of process variants—59,244—were computed. Subprocess B (Fig. 1) can be initiated by 736 variants, and the subprocess itself creates 80 variants as continuations of each of the incoming variants. Hence, the number of variants multiplies when subprocesses are included, leading to 58,880 variants after the subprocess is completed.

Along the process, we established several measurement points for which our monitoring system records the time and process data. Our monitoring solution allows us to compute the time period between two measuring points continuously to compare these metrics with threshold values, and to visualize the current and historic performance of a business processes. If the threshold value for a given metric is exceeded for a certain number of instances, the system notifies affected personnel.

As we show in the remainder of this chapter, the number of variants is an upper bound that can be significantly reduced.

3 Action Taken

The methods presented in this chapter refer to the discovery of process variants in business process models. The literature advocates two approaches: The multi-model approach uses a number of related process models to capture variants, typically as a result of manipulating one central reference model (Li et al. 2011; Sakr et al. 2011), while the single-model approach consolidates all possible variants into one process model that offers different configurations for a particular variant (Hallerbach et al. 2010; Rosemann and van der Aalst 2007). In the second approach, some gateways are marked as configuration points, where different variants follow different branches. Still, in both cases, a process variant is a complete business process model that includes control-flow branching structures.

In this chapter, variants are understood as distinct sequences of activities and events, similar to the notion of traces in process mining (cf. Dumas et al. 2013; van der Aalst 2011). Process mining analyzes the logs of business process executions and strives to define process models by reverse-engineering ordering relationships between activities and detecting where a path in a process might diverge. In contrast to process mining, our approach does not use process logs as the basis on which to generate a process model but starts with the model itself to reveal all possible variants. The number of variants is related to the cyclomatic number of programs (McCabe 1976; Myers 1977). However, in our case, iterations of the same process model fragment are also considered individual variants.

Based on the variants discovered, this work seeks to improve the quality of a process model by reducing the number of variants and increasing the consistency within it. Model quality has been the focus of a wide range of research, as an overview of the factors that affect process models' quality shows (Mendling et al. 2009). Our primary focus is on the process models' semantic and pragmatic quality (Reijers et al. 2010).

One particular issue that has not been addressed in the literature is the consistency of the configuration of points in business process models, where process execution diverges. We refer to these points as *trigger parameters for variants of a process model*. For instance, if two distinct exclusive-choice gateways model the same decision, they should be labeled identically. The following sections present our approach to discovering, characterizing, and reducing process variants and to normalizing choices within a process model.

Other proposals related to increasing the quality of process models include Mendling's Seven Process Modeling Guidelines (Mendling et al. 2010), which introduces rules based on empirical research to keep process models simple, consistent, and easily comprehensible. While these guidelines can improve a single model and reduce its cognitive complexity, refactoring of process models (Weber and Reichert 2008) strives to increase the consistency among several models in a collection, such as through consistent labeling of activities across all models. Weber and Reichert (2008) use of the term *variants* uses a different meaning than we use here.

Many of these approaches to increasing process models' quality had already been applied when our business processes were modeled, such as the labeling of objects and the extraction and linking of common subprocesses. Figure 1 illustrates the linking of processes, subprocess C is linked to processes A and B. However, these approaches do not change the semantics of a business process model but their organization, so they have no impact on a process model's number of variants.

3.1 Variants in Business Processes

In contrast to the related work discussed in the previous section, where process variants refer to different versions of a complete business process model, we define a process variant as a class of process instances:

> A **process variant** is a complete and unique sequence of activities, events, and decisions carried out in compliance with a business process model. Every process instance of this model belongs to exactly one process variant.

Zalando's order-to-cash process is executed among a number of independent and distributed software systems, each of which adds fragments and execution alternatives to the process. Our definition of a business process variant embraces this aspect of distributed IT environments and captures one variant of the overall process as a particular ordering scenario. Variants must be complete with regard to the start and end of the process.

3.2 Identification of Process Variants

Having defined the term *process variant*, we ask how variants can be identified. Business process mining offers a straightforward solution to the identification of unique variants—examining a process log—but in our scenario, such a log is not available, as our goal is to set up a monitoring solution prior to the rollout of a business process. Even so, it is possible to derive process variants from a process model if it is normative and sufficiently detailed, that is, if it is on an executable level. Essentially, all model constructs that yield alternative outcomes lead to a set of process variants such that each alternative adds another process variant. In the case of BPMN, such constructs can include exclusive gateways and interrupting boundary events.

Our approach to computing the number of variants in a process model is based on Sadiq and Orlowska (2000), who present an approach to identifying behavioral anomalies in sequential process models by iteratively eliminating paths in the model that are correct. For instance, a set of *n* alternative paths that are split and joined in a well-structured fashion are reduced to a single path. If the remaining model only contains single paths, then the original model was correct. Models that show deadlocks or lack of synchronization cannot be reduced completely.

In our case, the process models underwent a verification process a priori, so they are considered to be correct, but we reused the iterative reduction technique to identify variants in process models. For every reduction, we counted the number of variants that were created by the reduced fragment. Given the aforementioned set of alternatives, we would infer *n* variants and then annotate the number of variants to the outgoing control flow sequence. The number of variants is the input for the next fragment to be reduced. Subprocess C in Fig. 1, shows two fragments, each with two alternatives, which results in an overall count of four variants. Similarly, hierarchical decomposition in process models—that is, the use of subprocesses—adds significantly to the number of the business process's variants.

This method for deriving process variants is applicable only with well-structured, sequential process models (van der Aalst et al. 2002). Furthermore, the interwoven execution of parallel paths quickly explodes the number of process variants (Valmari 1998). In our case, the prerequisites of having well-structured models and sequential execution of activities apply because all parts of the end-to-end business process are carried out sequentially by different IT systems.

3.3 Characterizing Process Variants

A small number of process variants—perhaps around 500—is not problematic for process monitoring, as not every activity, event, or decision is tracked by a monitoring system. In our example, we computed the number of variants according to the method described above for the first part of our end-to-end business process, which resulted in 59,244 process variants, a number that becomes unmanageable if our monitoring system is configured manually. The high number of variants was not expected, but it confirmed our initial concerns about process complexity.

As shown in Fig. 1, only 360 variants are successful—that is, only 360 lead to the order-to-cash process's continuing to the next subprocess—which is often referred to as "the happy path." Comparing this number with the overall number of variants shows that most variants address deviations from the happy path, and a semantic analysis shows that almost all other variants cover parts of the process for error-handling and customer interaction, such as order cancellations triggered by customers.

3.4 Reducing Process Variants

With 59,244 process variants for only part of an end-to-end business process, we sought to determine why variants are triggered. To this end, one goal was to remove variants whenever possible to ease process monitoring. Such a large number of variants may also be a sign of the potential to increase the quality of our process model. In this section, we report on the approaches to reducing variants that we identified by studying the process model and related information.

3.4.1 Zero Variants

One of the first reasons that process variants are triggered is paths in the process model that can never occur, which we call *zero variants*. Although we reviewed all of our process models prior to the variant analysis, our review was flawed from a semantic point of view. An example from subprocess B (Fig. 1, and shown in detail in Fig. 2) internally handles an error before escalating that error to the parent scope.

The process path identified by the outgoing blank end event of the subprocess is unreachable because the subprocess always terminates with an error event. An analysis of this path indicates that it increases the effort required in understanding the model and may lead to misinterpretations. Hence, all paths with zero variants must be refactored to increase model quality.

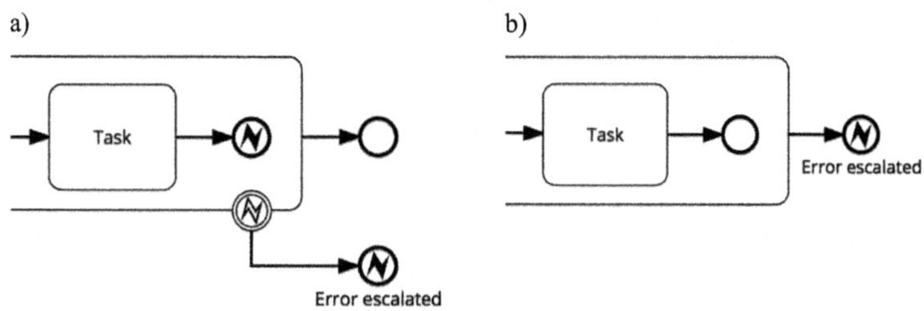

Fig. 2 Zero variants. (**a**) Original model (**b**) Refactored model

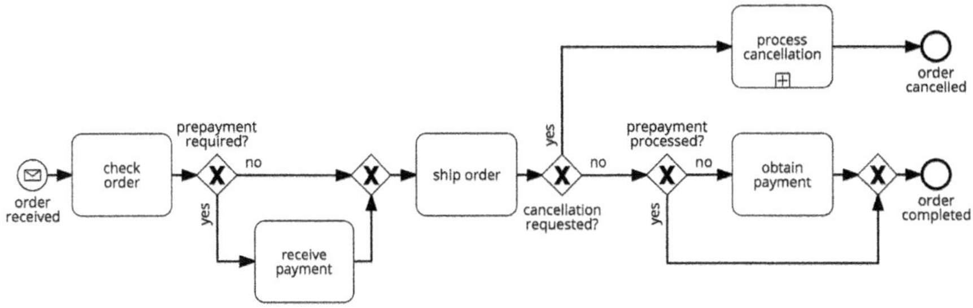

Fig. 3 Non-normalized decision

3.4.2 Duplicate Variants

The semantic analysis of process models—that is, the matching of model elements like activities, events, and decisions to their counterpart in our business—revealed a second opportunity to improve the quality of the process model and reduce the number of variants. Choices from among a set of alternatives in the process models are frequently not made completely independently; that is, the choice made at one point may depend on a choice made earlier in the course of executing the process. Figure 3 illustrates this factor with a fictitious example.

The business process shown in Fig. 3 contains a number of decisions. Two of them, *prepayment required* and *prepayment processed*, refer to the point at which the payment for an order is carried out. If the customer chose a form of prepayment, payment will be carried out before the order is shipped, but if the customer did not choose prepayment, the payment must be obtained after the order is shipped.

Looking only at the model, the process produces six variants, one for each combination of alternative paths. Taking into account the actual implementation of these decisions, we discovered that both decisions regarding payment are based on the customer's chosen method of payment. From a set of payment methods, one part qualifies for prepayment, whereas the remaining part does not. Hence, these two decisions are based on the same semantic context, so there are actually only four variants in the process model.

We introduce *trigger parameters*, *configuration parameters*, and methods to identify such dependencies and resolve them.

A **configuration parameter** (CP) is a variation dimension—that is, a set of values that denote alternatives.

A **trigger parameter** (TP) denotes a variation point in the process model that uses CPs that specify how to choose from among alternatives.

TPs characterize variants based on either conditions, such as at an XOR gateway, or based on events, such as at attached intermediate boundary message events, so they correlate process variants with elements of the process model. To identify duplicates, all TPs are listed separately with unique IDs, the condition of a gateway or the name of the event, and the process in which it is contained. Then a number of checks are carried out to identify duplicate and redundant TPs, duplicate trigger configurations, and merging of events.

3.4.3 Duplicate Trigger Parameters

Duplicate labels of TPs are identified and marked, but corresponding points in the model are not yet refactored, as there is a chance of finding replicas of the TP, and duplicate labels do not necessarily imply duplicates, as the CPs for these TPs must also coincide.

Currently, the duplicate detection uses only a simple string comparison, and language processing is done by a domain expert to identify duplicates. In the future, natural language processing could assist (cf. Leopold 2013). A second quality check focuses on labels assigned to TPs—that is, their corresponding conditions and event names. TPs' labels should comply with a style that ensures that readers can quickly comprehend the semantic information. As a labeling style, we focus on a best-practice approach. See, for instance, Mendling et al. (2010):

for events: object + past perfect verb

for gateways: a question attached to the gateway; condition expressions must be an answer to the question stated at the corresponding gateway; both question and answers are brief and precise.

The result of these checks is stored along with the specification of TPs. Labels that violate these standards are marked for refactoring. However, refactoring labels is still postponed because of the need for additional checks. Moreover, not all labels may be refactored, as some are used in a close business-IT alignment. Thus, some labels, particularly event names, are also used in the implementation of IT systems and are used for monitoring. Hence, best practices may be neglected to keep models and implementations in sync.

3.4.4 Redundant Trigger Parameters

The next check focusses on TPs that can be eliminated, which will decrease the number of variants. The check determines whether a process model can be refactored in such a way that the TP is eliminated without changing the process semantics, as otherwise the process logic would change. This task is performed by process experts and domain experts to ensure consistency. A reduction in the number of TPs improves the model's comprehensibility and increases its quality.

Figure 4, which shows an excerpt of our example process, illustrates the check for redundant TPs, with one fragment showing a split XOR-gateway that corresponds to a TP. Assuming that only a single variant is provided as input, there will be two variants—one that includes the timer event and one that does not. The question addressed at the split gateway and the condition at the intermediate timer event are similar, so from a semantic point of view, the condition is checked twice: If the time has not progressed far enough, the process will wait for it using a timer event. An equivalent logic is also shown in Fig. 4, where only the

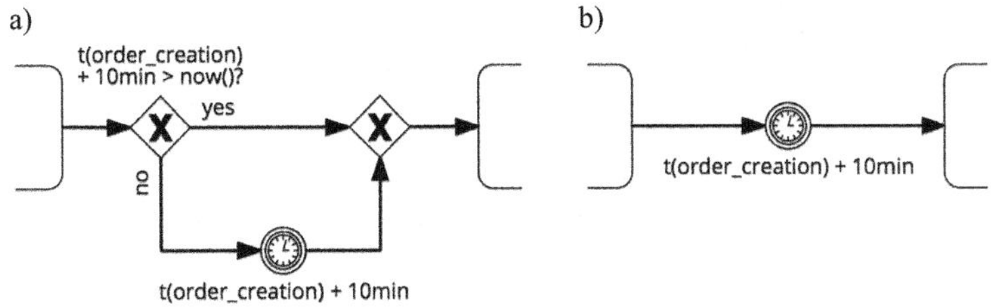

Fig. 4 Redundant trigger parameters. (**a**) Original model (**b**) Refactored model

intermediate timer event is used. The TP is avoided, reducing the complexity of the model and eliminating another variant.

3.4.5 Duplicate Trigger Configurations

Identification and documentation of duplicate and redundant TPs are the first steps toward understanding why variants occur. Information on TPs already supports the analysis of variants, and actions can be derived from the analysis results that can lead to removal of TPs and, consequently, decrease the number of process variants and increase the model's quality.

The next step toward reducing process variants is analysis of CPs, which are used to split up a business context, such as payment methods in the order-handling process. CPs are bound to TPs by assigning information about the business context. A TP that is linked to a specific process model element determines the process' behavior based on the information from a CP.

In the example shown in Fig. 3, the decision concerning which path is chosen is based on the customer's choice of a payment method for two out of three gateways. However, the information in the process model alone is not sufficient to determine whether these decisions are made under identical conditions. In practice "yes" and "no" do not determine which path to choose; instead, the actual selection of the payment method is required. In the future, it could payment methods that require both a prepayment before and a final payment after the shipment could be possible, but here CPs come into play, as they bind the actual conditions of TPs to values from a business context. For each CP, we store a unique ID, its name, and all of its unique values.

We distinguish among three types of CPs, which indicate how the value of the parameters is determined.

design-time CP: The parameter is static; for example it is used to configure an IT system.

a priori run-time CP: The parameter is determined at the creation of a process instance and does not change; for example, it is based on the received order that triggered a process instance.

live run-time CP: The parameter is determined during the run of the process instance; for example, it is the outcome of a human task or a value that is computed by an IT system.

These types of CPs are closely related to process variants. (See Sect. 3, where one variant is comprised of a complex model, including decisions.) Here, the *design-time CP* and *a priori run-time CP* can be used to exclude certain variants (in our definition) from the process model when a process is instantiated. *Design-time CPs* are comparable to configuration points in complex variant definitions.

In our example, the CP "payment method" consists of the values credit card, Paypal, invoice, and cash-on-delivery; the first two options are prepayment options, and the last two are payments after shipping. The type of CP is *a priori run-time* because it is based on the customer's choice of a payment method recorded in the incoming order. The CP is used for the TP of two gateways in the process model of Fig. 3.

The binding of a CP's values to the conditions of the outgoing paths of the gateway bridges the gap between domain knowledge, that is, the actual process execution and TPs in process models. Using this connection, we can identify TPs that use the same CPs. In combination with the search for duplicate TPs, we can normalize the process model by making decisions that are identical or similar consistent in their labelling.

First, we verify that all duplicate TPs are actually duplicates, that is, that they use the same CP values for the decision. If this is not the case, the labels in our model are ambiguous, which should be resolved by renaming one or both of the TPs in the model. Duplicate TPs with identical CP values are recorded as actual duplicates on the list of variants and are later refactored manually.

Second, we analyze TPs that have the same CP values. If a number of choices with semantically identical TPs and CPs occur in one process instance—that is, if they lie on a common path in a process model without concurrency—then a decision for one choice determines the decision in other choices, which reduces the number of variants.

3.4.6 Merging of Events

During our analysis of the process model, we found another opportunity to reduce the number of process variants. In some cases, variants were triggered by two or more message-receive events that indicated the same business trigger but differed in the data payload. Such variants can be treated as a single instance as long as some constraints are met:

All events must have the **same** scope; for example, boundary events are attached to the same scope.

The control flow of all events must be merged **directly** succeeding the message events.

These constraints ensure that different events, such as different messages, do not have different effects on the state of the business process. The decision concerning whether events can be merged must be made by domain experts, who must agree in terms of whether some events cannot be distinguished later on in the monitoring system. If they do not agree, the monitoring system must be configured in such a way that all events are monitored.

4 Results Achieved

We have presented several approaches to decreasing the number of process variants. We computed the number of variants for the first part of our end-to-end business process as 59,244, an unmanageable number if the monitoring system is configured manually.

As Fig. 1 shows, only 360 variants are successful—that is, only 360 lead to the continuation of the order-to-cash process. Comparing this number with the overall number of variants demonstrates that most variants address deviations from this "happy path." A semantic analysis shows that almost all other variants cover parts of the process for error-handling and customer interactions, such as order cancellations triggered by customers.

With the help of these approaches, we reduced the number of variants to 11,000. Because of the process hierarchy, the number of variants on the happy path dropped from 360 down to 120, significantly easing monitoring. This immense reduction was triggered by optimizing only two local areas, and the changes applied to the process model also reduced overhead, normalized decision labels, and increased the quality of our process model significantly.

4.1 Handling Zero Variants

Refactoring took place in the handling of "zero variants" and was performed without changing the process semantics from a business point of view. For instance, the quality of the process model in Fig. 2b increased without changing the number of variants. However, such may not be the case for process models that stem from other scenarios. We tested the approach presented here, and for several models the number of variants did change, even increasing in some situations, such as when the model contained boundary events. Hence, the number of variants must be computed again after model refactoring.

4.2 Handling Duplicate Trigger Parameters

Twenty-three duplicate TPs were detected in the first part of the order-to-cash process. An evaluation of these TPs for best-practice standards revealed that only four complied with best-practice naming standards, a very low success rate (~17%). Another 5 of the remaining 19 TPs could not be renamed because of their reuse in IT systems (~22%). The last 14 TPs (~61%) were adjusted according to best-practice naming standards.

4.3 Redundant Trigger Parameters

Although process models are checked for quality, TPs may be modeled in a redundant way, so our approach detects these triggers and applies remediation. The number of variants that are due to TPs can multiply throughout the process, such as when there are subprocesses, so saving even one variant locally can reduce the global number of variants significantly.

In fact, using our approach to eliminating redundant TPs decreased the number of variants to approximately 36,000, a 39.3% reduction. We had not been aware that such large reductions could be achieved in practice, but the effect is so large because the removal of a single TP may affect the complete process hierarchy. When processes or parts of processes are scoped by boundary events, the decrease in local variants might also significantly decrease variants on a global scale, as our example shows.

4.4 Duplicate Trigger Configurations

Variants are created based on TPs, so the evaluation of process variants also includes determining the configuration of those TPs, revealing the underlying conditions. Upon applying our approach, we found two TPs tagged with "gift voucher" and "gift voucher bought," suggesting a potential duplicate. However, the values of the corresponding CPs revealed that the first one addressed the payment of an order using a gift voucher, whereas the second one incorporated the purchase of a gift voucher. This example highlights the importance of verifying duplicates using CPs.

In order to refactor the process model, one must determine why the same business context, that is, the set of CPs, is applied to TPs with different labels. In our case, the main reasons were errors in process models and a gap or mismatch between modeling and interpreting business information. Process experts and domain experts clarified how to remediate this discrepancy by deciding upon the TP and updating the label of the other to match the context if necessary. Then duplicate TP entries can safely be eliminated, which reduces the number of variants.

Another example is that of TPs tagged with "articles exist" and "article exists." The first conveys the impression that *all* articles must be available, whereas the second suggests only *one* article was sufficient. However, consulting domain experts and CPs led to the decision that the two TPs are identical, and one was renamed accordingly.

Out of the 23 TPs identified initially, 4 were removed because of duplicate TPs or duplicate CPs, which increased the consistency and reduced the ambiguity of the process model. The labels now better fit the domain knowledge. Even more important is that readers of the process model can determine which domain information is used in TPs and how variants are triggered. The semantic binding helped to increase the process model's quality significantly, even though the number of variants was not decreased in the real-world example for this approach.

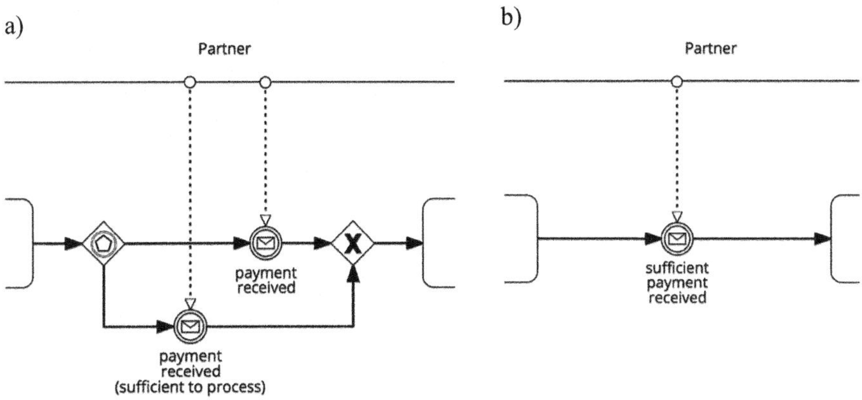

Fig. 5 Merging of events. (**a**) Original model (**b**) Refactored model

4.5 Merging Events

With regard to process monitoring, it is reasonable to merge events that fulfill the requirements stated in Sect. 3. In Fig. 5, we identified two variants that were triggered by two message events, respectively, of which only one is processed according to the event-based gateway that precedes these events. Both events indicate an incoming payment, but subtle differences led to their distinction in the model. After the issue was disclosed following the conditions above, domain experts confirmed that it was possible to merge the events for the purpose of monitoring. The original model was not changed in this case, and the refactored model is used only to configure the monitoring solution. This approach has the disadvantage of requiring that two models are in synchronization. Still, in many cases, the benefit of reducing variants outweighs the cost of maintaining two models.

5 Lessons Learned

We introduced an approach to characterizing and reducing variants in business process models based on the notion of TPs and CPs that provide insight into the data and logic that is applied when control flow diverges within the process model. Here we summarize our experiences and the insights gained during our study.

No Exclusion of Variants Implementing monitoring solutions often requires focusing first on important parts of a business process. Although we may not monitor all variants of a process, we cannot exclude any part of the process model from monitoring a priori. Even domain experts typically do not know which variants are infrequent without a proper throughput analysis, so it is virtually impossible to identify the most important parts upfront. The only chance is to enable monitoring in such a way that monitoring considers all variants. If variants are excluded from monitoring, experience has shown that process problems are detected late, if at all. One should carefully judge whether and why to exclude variants from monitoring.

Bias for the Happy Path In process analyses it is common to concentrate on the happy path first, but it is not sufficient to just focus on the most common and expected behavior if complete monitoring of a process is the goal; 100% of the process variants must be monitored. One important observation we made during the identification of process variants is that happy paths typically contain only a minor portion of all variants, so it is likely that most of the process errors or problems are ignored in the happy path, although they must be considered as well.

Automation for Analyses Currently, all of our approaches are based on manual work. Because of the manual effort and likelihood of errors, we sought to reduce the manual work in favor of automated solutions. For instance, we researched the automatic discovery of variants and focused on recommendations for reducing variants. We also considered concurrent activities on different process paths. Consequently, different orderings of interwoven activities must not be considered as distinct variants if they follow along the same paths in the process model. This conclusion is contrary to the notion of process variants that originate from process-mining scenarios, which has also been applied here.

High Number of Process Variants We did not expect such a high number of variants from applying our approaches to the first process, but they confirmed our initial concerns of process complexity. We used several process models to verify our approaches, and in all situations the final number of process variants was surprisingly high. Even domain experts and model experts were surprised, but they ultimately understood why reducing the number of variants is needed in order to activate process-monitoring solutions quickly and efficiently.

References

Dumas, M., La Rosa, M., Mendling, J., & Reijers, H. (2013). *Fundamentals of business process management*. Berlin: Springer.

Hallerbach, A., Bauer, T., & Reichert, M. (2010). Capturing variability in business process models: The provop approach. *Journal of Software Maintenance, 22*(6–7), 519–546.

Hammer, M. (2010). What is business process management? In *Handbook on business process management: Introduction, methods and information systems* (Vol. 1, pp. 3–16). Berlin: Springer.

Leopold, H. (2013). *Natural language in business process models – Theoretical foundations, techniques, and applications*. Lecture notes in business information processing (Vol. 168). Berlin: Springer.
Li, C., Reichert, M., & Wombacher, A. (2011). Mining business process variants: Challenges, scenarios, algorithms. *Data Knowledge Engineering, 70*(5), 409–434.
McCabe, T. (1976). A complexity measure. *IEEE Transactions on Software Engineering, 2*(4), 308–320.
Mendling, J., Recker, J., & Reijers, A. (2009). *Process modeling quality: A framework and research agenda* (BPM Center Report, BPM-09-02).
Mendling, J., Reijers, H., & van der Aalst, W. (2010). Seven process modeling guidelines (7PMG). *Information and Software Technology, 52*(2), 127–136.
Myers, G. (1977). An extension to the cyclomatic measure of program complexity. *SIGPLAN Notices, 12*(10), 61–64.
Reijers, H., Mendling, J., & Recker, J. (2010). Business process quality management. In *Handbook on business process management* (1st ed., Vol. 1, pp. 167–185). Berlin: Springer.
Rosemann, M., & van der Aalst, W. (2007). A configurable reference modelling language. *Information Systems, 32*(1), 1–23.
Sadiq, W., & Orlowska, M. (2000). Analyzing process models using graph reduction techniques. *Information Systems, 25*(2), 117–134.
Sakr, S., Pascalau, E., Awad, A., & Weske, M. (2011). Partial process models to manage business process variants. *International Journal of Business Process Integration and Management (IJBPIM), 6*(2), 20.
Valmari, A. (1998). The state explosion problem. In *Lectures on petri nets I: Basic models, advances in petri nets*. Lecture notes in computer science (Vol. 1491, pp. 429–528). Berlin: Springer.
van der Aalst, W. (2011). *Process mining – Discovery, conformance and enhancement of business processes*. Heidelberg: Springer.
van der Aalst, W., Hirnschall, A., & Verbeek, H. (2002). An alternative way to analyze workflow graphs. In *Advanced information systems engineering*. Lecture notes in computer science (Vol. 2348, pp. 535–552). Berlin: Springer.
Weber, B., & Reichert, M. (2008). Refactoring process models in large process repositories. In *Advanced information systems engineering*. Lecture notes in computer science (Vol. 5074, pp. 124–139). Berlin: Springer.

Matthias Schrepfer is a Senior Business Process Manager and Business Process Consultant in the Business Excellence team at Zalando SE. He drives initiatives to ensure reliable and superior performance of Zalando's operational business processes. Matthias is leading cross-departmental projects that apply continuous improvement methodologies to sustain and optimize business process performance. Besides that, he develops and adapts methodologies tailored towards specific goal and project scenarios within Zalando. Prior to his focus on operational excellence, he developed products and methodologies for business process monitoring at Zalando. Matthias implemented and established tools that monitor the process performance of core business processes in real time. This included the implementation of alerting capabilities and troubleshooting features to enable immediate impact detection and resolution. All tools were tailored for both business as well as technical teams. Matthias enabled these teams to effectively control and manage their business processes.

Matthias Kunze is a business process manager and business process consultant in the Business Excellence team at Zalando SE. The team is ensuring the reliable performance of Zalando's operations and business continuity, and enables stakeholders within Zalando to effectively understand, control, and manage their business processes. Before joining Zalando in 2015, he was a student, research associate, and postdoctoral researcher at the Hasso Plattner Institute in Potsdam. Besides his contributions to many practical aspects of BPM, his research work focussed on the behavioural analysis of business process models. Matthias Kunze received his PhD in 2013 for his dissertation on "Searching Business Process Models by Example". Together with Mathias Weske he published the textbook "Behavioural Models—From Modelling Finite Automata to Analysing Business Processes" in 2016.

Gunnar Obst is a passionated p-manager—all about processes, projects and (software) product development. After passing his diploma as business engineer he worked now for over 15 years in positions, where he connected business- and technology-stakeholders. At Zalando he worked over 6 years in the technology department heading different positions. Starting as responsible for the standard enterprise-resource-planning system Zalando used that days. After building a team of product-, process- and support-manager around the system, he drove the software-development of the own created ERP system ZEOS (Zalando E-Commerce-Operating-System)—full responsible for the wholesale part. Bringing the system live and handed it over to product management, he started to create a central team for process management within the technology department. This includes building up a process monitoring and anomaly detection system. After introducing "Radical Agility" in Zalando Tech, he worked as Delivery Lead Platform Excellence to ensure, the Fashion Platform work as expected.

Juliane Siegeris is a full professor in the school of computing, communication and business of the Hochschule für Technik und Wirtschaft (University of Applied Science) Berlin, Germany. She is head of the program computer science and business administration. Her main research interests are in business process modeling with a focus on correctness criteria. After her PhD "A Methodology for Workflow Modeling—from business process modeling towards sound workflow specification" she worked as business analyst at the Fraunhofer Institute for Software and System Engineering and as process manager at gematik. There she led the installment of a process map for the new process organization.

Adoption of RFID Technology: The Case of Adler—A European Fashion Retail Company

Roland Leitz, Andreas Solti, Alexander Weinhard, and Jan Mendling

Abstract

(a) **Situation faced**: Adler Modemärkte AG (Adler hereafter) is a fashion retailer that operates mainly in the German-speaking countries. At the beginning of the twenty-first century, first movers in the fashion retail sector began to adopt RFID technology. Adler monitored this new technology and decided to adopt it in 2010, even though it was not sure at that stage whether its use would be profitable. However, Adler hoped to improve process efficiency and effectiveness in the long run to increase customer satisfaction through faster checkout. Moreover, the company expected that RFID technology would help to prevent theft, and to provide better visibility of inventory.

(b) **Action taken**: Careful planning is required if the goals and promises of RFID are to be achieved. With the help of a consultancy, Adler managed the adoption of RFID as a project that spanned 2 years. The overall concept was first sketched and designed, followed by selection of a suitable provider for the required hardware and tag supply. Next, the concept was realized and prepared for rollout before employee training was provided and the new technology was rolled out in more than 170 stores.

(c) **Results achieved**: Most of the project's goals were achieved. Inventory accuracy and transparency of the flow of items contributed to an increase in

R. Leitz
Adler Modemärkte AG, Haibach, Germany
e-mail: roland.leitz@adler.de

A. Solti (✉) • J. Mendling
Wirtschaftsuniversität Wien, Wien, Austria
e-mail: solti@ai.wu.ac.at; jan.mendling@wu.ac.at

A. Weinhard
Universität Würzburg, Würzburg, Germany
e-mail: alexander.weinhard@uni-wuerzburg.de

J. vom Brocke, J. Mendling (eds.), *Business Process Management Cases*,
Management for Professionals, DOI 10.1007/978-3-319-58307-5_24

sales. RFID also improved the follow-up procurement of items, resulting in additional increase in sales. The efficiency of in-store processes was improved through faster item registration, and the speed of the customer payment process at the point of sale was significantly improved, thanks to parallel scanning by RFID-enabled cash desks. Finally, retail shrinkage was reduced.

(d) **Lessons learned**: Careful planning is required when conducting large improvement projects, including delegating responsibilities, as consultancy companies are specialized and experienced in managing such transition projects; doing an early check on the feasibility of process improvement projects; waiting for the right moment to conduct the project; and considering the project's critical risks and people's sensitivities.

1 Introduction

Adler Modemärkte AG (Adler hereafter) is one of the leading textile retail chains in Germany and one of the largest. At the end of 2015, the group operated 177 stores, 153 of which were in Germany, 21 were in Austria, 2 were in Luxembourg, and 1 was in Switzerland. With more than 4000 employees, Adler focuses on large stores with spacious sales floors, wide aisles, and spacious fitting rooms and rest areas. The company sells an average of around 27 million items per year. The company also operates an online shop at www.adlermode.com.

Adler's management first considered radio frequency identification (RFID) technologies in 2002, when they envisioned migrating to the novel and improved processes that advocates of RFID technology promised (Chappell et al. 2003). However, since preliminary estimations of the costs entailed in transitioning were high, the company's management put the idea on hold until 2005 when, encouraged by some early success stories, the company reconsidered the idea. Adler conducted a thorough feasibility analysis of a shift to the RFID technology, but the costs of equipping all of its products with RFID tags still outweighed the expected gains with respect to process optimization. The idea needed more time.

In 2009, after some changes in the company's management, Adler re-evaluated the issue (Adler Modemärkte AG 2015, p. 11). The new management recognized the potential of RFID to provide benefits like highly transparent logistical processes, improved in-store replenishment, and more effective electronic article surveillance (EAS) (Thiesse et al. 2009). As increasing numbers of the company's competitors transitioned to radio frequency technology for the purpose of source tagging and theft prevention and there was a dramatic drop in the cost of tagging items with RFID labels, the visionary ideas from 2002 finally became practicable in 2010. Changes in the company's infrastructure, such as replacing the exit gates, were overdue to improve theft prevention, so management decided to use the opportunity to make a full transition to RFID technology. In 2012 Adler invested roughly 3.4 million euros in its RFID project (Adler Modemärkte AG 2013, p. 39).

2 Situation Faced

The adoption of RFID technology at Adler was driven less by the need to solve problems than by the potential benefits of the new technology. We use the Business Process Management (BPM) Context Framework developed by vom Brocke et al. (2016) to describe the situation the company faced in Table 1.

The Goal Dimension Even though RFID is seen as an innovative technology, Adler's main goal was to improve its existing processes. Distinguishing between articles on the sales floor and articles in the stockroom had not been feasible because tracking transitions between the two areas would be slow and cumbersome if employees had to scan every item brought back and forth. Consequently, there was always a high risk that popular sizes and colors of high-volume articles were not available on the shelves, even though they were in stock. With an average of 70,000 items per store, Adler faced the potential of lost revenue (Adler Modemärkte AG 2015, p. 11). With RFID technology, a fixed scanner could be installed between the stockroom and the sales floor to scan the passing items automatically, requiring only that the employees traverse the gate carefully to ensure high accuracy in the system. In order to minimize errors, Adler conducted training sessions so that the employees knew how to pass through the gates correctly when they were carrying store items.

The Process Dimension Adler redesigned its structured *repetitive core processes* based on the needs of the RFID technology. At the start of the project, efficiency and standardization of the processes were in focus. Most processes were simple and

Table 1 BPM context framework (vom Brocke et al. 2016) applied to the Adler case

Dimensions	Characteristic	Value
Goal	Focus	Exploitation (Improvement, Compliance)
Process	Value contribution	Core processes
	Repetitiveness	Repetitive
	Knowledge-intensity	Medium knowledge-intensity
	Creativity	Medium creativity
	Interdependence	Medium interdependence
	Variability	Low variability
Organization	Scope	Intra-organizational processes
	Industry	Product industry
	Size	Large organization
	Culture	Culture medium supportive of BPM
	Resources	High organizational resources
Environment	Competitiveness	High competitive environment
	Uncertainty	Medium environmental uncertainty

had only a *medium level of knowledge-intensity*, and the process *variability* could be considered low because the processes were standardized across all Adler stores.

One potential process improvement was at the goods-receiving step. Before the use of RFID, the delivered merchandise had first to be removed from boxes. Then an employee checked to ensure that the delivery matched the order by scanning each item individually by hand. With RFID, apparel delivered on hangers are scanned with a handheld reader in an instant, and the stock management system captures the new goods (Adler Modemärkte AG 2015, p. 10). Boxed items can be scanned in one batch.

The RFID technology also promises significant process improvements for the point-of-sale process. Originally, barcodes of every item purchased were manually scanned at checkout with an installed or hand-held barcode scanner. Now, however, the RFID-enabled tags can be read in a batch when a number of items are placed on the checkout desk. The cashier needs only to count whether all items were detected by the system and does not have to look for barcodes.

Adler's previous electronic article-surveillance system relied on attaching bulky and expensive anti-theft hard tags. Employees and suppliers had to perform a time-consuming process to apply (and remove) the hard tags, which carried the risk of damaging the items if the employees executed the process incorrectly under time pressure. In addition, only 20% of the stores' articles could be secured this way, as the cost of this process was not feasible for items of lower value (Adler Modemärkte AG 2015, p. 12).

Finally, the RFID technology speeds up manual inventory counts, as RFID handheld scanners can simultaneously detect hundreds of items. Therefore, laborious and expensive manual counting can be reduced or eliminated in favor of more frequent inventory "sweeps."

The Organization Dimension Over 3 years, Adler invested 8 million euros into its RFID project. Thus, the resources allocated to the project can be characterized as high.

Intra-organizational processes were most of the project's focus. However, in order to fully leverage the benefits of RFID technology, some of the company's third-party suppliers also had to change their barcode-based processes.

The Environmental Dimension BPM is important for Adler because the high level of competitiveness in the retail fashion sector makes streamlined processes that waste no resources essential. Customer demand is difficult to forecast in the industry, which leads to some *uncertainty*. In addition, new developments in RFID technology require rapid modification of existing processes in order to realize the new technology's full benefits. For example, Adler is considering using robots equipped with RFID readers to perform the stock-taking. Consequently, the level of environmental uncertainty can be characterized as medium.

Another example of a source of uncertainty is new technological advancements that allow RFID tags to be integrated into sales articles, such as by being sewn into garments or placed in shoe soles, in order to make it difficult for a customer to leave

Table 2 Project goals and the corresponding KPIs supported in the RFID process-improvement project

Project goal	Supported KPI
Increased inventory accuracy and transparency of commodity flow	Turnover
Reduced “off of shelf” situations	Turnover
Parallelization of scanning activities	Processing time
Faster checkout process	Customer satisfaction
Increased anti-theft protection	Shrinkage

the store with unpaid items. These measures make it necessary for Adler to change the existing process but also help it to mitigate the problem of theft.

Table 2 summarizes the project’s goals and relates them to KPIs that benefit from the RFID technology. For example, RFID allows a retailer to conduct inventory checks more frequently using handheld devices, leading to earlier detection of misplaced, lost, or stolen items. In such cases, employees can replenish the missing items from the stockroom or order them. Consequently, the chance of lost sales opportunities is reduced, as customers are less likely to encounter situations in which the items they want are not on the shelf.

Not only is anti-theft protection increased because the RFID tags and can be attached to more items than was possible with the previous technology with hard tags, but the RFID tags are cheaper.

3 Action Taken

The first planning for the RFID project began in 2010, when Adler began to search for suitable software and hardware solutions. In order to manage the extreme complexity of such an RFID project, Adler needed qualified system-integration experts as well as software and hardware components that integrated well into its existing system (Adler Modemärkte AG 2015, p. 12).

The adoption of a new technology in multiple locations requires thorough coordination and planning, so Adler hired an independent consultancy to manage the transition project. The project was partitioned into three main phases, with an initial business case analysis and trailing economic feasibility studies. The project plan is outlined in Fig. 1. In the following subsections, we describe each phase in detail.

3.1 Concept and Provider Selection

In a first step, Adler’s project management team and a hired consulting firm analyzed the company’s and customer’s requirements, including an analysis of the existing ERP system (Adler Modemärkte AG 2014, p. 13).

The project management team screened potential suppliers of RFID equipment that were located in the vicinity based on Adler’s envisioned solution and required

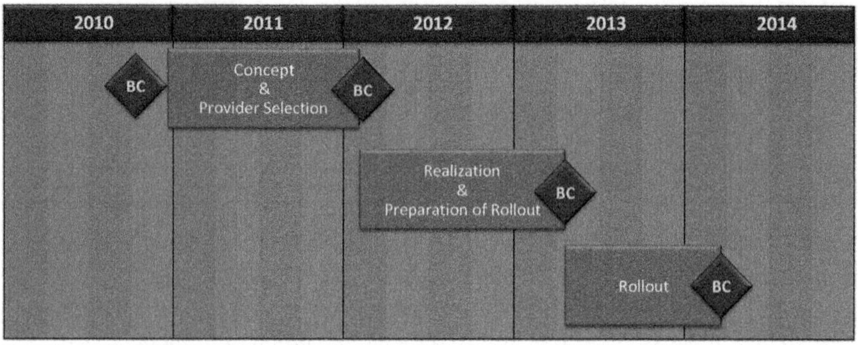

Fig. 1 Project plan for the adoption of RFID. Three main phases are depicted, each followed by a business case analysis

tools and processes. In addition to economic considerations, Adler had to consider the slight differences in the RFID reader technologies in selecting a provider. Spending time on the selection process is important because switching to another provider after installation might require replacing parts of the infrastructure at additional cost. In 2011 Adler selected its Weiterstadt store as a test store (Adler Modemärkte AG 2014, p. 13). First, it tested several software tools and hardware components in order to evaluate how well they interacted with each other. After a period of several months, Adler had a list of the most suitable hardware and software and corresponding suppliers (Adler Modemärkte AG 2014).

The conceptual design of the to-be processes requires a thorough understanding of the business and in-depth knowledge of the new technology's merits and potential pitfalls. For example, the company did not know initially to what extent RFID gates had to be physically shielded from the surrounding shop area to prevent false reads when store items passed near the gates. The cost of correcting an improper initial setup are much higher than the costs of adding extra shielding in the first place.

3.2 Concept Realization and Preparation for Rollout

Once the suppliers had been selected and planning of the placement of readers and processes had been set up, Adler was ready for the realization. To prepare for smooth rollout, feasibility of the new technology had to be tested. A conceptual prototype was set up in a test environment to validate that the components all worked together as expected and were ready for use in the stores. An example installation covering the focal points in a store with RFID readers is shown in Fig. 2. The figure shows a receiving cage, the replenishment gate between the stockroom and the sales floor, the checkout, and the EAS gate. The fitting rooms can also be equipped with RFID readers to offer customers additional information (available sizes, colors) about the products they bring to the fitting room.

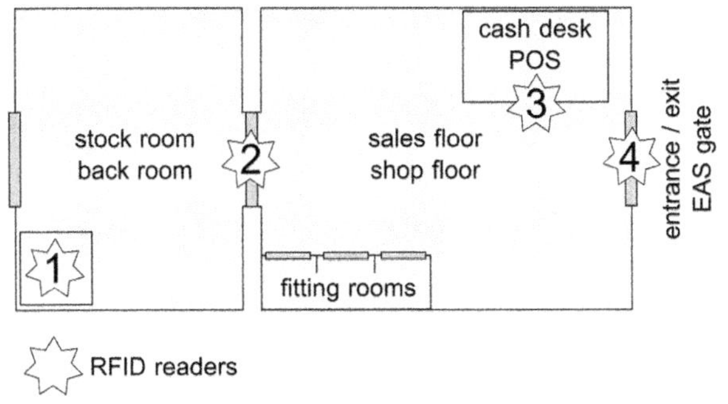

Fig. 2 Sketch of RFID gates and readers in a retail store

After selecting the supplier, Adler began the pilot project in Weiterstadt in the spring of 2012. The store was equipped with all systems, such as the chosen RFID-enabled handheld devices and RFID printers, and all garments were tagged with RFID transponders. The pilot was intended to demonstrate whether the assumptions the company had made about RFID were correct, whether the selected systems worked as expected, and whether the project's goals could be achieved. Months of testing preceded the pilot because employees had first to be trained on how to interact with the RFID infrastructure and systems and convinced that the new processes were better than the old ones so they would use them appropriately (Adler Modemärkte AG 2015, p. 13).

The pilot was expanded to five more stores in Germany and two stores in Luxembourg, all of which had different architectural layouts. This expanded testing provided a broad dataset that verified the positive results from the first pilot in Weiterstadt (Adler Modemärkte AG 2015, p. 14).

After briefly evaluating the feasibility and efficiency of the setup in the eight pilot stores, the upgrade was extended to six additional stores in late 2012. Meanwhile, tag delivery for source tagging was set up so the suppliers could integrate the tags required by Adler into their own processes. The IT infrastructure for handling the RFID events and providing monitoring and reporting was set up in summer 2013. Simultaneously, the stores were equipped with handheld devices for uses from inventory counting to tagging of new items.

The RFID gates and scanners were planned in autumn 2013. Important monitoring points for the processes in retail stores are points at which items enter and exit the store, the transition between the sales floor and the stockroom, and of course the point-of-sale counters.

The goods-receiving process was almost completely automated with scanners, as depicted in Fig. 3 for hanging garments and in Fig. 4 for boxed items. The automatic processing frees the staff to focus on core processes like assisting customers.

All required infrastructural changes were due to be implemented in January 2014 so a timely rollout could be ensured with subsequent tagging of the inventory.

Fig. 3 Receiving hanging garments

Fig. 4 Receiving boxed items

3.3 Rollout

One essential step in the use of RFID technology is the tagging of all the items in the store. This step required 9 months, from July 2013 until March 2014, and considerable effort. Meanwhile, the stationary readers were installed so employee training and go-live could be performed in succession.

The rollout was scheduled for a transition period from August 2013 to April 2014. Adler began by equipping four stores per week with RFID technology. Then, with more routine and first lessons learned, the company was able to double the pace to eight stores per week.

The rollout was smooth and saw no further delays or complications, so Adler stayed on plan and completed the rollout by April 2014, 5 months ahead of schedule (Adler Modemärkte AG 2015, p. 14).

After all of the stores went live, additional training and software releases that catered to Adler's specific needs took place from May 2014 to June 2014. The RFID adoption project was finalized by the end of June.

4 Results Achieved

The adoption of RFID technology at Adler was strategically relevant to the company's management. Besides economic factors, the modernization and the more efficient checkout process positively affects the company's brand image. In short, the improvement project was a success, with improved inventory accuracy, follow-up procurement, process efficiency, processing at the points of sale, and source tagging and theft protection. The following subsections discuss these results and how they contribute to the business goals.

Better inventory accuracy and transparency of the flow of items between the back of the store and the sales floor. The new technology makes it feasible to track items' movements in the stores in real time. The inventory management system can identify items that need to be replenished from the back of the store, reducing the chance that customers will miss a certain type or size of garment that is only in the back of the store. The higher inventory accuracy in the system supports an increase in the turnover.

Improved follow-up procurement is enabled by improved inventory accuracy. When items go missing from the sales floor because of theft, administrative mistakes, or other reasons, early detection of these issues can be improved by regular inventory "sweeps." In these inventory sweeps, employees walk around in the store with the handheld RFID devices to detect inventory anomalies. Adler assumes 99% accuracy for RFID-enabled stock-taking (Adler Modemärkte AG 2016) and has begun to test robotic counting in one of its flagship stores using an RFID-enabled robot that counts inventory on the sales floor each day. Even though stock-taking with an RFID-enabled handheld device is much faster than a bar-code-based inventory count, "it is manual work that ties up capacities of staff," according to the company's head of IT. With the help of the robot, RFID-enabled counting can be conducted more often to improve the accuracy of the inventory data and allow staff to focus on their core tasks of consulting and sales. Adler started the deployment of the robots in October 2015[1] and expanded its pilot to three more stores in 2016. Adler evaluates and analyzes the collected data and economic impact in 2017.

To illustrate the benefits, consider the example case of an item's having been stolen. Before the introduction of RFID technology, many of these cases could not be readily detected, so they led over time to a growing disparity between the store's theoretical and real inventory. With RFID and regular sweeps through the store, the inventory counts can be corrected, missing items can be detected earlier, and replacement orders can be made more accurately and timely, resulting in increased sales.

Increased process efficiency was achieved in the management of items. For example, the recording of incoming and outgoing items is now made in batches by packet, instead of having employees scan each individual barcode manually.

The process efficiency of full inventory counts also improved. The scanning speed of RFID sweeps beat that of manual scanning, so overall inventory accuracy has significantly improved using more regular sweeps. Full-inventory scans are still performed annually to verify the RFID accuracy and detect anomalies like destroyed tags.

Faster processing at points of sale. Faster processing at points of sale deserves separate discussion, although it also relates to the process-efficiency category. Efficiency at the points of sale are especially important, as customers must queue there in order to purchase their items. Studies have shown that waiting time impacts the perceived quality of service (Davis and Vollmann 1990), so speeding the point-of-sale process is more important than, for example, speeding the process of receiving items in the stockroom.

The speed-up in service at the points of sale was due to two changes in the process. First, the RFID tags allow the employee to batch-scan the customer's items instead of manually finding and scanning each item's bar code. Second, the manual step of removing hard tags is dropped with the introduction of RFID tags, which provide the EAS capabilities that the hard tags once provided. Consequently, the gain in efficiency at the points of sale results in lower queuing times and, thus, in *higher customer satisfaction*. In fact, most customers at the cash registers are amazed by the speed of item identification. The two most common questions the customers pose are: "Is that already the total amount?" and "Are you already done scanning everything?" (Adler Modemärkte AG 2015).

Source tagging and theft prevention by means of RFID technology. Instead of costly hard tags that were attached by suppliers and removed at the point of sale, lightweight and affordable RFID tags are mounted on each item's price tag. These tags and the tags sewn into garments allow for a broader coverage of article surveillance. More than 90% of the items at the Adler stores are equipped with

---

[1]http://www.rfidjournal.com/articles/view?14057/

RFID tags. In particular, the entire textile inventory is covered with this theft-preventing technology, in contrast to the costly hard tags that were used to secure only high-value items. The introduction of RFID technology clearly resulted in *reduced retail shrinkage*.

One of Adler's goals—improving the goods-reception process—was not completely achieved because of some of the suppliers' incomplete coverage of items with electronic product codes. Adler is currently working on this issue and will re-evaluate the potential for improvement when all of its suppliers have adopted the required tagging procedures. Meanwhile, this goal is excluded from the project's goals for evaluation purposes.

5 Lessons Learned

Realistic goals with respect to the expected benefits must be set when a company adopts a new technology. Otherwise, a bad impression remains even if the project succeeds despite its failure to meet overly optimistic goals.

There is often unreasonable hype around new technologies. RFID technology was hyped in the late 1990s (Sparks 1999), with all the promises and expected improvements of a new technology. Adler wisely resisted the urge to adopt RFID too early, when it was not yet economically feasible for the company with respect to its strategy, resources, and culture.

Once the decision to conduct the process improvement project was made, the support of specialists proved worthwhile, as did splitting the project into distinct phases with trailing evaluations, which helped to ensure that the project stayed on track.

Adopting a new technology requires not only economic feasibility and meticulous planning but also knowledge about the risks that are introduced with the new technology. For example, by thoughtlessly gathering unlimited (sensor) data in the current era of big data, we face potential privacy risks for employees and customers. To avoid this threat, Adler keeps its data in physically disconnected systems and participates in the SERAMIS research project, which researches privacy-related risks in this context.

When faced with process-related challenges in the course of an improvement project, companies must get their employees on board. To this end, it is better not to argue using the technology or its merits but to take a process-oriented view, where the technology is merely a means by which to achieve the process goals that will make their jobs easier. Process-improvement projects sometimes face reluctance or even outright rejection by the employees in large part because of cases in which employees have lost their jobs as a result of process improvements (Hammer and Champy 1993). For example, instead of telling employees that "we are adopting RFID to optimize our processes," make the goals and aims of the process improvement project transparent by asking employees, "How can we improve on the procurement of goods to prevent customers from being disappointed and moving to competitors when they can't find the items they want? How can we ensure that goods are always in reach of our customers?"

To conclude, the adoption of RFID has paid off for Adler and will serve as a basis for further process optimizations, such as robots that automatically perform stock-taking.

References

Adler Modemärkte AG. (2013). *Geschäftsbericht 2012*. https://www.adlermode-unternehmen.com/investor-relations/berichte-publikationen/geschaeftsberichte/

Adler Modemärkte AG. (2014). *Geschäftsbericht 2013*. https://www.adlermode-unternehmen.com/investor-relations/berichte-publikationen/geschaeftsberichte/

Adler Modemärkte AG. (2015). *Geschäftsbericht 2014*. https://www.adlermode-unternehmen.com/investor-relations/berichte-publikationen/geschaeftsberichte/

Adler Modemärkte AG. (2016). *Geschäftsbericht 2015*. https://www.adlermode-unternehmen.com/investor-relations/berichte-publikationen/geschaeftsberichte/

Chappell, G., Durdan, D., Gilbert, G., Ginsburg, L., Smith, J., & Tobolski, J. (2003). *Auto-ID in the box: The value of Auto-ID technology in retail stores*. Cambridge: Auto-ID Center, MIT.

Davis, M. M., & Vollmann, T. E. (1990). A framework for relating waiting time and customer satisfaction in a service operation. *Journal of Services Marketing, 4*(1), 61–69.

Hammer, M., & Champy, J. (1993). Reengineering the corporation: A manifesto for business revolution. *Business Horizons, 36*(5), 90–91.

Sparks, L. (1999). RFID: Transforming technology? In J. Fernie & L. Sparks (Eds.), *Logistics and retail management* (3 Ausg., S. 233–252). London: Kogan Page.

Thiesse, F., Al-Kassab, J., & Fleisch, E. (2009). Understanding the value of integrated RFID systems: A case study from apparel retail. *European Journal of Information Systems, 18*, 592–614.

vom Brocke, J., Zelt, S., & Schmiedel, T. (2016). On the role of context in business process management. *International Journal of Information Management, 36*, 486–495.

Roland Leitz is the Director IT of Adler Modemärkte AG. He holds a diploma in computer science, which he obtained at the university of applied sciences of Furtwangen in 1979. Afterwards, he was project development lead in various IT projects in the telecommunications, auto-mobile, and manufacturing domains. Roland worked as a freelancer for the consultancy company Mummert and Partner, before joining Adler Modemärkte GmbH in 1990. There, he worked as head of software development for two years, before entering his current position as Director IT in early 1992. He first investigated the opportunities of RFID technology in 2001, and conducted a feasibility study of RFID in 2005. Since then, he actively promotes the use of RFID in talks at conferences and workshops. He leads the RFID project at Adler. Since 2015, he also focuses on advanced use cases of RFID, like inventory robotics, and RFID-based intelligent fitting rooms.

Andreas Solti is a post-doc researcher at the Institute for Information Business at the WU Vienna, Austria. He completed his Ph.D. studies entitled "Probabilistic Estimation of Unobserved Process Events" in the business process technology group of the Hasso Plattner Institute of the University of Potsdam. Currently, he is working on the European FP7 project entitled "Sensor-Enabled Real-World Awareness for Management Information Systems" (SERAMIS) on topics of sensor data analysis. Andreas published more than 25 international research papers in journals and highly competitive conferences including such as Information Systems, BPM, CAiSE, ICSOC, EDOC. He served in several program committees including BPI, BPIC, EDOC.

Alexander Weinhard is a research assistant at the chair of information systems engineering at the Julius-Maximilians-Universität Würzburg, Germany. His research areas include simulation modeling, data science and technology acceptance. He is furthermore one of the coordinators of the EU research project SERAMIS that deals with the efficient usage of RFID technology in retail (seramis-project.eu).

Jan Mendling is a Full Professor with the Institute for Information Business at Wirtschaftsuniversität Wien (WU Vienna), Austria. His research areas include Business Process Management, Conceptual Modelling and Enterprise Systems. He has published more than 300 research papers and articles, among others in ACM Transactions on Software Engineering and Methodology, IEEE Transaction on Software Engineering, Information Systems, Data and Knowledge Engineering, and Decision Support Systems. He is member of the editorial board of seven international journals, board member of the Austrian society for process management (http://www.prozesse.at), one of the founders of the Berlin BPM Community of Practice (http://www.bpmb.de), organizer of several academic events on process management, and member of the IEEE Task Force on Process Mining. His Ph.D. thesis has won the Heinz-Zemanek-Award of the Austrian Computer Society and the German Targion-Award for dissertations in the area of strategic information management.

Automate Does Not Always Mean Optimize: Case Study at a Logistics Company

Jan Suchy, Milan Suchy, Michal Rosik, and Agnes Valkova

Abstract

(a) **Situation faced**: Dynamic growth of digitized information creates space for the systematic collection of data related to business processes. Extraction of this data is an enormous challenge because of the existence of many systems, which store data in many formats. The logistics company examined here has fully automated its Purchase Order and Invoice Approval processes, driven by a BPM system. Logistics always deals with optimization and cost reduction, and the company asked us whether it was possible to optimize its processes further.

(b) **Action taken**: In our work, we focus on the extraction, pre-processing, and analysis of data that is stored in BPM systems. We presented the methodology with which to extract business-related events from processes of the logistics company, analyzed the BPM system, deployed processes to develop a connector for extracting event data, and used process mining techniques to reconstruct processes from event logs. Advanced analytics techniques make it possible to present collected data in an "as-is" view of processes and to find bottlenecks, loops, delays, and deadlocks.

(c) **Results achieved**: We identified the structure for stored data and the attributes attached to the metadata of the processes. Then we imported newly created process logs into a process mining tool. Next, we introduced a process model and its statistics based on the extracted processes. Finally, we pointed out characteristics and points for improvement in individual human activity. As a result, we identified bottlenecks, loops, suppliers'

J. Suchy • M. Suchy (✉) • M. Rosik • A. Valkova
GRADIENT ECM, Kosicka 56, 82108, Bratislava, Slovakia
e-mail: Jan.Suchy@gradientecm.com; Milan.Suchy@gradientecm.com; Michal.Rosik@gradientecm.com; Agnes.Valkova@gradientecm.com

J. vom Brocke, J. Mendling (eds.), *Business Process Management Cases*,
Management for Professionals, DOI 10.1007/978-3-319-58307-5_25

characteristics, and found in the Purchase Order process over-allocated employees to dedicated tasks via the social network.

(d) **Lessons learned**: Today's businesses are process-driven; everything done in a business is a process. A process-driven application is a software that provides automatic execution of business processes and logs the executed activities. Most systems have design-time data that defines the processes and runtime data that includes information on executed activities. One can use connectors to extract the data in the desired process log structure. Process mining techniques allow us to reconstruct the process from logs, analyze it, and find optimization points. Processes can be analyzed from several perspectives: as human to human processes, human to system processes, and system to system processes.

1 Introduction

Most industries today automate their processes via workflow systems (van der Aalst and van Hee 2004). Efforts to capture and automate the desired behavior in industry processes can bring many benefits, but automation may also hide ineffective behaviors and instances. Therefore, when automating processes, companies must monitor them to see what takes place to enhance the processes so they meet changing business needs and eliminate risks.

Capturing processes' current conditions can be complicated and complex. What is needed is a team of people who will monitor all of the resource processes for each activity and record the individual steps that provide solutions to their problem areas. Thus, the team will be able to create a visible and interactive process model with dedicated timeframes for the people involved with each activity. The process model can be represented in a graph-based modeling language like Petri nets (van der Aalst 1998), BPMN (Wohed et al. 2006), or YAWL (van der Aalst and ter Hofstede 2005) so the resulting model holds all of the subjective views of the process analysts who contributed. On the other hand, process mining technology can reconstruct and visualize processes with an objective view in a fraction of the time. Reconstructing a process using process Mining technology requires acquiring all of the data recorded regarding all processes and transforming them into the structures needed for the reconstruction process to occur. Process mining makes it possible to reconstruct processes rapidly and to see the "as-is" reality of a process using a common and objective view. Process mining can reveal what actually goes on in an organization, providing a reality check that reveals the flaws and inefficiencies that must be worked out to enhance the firm's processes and the overall outcome.

Our goal was to show a precise picture of what really goes on in the Purchase Order and Invoice Approval processes. First, we became familiar with the specifications of the processes. Then we defined the structure in which we recorded the data. After familiarizing ourselves with the architecture of the BPM system, we developed a connector that extracts raw data and creates structured event logs. We then imported the event logs into a process-mining tool and introduced the process's basic statistics and characteristics. Finally, we focused on the key human activities, resources, and suppliers involved and gathered the knowledge and optimization points for both processes.

Our job was to provide to the logistics company tools for continuous business process improvement using three phases of the BPM Lifecycle (Dumas et al. 2013). Using the combination of the connector and the process-mining tool we developed, the company was able to perform the activities related to the phases of process discovery and process analysis, as well as the activities of the process monitoring and controlling phase. Using the connector makes exporting data in predefined intervals possible, and with the help of the process-mining tool, the company can analyze the variations in the process flow and the performance deviations in the set KPIs.

2 Situation Faced

Our logistics company is dealing with large numbers of invoices and purchase orders, covering their transportation business as well as overhead expenses. The number of invoices and orders was rising and the company was about to make several decisions related to hiring additional accountants, eliminating due dates, and loss of invoices. Scanning, automatic recognition, and data extraction and processing of invoices was the first solution the company needed. It was also important to implement a purchase order management system and document management system for storing, searching, and management of the documents. The key element of the solution that would be deployed was workflow automation for the Purchase Order and Invoice Approval processes based on the digitized version of the documents involved.

The benefits of implementing the solution were clear after short period of operation. The new invoice-approval process allowed the company to forego hiring the additional personnel and to process twice the number of invoices with the same personnel. The rate of lost invoices and invoices not approved on time fell to a negligible rate. The new purchase order approval process eliminated the need for double approval in most the cases.

Process automation introduced significant benefits, but it also raised the need for monitoring, controlling behavior, and searching for the additional optimization points. The company wanted to find out how to measure processes and how to measure the resources involved in the process execution. Its main interest was in controlling the fulfillment of enterprise-level KPIs and business rules, analyzing the purchase order process from the viewpoint of suppliers, and measuring discrepancies in the delivery of purchased goods. The increasing volume of rejected invoices was a concern. Data from active process instances were stored in a new system, but for analytical purposes a way to extract the historical data was needed as well.

2.1 Process Definition

To analyze and discover optimizations, we were provided with the Purchase Order process and the Invoice Approval process. Processes are implemented in a process-driven application and driven by a workflow engine. The Process Owner provided us with models and specifications of certain processes through which we became familiar with the individual steps and the process's attributes. The main objective in this part of work was to identify the flow of processes so we could validate the extracted process models.

2.2 Purchase Order Process

The Purchase Order process describes the creation and approval authority when orders are made. The system provides the users the ability to create a new order in the form of editable structured forms, so the user can fill any number of items ordered. Ordered items are defined by a set of attributes. After a new order is created, it is automatically launched into the Purchase Order process. The system then selects, based on the data entered, a tree of authorized users/group of authorities to approve the Purchase Order. Subsequently, the system assigns the approver/approvers tasks by email notifications. The approver may then approve orders or reject them. After the approval process, the system can decide, based on the financially authorized limit, whether the stock level is sufficient to approve the order and, if not, it initiates a reselection process from the existing tree of authoritative users/group of authorities. This process is repeated until all approvals have been acquired. If the order process is deemed approved in the system, the author will be notified of the outcome and the status will change to "Approved." If an order has been rejected, the system will change the status to "Declined," and a notification will be sent out to the appropriate author along with the reasons for refusal. If an order is rejected, the process and the order ends. With approved orders, the system identifies whether it is a cyclic order[1] and, if not, it continues and assigns tasks to those involved in the ordering process, who have been designated by the author of the order during its formation. In this part of the process, the user will have established and forwarded approved orders to its suppliers. The process then continues to confirm receipts of the ordered goods/services. The system then assigns tasks to authorized employees, who are given a chance to confirm a completed delivery order, confirm any partial deliveries, or cancel the order if the customer has cancelled the order. When a partial delivery takes place, the employee can wait for delivery of missing parts of the ordered goods or declare the order as partially delivered. Subsequently, the system marks the order as "Closed," and the process comes to an end.

[1]If the process is identified as a cyclic order, the system automatically declares it to have been delivered, and the process comes to an end. Cyclic orders are characterized by regular repetition.

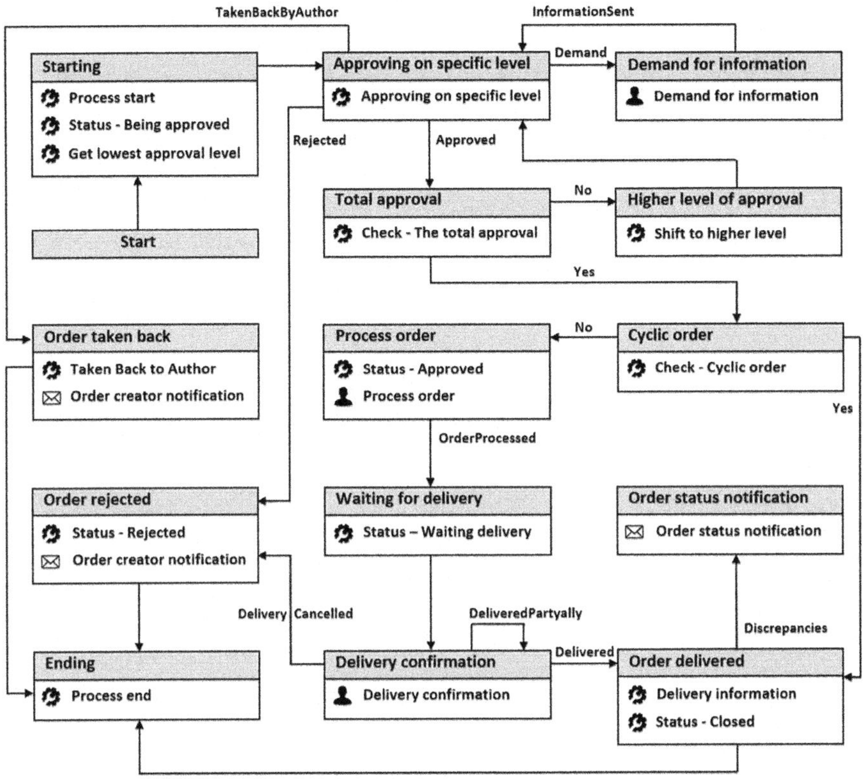

Fig. 1 Process diagram of the Purchase Order process

Figure 1 shows the process diagram for the Purchase Order process, which creates four human tasks and sixteen system tasks.

2.3 Invoice Approval Process

The Invoice Approval process is automatically prompted when an invoice is scanned/digitized. First, the system automatically assigns invoices to the correct order based on the order number. This solution was achieved by means of the combination of BPM and document-centric software. If the order is not found, the system will generate a task for manual entry of the order and assign it to a group known as "Accountants," whose goal is to find the order and pair it with its invoice. After assigning the order, the system automatically compares the total amounts, and if they do not match, the system checks the correctness of the cost center and continues to process the invoice in the approval process.

The Invoice Approval process has the same procedures as the Purchase Order process. The system generates tasks to confirm the accounted invoice. In this part of the process, the employee checks all other information pertaining to the invoice and, if the employee finds no discrepancies in the invoice, the system generates tasks to complete the accounting part/accounts payable process of the invoice, whereby the process will come to an end. However, if the employee finds irregularities, the process will continue, and the system will generate tasks to resolve them. At this point, the employee may reject the invoice and the process ends, or obtain missing data to enable the system to return the invoice to a re-approval state. Figure 2 shows the process diagram of the Invoice Approval process, which creates seven human tasks and thirteen system tasks.

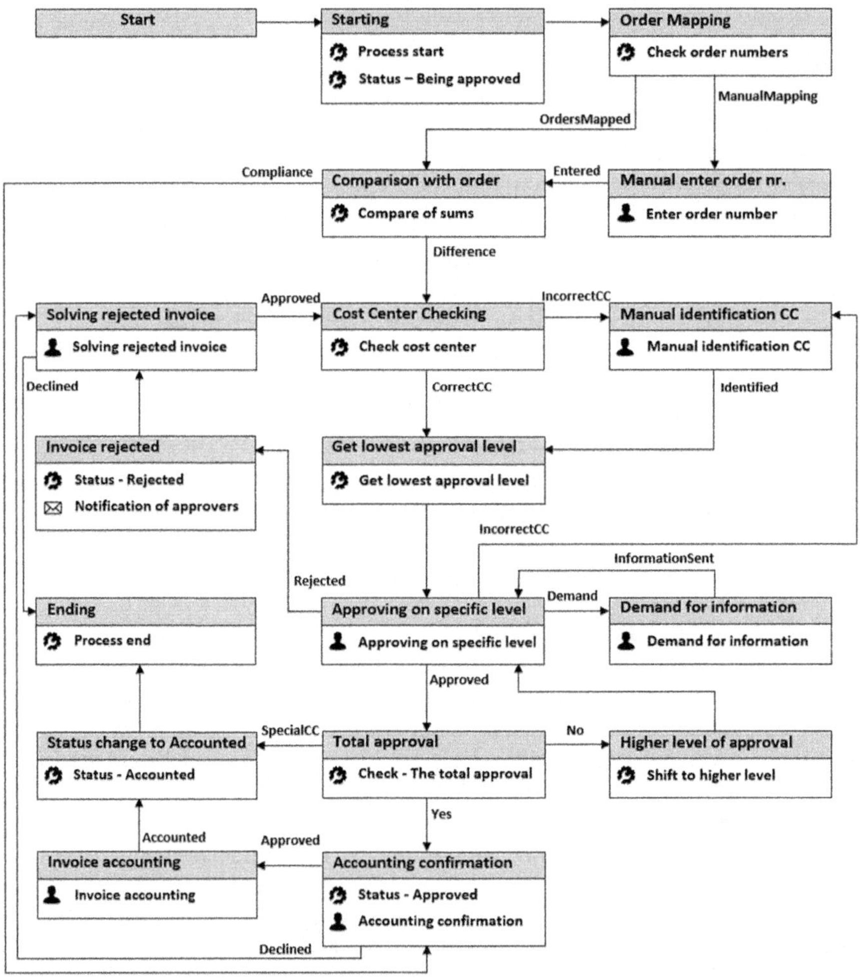

Fig. 2 Process diagram of the Invoice Approval process

3 Action Taken

In order for us to analyze the two processes and what takes place within them, we had to extract data from the company's databases and structure it. Data extraction is a challenge because data may be located in the database as well as in other formats (e.g., message logs, flat files, transaction logs, document management systems, ERP systems). Our main objective is to analyze the data obtained from a process-oriented perspective. In this section, we discuss information that should be present in such event logs.

Table 1 shows a fragment of an event log in which the information typically needed to analyze are presented. The main assumption is that the event log contains data related to a single process. Each event of the case is related to a single process instance, frequently marked as "case." Table 1 shows that Event ID 45678–45681 is related to Case 1. Another important factor is that every event must be related to an activity. As Table 1 shows, events refer to activities like Process Order, Being Approved, and Lowest level. In order for process analysis to take place, one must define the minimal requirements for the log: Case ID and Activity. If the log does not contain a timestamp, the correct chronological sequence must be secured at the first stage of events. Table 1 also indicates other information for each event, so we can see all events that have a timestamp. Without correctly ordered events we

Table 1 Fragment of the event log

Case ID	Event ID	Activity	Start timestamp	End timestamp	Event type	Resource
1	45678	Order delivered-	26.11.2014 12:51	26.11.2014 12:51	1	System
1	45679	Closed	26.11.2014 12:51	26.11.2014 12:51	1	System
1	45670	Waiting	23.10.2014 13:58	23.10.2014 13:58	1	System
1	45680	Approved	23.10.2014 13:25	23.10.2014 13:25	1	System
1	45681	Process order	23.10.2014 13:25	23.10.2014 13:58	2	USER2358
2	45682	Process start	23.10.2014 10:36	23.10.2014 10:36	1	System
2	45683	Being approved	23.10.2014 10:36	23.10.2014 10:36	1	System
2	45684	Lowest level	23.10.2014 10:36	23.10.2014 10:36	1	System
2	45685	Process end	25.11.2014 7:18	25.11.2014 7:18	1	System
2	45686	Approving	23.10.2014 10:36	23.10.2014 11:13	2	USER2358
2	45687	Approving	23.10.2014 11:13	23.10.2014 13:18	2	USER0357

would not be able to detect casual dependencies in process models. The number of timestamps recorded per event can be analyzed from a performance perspective, such as in terms of the duration between implemented events, where the activity itself has a duration value of zero; the duration of performed events, where the durations between events is zero; and the individual duration of that process instance, referred to as a throughput time. Other than the duration of events, we can further examine events between implementations, or waiting time. Table 1 also includes the resources attribute, which distinguish the personnel dedicated to specific activities. Attributes can be examined on two levels: an event-level attribute and a case-level attribute. A case-level attribute holds information regarding concrete process instances in which attributes' values are noted for all events corresponding to its case. Event-level attributes hold information that pertains to events within a case, so the values of these attributes are within a case within an event that may vary.

To be able to reason in regard to logs and to specify the requirements for event logs, we formalized several notions (van der Aalst 2011).

Definition 1 (Event, Attribute) Let E be the *event universe*, that is, the set of all possible event identifiers. Events may be characterized by *various attributes*, such as an event that has a timestamp, corresponds to an activity, is executed by a particular person, or has associated costs. Let AN be a set of attribute names. For any event $e \in E$ and name $n \in AN$, $\#_n(e)$ is the value of attribute n for event e. If event e does not have an attribute named n, then $\#_n(e) = \perp$ (null value).

Definition 2 (Case, Case Attribute, Trace, Event log) Let C be the *case universe*, that is, the set of all possible case identifiers. Cases, like events, have attributes. For any case $c \in C$ and name $n \in AN$, $\#_{\mathrm{n}}(c)$ is the value of attribute n for case c ($\#_n(c) = \perp$ if case c has no attribute named n). Each case has a special mandatory attribute *trace*: $\#_{trace}(c) \in E^*$. $\underline{c} = \#_{trace}(c)$ is a shorthand for the trace of a case. We assume $\#_{\mathrm{trace}}(c) \neq \langle\rangle$, that is, traces in a log contain at least one event.

A *trace* is a finite sequence of events $\sigma \in E^*$ such that each event appears only once; that is, for $1 \leq i < j \leq |\sigma|$: $\sigma(i) \neq \sigma(j)$.

An *event log* is a set of cases $L \subseteq C$ such that each event appears at most once in the entire log; that is, for any $c_1, c_2 \in L$ such that $c_1 \neq c_2$: $\partial_{\mathrm{set}}(\underline{c}_1) \cap \partial_{\mathrm{set}}(\underline{c}_2) = \varnothing$.

If an event log contains timestamps, then the ordering in a trace should respect these timestamps; that is, for any $c \in L$, i and j such that $1 \leq i < j \leq |\underline{c}|$: $\#_{\mathrm{time}}(\underline{c}(i)) \leq \#_{\mathrm{time}}(\underline{c}(j))$. Events and cases are represented using *unique* identifiers. An identifier $e \in E$ refers to an event, and an identifier $c \in C$ refers to a case. This mechanism allows us to point to a specific event or a specific case, as there may be many events with identical attributes; for example, the start events of activity *a* may have been recorded for other cases, and there may even be multiples of such events within a case. Similarly, there may be several cases that followed the same path in the process. These identifiers are just a technicality that helps us to point to particular events and cases, so they do not need to be present in the original data source but may be generated when we extract the data from the various data sources.

Extracted data from the data sources must be saved in a suitable format. The standard format for storing and exchanging event logs is Mining eXtensible Markup Language (MXML). Using MXML, one can store event logs like the one shown in Table 1 using an XML-based syntax.

Another format is eXtensible Event Stream (XES) (Günther 2009), which is the successor to MXML. The XES format has been made less restrictive and extendible based on many practical experiences with MXML.

The most widely used format used is comma separated values (.CSV). This format is less restrictive than XES, but it only enables one to store data, not to create one's own extensions.

We met many challenges when extracting the event logs (van der Aalst 2011). One of the challenges is known as *correlation* events, which are events that need to be related to each other. Dealing with legacy and a variety of interconnected systems requires additional effort to correlate events; see (Ferreira and Gillblad 2009) for an example of an approach with which to correlate events with no a priori information. Events must be ordered per case, which does not require timestamps in principle, but when merging data from different sources, one must typically depend on *timestamps* to sort events in order of occurrence. In extracted data, we can come across existing cases, which are still running, so event logs typically just provide a *snapshot* of a longer running process. Another challenge is the *scoping* of the event log. Information systems may have thousands of tables, so one must know which tables incorporate the relevant data and know how to locate the required data and scope it. The *granularity* of logged events is also an issue in the system, as some systems produce low-level events. There are several approaches to preprocessing these types of events; for instance, low-level patterns that appear frequently can be abstracted and merged into a new event that represents the performed activity (Bose and van der Aalst 2009).

3.1 Event Log Extraction

We designed and implemented a connector that extracts event logs from a process-driven application that ensures a proper process-monitoring functionality. All data is present in relational databases. We used design-time parts of the database to define processes, activities, events, cases, and case-level attribute data. Activity, events, and their metadata distinguish the monitored processes, and we extracted data from runtime parts in the database.

Design-Time Data The design-time data contains all process definitions. For the individual processes defined, information is available regarding the date of implementation, actual running versions, and the historical record of previously implemented versions. In addition, all process have defined their activity sessions/lines and their metadata. For individual activity, corresponding events are defined as one of two types: human or system. Information about the users who performed the human activities in the process was also available. The important information was that which involved the setup process concerning the amount of detail that will be logged, where the most necessary values represent complete logging. Throughout the process of logging all activities, attribute values pertaining to process instances regarding individual process activities were important for analysis.

Runtime Data The runtime data contains all the data for the running instances of processes and their components. Each released process instance contains unique identifiers. Unique identifiers and the foreign key for a process instance in which it took place are recorded for activities carried out in the process. Individual events are recorded for activities that contain unique identifiers that themselves contain a foreign key to an associated activity instance (which is specific to when an event instance occurs). For individual events, timestamps are recorded and the human activity type holds the employee that performed the activity. Metadata related to process, activity, and event instances are linked via specific foreign keys.

Figure 3 demonstrates a scheme for the processes extracted in an event log. Using the information about processes gained from the design-time areas of the database, we extracted data from the runtime parts of the database. Table 2 contains a list of attributes needed to reconstruct individual processes. The attributes "Resource" and "Event Type" are expandable attributes for reconstructed social networks and in respect to the server or human activity.

Data extracted from processes and supplementary information regarding suppliers were supplier name, supplier city, and supplier state as case attributes.

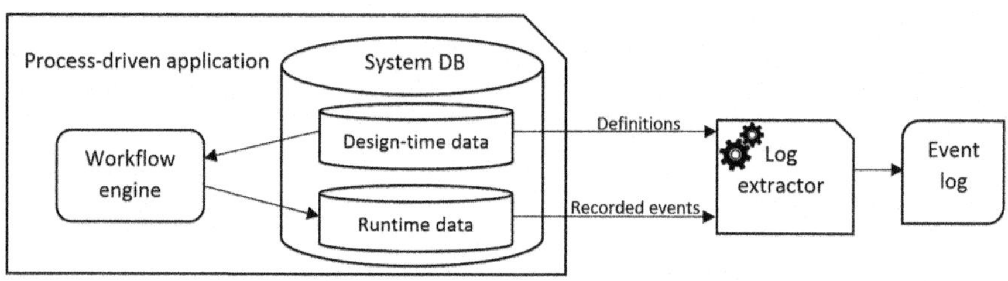

Fig. 3 Scheme of event log extraction

Table 2 Base extracted attributes

Attribute name	Orders	Invoices	Description
Case ID	✓	✓	Process instance identifier
Activity	✓	✓	Activity + event name
Start timestamp	✓	✓	Event start time
End timestamp	✓	✓	Event end time
Event Type	✓	✓	1 system, 2 human
Resource	✓	✓	Resource name

For the Invoice Approval process, user comments data was extracted to identify the most frequent reason for refusal of invoices. An additional case attribute was the case status, which helped to reveal the differences between completed, running, error, and deleted process instances. Analyzed data is provided only in regard to actual versions of processes.

Logs were stored in .CSV files. If we were to rate the quality of logs based on maturity levels (IEEE Task Force on Process Mining 2011), their rating would be five stars because logs are derived from a BPM system. Events are recorded in an automatic, systematic, reliable, and safe manner. Given such recording, the reconstruction of the processes did not require pre-processing of the data. The connector we developed enabled us to export the process instances according to the design-time information, which were completed and executed in the latest versions of both processes.

3.2 Process-Mining Techniques

We used a process-mining technique for reconstructed processes, as this technique can extract information from event logs. The goal of process mining is to discover, monitor, and improve processes. Process mining includes discovery process models, conformance checking (comparing model and log), social networking, organizational structure mining, case prediction, and history-based recommendations.

A number of tools for process mining is available for commercial and academic use. Commercial tools for process mining offer simple visualizations for end users and are significantly faster than other tools are in processing Big Data. Academic tools offer more algorithms, which may be difficult for less skilled users to apply. However, academic tools may have a wider range of use, and in the process of reconstruction they can expand support for concurrency (van der Aalst 2016). Because of the possibility of a large volume of data, we chose to use the commercial tool *Minit*[2] for the process analysis, as we are familiar with its functionality and it offers the most modern process-discovery algorithm, which is similar to fuzzy mining (Günther and van der Aalst 2007). With *Minit* we can import datasets for a wide range of possibilities in analyzing process models in a logistic company and their statistical characteristics. It was importance in our analysis to analyze the social network in order to bring out the fine details of each zoned resource in all processes.

After we imported the event log into *Minit*, identified process maps were created. Figure 4 shows a Purchase Order process map, and Fig. 5 shows an Invoice Approving process map. Both of the process maps[3] portrayed contain the case count metric.

[2]www.minitlabs.com

[3]Both process maps were redrawn for better readability after they were printed on paper.

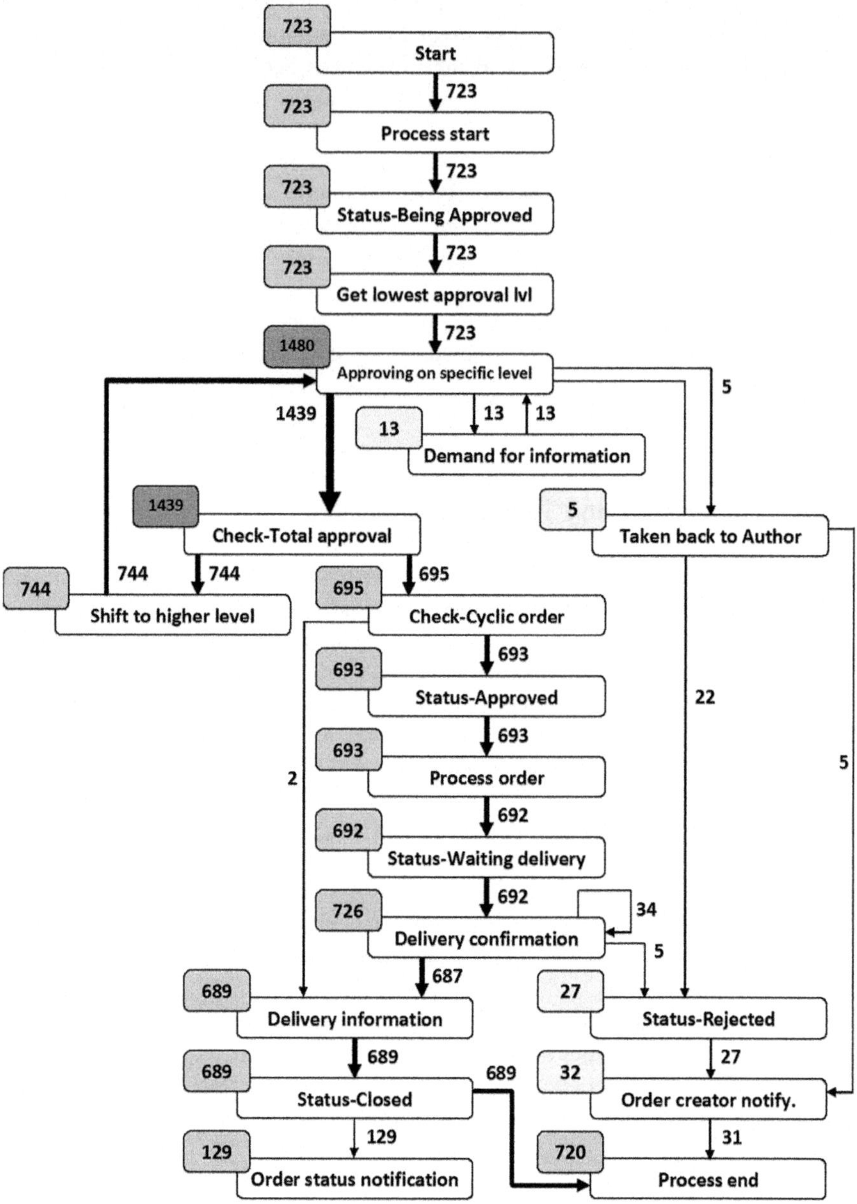

Fig. 4 Purchase Order process map

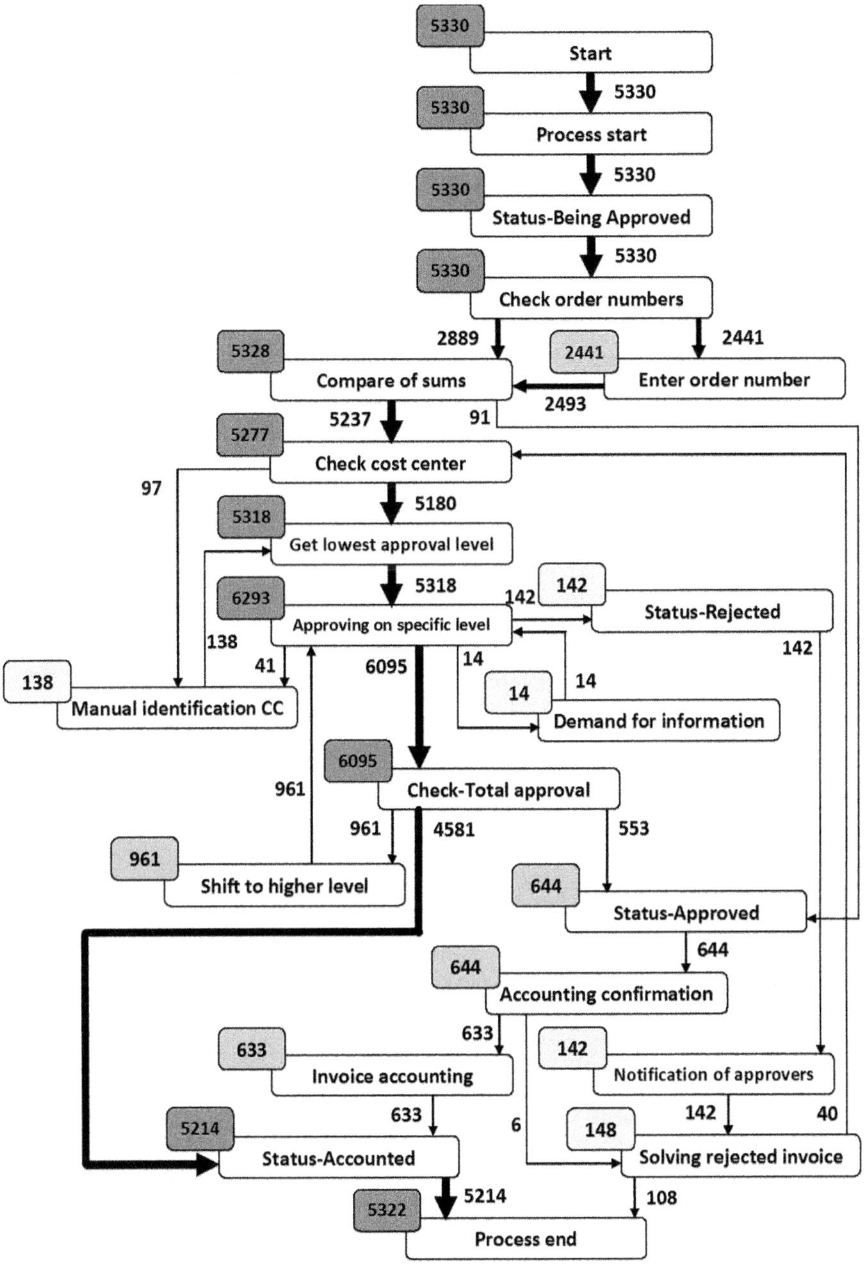

Fig. 5 Approve Invoice process map

4 Results Achieved

Our overall goal was to reconstruct and analyze process models from an event log. First, we identified the main process flows and their deviations. Then we analyzed social networks and selected activity processes. Statistical findings and analysis were performed only for completed process instances. Table 3 contains the basic statistics of the reconstructed processes.

4.1 Control Flow Identification

Processes' main streams were identified as their most numerous variants. A process variant is defined as the presence of unique activity sequences.

Purchase Order In the order-approval process, five of the most numerous variants accounted for 88% of the overall behavior. Table 4 indicates the basic characteristics of chosen variants. *Variant 1* describes when an order is approved on the second level, so "Approving on a specific level" occurs twice. Then orders are approved without additional activity; that is, an order is approved, processed, and its goods are delivered. *Variant 2* describes when a purchase order is approved without the approval of a higher-ranked individual, so they are approved once,

Table 3 Overview of processes characteristics

	Orders	Invoices
Timeframe	166 days 7 h	48 days 3 h
Cases	720	5322
Events	12,328	65,985
Activities	20	20
Event attributes	3	3
Case attributes	17	20
Variants	28	54
Resources	42	45

Table 4 Characteristics of the most numerous variants in the approval process of Purchase Orders

Variant ID	Cases coverage	Events per case	Events coverage	Mean duration
Variant 1	36%	17	35%	10d 23 h 15 min
Variant 2	20%	14	16%	5d 21 h 51 min
Variant 3	18%	20	21%	12d 21 h 34 min
Variant 4	11%	18	12%	8d 5 h 55 min
Variant 5	3%	21	4%	7d 9 h 2 min

Table includes how many cases and events are included in the monitored variants, along with information about their mean duration

Table 5 Characteristics of the most numerous variants of the Invoice approval process

Variant ID	Cases coverage	Events per case	Events coverage	Mean duration
Variant 1	50%	11	44%	1d 3 h 54 min
Variant 2	28%	12	27%	1d 11 h 46 min
Variant 3	8%	15	9%	2d 22 h 48 min
Variant 4	4%	18	6%	8d 10 h 45 min

This table indicates how many cases and events were obtained in the monitoring of variants, along with mean duration values

without any additional activities. The approval of the Purchase Order thereafter is completed upon delivery of all goods. *Variant 3* describes when a Purchase Order is approved in the third level, so "Approving on specific level" takes place three times. Purchase Orders are approved without carrying out any further activities, and the approval of the Purchase Order thereafter is completed upon delivery of all goods. *Variant* 3 and *Variant* 4 describe behavior when Purchase Orders are approved in the second (*Variant 4*) and third (*Variant 5*) level. These Purchase Orders are approved and processing takes place, but goods delivered are carried out with discrepancies.

Invoice Approving Four of the most numerous variants accounted for 89% of the overall behavior in the Invoice Approval process. Table 5 indicates the basic characteristics of the selected variants. *Variant 1* describes when an invoice is successfully mapped to compare the difference in prices found, followed by the cost center's verifying the data. The invoice is approved at the first level without the need for a higher authority, and no further activities take place at this stage. All invoices in this variant are directed to a special Cost Center (CC). *Variant 2* describes when the invoice does not have a purchase order labeled and one that is manually labeled must be secured to complete the invoice's missing data. Price comparison reveals a difference. The CC's checking takes place, and the center that will take further action to process the order is correctly defined. At the first stage, the invoice does not need the approval of a higher, so there is no further activity. All invoices in this variant are directed to a special CC. *Variant 3* describes when a purchase order number pertaining to the invoice is not labelled, so a manually labelled order must be secured. Price comparisons reveal a difference, and an inspection is followed by the CC's checking and defining which center will process further. The invoice at the second level is approved without the need of a higher authority or further activity. All invoices in this variant are redirected to a special division of the CC. *Variant 4* describes when an invoice that has an unlabeled order number requires that a manually labeled order number be secured. The prices comparison reveals a difference. The CC is correctly selected. Invoices are approved at the second level. Invoices are approved without further activity, and no invoices in this variant are directed to the CC but they are approved and sent to accounts payable.

The most frequent behavior and performance properties were revealed. Both processes have a common bottleneck, where multi-level approvals take place. Both processes had a remarkable growth in throughput time when multiple approvals took place. In the Purchase Order process, throughput times in the second-level approvals were 1.8 times higher than an approval on the first level, and they were 2.2 times higher in the third level. In the Invoice Approval process, throughput times on the second level were 2.5 times higher than an approval on the first level and 4.5 times higher on the third level.

4.2 Points of Interest in the Purchase Order Process

In this section, we tend to the possibilities of optimizing the Purchase Order process. We identify areas in which we see processes that hold statistical value or performance problems, focusing on the approval of purchase orders, the people involved in the process, and their social network.

4.2.1 Approval Level

Activity seen in this section pertains to the approval of purchase orders. All orders must be approved when the approver can do so the first time (or request additional information). A problem was discovered in the distribution of work, as the approver with the highest number of approvals approved 288 orders in an average of 20 h, while the approver with the second highest number of approvals approved 208 orders in an average of eight minutes.

For seventeen process instances, research found procedural irregularities, where one user approved on multiple levels, although the rules state that the approver cannot approve at multiple levels.

In one instance, 23 orders were approved for one supplier with the same amounts in each other and three users carrying out the same order of processing. Seeing this procedure take place allowed a cyclic procedure to be implemented to save time in process.

4.2.2 Resources in the Process

Over-allocated resources were discovered in the Purchase Order process. Resources in the process provide multiple tasks, where they carry out all or some of the required human activity. Unclearly defined working tasks for employees show strained and overworked employees comparing one another. Within the process, 42 resources were seen, but five employees performed 55% of all human activities and 57% of all process instances. Process owners were advised to relieve these over-allocated resources. The research also revealed that some employees had to communicate with a larger number/group of employees to process purchase orders and that a pair of resources shifted their work among other areas of work in 27% and 20% of process instances, respectively. Over-allocated resources are clearly shown in the social network of the Purchase Order process (Fig. 6). Their communication is also compared to that of others.

When purchase orders are created for individual resources, there is often insufficient knowledge regarding the work process. The slowest employee performed an

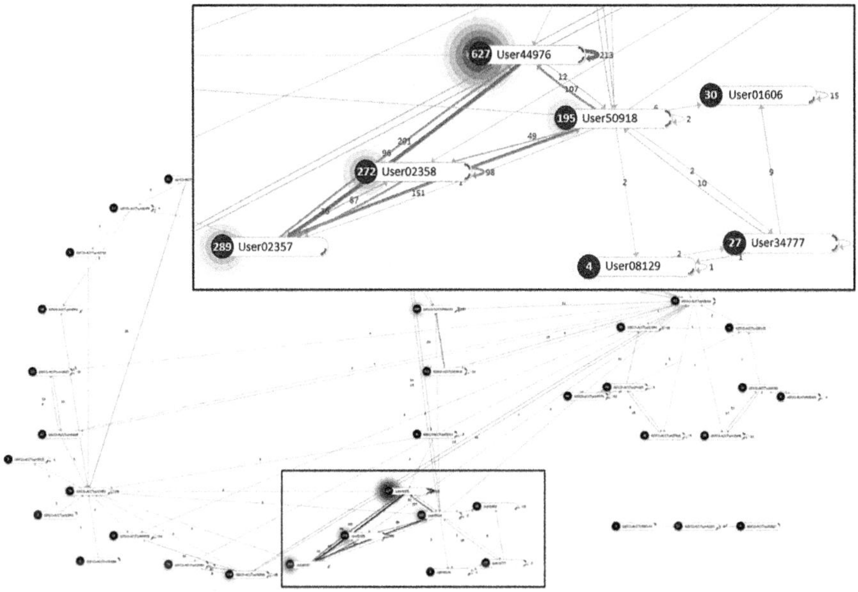

Fig. 6 Social network for the Purchase Order process with event-count metric

activity 30 times slower than the fastest employee. In addition, the duration of activities ranged widely, with the longest difference being 17 s for the shortest duration compared to 21 days and 18 h for the longest. Over-allocated resources were more likely to take longer than average to complete an activity.

4.2.3 Suppliers' Characteristics

Through the "Delivery confirmation" activity, we identified discrepancies in the delivery of goods/services for individual suppliers and information about the number of discrepancies that took place. Contractors were also identified who reported discrepancies in all of their deliveries of goods/services. From this information we were able to predict the time it would take to deliver goods/services for individual contractors together and the likelihood that the order would be completed. This information helps process owners accurately plan and schedule orders for the delivery of their goods/services.

4.3 Points of Interest in the Invoice Approval Process

In this section, we tend to the Invoice Approving process. We investigated activity that took place in "Manual enter order number" and saw that it accounted for approximately 50% of all process instances. Focusing on the "Solving rejected invoices" activity, we applied text-mining techniques to see the most common causes of rejected invoices.

4.3.1 Manual Entry of Order Numbers

The system identifies invoices with incorrect or missing IDs. For unidentified invoices, the system allocates tasks among the staff to enter correct order numbers manually. We identified the suppliers that needed the most such manual entries. By introducing these suppliers to the process owners, we reduced the number of invoices that had to be manually labeled, saving up to 7 h in invoice-processing time.

4.3.2 Resolving Rejected Invoices

Invoices can be rejected at the first level of approval or at the payment-processing stage. Rejected invoices are directed to a human activity that examines why the invoice was rejected and determines whether to end the activity (Decline the invoice) or to correct the problem and begin the process again. The process owner allocated three employees to complete the tasks involved in this activity, planning to divide tasks equally among the three. However, the reality was that the three employees differed in terms of how often they were assigned a task, as one performed 56% of all tasks, another performed 34%, and the third performed only 10%. The person with the highest number of tasks in this activity obtained the shortest average duration time in resolving rejected invoices, taking only 13 h, while the employee with the lowest percentage of assignments took an average of 15 days. These "reality checks" were presented to the process owner so the work habits of the most efficient employee could be presented to the other employees to improve their effectiveness.

Through analysis of this information, we found that, if an employee devoted less than 2 days to solving a rejected invoice, the invoice was declined 85% of the time and only 15% were approved. A ratio of 50% approved and 50% declined were obtained if an employee was solving a rejected invoice more than 2 days.

In order to establish the most common grounds for refusal regarding invoices, an expansion of the event log was made to contain "User comments." Data was extracted and reserved for this activity alone using a frequency analysis of phrases in the users comments to obtain the most common causes of rejection. The most frequent phrase was "wrong verification," which appeared in 29% of the rejections. The second most frequent phrase was "wrong amount," which appeared in 24% of the rejections. Less frequent phrases included "missing date" and "invoice in the wrong language." With these phrases identified, the process owner was able to address these frequent shortcomings and help the overall process to run more smoothly.

5 Lessons Learned

For analyses of processes to have value, the logs must be of high quality, so a significant challenge lies in pre-processing the data from multiple systems to create high-quality logs. All events and information that were recorded in the midst of all operations in processes had to be included, and the higher the quality of the information in the logs, the higher the quality of the resulting details about the processes.

We focused on the extraction, pre-processing, and analysis of data that was stored in a process-driven application. This software automatically executes business processes and logs the executed activities. In most of the systems, one can find design-time data, that is, process definitions and runtime data, including information on activities executed during the process. We defined the structure for stored data and defined the attributes attached to analyzing the processes.

Data was extracted using a connector we developed to identify design-time data automatically and extract runtime data into the desired process log structure, which must at least include an instance identifier and process steps in the form of an activity identifier to enable frequency analysis. If the process log does not include a timestamp attribute, events in the log must be ordered chronologically before the log is imported into a process-mining tool. Performance analysis can show the time between executions of two consecutive activities if at least one timestamp attribute is logged. However, when two timestamp values are logged—one describing the start and one describing the end of an event—we can reconstruct the process model, including the active time and waiting time for activities and the paths between them. One of the most important features of analytical tools is their ability to aggregate data, because sometimes the mean value does not have the same informative value as the median value. The process logs of two processes were exported using a comma-separated values format. Thus, we can gain insights using process-mining techniques for analyses and evaluations.

Process mining, along with business process modeling and analysis, provides an important bridge between computational intelligence and data mining. The idea of process mining is to discover, monitor, and improve real processes by extracting knowledge from event logs stored in information systems. One of the major benefits of using the technology is improved process transparency. By reconstructing the process models, we discovered the main process flow, as well as its deviations. Identified delays and bottlenecks become visible for both processes. Social networks were also reconstructed, and over-allocated resources were identified.

As process-mining techniques also include data mining, they can help to identify how input parameters influence process flow. Historical data can be used to predict the duration of process instances. We also focused on attributes that describe invoice rejections, where text-mining techniques helped to uncovered the most frequent reasons for rejecting an invoice.

Process discovery via process-mining methodology is faster and more cost effective than process reconstruction using a team of consultants. The goal should be use process mining and its advantages daily in order to conduct process-mining based on real-time event data. Using the real-time data makes it possible to enrich process model in several ways. For example, users involved in a process can navigate through the process in non-standard situations, and real-time data can be projected on process map to show a process's status, thereby informing employees about delays and other problems. Process mining should be viewed as a continuous process that provides actionable information.

One of the possibilities that was not pursued in this work is how to analyze processes within a BPM system. Our study analyzed primarily human activity, but system activities can also be analyzed to detect performance characteristics, communication, and bottlenecks that pertain to individual systems in a process. By modifying logs or using selected filters in the process-mining tool, we can select and analyze parts of processes that most needed attention.

References

Bose, R. P. J. C., & van der Aalst, W. M. P. (2009). Abstractions in process mining: A taxonomy of patterns. In U. Dayal, J. Eder, J. Koehler, & H. Reijers (Eds.), *Business Process Management (BPM 2009), volume 5701 of Lecture notes in Computer Science* (pp. 159–175). Berlin: Springer.

Dumas, M., La Rosa, M., Mendling, J., & Reijers, H. H. (2013). *Fundamentals of business process management*. Berlin: Springer.

Ferreira, D. R., & Gillblad, D. (2009). Discovering process models from unlabelled event logs. In U. Dayal, J. Eder, J. Koehler, & H. Reijers (Eds.), *Business Process Management (BPM 2009), volume 5701 of Lecture notes in Computer Science* (pp. 143–158). Berlin: Springer.

Günther, C. W. (2009). *XES Standard definition*. www.xes-standard.org

Günther, C. W., & van der Aalst, W. M. P. (2007). Fuzzy mining: Adaptive process simplification based on multi-perspective metrics. In G. Alonso, P. Dadam, & M. Rosemann (Eds.), *International conference on Business Process Management (BPM 2007), volume 4714 of Lecture notes in Computer Science* (pp. 328–343). Berlin: Springer.

IEEE Task Force on Process Mining. (2011). Process mining manifesto. In *BPM Workshops*, volume 99 of Lecture notes in Business information processing. Berlin: Springer.

van der Aalst, W. M. P. (1998). The application of petri nets to workflow management. *Journal of Circuits Systems and Computers, 8*, 21–66.

van der Aalst, W. M. P. (2011). *Process mining: Discovery, conformance and enhancement of business processes*. Berlin: Springer.

van der Aalst, W. M. P. (2016). *Process mining: Data science in action*. Berlin: Springer.

van der Aalst, W. M. P., & ter Hofstede, A. H. M. (2005). YAWL: Yet another workflow language. *Information Systems, 30*(4), 245–275.

van der Aalst, W. M. P., & van Hee, K. (2004). *Workflow management: Models, methods, and systems*. Cambridge, MA: MIT Press.

Wohed, P., et al. (2006). On the suitability of BPMN for business process modelling. In S. Dustdar, J. L. Fiadeiro, & A. P. Sheth (Eds.), *Business process management*. Berlin: Springer.

Jan Suchy is process and data analytic, while he is experienced in the field of development and implementation of the analytic algorithms. He focuses on the analysis of the data obtained from the enterprise systems, such as LOB, CRM, ERP and various BPM tools. Identification of "business values" of data, their extraction, transformation and processing by the means of Process Mining and Data Mining technologies are essentially covered by the analysis performed by Jan. Outcomes of his analysis form basis for optimisation, control and effective management of the processes. His experience consists of various analytical projects in different business sectors (Insurance, Banking, Public sector, Gaming industry, IT, Media, etc.). Jan contributes to academic publications and actively participates on the professional conferences in BPM sector. His added value lies in the prompt adaptation of the most modern analytical methods and their implementation in practice.

Milan Suchy is data analytic and expert in the field of process analysis. He has rich experience with extraction, processing and visualisation of data. In the past he participated on projects focused on reconstruction and optimisation of business processes, creation of machine learning models and identification of patterns in data. His strong areas include ability to apply data science and process science methods to various business sectors and provide to the clients valuable information hidden in data.

Michal Rosik As Product Visionary for Minit, he defines the Research & Development direction for this process mining solution, develops close ties to the academic community in this area and evangelises process mining benefits to enterprises worldwide. He received his master's degree in Management of Information Systems and Banking and Finance at Comenius University in Bratislava, Slovakia. Michal previously lead Microsoft Consulting department in Siemens and was involved in several large enterprise projects as a consultant and project manager. In his free time, he is a passionate trail runner.

Agnes Valkova is the head of marketing at Resco.net. With over thirteen years of experience in the Sales/Marketing industry and 10 years of direct experience in the field. She is an award winning sales/marketing executive with extensive global online, digital, and entertainment expertise. Proven success in developing cross platform content and marketing strategies, which exceed industry standards and deliver significant ROIs. A multi-disciplinary with a unique combination of creative, commercial, lingual and technical acumen. Skilled at high-level strategy, as well as tactical implementation. Agnes is also a public speaker at many worldwide conferences pertaining to her field in IT—Microsoft Envision, European SharePoint Conference, and more.

Integrate Your Partners into Your Business Processes Using Interactive Forms: The Case of Automotive Industry Company HEYCO

Bernhard Schindlbeck and Peter Kleinschmidt

Abstract

Situation faced: The automotive industry company HEYCO-WERK Heynen GmbH & Co. KG (HEYCO) wanted to improve how it handled purchase order confirmations. Its purchase department spent a lot of time entering incoming purchase order confirmations from its vendors into its SAP system. This process had to be automated with the most suitable technology to make it more time- and cost-efficient.

(a) **Action taken**: Before doing anything else, we had to choose the technology to support the process. Based on an empirical study, we developed a comparison scheme for business-to-business (B2B) technologies. We considered three types of technology, electronic data interchange (EDI), online portals, and interactive forms. Unlike the first two categories, interactive forms are seldom considered in the literature as an alternative B2B technology, but they turned out to be the best technology to support the purchase order confirmation process. Therefore, we chose them to support the process.
(b) **Results achieved**: With the implementation of interactive forms as a B2B solution to process purchase order confirmations, we achieved essential efficiency gains in time and quality. Working with interactive forms is well accepted by the process owners in the purchase department, who were able to automate the recording of purchase order confirmations with more than 100 vendors within 6 months.
(c) **Lessons learned:** Interactive forms turned to be a highly flexible and powerful tool in avoiding media breaks in document-driven processes.

B. Schindlbeck (✉) • P. Kleinschmidt
4process AG, Passau, Germany
e-mail: bernhard.schindlbeck@4process.de; peter.kleinschmidt@4process.de

J. vom Brocke, J. Mendling (eds.), *Business Process Management Cases*, Management for Professionals, DOI 10.1007/978-3-319-58307-5_26

We present the results of a feedback round with HEYCO's process owners, which was carried out 9 months after the introduction of the new procedure. Based on the input from those interviews, we discuss useful enhancements for the application to meet changed requirements and to accelerate technology adoption.

1 Introduction

For some time, companies have been using information technologies (IT) like EDI and online portals to support the exchange of data with their business partners (Allen et al. 1992; Hart and Saunders 1998). The benefits of using IT in B2B have been confirmed by many studies (Schindlbeck 2015). For example, IT improves collaboration between firms (Campo et al. 2010), inventory turnover and delivery performance (Li et al. 2009), and performance indicators of the supply chain like time, cost, quality, and flexibility (Wecker 2006). In spite of these positive impacts, many companies are still focusing on integrating a small portion of their partners into their business processes. Instead, the focus could be on achieving a high level of technological diffusion to support data exchange with as many of them as possible (Schindlbeck 2015). Hence, there is room for new technologies that can automate data transfer between firms so companies can integrate more of their partners.

One of the technologies of interest is interactive forms. Unlike electronic data interchange (EDI) and online portals, interactive forms are seldom discussed in the scientific literature as a technology to support B2B processes. We define interactive forms as electronic forms that can be generated from an enterprise application like enterprise resource planning (ERP) or customer relationship management (CRM), enriched with application-specific data. The form can be sent by e-mail to an external recipient, who completes it with the requested data using free software and sends the form back to the application, where the data are extracted and processed automatically. Additional processes can also be initiated.

This article presents a real-life scenario in which interactive forms are used to redesign an automotive-industry company's purchase order (PO) confirmation process by automating the recording of PO confirmations in the ERP system. The scenario was implemented as a prototype, and 9 months later feedback was solicited from the process owners in the purchasing department. Therefore, this paper discusses:

- how well the technology was established after 9 months in operation,
- what lessons can be learned after 9 months of operation, and
- what improvements can be made to accelerate technology adoption.

2 Situation Faced

The scenario took place in the company HEYCO-WERK Heynen GmbH & Co. KG (http://www.heyco.de/) (HEYCO hereafter). Founded in 1937, HEYCO employs about 900 people at production sites in Germany, Ireland, and the Czech Republic. The company, a supplier for the automotive industry, produces hand tools, plastic parts, and forgings. Many components from various vendors at home and abroad are needed for the manufacturing process, and goods for maintenance, repair, and operations (MRO) are purchased from a number of suppliers. The company has integrated some of its most important vendors into its business processes using EDI solutions, but PO confirmations for delivery dates and quantities were not yet processed automatically. In fact, the data transfer by EDI supported less than 2% of all current suppliers. A solution for a more efficient handling of confirmed delivery dates and quantities in the ERP system was needed.

Figure 1 shows the steps of the original version of the PO confirmation process before interactive forms were implemented.

The PO confirmation process starts when a HEYCO purchaser enters a PO in the company's SAP ERP system. When creating the PO, the purchaser determines the vendor and enters the articles, the requested quantities, and delivery dates. After saving the PO, the system generates the PO form as a PDF document and sends it to the supplier, which checks for the availability of the requested articles. Depending on the ATP (available-to-promise) situation, the supplier confirms or changes the quantities and delivery dates and sends a PO confirmation document by surface mail or e-mail to HEYCO. Then the purchaser finds the corresponding PO in the SAP system and enters the confirmed data (quantities, delivery dates, and the

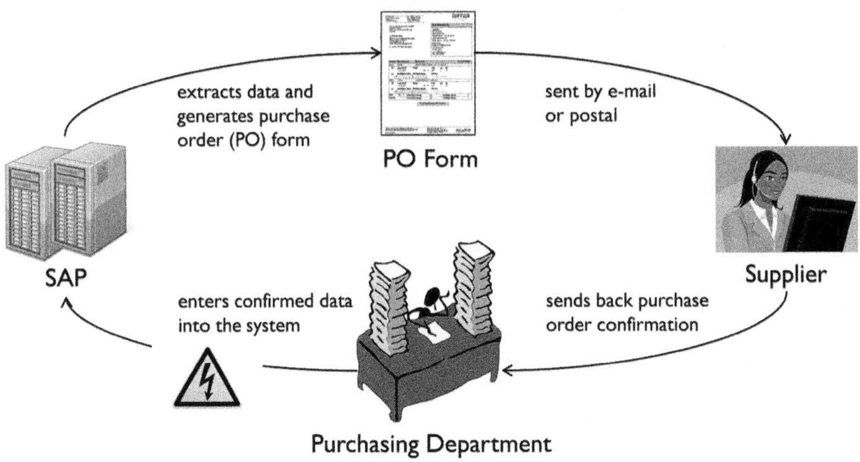

Fig. 1 Original process for purchase order confirmation

vendor's PO confirmation number) for each item on the PO. The material resource planning (MRP) module in SAP uses the confirmed data, not the requested data, for its computations. Finally, the purchaser archives the PO confirmation document for controlling purposes.

Because of its impact on MRP, the original process required accurate handling to guarantee high-quality data for planning purposes. The time required to enter a confirmation for one PO item averaged 150 s, so based on more than 12,000 PO confirmations entered in 2012, more than 500 h of work could be saved per year by automating this process.

3 Action Taken

The first step was choosing a suitable technology to support the process with as many vendors as possible. We considered three types of solutions for automating the process, which can be categorized as one-to-one technologies, one-to-many technologies (Wirtz and Bronnenmayer 2011), and interactive forms.

3.1 One-to-One

One-to-one technologies include those that are used to integrate each partner individually. These connections are characterized by a mutual exchange of information and efficiency gains for both sides. However, establishing these connections requires that each partner make certain investments. A typical example of a one-to-one technology is the automated exchange of business documents between two partners' ERP systems using EDI or extensible markup language (XML) messages (Wüstner 2005).

3.2 One-to-Many

One-to-many technologies enable companies to integrate their partners in a flexible way, without extensive coordination. These technologies can be implemented by portals (Gmelch 2012), online platforms, or e-marketplaces (Petersen et al. 2007) integrated into the enterprise's ERP system. However, these technologies usually force the interacting partner to enter the required data into a web form manually, so efficiency gains from eliminating a media break are mostly those of the company that implemented the technology.

3.3 Interactive Forms

Interactive forms are electronic forms generated from an enterprise application (Hauser et al. 2011) that contain both application-specific data and interactive elements like input fields and dropdown lists. Users can enter data into the forms and save them in a structured way (mostly technically in XML structures). Because of the structured storage of information, the data entered can be extracted and automatically processed in the source application to eliminate media breaks and initiate other processes. Interactive forms can also be dynamic in that they can change their layouts depending on the user's actions (e.g., making it possible to provide a user-friendly form). Certain areas are hidden until the user needs them. Embedded scripting allows the system to react to users' actions by means of warnings and error messages, and to calculate key figures based on the values entered. Examples of providers of interactive forms are Adobe, with its product Adobe Interactive Forms, and LUCOM, with the application FormsForWeb.

One may argue that interactive forms belong among the one-to-many technologies, as they share a number of characteristics, including integrating partners in a flexible way without any individual implementation effort and eliminating the media break in the process only for the company that generates the form and processes it in its ERP after it is completed. However, it seems justified to put interactive forms in a category of its own because of some unique characteristics, including the offline capability of interactive forms. In contrast to the web forms that are used in typical one-to-many scenarios, completing an interactive form does not require an internet connection, as all data and scripting are usually embedded in the form. Offline capability generally goes hand in hand with the possibility of saving intermediate results and of printing the form, so users can interrupt the data-entry process, save the form, and complete it later and can retain a paper copy for their own controlling purposes. Hence, interactive forms have advantages in converting paper-based scenarios to electronic processes. What's more, most users are well acquainted with Adobe forms.

3.4 Comparison of the Technologies

We set out to find the most suitable technology by comparing the three categories with respect to the requirements of HEYCO's purchase department. Relevant entry barriers for one-to-one and one-to-many technologies were identified by an empirical study with 95 German manufacturing companies (Schindlbeck 2015). Based on the most important barriers determined in the study and the characteristics of the technologies, a comparison scheme was developed consisting of six indicators.

- Evaluation of Return on Investment (ROI)
- Process Expertise and User Acceptance

- Flexibility
- Partner Acceptance
- Possible Level of Automation
- Possible Functional Scope

Evaluation of ROI: Project managers must always be able to explain how a new solution generates significant benefits for the company, but depending on the technology, it may be more or less difficult to calculate the solution's ROI. One-to-one technologies are usually used to support one specific process, such as when enterprises exchange orders with their partners electronically using EDI. It is comparatively easy to determine the costs and benefits of the implementation because orders would not have to be entered into the system manually anymore. Like one-to-one technologies, interactive forms usually support a single process and can be evaluated well. In contrast, one-to-many technologies like online platforms and portals frequently provide a wider range of functionalities and are implemented to support a wide range of scenarios. Therefore, it is more difficult to estimate all costs and benefits and to break them down to the supported processes. Consequently, one-to-one and interactive forms have advantages over one-to-many technologies the ability to evaluate ROI.

Process Expertise and User Acceptance: The use of technologies in B2B often leads to significant changes in the process. With our example of orders exchanged by means of EDI, the purchaser creates the PO in the system, prints it, and sends it to the vendor, and after the vendor enters the PO, a sales order is automatically created in the vendor's system. The PO form used in the original process is obsolete. In addition, one-to-many solutions often replace paper-based or electronic forms with web forms, so users must be trained in the new process, and resistance to the technology can occur because of the changes in the process flow. Interactive forms usually do not touch the process and are similar to paper documents because of they can be handled offline, so they do not require much training and are likely to be more readily accepted by users than are other B2B technologies.

Flexibility describes how easily a new partner can be integrated using the solution. The integration of a partner with one-to-one technologies requires individual coordination: data structures have to be mapped, interfaces must be implemented, and communication channels for the data exchange have to be established. Therefore, previous investments are lost (sunk costs) when the transaction is no longer executed. Implementation makes sense only if a high volume of data is exchanged between partners and if the business relationship is stable, so one-to-one is preferred for strategic partners. For partners to participate in a one-to-many solution, it is usually sufficient that they log on to an online platform with a provided user name and password, which is even easier with interactive forms, as everyone who receives and completes a form can take part in the process.

Partner Acceptance: There are (at least) two sides in B2B, so the partner must willing to take part in the process. In dealing with one-to-one technologies the partners faces the same challenges as the company itself, so only partners with a high volume of data exchange are likely to accept the investment required to establish a one-to-one connection. On the other hand, one-to-many technologies eliminate media breaks only on the side of one company, so these technologies may make even higher demands on the partners in a process supported by a one-to-many technology because they have to enter data into a web form manually. Like one-to-many technologies, interactive forms avoid media breaks only for the company that generates and processes them, but interactive forms' ability to be managed offline gives them some advantages over web forms (one-to-many). For example, the partner can keep a copy of the form for its own controlling purposes, it does not have to enter all of the data in one step but can save intermediate versions and complete the form later, and it does not have to log on to a platform but can provide data as soon as it has received the interactive form.

The highest *Level of Automation* can be achieved by one-to-one technologies, as data exchange that is free of media breaks can be possible if the systems of both transaction partners are integrated with each other. On the other hand, one-to-many technologies have limited capabilities to automate processes because data processing is automated on only one side, although it is at least possible for the user to execute more than one process step when using a web form. Web forms are usually connected to a database, so the information entered can be handled immediately in the backend systems and additional steps can be initiated based on the input. Interactive forms perform poorly in this regard. Because interactive forms can be processed offline, all the information that is needed during the data entry, such as data for validation, different layouts, and data screens, has to be stored in the electronic document. A document can never compete against a database in that respect.

Functional Scope describes the range of functionalities offered by a technology to support the interaction between companies. One-to-one technologies are powerful in automating on both sides, so they can optimize process flows across companies, but their functions are generally limited to the transfer of data. Limited resources due to the offline capability force developers to keep interactive forms simple so the forms are used primarily as data collectors with basic functions like validations and the ability to change their layout. One-to-many technologies are the most powerful in terms of functional scope, as they run on servers and are connected to databases, so they have access to almost unlimited resources. Nearly every type of application could be developed based on these platforms, including the integration of media files, data sharing, collaboration rooms and much more.

Based on this analysis, we visualize the evaluation of the three technology categories as network diagrams in Figs. 2 and 3.

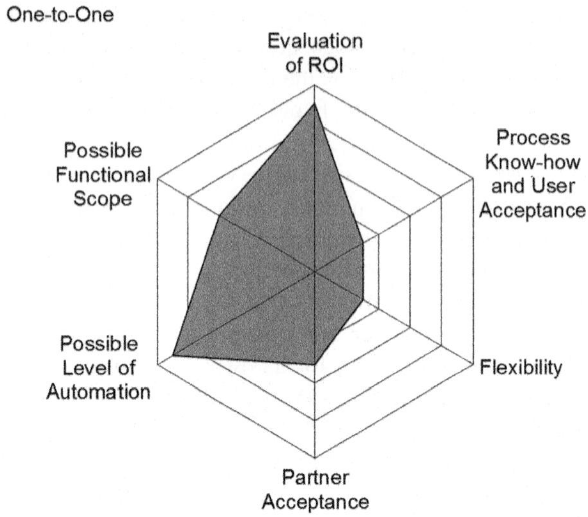

Fig. 2 Evaluation of one-to-one technologies

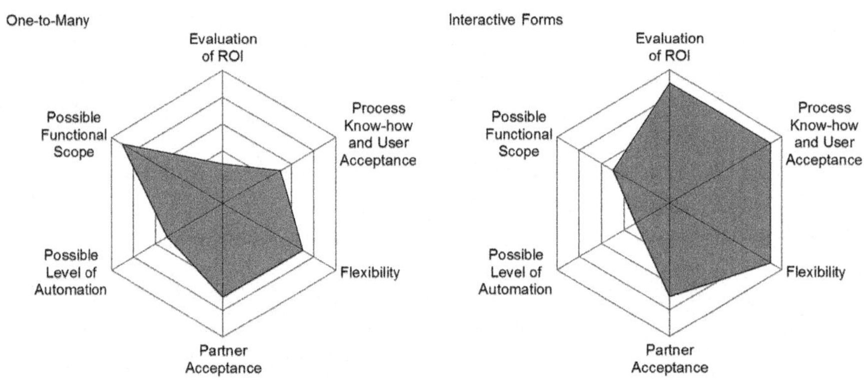

Fig. 3 Evaluation of one-to-many technologies and interactive forms

HEYCO's requirements for choosing a software were that:

- the necessary investments be justified by means of a qualified calculation of ROI;
- purchasers could use the technology without intensive training, so the new process had to be as similar to the old process as possible;
- nearly every partner could be integrated into the system, even B- and C-partners with low volumes of data to exchange.

We first excluded one-to-one technologies because of their lack of *flexibility*. The individual coordination required with each partner would be profitable only when a high volume of data is exchanged, so businesses with less data to exchange would not agree to make the necessary investments.

As Fig. 3 shows, one-to-many technologies and interactive forms can integrate all types of partners because of their advantages in terms of *flexibility* and *partner acceptance*. While a portal solution and interactive forms were both shortlisted for HEYCO, purchasers preferred interactive forms because of the ROI. While there were expenses for implementation, infrastructure, and licenses, the estimated time savings were sufficient for the solution to be profitable. The portal solution would have provided some additional functions for the vendor, such as the possibility of printing HEYCO-compatible delivery notes, it was more important to HEYCO to support the core process with a computable cost-benefit ratio.

In addition, with interactive forms the original process flow changes very little. The PO confirmation document is replaced by the interactive form, but the procedure remains the same, so purchases do not need much training. With the portal, the PO confirmation form would have been replaced by a web form, and instead of just completing the PO confirmation document, the vendor would have had to log on to the portal, search for its POs, and enter the confirmations. Therefore interactive forms are better in terms of the second requirement because of the advantages indicated by *process expertise* and *user acceptance* (Fig. 3).

Finally, higher ratings in terms of *flexibility* and *partner acceptance* make interactive forms more suitable for integrating nearly every partner. The supplier does not need any specific technical skills but just completes the received form and sends it back.

The new PO confirmation process is a simple, linear procedure: The vendor enters the confirmed delivery dates, quantities, and its order confirmation number, so the interactive form covers only one process step (entering the confirmations). Therefore, interactive forms' lower ratings for *level of automation* and *functional scope* compared to the ratings for one-to-many technologies do not matter in this scenario.

3.5 Implementation of the Scenario with Interactive Forms

The solution was created using a rapid prototyping approach. A first prototype was presented to HEYCO's main actors that was based on the company's initial requirements. Then their feedback was integrated into the prototype to refine it step by step. In the end, the solution consisted of four main components:

- Form processing module
- Status management module
- Inbound processing module
- PO confirmation monitor

The *form processing* module generates an e-mail with the interactive PO confirmation form as an attachment as soon as a purchaser creates a PO in the system. The module selects the application data in SAP ERP, implements the interface for the transfer of the application data to the interactive form, and provides the form layout of the PO confirmation.

The *status management* module tracks the status of each form. Every mailed form is identified by a globally unique identifier (GUID) that is generated from the *form processing* module. With its own data model developed in SAP, the *status management* module documents (among other things) the timestamps

- when the form was sent to the supplier
- when the form was received back
- when the form was processed by the purchaser in SAP with regard to that GUID.

Possible statuses are *confirmation not received yet*, *ready to process*, *completed*, and *form received multiple times*.

The *inbound processing* module extracts the data from incoming forms, validates it, and updates the *status management* module's database tables. The module also archives received forms in a content server.

The *PO confirmation monitor* reports on the content of the *status management* module's tables so the user can display all generated forms and their statuses. The user can also choose to see the archived PO confirmation.

4 Results Achieved

The flow of the PO confirmation process with interactive forms (Fig. 4) is similar to that of the original procedure (Fig. 1), as only the manual transfer of the PO confirmation form to the SAP system is replaced by the automatic processing of the interactive form.

Saving the PO in SAP ERP generates, in addition to the PO document, an interactive PO confirmation form that is sent to the supplier. It looks similar to the PO document and contains the requested delivery dates and quantities for each PO item. Interactive input fields allow the user to enter the confirmed dates and quantities and the vendor's order confirmation number. Mandatory fields are marked by a red frame, which disappears as soon as the field is filled, so the user can easily identify the fields that still require values.

Figure 5 shows a plain example of a PO confirmation with one item. The company requests 80 pieces of a material to be delivered on 18 December 2015. In our example, the supplier confirms the quantity and the delivery date and then sends the form back to HEYCO's SAP system using a send button in the form. With a click of that button, a number of validations are performed. For example, the system checks to ensure that all mandatory fields are filled in, after which the form's interactive functions are switched off, and no changes are possible, so the document can be used for audit-proof archiving. In addition, an e-mail is created

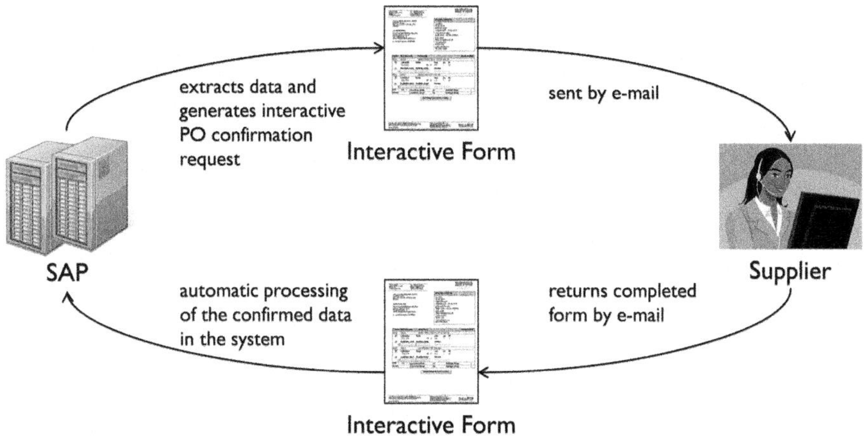

Fig. 4 Process for PO confirmation with interactive forms

automatically that contains the SAP system's email address as the receiver and the completed PO confirmation form as an attachment. As soon as the e-mail is delivered to HEYCO's SAP ERP, the data entered are extracted by the *inbound processing* module and stored in the system's database. The form is also automatically stored in the content server with a link to the PO in SAP.

The purchaser can use the *PO confirmation monitor* to display received PO confirmations. The monitor shows one reporting line for each confirmed delivery date, along with information like requested and confirmed delivery dates and quantities, vendor name, material, related PO number and item, and timestamps for sending and receiving.

Possible exceptions are:

- The confirmed quantity or delivery date deviates from the requested one.
- The vendor rejected the confirmation.
- The related PO item is already confirmed in SAP ERP (e.g., because someone had already entered the confirmation manually).
- The related PO item was deleted in SAP ERP in the meantime.
- The confirmation is not up to date because the requested quantity or delivery date of the related PO item was changed in SAP ERP in the meantime.

With the monitor, the purchaser can check all of the confirmations at a glance, and the exception groups identify problematic confirmations so the purchaser can clarify deviating confirmations with the vendor. All of the accepted confirmations can be selected and processed with one click, at which time the confirmations are transferred to the related PO items in SAP ERP. Henceforth, SAP MRP considers the dates and quantities to be confirmed. In addition the purchaser no longer has to

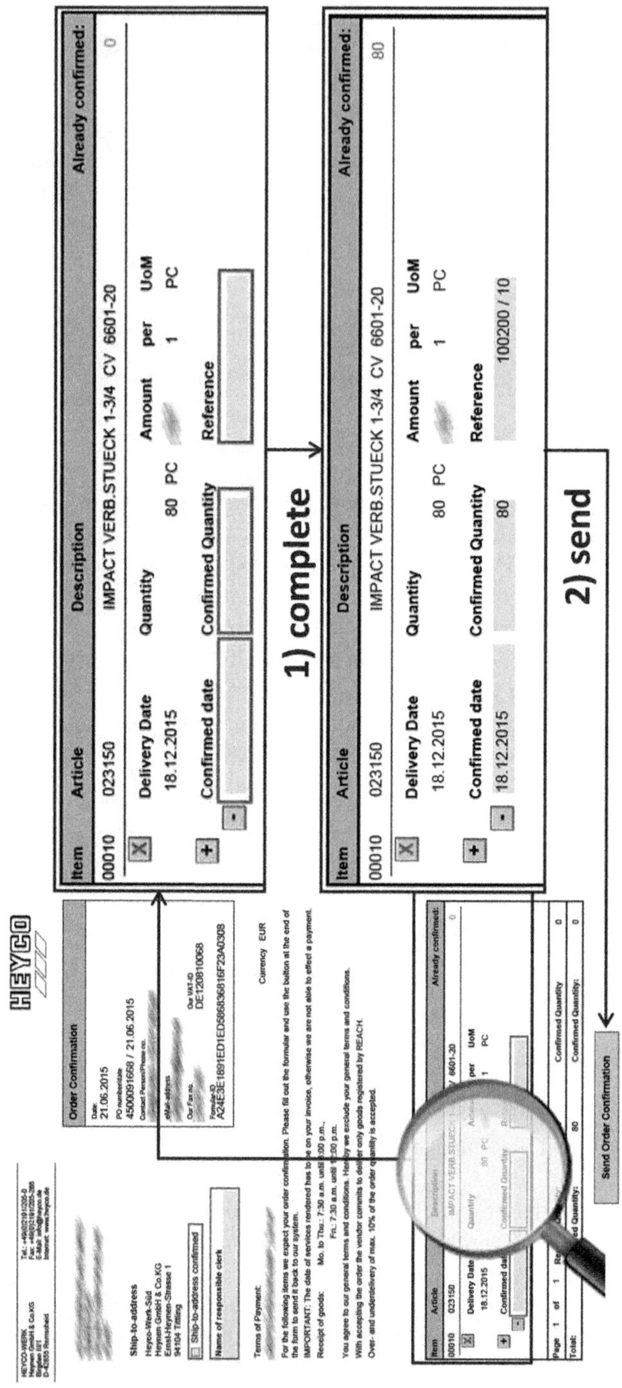

Fig. 5 Example of a completed interactive PO confirmation form.

enter confirmations manually. The archiving of the form is also obsolete, as all confirmations can be monitored easily and are well arranged.

4.1 Extent of use

In September 2014, HEYCO's purchasing department began using interactive forms to automate the PO confirmation process with its vendors. Nine months later, feedback was solicited from purchasers to discuss their experiences in using the application. In general, the purchasers were convinced of the quality of the solution, mentioning several advantages:

- The solution simplifies the process of recording PO confirmations in SAP ERP, so it is helpful in daily business.
- From the point of view of most vendors, it is a low-tech-solution that required only a slight modification from the original process, so many suppliers were easily convinced to accept the new procedure.
- Vendors who have used interactive forms once work with them in a reliable way.
- The *PO confirmation monitor* is easy to use. It provides a good overview of sent and outstanding PO confirmations, and received data can be handled efficiently. Critical PO confirmations are easily identified by the exception groups, while the rest can be processed with one click.
- The transparency of the process is improved because incoming forms are archived with a link to the PO in SAP ERP.

In the first month of use, 45 vendors confirmed POs with interactive forms, and about 15 new vendors were integrated every month thereafter (Fig. 6). Figure 6 also shows that the average number of suppliers that actually used the interactive forms

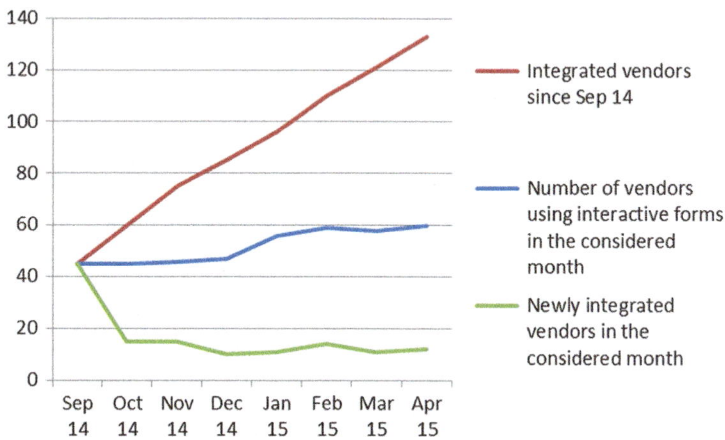

Fig. 6 Number of vendors who participated in the new process since September 2014.

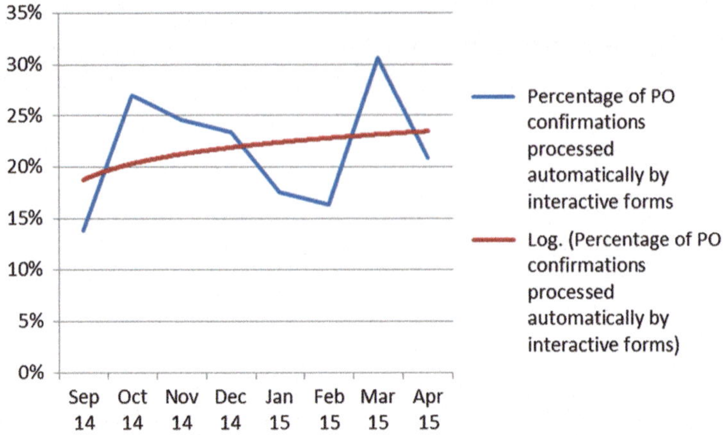

Fig. 7 Percentage of the PO confirmations processed with interactive forms.

during a 1-month period grew slowly, from 45 in September 2014 to 60 in April 2015. Therefore, vendors with less than one PO per month (and, therefore, a comparatively low volume of data) use the solution, too, so the solution is suitable for all types of vendors.

Figure 7 describes the percentages of PO confirmations processed with interactive forms in relation to all recorded PO confirmations in SAP ERP. The blue line shows the percentage for each month. The red line is a logarithmic trend line, which was calculated with the monthly data. In the first month (September 2014), 14% of the data volume was already processed with interactive forms. The coverage increased strongly in October 2014, but then it declined again and settled at a level of around 23%, in part because the solution is also used with C partners, so an increase in the number of participating vendors did not lead to a commensurate increase in the monthly data exchanged using the system.

5 Lessons Learned

While the automated recording of 23% of the PO confirmations makes a strong contribution to improving process quality and efficiency, we expected more vendors to adopt the solution during the first 8 months. Therefore, we asked HEYCO's purchasers why the percentage did not increase faster. It turned out that, even with the simplicity of interactive forms, there are some barriers to adoption and some challenges in convincing vendors to work with the solution. Before a vendor receives its first interactive form, the responsible purchaser explains the new procedure in order to obtain the vendor's commitment. Some vendors try to avoid even small change in processes because of a general mistrust of process changes. A good way to support purchasers in their attempts to remove their vendors' concerns is to provide purchasers with a conversation guideline and to provide vendors with a short documentation of the PO confirmation process with interactive forms so communication with vendors is standardized.

A second reason that vendors resisted working with the interactive forms was that they could not confirm a HEYCO PO if purchase prices had changed and the prices on the interactive PO confirmation were not up to date. Therefore, the solution would be enhanced by a function that could change and confirm prices in the interactive form.

Users also suggested implementing a way to report statistics regarding the extent of the use of interactive forms in SAP ERP, including:

- the monthly percentage of received PO confirmations via interactive forms in relation to sent interactive forms for each vendor (response rate)
- the monthly percentage of PO confirmations processed by interactive forms in relation to all the recorded PO confirmations for each vendor (coverage of data volume)
- the monthly percentage of PO confirmations processed by interactive forms in relation to all the recorded PO confirmations for each purchaser (internal adoption)

The first two vendor-specific figures, which are generated automatically in SAP ERP, can be used in periodical reviews and evaluations with the suppliers. As part of the evaluation, the supplier can be encouraged to use the technology by using the third key figure to agree on purchaser-specific targets for process automation.

With these activities, the technology adoption can be accelerated and the percentage of PO confirmations processed by interactive forms increased.

5.1 Conclusion

We described some challenges in the process of introducing HEYCO's technology changes, but the general results of the first 8 months are satisfactory for a medium-sized company like HEYCO, with up to 31% of PO confirmations processed by interactive forms and 133 vendors working with the solution.

The main process actors gave positive feedback, and they are confident that implementation of the planned improvements will result in even better and faster adoption of the technology.

Interactive forms were evaluated as a suitable way to integrate all types of B2B partners into business processes. The positive experience with the PO confirmation scenario underscores these forms' ability to enable companies to automate more of their processes with a larger number of their partners. The comparison scheme we developed can help decision-makers choose the appropriate technology for their particular situations.

The feedback round also resulted in discussions about other processes that could be supported by interactive forms, such as requests for quotations, 8D reports, and suppliers' declarations. Other projects with interactive forms are planned.

Because of the platform independence of PDFs and low entry barriers, interactive forms can help to integrate all types of partners (A/B/C). However, all barriers and characteristics of technologies should be considered with respect to the requirements of the process before choosing a technology for automation. The comparison scheme developed here helps companies to choose the best technology for their needs.

References

Allen, B. J., Crum, M. R., & Braunschweig, C. D. (1992). The US motor carrier industry: The extent and nature of EDI use. *International Journal of Physical Distribution & Logistics Management, 22*(8), 27–34.

Campo, S., Rubio, N., & Yagüe, M. J. (2010). Information technology use and firm's perceived performance in supply chain management. *Journal of Business to Business Marketing, 17*(4), 336–364.

Gmelch, O. (2012). User-Centric application integration in enterprise portal systems. Dissertations University of Regensburg. Lohmar: Eul.

Hart, P. J., & Saunders, C. S. (1998). Emerging electronic partnerships: Antecedents and dimensions of EDI use from the supplier's perspective. *Journal of Management Information Systems, 14*, 87–111.

Hauser, J., Deutesfeld, A., Rehmann, S., & Szücs, T. (2011). *SAP interactive forms by Adobe* (2nd ed.). Bonn: Galileo Press.

Li, G., et al. (2009). The impact of IT implementation on supply chain integration and performance. *International Journal of Production Economics, 120*(1), 125–138.

Petersen, K. J., Ogden, J. A., & Carter, P. L. (2007). B2B e-marketplaces: A typology by functionality. *International Journal of Physical Distribution & Logistics Management, 37*(1), 4–18.

Schindlbeck, B. (2015). Verbreitung und Durchdringung von Business-to-Business Technologien. Interaktive Formulare als alternative Technologie zur Unterstützung des Informationsaustauschs zwischen Unternehmen. Dissertations University of Passau. Berlin: Logos Verlag.

Wecker, R. (2006). Internetbasiertes supply chain management. Dissertations University of Witten/Herdecke. Wiesbaden: Deutscher Universitäts-Verlag.

Wirtz, B. W., & Bronnenmayer, M. (2011). B2B-Geschäftsmodelle im Electronic Business. *Wirtschaftswissenschaftliches Studium, 40*(9), 454–461.

Wüstner, E. (2005). *Standardisierung und Konvertierung: Ökonomische Bewertung und Anwendung am Beispiel von XML/EDI*. Aachen: Shaker.

Bernhard Schindlbeck is project manager at 4process AG—a SAP consulting company. He has more than 10 years of experience in the SAP environment. He was active in and responsible for national and international SAP projects in various countries (Argentina, Dubai, France, Hungary, USA and others). He is SAP expert in the logistics area (Sales & Distribution, Logistics Execution, Material Management, Production Planning and Equipment & Tools Management). Furthermore, he analysed the capability of interactive forms as an alternative B2B technology in his dissertation. The results are fed into current projects on his responsibility in which processes are improved by using interactive forms.

Peter Kleinschmidt
Education:
Undergraduate and graduate studies at the University of Bochum in Mathematics and Business
Administration and Economics, 1968–1974:
Degrees: Dipl. Math, Dr. rer. Nat., Priv. Doz.
Appointments as visiting Professor: University of Washington, Seattle
University of Siegen
University of Augsburg
Permanent positions as professor: University of Bochum (Department of Mathematics) 1985–1986
University of Passau (Department of Mathematics and Computer Science) 1986–1992
University of Passau (Department of Business Administration and Economics, Chair of Business Information Systems) 1992–2015
Retirement: 2015
Various positions on the board of several IT companies
Founder of the first SAP University Competence Center in Germany
Current: Head of the supervisory board of 4process AG

Part IV

People and Culture

Leading 20,000+ Employees with a Process-Oriented Management System: Insights into Process Management at Lufthansa Technik Group

Mirko Kloppenburg, Janina Kettenbohrer, Daniel Beimborn, and Michael Bögle

Abstract

(a) **Situation faced**: Structured documentation of an aviation company's processes is a prerequisite to gaining an authority's approval for aircraft maintenance, repair, and overhaul. Processes had been documented in a continuously growing number of PDF-based text documents, but the growing complexity of processes meant that this approach to process documentation no longer provided easy-to-understand work instructions for employees that fulfilled the authorities' requirements.

(b) **Action taken**: Lufthansa Technik Group implemented a process-oriented management system called IQ MOVE, the goal of which is to provide concise, easy-to-read documentation of processes in the form of process maps and swim-lane-based process descriptions. The system is designed to ensure seamless integration of normative and legislative requirements into the processes to avoid cross-references and to separate process documentation into multiple points of view. Moreover, IQ MOVE applies the "Framework for Assignment of Responsibilities" (FAR+) to strengthen process-management roles and increase employees' acceptance of the system.

(c) **Results achieved**: 20,000+ employees at Lufthansa Technik use IQ MOVE in their daily work. A periodically performed employee survey shows a

M. Kloppenburg (✉) • M. Bögle
Lufthansa Technik AG, Hamburg, Germany
e-mail: Mirko.Kloppenburg@lht.dlh.de; Michael.Boegle@lht.dlh.de

J. Kettenbohrer
University of Bamberg, Bamberg, Germany
e-mail: Janina.Kettenbohrer@uni-bamberg.de

D. Beimborn
Frankfurt School of Finance & Management, Frankfurt, Germany
e-mail: d.beimborn@fs.de

J. vom Brocke, J. Mendling (eds.), *Business Process Management Cases*, Management for Professionals, DOI 10.1007/978-3-319-58307-5_27

high level of acceptance by the employees and increased awareness of the process-management roles (e.g., Process Owner, Process Architect, and Process Manager) based on the implementation of FAR+ and the integrated BPM Lifecycle approach.

(d) **Lessons learned**: Key success factors of the system are the easy-to-understand process-modeling notation, the seamless integration of normative and legislative requirements into processes, the clearly defined process-management roles, the holistic process-modeling team, and the comprehensive process operations concept that Lufthansa Technik Group applied.

1 Introduction

The Lufthansa Technik Group, the technical division of Lufthansa Group, provides aircraft maintenance, repair, and overhaul (MRO) services to about 800 customers around the world. At its 30 subsidiaries worldwide, more than 20,000 employees perform tasks like aircraft overhaul, component maintenance, and V.I.P. cabin completion. The basis for all aircraft-related tasks are the approvals of the respective aviation authorities from 69 countries. To gain these approvals, Lufthansa Technik must demonstrate to these regulatory authorities its compliance with international laws and standards. The company accomplishes this requirement based on the process-oriented management system called IQ MOVE.

IQ MOVE consists of a web application with two modules. In the background, "requirement management" covers all applicable legislative and normative requirements (e.g., EASA Part-145, EN 9110), which are interpreted and assigned to all processes to which they are relevant. At the front-end, these processes are presented to the users in the system's process-management module, in which all relevant processes are mapped in concise and easy-to-read process-modeling language that is designed to fit to the employees' needs.

Since the beginning of the IQ MOVE implementation in 2002, "Finding all relevant procedures quickly and easily" has been the guiding vision of the development and operation of the system. Its acceptance by the employees is the key indicator of the success of the IQ MOVE implementation.

Today, IQ MOVE covers a wide range of processes, from production to administration. In the beginning, the implementation project focused on modeling processes that are under regulatory supervision, but processes from areas like human resources, accounting, and innovation were also included. Regarding employees' acceptance of the system, most of the efforts was directed toward production processes, particularly the repair and release-to-service of aircraft and aircraft parts processes, which are performed by about 12,000 mechanics all over the world.

An essential step in increasing employees' acceptance was the introduction of a process-management role concept that facilitates clear assignment of management responsibilities to specific roles, such as Process Owner, Process Architect, and Process Manager (for process responsibility) and Line Manager (for disciplinary responsibility). Intensive training and coaching for these roles has helped to improve the operation of processes by, for example, keeping processes up-to-date and providing process training to employees.

2 Situation Faced

Performing aircraft MRO requires the approval of the respective customer's aviation authority. For example, to provide aircraft maintenance to a customer with U.S. registered aircraft, approval by the Federal Aviation Administration (FAA) for performing the corresponding tasks is a prerequisite. To gain approval, the company has to prove its processes' conformity with the respective law in terms of both process documentation and the practical execution of processes.

Prior to the implementation of IQ MOVE, the company demonstrated its procedures' conformity with international laws and standards in a conventional way using more than 360 PDF documents issued by multiple departments and developed by about 250 employees across the company. These documents varied in length from 2 to 120 pages, contained a large number of cross-references, and described procedures from multiple points of view. For example, the process of "Creating quotations for the repair of aircraft components" was described from the workshop's point of view as well as from customer service's point of view. The two responsible departments issued separate procedure documentations that described the specifics of the process, often without matching the content.

Therefore, when an employee wanted to perform a specific activity, he or she had first to identify the relevant procedures and then to look up the relevant content. Because of the continuously growing number of documents written from multiple points of view and containing numerous cross-references, it was challenging to take all relevant procedures into account, and increasing numbers of inconsistencies caused coordination issues, not to mention irritation. As a consequence, the system had to be redesigned.

3 Action Taken

The core idea of the new system was to replace the existing documentation by means of a process-oriented, integrated management system that provides in one place all relevant information to performing an activity, taking all applicable norms, standards, and internal and external regulations into account. To implement this idea, a web-based application was developed in close cooperation with the future users of the system, particularly employees from production, such as aircraft mechanics and engineers.

This system was named IQ MOVE. "IQ" reflects the "integrated quality management" approach of combining several requirement disciplines in one system, while "MOVE" represents the flexibility and the ongoing development of the system and its content.

The overall target of the IQ MOVE implementation was—and is—to ensure the "safety first" principle by providing to employees around the world all of the information that is relevant to the safe execution of processes and informed decision-making.

3.1 Requirement and Process Management Form the Basis of IQ MOVE

The IQ MOVE application consists of two major modules: A "Requirement Management" module and a "Process Management" module. The Requirement Management module is designed for the implementation of all requirements, such as EASA Part-145, EN 9110, and OHSAS 18001.[1] Target groups for this area are authorities, certification bodies, and customers' auditors. To build the content of the requirement database, internal Requirement Managers interpret all applicable requirements into actionable tasks and document these tasks in the requirement database.

The Process Management module contains the organization's processes. All processes are modeled so they are easy for employees to understand. Processes are stored in IQ MOVE's Process and Document Database.

To connect requirement management and process management, tasks that result from requirements are assigned to processes in the course of the Requirement Manager's "conformity check" and integrated into processes by process modeling teams before the processes are published. Figure 1 provides an overview of the connection between these two modules.

3.2 Process Modeling in IQ MOVE

The integration of requirements into processes is enabled by the application of a concise process-modeling methodology that consists of multiple modeling levels with increasing levels of detail. The highest level of the "process world"—the level with the least detail—consists of "process maps" that structure processes from a process-oriented organizational perspective. This structure is detailed by several levels of process maps until the next-highest level, a "process display," is reached. A process display consists of six swim lanes that contain the process's roles and activities and provide an overview of the process flow and how the roles interact. Every activity in the process is further explained by "info boxes," the third level, which present detailed information on how to perform the respective activity on

[1]EASA Part-145 describes the requirements for achieving and maintaining the aviation authority's approval as a maintenance organization for aircraft and aircraft components in the EU. EN 9110 describes the requirements for a quality-management system of the EN 9xxx family, with specific requirements for aviation and aerospace maintenance organizations. OHSAS 18001 describes requirements for an occupational health and safety management system to eliminate or minimize risks to employees.

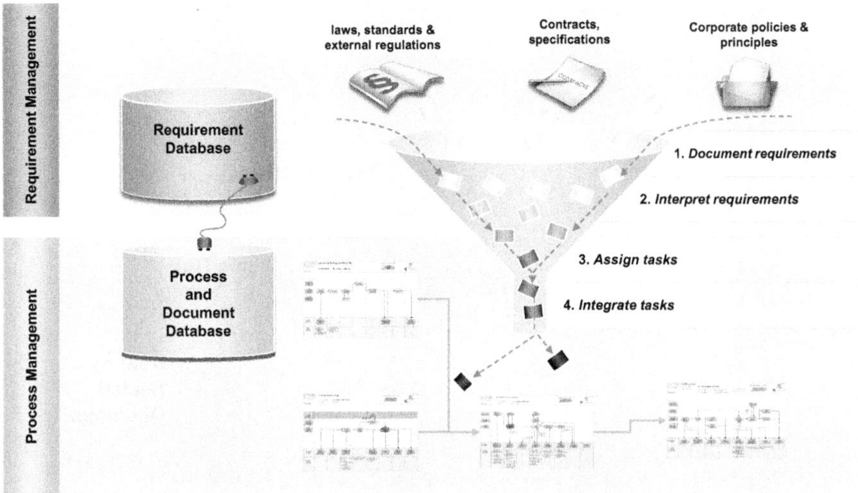

Fig. 1 Processes and requirements are connected by tasks in IQ MOVE

responsible roles, applicable IT systems, and related documents. These "activity-related documents" are the lowest level of the documentation and provide the highest level of detail in terms of checklists, forms, examples, and so on (Fig. 2.).

A closer look at the design of process displays in IQ MOVE is shown in Fig. 3, which shows an example of a process display. A swim lane consists of nine cells. The first cell is reserved for the role that executes the activities and decisions placed within the remaining eight cells of the swim lane. Activities and decisions are connected by either the standard workflow or by optional (alternative or additional) connections. Roles, activities, decisions, and connections are the core elements of the modeling notation used in IQ MOVE. Two swim lanes at the bottom of the process refer to upstream and downstream processes for navigation between process displays and to activity-related documents for quick access to more detailed information. An end-to-end process initiated and ended by the customer (internal as well as external customers) can be modeled along several process displays.

The reduced modeling methodology IQ MOVE uses is the result of several workshops with about 100 employees during the design phase of the IQ MOVE development project. The goal of these workshops was to identify a way to do process modeling that employees can understand easily. As a consequence, more complex modeling elements, such as operators, events, and interfaces, were abandoned. Workshop participants evaluated notations like UML[2] activity diagrams and Event Driven Process Chains. (BPMN[3] was not available in 2002.)

Not only the process maps but also other paths enable the users of IQ MOVE to access the process world. Because of the assignment of roles to an organization's

[2] UML = Unified Modeling Language.

[3] BPMN = Business Process Model and Notation.

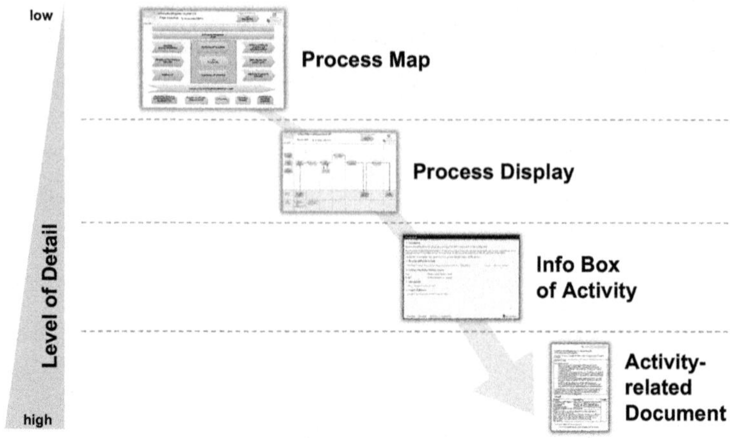

Fig. 2 Four levels of detail are used to describe processes in IQ MOVE

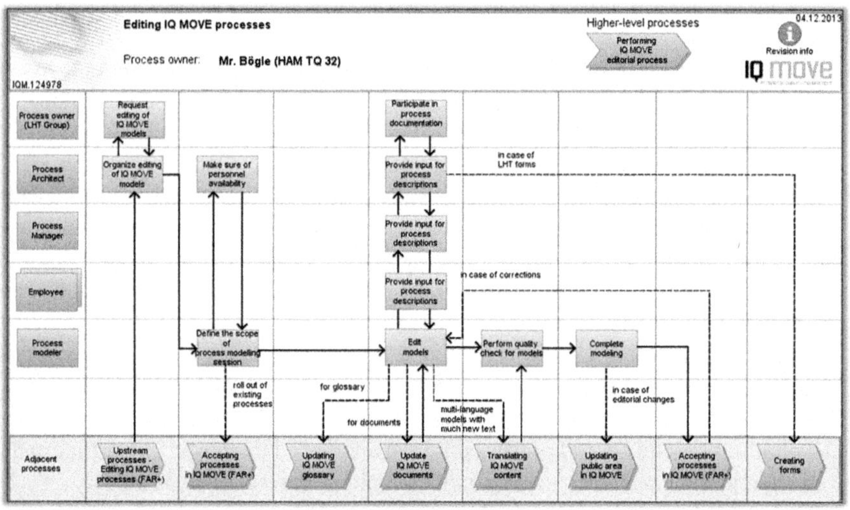

Fig. 3 Example of a process display in IQ MOVE

structure, visual organizational charts can be used to open up the processes that belong to specific roles. Personalized bookmarks also enable direct access to frequently used processes and documents, and a search function makes it possible to look up information throughout the whole process world. Based on the role-based modeling approach, it is possible to limit content (e.g., within search results) to processes in which a user is involved. Figure 4 shows the interconnections based on the integration of roles and activities into IQ MOVE's process database.

To explain the difference between management system documentation and operational information, Fig. 5 presents the characteristics of both levels of

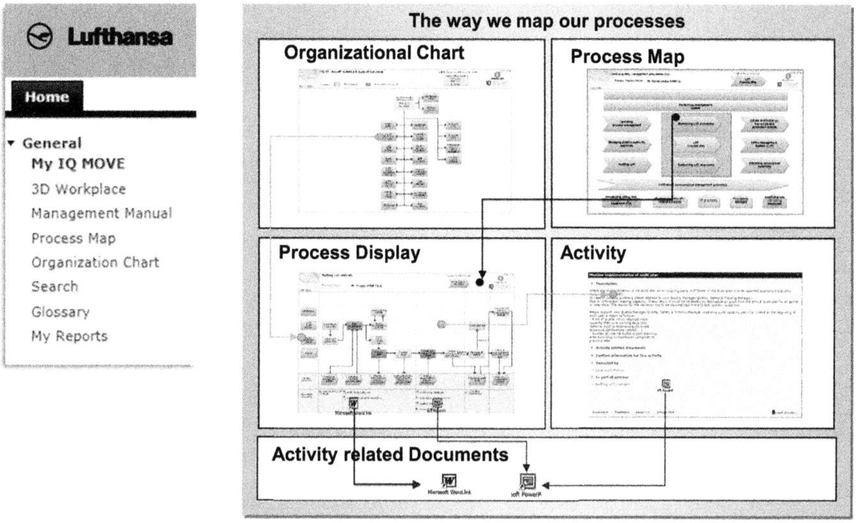

Fig. 4 Interconnection of elements in IQ MOVE

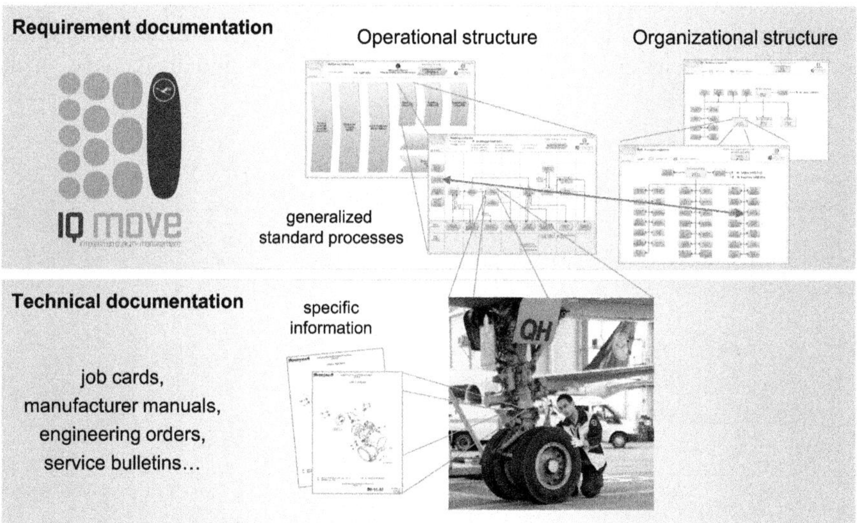

Fig. 5 Differentiation between management system and operational documentation

information. IQ MOVE focuses on generalized standard processes—that is, it avoids modeling product, customer, and location specifics. The specific information related to a process (e.g., detailed technical documentation for the maintenance of all of an aircraft's components) is provided by operational systems (e.g., a document management system called eDoc for the distribution of component maintenance manuals). Therefore, the detailed description of an activity contains a reference like "Please repair the component according to the applicable component maintenance manual in eDoc."

3.3 The IQ MOVE Editorial Process

In addition to processes from production and administration, also the way how Lufthansa Technik creates its process documentation is modeled in IQ MOVE. Figure 6 presents the process map of the editorial process in IQ MOVE.

The beginning of the process reflects the two areas of IQ MOVE: The process "Editing regulations in IQ MOVE" explains how to update the requirement database by registering and revising all relevant requirements as the basis for the subsequent conformity check. In parallel, the process documentation is created as described in the two processes "Editing IQ MOVE processes" and "Accepting processes in IQ MOVE."

Before they are published, all new processes and selected updated processes have to pass a conformity check to ensure compliance with all applicable norms and laws. The conformity check is split into an internal check and an external check. The internal conformity check is performed by the internal Requirement Managers, who specialize in interpreting and company-specific implementation of laws and standards. To demonstrate compliance, tasks that were initially created in the

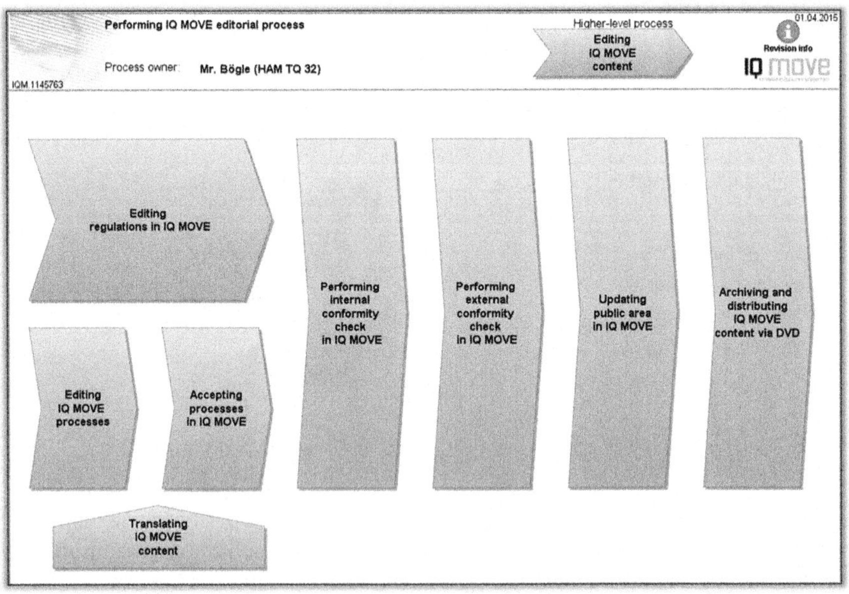

Fig. 6 Process map of the editorial process in IQ MOVE

process "Editing regulations in IQ MOVE" are assigned to all relevant processes, content is integrated into the process models, and a "conformity confirmed" or "adjustment necessary" status is set. Only with a confirmed conformity check can a process proceed in the editorial process.

Most processes will be published right after successful completion of the conformity check, but some processes require an external conformity check by a supervisory authority, such as the Luftfahrt-Bundesamt, the German aviation authority.

The process "Updating public area in IQ MOVE" explains the weekly and monthly activities for publishing processes in IQ MOVE. Finally, all IQ MOVE revisions are archived for later reference.

The process map of the IQ MOVE editorial process is completed by means of a support process for translating processes. The goal of this part of the editorial process is to ensure that all processes provide their information in English and any other languages made mandatory by the respective authorities. Mandatory languages are defined for each legal entity according to local requirements. For example, Lufthansa Technik AERO Alzey GmbH provides processes only in English, but Lufthansa Technik AG provides processes in both English and German as a result of coordination with the worker's council.

3.4 BPM Governance Based on the Framework for Assignment of Responsibilities (FAR+)

An adapted version of the Framework for Assignment of Responsibilities (FAR+) was implemented in 2014 as the basis for the operation and improvement of processes (Kettenbohrer et al. 2013, 2014) to enforce process governance. The underlying idea of the FAR+ concept is the split of managerial responsibility into "process responsibility," which defines *how* employees are supposed to perform processes, and "disciplinary responsibility," which defines *what* employees are supposed to do. Both responsibilities must be defined for every position.

The core role in process responsibility is that of the Process Owner. According to a RACI classification[4] (Loshin 2008), the Process Owner is accountable for defining, improving, and coordinating the process on the level of detailed processes described by one or more process displays. The Process Architect role is assigned to specialized employees who are responsible for defining and improving the process. The Process Manager role is assigned to persons who are responsible for coordinating process execution inter-organizationally in the various process instances (e.g., location-specific, customer-specific, product-specific process execution). The fourth role in the realm of process responsibility is that of the Process

[4]R = the role is responsible for an activity; that is, the role performs an activity. A = The role is accountable for an activity; that is, the role is ultimately liable for an activity. C = The role has to be consulted. I = The role has to be informed. Only R and A are applied in this example.

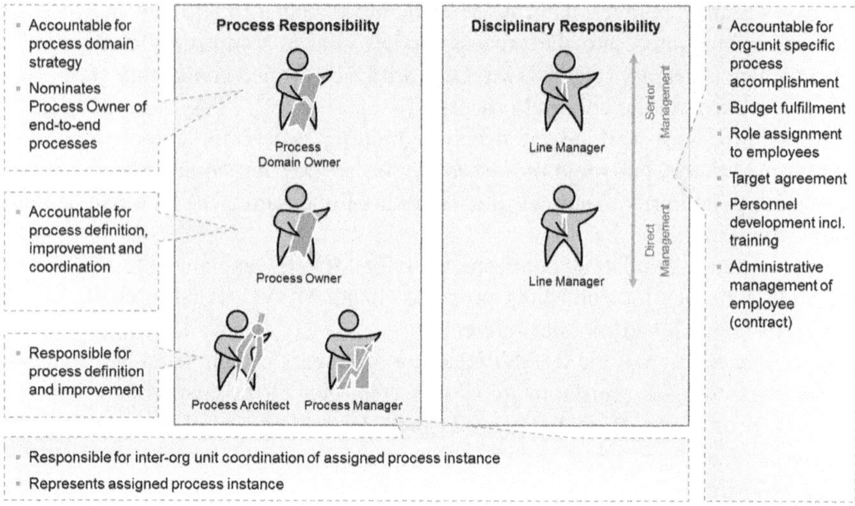

Fig. 7 Roles of the Framework for Assignment of Responsibilities (FAR+) (Kettenbohrer et al. 2013, 2014)

Domain Owner, who is accountable for the strategic direction of the processes and sub-domains in the respective process domain.

In the realm of disciplinary responsibility, the Line Manager is accountable and responsible for the assigned organizational unit's accomplishing the process, including organizational-unit-specific budget fulfillment, assignment of roles to employees in the organizational unit, coordination of target agreements, and personnel development (Kettenbohrer et al. 2013, 2014). In contrast to the theoretical FAR+ concept, Lufthansa Technik did not implement a separate role for the administrative management of employees (e.g., signing of work contract) but integrated this responsibility into to the Line Manager's role for the time being. The Line Manager role is assigned to managers of organizational units on all hierarchical levels. Figure 7 provides an overview of the roles.

In addition to the roles, structured communication flows between the roles ensure the smooth operation of processes, provide a platform for decision-making, avoid unstructured escalation in case of a dispute, and align process strategy (assigned to process responsibility) with business strategy (assigned to disciplinary responsibility).

3.5 The Procedure of Process Modeling in IQ MOVE

To ensure the applicability of process documentations, modeling of the processes in IQ MOVE is performed by three parties in joint process modeling sessions, based on the FAR+ concept. As the first party, the Process Owner and Process Architect represent the mandate of defining a process. As the second party, Process Managers

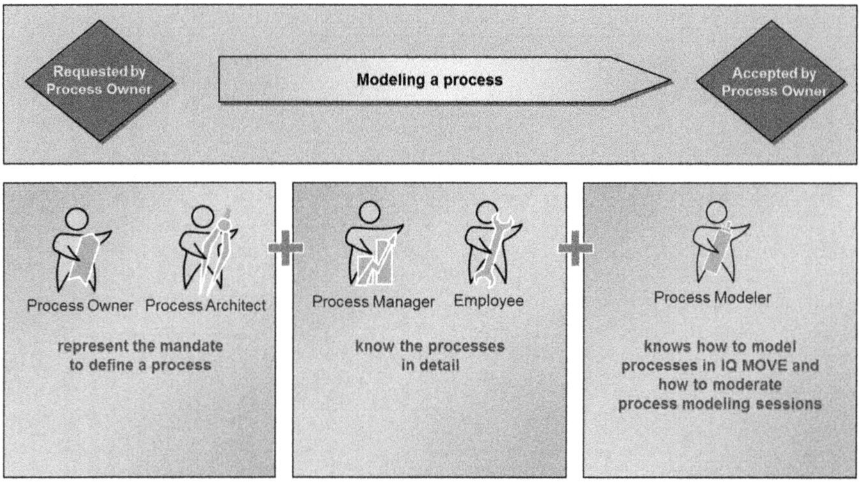

Fig. 8 Three parties participate in IQ MOVE process-modeling sessions

and/or employees participate in process-modeling sessions to bring in the detailed expertise of real-life process execution. As the third party, a Process Modeler moderates the process modeling session and handles the actual documentation in the system. The Process Modeler is experienced in Lufthansa Technik's process-modeling methodology and has completed moderator training (Fig. 8).

Process modeling itself is initialized by the Process Owner, who contacts the Process Modeler to request a process modeling session. The Process Owner (supported by Process Architect) and the Process Modeler agree on the scope, timeframe, and participants of a process-modeling session. During the meeting, the process is modeled live in the system, although several sessions are often required. In the end, the Process Owner is asked to accept the new process within a workflow in IQ MOVE.

3.6 IQ MOVE's Operational Concept

To protect the investment in IQ MOVE and to improve the system, at the end of the project the project's review board requested a concept for the system's operations. As a result, the IQ MOVE's Operational Concept shown in Fig. 9 was developed. Then operation of the system and the editorial process were handed over to the Process Owner of IQ MOVE's editorial process.

The concept is structured as a Plan-Do-Check-Act cycle. The core of the "Do" phase is the process "Performing IQ MOVE editorial process", which summarizes all processes that relate to the editing of content in IQ MOVE. To fuel this process, those who hold the editorial roles of the system (e.g., Process Modelers, Requirement Managers) must be trained, while user roles like those of employees, Line

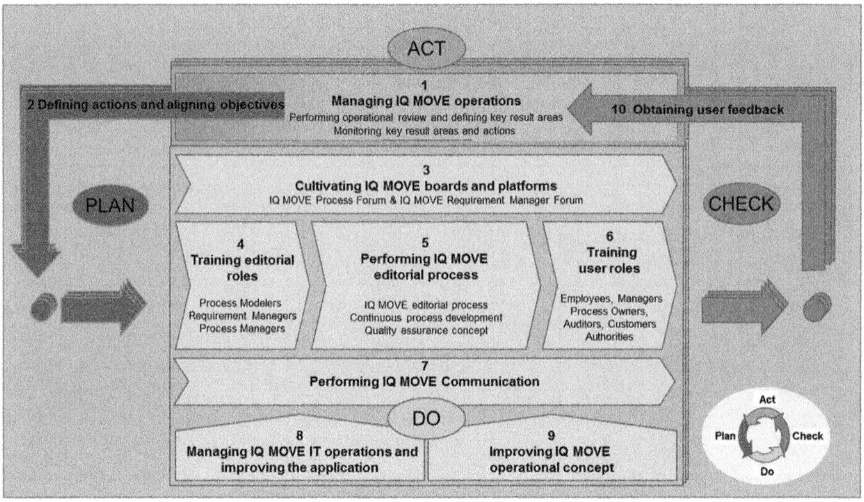

Fig. 9 IQ MOVE's operational concept

Managers, Process Owners, and External Auditors have to be trained in the use of IQ MOVE. In parallel to these core processes, the Process Owner of the IQ MOVE editorial process cultivates the IQ MOVE community by facilitating the exchange of experiences by those who hold the roles involved. For example, all Process Modelers are invited to a yearly "IQ MOVE Process Forum," the goal of which is facilitate their getting to know their colleagues, to train Process Modelers on changes in the editorial process, and to identify ideas for improving the system. The "Do" phase is completed by undertaking processes to define activities for internal and external communication related to IQ MOVE and processes to improve the IQ MOVE IT application and the IQ MOVE Operational Concept itself.

Every 2 years, as part of the "Check" phase, all users of the system—that is, participants in the IQ MOVE editorial process, such as employees, Process Owners, Line Managers, and Process Modelers—provide feedback concerning IQ MOVE's strengths and weaknesses. Based on this IQ MOVE user feedback, key result areas for improving the system are identified and measures for implementing these improvements are developed. The IQ MOVE user feedback is also used to evaluate the system's acceptance by the users with regard to the system's vision of "finding all relevant procedures quickly and easily."

Finally, in the "Act" phase, the developed measures are presented to the Process Domain Owner and the process participants' senior management (i.e., the Lufthansa Technik Board) for approval. Based on this committee's decision, measures are implemented in the "Plan" phase.

4 Results Achieved

Results of the biannual IQ MOVE user feedback (according to the IQ MOVE Operational Concept) indicate a constant level of acceptance by the employees, but ensuring the IQ MOVE vision of "finding all relevant procedures quickly and easily" is met in daily work remains a challenge.

In general, the results of IQ MOVE user feedbacks confirm that the implemented process modeling methodology, with its varying levels of detail (i.e., process maps, process displays, info-boxes of activities, and activity-related documents) and reduced number of process modeling objects (i.e., roles, activities, and decisions), is easily understood and simple to use. However, because of the complexity of the real-life processes, the complexity of process documentation increases over time, and Process Owners, Process Architects, and Process Modelers must work to keep documentation as concise as possible.

The development and implementation of FAR+ was initialized as result of IQ MOVE's 2011 user feedback to strengthen the role of the Process Owner, facilitate continuous process improvement, ensure proper accomplishment of processes at all locations, and provide comprehensive training of process participants. First results of the evaluation of the FAR+ implementation confirm that the concept helps to improve the system in these ways, but it is clear that the assignment of the FAR+ roles alone does not fully enable all employees to perform their roles. As a result, additional workshop series have been started, especially to support Process Owners and Process Architects by offering a structured process-operation concept. This concept was developed based on the generalized IQ MOVE operational concept, and training will be offered to all Process Owners in the near future. The core of this generalized process operations approach is a simplified BPM lifecycle based on Dumas et al.'s (2013) BPM Lifecycle, which is supported by BPM tools and methodologies. To apply this concept to the individual processes, the workshop series will guide Process Owners and Process Architects through the individual setup of operational concepts. For example, it will provide tools and methodologies with which to develop a process strategy based on the corporate strategy, to innovate processes, to implement process changes, to steer processes based on indicators, and so on.

5 Lessons Learned

Even after 10 years of BPM at Lufthansa Technik, the vision of "finding all relevant procedures quickly and easily" still drives all BPM activities. Along the journey to fulfilling this vision, key factors to increase the system's acceptance by the employees were identified.

How process modeling is done in IQ MOVE is a core element of the project's success. The four modeling levels (i.e., process maps, process displays, info-boxes, and activity-related documents) offer a flexible approach to mapping processes and provide easy access to the documentation, while the concise process-modeling language for process displays (i.e., swim lanes with roles, activities, and decisions only) increases the readability and usability of the process documentation in IQ MOVE. Both of these aspects of the system positively influence its acceptance.

The seamless integration of legislative and normative requirements into process descriptions also helps to increase employees' acceptance of the system because it reduces the complexity of process documentation. In the IQ MOVE editorial process, specialized experts check all process models for compliance before publication and ensure that all requirements are integrated into the process descriptions. Therefore, employees can work according to the process descriptions without worrying about all the requirements in the background.

In addition, the clear definition of process-management roles (i.e., Process Domain Owner, Process Owner, Process Architect, and Process Manager) increases employees' awareness of process management and facilitates the precise assignment of process-management activities to positions. In particular, the differentiation of roles related to process responsibility vs. disciplinary responsibility according to FAR+ was a major step in promoting process management and strengthening the role of the Process Owner. In an additional step, the introduction of BPM role-oriented training modules contributed to the professionalization of process management in the organization by providing tools and methodologies along the process lifecycle.

The role concept also helps to improve process modeling by bringing the right parties together: Process Owners and Process Architects represent the mandate to define the process and drive process improvement, while Process Managers and employees bring practical experience into process modeling. The Process Modeler has the expertise to moderate process modeling sessions and to map processes in an easy-to-understand way.

Finally, the key to keeping the process management system on track is the IQ MOVE operational concept, which is the basis for the system's continuous improvement and that helps to structure and steer its global operation. The underlying Plan-Do-Check-Act cycle collects the users' feedback and integrates their needs into the system's development. In addition, the integration of top management into the system's development is ensured by regular reporting to and discussion with the organization's senior line managers.

These key factors, which enabled Lufthansa Technik Group to implement a stable and robust process-oriented management system that is used by 20,000+ employees and managers around the world, may also help other organizations to strengthen their process management systems.

References

Dumas, M., La Rosa, M., Mendling, J., & Reijers, H. H. (2013). *Fundamentals of business process management*. Berlin: Springer.

Kettenbohrer, J., Beimborn, D., & Kloppenburg, M. (2013). Developing a governance model for successful business process standardization. In *Proceedings of the 19th Americas Conference on Information Systems (AMCIS)*, Chicago, IL.

Kettenbohrer, J., Kloppenburg, M., & Beimborn, D. (2014). Driving process innovation: The application of a role-based governance model at Lufthansa Technik. In J. vom Brocke & T. Schmiedel (Eds.), *BPM—Driving innovation in a digital world, management for professionals* (pp. 275–286). Switzerland: Springer.
Loshin, D. (2008). *Master data management*. Burlington, MA: Morgan Kaufmann.

Mirko Kloppenburg is head of IQ MOVE Process Center at Lufthansa Technik AG and is responsible for the operations and improvement of the company's process management system IQ MOVE. Before, he held various positions in the context of process management within Lufthansa Group. He holds a diploma in Business Information Systems from the University of Cooperative Education Mannheim, Germany, and a Master of Business Administration from University of Louisville, USA. Mirko is co-founder of the Process Management Alliance e.V. which facilitates the identification of Best Practices in Process Management (BPinPM.net) as well as the transfer of BPM knowledge to the social and education sector.

Janina Kettenbohrer is research assistant and PhD student at the Department of Information Systems and Services at the University of Bamberg and affiliated researcher at the ProcessLab at the Frankfurt School of Finance & Management. She holds both a Master of Science and a Bachelor of Science in Information Systems from the University of Bamberg. Additionally, she is an external consultant at Lufthansa Technik AG and works in the context of process management operations and improvement. Her research focuses on employees' acceptance of business process change and individual workers' process orientation. Her work has been presented at several international conferences (e.g. AMCIS, ECIS, and ICIS).

Daniel Beimborn is Professor of Information Systems at the Frankfurt School of Finance & Management. Before, he held a PostDoc position at the University of Bamberg, Germany, and received his PhD from Goethe University in Frankfurt. He was Visiting Researcher at Georgia State University, Louisiana State University, and Microsoft in Redmond. At Frankfurt School, he is heading the Digital Business concentration of the Master in Management and he is co-head of the ProcessLab research center. He teaches courses on Strategic IS Management, Enterprise Systems, and Enterprise Architecture Management. His research focuses on outsourcing, business process management, digital transformation, and business/IT alignment. He has published in various internationally renowned journals, such as MIS Quarterly, Journal of Management Information Systems, Journal of Strategic Information Systems, and Journal of Information Technology. Services to the academic community include, among others, being associate editor of BISE and member of the Editorial Review Board of JAIS.

Michael Bögle is currently head of Management System at Lufthansa Technik AG. In the past he has held various positions within Lufthansa which include work planning, technical inspection, training and auditing. He was part of the project management team which developed and implemented the company's process management system IQ MOVE. Michael holds a diploma in Aeronautical Engineering from the University of Applied Sciences in Hamburg. He is also co-founder of the Process Management Alliance e.V. which facilitates the identification of Best Practices in Process Management (BPinPM.net) as well as the transfer of BPM knowledge to the social and education sector.

"Simply Modeling": BPM for Everybody-Recommendations from the Viral Adoption of BPM at 1&1

Florian Imgrund, Christian Janiesch, and Christoph Rosenkranz

Abstract

(a) **Situation faced**: 1&1 is a German Internet service provider that embraced business process management (BPM) in 2010 as a way to optimize its processes. The company expected BPM to increase corporate performance by realizing such customer-centric goals as high quality standards, reduced set-up times, shortened time-to-market cycles, and increased adaptability to changing customer requirements. 1&1 decided to use the Business Process Model and Notation (BPMN) for its business process models, but the specification offers no pragmatic advice on how to introduce and adapt the modeling method in a company. 1&1 started with a conceptual process architecture—a lightweight process modeling infrastructure—and invested in a BPM initiative using a bottom-up approach. The resulting viral spread of BPM led to a "success disaster" with a high adoption rate and a high number of models but low model quality.

(b) **Action taken**: 1&1 turned around the proliferating trend of low quality and barely usable process models by means of carefully targeted decisions. An initial analysis showed that the key factors in the disastrous situation were insufficient training and the lack of modeling conventions. While no changes were made to the process architecture, the company increased the integration of system architecture components, resulting in improved knowledge management as increasing amounts of information became retrievable through the enterprise information portal. Quality assurance

F. Imgrund (✉) • C. Janiesch
University of Würzburg, Würzburg, Germany
e-mail: florian.imgrund@uni-wuerzburg.de; christian.janiesch@uni-wuerzburg.de

C. Rosenkranz
University of Cologne, Cologne, Germany
e-mail: rosenkranz@wiso.uni-koeln.de

J. vom Brocke, J. Mendling (eds.), *Business Process Management Cases*, Management for Professionals, DOI 10.1007/978-3-319-58307-5_28

was mandated through a few selected modeling conventions to guide and constrain but not restrict the modelers. Finally, the BPM initiative grew larger with more volunteer trainers and more differentiated courses that helped to ensure an appropriate level of process modeling competence for each employee's tasks.

(c) **Results Achieved**: Because of its lightweight implementation, BPM at 1&1 can enable continuous process adjustments triggered by any employee at any time and on every level, so it can achieve short time-to-market for core business products and services, as well as rapid changes in business processes. Business knowledge and expertise is extracted from all of the company's corporate levels and is merged and presented in the process models. The company currently uses as its production environment the Signavio Process Editor, which relies on a repository of more than 12,000 process models and more than 1800 active process modelers.

(d) **Lessons learned**: The BPMN specification provides no guidance on how to introduce and use BPMN in the individual corporate context. While it is often useful to follow a reference approach for the adaptation and use of a modeling method and the associated IT infrastructure, there is none available for BPMN. Based on the 1&1 case, we present recommendations that can be considered best practices for setting up and steering a large-scale BPM initiative based on process modeling that emphasize process modeling technology, user training, modeling regulations, employee management, and time management.

1 Introduction

On March 29, 2016, Martin Petry, expert in business process management (BPM) at 1&1, gave another training course on Business Process Model and Notation (BPMN). Petry's training courses, which contain a high degree of interaction between trainer and participants, had been held since 2010, but this one was different. At the beginning of the course, Petry often asks attendees to say in what department they work, and the participants often answer that they work in such departments as finance, human resources, and customer support, but most of them work in one of the technology and development departments. On that day, however, not a single person with a technical background was in the room. Although the number of participants from non-technical departments had been increasing, this was unusual because the historical nucleus of BPM was the technology and development department, which had a clear focus on executable processes. "This has never happened before," Petry pointed out, going on to associate this phenomenon with how process modeling has spread in the company. Apart from the introductory event in which new employees learn about the availability of the BPMN training courses, there is no central initiative or dedicated program that obligates employees to take part. Instead, Petry likens the situation to a *viral dissemination* of modeling in 1&1.

In this context, "viral" refers to a behavior that spreads quickly and widely using person-to-person communication (Merriam-Webster Online Dictionary 2016). Translated to 1&1, "viral" behavior means that there is no need to motivate people to take part in such training nor to increase participation levels by stressing the value of modeling because, as employees who have participated in the trainings have observed, "We make full use of process models in our finance department [so] I need to deal with them" and "Processes are ubiquitous in meetings, working instructions, etc., [so] when I became aware of that, I enrolled in the next BPM training immediately."

Of course, this viral behavior was not present from the outset; it was a gradual process that started with a customer-facing project. As a turning point while progressively developing BPM, 1&1 experienced a "success disaster," as Petry calls it. Because of the lack of pragmatics in the BPMN specification, large quantities of qualitatively low-quality process models spread throughout the enterprise. The models could not be executed within the BPM environment, and continuous maintenance of such a large quantity of process models was out of the question. However, despite these difficulties in the adoption of BPM in the initial few years, 1&1 has managed to institutionalize BPM in a way that not only overcame these difficulties but also increased the company's efficiency and led to the rise of a community of cooperative process modelers who virally spread the idea of process modeling throughout the entire enterprise.

Several factors were decisive, including adapting a process architecture, interventions in the training concept, and adjusting the level of governance. Therefore, the case of 1&1 offers a set of best practices on how to adopt BPMN in large companies and how to support the development of a collaborative community of process modelers. In order to depict the development as a whole, we first recapitulate the prerequisites for BPM when it was first implemented at 1&1. We then detail the adjustments that were introduced in response to the "success disaster." Finally, we describe a set of best practice recommendations, which are discussed in the lessons learned section. This case shows that even large companies can implement BPM in a bottom-up and lightweight way that neither restricts modeling nor leads to inflexible structures.

2 Situation Faced

2.1 Origin of BPM at 1&1

1&1 is a German Internet service provider whose head office is in Montabaur, Germany. It specializes in Internet-access products and hosting and e-business solutions in the cloud. Companies like 1&1 operate in highly competitive and dynamic markets that are characterized by rapid price changes, increasing interchangeability of products, and/or short product lifecycles. Participants in such markets have no guarantee of long-term prosperity, so enhancing productivity increasingly appears to be a key factor to success. As a result, companies began to reflect on their business processes to maximize their performance (Dumas et al. 2013). To provide companies with the ability not only to depict process models but also to analyze and improve them, the Business Process Management Initiative (BPMI) and later the Object Management Group (OMG) published BPMN in 2004. The notation has evolved to become today's de-facto standard for process modeling and is used in companies all over the world (Recker 2010). Its current version also includes execution semantics (OMG 2013).

1&1 acknowledged the merits of BPMN's graphic representation in managing business processes when the enterprise delved into BPM as a way to optimize its processes in 2010. Gradually superseding a function-oriented management approach implemented by an enterprise resource planning system, BPM was initially intended to support the simultaneously launched Customer Satisfaction Offensive (CSO). (This approach is common in other companies as well.) In doing so, 1&1 sought to increase corporate performance by realizing such customer-centric goals as high quality standards, reduced set-up times, shortened time-to-market cycles, and increased adaptability to changing customer requirements. The CSO primarily dealt with process standardization and automation with the initial goal of making processes executable, but over time it became key to promoting BPMN as the graphic representation of business processes. Employees recognized the ease of using process diagrams as a means of communication in a process-oriented enterprise.

BPMN became a popular means of communication, although using the notation was not always straightforward. A lack of clarity concerning linguistic subtleties yielded to uncertainty, redundant design, and even low-quality process models, partly because, in contrast to its well-defined syntax, the BPMN specification (BPMI 2004; OMG 2013) offers no pragmatic advice on how to introduce and tailor the modeling method to a company's needs. Several general purpose frameworks are available (e.g., Becker et al. 2011; Rosemann and vom Brocke 2010), but not all were as refined in 2010 as they are today, and they often do not focus on modeling or BPMN. Specific advice on how to adapt and institutionalize BPM(N) outside a consulting project is scarce, so 1&1 had to take matters in its own hands.

2.2 Prerequisites and Early Decisions at 1&1

Here we introduce 1&1's process architecture and its IT infrastructure. Figure 1 shows the *system architecture*, which consists of a *Process Editor*, a *Business Process Management System (BPMS)* for executing processes, an *Enterprise Information Portal (EIP)* for gathering and analyzing information from across the enterprise, and a connection to the organizational user management using an *Identity Management System (IMS)*. The EIP is a tailor-made portal for importing data from other systems and providing data via sophisticated information-retrieval options. The EIP also takes care of in-house knowledge management. We refer to knowledge management at 1&1 as "the systematic and explicit management of

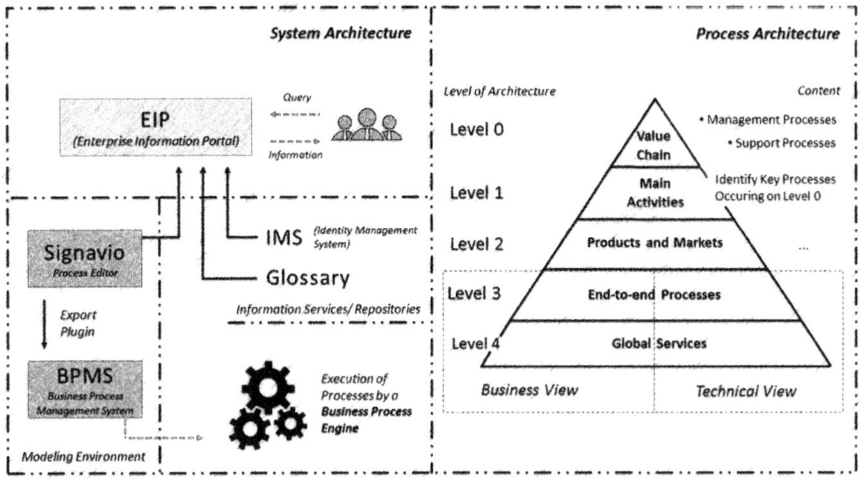

Fig. 1 System architecture and process architecture at 1&1

knowledge-related activities with the goal to build and exploit intellectual capital effectively and gainfully" (Wiig 1999, p. 3–3).

The five-level *process architecture*, which provides an overview of the existing processes by classifying them into levels of abstraction, is depicted symbolically as a pyramid. The interplay between the system architecture and the process architecture helps to integrate an intuitive-to-use modeling environment in order to integrate BPM fully into the company.

However, in order for the architecture to function as intended, 1&1 had to meet five prerequisites. First, 1&1 had to identify the value-adding processes and map them in an overall framework. At 1&1, the process architecture starts with *level 0*, the highest level of abstraction, where management and support processes are displayed as value chains and the management processes are kept simple and functional. They are based on four core activities, which cover the full spectrum of added value, such as *Offer to Order* and *Order to Fulfillment*. Each management process has sub-processes, such as the new orders, tariff change, and termination of a contract sub-processes for *Order to Fulfillment*. The main activities on *level 1* identify the key processes that complete the business transactions that occur in the value chains (level 0). *Level 2* clarifies which product- and market-specific variants exist to implement the main processes. *Level 3* is the most important layer for modeling, as it covers the end-to-end processes. On this level, specific tasks are depicted that describe how a specific business case is performed. On *level 4*, global services, which support the execution of level 3 processes, are detailed.

Management processes are clearly communicated to employees, but there is no substantial limitation or constraining guidelines for modeling on lower levels, especially on level 3. The process architecture is neither fully or centrally managed nor—with the exception of level 0 and level 1 processes—prescribed in its structure and content. The process architecture with all its processes is often referred to as a process map or a *process house*. (The meanings of the terms *process architecture* and *process house* differ only slightly at 1&1, where the process architecture describes the overall structure of the five levels of processes in the enterprise, and a process house is a running instance of the process architecture that is adapted to the needs of the particular department to which it is applied. Consequently, each department has its own process house that adopts its activities on level 0 and level 1 from the overall architecture but acts independently on levels 2, 3, and 4.)

As a second prerequisite, 1&1 had to develop a suitable *system architecture* to support the modeling and execution of processes (Fig. 1). For modeling purposes, 1&1 uses the *Signavio Process Editor* (Signavio GmbH 2016), which can be used either as software as a service (SaaS) or as on-premises software. 1&1 runs the latter, a self-hosted deployment model, to escape receiving the automatic updates of SaaS applications that are subject to increased risk of integrity issues with pre-existing models (Cheng et al. 2010). Such is the case in particular for executable process models. Signavio's process model editor appealed to 1&1 because of its ease of access and ease of use.

Third, 1&1 had to decide which management approach to apply for BPM: a *bottom-up approach* or a *top-down approach*. The OMG offers no official support regarding how to implement BPMN and its methods and procedures into an individual business environment—the *pragmatics* of modeling (Freund and Rücker 2014; Imgrund and Janiesch 2016; Zur Muehlen et al. 2010)—so 1&1 had no substantial advice on implementing its process architecture, ensuring the system architecture's integrity, or selecting an appropriate direction of action. The last is the reason for highly varying application scenarios in practice (Bjeković et al. 2014), which focus on either strong top-level management support or a more user-oriented bottom-up approach.

Fourth, 1&1 had to choose between a top-down or a bottom-up approach for BPM. It chose a bottom-up approach in part because it did not want to create only a small user base that can read and create process models, but instead wanted to make the capability of modeling available to a large number of employees. When 1&1 decided to apply a bottom-up approach, it was aware of its large number of product-specific processes with a strong focus on technical feasibility using the BPM system, but the company follows a highly user-oriented modeling approach and does not want to neglect the actual users' needs. Furthermore, 1&1 considers activities on level 3 as its starting point for each modeling activity, so it rejected a fully managed process architecture and accepted the risk of isolated, stand-alone solutions for specific problems.

Finally, 1&1 started a small *BPM initiative* to provide governance, to keep the technical infrastructure operative, and to teach modeling by providing training. Even if processes play a central role and can be found everywhere in the enterprise, Petry is the only person who is responsible for BPM full time. All other BPM coaches are volunteers a variety of divisions, although most are from the technology department.

2.3 The *Success Disaster*

As a result of its bottom-up approach, 1&1 observed a rapid spread and popularity of process modeling in the enterprise shortly after it was introduced—that is, BPM "went viral." However, this development did not provide only benefits for the company. What at first seemed positive when thinking about 1&1's objectives emerged as problematic in 2013, when the enormous number of new users (i.e., process modelers) and new process models became a serious organizational and administrative challenge. As Petry explains, "In light of the significant number of process models, in a certain sense it was not clear whether this was a success, a disaster, or both." The reasons for this initially mixed assessment of the approach's outcome were closely related to the quality of these models.

3 Action Taken

3.1 Identification of Issues and Associated Responses

1&1 has an operational system architecture and a well-structured process architecture that carry the company's vision. At first glance, neither the process architecture nor the system architecture differs significantly from that found at its peer companies. 1&1 provides training to enhance its employees' modeling capability, but it faced serious organizational and administrative problems with BPM in 2013. However, during this success disaster, another unplanned effect of the approach became apparent: the employees at 1&1 used almost every opportunity to share process models. Despite the suboptimal quality of some of these models, 1&1 identified a promising advantage in this mentality of "simply modeling" as offering the potential and opportunity to transform 1&1 into a highly process-oriented enterprise. Consequently, the first activity in addressing the success disaster was to identify causes that contributed simultaneously to the initiative's success and failure. 1&1 also sought to identify effective countermeasures for the issue of poor-quality models while retaining the drive of the grass-rooted viral effect. Naturally, the number of users—about 2000 process modelers by 2016—and the approximately 12,000 shared process models were a main reason for the models' erratic quality. Variance is to be expected with such numbers because, as Petry puts it, "At 1&1, you can compare the creation of process models with the creation of a PowerPoint presentation: no one asks for a specific use case of a single model. No matter if a process model maps an executable process or if it is just for individual use or serves as a basis for discussion, there is virtually no limitation for the case of process modeling."

Despite the resulting low quality of many process models, 1&1 did not want to reduce or limit this development, as it considered employees' eagerness to engage in modeling as a highly positive improvement and provided access to every employee who was interested in modeling. Hence, 1&1 tried to strengthen this

Table 1 Objective of actions taken, divided by area

Area	Actions	Objective
Process architecture	None	– Five-level architecture with end-to-end processes on level 3 – Adoption of a bottom-up approach to guarantee an open system architecture
System architecture	Minor adjustments	– Full integrity and availability – Full interoperability of all software programs and tools
Quality assurance	Minor adjustments	– Improved training system – Increased number of volunteers – Enterprise-specific modeling conventions without too many restrictions
BPM initiative and governance	Minor adjustments	– Ensuring both the quality of modeling and the functioning of the overall process architecture, without enforcing overly restrictive quality rules – Maintaining the quality of BPM in full at a high level using volunteers and by spreading important content throughout the enterprise
Knowledge management	Major adjustments	– EIP as a central operational database that is fed with data from all relevant systems – Availability of structured data – Availability and company-wide access

phenomenon with several adjustments, such as automated rule checks, that were intended to improve quality while not constraining users with too many guidelines.

At first glance, insufficient training may have been seen as the only cause of poor-quality models and as a bottleneck for improving model quality. However, a detailed investigation of possible reasons revealed that the causes for the situation were more complex. Hence, 1&1's sophisticated reaction multiple interdependent factors into consideration.

Table 1 displays each area that is associated with process modeling activities and the important adjustment opportunities for improving the quality of modeling in a process-oriented enterprise like 1&1. In the case of the process architecture, 1&1 decided that no further adjustments were necessary.

3.2 The Technical Baseline: Process Architecture and System Architecture

The general *process architecture* outlined above worked well and was not affected by the changes made to increase model quality, so no action was taken.

The *system architecture* is the process architecture's technological counterpart. The four core applications—the Signavio Process Editor, the BPM system, the EIP, and user management—have to be synchronized, which entails a full integration of and interchangeability between the tools. Therefore, a primary focus lies on the EIP, as it may be represented as the nerve center of the enterprise. All information that is relevant to the day-to-day business is gathered or linked here, so not only are access and links made to all shared process models from Signavio, including metadata and information about employees and their organizational units, etc., but the EIP is fed through interfaces to almost all of 1&1's systems (e.g., tracking and project management tools, intranet, contact databases). The minor adaptions mentioned in Table 1 deal with interface-connection optimizations to the applications. For example, the attachment of an extended glossary to the system architecture enables Signavio to reuse document templates or system-specific information.

3.3 Improving Process Modeling Quality: Quality Assurance

Meaningful data is the backbone of today's enterprises, as there are strong relationships between data quality and system quality (Wixom and Watson 2001). However, because of 1&1's user-oriented approach to modeling, it is a major challenge to have not only quantitative data but also qualitative data. To improve data quality sustainably, 1&1 had to put several measures into place. The *quality-assurance measures* included training and the nature and content of modeling conventions.

Concerning the organization of *training*, 1&1 increased both the number of trainers and the frequency of training. The main topics in the 1-day basic course on BPM—"Introduction to BPM and BPMN," "Introduction to Signavio," and "Modeling with Signavio (hands-on)"—have not changed much, but short, 2-h courses offer interested employees the opportunity to deepen their knowledge by learning how to build high-quality process models and learning about topics like release notes on new Signavio versions.

Petry has remained the only full-time employee responsible for BPM, while each of the other eleven trainers teaches voluntarily. Course announcements and the internal marketing also remain unchanged; only new employees are specifically made aware of the courses in their introductory event. There are other ways employees can be informed about courses, although none is actively promoted. Even incentives to take part in such courses barely exist.

At the same time, the *modeling conventions* have been tightened. 1&1 takes a clear stand in giving as much freedom as possible and constraining or restricting only where it is deemed necessary and/or useful to do so, such as in providing conventions that prevent common pitfalls. Signavio distinguishes between "errors" and "warnings," as the software's rule engine recognizes both but treats them differently in the conventions: if the process model contains one or more errors, the modeler is required to correct them in order to save the diagram, but if the process contains warnings, the software tool merely warns the modeler with a listing of the findings. While warnings might be incorrect or missed labels, errors might refer to mandatory fields or type definitions in the process model. For example, if the type of the process model is missing, the modeler can choose the process to be a level 3, a level 4, or a sub-process. If nothing is suitable, the process model can be clarified as unofficial. If the modeler chooses level 3, the process has to be associated with the appropriate part (or sub-part) of the value chain, and if a process is declared to be executable, an operator has to be clarified.

Beyond errors, 1&1's modeling conventions advise its process modelers that a task should have only one input and one output, that an AND gateway should not merge with multiple conditions, and that a process name should follow a specific format. Other than errors, recommendations do not prevent the modeler from storing the process model but indicate that there are shortcomings in the model, as minor conventions have been violated.

However, 1&1 does not restrict the modeler in other areas, such as regarding limitations on a process's granularity, which is directly dependent on the objective of the model. Because of the variety of modeling cases in the enterprise, 1&1 sees no value in limitations on that level. The same applies to the folder structure in the modeling tool, as there is no higher-level control system on the naming or the structure of folders and no restriction on how to classify process models. The adjustments in response to the success disaster tended to be subtle changes that took the form of minor adjustments to the conventions.

3.4 The BPM Initiative's Lean Governance

The main task of the BPM initiative at 1&1 is to guide the development of BPM and process modeling to ensure transparent and high-quality processes with a focus on practicability. It is fair to assume that the workload increased significantly after the activities related to the quality-assurance measures were introduced, yet there were no changes in support for Petry. Petry's main duty is to coordinate and execute governance activities and to increase the quality of modeling sustainably. However, to meet the increasing demands, Petry is supported by a growing number of qualified volunteer trainers, who deliver, according to their skills, basic courses, advanced courses, or intensive (short) courses on selected topics. Since all courses could hold interest for each of 1&1's employees, there are no barriers to participation—but there is also no obligation to participate.

For their part, the approximately 50 BPM coordinators, act as multipliers in the enterprise by attending regular meetings and spreading news concerning BPM or modeling to their departments. While the BPM initiative coordinates the overarching governance at 1&1, the same activities on the department level are left to the multipliers, who decide what information is relevant to their particular departments.

3.5 Making Knowledge Visible

Knowledge management is increasingly critical in the management of an enterprise's corporate memory and intellectual assets (Geisler and Wickramasinghe 2015). The purpose of knowledge management is to generate and provide meaningful information to the right people at the right time (Duffy 2001). 1&1 is aware of the need for a high-quality knowledge database to prevent another proliferation of low-quality process models.

The main focus and effort in this area was to make knowledge centrally and transparently available. In doing so, knowledge management provides a way to make employees' tacit process knowledge retrievable by other colleagues. The increased networking of systems plays a major role in this context, as the system architecture provides the basic building block of any activities in this area. Knowledge management was also already available to employees who regularly used Signavio. The necessary skills consist merely of identifying and structuring important knowledge and making it available to stakeholders, the latter of which was achieved by using the centrally available EIP as the access point. Actions like introducing a ranking algorithm for processes and an intelligent search function now assist in the purposive representation of the desired information, helping the users.

1&1's primary concern was to develop a sophisticated concept to improve the quality- and quality-assurance of models. Although the individual changes described here were minor, the result was more than the sum of the actions taken. Multi-annual and always progressing adjustments were necessary to sustainably increase the quality of modeling. 1&1 took the situation seriously, responded with focused actions while retaining the positive viral effect, and achieved not only a wealth of knowledge and experiences, but also the valuable results that are described in the next section.

4 Results Achieved

In 2013, 3 years after the introduction of BPM, 1&1 was in the middle of its success disaster. Today, after about 5 years of continuous adjustments and improvements, the enterprise sports a high-quality, mostly maintenance-free BPM approach that has created a highly dynamic and innovative process-oriented environment. A closer examination reveals two key aspects of the company's success in particular: An unusually strong viral spread of *modeling ability* and substantially improved *architecture*, *governance*, *quality assurance*, and *knowledge management*. "To be frank," Petry says, "neither development was expected on this scale, [but] [because of] the way BPM evolved and is applied, it is now an irreplaceable capability in the enterprise."

4.1 Benefits of Today's Situations

Here we explain the value of BPM from a user-centric perspective, taking the viewpoint of Ana-Maria, a *Solution Designer* at 1&1. We start from her first day at the enterprise:

"I already knew that 1&1 was a very process-oriented enterprise. Both my vocational education and my personal interests focused strongly on BPM. It did not surprise me when I heard that there was a "BPM basic course" and the "availability of short courses on priority topics." However, the information that each employee could apply to be a potential trainer did. But after a few weeks at the enterprise and after completing the first two training sessions on BPM (basics) and BPM (advanced), the overall situation became clear. BPM can be found almost everywhere at 1&1 and it is on virtually everyone's lips. It's like, "Hey, how was that again with that order process?" and the answer is "Have a look at the process model; EIP or Signavio will link you, and you will find everything you need," or even "What do I have to do to in order to get my business trip approved?" and anyone would reply something like, "Search for 'business trip' in the intranet. The search results will link you to the process that describes how to apply and which documents to fill in. Don't forget to search for 'travel expense accounting.'" Almost any information you do need for your day-to-day business can be acquired through tool-based process models. The EIP is particularly useful when seeking helpful information."

In fact, asking questions using the EIP yields consolidated search-and-retrieve results from 1&1's distributed databases. Its index and data are updated every night. Without the need for additional input, this new solution designer can learn about literally every process that occurs in the enterprise. This structured and explicit knowledge base is also a useful tool to document tacit procedural knowledge, as another positive impact of the widespread use of modeling is the spread of modeling capability. Process innovation can occur at any employee level in 1&1's large and proactive user community, where everyone can help everyone. As a result, the company is a strong, cooperative workplace and has a high level of expertise regarding process modeling. The strong viral effect and the improved knowledge management is the overall outcome from the implementation of several sub-targets. We illustrate them using again the example our new process designer at 1&1.

The basic training on BPM taught Ana-Maria a lot about the basic infrastructure at 1&1. She learned about the activities in the value chain and their levels of abstraction, which form the enterprise's process architecture. At this point, she observed an important characteristic regarding the direction of action, as 1&1 uses both top-down and bottom-up approaches. While the activities of the value chain are prescribed using the top-down manner, the employees' activities, i.e. level 2 to level 5 processes, follow a bottom-up approach. Metaphorically speaking, drawers are provided that build the classification framework for activities on lower levels of the process architecture, and other activities are coordinated and carried out at the employee level. This approach not only reduces the administrative effort considerably but also gives the employees with a high level of responsibility. Therefore, it is up to the departments to optimize their functions and to build and manage their own processes and even their process house, which contributes to the value of the enterprise. Effectively, this approach for 1&1 applies to function-oriented departments like HR and finance as well as to departments that have to demonstrate consistency for auditing purposes.

Moreover, the direction of action affects how modeling is done at 1&1. As there is neither regulation nor restriction on the use case of modeling, once an activity *can* be supported by creating a process model, it *is* supported by creating a process model. By now, the resulting process models fulfill the quality requirements, demonstrating the success of the training courses and the viral spread of modeling capability.

Now that Ana-Maria has learned about the basics of BPM, she takes a short course that deals with the EIP. Once she hears a short explanation of the system architecture at 1&1 and a more detailed one on the EIP, she understands that the interplay between the components is a prerequisite for requests like "What systems are relevant to or affected by the process XY?," "To which processes am I linked?," "In which processes is System X used?," "In how many (and which) processes is my department involved?," or even "How many findings/errors (syntactical or semantical) do my process models include?." The high degree of crosslinking between the underlying systems makes the EIB a highly effective knowledge-management tool. Ana-Maria remembers the unguided folder structure in Signavio, which she at first interpreted as an obstacle to the management of processes and as difficult to understand for employees from other departments. However, in combination with the EIP, which sorts processes clearly, and depending on the needs of the user, the unguided folder structure turns out to be more advantage than disadvantage. Without an enforced structure, similar to a process house, the folders are governed by their users and so are generally up-to-date. The short course concludes with the statement that the EIP obtains its power by evaluating structured information from various data sources and providing bundled information in a central location—an added value that a tool run in isolation could not provide.

4.2 Capabilities Necessary for Success

On completion of the advanced training, Ana-Maria seized the opportunity to ask the trainer some questions. She wanted to know how a company with about 2000 process modelers could employ just one person working full time to coordinate the BPM efforts. The answer describes one significant characteristic that is most responsible for the whole concept's ability to work: everyone realizes that process modeling supports his or her daily work, so they not only use BPM but are also willing to help others directly or by delivering training courses. In addition, the lightweight restrictions imposed by the *modeling conventions* increase the *quality of modeling*. As Petry argues, "While it was almost impossible for a token in a process model to move from left to right a few years ago, today these errors happen rarely. Moreover, not only the quality of the process model is improved, but also its administrative management. Signavio forces the modeler to declare the type of the process so it can be classified and found more easily."

These lightweight adjustments entailed not only a viral spread of the models themselves but also a viral distribution of modeling capability. As Petry also notes, "The spread of BPM capabilities has accelerated at a rate no one expected. After

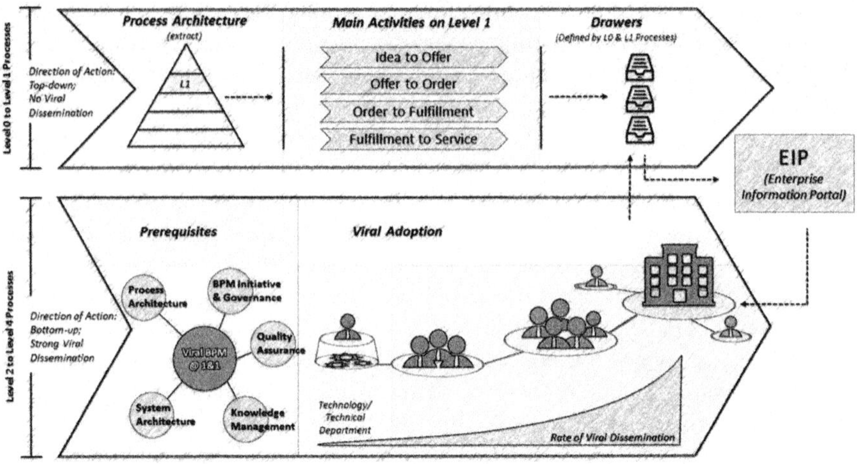

Fig. 2 Viral BPM adoption at 1&1

facing this situation barely 3 years ago, today it is not necessary to constantly remind employees to take part in training courses. Process modeling has penetrated various application contexts, and the majority realized quickly that they have to learn the skill of modeling in order to boost their efficiency." In particular, widespread tool support and meaningful modeling conventions that enabled a less formal interpreted governance that was not prone to inflexible regulations and so retained a high degree of flexibility laid the groundwork for the viral spread of BPM at 1&1.

Figure 2 provides a summary of how process modeling went viral at 1&1 and indicates how knowledge was made transparent and available in the company. The system architecture provides the required infrastructure, the process architecture provides the framework for structuring or classifying the process information through the process house, the quality assurance ensures meaningful content, and both the BPM initiative and lean governance ensures the sustainability of the whole. Bringing these factors together allows employees to find high-quality information using the EIP. 1&1 created both the opportunity and incentives for modeling. While a proper system architecture and process architecture served as enablers of process modeling, the ease of use and increasing acceptance of process models as a standard of communication encouraged use of the notation. Eventually, the presence of a large number of potential process modelers promoted the viral dissemination of BPM. At 1&1, the adoption and use of process modeling spread exponentially in several stages, starting in the technical department and then penetrating departments involved in business analysis, requirements measurement, and enterprise business intelligence before reaching departments with broader operational and business-oriented orientations, such as finance and human resources.

1&1's BPM approach has been successful and has helped the company to increase its efficiency in many ways. The organization was able to adopt and use BPM(N) holistically in its entire value chain. With a deliberately lightweight implementation, the approach is highly responsive to change from inside or even outside the enterprise and enables continuous process adjustments triggered by nearly any employee on every level while also providing top management support and respecting the users' requirements and those of the integrated BPM system. As Petry explains, "This approach offers several advantages for us: from a macroeconomic perspective, the efficiency promises short time-to-market cycles and the ability to make rapid changes in organizational processes. 1&1 is globally competitive and can adapt quickly to changing customer needs. Although virtually all activities in the organization are mapped by processes, the administrative effort is still kept at a minimum." BPM became a highly valuable asset in creating a dynamic and innovative process environment. In short, BPM has become indispensable for 1&1.

5 Lessons Learned

The case of 1&1 provides useful insights that can be summarized in recommendations for the adoption of BPM as a paradigm. Figure 3 provides a graphic overview and structure. The list of recommendations is in no particular order of importance or urgency, but all can be related to the five areas of improvement that were introduced in Table 1.

(a) **Create a working process-modeling environment.**

Creating new knowledge by modeling is the first and most important use case, so users should be able to start modeling whenever they see the need to do so.

- Provide a sound and integrated infrastructure that facilitates the creation, viewing, and sharing of the result. Ensure that all conditions for implementing a BPM modeling tool are met.
- Provide a sound BPM modeling platform that is well integrated into the existing system infrastructure. Ensure that the tools in the system architecture do not interfere with each other.
- Consider separating executable and non-executable processes with at least one lightweight modeling environment for casual users and a BPM system for technical users. If you use SaaS, consider that executable processes can be fragile and can break after (automatic) updates.

(b) **Create a working process-viewing environment.**

Process models provide value to a BPM initiative only if they can be found, retrieved, and viewed at high quality. Modeling is not an end in itself but can be used to support communication, training, and automated execution. The modeling software alone often cannot ensure this level of service.

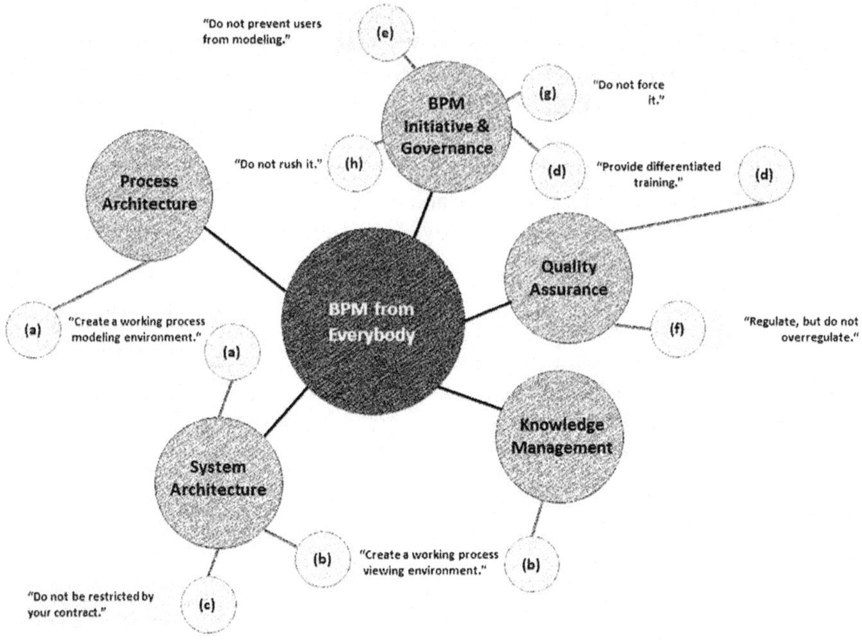

Fig. 3 Overview of guidelines for adoption of BPM

- Evaluate modeling software for its ability to structure and present process models, including both online viewing and export functionality.
- If additional systems must be integrated, consider an information portal as an aggregator to consolidate information in one place, index it, and disseminate it.
- Similar to the modeling recommendations, lightweight approaches make it easier for the casual user to get started and to be won over to BPM.

(c) **Do not be restricted by your contracts.**

Use software that enables everybody to create and access models. Software with tight user restrictions does not allow everybody to model, or logins have to be shuffled around. It does not create a free and open environment that enables creativity.

- Ensure that your software comes with a license that enables everybody to model and access the information.

(d) **Provide differentiated training.**

Not everybody knows the basics of BPM or BPMN or how to use a particular BPM software. Differentiated training is the key to raising everyone's level of expertise. Straightforward application procedures and cost center allocation, if any, will help spread acceptance.

- Provide basic and advanced courses for those who are new to the company or unaccustomed to BPM and those who know their way around, respectively. Advanced courses should be differentiated into smaller and more targeted courses.

- Provide short, long, and intense courses. Every employee has a different time budget to spend on BPM. Cater to those with only a few hours as well as to those who can spend a full day or two.
- Empower employees to teach. While a professional teacher may be a good start, grow the capability to teach about modeling in-house. Employees who teach learn when teaching too (Cau 2015).

(e) **Do not prevent users from modeling.**

Process modeling can only work for everybody if all interested users can benefit from it and incite others' interest in using it. It is impossible to centralize this dissemination of interest, so do not try to prevent anyone from creating a model.

- Process modeling should be like creating a PowerPoint presentation: while it is not perfect for knowledge management, it is better than chasing tacit knowledge.
- The model that was useless today may be important tomorrow. As it is impossible to foresee all use cases for process modeling in a company, it is similarly impossible to judge a model in advance.

(f) **Regulate but do not overregulate modeling.**

Process modeling, like any other modeling activity, requires some framing; otherwise, the resulting models will not be useful to anyone—not even the person who created them. However, do not overregulate how models can be designed. Based on the experience of the 1&1 case, we suggest six guidelines for regulating models:

- Provide a high-level structure into which all models should fit, whether the five levels of modeling 1&1 used or another kind of structure.
- Anchor all models within this structure through naming and conventions on how to name and/or categorize/tag the models.
- Provide a managed glossary, rather than an open, wiki-like glossary. Central terms should be managed centrally.
- Do not restrict modeling to specific purposes. Models may be created for a purpose you do not yet know, and departments may try to use process modeling in ways other than those initially anticipated.
- There is no "one size fits all" approach or solution. There are different views and, therefore, different versions of one use case or of processes that have the same sequence/effect. Do not limit the number of concurrent versions to one.
- Allow the creation of technical and non-technical process models. While BPM initiatives often originate from technical departments, much of its potential lies in other departments. Not every model has to be executable.

(g) **Do not force it.**

After experiencing the viral spread of BPM at 1&1, we are sure that a similar adoption elsewhere will work only if the employees see the benefits of process models for themselves. While employees should be encouraged to become process modelers, do not to force this concept.

- Do not force users who do not see the immediate benefit of using process modeling use it. They will not see the benefit after creating an uninspired model.

(h) **Do not rush it.**

In contrast to research facilities or universities, initiatives in enterprises often have to demonstrate success within the fiscal year, rather than a couple of years, or the project will be scrapped. BPM initiatives need some time to get rolling. A viral spread always starts with a small population and experiences slow growth in the early stages before reaching observable exponential growth.

- Give your BPM initiative enough time to get started so you can set up technology and training and start creating content before you expect a return in investment through your employees' mind shift. All exponential curves are slow starters, while logarithmic curves have a ceiling.

Much of our private lives are impacted by the Internet and social technologies, which build on the Web 2.0 principle of user content creation. It is difficult to incite this viral behavior in a business context, and many enterprises have failed in doing so (Turban et al. 2011). 1&1 provides a working example of where user content co-creation was successful despite initial setbacks and only moderate incentives. The recommendations given above can assist other enterprises to enjoy similar benefits when introducing or improving their BPM initiatives. Viral adoption is difficult to incite and predict, and research on its context (particularly with respect to BPM) is scarce, so there are no guarantees.

References

Becker, J., Kugeler, M., & Rosemann, M. (2011). *Process management: A guide for the design of business processes* (Vol. 2). Berlin: Springer.

Bjeković, M., Proper, H. A., & Sottet, J.-S. (2014). Embracing pragmatics. In E. Yu, G. Dobbie, M. Jarke, & S. Purao (Eds.), *Conceptual Modeling: 33rd International Conference, ER 2014, Atlanta, GA, USA, October 27–29, 2014. Proceedings* (pp. 431–444). Cham: Springer International Publishing.

Business Process Management Initiative. (2004). *Business process modeling notation (BPMN). Version 1.0*.

Cau, L. (2015). Lernen durch Lehren: Ganz Korrekt. *Pädagogik* (2), 20–23.

Cheng, G., Jin, H., Zou, D., & Zhang, X. (2010). Building dynamic and transparent integrity measurement and protection for virtualized platform in cloud computing. *Concurrency and Computation: Practice and Experience, 22*(13), 1893–1910.

Duffy, J. (2001). The tools and technologies needed for knowledge management. *Information Management Journal, 35*(1), 64–67.

Dumas, M., Rosa, M. L., Mendling, J., & Reijers, H. A. (2013). *Fundamentals of business process management*. Berlin: Springer.

Freund, J., & Rücker, B. (2014). *Praxishandbuch BPMN 2.0* (Vol. 3). München: Carl Hanser Verlag GmbH & Co. KG.
Geisler, E., & Wickramasinghe, N. (2015). *Principles of knowledge management: Theory, practice, and cases*. New York: Routledge.
Imgrund, F., & Janiesch, C. (2016). Vom Standard zur Anwendung: Ein Blick in Syntax, Semantik und Pragmatik der Adaption von BPMN. In *Proceedings of the Multikonferenz Wirtschaftsinformatik (MKWI) – Poster Track* (pp. 99–110), Ilmenau.
Merriam-Webster Online Dictionary. (2016). *viral*. Accessed April 12, 2016, from http://www.merriam-webster.com/dictionary/viral
Object Management Group. (2013). *Business process model and notation (BPMN). Version 2.0.2*. Accessed July 26, 2016, from http://www.omg.org/spec/BPMN/2.0.2/PDF
Recker, J. (2010). Opportunities and constraints: The current struggle with BPMN. *Business Process Management Journal, 16*(1), 181–201.
Rosemann, M., & vom Brocke, J. (2010). The six core elements of business process management. In J. vom Brocke & M. Rosemann (Eds.), *Handbook on business process management, Introduction, methods, and information systems* (Vol. 1, pp. 107–122). Berlin: Springer.
Signavio GmbH. (2016). *Signavio Process Editor*. Accessed April 15, 2016, from http://www.signavio.com/products/process-editor
Turban, E., Bolloju, N., & Liang, T.-P. (2011). Enterprise social networking: Opportunities, adoption, and risk mitigation. *Journal of Organizational Computing and Electronic Commerce, 21*(3), 202–220.
Wiig, K. M. (1999). Introducing knowledge management into the enterprice. In J. Liebowitz (Ed.), *Knowledge management handbook*. Boca Raton: CRC Press.
Wixom, B. H., & Watson, H. J. (2001). An empirical investigation of the factors affecting data warehousing success. *MIS Quarterly, 25*, 17–41.
Zur Muehlen, M., Wisnosky, D. E., & Kindrick, J. (2010). Primitives: Design guidelines and architecture for BPMN models. In *Proceedings of the 2010 Australasian Conference on Information Systems (ACIS 2010)*, Brisbane.

Florian Imgrund is a researcher and Ph.D. candidate at the Junior Professorship for Information Management at the Julius-Maximilians-University of Wuerzburg. He received his Master's degree in Business Information Systems from the University of Wuerzburg. His research areas include Business Process Management, E-Business and Complex Event Processing. His work appeared in conferences like the International Conference on Wirtschaftsinformatik (WI) or the Multikonferenz Wirtschaftsinformatik (MKWI).

Christian Janiesch is Assistant Professor at the Julius-Maximilians-Universität in Würzburg, Germany. He received his Ph.D., MSc, and a BSc in Information Systems from the University of Münster. Christian worked full-time at the European Research Center for Information Systems (ERCIS) in Münster, at the SAP Research Center Brisbane at SAP Australia Pty Ltd, and at the Karlsruhe Institute of Technology (KIT). His research is at the intersection of BPM and BI with a current focus on real-time, event-driven applications. Christian has been reviewing for various ACM and IEEE journals as well as BPMJ. He is on the Department Editorial Board for BISE. He has authored over 100 scholarly publications. His work has appeared in CAIS, BPMJ, BISE, FGCS as well as various major international conferences including ICIS, ECIS, and HICSS and has been registered as U.S. patents.

Christoph Rosenkranz is a Professor of Integrated Information Systems at the University of Cologne. He holds a diploma degree from the University of Münster, Germany. He received his doctoral degree and his habilitation from Goethe University of Frankfurt, Germany. He has collaborated and worked with leading organizations such as SEB, zeb, Woolworth's, Lufthansa, e-Spirit, and SAP. His research interests focus on designing, building, and managing integrated information systems, on business process management, on systems development, and on online communities, with an interest on the general question of how organizations can design, build, and manage integrated information systems. His work has been published in leading academic journals such as the Journal of Information Technology, Information Systems Journal, Business & Information Systems Engineering, Journal of Database Management, Supply Chain Management, and Journal of the Association for Information Systems.

Supporting Process Implementation with the Help of Tangible Process Models

Thomas Russack and Susanne Menges

Abstract

(a) **Situation faced**: Companies invest considerable resources in the elaborate design of computer-based process models. Because of these models' inherent complexity, they are not necessarily suitable for communicating with and training the employees who are supposed to apply them, but their understanding the processes is essential for efficient and effective work. Hence, creative, innovative methods are needed to bring these abstract models to life and increase their adoption by employees who typically have a low affinity for IT-related tools. Therefore, the methods that are developed should require little previous knowledge, (ideally) should not be IT-based, and should stimulate creativity, collaboration, and discussion. They should also create a playful experience while still offering guidance and overview of existing processes.

(b) **Action taken**: The company considered in this case searched for new, playful ways of communicating existing processes to employees who have little knowledge about process operations or process management. Two methods, a process card game and a process board game, were chosen and implemented. The card game conveys the most important process steps and process characteristics in a playful manner, providing a positive experience for the training participants and, thus, being memorable. The process board game complements the card game by conveying deeper knowledge about,

T. Russack (✉)
FOM Hochschule für Oekonomie and Management, Essen, Germany

Hochschulzentrum Münster, Münster, Germany
e-mail: Thomas.russack@fom.de

S. Menges
Curacon GmbH, Münster, Germany
e-mail: Susanne.menges@yahoo.de

J. vom Brocke, J. Mendling (eds.), *Business Process Management Cases*, Management for Professionals, DOI 10.1007/978-3-319-58307-5_29

for example, incidents that had in the past had positive or critical influences on the process. Both methods were developed in theory, both have been implemented as prototypes, and both have been tested in training new employees and during simulations, after which they were evaluated based on predefined requirements.

(c) **Results achieved**: The participants in the training were interviewed orally and in written form to evaluate the methods' benefits. Feedback from the trainers was included as well. These participants evaluated the methods positively, as both the participants and the trainers attested to the methods' ability to provoke discussions and stimulate creativity. Both methods are applicable to a variety of processes with reasonable effort.

(d) **Lessons learned**: Creative models demand the ability to abstract from business processes that are normally filled with details, so a clear business outcome and target group must be in mind when the new methods are first set up. However, since they do not provide a complete presentation of a process, additional methods should be used as complements. It is advisable to focus on one process that matters most to the target group at the beginning and to concentrate on the basic process features while designing the creative methods. Moreover, the degree of creativity should fit the company and its corporate culture.

1 Introduction

The benefits reaped by Business Process Management (BPM) are well understood, and many companies use computer-based models to document their procedures (Liebert 2012; Vlahovic et al. 2010). However, these models should be more than a documentary tool, as other benefits unfold when employees apply the process models and draw information for their daily work from them. However, domain experts are not typically sufficiently familiar with process models to understand and interpret them fully, so they are not willing to apply them (Bandara et al. 2007; Grosskopf et al. 2010).

The company that is the focus of this case searched for new ways to communicate existing processes to employees. This case study, conducted in cooperation with the FOM Hochschule für Oekonomie and Management, deals with the design and implementation of innovative training methods that help to impart knowledge about processes to employees. The two approaches presented in this paper help employees to understand process models and convert them into operational procedures.

This paper deals with a medium-sized German auditing, tax, and management consultancy called Accounting&Tax (A&T) that executes audits and consultancy mainly within the health, social services, and public sectors. A&T employs approximately 250 employees at ten locations in Germany. The prevalent business processes are highly knowledge-intensive, so they are usually complex and unpredictable and require precise interactions between a variety of departments and functions involved.

These procedures have a substantial impact on the quality perceived by the customers, which significantly affects customer satisfaction and the economic success of the company as a whole.

In the audit industry, efficient processes are crucial not only for economic reasons but also because legal and self-regulatory professional standards dictate a narrow framework and faultless processes. Even though the firm made detailed, computer-based process models accessible via its intranet, the rate at which these models were applied remained low. The *Knowledge Management* department deduced that this problem was due to the models' complexity, which might be difficult for non-experts in BPM to understand. As described in the BPM lifecycle model (Dumas et al. 2013) the "process implementation" phase also covers the aspect of organizational change, and organizational change management was required to enable employees to adapt to the scheduled processes.

Negative attitudes toward process implementation and the resulting lack of applications of the implemented models significantly affect BPM's benefits. Difficulties arise when management and the process management department assume that the mere presence of IT-based models will result in the required changes.

In order to address these "human" issues in the process implementation phase of BPM, the company developed creative methods from the IT-based models to convey process knowledge playfully. This rejection of opaque, businesslike process models changed the employees' attitudes, and the processes suddenly became understandable. When employees were provided with the precise, targeted information they needed to perform and prioritize their tasks, the presented process became tangible for them.

2 Situation Faced

Because of the importance of its business processes, the enterprise represented them in IT-based process models created using the modeling language BPMN 2.0. These models serve the purpose of providing training and instruction and are the basis for analyses/improvements and external certifications. In addition, a process-oriented job control supported by a dedicated IT system is based on these models (Russack 2013). The multifaceted areas of application assumes that the process models depict a comprehensive and complete picture of all the affected activities, resources, and coherencies. The respective sub-processes, as well as each single activity, have to be coordinated effectively, and the required information must be provided completely and on time, so the process models are relatively complex.

The staff turnover in A&T is relatively high, which is common in the industry, but in increasingly competitive markets, professional service firms should work continuously to improve the efficiency of their job executions. Consequently, new employees must be trained often and quickly.

3 Action Taken

New staff members must capture and process a large amount of information quickly, so the department of Knowledge Management at A&T searched for suitable training methods that would help new employees understand the company's business processes.

Management wanted these methods to be an alternative to extensive texts and ordinary process models, which had not proven to be sufficient training tools, as the more extensive and accurate the descriptions and process flow charts, the less they were used. At the same time, management knew that efficient communication of processes is a key success factor for establishing process thinking in an organization (Dombrowski et al. 2015; Bandara et al. 2009).

While process models and process descriptions are geared toward perfection and completeness, discussions with, informal interviews with, and observations of employees indicated that it was exactly those attributes that caused uncertainty and a feeling that one could not cope with the complexity these models imply. Therefore, while searching for new ways to improve the application of the process models, "imperfection" was the first requirement directed at the new training method.

What seems paradoxical has proven to be useful: Obvious incompleteness and gaps in descriptions in process models promoted creativity in the beholders and motivated them to think about changes, additions, and variations (Herrmann 2012). Completeness is not necessarily as advantageous for the success of training as is employees' actual application of the models, which are important if the company is to reap the benefits of any BPM implementation (Dumas et al. 2013). The company's Department of Knowledge Management knew it had to convince employees of the necessity and desirability of such tools and of their ability to apply them, so it needed new training methods that appeal to both the factual and the emotional parts of the employees' perceptions. Hence, the department sought to create training methods that combine the logical, abstract process models with emotional, symbolic elements in order to facilitate the learning success. Since new employees in the enterprise typically have a low affinity for IT-related tools, the department also wanted to use methods that were not IT-based.

These requirements were converted into a framework that is summarized in Fig. 1.

3.1 The Process Card Game

Starting from the requirements presented in Fig. 1, the core team of the knowledge-management project identified several suitable methods and elaborated on them during an intensive brainstorming session. One of these methods, the process card game, is based on traditional card games that are often used for comparisons of, for example, cars, airplanes, and ships. The cards typically show pictures of the objects, each with a number and letter on top (e.g., 1A, 1B, 1C, 1D). Attributes like speed,

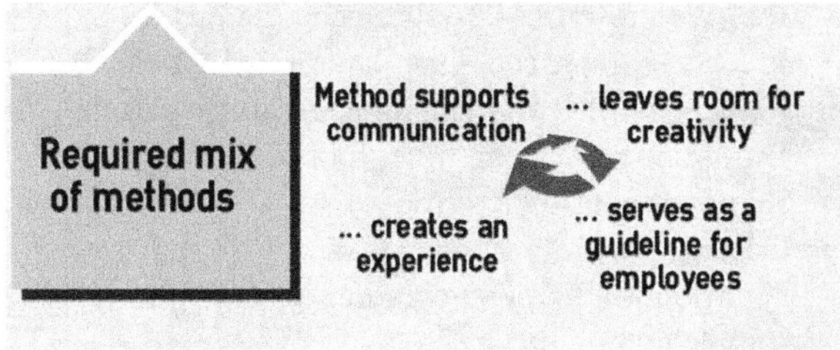

Fig. 1 Framework: Requirements for an ideal mix of methods

power, price, and weight are also given. Each player receives an equal number of cards and is allowed to play only the top card of his or her own cards, from which the player chooses an attribute and reveals the associated value (e.g., price). The player with the best value wins and is awarded with the other player(s)' card(s). The goal is to win all the cards.

Based on this game, the single process steps of a process (e.g., "Send the audit report") were portrayed on the cards. An image was assigned to each step, and each process step was given selected attributes and characteristic values (e.g., attribute: handling time; value: 0.25 h). Thus, a card game consisting of the individual process steps of a business process emerged.

The cards offer the advantage of making immediately visible the relevant process characteristics, as they constitute the central element of each card. In IT-based process models, the visualization of the process flows is often at the core, so even though a variety of process attributes can be attached to the models, this important information is often not immediately visible.

For the sake of clarity, no more than six features should be displayed on each card, so the features should be selected carefully with reference to the training's objective and the target group (For example if the participants are asked to reconstruct the sequence of the process at the end of the training, showing the attributes "predecessor" and "successor" on the cards would reveal too much beforehand). Suggestions for useful process characteristics can also be taken from the BPM context framework (e.g., based on the process dimensions of value contribution, knowledge intensity, creativity, interdependence, and variability) (vom Brocke et al. 2016).

Potentially meaningful process attributes are:

- Necessity of the process step (mandatory vs. optional)
- Roles: Who is responsible? Who accomplishes the tasks (customers, suppliers etc.)?
- Characteristics: Planning, execution, control, rework, feedback, mental activities, physical activities, etc.
- Qualifications and/or competencies required
- Development perspectives for those involved
- Input/Output
- Scope/Objectives
- Customer expectations regarding output (quality of results)

- Required resources, tools, specifications
- Predecessors, successors, parallel activities
- Frequency of repetitions of each process cycle
- Duration (processing time, transition time)
- Required control activities
- Cost
- Contribution to value creation
- Impact on quality
- Risks (e.g., risk of shortage)
- Degree of IT support, IT tools used
- Workload: time pressure, quantities
- Predictability/leeway in decision-making/structuring
- Transparency
- Communication and interaction
- Spatial arrangement
- Potential conflicts
- Outsourcing potential

We next describe one example of the process card game. Six process attributes were selected:

- **Necessity of the process step**—mandatory versus optional. This aspect of a process is important for new employees since they need to know in which cases a process step may be omitted (e.g., for economic reasons).
- **Interactive partners**—the number of functions that work together to complete the process step, not including those who work on the upstream and downstream process steps. New employees learn which colleagues and departments to involve in their activities and decisions and in which situations and sequences their support is needed. This process attribute indicates the degree to which the specific process step depends on other functions ("degree of dependence") and, in so doing, become aware of some of the reasons for delays in the process flow.
- **Description/value contribution of the process step**—proportions and degree (share, percentage) of service/production/review/rework in the process step. While the service and production part of a process usually adds value directly, non-value-adding parts like control and rework activities should be reduced to a minimum.
- **Estimated average duration/processing time measured in hours**—provides an idea of what the single process step contributes to the overall processing time.
- **Impact on the overall process quality**—the quality of results based on content quality, formal quality, and timeliness. The impact of the process steps on each of the three building blocks of quality (ranging from 0 = no impact, 5 = high impact) can be objectified, giving new employees who are willing and motivated to increase the quality of their work an idea of where to start. This knowledge also helps them to set the right priorities in their daily work.

B2 Send the final audit report

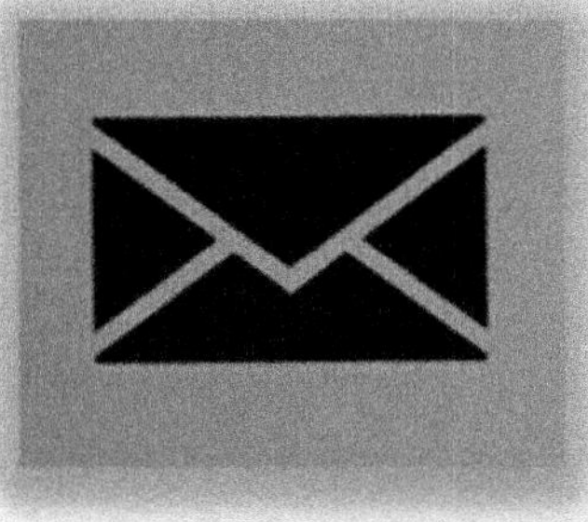

Execution	Office mandatory
Number of interaction partners	0
Description:	
Service/Manufacturing:	90 %
Control/Authorization:	10 %
Rework/Revision:	0 %
Average processing time:	0,25 h
Influence on quality of results (0-5)	
Contentual:	0
Formal:	1
Adherence to schedules:	4
Risk of shortage (0-5)	1

Fig. 2 Example: Card portraying the process step "Send the final audit report"

- **Risk of shortage/bottleneck**—sensitizes new employees to risks so they can plan for them. The higher the risk, the higher the chances that this process step might cause delays (ranging from 0 = no risk, 5 = very high risk) in the whole process.

An exemplary card from the game is shown in Fig. 2.

The process card game is used as a part of the initial 5-day training for new employees at A&T. The attendees get subject-specific input and learn about important business processes. The IT-based process flow charts are shown initially as an introduction to give the new hires a rough overview. Then, at the end of a training day or the beginning of the next one, the card game comes into action. Participants play in groups of two to four people, comparing the values of the attributes and collecting their opponents' cards when the "better" value wins. This approach also leads to lively discussions related to, for example, "Is a higher value at 'risk of shortage' really the winning value?" The participants are intended to reflect on the process and discuss the steps with their attendant values, thereby playfully deepening their knowledge about the process. After playing a few cards, the trainees often pose questions about the process steps, and the characteristics and values are clarified with the help of the trainer. Finally, the attendees model the complete process with the cards by placing the individual process steps in the correct order based on the "swim lane" method in which each department has its own "lane".

The card game can also be used for process modeling on a highly abstract level. The amount of time it takes the attendees to model the process, along with the accuracy of the results, indicates how well the participants understand the whole process, providing important feedback and insight for the trainer.

3.2 The Process Board Game

The process board game is a playful way to communicate extensive information about the processes, so it is a useful complement to the card game. Compared to the card game, though, the board game has fewer process steps, as the level of abstraction is higher so it does not take some details into account. The process example portrayed here consists of seven steps, but its content is identical to the process described and used in the card game, which consists of 20 steps. The game can be played by two or three teams of 1–4 players (2–12 players in total). A trainer directs the game and moderates discussions (especially those provoked by the "chance" cards).

The aim of the game is to produce as many products as possible within a predetermined time (45–90 min). Since A&T produces a service, rather than a product, the "product" is a completed audit report that is sent to the customer at the end of the annual audit. Each completed audit report brings money at the end of the process but only as long the required level of quality is achieved. There is also competition among the teams, as the team that finishes a report faster than the other teams receives significantly more "money." If a team's product quality is lower than required, there are significant deductions in revenues, while exceeding the quality requirement results in a bonus payment. In the end, the team that generated the highest revenues wins.

The groups go through the necessary process steps to complete and deliver the audit, rolling dice in order to move forward. Each process step is divided into six sub-steps. One dimension, employee satisfaction affects the pace of the game, and this feature (employee satisfaction) is displayed on a scale from 1 to 15. If employee satisfaction falls to a score of seven or lower, the operating speed also falls, and one point is subtracted from the dice's value. Conversely, employee satisfaction at a value of 12 or higher means a better operating speed, and the team adds a point to the value of the dice. There is also a connection between satisfaction and quality, as dissatisfied employees reduce quality while satisfied employees boost it. The higher the quality, the higher the revenues in the end.

Employee satisfaction and quality are also influenced by "chance" cards, which increase excitement and provide opportunities to gain new experience-based knowledge. Before entering a new process step, a new "chance" card is removed from the stack read aloud. These "chance" cards present typical issues that have occurred repeatedly in the course of the real process in the past. These incidents result in either positive or negative impacts for the group, as they influence employee satisfaction and quality positively or negatively. The chance card describes the situation and its impact on employee satisfaction and quality are briefly described on the cards. For example:

- Parts of upstream process steps have not been completed: Negative impact → quality decreases → total quality points are reduced.
- Required information is not yet available/required documents are not available: Negative impact → quality decreases → total quality points are reduced.
- Information is entered incorrectly in an IT system: Negative impact → quality decreases → total quality points are reduced.
- Employees from upstream process steps have already completed parts of the work of the process: Positive impact → satisfaction increased → dice number is raised → team is faster.
- An intern or an employee from another department supports the team: Positive impact → satisfaction increased → dice number is raised → team is faster.
- Deadline is moved up: Negative impact → quality decreases → total quality points are reduced.
- There are customer complaints: Negative impact → satisfaction decreases → dice number is reduced → team is slower.
- Customers are satisfied: Positive impact → satisfaction increased → dice number is raised → team is faster.
- Time pressures forces the team to work more quickly than under normal circumstances: Negative impact → quality decreases → total quality points are reduced + Negative impact → satisfaction decreases → dice number is reduced → team is slower.
- An employee becomes ill: Negative impact → satisfaction decreases → dice number is reduced → team is slower.
- A machine is broken: Negative impact → quality decreases → total quality points are reduced + Negative impact → satisfaction decreases → dice number is reduced → team is slower.
- A process step is automated: Positive impact → satisfaction increased → dice number is raised → team is faster.
- Few errors found by the quality-control audit: Positive impact → satisfaction increased → dice number is raised → team is faster + Positive impact → quality increases → total quality points increase.

These incidents and their impacts are identified with the help of employees who are experienced in the process. This effort also assists in process analysis since this group searches for typical incidents and possible solutions, albeit under playful, cheering conditions—in contrast to the more somber attempts for continuous improvement.

In the course of the game these incidents are discussed with the participants: Do those things really happen? Are the effects portrayed correctly? What events lead to the problems presented? How could they be prevented? By doing this, information about the process is communicated to the new employees in an entertaining manner.

4 Results Achieved: Critical Reflection and Evaluation of the Methods

The goal was to determine the effectiveness of the method, which is deemed successful if it meets the requirements formulated and summarized in the initial framework (Fig. 1). Based on this framework, an ideal method promotes creativity, supports communication, and combines abstract artifacts with symbols and vivid descriptions to reduce complexity. These attributes led to the specific requirements: a method that stimulates creativity among the participants, is neat and instructive, helps employees understand the process, creates a playful experience, promotes discussions and participation, and considers varying levels of expertise. Even so, it is unlikely that one method would meets all requirements completely.

4.1 Evaluation of the Process Card Game

After the training of new staff members had been running for several cycles, the participants, including the trainers, were invited to complete a survey that asked them to reflect on the process card game. This survey was supplemented with a personal interview in order to uncover the reasons for the results. The evaluation results for the process card game are shown in Fig. 3.

As Fig. 3 shows, the card game was assessed as a method that stimulates discussion and creates an experience, primarily because of the playful contest in which the attendees participated. Comparing the processes' attributes and their values, discussing why the "enemy's" value is higher than one's own, winning and losing—such emotional moments stay in one's memory. In addition, playing cards against each other creates a relaxed atmosphere, a welcome change during a week full of teacher-centered training. Moreover, playing cards is connected to childhood memories, which promotes a comfortable feeling throughout the event which is beneficial for training's success. The criteria "Stimulates creativity" and "Encourages participation" were rated high, with four out of five points each, probably because it is an interactive game. In addition, the final modeling of the process demanded a high degree of creativity and provoked discussions among the attendees.

The card game neither constitutes a complete process model nor a complete process documentation, which helps to explain the low ratings with respect to the criterion "Is the method neat and instructive?" The card game can always be seen as a supplement to existing (often IT-based) process models and other methods that help to communicate the process.

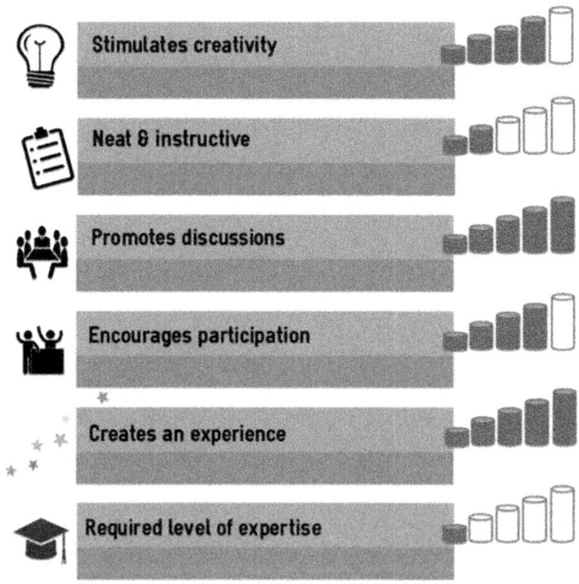

Fig. 3 Evaluation results for the process card game

The ratings on previous knowledge and level of expertise required are relatively low in terms of both the difficulty of understanding the method itself (the card game) and understanding the process the card game depicts. The participants reported that, even though the process had been explained theoretically, the relationships between the steps, roles, and activities become most apparent during the game.

The evaluations confirm the expectations for this method, as it improves the communication of processes and related information, so it improves the new employees' ability to apply the implemented process models.

4.2 Evaluation of the Process Board Game

In order to evaluate the quality of the board game method, the participants and trainers were invited to complete a survey that asked them about their opinions and perceptions of the board game. The survey was supplemented by a personal interview in order to determine the causes for the results.

Figure 4 summarizes the evaluation results for the process board game method.

As Fig. 4 shows, the board game was perceived as stimulating discussions, creating an experience. It was also rated as being relatively instructive, perhaps because of the "chance" cards and the incidents they contain, which make problems and real operational coherences more tangible. Only one person perceived the game as useless. The participants also testified that the knowledge

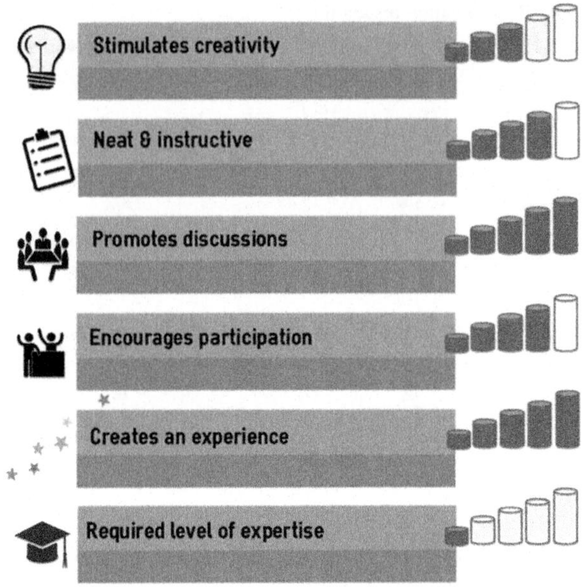

Fig. 4 Evaluation results for the process board game

required to play the game is low—referring to both the game's rules and knowledge about the process. In summary, the evaluation results confirm the expectations.

4.3 Summary of the Results Achieved

The problem A&T encountered with implementing detailed business process models was that high complexity often interfered with comprehensibility. In order to turn complexity into something understandable, the company created new tools to support communication of the processes. The innovative, game-based methods helped A&T handle the trade-off between the completeness and intelligibility. With reference to the BPM framework (Dumas et al. 2013), we argue that successful implementation of a process also requires sufficient training of the affected employees, which was especially true in the case of knowledge-intensive service and high fluctuation in processes. The human side of implementation must be kept in mind by considering how plain process models can be turned into something vivid with which an employee *wants* to deal? In the case presented here, these models were used as a foundation for new methods that are adapted to "arouse" the process, turn it into something tangible, and thereby serve as a supportive communication tool.

The card game and the board game helped to change the prevailing attitudes of new employees toward the existing process models: The playful approach led the employees to want to deal with the IT-based models, as once they understood the procedures, they lost their timidity about asking for additional details. In the protected, playful classroom environment, the employees realized that it is not a sign of weakness to ask questions. Their basic understanding of the processes that was acquired during the training and with the help of the two games helped them to understand the processes' complex interrelationships. The board game in particular highlighted dependencies between departments and the effects of historically accurate incidents. Understanding the degree to which their work affects others also improved the attitude in the departments that participated in the training.

In short, the number of employees who retrieved the IT-based models on the firm's intranet increased, while requests for additional information on individual process steps declined.

5 Lessons Learned

Process models have to serve multiple areas of application (e.g., process analysis, process improvements attempts, documentary purposes, form the basis for certifications, trainings, communication), which tends to make these models inherently complex. However, employees who are not familiar with process thinking might be overwhelmed by this complexity. The benefits of BPM implementations can be negatively affected if employees do not apply the available models to the desired extent.

One important finding of the case presented is that the newly introduced methods should be seen as enhancements of, rather than as substitutes for, the computer-based models (e.g., based on BPMN 2.0). In other words, the computer-based models should be the basis for supplementation by the new methods.

A clear business outcome and target group should be in mind when new methods are first set up. Designing these creative methods demands time, so it is advisable to start with a maximum of three core processes that are particularly important to the target group. Once employees have gained an understanding of process thinking and changed their attitudes toward the topic, they will be more willing to deal with the existing process models. Therefore, it may not be necessary to represent all existing processes in the new, creative form.

The advantage and the "core" of the new methods are their level of abstraction. Both the card game and the board game help employees to understand the basic sequence of the process by omitting details. With the target group and the business outcome in mind, the designers of the methods should focus only on the handful of details that will be presented. Feedback loops with participants in the training and other employees involved in the processes will help the designers to stay focused.

Such new, creative methods work only so long as they fit the prevailing corporate culture. The level of creativity and playfulness should always be aligned with the company's values and "unwritten rules."

The two new methods closed a gap between business analysts (experts in process modeling) and specialty departments (experts in their fields who often lack a deep understanding of process management methods).

References

Bandara, W., Indulska, M., Chong, S., & Sadiq, S. (2007). Major issues in business process management: An expert perspective. *ECIS 2007 Proceedings*, Paper 89.

Bandara, W., Alibabaei, A., & Aghdasi, M. (2009). Means of achieving business process management success factors. In *Proceedings of the 4th Mediterranean Conference on Information Systems*.

Dombrowski, U., Grundei, J., Melcher, P. R., & Schmidtchen, K. (2015). Prozessorganisation in deutschen Unternehmen, eine Studie zum aktuellen Stand der Umsetzung. *Zeitschrift für Organisation (ZFO), 01*, 63–69.

Dumas, M., La Rosa, M., Mendling, J., & Reijers, H. (2013). *Fundamentals of business process management*. Berlin: Springer.

Grosskopf, A., Edelmann, J., & Weske, M. (2010). Tangible business process modeling. Methodology and experiment design. *Business Process Management Workshops, Lecture Notes in Business Information Processing* (Vol. 43, pp. 489–500). Springer.

Herrmann, T. (2012). *Kreatives Prozessdesign, Konzepte und Methoden zur Integration von Prozessorganisation*. Berlin: Technik und Arbeitsgestaltung.

Liebert, T. (2012). *Prozessorientierung in der Unternehmensorganisation – Eine empirische Untersuchung in deutschen Industrieunternehmen*. Wiesbaden: Gabler Verlag.

Russack, T. (2013). Prozessorientierte Auftragssteuerung. *Industrie Management, 29*(4), 61–65.

Vlahovic, N., Milanovic, L., & Skrinjar, R. (2010). Turning points in business process orientation maturity model. An East European survey. *WSEAS Transactions on Business and Economics, 7*(1), 22–32.

vom Brocke, J., Zelt, S., & Schmiedel, S. (2016). On the role of context in business process management. *International Journal of Information Management, 36*(3), 486–495.

Thomas Russack is a Professor of Strategy and Organization at the FOM University of Applied Sciences (FOM Hochschule für Oekonomie & Management) in Münster, Germany. His research areas include Business Process Management, Change Management, Innovation Management, Organizational Culture and Quality Management. He also works as a management consultant in the fields of strategy and organization. Previously, he headed the department of quality and process management in an accounting firm.

Susanne Menges After graduating from the University of Applied Sciences in Muenster with a Master‘s degree in International Management (M.A.), Susanne Menges started in the department of quality and process management in a medium-sized accounting firm. In her 3 years with this company she accompanied the digital transformation of this enterprise: She headed a project to introduce a social collaboration platform and also coordinated various projects to improve internal process flows. In the meantime, she works in the Human Resources department and uses her creative potential to run the company's recruitment marketing activities.

Business Process Modeling of a Quality System in a Petroleum Industry Company

John Krogstie, Merethe Heggset, and Harald Wesenberg

Abstract

(a) **Situation faced**: The petroleum industry is characterized by increased focus on safety and compliance with regulations, in addition to efficient operations. Earlier quality systems were represented in large binders of textual documents, which made important governing documentation difficult to access and unusable for operational personnel who wished to gain an overview.

(b) **Action taken**: Based on the existing quality system, a new way of structuring and accessing the material was developed as a collection of 2000 process models with navigational support through an intranet solution whose use was mandatory in the workplace.

(c) **Results achieved**: Improved compliance with regulations and reduction in the number of accidents were observed. This improvement is not attributable only to the restructuring and presentation of the quality system through process models, but the process models are a visible sign of the organization's focus on safety and compliance, and it has made it easier for workers to find relevant regulations and requirements when dangerous work is to be undertaken.

J. Krogstie (✉)
Norwegian University of Science and Technology—NTNU, Trondheim, Norway
e-mail: krogstie@idi.ntnu.no

M. Heggset
SopraSteria, Oslo, Norway
e-mail: merethhe@gmail.com

H. Wesenberg
Statoil ASA, Trondheim, Norway
e-mail: hwes@statoil.com

J. vom Brocke, J. Mendling (eds.), *Business Process Management Cases*,
Management for Professionals, DOI 10.1007/978-3-319-58307-5_30

(d) **Lessons learned**: Although good results have been achieved, there is room for improvement in this large-scale example of the use of process models to structure a company's quality system. Ensuring that all employees can find all the models they need and that the models are kept up to date based on practice are important challenges. In addition, handling the trade-offs among goals for safety, efficiency, and compliance is a challenge. Modeling practices that were regarded favorably at an earlier stage might come to be seen as insufficient for the future needs. Therefore, professional long-term use of models must be conscientiously pursued over time.

1 Introduction

The case organization, which operates in the oil and gas sector, has more than 24,000 employees and approximately the same number of external contractors. It operates in 37 countries, although main operations are in the company's home country. Permanent employees are divided among organizational units of varying size, with Development and Production (DPN) and Technology, Products, and Drilling (TPD) the largest. The company operates worldwide and, particularly over the last decade, it has used process modeling to structure its massive amount of organizational knowledge.

As an advanced technology company, the organization has a long tradition of adopting new approaches to IT and organizational development. In the 1980s, the organization experimented with the use of process and data modeling in connection with the application of what was then called CASE tools (Solum and Østerud 1989). In the 1990s, modeling was used for a broader set of tasks. As summarized in Christensen et al. (1995), the use of process and enterprise models in the company was divided into three purpose-based categories:

1. Construction of reality: modeling as a technique for creating a common understanding among people whose cognitive models do not necessarily coincide.
2. Analysis and simulation: making changes to simulated enterprise models and monitoring the consequences to determine whether a change should be implemented.
3. Model deployment and activation: the use of an enterprise model for controlling and performing work.

These areas for the use of models are still central for enterprise process modeling (Krogstie 2016). Although the notations used in the various early projects differed and covered a larger part of the enterprise than business processes, the company developed a standardized process-modeling notation. In 2001 (when BPMN was not yet available) this notation was evaluated and compared with other notations (Krogstie and Arnesen 2005) and the "home-brew" notation was kept, albeit with some changes. Some years later, when BPMN arose as a standard, the company adopted it, and in 2004 the company began using enterprise process models as part of its corporate management system. According to Wesenberg (2011) the company "achieved a fair [amount of] success with enterprise modeling in its corporate management system where workflow models are used extensively to communicate requirements and best practices throughout the enterprise."

Classifying the case according to the BPM Context Framework (vom Brocke et al. 2015), we find the following:

- Goal
  - Focus: The focus is on exploitation of the framework to support compliance and improvement.
- Process:
  - Value contribution: The main value is the standardization of core processes, although the overall framework also supports management and support processes on a less detailed level, since there are fewer compliance rules and virtually no dangerous work situations in these areas.
  - Repetitiveness: The focus on the core processes is on repetitive processes, but the framework also represents non-repetitive processes on a high level.
  - Knowledge intensity: Similarly, the framework covers processes of both low, medium, and high knowledge intensity.
  - Creativity: Similarly, the framework covers processes of low, medium and high creativity.
  - Interdependence: Processes with low, medium, and high interdependence are covered in the framework.
  - Variability: Processes with low, medium, and high variability are covered, although the level of detail differs based on knowledge intensity, variability, and creativity.
- Organization
  - Scope: intra-organizational processes.
  - Industry: product (resources) industry.
  - Size: large organization.
  - Culture: highly supportive of BPM (at least in large parts of the organization, although some parts are only moderately supportive).
  - Resources: high levels of organizational resources used.
- Environment
  - Medium competitive environment.
  - Medium level of environmental uncertainty, although a high level of uncertainty is soon likely given the significant changes in the energy area.

2 Situation Faced

Although the case organization works across a number of fields, the main activity is off-shore oil and gas production. This area focuses on safety and on compliance with the regulations in the country of operations (which are often there to ensure safe production). Offshore work, such as that in the North Sea, is also characterized by workers' working in shifts (e.g., 2 weeks on and 3 weeks off). When returning to the platform after 3 week off, workers must be able to work according to the procedures from the first minute to ensure safety and compliance.

The organization has a detailed management system, described as "the set of principles, policies, processes and requirements which support the organization in fulfilling the tasks required achieving our goals" (Statoil 2016). The management system defines how work is done in the company, and all employees are required to act according to its relevant governing documentation (GD).

The three main objectives of the management system are:

1. Contributing to safe, reliable and efficient operations and enabling compliance with external and internal requirements.
2. Helping the company to incorporate its values, its people, and its leadership principles into everything it does.
3. Supporting business performance through high-quality decision-making, fast and precise execution, and continuous learning.

GD describes what is to be achieved and how to execute tasks, and it ensures standardization.

The management system's organizational function, Corporate Security and Safety—Corporate Management System (the CSS-CMS unit) is responsible for creating and improving the management system based on business needs, ensuring that the GD is understood and used, and monitoring compliance with work requirements. Around 50 persons work in this function, and an additional 15 or so persons from other parts of the organization, most notably from Corporate Audit (COA) work daily to ensure the quality and compliance of the quality system. The CSS-CMS function's work follows a five-step cycle:

1. Assess and plan changes to the GD: When a change or update to the GD is needed, a lead nominated by the owner of the GD which often is the same as the owner of the process performs a stakeholder analysis to identify all roles involved. A work group is established to perform the planning and scoping of the work to be done. The plan is then evaluated, and when agreed upon, the design step begins. This step relates to Process Discovery and Process Analysis in the BPM Lifecycle (Dumas et al. 2013).
2. Design the GD: A workflow model (or a detailed textual GD or both) is created as described in a predefined workflow. This work includes describing the process's purpose and triggers, identifying activities, checking its business value, assigning roles, and identifying risks. External consultants usually facilitate the modeling activities, while the process owner and representatives from the stakeholder groups identified contribute in participative modeling sessions (Gjersvik et al. 2005). This step relates to Process Redesign in the BPM Lifecycle (Dumas et al. 2013).
3. Implement the GD: When the GD is ready, the implementation is planned and executed. The local process manager acts as a facilitator, the scope of the implementation is assessed, and a plan for the implementation is established. The local process manager then performs the activities needed in order to prepare for the implementation of the new GD in his or her area. If needed, employee

training is prepared and conducted. When ready, the local process manager sends a confirmation to the lead of the implementation planning, who passes the confirmation on to the GD's owner. The GD is then ready for publication. This step relates to Process Implementation in the BPM Lifecycle (Dumas et al. 2013).

4. Use the GD: GD is intended for use by its target group, according to its purpose and validity (i.e., to whom it applies). Before dangerous work begins, the actor responsible for the process must go through the documentation/process model, and before getting a work order accepted, the employees acting in each role defined in the process must consult the model. Employees can apply for a permission to deviate from a requirement in the GD, and upon registration of such an application, an initial consideration is performed, where the line manager and local process manager give comments and advice, and relevant contributors propose additional actions. When the application is submitted, the process owner decides whether to submit the application for implementation approval or to terminate it. The line manager then rejects or approves the implementation. Information on the result is then sent to the applicant, and if approved, the deviation permit is ready for use. As part of this process, any employee might also suggest improvements to the general process.
5. Monitor and control use of the GD: The purpose of monitoring use of the GD is to reduce risk, drive performance, and ensure compliance. Monitoring can be carried out by internal or external parties. Activities performed in internal monitoring include:

   - Follow-up: ensuring that strategies and tasks are executed according to plan.
   - Verification: confirming through objective evidence that work has been done in compliance with requirements.
   - Internal audit: evaluating and improving the effectiveness of performing a process with a formal mandate from the board of directors to, for example, ensure that projects are properly organized and managed.

The last step relates to Process Monitoring and Control in the BPM Lifecycle (Dumas et al. 2013).

Until 2004, the company's quality system was text-based and was found in binders around in the organization. After an accident in which the procedures were not followed, it was determined that employees had not been able to identify all relevant procedures. At the same time, the organization merged with another organization that used process modeling more actively for structuring its quality system, and the merged organization was able to build on this example.

3 Action Taken

Over the last decade, the company's quality system has been restructured and maintained in the form of an integrated collection of process models. The general requirements for the quality system were described above, but five more concrete areas of use are also important:

1. Compliance management: Monitor and control how and whether the work performed complies with the standards set for how to work to ensure the production of predictable output from work.
2. Competence management: Document the competency profiles needed to perform tasks, compare required competency profiles with the competence represented in the organization, and manage the competency gap.
3. Portfolio management: Gain an overview of the current portfolio of, for example processes, information systems, and technologies in order to provide opportunities to determine whether the existing portfolio will meet future needs and to plan the roadmap to move from the current to the future portfolio.
4. Analysis and decision-making: The model and its sub-models enable an analysis of the relationships among the objects in the models and how changes to one object (e.g., a process) will impact other objects (e.g., the information systems used by that process or relationships among work processes).
5. Performance analysis: Monitor results to obtain experience and data related to quality in order to determine whether the method of working produces the best possible result.

Even if several possible purposes are listed, a model always has one primary purpose, although it may have a number of secondary purposes. The current primary purpose of the enterprise process model is compliance management, so priority is given to achieving an acceptable level of quality for the GD models, along with their corresponding governing elements, roles, and responsibilities. The process owners decide what is the right level of quality based on the use of and feedback related to the models. Guidelines for the quality of the models, including a balance among the syntactic, semantic, and pragmatic quality of the models (Krogstie 2016), are described in the GD, TR0002 (Statoil 2013). Two of the five concrete goals, competency management and performance management, were not included in version 1 of the requirements (Statoil 2009). This change is not an example of "goal creep" [i.e., the use of models for purposes that were not originally envisioned (Krogstie et al. 2008)], but it results from the requirement that the models be current as-is models because of the focus on compliance. Recently, the underlying infrastructure to support the areas of competency management and performance analysis was put into production in the organization.

The model-based management system consists of three main parts:

- The end users assess the process models using a restricted subset of BPMN (Silver 2012) that is represented in the ARIS tool, the modeling solution that all of the GD in the models and in accompanying detailed documents uses. The models are as-is models that are manually activated; that is, they represent how people are expected to work at the company and also support checking adherence to the models at times such as when employees are doing dangerous work or submitting new work orders.

- Docmap is used for handling and publishing textual GD. These more detailed documents are directly accessible from the process models in ARIS, where they are relevant.
- Disp is a tool that supports the process of handling applications for deviation permits when compliance with a requirement is difficult or impossible to achieve. Disp is also accessed directly from the ARIS process models. It is also possible to add suggestions for process improvements directly in the ARIS tool.

There are three levels of abstraction in the enterprise process model—the contextual level, the conceptual level, and the logical level—which include the interrelated diagrams illustrated in Fig. 1. Examples of each diagram-type are found in Figs. 1, 2, 3, 4, 5 and 6. The example diagrams provide a "flavor" of the types of models on the various levels and are not meant to be read.

- The top-level diagram (Fig. 2) is a mandatory navigational diagram that visualizes core value-chain processes, management processes, and support processes, capturing what the company terms "the contextual level." This diagram is similar to a process map (Malinova et al. 2014), as it depicts core, support, and management processes at the highest level.

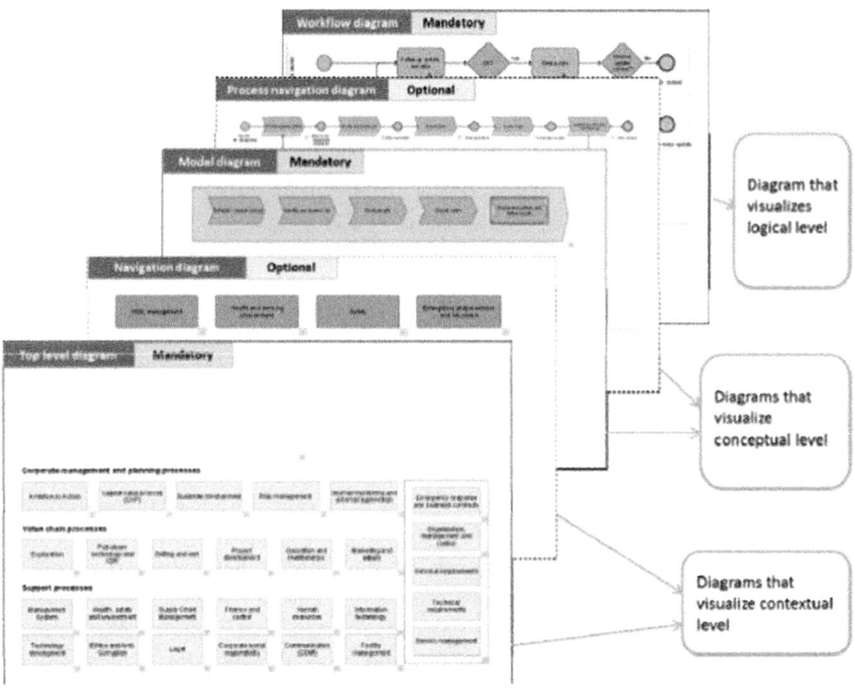

Fig. 1 Structure of models in the management system

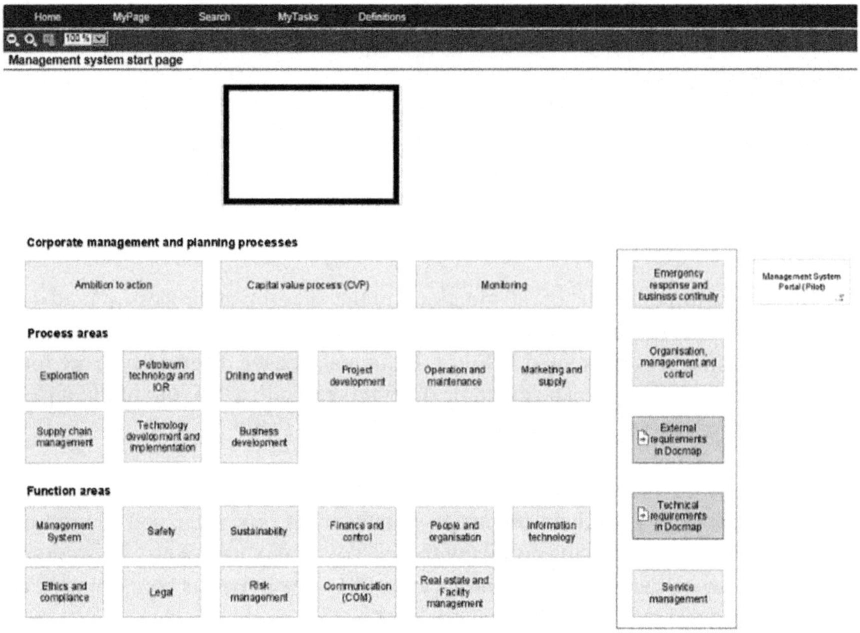

Fig. 2 Top-level diagram, a.k.a. company process map

- The navigation diagram(s) (Fig. 3) are optional diagrams that support more tailored access to the processes for users in various parts of the organizations than is provided by the top-level diagram. All models show validity (i.e., relevance) for all business and organizational units, so a person has access only to the part of the model that is relevant to him or her based on the organizational unit to which he or she belongs.
- The model diagram (Fig. 4) is a mandatory diagram that visualizes the model of one process area in the organization.
- The process navigation diagram (Fig. 5) is an optional model for navigational support on the conceptual level.
- The workflow model (Fig. 6) contains BPMN models on the logical level. This model is similar to what others term "the descriptive level" (Silver 2012). The quality system contains approximately 2000 BPMN models at this level, qualifying the case as BPM-in-the-large (Houy et al. 2010).

The contextual level consists of a top-level diagram and navigation diagrams and provides a high-level overview of the enterprise. The top-level diagram, which is mandatory, contains a model of the enterprise in terms of both process areas and function areas. The management system's start page, shown in Fig. 2, is a top-level diagram.

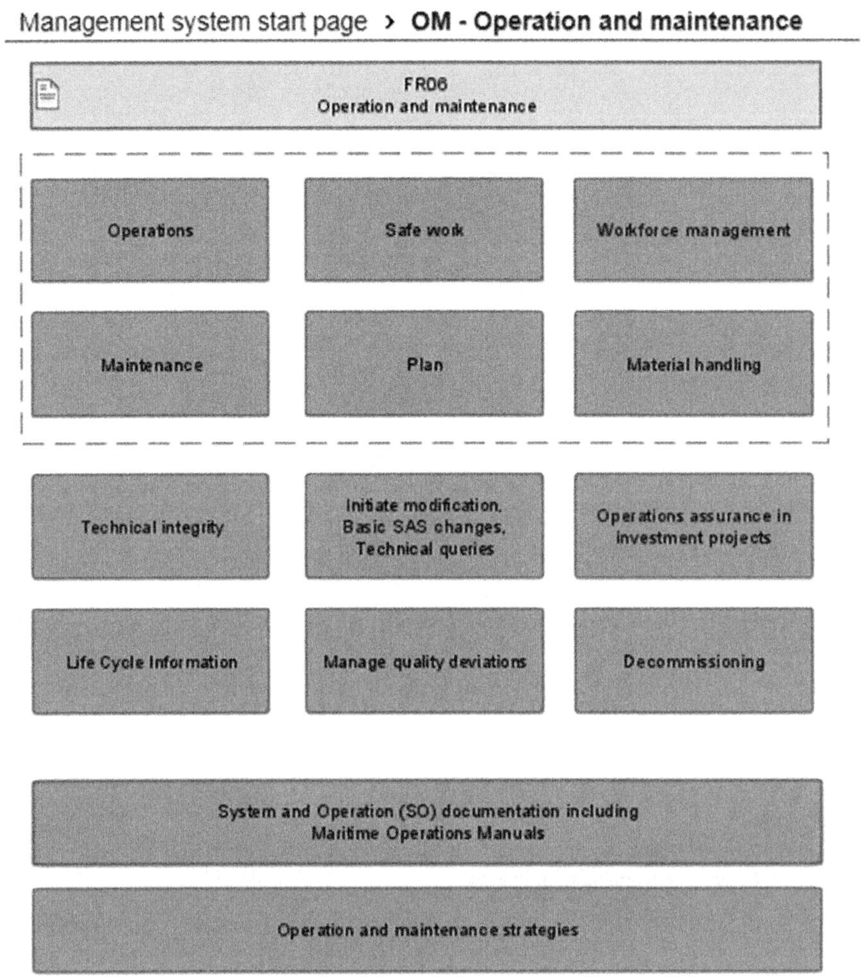

Fig. 3 Navigation diagram

The purpose of the navigation diagrams, which are optional, is to help the user navigate to the correct model by structuring and detailing the content in a process area. The navigation diagram can contain symbols that represent closed content groups, document model groups, and document models. A stippled rectangle can be used to group a set of closed content groups. An example of a navigation diagram is given in Fig. 3.

The primary purpose of the conceptual level, which provides a conceptual view of the enterprise as model diagrams and process navigation diagrams, is to show relationships between or within models.

The model diagram in Fig. 4 is a mandatory diagram that shows the content of a closed content group or a process area. It may contain collapsed workflow models,

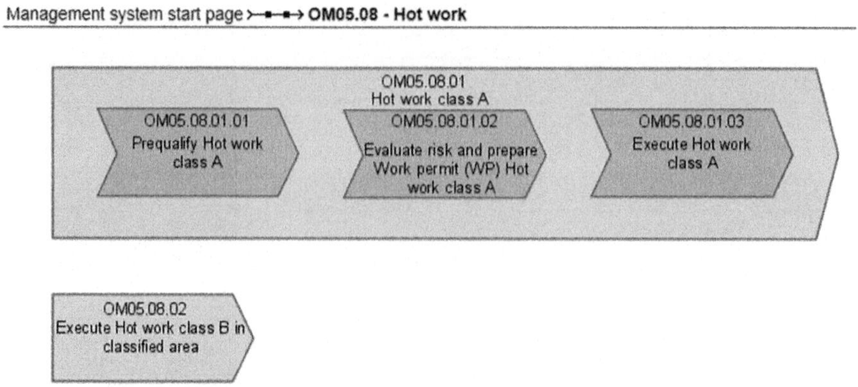

Fig. 4 Example of a model diagram

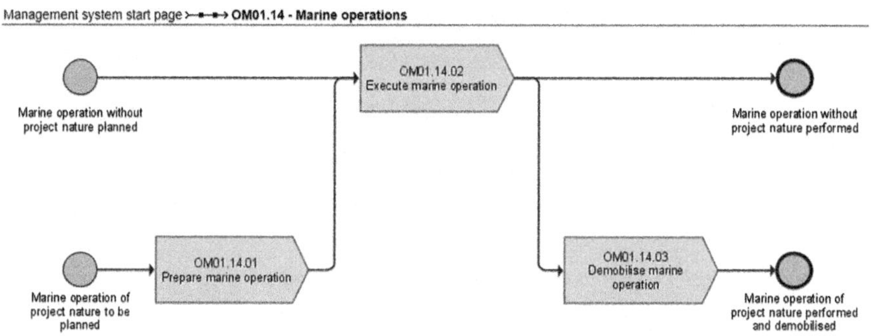

Fig. 5 Optional process-navigation diagram

process models, and document models. A rectangle can be used to group a set of collapsed process models, and for quicker navigation, collapsed workflow diagrams can be placed inside a collapsed process model symbol.

The optional process-navigation diagram (Fig. 5), which is used to show how workflow models are related to each other, uses collapsed workflow models, start events, end events, and intermediate events. A sequence flow in the form of an arrow visualizes the order in which the workflow models are to be executed.

The logical level shows the breakdown of the enterprise model into generic elements. The only diagram that visualizes the logical level of the enterprise model is the workflow diagram, a mandatory diagram that is modeled using an adapted subset of BPMN 2.01. This diagram has several activities and may have decision gateways arranged in a sequence within lanes that represent the process role that is responsible for those activities. The activities, which are carried out by someone who represents the process role, are represented by a task symbol. Activities can be either mandatory or

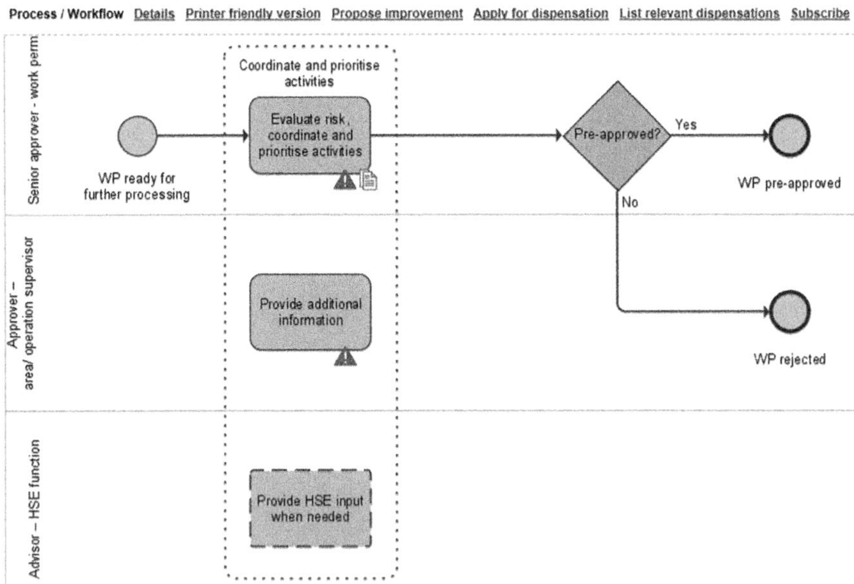

Fig. 6 Example of workflow diagram

optional. A set of task symbol with a stippled line around them is used to represent a collaboration activity that includes more than one role. (This is a modeling mechanism not found in core BPMN.) The diagram can also contain either collapsed sub-processes that lead to another workflow diagram that details the sub-process or call task symbols that refer to a workflow model in another process model. The workflow diagram also contains start and end events and various types of standard gateways ("and" and "xor"), but not intermediate events or complex gateways.

An example of a small workflow diagram is given in Fig. 6, which shows the interactions among three roles (as swimlanes) relative to a coordination activity that involves risk assessment and activity approval. The approver and senior approver are mandatory participants in the task, whereas the advisor is an optional participant. When the coordination activity is complete, the task ends successfully if pre-approval has been made. This example follows the version of BPMN the company uses (Statoil 2013; Heggset et al. 2014), which differs somewhat from the official BPMN definition (e.g., including special semantics in the grouping mechanism) and links to extra requirements and guiding documentation from the models (stored in the Docmap tool). The use of restricted and tailored subsets of BPMN is common in practice (Aagesen and Krogstie 2015).

There are several ways for users to access GD:

- Navigating through process areas: When a user accesses the ARIS start page, he or she gets an overview of all process areas and can click one for an overview of the content in it. From there, the user can access work processes, documents, workflow models, and other information.

- Using the navigation history: The user can use the dropdown menu to access his or her navigation history from anywhere in ARIS. This menu displays the pages in the management system that the user previously visited.
- Using "breadcrumbs": From any but the top level in the hierarchy users can navigate to higher levels using "breadcrumbs" located at the top of the page. (See, e.g., Figs. 3, 4 and 5) The "breadcrumbs" also help users keep track of where they are in the process hierarchy.
- Searching: ARIS search is a simple search interface into which the user can put search words and then use a drop-down menu to choose the type of GD that they seek. The results appear as a list of full or partial hits that is updated as the user types.
- Using "MyPage": Each user has a personal space, called "MyPage," which is accessible on each page. Beginning from a workflow model page, the user can click the "Subscribe" tab and confirm that he or she wants to subscribe to that particular model. Within a short time, a direct link to the model will be available in the Subscriptions section of the user's MyPage.

4 Results Achieved

The company's quality system had been text-based and stored in large binders before it was restructured as a network of process models. Our contact in the company claimed that the process modeling approach provided the employees the ability to structuring the quality system in manageable pieces that, together with good tool support for accessing the models and detailed requirements for the process, made it much easier to find relevant parts of the process, thus doing a better job of supporting the work to be done. One KPI in particular that improved after the introduction of this new way of structuring the quality manual is the Serious Injury Frequency (the SIF-index). Figure 7, which is based on the

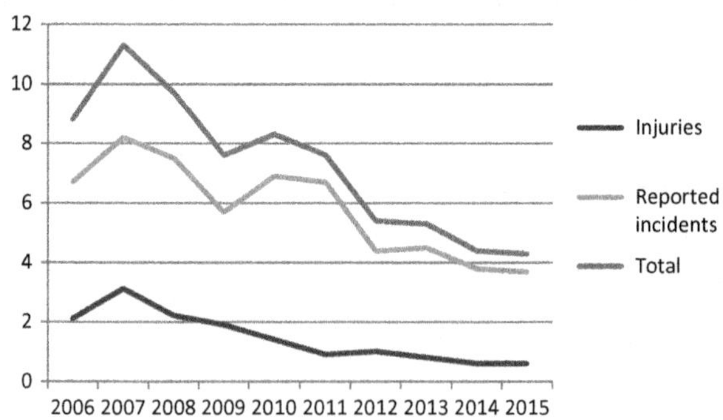

Fig. 7 Development of the SIF-index over the last decade. The *red line* in the *bottom* indicate the trends for injuries, whereas the *yellow middle line* indicate the trend for reported incidents, i.e. dangerous situations (without physical injuries)

company's yearly sustainability report (Statoil 2015), provides an overview of the positive development in the company's injury frequency over the last decade.

To investigate how the improvments in the SIF-index might be related to the models, we looked at actual model use. Using the models as a checklist before starting dangerous work (safe job analysis) and before getting work orders accepted (work permits), including daily work-permit meetings, is mandatory. In recent years, the company has been using the Splunk Enterprise tool, a platform for collecting and indexing machine-generated data such as click-streams, to monitor the use of the management system. The data collected by Splunk are indexed as events and can be searched using the Search Processing Language (SPL), a query language developed by Splunk. The search results in Fig. 8, which are based on around a half year of usage data, provide information on how employees use the enterprise model, such as how often a certain page or model is accessed and how users navigate through the enterprise process model. According to the results collected from Splunk and a user survey fielded in the company, Operation and Maintenance (O&M) is the process area that uses the management system most frequently. The number of navigational elements and levels in ARIS vary widely by process area, so the search included only clicks on workflow models at the bottom level and excludes events that lack the "process area" field. Therefore, the calculated percentage for each process area is the percentage of the total number of events that do contain the field for process area.

Table 1 lists the ten most frequently used workflow models. Twelve of the 20 most frequently used models deal with safety-critical processes; that is, either they are classified as Safe work (a sub-category of O&M) or they belong to the Safety process area. The high number of distinct users over the half-year period indicates the models' high level of use, which occurs at least in part because their use is mandatory in many operational areas.

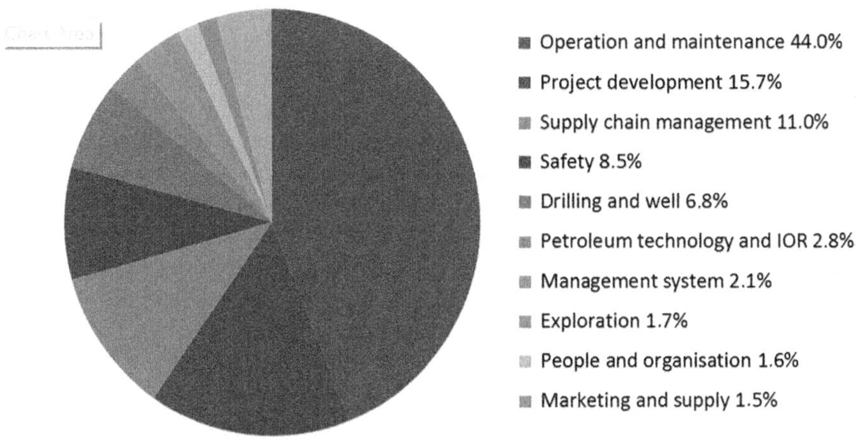

Fig. 8 Process areas' system use

Table 1 The ten most frequently used process models

Workflow model	Distinct users	Hits per user
Prepare isolation plan	4054	8.5
Apply for and evaluate work permit	4145	5.9
Initiate modification	2342	9.8
Perform work at night	3953	5.1
Commission and hand over systems	2308	7.9
Checklist for safe work	3572	4.6
Safety incident	1628	9.6
Prepare for activity that weakens safety system	3438	4.5
Execute mechanical completion	1993	4.5
Perform bolt tightening	2076	6.3

Table 2 Workflow model hits per organizational unit

Organizational unit	Percentage of hits	Workers in total	Hits per worker
Development and Production (DPN)	44.80	8954	73.00
Technology, Projects and Drilling (TPD)	32.27	6778	69.50
Marketing, Processing and Renewable Energy (MPR)	13.23	3526	54.60
Chief Financial Officer (CFO)	6.41	2124	44.00
Development and Production International (DPI)	1.40	736	27.90
Exploration (EXP)	1.36	969	20.40
Development and Production North America (DPNA)	1.07	757	20.60
Corporate Audit (COA)	0.63	49	186.80
Corporate Security and Safety (CSS)	0.57	60	138.00
Global Strategy and Business Development (GSB)	0.32	262	17.80
Total		24,215	

Table 2 lists the total number of clicks for each organizational unit for the 6-month period, along with the average number of clicks per user. (This value was calculated only for organizational units with more than a thousand total clicks.) As the table shows, DPN is the organizational unit responsible for the largest number of workflow hits, although both COA and CSS have much higher average hits per employee, with 186.8 and 138, respectively. This result is not surprising because one of COA's primary responsibilities is to evaluate and improve the management systems' effectiveness. CSS's sub-unit, CSS-CMS, is responsible for the corporate function described in Sect. 2, related to the management system. Therefore, although employees in these units work directly with the management system, they are not its primary end users.

Although used in various ways and at various levels, the models were visited and searched for extensively and by more than 24,000 individual people over the 6-month period (i.e., almost all employees). One can use various methods to access the workflow model of interest, and a clickstream analysis enables a more detailed study of this phenomenon.

A path analysis for the most frequently used workflow model, "Prepare isolation plan," shows that the most common path corresponds to navigating from the start page directly down through all of the layers above the model page, which indicates that 38.8% of those who used this model knew exactly what they were looking for and where to find it. That so many users went directly to the model via the navigational pages is unsurprising considering that this model is the most-used workflow model, so most of its users probably use it frequently and have learned where it is located. Even so, although they use it often, these users do not use "My Page:" or bookmarks to access it directly. However, 15.1% of those who use this model either do that or access it through the search function, because the second most-popular path contains only one click—to the model itself. The fifth most-common path is the only one in the top five that suggests that the user looks for the model in several places before locating it.

Another example process is "Chemical management". Whereas 11,753 sessions ended with a view of "Prepare isolation plan," only 2096 ended with "Chemical management." However, as many as 42.4% of users went directly to "Chemical management," whereas only 15.1% accessed "Prepare isolation plan" directly. The number of sessions in which the workflow model is accessed directly varies widely by sub-model, perhaps in part because awareness of the "MyPage" functionality is higher in some parts of the organization than it is in others. The intuitiveness of the model's placement in the hierarchy is another possible explanation. Users might use the search function when they feel that it is difficult to locate the model using their intuition and knowledge about the process area.

Diagrams that are designed in the enterprise process model must meet specific company requirements. Heggset et al. (2014) provides an overview of the company's modeling requirements structured according to SEQUAL's model quality levels (Krogstie 2012).

5 Lessons Learned

Although the models in the quality system are widely used and likely contribute to the improved safety and compliance of company operations, there is also room for improvements in the approach.

A large-scale user survey was conducted in the company to clarify users' experiences and opinions related to the management system and GD. The survey was completed by 4828 employee participants, approximately half of those invited to respond (Heggset et al. (2015a)). The results of the survey revealed many challenges related to the management system itself, as well as educational processes and work practice, all of which contribute in some way to the management system's goals of safety, reliability, and efficiency. Some important points from the survey revealed that:

- Many of the employees have trouble finding what they need when they look for GD, although the clickstream analysis indicates that the level of difficulty varies in different parts of the organization. Moreover, when users do find the relevant documentation, many are unsure that they have found all of it.
- Many are not satisfied with how changes to the GD that affect their work are communicated, which makes it difficult to know whether their information is current. Fourteen percent of the respondents report using paper copies to access GD in part because of limited access to IT systems on the oil-platforms; therefore, unless employees are notified of changes, they might continue to use old versions. This situation has improved, though, so the quality system is used as a work tool for preparing the tasks to do out on the platform deck.
- The models use too many abbreviations. Although the guidelines for modeling explicitly discourage the use of abbreviation (Heggset et al. 2014), these guidelines are not always followed.
- There are many guidelines for the correct use of the modeling language and many examples of those guidelines' being only partly obeyed. Although this issue was not explicitly mentioned in the survey, when a large number of syntactic errors are found in the models, comprehension can be affected (Heggset et al. 2015b).
- The process of handling improvement proposals is experienced as being too slow for some users.
- Sixty-eight percent of those who responded to the survey feel that the GD has the right amount of detail, although they are seen as too rigid or general to account for local needs and variations in some cases, leading to many requests for deviations because the models are not seen as properly fitting the domain of the specific sub-process.
- Approximately half of the respondents feel that the GD is easy to understand, but others perceived it as vague and ambiguous, especially with respect to authorities and responsibilities. Approximately half of the respondents have participated in organized training related to the use of GD. These respondents have a higher score for confidence in, use of, and compliance with the GD than the respondents who have not participated in a training program.
- The survey showed that good leadership support has a strong positive effect on use.
- Considering how GD contributes to the management system's goals, the results from the survey indicate that it makes a substantial contribution to a high level of safety (as confirmed by 75% of the respondents) and to a moderate to high effect on reliability, but not to high efficiency (37%). One in five of the respondents feel that safety and efficiency is not properly balanced. Reasons for this imbalance include that the GD is experienced as too focused on safety, which sometimes results in longer task-execution times, and that local best practices

are not always reflected in the GD. Even so, safety was a main driver for restructuring the quality system in the first place.

The quality system was developed especially to support compliance with requirements in order to reduce risk, an area in which large improvements have been observed over the last decade. Still, there are challenges related to, among other things, finding all relevant information, the comprehensibility of some of the models [although the pragmatic quality of models has been emphasized (Wesenberg 2011)], the update of models based on local needs, and the combined focus on compliance, safety, and effectiveness. The need for training is also emphasized.

Through the Splunk analysis, the user survey, interviews, and conversations with company employees we have gained valuable insights into how users experience the management system. Some measures can be taken to achieve higher model quality, as some users in the user survey report that the GD is difficult to understand, and improved understanding is a necessity if 100% compliance is the goal. Measures that can contribute to increased understanding include strictly applying the language guidelines and naming conventions and tailoring model complexity to the needs of the target audience. Processes for including employees' knowledge more directly in the loop, such as the AKM approach (Lillehagen and Krogstie 2003) and the use of interactive models (Krogstie and Jørgensen 2004), and for clearer model governance are also important. Changing the organization's emphasis to focus more on efficiency, rather than only on safety and compliance may influence the perception of quality.

The company's use of modeling has evolved over the years, and models and modeling practices that were once regarded favorably might come to be seen as insufficient later. As in many companies (Krogstie 2008) one see a need to integrate also other type of modeling perspective than process models. Therefore, the serious long-term use of models must be conscientiously followed up over time as the organization's context and need for modeling changes.

References

Aagesen, G., & Krogstie, J. (2015). BPMN 2.0 for modeling business processes. In J. vom Brocke & M. Rosemann (Eds.), *Handbook on business process management*. Berlin: Springer.

Christensen, L. C., Johansen, B. W., Midjo, N., Onarheim, J., Syvertsen, T., & Totland, T. (1995). Enterprise modeling-practices and perspectives. *Computers in Engineering*, 1071–1084.

Dumas, M., La Rosa, M., Mendling, J., & Reijers, H. (2013). *Fundamentals of business process management*. Berlin: Springer.

Gjersvik, R., Krogstie, J., & Følstad, A. (2005). Participatory development of enterprise process models. In J. Krogstie, K. Siau, & T. Halpin (Eds.), *Information modelling methods and methodologies*. Hershey, PA: Idea Group Publishers.

Heggset, M., Krogstie, J., & Wesenberg, H. (2014). Ensuring quality of large scale industrial process collections: Experiences from a case study. In *The practice of enterprise modeling* (pp. 11–25). Berlin: Springer.

Heggset, M., Krogstie, J., & Wesenberg, H. (2015a). Understanding model quality concerns when using process models in an industrial company. In *Proceedings from EMMSAD 2015*. Berlin: Springer.

Heggset, M., Krogstie, J., & Wesenberg, H. (2015b). *The influence of syntactic quality of enterprise process models on model comprehension*. CAiSE Forum. CEUR: Stockholm.

Houy, C., Fettke, P., Loos, P., van der Aalst, W. M. P., & Krogstie, J. (2010). BPM-in-the-large – Towards a higher level of abstraction in business process management. In M. Janssen et al. (Eds.), *EGES/GISP 2010, IFIP AICT 334* (pp. 233–244). Berlin: Springer.

Krogstie, J. (2008). Integrated goal, data and process modeling: From TEMPORA to model-generated work-places. In P. Johannesson & E. Søderstrøm (Eds.), *Information systems engineering from data analysis to process networks* (pp. 43–65). Hershey, PA: IGI.

Krogstie, J. (2012). *Model-based development and evolution of information systems: A quality approach*. London: Springer.

Krogstie, J. (2016). *Quality in business process modelling*. Cham: Springer.

Krogstie, J., & Arnesen, S. (2005). Assessing enterprise modeling languages using a generic quality framework. In J. Krogstie, K. Siau, & T. Halpin (Eds.), *Information modeling methods and methodologies*. Hershey, PA: Idea Group Publishing.

Krogstie, J., & Jørgensen, H. D. (2004). Interactive models for supporting networked organisations. In *16th Conference on advanced information systems engineering*. Riga, Latvia: Springer.

Krogstie, J., Dalberg, V., & Jensen, S. M. (2008). Process modeling value framework. In Y. Manolopoulos, J. Filipe, P. Constantopoulos, & J. Cordeiro (Eds.), *Selected papers from 8th international Conference, ICEIS 2006* (Vol. LNBIP 3, pp. 309–321). Paphos, Cyprus: Springer.

Lillehagen, F., & Krogstie, J. (2003). Active knowledge modeling and enterprise knowledge management enterprise inter- and intra-organizational integration. In *Volume 108 of the series IFIP—The international federation for information processing* (pp. 91–99). Boston: Springer.

Malinova, M., Leopold, H., & Mendling, J. (2014, June 16–20). *A meta-model for process map design*. CAiSE Forum 2014. Thessaloniki, Greece.

Silver, B. (2012). *BPMN method and style*. Aptos, CA: Cody-Cassidy Press.

Solum, P. E., & Østerud, M. (1989). *Integreret CASE-verktøy. Kartlegging av teknologien og problemer i forhold til tradisjonell systemutvikling*. Master Thesis NTNU. Trondheim, Norway.

Statoil. (2009). *TR0002 enterprise structure and standard notation. Version 1*.

Statoil. (2013). *TR0002 enterprise structure and standard notation. Version 3*.

Statoil. (2015). *Statoil sustainability report*. http://www.statoil.com/no/environmentsociety/sustainability/Pages/SustainabilityReporting.aspx

Statoil. (2016). *The Statoil book (2016)*. http://www.statoil.com/no/about/thestatoilbook/Pages/TheStatoilBook.aspx

vom Brocke, J., Zelt, S, & Schmiedel, T. (2015, December 1). Considering context in business process management: The BPM context framework. *BPM Trends*.

Wesenberg, H. (2011, November 2–3). Enterprise modeling in an agile world PoEM 2011. In *Proceedings of the 4th Conference on Practice of Enterprise Modeling*. Oslo, Norway.

John Krogstie (1967) received a M.Sc. in Information Systems from IDT, NTH in 1991 and has a Ph.D. in Information Systems (IDI, NTNU) from 1995. He was employed as a manager in Accenture 1991–2000. In 2000–2005 he was employed by the research institute SINTEF as senior researcher. Since 2005 he has been Full Professor at IDI, NTNU, focusing on enterprise and process modeling, quality of models and modeling languages, eGovernment, digital ecosystems, and mobile and ubiquitous information systems. Krogstie leads the faculty lighthouse on Open, Autonomous Digital Ecosystems (OADE), and the Wireless Trondheim Living Lab. Krogstie is currently secretary of IFIP WG 8.1 on Design and Evaluation of Information Systems (chair 2010–2015, vice-chair 2004–2009), and vice-chair of IFIP TC8. John Krogstie has published around 200 refereed papers in journals, books and archival proceedings since 1991.

Merethe Heggset is a former student of Informatics at the Norwegian University of Science and Technology (NTNU) in Trondheim. She currently works as a Software Engineer and IT consultant in the company Sopra Steria in Oslo. Her Master's Thesis from NTNU, entitled "Achieving Long-Term Value of Enterprise Models—A Case Study" formed the basis for the work presented in this book.

Harald Wesenberg tok his Master in Computer Science in 1996. Since then he has worked in Statiol with a total of 20 years experience as a professional software engineer specializing in software for the oil and gas industry, with the last 6 years spent working as an solution architect with focus on researching large scale software solutions for the oil and gas value chain.

Business Process Management in German Institutions of Higher Education: The Case of Jade University of Applied Science

Jan Bührig, Thorsten Schoormann, and Ralf Knackstedt

Abstract

(a) **Situation faced**: Faced with challenges like heterogeneous processes across three campuses, a campus management system that was not up to date, and loss of knowledge because of demographic changes and undocumented, inconsistent processes, Jade University of Applied Science implemented a campus-management system developed by HIS. This system includes an integrated reference model for processes that are related to campus management. The university wanted to use common standards and needed a guide based on best practices. Implementing business process management (BPM) provides an opportunity to document, standardize, and centralize processes across their campus locations.

(b) **Action taken**: Implementation of the campus management system and reference processes was structured in steps that can be described using a BPM lifecycle model: (I) initialization, (II) process identification, (III) process discovery, (IV) process analysis, (V) process redesign, (VI) process implementation, and (VII) process monitoring. Each of these steps is directly related to using the HISinOne reference model to obtain recommendations based on best practices.

(c) **Results achieved**: Both expected and unexpected results were obtained from implementing the campus management system: (I) the standardization of processes across three campus locations was improved

J. Bührig (✉)
Hochschul-Informations-System eG (HIS), Hanover, Germany
e-mail: buehrig@his.de

T. Schoormann • R. Knackstedt
Institute for Economics and Information Systems, University of Hildesheim, Hildesheim, Germany
e-mail: thorsten.schoormann@uni-hildesheim.de; ralf.knackstedt@uni-hildesheim.de

J. vom Brocke, J. Mendling (eds.), *Business Process Management Cases*, Management for Professionals, DOI 10.1007/978-3-319-58307-5_31

by (II) adopting best practices, and internal workshops to standardize processes (III) strengthened Jade University's overall team spirit. In general, (IV) individual barriers to using process models and process documentation were reduced, and a BPM-supportive culture was developed such that some departments have begun to document other processes and to consider the implementation of a broader BPM department.

(d) **Lessons learned**: Five primary lessons were learned during the project: (I) orienting to existing solutions like process reference models supports the initialization of new projects, and (II) standardization limits the involved stakeholders' creativity. In addition, (III) guidelines for consistently documenting the implementation's progress are important to easily provide relevant information to all stakeholders at all times, (IV) integrating relevant stakeholders into the process enables the standards across different locations to be determined, and (V) limited project resources must be taken into account in order to plan suitable and feasible actions.

1 Introduction

Business Process Management (BPM) is increasingly used to improve companies' operations (e.g., Malinova and Mendling 2015), but constantly increasing competitiveness has led to its becoming more important in fields like education. Process-oriented information systems could be implemented to facilitate the efficient management of such institutions' resources (Bob-Jones et al. 2008). Information systems (IS), such as campus management systems, can illustrate students' entire educational lifecycle, from application to ex-matriculation (Sprenger et al. 2010). A study in campus management indicates that about 50% of the involved institutions see implementing a campus management system as not just an IT project but as a project for the entire organizational structure (Ernst & Young 2012). Hence, the aim of this case study is to report *how BPM and IS are used in the education sector*, specifically at Jade University of Applied Science.

Because of challenges related to such issues as being competitive, protecting knowledge, standardizing work operations, and being sufficiently digital and modern for students, Jade University needed a campus management system that would support *documenting and standardizing processes across three campus locations. The system in use was out of date, and the provider would soon stop supporting it.*

Because campus structures are complex and Jade had no documentation of its processes, the determination of relevant processes for implementing a campus IS was to be based on best practices. HISinOne is an established campus management system that provides preconfigured process-oriented settings based on a process reference model. The system is used by about 50 German universities (HISinOne 2016). Reference models, which (usually) describe the best practices in a specific domain, can be reused and adapted to other contexts (e.g., vom Brocke 2007; Fettke and Loos 2003; Rosemann and van der Aalst 2007). They also provide benefits like efficiency and effectiveness in respect to costs, time, quality, and risks (Becker et al. 2007).

Implementing a new campus management system was the institution's biggest (IT) project and the first that related to BPM. Several departments, including the centralized IT department, were involved, and a project team was created. A professional project management were established that consisted of two employees to manage the project and two other employees to execute the daily work.

The next section uses the BPM context framework (vom Brocke et al. 2015) to provide details about the situation Jade University and its project management team faced. Then Sect. 3 describes the actions taken by adapting Dumas et al.'s (2013) life cycle model. Finally, based on the archived results (Sect. 4), we outline the lessons learned from the project (Sect. 5).

2 Situation Faced

Based on challenges like an obsolete campus management system, heterogeneous processes across three campus locations, loss of knowledge because of demographic changes, and the need for digitalized and documented processes, Jade University decided to implement HISinOne and the integrated software reference model. Jade wanted to use common standards and needed a guide based on best practices and saw the implementation of the system and a BPM as an opportunity to document and standardize its processes.

We describe the characteristics of our case first because one critical principle for successful BPM is context awareness (vom Brocke et al. 2014). In describing them, we use the *BPM Context Framework*, which presents the contextual factors of a BPM project (vom Brocke et al. 2015). Our assessments in defining these factors are based on our own project experiences, interviews with experts (particularly the head of BPM at Jade University), analysis of documents, and analysis of conceptual project papers (Table 1).

Goal-Dimension Jade University sought to *improve* aspects of its processes, such as (a) managing and protecting internal knowledge, (b) standardizing processes across all campus locations, and (c) orienting to the best practices relating to campus management (system) processes.

Jade wanted to focus on *(a) managing current knowledge to ensure that future generations have access to that knowledge*, particularly because of demographic changes. In addition, Jade wanted to make the knowledge more transparent and accessible to all employees and campus locations. Hence, one of the essential objectives was *(b) standardizing these processes* across all locations and departments, for which Jade needed a consistent BPM. Moreover, Jade wanted the implemented standards to be based on *(c) best practices and recommendations* for using a campus management system. Initially, Jade focused on implementing processes that were related to campus management because of limited project

Table 1 Contextual factors (vom Brocke et al. 2015)

Dimension	*Characteristic*	*Characteristic value*		
Goal	Focus	Exploitation (Improvement, Compliance)		Exploration (Innovation)
Process	Knowledge-intensity	Low	Medium	High
	Creativity	Low	Medium	High
	Interdependence	Low	Medium	High
	Variability	Low	Medium	High
Organization	Scope	Intra		Inter
	Industry	Product	Service	Product & Service
	Size	Start-up	Small/Medium	Large
	Culture	Highly supportive of BPM	Medium supportive of BPM	Non-supportive of BPM
	Resources	Low	Medium	High
Environment	Competitiveness	Low	Medium	High
	Uncertainty	Low	Medium	High

Note: Gray cells represent the results of our case study

resources, so the focus on goals like optimizing processes and developing actions for the organizational structure were also limited.

Furthermore, Jade's employees expected *(d) full documented guidance* on how they should do their work. There were no goals related to monitoring archives, measurements, or controlling, such as analyzing times and costs.

Overall, Jade intended to implement processes and preconfigured settings in the standard software using the HISinOne recommendations to reduce the project delays that often accompany the development of new tasks.

Process Dimension In general, universities like Jade University that have multiple campus locations have heterogeneous types of processes that are not distinctly assignable to a specific characteristic value. For example, the *knowledge intensity* of the processes considered varies widely. Most of the processes are complex, requiring training for up to 2 years because understanding and executing these processes requires knowledge. There are also some simple processes (e.g., administrative work) that are not difficult to understand and execute.

The level of processes' *creativity* ranges widely. Simple processes like stamping letters go side by side with processes of medium difficulty (e.g., managing applications) and highly creative work (e.g., building examination regulations and managing courses). Many of the processes in the campus management system are highly *interdependent*, with processes and flows linked to previous or subsequent processes, but starting and ending points are defined precisely and connectable via integrated interfaces. These processes' *variability*, however, is low because there are usually only a few small changes in each process over time, except for some irregular legal terms.

Organization Dimension Jade University, established in 2009, has three campus locations, one each in Wilhelmshaven, Oldenburg, and Elsfeth (Germany). The *scope* of this BPM project embraces the processes that are related to campus management in each of the campus locations, as well as those that occur in all three locations. Implementing HISinOne (including the reference model) is the biggest (and first) project related to the field of BPM undertaken by this institution. Therefore, a project team was created and a professional project management was established.

Jade University is a *small to medium-sized* institution of higher education, with 500 employees and 180 professors across six faculties: architecture, civil engineering, engineering sciences, maritime management, business sciences, and management/information/technology. It offers 37 bachelor's degrees and eleven master's degrees and has about 8000 students (Jade University 2016).

The *industry/sector* can be defined as service because Jade offers educational services. Because of the importance of this implementation, Jade hired two employees to manage the project and two additional employees to execute the daily work. However, very limited *resources* were available, especially considering the complexity and the objective of the project.

At the beginning of the project, the limited expertise in BPM that was available was a risk factor (Rosemann and vom Brocke 2015). Most employees were open-minded and supportive of BPM, but there were some skeptics who were only moderately supportive. In general, the *culture* was characterized by employees who were highly and medium supportive of BPM. Some departments documented their processes in mixed and inconsistent forms, such as checklists, text, and sequence diagrams, and some employees did not even know what a flowchart is. Hence, one issue was to create acceptance, a BPM-supportive culture, and expertise.

Environment Dimension BPM is becoming important for Jade University because of the rising *competitiveness* that makes it essential that the university be up to date and interesting to applicants and researchers. The level of *uncertainty* in this sector is low.

3 Action Taken

BPM can be understood as all of the management tasks that are related to business processes. BPM-related tasks are often described as a lifecycle model that is based on general plan-do-check-act models (Malinova and Mendling 2015). Because of complex structures in campus management systems and processes, Jade University needed guidelines and references for how processes could be undertaken or executed. For this reason, they decided to get an orientation by using the HISinOne reference model and the recommended HIS approach to how related processes can be implemented in universities.

The HIS approach to implementing processes is based on guidelines like BPM lifecycle models (e.g., Dumas et al. 2013), domain-specific requirements, and experiences. We use Dumas et al.'s (2013) framework for describing the steps taken in our case (Fig. 1) This framework has six main steps: *process identification*, *process discovery*, *process analysis*, *process redesign*, *process implementation*, and *monitoring/controlling*.

Our description adapts these steps and complements them by adding project-specific actions like *(a) initialization* and *(b) interdependency between process analysis and process redesign.* Jade University had to create an environment that allows BPM to be implemented, which included hiring professional staff. There was also a loop between analysis and redesign and some discussions and workshops regarding standardizing processes that did not lead to a result because of insufficient information or expertise. The project team had to reanalyze these cases in detail before the next step, redesign, could be taken.

Initialization A project team and project management were established to support implementing the campus management system and the BPM. These people sought to improve performance by, for example, educating all stakeholders (Rosemann and vom Brocke 2015) and creating a BPM-supportive culture. HIS also conducted an

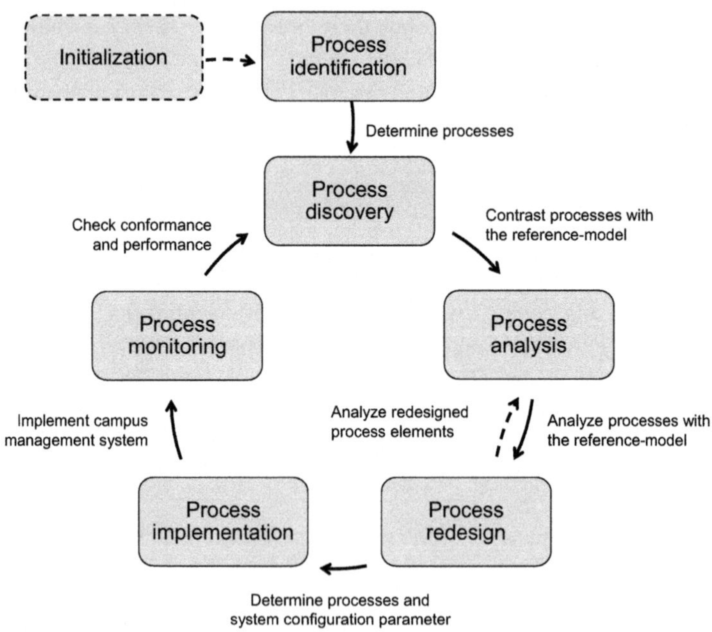

Fig. 1 Overview of action taken (Dumas et al. 2013). Note: *Dotted lines* and *boxes* represent additional steps and flows

initial workshop to determine how process management should be integrated into the university, and based on this workshop, HIS designed training concepts that were customized according to the requirements of the individual employees involved and the university's needs.

Process Identification Jade determined the processes that would be used based on the best practices of the education sector so it put a strong focus on the reference model's suggested flows. Therefore, the identification of processes was based on the HISinOne reference model, which offers models described in the Unified Modeling Language (UML) for all processes that can be supported by the HISinOne campus management system. The reference model is structured in five levels, each with its own perspectives and details (Fig. 2).

The structure follows the object-oriented BPM (OOBPM) approach (Oestereich 2003). In contrast to a holistic approach for major university processes (Petkovics et al. 2014), all levels are focused on campus management-related processes to cover the students' educational lifecycle. The process map (level I), which includes all campus management processes and is the starting point for the process identification, defines the modeling scope, such as application management, student management, or examination management. Level II uses UML use case diagrams, which are related to the elements of the process map. For each process area, the actors and their use cases are visualized so the process manager can identify relevant stakeholders. Level III structures the use cases into business processes, focusing on *what* has to be done to reach the process goals. Here, no executing actors are modeled because the sequence of actions is the focus. This level is often used to structure workshops and discussions. Each of the actions of the business process is described in detail by a workflow in level IV, which focuses on *how* the actions will be done and assigns the defined actors of the use case diagram to actions. According to the OOBPM, there is a link from workflow to system processes, so level V shows which actions the system can support (level V),

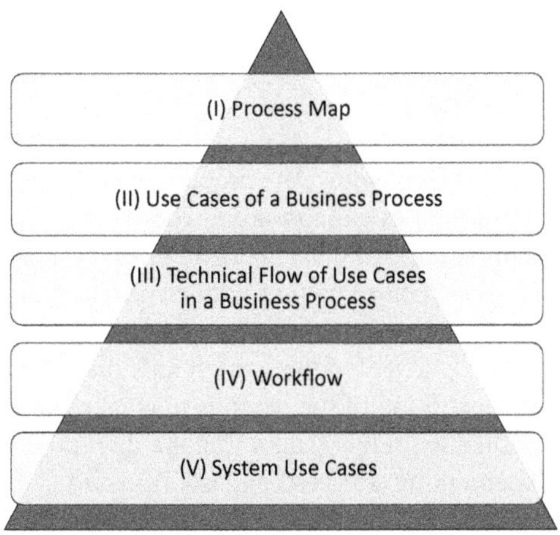

Fig. 2 Five levels of the HISinOne reference model (Bührig 2011)

based on which, workshops with specialists and relevant stakeholders of the university can be conducted. The stakeholders describe their daily work, and the processes link to the system configuration.

Process Discovery Derived from the determined objectives (Sect. 2) the project team had to define maximally efficient actions because resources were limited. In order to achieve the high standards that are related to best practices, the project team decided not to identify and document the current state of their own processes, so the discovery started without a current overview. Instead, the documentation of individual processes was done only in special cases that needed further analysis in order to be implemented.

The implementation of the software and the identification of processes occurred step by step analogous to HISinOne's software products. After defining each process area, the process management team determined the relevant processes based on the reference model and discussed relevant processes with accountable stakeholders in interviews and workshops. Some employees and departments already had a few rudimentary (flow) diagrams of or textual information about their workflows, although these tended to be heterogeneous and to focus on an individual employee's perspective. In order to create generalized processes for all three campus locations, all stakeholders involved discussed the processes and determined what they should be together.

Process Analysis The process analysis step is workshop-oriented. In these workshops, the Jade University's process manager discussed the reference processes with the relevant stakeholders, taking three primary questions into account: Do the processes map to our current operational sequences? What needs to be improved? What should be changed? As a result of the workshops, process models of the reference model were annotated with Jade's individualized requirements. Then these models were sent to the HIS specialists who prepare the redesign phase. Using the reference model, the process modelers began building models on existing, best practice processes. This work could not have been done by a process manager who was working on the project part-time. Another benefit of the workshops was that all relevant stakeholders were familiar with the reference processes.

Process Redesign The process modeler, relevant stakeholders, and HIS specialists determined in collaborative workshops how the processes should be executed. For example, one of these workshops dealt with all of a process's sub-workflows (level III). Based on sequential implementation, this step is repeated for each process area mentioned in level I. Thus, process-related questions had to be clarified.

In the next step the participants discussed relevant system processes using a live demonstration of the campus management system. If any deviations occurred, they handled them by (I) adopting the deviation into the configuration of the system and documenting all fixed and coordinated steps in an additional business concept. If this approach was not possible, (II) they verified whether existing work practices could be changed to fit the reference model, with adjustments to the organizational structure if necessary. In such cases, extra workshops were conducted to define new processes across the three locations. Finally, (III) software requirements were defined to adjust the software according to the individual university process.

For example, Fig. 3 shows a schematic representation of designing processes based on the reference model for campus management, including the original reference process given by HISinOne and the adjusted (individual) process model. Because new actions and eliminated actions are highlighted, the reader can identify changes at a glance. The three types of adjustments to a process are changes in responsibilities and re-assignment of actors to existing actions, eliminating unnecessary actions, and adding new steps.

The results of the process redesign were documented. An essential part of this document is the definition of the adjusted process model. This document is revised by the responsible committees and represents the basis for the following process implementation.

Process Implementation The implementation was realized with configurations of the HISinOne system based on individual specifics of Jade University. No static

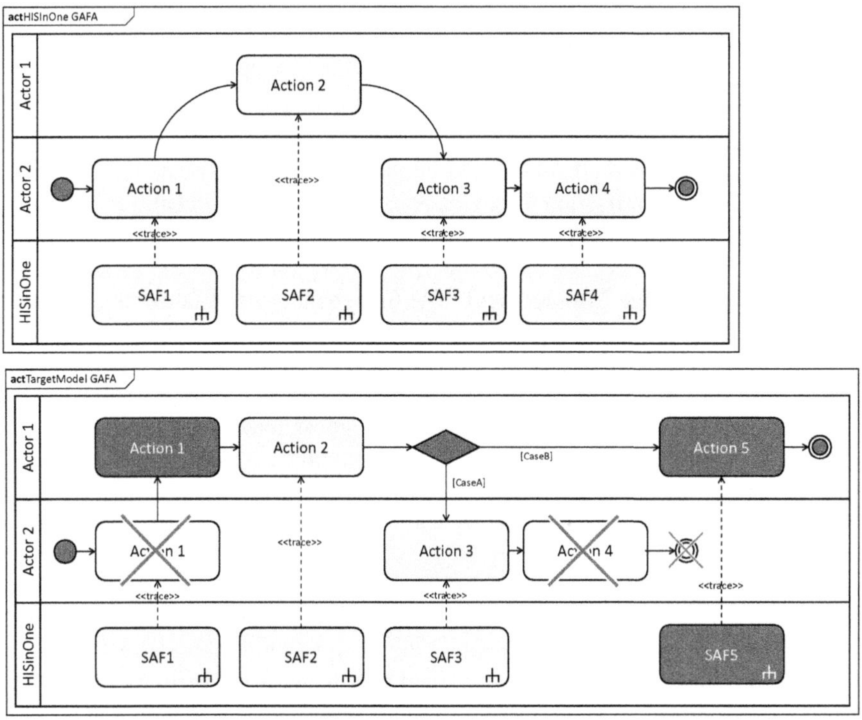

Fig. 3 Schematic representation of designing processes based on HISinOne. Note: *SAF* system use cases; *above* original reference model; *bottom* changed model; *dark gray* additional action; *light gray* reference action; *crossed* eliminated action

workflows were defined in order to allow for necessary flexibility in the daily work, so automatic adoption of the processes in the software was not possible. In fact, existing functions had to be configured, reports adapted, and the interface adjusted to allow for future executions of the processes. In the next step, the users were trained in using the software, and intensive quality management was carried out to test relevant software functions and the standardization of processes. If there were no further adjustments, the software went live and the processes were implemented.

Process Monitoring There was no explicit mechanism with which to measure, monitor, or control the project's performance, but the achievement of goals was rated using other methods. For example, the number of requests received in the student service center was analyzed, suggesting that new processes with more self-service functions reduced the number of requests. Moreover, regular feedback meetings with stakeholders were conducted to analyze the new processes and the use of the system. These meetings allowed the users to share experiences and issues, and some issues were considered in further steps of the implementation. Other issues served as starting points for the continued improvement. As part of the project, Jade established a department especially for BPM.

4 Results Achieved

Because there was no explicit mechanism with which to measure, monitor, or control the university's and its processes' performance, we focus on the qualitative statements of the experts involved. The initial objectives were related to knowledge management, standardization of processes across the campus locations, and application of best practices in campus management processes.

Ensuring Knowledge Management The first goal, ensuring knowledge management, can be rated as having been achieved. Jade University wanted to protect existing knowledge and to make it more transparent for the entire campus management and staff. At present, all processes that are relevant to the campus management system are documented, and a wide range of other knowledge across the campus locations is saved and accessible to the employees. Some departments have also started to describe their own processes in order to standardize them and make them more transparent to their colleagues.

Standardizing Processes The second issue was related to the standardization of processes across Jade's three campuses. This objective was definitely achieved, considerably improving the university's initial situation. Internal effects like consistent workflows and handling the campus IS have been positive, and external stakeholders have seen standardized applications for academic studies and applications for semesters on leave.

To show what kinds of improvements were achieved, we focus on the process for the application for a leave of absence as representative of the results. Before starting the implementation of the new process, there was no standardized or explicitly described process. Jade used the HIS reference model to identify 17 actions. In workshops and discussions held to identify and analyze processes, Jade added six new, individual elements that related to, for example, the reregistration barrier and fees charged for a semester on leave. In these workshops with consultants, seven agreements were made and documented. Subsequent workshops were held to discuss processes across all three locations, and a standardized process was defined that is close to the one suggested in the reference model: Just two of the 17 actions were eliminated, and some comments were added that help to clarify individual requirements for specific actions. This example shows how the university adapted the processes of the reference model.

Adopting Best Practices for Higher Education This result overlaps with the third objective regarding achieving an orientation that is based on best practices for higher education. An essential result was achieved by the creation of an adapted process model for Jade's essential campus management processes. Furthermore, concepts for all software modules were created, and the process areas for application management and student administration were analyzed, redesigned, and implemented. The consequent use of the reference model and the discussion across the campus locations contributed to achieving this goal. In addition, the example of applying for a leave of absence shows how Jade adapted the processes of the reference model in order to obtain a standard that is closely related to the suggested best practice. Instead of changing many recommended actions, Jade changed only some organizational dimensions, such as mapping and relocating employees and operations.

Developing a BPM-Supportive Culture The acceptance of BPM was achieved, which has a strong impact on the success of a BPM project (e.g., Rosemann and vom Brocke 2015; Schmiedel et al. 2013). In general, barriers to using and dealing with process models were significantly reduced. The effects of the implementation as they related to the employees and users included greater acceptance of process models, which acceptance played an important role over time. Some departments began to document and standardize their own processes that were not related to the campus management system using the same approach. They started to "think in processes," and took the opportunity to save knowledge about their own and their colleagues' processes. However, four types of users were observed: (I) those who use process models voluntarily, and those who try to avoid process models because (II) they see no additional benefit in using them, (III) believe that they are already transparent in what they are doing, or (IV) fear that they will have a heavier workload because of the required documentation.

Improving Team Spirit According to Schmiedel et al. (2015), teamwork—particularly collaboration across functions—is an essential value that contributes to successful BPM. In our case, team spirit improved over time. Internal workshops and discussions to standardize processes across the campus locations strengthened the entire university staff's team spirit. Despite the separate locations, the departments involved started to grow together and to be more unified; that is, they began to be "one university," rather than three locations of a university.

5 Lessons Learned

This project provided some lessons learned that affected Jade University, the project team, and the campus management system provider, HIS, related to editing documentation, conducting workshops and interviews for designing process standards, and (mainly) applying the software reference model HISinOne. We can conclude that Jade University would choose the same approach for similar situations, such as implementing software and other processes by considering a reference model, but five lessons in particular stood out.

Orient to Existing Solutions vs. Starting from Scratch The integrated software reference model HISinOne helps universities to navigate through processes in complex structures, such as campus management. Based on this navigation, the process management team can consider their own processes and compare them to what is suggested as the best practice. Before this project started, Jade University had only a few types of documentation of processes in the form of textual description or simple flowcharts, so it needed a guide to help it navigate through the process areas and single processes. Orientation to the reference model gave it such an opportunity. The employees involved analyzed their processes and continuously asked themselves how do other institutions do it, what has to be improved, and which of their own process elements should not be changed. Without the reference model, process management on this level with the available resources would not have been possible. The reference processes mostly fit with to the university's processes or could be adjusted, but some single actions in the workflow and some details were the subject of intensive discussion. Good moderators and different formats for the workshops and documentation would help to support these discussions.

Maintain Awareness About Tradeoffs in Standardizing vs. Allowing Total Creativity Regarding Process Management In addition to positive effects, there were also some negative aspects of using process reference models. Some employees developed creative ideas about how their work should be done during workshops and discussions when defining processes. The reference model opened their minds to new suggestions because they were thinking of what was possible. Unfortunately, these suggestions were often too big because the available resources (e.g., software and manpower) were limited. In addition, the university's complex structures had to be respected. Therefore, in some situations the standards limited the users' creativity, and there was a conflict between the pattern and the structure of the campus and the university management system and new ideas for how to design processes. Some of the participants recommended introducing the campus management system before introducing the reference model to minimize this effect. Following this recommendation, the employees could start to determine process ideas based on the system instead of the reference model.

Develop Guidelines for Consistently Documenting vs. Omitting this Step to Speed the Project This lesson learned deals with the improvement of documentation during the project. For future projects, the project team recommended reserving more time for continuous documentation of relevant information, such as realized changes, ongoing discussions, and the status of implementation steps. Because of the tight schedule, the project team focused on the process area that would be implemented next instead of using time to reflect on the results in documentations. Ongoing changes in the process areas that were already implemented were not completely documented. Participants suggested establishing a process management team at Jade University that is independent and accountable for their work.

Develop Concepts for Bringing People Together vs. Implementing BPM Without All Stakeholders A challenge as well as a significant opportunity for implementing BPM was bringing all the employees and users involved together. This involvement was helpful in standardizing processes across the three campus locations, which standardizations were based on best practices at each location. Conducting comprehensive workshops and discussions also contributed to the team spirit. Despite the spatial separation, the participants began to unify based on the collective agreement related to their processes during workshops as well as the implemented standards, which allowed them to do their work in a consistent way. Both internal and external appearances of the processes implemented became consistent.

Consider Limited Resources vs. Unplanned Conducting of Activities Another important lesson was to consider the available resources for the project. Although some steps, such as bringing together all relevant stakeholders, are helpful in achieving objectives, limited resources must be considered. Hence, the process management team suggested care in selecting methods (e.g., interviews and workshops) for determining processes because they can be time-consuming and expensive.

Comparability of this Case We compared our results and lessons with existing cases in the education sector. For example, Bührig et al. (2014) investigated the deployment, application, and impact of BPM approaches in the context of a process-oriented implementation of a campus management IS by conducting interviews with 37 experts from 16 German institutes of higher education. The Jade case fits well into the results of the other study, which showed that the implementation of a process-oriented IS leads to the establishment of process management in the domain of higher education. The use of the BPM lifecycle and the limitation to the BPM in the context of smaller institutes of higher education can be seen in the Jade case, making it comparable to other BPM projects in the field of higher education.

Acknowledgments This case study was supported by the project team, which consisted of members of Jade University of Applied Science and HIS. We thank them for their support.

References

Becker, J., Delfmann P., & Knackstedt R. (2007). Adaptive reference modeling: Integrating configurative and generic adaptation techniques for information models. In *Reference modeling* (pp. 27–58). Physica-Verlag HD.

Bob-Jones, B., Newman, M., & Lyytinen, K. (2008). Picking up the pieces after a "Successful" implementation: Networks, coalitions and ERP systems. In *Proceedings of the Fourteenth Americas Conference on Information Systems (AMCIS)*, Toronto, ON, Canada.

Bührig, J. (2011). Referenzmodelle in IT-Einführungsprojekten: Anforderungs-orientierte Gestaltung des HISinOne Referenzmodells. In A. Degkwitz & F. Klapper (Eds.), *DINI-AG E-Framework Prozessorientierte Hochschule* (pp. 51–66). BOCK + HERCHEN.

Bührig, J., Ebeling, B., Hoyer, S., & Breitner, M. H. (2014). Process-oriented standard software – An impulse for sustainable business process management at higher education institutions? In: D. Kundisch, L. Suhl, & L. Beckmann (Eds.), *Proceedings Multikonferenz Wirtschaftsinformatik 2014 (MKWI)* (pp. 558–570), Paderborn, Germany.

Dumas, M., La Rosa, M., Mendling, J., & Reijers, H. (2013). *Fundamentals of business process management*. Berlin: Springer.

Ernst & Young. (2012). *Campus management between university autonomy and the Bologna reform*. Results of the Ernst & Young Campus-management-study. www.ey.com/Publication/vwLUAssets/Campus-Management_zwischen_Hochschulautonomie_und_Bologna-Reform_2012/$FILE/ErnstYoung_Campus-Management-Studie.pdf

Fettke, P., & Loos, P. (2003). Classification of reference models: A methodology and its application. *Information Systems and e-Business Management, 1*(1), 35–53.

HISinOne. (2016, April 29). *HISinOne reference model*. www.his.de/produkte/hisinone/management/referenzmodell.html

Jade University. (2016, April 24). *University of applied science – facts and figures*. https://www.jade-hs.de/en/university-of-applied-sciences/university-of-applied-sciences/

Malinova, M., & Mendling, J. (2015). Leveraging innovation based on effective process map design: Insights from the case of a European insurance company. In *BPM-driving innovation in a digital world* (pp. 215–227). Cham: Springer International Publishing.

Oestereich, B. (2003). *Objektorientierte Geschäftsmodellierung mit der UML* (1. Aufl). Heidelberg: Dpunkt-Verl.

Petkovics, I., Tumbas, P., Matkovic, P., & Baracskai, Z. (2014). Cloud computing support to university business processes in external collaboration. *Acta Polytechnica Hungarica, 11*(3), 181–200.

Rosemann, M., & van der Aalst, W. M. P. (2007). A configurable reference modelling language. *Information Systems, 32*(1), 1–23.

Rosemann, M., & vom Brocke, J. (2015). Six core elements of business process management. In J. vom Brocke & M. Rosemann (Eds.), *Handbook on business process management: Introduction, methods, and information systems (International handbooks on information systems)* (Vol. 1, 2nd ed., pp. 105–122). Berlin: Springer.

Schmiedel, T., vom Brocke, J., & Recker, J. (2013). Which cultural values matter to business process management? Results from a global Delphi study. *Business Process Management Journal, 19*(2), 292–317.

Schmiedel, T., vom Brocke, J., & Recker, J. (2015). Culture in business process management: How cultural values determine BPM success. In *Handbook on business process management* (Vol. 2, pp. 649–663). Berlin: Springer.
Sprenger, J., Klages, M., & Breitner, M. H. (2010). Cost-benefit analysis for the selection, migration, and operation of a campus management system. *Business & Information Systems Engineering (BISE), 2*(4), 219–231.
vom Brocke, J. (2007). Design principles for reference modeling: reusing information models by means of aggregation, specialisation, instantiation, and analogy. In P. Fettke & P. Loos (Eds.), *Reference modeling for business systems analysis* (pp. 47–75). Hershey, PA: Idea Group Publishers.
vom Brocke, J., Schmiedel, T., Recker, J., Trkman, P., Mertens, W., & Viaene, S. (2014). Ten principles of good business process management. *Business Process Management Journal, 20* (4), 530–548.
vom Brocke, J., Zelt, S., & Schmiedel, T. (2015). Considering context in business process management: The BPM context framework. *BPM Trends, 1*.

Jan Bührig is a Ph.D. student at the department of Enterprise Modeling and Information Systems which is part of the Institute for Economics and Information Systems at the University of Hildesheim, Germany. And head of project- and process management at Hochschul-Informations-System eG (HIS). His current research interests include business process management and IS implementation in the higher education domain. His work appeared in conferences like the European Conference on Information Systems (ECIS) or the Multikonferenz Wirtschaftsinformatik (MKWI).

Thorsten Schoormann is a Research Assistant and Ph.D. student at the department of Enterprise Modeling and Information Systems which is part of the Institute for Economics and Information Systems at the University of Hildesheim, Germany. Previous to his work at the institute he studied Information Systems at the University of Hildesheim, where he received his Master's degree (M.Sc.) in 2015. His current research interests include business process management, business model frameworks and sustainability.

Ralf Knackstedt is Full Professor of the Institute for Economics and Information Systems, department for Enterprise Modelling and Information Systems at the University of Hildesheim, Germany. His research areas include Reference Modelling, Product Service Systems, Conceptual Modelling and Business Process Management. Previous to his work at the institute, he received his doctoral degree and his habilitation at the University of Münster, Germany and worked at the European Center for Information Systems (ERCIS). His work has been published in leading academic journals and conferences such as *Business Information Systems Engineering*, *IEEE Transactions on Engineering Management*, *Communications of the AIS*, *Scandinavian Journal of Information Systems* and *Enterprise Modelling, and Information Systems Architectures.* His Ph.D. thesis has won the dissertation award from the Westfälischen Wilhelms-Universität Münster, Germany.

Exploring the Influence of Organizational Culture on BPM Success: The Experience of the Pernambuco Court of Accounts

Carina Alves, Iveruska Jatobá, George Valença, and Glória Fraga

Abstract

(a) **Situation faced**: This chapter presents a cultural analysis of the BPM initiative conducted by a public organization, the Pernambuco Court of Accounts (TCE-PE). In particular, we look at how organizational culture influences the evolution of our BPM initiative.

(b) **Action taken**: We conducted in-depth interviews, observations, and documentation analyses in order to understand each interviewee's organizational culture. Then we analyzed the extent to which the TCE-PE culture is aligned with a BPM-supportive culture, as represented by the CERT values (Customer orientation, Excellence, Responsibility, Teamwork).

(c) **Results achieved**: We identified a set of cultural values, practices, and organizational characteristics at TCE-PE that may influence the BPM culture—that is, the aspects of the organizational culture that would act as facilitators of or barriers to our BPM initiative. We present a set of strategies that nurture the cultural values that are supportive of BPM and hinder those that are obstacles of BPM.

(d) **Lessons learned**: During our journey toward establishing a BPM-supportive culture at TCE-PE, we learned that key success factors

C. Alves (✉) • I. Jatobá
Centro de Informática—Universidade Federal de Pernambuco, Recife, Brazil
e-mail: cfa@cin.ufpe.br; icjba@cin.ufpe.br

G. Valença
Departamento de Estatística e Informática, Universidade Federal Rural de Pernambuco, Recife, Brazil
e-mail: george.valenca@ufrpe.br

G. Fraga
Tribunal de Contas de Pernambuco (TCE-PE), Recife, Brazil
e-mail: glorinha@tce.pe.gov.br

J. vom Brocke, J. Mendling (eds.), *Business Process Management Cases*,
Management for Professionals, DOI 10.1007/978-3-319-58307-5_32

include investing heavily in communication, understanding who the stakeholders are and what they want, and creating a long-term vision of BPM goals and articulating them with future sponsors. We believe the experience presented in this chapter has value for public organizations that face challenges in aligning their organizational culture with BPM principles.

1 Introduction

Business Process Management (BPM) is a holistic management approach that includes the dimensions of strategic alignment, governance, methods, people, culture, and information technology (Rosemann and vom Brocke 2015). In particular, organizational culture, as a pattern of basic assumptions discovered or developed within a group (Schein 2010), is a key factor in the success or failure of BPM initiatives (Schmiedel et al. 2015). If the culture's basic assumptions prove of value, they are communicated to new members of the group (Grau and Mörmann 2014). Therefore, organizational culture can change when the shared values, beliefs, and procedures that prove successful change and are asserted over time. According to Schein's (2010) model, organizational culture can be analyzed on three levels—observable artifacts, values and norms, and underlying assumptions and premises–depending on their degree of visibility and consciousness.

We have observed an increasing interest in BPM by the public sector (Valenca et al. 2013). Three main factors motivate public organizations to embrace a process-centric perspective: the first motivation involves citizens' demands for improved quality of public services, the second involves the need to adopt information technologies to support e-gov solutions, and the third involves the continuous pressure for accountability and transparency of their activities that public organizations face (Alves et al. 2014).

This chapter investigates the BPM experience of the Pernambuco Court of Accounts (TCE-PE). We look at how the organization's culture influences the BPM initiative's evolution both positively and negatively.

TCE-PE is a public organization with around 900 employees who are responsible for auditing state and municipalities accounts. The organization's mission is to monitor and guide public management for the benefit of society, and its vision is to be recognized as an effective instrument for improving public management in defense of social interests and prevention of corruption. The espoused values present in the mission statement are ethics, transparency, commitment, effectiveness, coherence, and impartiality.

The aim of the BPM initiative is to standardize and automate key business processes in order to improve productivity and quality. The BPM initiative is supported by well-established project and strategic-planning principles, and top management trusts that it can help them implement their strategic plan. TCE-PE has a culture similar to those of other Brazilian public organizations—hierarchical structures, low levels of flexibility, and a strong influence of political factors—so it presents a rich case with which to investigate the role of culture in BPM projects. In particular, the TCE-PE case can provide inspiration and insights for public organizations around the globe that are undertaking BPM initiatives.

In this chapter, we present the journey of TCE-PE toward understanding and transforming the organizational culture to nurture values that are supportive of BPM and limit the effects of the cultural values that act as obstacles. By identifying the facilitators and barriers that affect BPM, we were able to define effective strategies that foster a BPM-supportive culture (vom Brocke and Sinnl 2011) at the organization.

The next section uses the six core elements framework from Rosemann and vom Brocke (2015) to describe the situation TCE-PE faced. Section 3 explains how we adopted the BPM-Culture Model from Schmiedel et al. (2015) to analyze the alignment between TCE-PE's corporate culture and BPM culture. Then Sect. 4 presents the results obtained so far from attempts to foster BPM-supportive cultural values at TCE-PE. Finally, Sect. 5 describes lessons learned during our BPM culture transformation journey that may be useful to other organizations with similar contextual factors and cultural values.

2 Situation Faced

Given its disciplinary role of ensuring that public organizations act in a transparent and ethical manner, TCE-PE operates in accordance with the principles of legality, morality, impartiality, and honesty. An early driver of the BPM initiative at TCE-PE was its solid strategic planning and project-driven culture. The organization's strategy monitoring includes follow-up bimonthly meetings with departments and annual summits with the board of directors and managers.

In 2001, the organization made preliminary attempts to build a strategic map. The departments created plans, but most of them were not related to strategic goals. Moreover, there were neither indicators nor operational processes to monitor these plans systematically. At the end of 2003, the first strategic plan was built for the period 2004–2008, after which the plan became an institutionalized management practice. The current strategic plan is based on SWOT analysis and Balanced Scorecard (BSC), comprising the period 2013–2018. The goals of the strategic plan include increasing the effectiveness of external control, improving public management, strengthening the institution's image in society, obtaining agility in judgment processes without compromising quality, encouraging innovation and knowledge management, and consolidating public sector governance.

TCE-PE introduced BPM practices in 2012 and instituted a Business Process Management Office (BPMO) a year later. At that time, the leaders of the initiative realized that they didn't have sufficient expertise in process improvement, so the board of directors established an R&D partnership with researchers from UFPE, a local university. Today the BPMO team is composed of nine professionals: two internal staff, four researchers with practical and academic experience in BPM, and three undergraduate students. Researchers and students work part-time (15 h and 20 h, respectively). Two of the authors jointly manage the BPMO, one as an employee of TCE-PE and the other as the coordinator from the university. These two managers make all decisions together and report the results of process improvement initiatives to TCE-PE's top management. The other two authors play the role of process analysts. Researchers and students are all considered parts of the BPMO's active workforce; they are employed to conduct activities such as, process modeling, analysis and implementation. This case is presented from the viewpoint of TCE-PE's BPMO team.

To clarify the context of the BPM initiative at TCE-PE, Table 1 presents an overview of how the organization handles the six core elements of BPM (Rosemann and vom Brocke 2015). One of the initial projects we performed in 2013 was an organizational diagnosis using system dynamics (Senge 2006) to analyze the key barriers to and facilitators of the BPM initiative at TCE-PE. We conducted interviews and observations to build systemic archetypes, the detailed results of which

Table 1 BPM six core elements identified at TCE-PE

Factor	Context
Strategic alignment	The BPMO is a formal unit of the governance and management department, a position that ensures its direct alignment with strategic goals. According to the strategic planning for 2013–2018, the BPM initiative is a strategic action. All process improvement projects are aligned with and monitored in terms of the organizational strategy. The president and directors actively sponsor the BPM initiative
Governance	Corporate governance is a main concern for the organization because of its role as public accounting auditor. We developed a BPM governance model to guide the initiative and ensure its alignment with the strategy. We also modeled the value chain to represent key business processes. The scheme associates each process with specific values and clients. The TCE-PE value chain contains 22 processes
Methods	A specific BPM methodology was created to suit the purposes of the organization and the characteristics of its business processes. The methodology, which has well-defined phases, templates, and procedures, has been used in four process-improvement projects to date. The core process of compliance audit has been fully implemented
IT	Bizagi is the tool adopted for process modeling. TCE-PE also acquired a customized electronic process tool with which to implement business processes. Process automation is a way to standardize and control core activities and ensure service quality
People	Public servants have permanent job stability, and staff is resistant to change, preferring to retain established work practices. An intensive training program is underway to ensure that BPM knowledge is well-disseminated throughout the organization
Culture	TCE-PE has a strong hierarchical structure, mature strategic-planning, and a project-oriented culture. The main publicly expressed values are those of ethics, transparency, formality, and legality. A key unwritten value is a paternalistic vision in the benevolent way the organization deals with staff and the public organizations it audits

are available in Alves et al. (2014). This diagnosis allowed us to analyze facilitators and barriers as factors that can interact with each other to create patterns of functional and dysfunctional systemic behaviors that may foster or inhibit the BPM initiative's success. We observed that the strong sponsorship of the project from the president and influential directors was the most influential facilitator in promoting the BPM initiative. They were committed to and always supportive of the implementation of new process-centric ideas.

During the systemic analysis, we identified that a major barrier was employees' resistance to change. Staff reported that they had seen similar management projects fail and that they perceived such efforts as fruitless and as bringing little more than extra work for them. This view reflects the fear of change that is common in the local public sector's culture. An important contextual factor of the Brazilian public sector is that staff has permanent job stability, so public servants often prefer to maintain established practices instead of experimenting with innovative ideas. Another barrier identified was the staff's poor understanding of BPM, as they did not understand the concepts related to it nor did they recognize its relevance to them. Therefore, it was clear that strong sponsorship was a key asset but that the people and cultural factors had to be addressed in order to ensure a sustainable organization-wide BPM initiative.

This diagnosis was a fundamental tool in understanding the current situation, identifying the main goals of adopting BPM, and planning its evolution. An important outcome was the conclusion that, in order to disseminate BPM successfully, the members of the BPMO team had to investigate the organizational culture sufficiently to improve the alignment between BPM principles and internal cultural values and practices.

3 Actions Taken

Considering the TCE-PE organizational context, we used the BPM-Culture Model proposed by Schmiedel et al. (2015) to address the culture and people factors as key issues in ensuring consolidation of the BPM initiative. The model presents the notion of BPM culture and how the organization can align the organizational culture and its values to achieve BPM objectives. Figure 1 presents an overview of the model.

The model explains the interdependency between BPM and organizational culture by providing guidance for identifying what cultural changes the organization needs to accomplish in order to promote a successful BPM initiative.

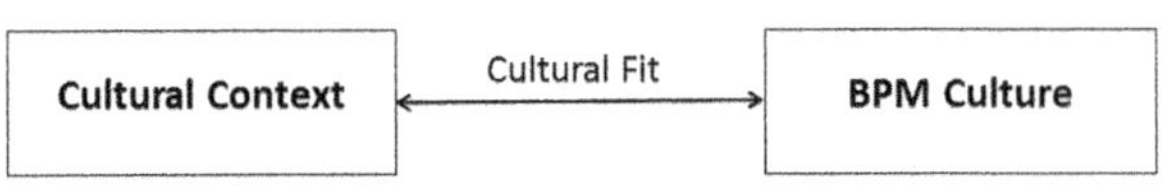

Fig. 1 BPM-culture model (adapted from Schmiedel et al. 2015)

Schmiedel et al. (2012) conducted a Delphi study to identify cultural values, called CERT values, that are supportive of a BPM culture. The CERT values are:

- ***Customer Orientation (C)***—Focuses on customer needs and expectations regarding the process's outputs.
- ***Excellence (E)***—Refers to the direction toward continuous improvement and innovation as a way to improve business processes' performance.
- ***Responsibility (R)***—Involves attitudes and committed actions to achieve process objectives, as well as accountability and transparency regarding process decisions.
- ***Teamwork (T)***—Refers to an open mindset to cross-functional collaboration.

We also used the framework proposed by Grau and Mörmann (2014), which presents the interrelationship between BPM and organizational culture in terms of its influence on the organization's performance. The authors claimed that, in order to implement BPM successfully, the organization's culture must be influenced or changed for the better. To achieve that goal, the BPM team must understand the organization's visible artifacts, values, and basic assumptions.

To gain an understanding of TCE-PE culture, we conducted nine in-depth interviews with staff from a variety of areas and in a variety of hierarchical positions. The interviewees were sponsors, process analysts, internal clients of the BPMO, and stakeholders from key process areas. In addition, several documents were analyzed, including the organizational strategic plan (2013–2018), the BPMO's communication and training plan, and an organizational climate survey. We also performed non-structured observations over the course of a year. One of the authors conducted the observations as part of the author's work routine at the BPMO. All relevant episodes, opinions, behaviors, and interactions observed during meetings and daily activities were documented, and the authors discussed the resulting notes to share their perceptions regarding the visible actions and values. The authors also analyzed the underlying assumptions embedded on the organization's invisible culture, where support from a BPMO manager and co-author of this chapter was critical. This manager has worked at TCE-PE for 20 years and has significant experience in several organizational areas. This experience was valuable in clarifying ambiguous observations and confirming impressions from the interviewees' discourse. The result of this study was a set of cultural values, practices, and organizational characteristics that may directly or indirectly act as barriers or facilitators of the BPM initiative. Armed with this knowledge, we could create strategies to promote necessary cultural change.

Figure 2 presents the main cultural values and organizational characteristics of TCE-PE that are captured in this study. The figure also represents the CERT values, which were important elements of the analysis. Each cultural value observed at TCE-PE contributes positively or negatively to the CERT values. Next, we describe the organizational context and present excerpts from interviewees' discourse that help to portray the organizational culture.

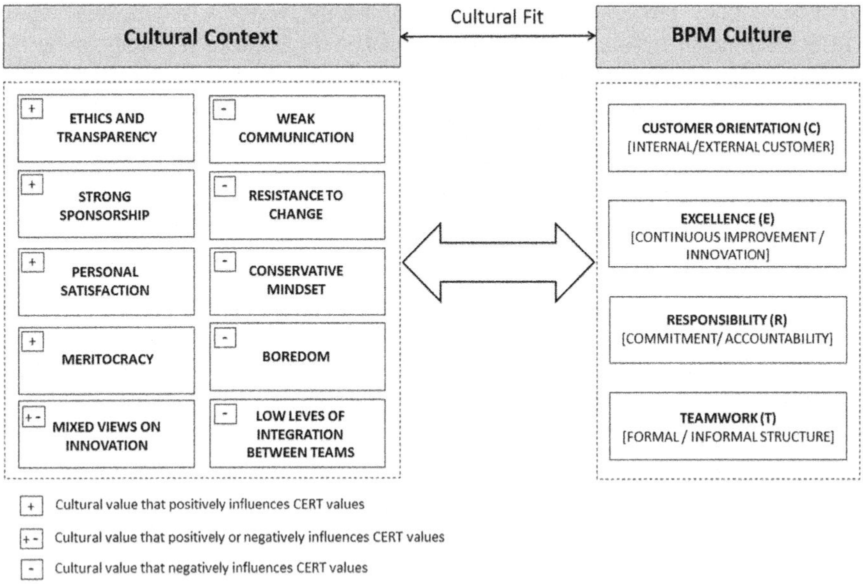

Fig. 2 Interrelationship between TCE-PE's cultural context and the BPM culture as represented by CERT values

3.1 Weak Communication

We perceived that both internal communication (between departments) and external communication (between TCE-PE and other public organizations or society) is weak. The public has no clear understanding of the role and the activities undertaken by a Court of Accounts, and staff often fails to comprehend who the internal clients are and, consequently, with whom they must interact. Interviewees reported that the organization has inefficient communication channels and needs to improve communication by creating new channels or improving existing ones. The increasing demand for public administration to act efficiently and transparently reinforces the criticality of the weak communication channels. As one business analyst argued, *"The communication with the external public has improved a lot, but I think we have to change radically; people want faster answers [and] full transparency. I think the communication is still very slow."* The organization is currently trying to improve external communication by advertising its activities in local newspapers and improving its Web portal.

The weak internal communication raises the need for mechanisms that will improve employees' understanding of BPM practices. Effective communication strategies (e.g., internal publicity about process-improvement results) can improve staff awareness of BPM as an approach to transforming the organization by helping staff understand what BPM means and how process-oriented practices may help them in their daily activities. Moreover, staff must be informed about how BPM can promote agility and efficiency for the organization, which will positively affect TCE-PE's image in society. As a systems analyst explained, *"If people believe in [BPM], they will help [to implement it]; they need to believe that it will bring results and make the organization more agile, [to] see that we are providing information for society... The dream of the public servant is that people believe what we do is important."*

Weak communication is a cultural characteristic of the organization that hampers its orientation toward satisfying clients. This cultural flaw limits the understanding and responsive treatment of clients' expectations and has a negative influence on the CERT value of *customer orientation*. In addition, inadequate internal communication is a barrier to sharing information between departments and limits cross-functional collaboration, which affects the development of *teamwork*. Finally, weak communication channels negatively affect the *responsibility* of staff, who may not perceive the importance of their commitment to process outputs and their accountability to the achievement of process goals.

3.2 Resistance to Change

From the beginning of our BPM initiative, we observed resistance to change, especially from older staff, who expressed a feeling of distrust regarding any new managerial approach. They frequently mentioned that they had seen many innovative approaches that failed. This resistance stems primarily from the fact that changes may take them away from their comfort zones. As a systems analyst explained, "*For everything that we are implementing here there is a resistance: [people think] why change? This will bring more work for me.*" Therefore, there was some resistance to embracing BPM principles since BPM fundamentally promotes organizational change (Baumol 2014), as the director of corporate governance observed in saying, *"The excess of formalism and the resistance to change may affect the BPM initiative."* On the other hand, we observed a counter-culture among younger employees, who are eager for change and receptive to co-creating a modern public administration. This young generation became allies of the BPMO in promoting a process-centric view. The director advised us to simplify our discourse whenever possible so the BPMO would "speak the same language" of staff from all departments and cohorts.

Fear of change and mistrust may hinder the development of cultural values related to innovation and continuous improvement, which are sub-dimensions of the CERT value of *excellence*, and the generational conflict at the organization may negatively impact the creation of *teamwork*. We also found that, if the initiative confronts highly ingrained cultural values, it may not be easily assimilated or may even be boycotted, which may lead to failure. This resistance may occur even if the proposed actions promise to improve organizational results. In our case, we had to convince key people who had legitimate or referent power at the organization to implement changes so they could act as facilitators of process-centric principles.

3.3 Strong Sponsorship

Despite being an embedded value of organizational culture, resistance to change can be minimized by political power. Top management sponsors must support strategic changes, because, as the IT director contended, *"If there is no sponsorship from the president or key directors for a substantial change, it does not occur."* We identified an interrelationship between sponsorship and the development of the *excellence* and *responsibility* values of a BPM culture. When we were implementing significant changes related to quality indicators and more radical innovation on the compliance audit process, we knew that active sponsorship was critical to their success. The commitment and responsibility of key employees also contributed to achieving desired results. on several occasions we relied on process owners to endorse BPMO proposals during strategic meetings. We recognize that such strong sponsorship has been a key factor in the success of our BPM initiative at TCE-PE.

3.4 Low Levels of Integration between Teams

In general, employees do not have a holistic perception of the services the organization offers and do not understand what their contributions to business process improvement are. Departments work as isolated islands; they carry out disconnected activities, and teams from different departments do not work as a cohesive team. Poor internal communication intensifies this problem. Poor handoffs between involved departments may hinder the effective execution of business processes. Effective collaboration among teams often requires explicitly requesting cooperation from the teams' managers.

The low level of integration between teams is part of the organizational culture at TCE-PE, and it represents a critical issue, as a project manager observed:

> I think that teams from business areas may not truly understand the strategic goals. Sometimes it is not clear for people what the changes decided at the strategic level are. They have certain distance from the organizational goals. Although there is investment on BPM courses, campaigns about organizational indicators, and achievement of goals, people do not feel [like they affect organizational goals], and this can negatively impact the change that is arriving.

The fact that employees often do not feel like parts of a single integrated team and do not understand the relevance of their work to achieving strategic goals negatively influences the CERT values of *teamwork* and *responsibility*.

3.5 Mixed Views on Innovation

Formality and conservatism are strong cultural values at TCE-PE in large part because of the organization's central role as auditor of public accounts. These values may be barriers to innovation and change, but there is an increasing awareness of the need to promote innovation at the institutional level. As a process analyst observed, *"No doubt the innovation award is an incentive policy; however, at the same time, the institution is very conservative in the face of innovation. [...] People talk a lot about previous projects that failed, and they fear being stigmatized."* Incentives like the innovation award are important instruments with which to promote innovative thinking, but we observed that innovative actions are not widely spread at the organization and that some people still perceive innovation as risky. In addition, as the same process analyst remarked, "*We don't have practices to understand why errors occurred and how to prevent them. We can learn a lot from our mistakes.*"

In sum, we perceived that the staff has mixed views toward innovation. A positive aspect of the culture is that, at the strategic level, the staff is open to innovation. During our strategic meetings with sponsors of the initiative, we concluded that the BPMO plays an important role in disseminating an innovation culture throughout the organization. Such actions will foster the CERT value of *excellence*.

3.6 Conservative Mindset

Aspects of the existing organizational culture, such as bureaucracy, legalism, and resistance to change, are barriers to implementing a modern management model. Especially during process analysis meetings, we identified a conservative mindset that hinders organizational ambitions to establish a new management model that is focused on goals and supported by BSC. The BPMO manager illustrated this observation: *"Many of the modern attitudes toward building a better organization clash with the conservative culture that exists here."* The president's assistant remarked that "*the organizational culture expects to see concrete results [if it is] to believe in new things.*" Therefore, only when novel ideas prove to be successful does staff start to accept and support change. Although TCE-PE works hard to consolidate a goal-oriented management model, we identified unconscious, obsolete cultural values that are embedded with bureaucracy, political influence, and inefficiency. This situation may hinder the development of *customer orientation*, *responsibility*, and *excellence*.

3.7 Personal Satisfaction

We perceived that the staff is personally satisfied with working at TCE-PE because of the organization's mission to inspect the correct use of public funds, which is considered a noble job. The staff is pleased to contribute directly to combatting corruption and promoting the efficiency of public administration. They are proud of the organization's technical excellence, their autonomy in executing their work, and their high salaries (which are above the average in the Brazilian public sector).

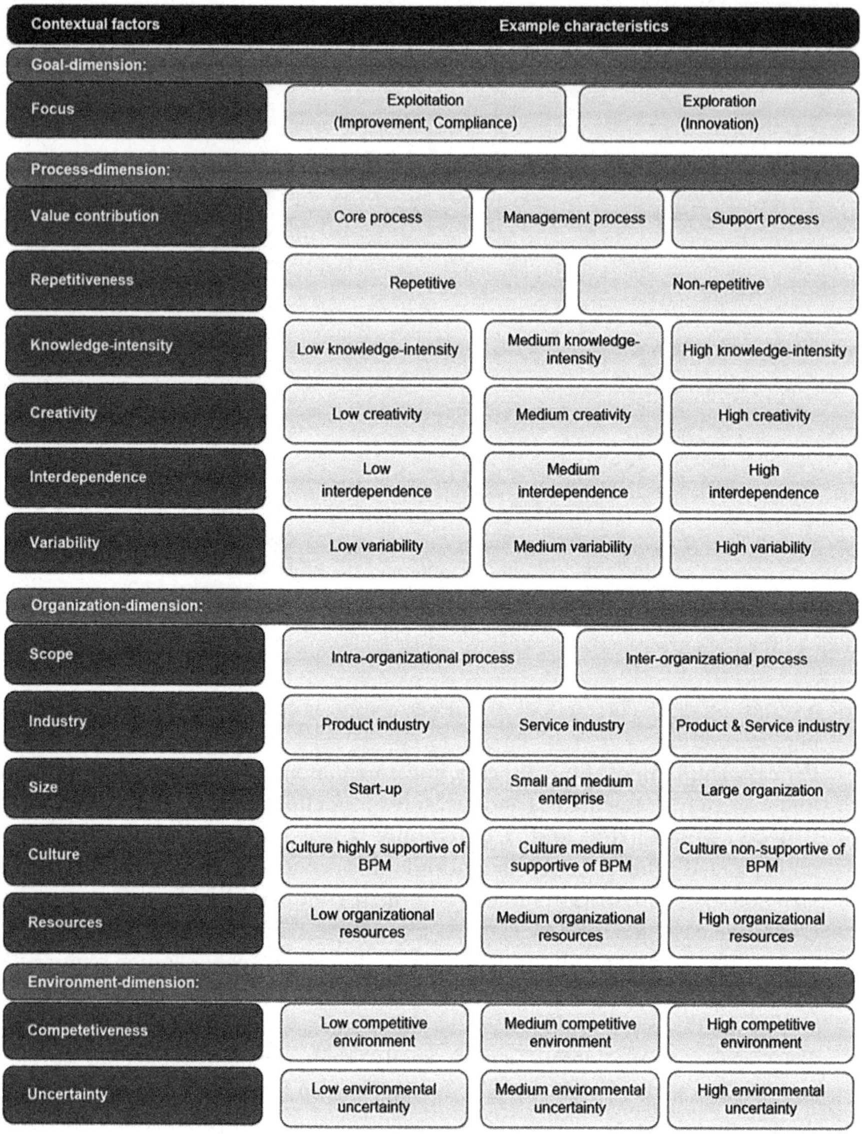

Six primary tasks were defined for the new BPM department:

(a) Assure processes' compliance with industry-specific reference models (e.g., eTOM).
(b) Manage the detailed design of process flows in all functional areas.
(c) Define and monitor process performance indicators and their respective performance targets.
(d) Manage process implementation initiatives.
(e) Develop and conduct process-related trainings and communications.
(f) Continuously improve processes based on performance figures.

A major challenge was distinguishing between the central governance of processes from a methodical perspective and the responsibility for the design and execution of individual processes. Therefore, a detailed ownership model was developed in order to ensure that the responsible persons from the line organization were involved (cf. Fig. 5). The ownership model followed a top-down approach

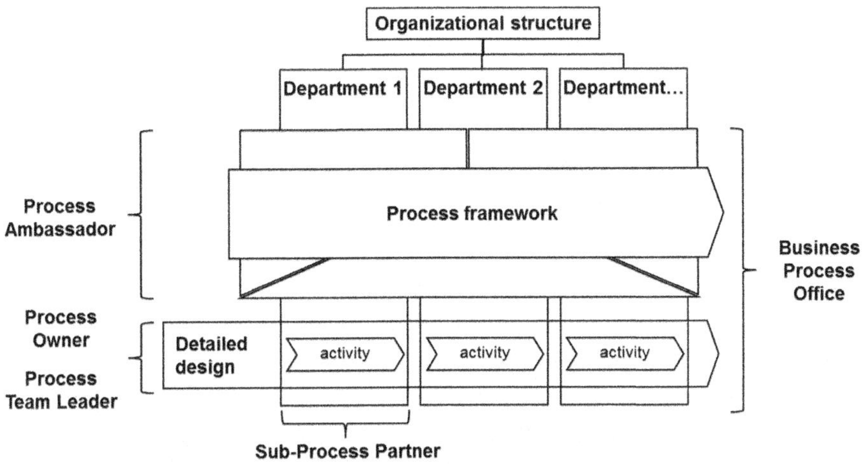

Process Ambassador	▪ Communication of process concept within the entire organization ▪ Quick response on escalations and enforcement of needed decisions
Business Process Office	▪ Assuring compliance of processes with industry-specific reference models (e.g. eTOM) ▪ Management of detailed design of process flows in all functional areas ▪ Definition and monitoring of process performance as well as continuous improvement ▪ Management of process implementation initiatives ▪ Development and conduction of process-related trainings and communications
Process Owner	▪ Leadership for the related process (level 1 or 2) from an end-to-end perspective ▪ Overall coordination of process design and implementation ▪ Decision-making and communication
Process Team Leader	▪ Coordination of process design and implementation as assistance to process owner ▪ Management of process-related activities on an operational level (level 3 and 4)
Sub-Process Partner	▪ Responsibility for the functional organization which is involved within the sub-process ▪ Support of detailed design and implementation on an operational level (level 3 and 4)

Legend: [grey box] = focus on process governance [white box] = focus on single processes

Fig. 5 Ownership model

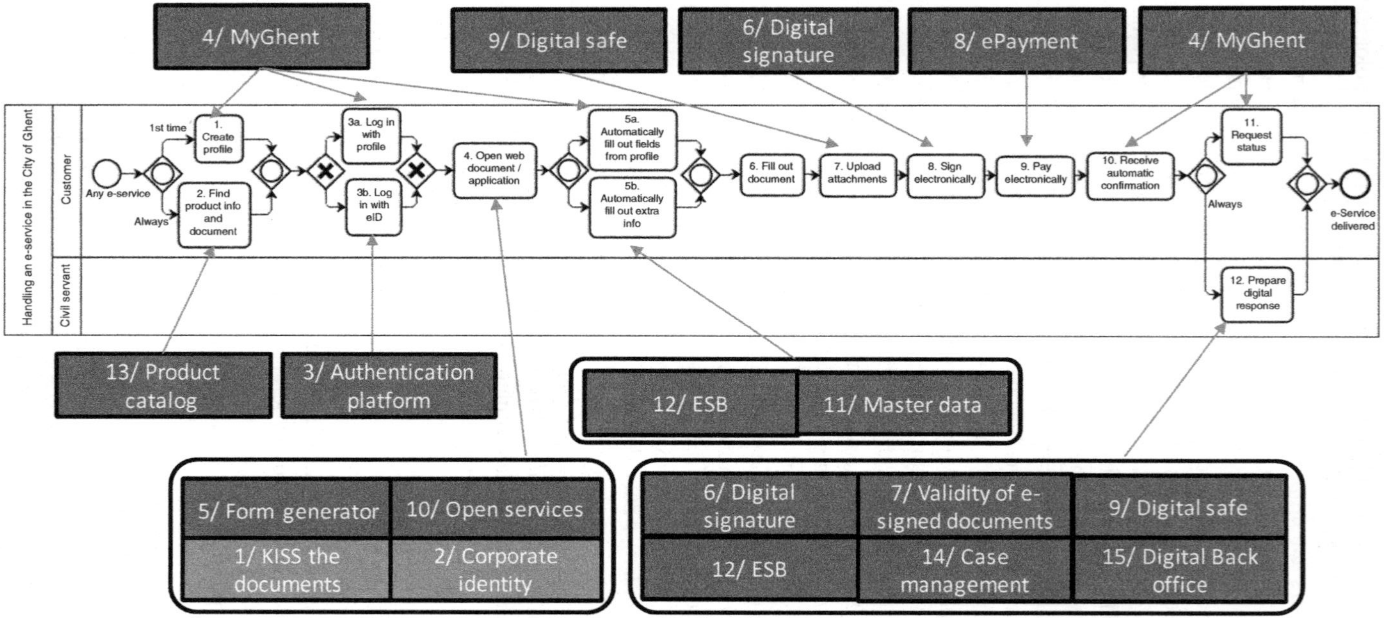

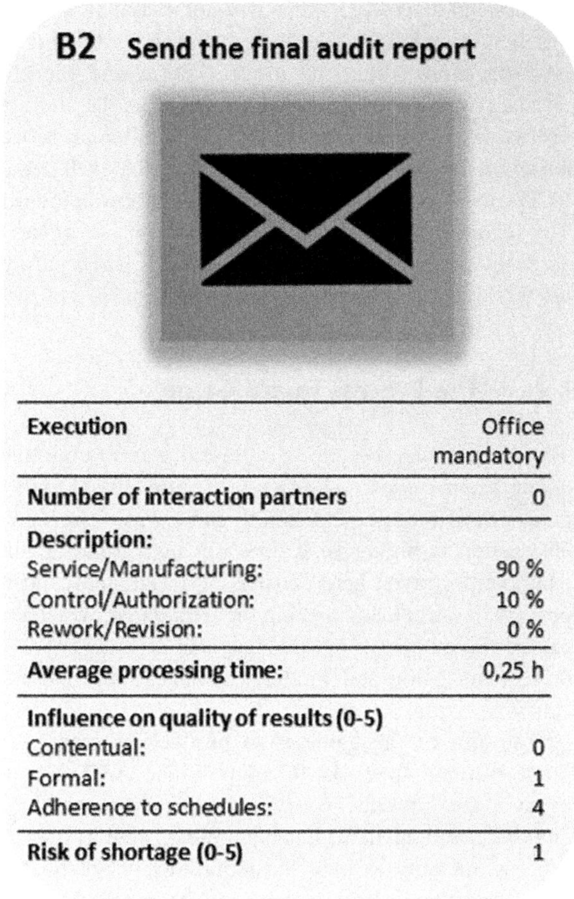

The cultural value of personal satisfaction positively influences the CERT values of *excellence*, *responsibility*, and *teamwork*.

3.8 Boredom

Despite being proud of working at the organization, some employees show a level of boredom. They are tired of the bureaucratic work and often do not see the results of their efforts. Similar attitudes frequently occur in other public organizations in Brazil, so the nature of bureaucratic work and traditional public sector management styles are likely key reasons for this attitude. We found that the infrequent rotation of employees across departments and repetitive tasks at TCE-PE are sources of their apathy. As the president assessor remarked, *"The institution does not promote job rotation; it leaves people too long at one place, doing the same task. For people who want to be relaxed at work, it is very convenient."* Job stability is a key factor that may negatively affect the staff's commitment to achieving organizational goals. The cultural aspect of boredom can be a barrier to achieving a BPM supportive culture, as it negatively affects all four of the CERT values—*customer orientation*, *excellence*, *responsibility,* and *teamwork.*—Employees may not be motivated to leave their comfort zones because their salaries are guaranteed for the rest of their lives, so we saw the need for a results-driven management model that reinforces reward and promotion policies based on employees' performance.

3.9 Meritocracy

Aware of the problem of employees' boredom, TCE-PE established a financial reward system that evaluates employees' individual performance based on their individual achievement of goals defined by their managers. The organization is also trying to reduce political appointments to key positions. The results-driven model raises the need to appoint employees with proven competence and commitment to strategic roles, illustrating the organization's effort to inculcate meritocracy as an important cultural value. We observed this fact in a statement from a process analyst: *"As the organization reinforces the importance of a results-driven model, managers are seeking to assign competent people; since people in leadership positions play a great influence on the achievement of these goals, there is even more attention to meritocracy."* As a cultural value that has been strengthened at TCE-PE, meritocracy can foster all four CERT values.

3.10 Ethics and Transparency

Ethics and transparency are public values described in the TCE-PE strategic plan. These values are respected, and they play an important role in the employees' identities, as a systems analyst explained: "*Honesty is a very strong value. People [are concerned with whether] someone is honest [and] if it is correct to do something from the point of view of the external public."* The values of ethics, transparency, and honesty positively influence the CERT values of *responsibility* and *excellence* since they stimulate commitment, continuous improvement, and especially accountability.

Based on the cultural analysis presented above, we identified and nurtured cultural values that are supportive of BPM and created strategies to hinder the values that are obstacles. The key actions taken by the BPMO are centered on two pillars:

- Ongoing and appropriate communication is essential to ensuring the dissemination of BPM-supportive cultural values. Communication also plays a central role in minimizing cultural values that hamper a BPM culture (Fig. 2).
- Staff motivation and engagement strategies drive the transformation of the negative cultural values identified at TCE-PE, such as *resistance to change*, *a low level of integration between teams*, *a conservative mindset*, and *boredom*.

4 Results Achieved

This section reports the results obtained by TCE-PE's BPMO to align the current organizational culture with values that foster a BPM-supportive culture. We analyzed to what extent the cultural values identified at the organization can act as facilitators of or barriers to the BPM initiative. We defined a set of strategies to nurture desirable cultural values and to change the values that hamper a BPM culture. Here, we discuss the results obtained so far in light of the *six core elements of BPM* (Table 1).

In the early years of the BPMO, we focused on establishing internal *BPM methods* and organizing the IT infrastructure. Substantial effort was put into creating a methodology that covered the whole BPM cycle. The BPM methodology is based on good management practices (vom Brocke et al. 2014) but also takes into account the specific characteristics of the organization, its internal staff, and the nature of its business processes. This action is aligned with advice from vom Brocke et al. (2016) that BPM projects that adopt a one-size-fits-all approach are likely to fail. The methodology has well-defined steps, procedures, and documentation templates. We created the methodology iteratively, using and evaluating it on four pilot BPM projects to date. In addition, we presented the methodology at several local events in order to disseminate BPM practices. Another important action related to methodology was the definition of the BPMO structure, which included descriptions of the roles, activities, and services provided by the BPMO (Jesus et al. 2015).

Regarding the *IT infrastructure*, the TCE-PE acquired a bespoke solution for an electronic process that we used to implement the business processes. We acknowledge that the solution is not exactly a Business Process Management Suite (BPMS), but acquisition of the tool was an executive decision motivated by other public organizations' adoption of similar solutions from the same supplier. This decision was a clear illustration of the *conservative mindset* and *mixed views toward innovation* cultural values in place.

Since the beginning of the initiative, we have emphasized *strategic alignment*. We have regular meetings with sponsors of the BPMO and direct our efforts in such a way as to materialize the top management's strategic vision and goals. Given that the managerial staff are eager to implement innovative ideas at TCE-PE, we recognized they are our key partners in achieving our goals of implementing a BPM culture organization-wide. Initially, we perceived that employees did not understand the BPM jargon, so we conducted several training courses for employees that explained the basic concepts of BPM and promoted workshops and open events to publicize our BPM results.

In parallel, we developed a *BPM governance model* as part of a Ph.D. thesis from one of the collaborators with the BPMO. The model served as guidance in developing our maturity model, which is currently being produced.

In sum, our initial efforts targeted the core elements of methods, IT, strategic alignment, and governance. Our rationale in choosing this direction was based on its being the safest path. Since the beginning of our initiative, we have been aware that the culture and people factors were complex to treat, so our strategy was to pursue some "quick wins" before dealing with them. The trainings and events were a way to inspire and engage employees who were already open to changes, but we knew that these actions would reach only the tip of the cultural iceberg. Another result refers to the corporate governance model that TCE-PE implemented, which has facilitated its organizational development and modernization in recent years. The consolidation of the strategic plan with well-defined goals to guide improvement actions, and strong project-driven practices are drivers of the BPM cultural transformation at TCE-PE. We are conscious that, if the organization were not undergoing such remarkable management improvements, our efforts to disseminate BPM would be much harder, given the cultural context of Brazilian public sector.

By the end of 2015, the core business process of compliance audit was fully implemented. This achievement was publicized in external and internal media, as it was a key goal of TCE-PE's president. The publicity was beneficial in disseminating the relevance of BPM, and we perceived that it was the right time to initiate more aggressive actions that would handle the people and cultural factors. At that time, the BPMO had already obtained recognition within the organization as a hardworking and committed team, so the employees who feared failure and were *resistant to change* started to understand and trust BPM. The *cultural* analysis presented in this case is a key outcome for the BPMO in improving the cultural fit. We believe that, by understanding this cultural panorama, we obtained a holistic vision of how to evolve our BPM initiative in a sustainable manner. To direct our next steps, we built a BPM maturity model using the proposal from Rosemann et al. (2006) as a reference model. Linked to the organizational strategic map, the model follows the five maturity levels and defines concrete goals that must be achieved in order to reach higher maturity levels. A change-management plan guides all actions the organization and the BPMO in particular must accomplish.

To address the *people* factor more objectively, we created a stakeholders' matrix that classified internal and external customers. This instrument supported the identification of key stakeholders who may influence the business processes under improvement. For instance, we classified stakeholders' legitimate (related to their formal position), expert (related to their knowledge regarding BPM and/or TCE-PE core activities), and referent (related to their respect among their peers) power. During process improvement projects, we also worked to build closer relationships with stakeholders in order to understand their motivations and needs. The classification enabled the BPMO to define specific strategies to promote the positive engagement of stakeholders who can influence the success of our actions. By clarifying the stakeholders' expectations and levels of power, we can mitigate the negative outcomes of the cultural values of *weak communication*, *boredom*, *conservative mindset*, and *resistance to change*.

In regard to communication, TCE-PE has already included the goal of improving internal and external communication in the strategic map. The strategic action involved the creation of an institutional communication plan and restructuring the communication department. In so doing, the organization created TCE-TV, an internal channel with videos showing the activities of departments and relevant news; placed weekly columns in local newspapers that informed the public about the main activities underway, redesigned the corporate website, and created institutional profiles on Facebook and Twitter. In addition, the organization introduced a series of short videos called "A Minute with the President" on the company's Intranet to share information about top management's decisions. The organization also invested in internal marketing campaigns called "Digital Windows" to promote strategic projects on digital screens throughout the buildings' corridors and elevators.

The BPMO also created its own strategic communication plan that presents communication goals for disseminating BPM knowledge, describes potential risks and problems faced by the initiative, and proposes actions to address them. The plan covers the organizational strategic cycle (2013–2018), is updated biennially, and is linked to the BPM Maturity Model. Therefore, when defining change-management activities, the BPMO also determines the required communication actions.

By improving both internal and external communication using these actions, the organization can foster the consolidation of positive cultural values that are aligned with CERT values. Effective communication strategies can reduce *resistance to change*, improve *integration between teams*, and demystify *innovation*. In addition, internal and external communication efforts have direct effects on *personal satisfaction* and on *ethics and transparency*, respectively.

When the current organizational strategic plan was created, managers and their subordinates had difficulty understanding how their routine activities would contribute to strategic goals. To handle this problem, the organization defined employees' individual performance indicators that were associated with strategic goals. These goals are measured by means of deliverables specified in performance agreements for each department and each employee. The definition of clear individual, departmental, and organizational goals and the transparency of results are intended to encourage staff engagement and motivation, leverage *meritocracy* and minimize staff *boredom*. However, since this initiative started only a few months before this article was written, we cannot yet measure its impact.

5 Lessons Learned

During our experience of developing cultural values that foster a BPM philosophy at TCE-PE, we faced several challenges and opportunities that we report here as lessons learned. We believe that these findings can be helpful for other organizations that have similar cultural values and contexts. We learned four primary lessons during our journey as members of the BPMO at TCE-PE are:

- **Associate the BPM maturity model with the organizational strategic map**: Using the organizational strategic map, we built a sectorial strategic map for the BPMO. We identified actions related to specific strategic goals that should be the BPMO's responsibility, and completing these actions became the mission of our sectorial strategic map. Then we linked the requirements of the BPM maturity model that would support the achievement of the organizational mission with the strategic map. We organized corresponding projects and action plans, which were monitored by means of specific indicators.
- **Invest in communication strategies**: Appropriate and timely communication is a key success factor for any novel management approach. Since TCE-PE has been undergoing significant managerial transformations by means of initiatives in several areas, including the BPMO, it was necessary to invest heavily in communication. Our communication actions disseminated basic concepts, addressed unfounded fears and resistance, and advertised results both internally and externally. Positive BPM marketing was an essential strategy in fostering the organization-wide evolution of our initiative.
- **Determine who the stakeholders are and what they want**: At the beginning of our BPM initiative, we convinced strategic staff to attend our training courses and to participate in important process-analysis meetings. These staff members can be considered the first "ambassadors" of BPM. We performed these actions intuitively, inviting the most receptive, curious, and communicative staff members and then seeing how their sponsorship would be fundamental to our ability to articulate our goals and actions with resistant employees. To capture the influence and power of stakeholders from various departments and hierarchical positions, we created the stakeholders' matrix. This instrument helped us to identify the key staff that, because of their positive influence and expertise, should actively participate in process-improvement initiatives. The instrument also identified those individuals who were most likely to obstruct, either consciously or unconsciously, the diffusion of a BPM culture.
- **Create a long-term vision of BPM goals and communicate them to future sponsors**: The public sector is affected by regular elections and frequent changes in managerial positions. Therefore, current initiatives are often discontinued by new leaders whose agendas may differ from those of their predecessors. Aware

of this intrinsic condition of public organizations, we articulated the evolution of the BPMO with the whole board of directors and counselor cabinet. Ensuring the initiative's strategic alignment with current and future leaders was an important strategy in guaranteeing the sustainable evolution of BPM at TCE-PE.

References

Alves, C., Valença, G., & Santana, A. F. (2014). Understanding the factors that influence the adoption of BPM in two Brazilian public organizations. In Bider et al. (Eds.), *BPMDS 2014 and EMMSAD 2014* (pp. 272–286). Berlin: Springer.

Baumol, U. (2014). Cultural change in process management. In J. vom Brocke & M. Rosemann (Eds.), *Handbook on business process management. Introduction, methods and information systems* (Vol. 1, 2nd ed., pp. 665–692). Berlin: Springer.

Grau, C., & Mörmann, J. (2014). Investigating the relationship between process management and organizational culture: Literature review and research agenda. *Sciedu Press, 1*, 1–17.

Jesus, L., Macieira, A., Karrer, D., & Caulliraux, H. (2015). BPM center of excellence: The case of a Brazilian company. In J. vom Brocke & M. Rosemann (Eds.), *Handbook on business process management. Introduction, methods and information systems* (Vol. 1, 2nd ed., pp. 105–122). Berlin: Springer.

Rosemann, M., & vom Brocke, J. (2015). The six core elements of business process management. In J. vom Brocke & M. Rosemann (Eds.), *Handbook on business process management. Introduction, methods and information systems* (Vol. 1, 2nd ed., pp. 105–122). Berlin: Springer.

Rosemann, M., de Bruin, T., & Power, B. (2006). A model to measure business process management maturity and improve performance. In J. Jeston & J. Nelis (Eds.), *Business process management: Practical guidelines to successful implementations* (pp. 299–315). Burlington, VT: Butterworth Heinemann.

Schein, E. (2010). *Organizational culture and leadership* (4th ed.). San Francisco, CA: Jossey-Bass.

Schmiedel, T., vom Brocke, J., & Recker, J. (2012). Which cultural values to business process management? Results from a global delphi study. *Business Process Management Journal, 19*, 292–317.

Schmiedel, T., vom Brocke, J., & Recker, J. (2015). Culture in business process management: How culture values determine BPM success. In J. vom Brocke & M. Rosemann (Eds.), *Handbook on business process management 2—Strategic alignment, governance, people and culture* (Vol. 2, pp. 649–663). Berlin: Springer.

Senge, P. M. (2006). *The fifth discipline: The art and practice of the learning organization*. New York: Crown Publishing Group.

Valenca, G., Alves, C., Santana, A. F., Oliveira, J., & Monteiro, H. (2013). Understanding the adoption of BPM governance in Brazilian public sector. In *Proceedings of the 21st European Conference on Information Systems*, Utrecht, Netherlands.

vom Brocke, J., & Sinnl, T. (2011). Culture in business process management: A literature review. *Business Process Management Journal, 17*, 357–378.

vom Brocke, J., Schmiedel, T., Recker, J., Trkman, P., Mertens, W., & Viaene, S. (2014). Ten principles of good business process management. *Business Process Management Journal, 20*, 530–548.

vom Brocke, J., Zelt, S., & Schmiedel, T. (2016). On the role of context in business process management. *International Journal of Information Management, 36*, 486–495.

Carina Alves is Associate Professor at Centro de Informatica, Universidade Federal de Pernambuco, Brazil. She received her Ph.D. in Computer Science from University College London and spent a sabbatical period at Utrecth University. She has expertise in Business Process Management, Software Ecosystems and Requirements Engineering. She coordinates the Business Management and Innovation research group. Her group conducts several R&D projects with local companies and public organizations. In particular, she coordinates the team of researchers and is advisor of the Business Process Management Office at Pernambuco Court of Accounts (TCE-PE).

Iveruska Jatobá is systems analyst at Pernambuco Justice Court, where she has served as director of information systems for 10 years. Currently, she is head of the Project Management Office there. She received a M.Sc. degree from Universidade Federal de Pernambuco. Her dissertation investigated cultural values in Business Process Management initiatives. Moreover, she is business process analyst of the Business Process Management Office at Pernambuco Court of Accounts (TCE-PE) and conducts research in BPM culture there. She holds CBPP and PMP certifications.

George Valença is adjunct professor at Departamento de Estatística e Informática at the Universidade Federal Rural de Pernambuco, Brazil. He received his Ph.D. and M.Sc. degree from Universidade Federal de Pernambuco. In particular, his Master's thesis explored the phenomenon of business process variability by means of a systematic mapping study. He is member of the Business Management and Innovation research group. Moreover, he is business process analyst of the Business Process Management Office at Pernambuco Court of Accounts (TCE-PE) and conducts research in process governance there. He also acted as business analyst at the Federal Data Processing Service, the largest government-owned corporation of IT services of Brazil. His research interests include Business Process Management, Requirements Engineering, Software Ecosystems and Empirical Software Engineering.

Glória Fraga holds a law B.Sc. degree from Universidade Federal de Pernambuco and a M.Sc. degree in Juridical-Political Sciences from Universidade de Lisboa (FDUL). Since 2012, she manages the Business Process Management Office at Pernambuco Court of Accounts (TCE-PE). Previously, she worked at the audit division for 16 years at TCE-PE.

Printed by Printforce, the Netherlands